Entrepreneurship in Theory and Practice

SECOND EDITION

Entrepreneurship in Theory and Practice

PARADOXES IN PLAY

SECOND EDITION

Suna Løwe Nielsen, Kim Klyver, Majbritt Rostgaard Evald and Torben Bager
University of Southern Denmark

Case writers:
William B. Gartner, Saras Sarasvathy, Alain Fayolle, Benson Honig et al

Cheltenham, UK • Northampton, MA, USA

Published by
Edward Elgar Publishing Limited
The Lypiatts
15 Lansdown Road
Cheltenham
Glos GL50 2JA
UK

Edward Elgar Publishing, Inc.
William Pratt House
9 Dewey Court
Northampton
Massachusetts 01060
USA

A catalogue record for this book
is available from the British Library

Library of Congress Control Number: 2016962552

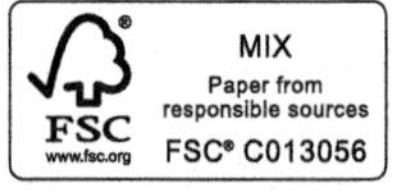

ISBN 978 1 78536 445 7 (cased)
ISBN 978 1 78536 447 1 (paperback)
ISBN 978 1 78536 446 4 (eBook)

Typeset by Servis Filmsetting Ltd, Stockport, Cheshire

Printed and bound in Great Britain by TJ International Ltd, Padstow

Contents in brief

Preface xiv
Introduction xvii

SECTION 1: WELCOME TO ENTREPRENEURSHIP

1 What is entrepreneurship? 3
2 Who is the entrepreneur? 21

SECTION 2: THE ENTREPRENEURIAL PROCESS

3 Emergence of opportunities 47
4 Evaluation of opportunities 67
5 Organisation of opportunities 89
6 Nascent entrepreneurship 113

SECTION 3: THE ENTREPRENEURIAL CONTENT

7 Resources 137
8 Networks 157
9 The business plan 179
10 Design thinking 201

SECTION 4: THE ENTREPRENEURIAL CONTEXT

11 Intrapreneurship 227
12 Social entrepreneurship 252
13 Public entrepreneurship 269
14 Entrepreneurship policy 294
15 Synthesis and recap 316

Index 325

Full contents

Preface xiv
Introduction: the ideas behind the book xvii
The audience xviii
Basic concept: theory and practice in action xix
The chapters' fourfold structure xx
Entrepreneurship: a world of paradoxes xxi
The book's structure xxiii

SECTION 1: WELCOME TO ENTREPRENEURSHIP

1 What is entrepreneurship? 3
An elevator pitch for entrepreneurship 4
Elevator pitch for you 4
Elevator pitch for existing organisations 5
Elevator pitch for society 5
A historical flashback 6
The economic tradition 8
The social-psychological tradition 9
The emergence tradition 10
The opportunity tradition 11
The book's starting point 12
A complementary approach 12
Central themes 14
The significance of context 16
The international variation 17
Ready for departure 18

2 Who is the entrepreneur? 21
Entrepreneurship in practice 21
Case study: a taste of the French wine business 22
(Devised by Alain Fayolle)
Your immediate interpretation 25
Theories of entrepreneurship 25
Types of entrepreneurs 26
The entrepreneur is born 27

The entrepreneur is made 30
Entrepreneurs: born or made? 37
A theoretical interpretation 39
The born perspective 39
The made perspective 40
Testing the theory 42

SECTION 2: THE ENTREPRENEURIAL PROCESS

3 Emergence of opportunities 47
Entrepreneurship in practice 47
Case study: serving the Starbucks coffee story 47
(Devised by Saras Sarasvathy)
Your immediate interpretation 50
Theories of entrepreneurship 51
Opportunity versus idea 51
The extent of intentions and capabilities 52
Types of opportunities 55
Discovering opportunities 57
Creating opportunities 60
Opportunities: discovered or created? 62
A theoretical interpretation 63
The discovery perspective 63
The creation perspective 64
Testing the theory 65

4 Evaluation of opportunities 67
Entrepreneurship in practice 67
Case study: 'The sky is the limit' 68
(Devised by the authors)
Your immediate interpretation 71
Theories of entrepreneurship 72
What is evaluation? 73
The instrumental evaluation 74
Evaluation through the creation of legitimacy 79
Evaluation: instrumental or legitimate? 83
A theoretical interpretation 84
The instrumental perspective 84
The legitimacy perspective 85
Testing the theory 87

5 Organisation of opportunities 89
Entrepreneurship in practice 89
Case study: a famous chef, 'It just happened' 90
(Devised by the authors)
Your immediate interpretation 93
Theories of entrepreneurship 93
What is an organisation? 94
What does organising involve? 96
Organising is not always a success 99
Organising can be planned 101
Organising is all about improvisation 103
Organising: planning or improvisation? 107
A theoretical interpretation 108
The planning perspective 108
The improvising perspective 109
Testing the theory 110

6 Nascent entrepreneurship 113
Entrepreneurship in practice 113
Case study: ADAM: community entrepreneurship 114
(Devised by Benson Honig)
Your immediate interpretation 117
Theories of nascent entrepreneurship 117
Entrepreneurship, self-employment and nascent entrepreneurship 118
Institutional factors influencing nascent entrepreneurship 119
Individual factors influencing nascent entrepreneurship 120
Life events influencing nascent entrepreneurship 122
Hybrid entrepreneurship and freelancers 125
The start-up process 125
Necessity perspective of nascent entrepreneurship 128
Opportunity perspective of nascent entrepreneurship 129
Nascent entrepreneurship: necessity based or opportunity based? 130
A theoretical interpretation 131
The necessity perspective 131
The opportunity perspective 131
Testing the theory 132

SECTION 3: THE ENTREPRENEURIAL CONTENT

7 Resources 137
Entrepreneurship in practice 137

Case study: the idea of 3D carpets 138
(Devised by the authors)
Your immediate interpretation 140
Theories of entrepreneurship 141
From a market to a resource focus 142
A three-way split of resources 145
Resource exploitation 150
Resource exploration 151
Resources: exploit or explore? 152
A theoretical interpretation 153
The exploiting perspective 153
The exploring perspective 154
Testing the theory 155

8 Networks 157
Entrepreneurship in practice 157
Case study: a hip hop entrepreneur 158
(Devised by the authors)
Your immediate interpretation 161
Theories of entrepreneurship 162
Theory of entrepreneurship and networks 162
The heterogeneity argument 163
The homogeneity argument 166
Effective networking is situation dependent 169
Networks seen as a rational tool 171
Embedded in networks 173
Network: rational or embedded? 174
A theoretical interpretation 175
The rational perspective 176
The embedded perspective 176
Testing the theory 177

9 The business plan 179
Entrepreneurship in practice 179
Case study: Mobitrix: a start-up company in the medical software industry 179
(Devised by Thomas Cooney and Anita Van Gils)
Your immediate interpretation 183
Theories of entrepreneurship 184
The business plan: context, content and process 184
Written document or thought process 186
Planning 188

The plan's content 191
The business plan as a management tool 192
The business plan as a creativity curb 194
Business plan: management tool or creativity curb? 196
A theoretical interpretation 197
The management tool perspective 197
The creativity curb perspective 198
Testing the theory 199

10 Design thinking 201
Entrepreneurship in practice 201
Case study: kicked out of the comfort zone 201
(Devised by Birgitte Norlyk)
Your immediate interpretation 205
Theories of entrepreneurship 205
Three views of design thinking? 206
The design thinking process 209
Design thinking methods 212
Entrepreneurial thinking 213
Design thinking 215
Entrepreneurship: entrepreneurial thinking or design thinking? 218
A theoretical interpretation 220
The entrepreneurial thinking perspective 220
The design thinking perspective 221
Testing the theory 222

SECTION 4: THE ENTREPRENEURIAL CONTEXT

11 Intrapreneurship 227
Intrapreneurship in practice 227
Case study: Man on the Moon – a business case competition in a global company 228
(Devised by William B. Gartner and Ann Højbjerg Clarke)
Your immediate interpretation 232
Theories of entrepreneurship 232
Background story 233
A diverse concept 235
The process behind intrapreneurship 239
Top-down intrapreneurship 242
Bottom-up intrapreneurship 242
Top-down and bottom-up 243
Intrapreneurship: top-down or bottom-up? 245

A theoretical interpretation 247
The top-down perspective 247
The bottom-up perspective 248
Testing the theory 249

12 Social entrepreneurship 252
Entrepreneurship in practice 252
Case study: the parable of the teepee 253
(Devised by Kevin Hindle)
Your immediate interpretation 256
Theories of entrepreneurship 257
Introduction to social entrepreneurship 258
Social entrepreneurship as a continuum 259
Creating a better world 260
At the intersection of social and financial goals 261
Social entrepreneurship as business 262
The emergence tradition and the opportunity tradition 263
Social entrepreneurship: business or better world? 264
A theoretical interpretation 265
The business perspective 265
The better world perspective 266
Testing the theory 267

13 Public entrepreneurship 269
Entrepreneurship in practice 270
Case study: faster transport of blood samples from patients to the laboratory 270
(Devised by the authors)
Your immediate interpretation 273
Theories of public entrepreneurship 274
The public sector's characteristics in Western countries 275
Differences between the private and public sectors 277
Scarce financial resources call for entrepreneurship 279
New ways to understand the public sector today 279
Public sector entrepreneurship antecedents 282
Closed perspective of public entrepreneurship 284
Open perspective of public entrepreneurship 286
Public entrepreneurship: closed or open perspective? 288
A theoretical interpretation 288
The closed perspective 288
The open perspective 290
Testing the theory 291

14 Entrepreneurship policy 294
Entrepreneurship in practice 294
Case study: Enspire EU 295
(Devised by Pia Schou Nielsen)
Your immediate interpretation 298
Theories of entrepreneurship 298
The growth of the entrepreneurship policy field 299
The rationale for entrepreneurship policy 300
The institutional anchoring of entrepreneurship policy 303
Target groups 304
Entrepreneurship policy areas, objectives and measures 306
Entrepreneurship policy from a wealth perspective 309
Entrepreneurship policy from a welfare perspective 310
Entrepreneurship policy: wealth or welfare? 310
A theoretical interpretation 311
The wealth perspective 311
The welfare perspective 312
Testing the theory 314

15 Synthesis and recap 316
The book's paradoxes 316
A synthesis of the paradoxes 318
An objectivist approach 318
A subjectivist approach 320
The relevance and possible combination of the approaches 321
Your journey is just beginning 322

Index 325

Preface

We wanted to write a different kind of entrepreneurship textbook, a textbook that embraces the messy and paradoxical world of entrepreneurs. In this world where fixed plans tend to be swept away overnight, textbooks with unambiguous guidelines and clear answers are of limited use. Certainly, there are bodies of knowledge and useful methodologies that students and entrepreneurs can and should learn from, but an entrepreneurship textbook should not pretend that there are clear answers and a predictable journey ahead. An entrepreneurial journey is never predefined so it is imperative to be prepared for complexity and uncertainty, as well as for continuous bombardment from new challenges and opportunities along the road.

Getting close to the paradoxical world of entrepreneurs in a textbook is a challenge; in fact, a paradox in itself. One way to get close to entrepreneurs and entrepreneurial processes is through cases. However, the normal use of cases in textbooks as end-of-chapter illustrations to theories and models is not very helpful. Therefore we try something else. In each chapter the point of departure is an interesting case with an immediate interpretation. Then theories and models are introduced and discussed, and at the end of each chapter we turn back to the case to look at it again at a theoretically informed level, and with a selected paradox in mind. We hope this case structure creates an element of learning-by-doing-and-reflecting throughout the book. In this book you will find cases from many countries around the world. We asked entrepreneurship colleagues for interesting case contributions and William B. Gartner, Saras Sarasvathy, Kevin Hindle, Alain Fayolle, Anita Van Gils, Thomas Cooney, Benson Honig, Ann Højbjerg Clarke, Pia Schou Nielsen and Birgitte Norlyk contributed with a selection of valuable cases – many thanks!

In this second edition of the textbook we have included four new chapters. As venture creation is core to the entrepreneurship field we decided to include a specific chapter on this. A fresh new challenge is design thinking and its contribution and challenge to the entrepreneurship field. Another recent development calling for a new chapter is the emergence of public entrepreneurship as a new research area. Finally, we have added a new chapter on

Figure I.1 The authors balancing and cooperating on their entrepreneurial journey entrepreneurship policy, which since the 1990s has established itself as a recognized sub-discipline.

The book is co-authored by four entrepreneurship colleagues at the University of Southern Denmark. We wanted to produce a textbook where readers, in spite of the fact that we are four authors, would not experience four different writing styles. This required close collaboration and a double writing process. Each chapter was drafted by one author, then discussed with the group and then revised by another author – and in many cases revised once more by a third author after a new round of discussion. This helped to align the writing styles, but the translation process was probably more important. We decided to draft the manuscript in our mother tongue and then ask a good translator to produce an English version. Here we were lucky to engage Mick Hancock who knows the entrepreneurship field well and is a good writer – thanks Mick! Also, a big 'Thank You' to Lennart Schlüter for your complete and beautiful graphic design of the book's models. Finally, thanks to Edward Elgar Publishing for a smooth collaboration during the publishing process.

Introduction: the ideas behind the book

Entrepreneurship is an important and exciting field of study. The creation of new organisations along with the renewal of existing organisations is the key to job creation and growth in modern society. Entrepreneurs are exciting people who make a difference.

This textbook in entrepreneurship differs in many ways from typical textbooks on the subject.

First and foremost, we define entrepreneurship as a broad phenomenon: fundamentally about the birth of new methods and processes, their evaluation and organisation. Whilst typical textbooks are limited to understanding entrepreneurship as the creation of new and independent organisations, this book shows that entrepreneurial behaviour can also take place and be manifested within many other organisational contexts (associations, government agencies, existing businesses, etc.).

Secondly, most books focus on 'How to' develop and operate new and small businesses by referring to theory, which is already familiar from the management literature. In this book, we highlight the theory and knowledge that are unique to entrepreneurship.

Thirdly, we want to give students a global perspective, using case studies from several countries, written with the cooperation of world-renowned entrepreneurship researchers. Many textbooks use only cases from a single country, thereby failing to achieve a global view.

Of course the challenge is, in many ways, the same for an entrepreneur in Europe, the USA and other parts of the world, but the context makes a difference to particular entrepreneurial opportunities. This applies to both soft variables such as culture and hard variables such as legislation.

Last but not least, we offer an exciting, but alternative pedagogical approach to entrepreneurship education. The traditional pedagogy underpinning other textbooks typically focuses primarily on presenting the theory, which is peppered with empirical examples and cases.

The approach taken in this book is different and significant because it is based on actual entrepreneurial stories. You will meet 'real entrepreneurs' in many different contexts, and you will be challenged to make decisions on their behalf – to put yourself in their place. Only after that will you be introduced to the theories and concepts of entrepreneurship. The approach also includes carrying out exercises and investigations on your own to test the established theory and knowledge in new entrepreneurial situations.

Below we introduce the audience, ideas, content, structure and pedagogical approach. When we use the term 'entrepreneurship', we refer generally to a broad concept that captures the book's subject area as a whole. Entrepreneurship is defined as the initial emergence of new opportunities being evaluated and utilised through organising. Closely related to the concept of entrepreneurship is the concept of 'the entrepreneurial process'. We define process as the movement from discovering or creating an opportunity, evaluating it and finally exploiting it through organising. As such, the organising may lead to a new organisation, which can either be an independent organisation or a new organisation within the framework of an existing association, public institution or company. A third recurring concept is 'entrepreneur'. The concept refers to the individual who initiates, pursues and creates entrepreneurship. Many other concepts are regularly featured in the book.

The audience

Who is the audience? This book, being introductory in its nature, is aimed at all of you students who have no previous education in entrepreneurship. It is a book that is equally suited to all and not just 'would-be' entrepreneurs. So, it is equally suitable for a specific audience who want to start a business and a wider audience who wish to develop their entrepreneurial mind-set. If you are a member of the first group, the book will give you a great insight into how entrepreneurs act and create value. You will gain an understanding of the start-up process and among the learning points you are probably searching for, are instrumental and very specific entrepreneurial skills. On the other hand, if you are a member of the latter, broad audience, the book's value is that it introduces a set of principles to be applied in most situations that concern the creation of something new. Regardless of whether the situation is associated with design, humanities, political science or some other field, you will hopefully become more entrepreneurial in your thinking and learning. You will probably improve your ability to identify or create, evaluate and organise opportunities. Table I.1 shows some basic differences between the two groups.

Table I.1 Differences between audiences

	Specific audience	Broad audience
Career ambition	Have real ambition to start a business	Has ambition to work with entrepreneurial issues
Overall rationale	To understand start-up processes	To develop an entrepreneurial mind-set
Learning needs	Seeking practical and instrumental skills	Seeking an ability to identify/create, evaluate and organise opportunities

Regardless of which audience you belong to, teaching in entrepreneurship is important to you. Students who have received this type of teaching are different from their fellow students and have a greater tendency to start new organisations compared with students in general. Furthermore, they are more efficient in accumulating financial assets, they receive higher wages and participate more in product development and other research and development activities than other students (Autio 2007).

Basic concept: theory and practice in action

There is strong evidence that entrepreneurship education should be different from normal teaching because it's about teaching you to create something that does not yet exist. Traditional teaching typically concerns how one conducts oneself within something that has already been created; for example, how to act within an existing organisation or a known market. In the teaching of entrepreneurship there needs to be room to stimulate entrepreneurial imagination, risk taking, action orientation and occupational independence. Therefore, gaining technical knowledge and skills is not enough. You also need the ability to use and create knowledge and link it to your own situation, activities, experiences and creativity. This book supports you in capturing the essence of entrepreneurship's complex, creative and transformative nature.

The book's concept is inspired by Kolb's (1984) learning cycle, a cycle that pushes you into entrepreneurial practice rather than simply reading about it. The cycle also means that you will be introduced to entrepreneurship from an in-depth and theoretical angle. Practice, theory, experimentation and reflection are all parts of the learning game... So enjoy it!

Kolb's learning cycle consists of four activities:

1. Its starting point is the practice-oriented stories of entrepreneurship, which, in this book, take the form of text. This activates your learning process.
2. Next, it focuses on your immediate reflection and interpretation of what happens in the story and why.
3. Only at this stage are the relevant theories introduced, and we also give you a taste of how the stories can be interpreted in light of the theory.
4. Based on these three learning activities you are finally ready to experiment with the knowledge you have gained by reading the chapter.

We offer some exercises that you can review to test your new knowledge. The learning cycle, which is illustrated in Figure I.2, can thus start a new learning cycle.

The chapters' fourfold structure

The book's chapters are structured based on the learning cycle's logic. This means that each chapter uses a very different language that spans theoretical as well as everyday language. Finally, each chapter of the book is divided into

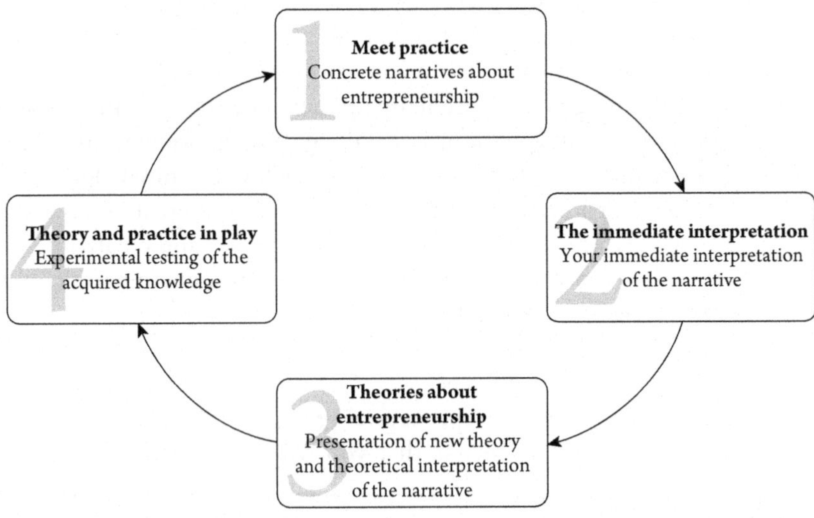

Source: Inspired by Kolb (1984).

Figure I.2 The use of the learning cycle in the book

four sections, corresponding to the learning cycle's key areas. The four sections are as follows:

- *Practical cases.* The chapters open with actual stories about entrepreneurship in the form of cases.
- *Your immediate interpretation.* This is followed by exercises that guide you to reflect on and create your initial interpretation of the entrepreneurs' stories: what happens and why does it happen?
- *Theories of entrepreneurship.* Here, relevant theories of entrepreneurship are introduced to interpret the stories further and to add theoretical angles to them. This part focuses on presenting the theory in a nuanced fashion. Therefore, the theory's presentation is built around a paradox. The paradox gives you versatile and exciting theoretical tools to interpret the entrepreneurial stories.
- *Testing the theory.* The last part of the chapter provides suggestions on how the knowledge and theory that have hitherto been discussed in the chapter may be tested in another entrepreneurial context. How can we understand the acquired knowledge and theory in light of situations other than just those outlined by the stories that were initially presented in each chapter?

Entrepreneurship: a world of paradoxes

Theories of entrepreneurship are filled with tensions and dilemmas that at first glance may seem contradictory. For example, many theories present the entrepreneurial process as a determined act that the entrepreneur can plan in advance. The entrepreneur can then predict the process, and thus what steps he or she must move through in order to achieve the goal: like a kind of jigsaw puzzle (Figure I.3). These theories assume that from the beginning of the entrepreneurial process, a picture of the completed puzzle exists. The entrepreneurial process is then about making the right plans and taking the optimal decisions, so that the pieces can be put together in such a way that the puzzle is completed according to the picture.

Other theories take the line that that the entrepreneur does not *a priori* predict which goals are to be achieved, and how he or she can achieve them. The picture of what the entrepreneur will create does not yet exist. Entrepreneurship is simply too unpredictable to be able to plan everything in advance – it's all about creating a future in the form of a product, organisation, market or something else, that is, as yet, unknown. Therefore, an entrepreneur needs to take an improvisational approach moving step

Figure I.3 The puzzle

by step: like making a kind of patchwork quilt (Figure I.4). Such a quilt is created by gradually gathering a lot of new and old materials (fabrics, ribbons, embroideries, buttons, etc. that exist in a variety of colours and qualities) into a meaningful pattern. From this, many different beautiful, and less beautiful, patchwork creations are produced. Seen in this light, the entrepreneur through small steps and improvisation creates an entrepreneurial process with the materials that he or she can obtain. The results depend on the process and can be many different organisations, products or markets.

In this way the book presents theories of entrepreneurship as a collection of paradoxes. Generally, a paradox is a contradictory statement that in this book is introduced as two conflicting theoretical perspectives. The perspectives can be viewed as opposites. In this way we want to illustrate the tensions within theory, which in turn reflect the dilemmas that the entrepreneur meets in his everyday life. As an entrepreneur you will often be left in a perplexing situation where you must make up your mind on paradoxical perspectives. You must be critical and decide for yourself.

Figure I.4 Patchwork quilt

Paradoxes in the book are not only 'either-or' paradoxes, despite the fact that they are often presented in relatively extreme versions. The purpose is to distinguish the paradoxical perspectives from each other. It is easy to talk of them as stylised interpretations, but in practice a combination of both perspectives applicable to the paradox is extremely useful in terms of understanding what's happening in the entrepreneurial process.

The book's structure

You can choose to read the book in its entirety. However, its structure also allows you to select the parts of the book that you find most relevant in light of your academic skills and interests. Thus, the book is structured around four main sections, each of which can be used independently. The sections are:

1. Welcome to entrepreneurship;
2. The entrepreneurial process;
3. The entrepreneurial content;
4. The entrepreneurial context.

Each section consists of a small group of chapters. These chapters contain a core subject area in entrepreneurship. As you can see from Table I.2, we have selected key theoretical paradoxes that are related to each subject.

Section 1: Welcome to entrepreneurship

In the book's first section you will be confronted with two chapters. Chapter 1 introduces the entrepreneurial phenomenon. Why is it important from an

Table I.2 The book's sections, chapters and paradoxes

Sections	Chapters	Paradoxes
Welcome to entrepreneurship	1 What is entrepreneurship?	Introduction – no paradox
	2 Who is the entrepreneur?	Born or made?
The entrepreneurial process	3 Emergence of opportunities	Discovered or created?
	4 Evaluation of opportunities	Instrumental or legitimate?
	5 Organisation of opportunities	Planning or improvising?
	6 Nascent entrepreneurship	Necessity or opportunity?
The entrepreneurial content	7 Resources	Exploit or explore?
	8 Networks	Rational or embedded?
	9 The business plan	Management tool or creativity curb?
	10 Design thinking	Entrepreneurial thinking or design thinking?
The entrepreneurial context	11 Intrapreneurship	Top-down or bottom-up?
	12 Social entrepreneurship	Business or better world?
	13 Public entrepreneurship	Closed or open?
	14 Entrepreneurship policy	Wealth or welfare?

individual, organisational and societal angle, and how has the phenomenon been seen in a historical perspective? Last but not least the chapter provides an insight into the key concepts that underpin the book.

Chapter 2 looks at the decision to embark on an entrepreneurial career path. Why do some people decide to become entrepreneurs and not others? Who is the entrepreneur? Can you identify him or her in the crowd? Is an entrepreneur something you are born to be, or something we all have the potential to become? Here we expressly discuss the paradox: Born or made?

Section 2: The entrepreneurial process

Discovering/creating, evaluating and organising new opportunities are three key activities related to the formation and realisation of the entrepreneurial process. The book's second section contains four chapters. The first (Chapter 3) discusses the circumstances that lead to the emergence of a new opportunity. Specifically, there is discussion about whether opportunities exist around us at all times and are just waiting to be discovered, or whether opportunities are created by the individual? The paradox is: are opportunities discovered or created?

The section's second chapter (Chapter 4) provides an insight into how the entrepreneur can evaluate his or her opportunity(ies). Evaluation refers to the process associated with assessing whether the opportunity makes sense in the market, or what action is needed to make it viable. We also discuss whether evaluation of opportunity(ies) is a systematic and analytical process or whether the evaluation is better understood as a legitimisation process where the entrepreneur, through interaction with the market attempts to gain legitimacy for his or her activities. Thus, the chapter presents opportunity evaluation in light of the paradox: instrumental or legitimate?

The third chapter in this section (Chapter 5) focuses on how opportunities can be organised. Opportunities are only really visible to investors, customers, etc., when they are organised. So, every entrepreneurial process develops structures and routines that can support the organising process, which can lead to an independent organisation or a new organisation within an existing organisation. Can this organisational effort be planned and predicted, or is the process characterised by being improvisational? This is a question we will address in this chapter during the discussion of the paradox: planning or improvisation?

Like the cherry on the top of the cake, the final chapter of this section (Chapter 6) restricts your attention to a specific and frequently used view of the entrepreneurial process. It deals with entrepreneurship as a process of venture creation, which is closely associated with the term nascent entrepreneurship. The chapter aims to present the key issues and activities leading to the start-up of a new business. It starts from an appreciation that whilst some people are drawn to attractive business opportunities, and therefore choose to start a new business, others are pushed into starting a new business out of necessity because they do not really have any other options. The chapter therefore discusses the paradox: necessity or opportunity?

Section 3: The entrepreneurial content

The book's third section focuses on four key subjects that can assist entrepreneurs in enabling the discovery/creation, evaluation and organisation of the entrepreneurial processes. In the section's first chapter (Chapter 7) you will be confronted with the issue of resources. The chapter divides resources into three types: financial resources, human resources and social resources. It discusses how the value of a resource can be assessed. It also discusses whether the entrepreneur must use the resources he or she has control over, at any given time, to exploit an opportunity, or whether the entrepreneur must use these resources to explore new and more resources. This examines the following paradox: exploit or explore?

The following chapter (Chapter 8) deals with networks and networking. The entrepreneur's social and business network is important. The chapter examines the different types of networks utilised by the entrepreneur and how various challenges in the entrepreneurial process expose a need for different types of networks. Should networks be understood as rational tools that are available to the entrepreneur, or as the 'hard to manage' conditions surrounding the entrepreneur? The paradox discussed therefore is: rational or embedded?

Chapter 9 gives an insight into the business plan, which is a central element in entrepreneurship. The plan's role in the entrepreneurial process and its importance is discussed. Here we address questions such as: is the business plan a valuable management tool in the often chaotic entrepreneurial process, a tool that supports and promotes the entrepreneur in a structured and holistic understanding of the idea and its potential? Or, is the business plan an impediment to the maturing of the idea and to the consideration of new opportunities during the process? The paradox is, in other words, is the business plan a management tool or a curb on creativity?

The final chapter of this section (Chapter 10) is concerned with design thinking, which is a unique approach to entrepreneurship that draws on the designer's methods and creative ways of solving problems. Design thinking refers to a creative, iterative and collaborative, problem-solving approach to launching and developing entrepreneurship. Empathic engagement, rapid prototyping and co-creation are key elements of the design-thinker's entrepreneurial process. An important issue in the chapter revolves around the differences between design thinking and more classical entrepreneurial thinking. To some extent the basic ideas of design thinking run contrary to much of the entrepreneurial literature, and thus the paradox to be discussed in this chapter is: entrepreneurial thinking or design thinking?

Section 4: The entrepreneurial context

The final section emphasises that the entrepreneurial process does not take place in a vacuum. Different contexts help to shape the process. The section examines four interesting contexts for entrepreneurship. The first chapter

(Chapter 11) introduces entrepreneurship within the context of an existing organisation. This phenomenon is often called 'intrapreneurship'. New ideas to be discovered or created, evaluated and organised, also occur within the framework of existing organisations, just as they do in the start up of new independent organisations. The question is whether this happens through management-led initiatives and supported processes, or whether it is initiative and commitment on the part of employees that creates intrapreneurship. The focus of the chapter is thus the discussion of the paradox: top-down or bottom-up?

Chapter 12 gives an understanding of the social entrepreneur who provides or creates a new organisation in an effort to achieve social objectives or to contribute to social activities, creating better conditions for people locally or globally. The title of the chapter is social entrepreneurship, but how can social entrepreneurship be created? Is social entrepreneurship a matter of creating a better world where social objectives are the social entrepreneur's only objective? This implies that profit and commercial exchanges are unheard of. Or does the creation of a better world require an economically sustainable business to be established so that the social entrepreneur can contribute to social activities? This means that social objectives are no longer the primary, but only secondary objectives because the first priority is profit and commercial exchange. The paradox of the chapter is: business or better world?

Whilst the book has, up to this point, primarily linked entrepreneurship to the private sector, this section's third chapter (Chapter 13) is devoted to showing that entrepreneurship is a phenomenon that also unfolds within the public sector. The specific conditions that the public sector operates under, such as the political context and the attention to the common good in providing welfare services, influence the entrepreneurial process in both restricting and enhancing ways. A dichotomy between two different perspectives on public entrepreneurship is introduced, one closed and one open. The closed perspective highlights that public entrepreneurship unfolds within public organizations with minimal inputs from the external environment. The open perspective points out that public entrepreneurship can, alternatively, be developed from complex processes involving a number of different stakeholders from the public, private and voluntary sectors, as well as from civil society. The paradox presented is: closed or open?

The final chapter of the section (Chapter 14) makes a strong case for entrepreneurship policy playing an important role in understanding entrepreneurial processes. Worldwide, and at several other levels (EU, national government etc.), entrepreneurship is encouraged through different policies. The many potential societal advantages of entrepreneurship mean that it is worth paying political attention to the phenomenon. The chapter emphasises the importance of two perspectives on entrepreneurial policy. One based on the idea that the main aim of entrepreneurial policy is to achieve economic growth, and another that emphasises the role of entrepreneurship in assisting the development of the welfare system, for example as a way to involve disadvantaged and marginalized groups in the economy. Thus, the chapter presents the paradox: wealth or welfare?

In addition to the 14 central chapters, the book contains a summary (Chapter 15) of the book's discussions, emphasising the paradoxes that have been addressed. This chapter discusses whether there is a stronger correlation between the presented paradoxes, which can further support our understanding of entrepreneurship.

LITERATURE

Autio, E. (2007) *Entrepreneurship Teaching in Öresund and Copenhagen Regions*, Copenhagen: Danmarks Tekniske Universitet.

Kolb, D.A. (1984) *Experimental Learning: Experience as the Source of Learning and Development*, Englewood Cliffs, NJ: Prentice-Hall.

Section 1

Welcome to entrepreneurship

1

What is entrepreneurship?

Entrepreneurship is around us all the time and often talked about. But what exactly is it? How would you define entrepreneurship? This might seem an easy task, but it certainly is not. Reading the newspaper or watching TV, it's easy to get the impression that entrepreneurs are today's heroes. You will encounter stories of the resourceful hero or heroine, who starts his or her own organisation, and as a result, becomes rich and famous, e.g. Henry Ford's creation of the Ford motor company and Bill Gates' creation of Microsoft. This book's message is that entrepreneurship is much more than just starting an independent organisation. Entrepreneurship is a complex phenomenon that occurs in many different contexts, and varies in terms of its scope, process and output.

The primary purpose of this chapter is to address the question: what is entrepreneurship? There is no one answer to that question. The entrepreneurial phenomenon is broad and has many facets: 'there are many entrepreneurships in terms of focus, definitions, scope and paradigms' (Steyaert & Hjorth 2003: 5). One reason for the existence of many different 'entrepreneurships' is that entrepreneurship is studied within many different disciplines (economics, psychology, sociology, management, etc.). In fact, each author seems to have his or her own definition of entrepreneurship. With reference to Saxe's (1872) story about the blind men touching different parts of an elephant (trunk, tail, etc; Figure 1.1) and as a result telling different stories about it, Gartner (2001) asks: 'Is there an elephant in entrepreneurship?'

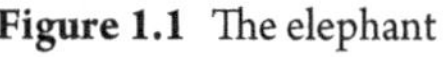

Figure 1.1 The elephant

An elevator pitch for entrepreneurship

Before we start defining entrepreneurship, we will first provide you with a short 'elevator pitch'. This term is often used in entrepreneurship. The term usually refers to a short sales pitch or oral monologue from one person to one or more people, where a given theme is introduced in the timespan of an elevator ride. The concept is American and is frequently used in networking at various business events. Here you have just a few seconds to efficiently and quickly arouse interest in your idea, product or the like.

In the following we will stimulate your interest in the idea of studying entrepreneurship. However, there will be no question of an 'elevator pitch' in the formal sense, but it is nevertheless a relatively short sales pitch for entrepreneurship. Entrepreneurship has great value for the individual, existing organisations and society. It therefore has value for you as an individual, the organisations that you may create or work within, and the people around you.

Elevator pitch for you

Entrepreneurship has different values for different people. What value would you place on becoming an entrepreneur? Surveys among students and other populations show that it is not only the prospect of making money that motivates entrepreneurs. It is more the desire for 'independence' and the need for 'achievement' that drives the potential entrepreneur (Naffziger et al 1994; Shane et al 2003). This does not mean that making money can be ignored. In order to implement their entrepreneurial processes entrepreneurs are required to establish an organisation that is commercially viable. This means that they must, at least, earn enough money to pay necessary expenses, including remuneration for their own efforts.

You might think that entrepreneurship is of no direct value to you, but think of the changes taking place in the labour market. The trend is towards more free agents, more frequent switching between jobs, faster technological development, more choice and more ambiguous job structures. Effectively this requires each of us, to a greater extent than ever before, to act as entrepreneurs in the context of our own education and careers. We must to a greater extent create a career instead of just having a career. We can usually choose from many educational opportunities and there are often multiple career tracks to pursue after graduation, including the choice between different forms of wage earning and a career as self-employed. In the past, it was common for children to follow the same career as their parents: one was almost born to follow a particular career. Although such a career path is still to be found today, younger generations are now much more challenged to create their own future. As Down said: 'We are entrepreneurs of the self' (Down 2006: 5). Therefore it is crucial for young people, generally, to know what entrepreneurship entails and to be trained in it.

Last but not least, entrepreneurship is exciting. As an entrepreneur, you are helping to create something new, typically together with others. It is a challenging and educational experience to work in the pioneering phase, bringing new things into being.

Elevator pitch for existing organisations

Entrepreneurship is also of great value to existing organisations. Organisations may find it difficult to survive if they fail to differentiate and innovate in what is essentially a globalised world. Here there is more competition for everything from everywhere; it is also a world that seemingly has no speed restrictions (Nordström 2000). Technological advances mean that organisations' products and services constantly become obsolete. Therefore, organisations must continually renew themselves and innovate across the board (new products, materials, markets, technologies, processes, etc.).

Differentiation and renewal requires that organisations are able to create or discover new opportunities and pursue them, which is precisely the core of entrepreneurship. Therefore you see more and more organisations seeking employees who can do something beyond traditional management skills with a focus on the ability to plan, organise and coordinate; they are looking for employees who are entrepreneurial, innovative and creative. Entrepreneurship is therefore also of value for those of you that take employment in an existing organisation.

Elevator pitch for society

The value of entrepreneurship to society as a whole should not be forgotten. Especially since the 1970s, entrepreneurship has been seen as a means to generate jobs, economic growth and prosperity. In the 1970s, Bolton (1971) and Birch (1979) in particular, focused on the revolutionary idea that small businesses are more important to the economy than large businesses when it comes to creating economic growth. The idea still has currency, and the importance of entrepreneurship in a socio-economic perspective is often singled out by politicians and researchers the world over.

Seen in this light it is no wonder that in many countries there is a policy objective to increase the number of growth-oriented entrepreneurs. Globally, there is great variation in the proportion of the total population that are active entrepreneurs. Generally, the prevalence of the entrepreneurially active population is higher in developing countries than in developed countries, but there is also wide variation within groups of countries. Explanations are many: culture, framework conditions, industrial structure, etc. (Kelley et al 2016). It is this proportion that politicians are trying to change in order to achieve a better level of entrepreneurial activity, both in terms of quantity and quality, which we discuss further in Chapter 14 Figure 1.2 shows examples of the various levels of entrepreneurial activity across a number of selected countries. It shows the percentage of adults who are in the process of starting a business. As we see, variation occurs not only between developed and less developed countries, but also within each group; thus, there is also a variation among developed countries and variation among less developed countries. In Bulgaria just 2 per cent of adults were in the process of starting an enterprise in 2015 but the percentage in the US was 8.3 per cent against 25.9 per cent in Ecuador (Kelley et al 2015).

Entrepreneurship is also acknowledged as helping to develop healthy competition in the economy, as the entrepreneur constantly pushes new ideas, products, services and processes into the market. Yes, entirely new industries and markets arise as a result of the activities of entrepreneurs. Alternative energy from wind turbines is an example of a Danish entrepreneurial adventure, which has created a new industry with great impact on our ability to solve present and future environmental and climate problems.

Therefore, through the study of entrepreneurship you achieve an understanding of a phenomenon that is interesting and important both for you, existing organisations and society. Need we say more? Entrepreneurship is worth studying.

A historical flashback

Nothing comes to this world from nothing, and most phenomena are part of a longer historical process of learning. Entrepreneurship also has a story. Let's go back in time and delve into this story; it will give you a better understanding of what entrepreneurship is and how this phenomenon can be defined. We've divided the field into four traditions:

- the economic tradition;
- the social-psychological tradition;

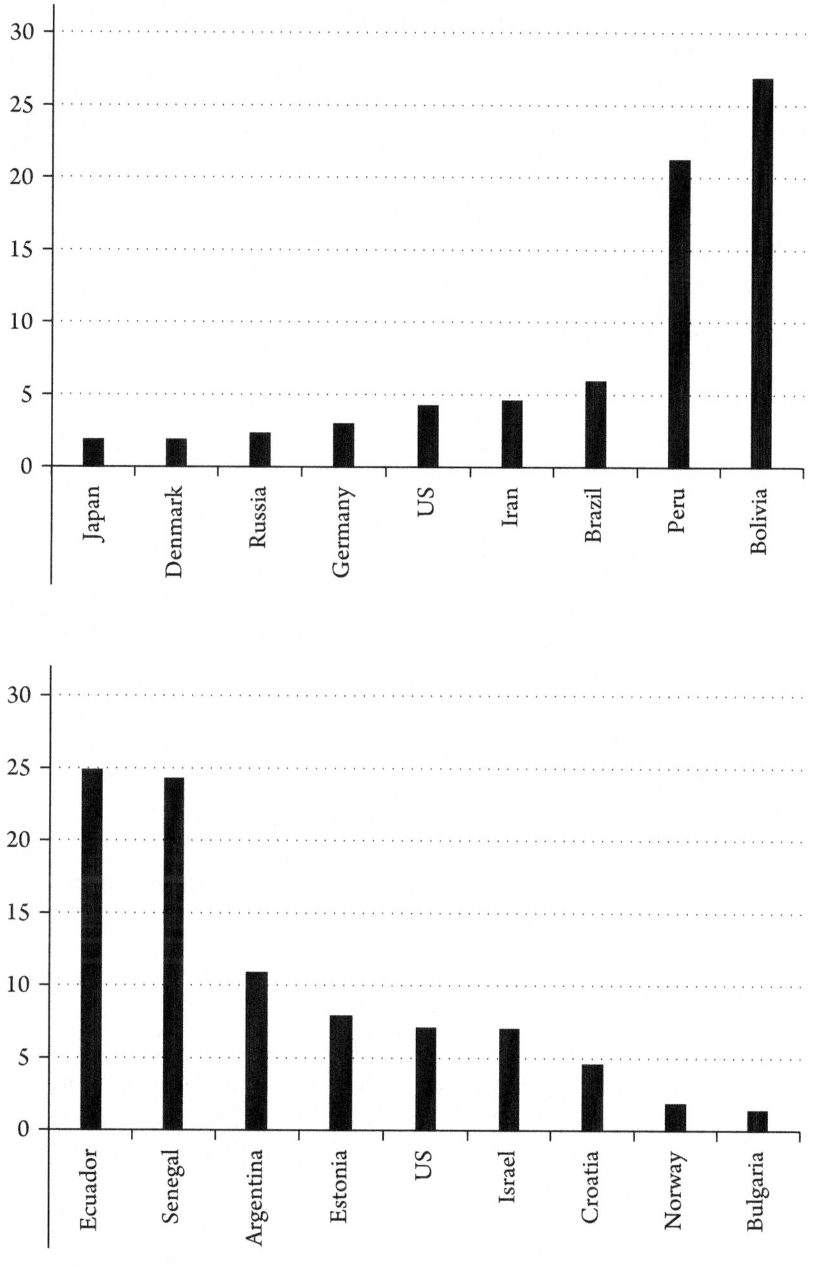

Source: Kelley et al (2016).

Figure 1.2 Percentage of adult population actively engaged in start-up activity in 2015

- the emergence tradition; and
- the opportunity tradition.

The economic tradition

Entrepreneurship is an old phenomenon. Going way back, warfare in particular, including the conquest of countries, was regarded as a form of entrepreneurship. Conquest and acquisition of resources was considered then as a natural part of efforts to discover and exploit new opportunities (Baumol 1990).

We have to wait until about 1755 before the entrepreneurial phenomenon is formally introduced into the literature on trade, economy and business. Cantillon (1680–1734) is often seen as an important pioneer in the field (Landström 1999). For him, the entrepreneur's function was to compensate for discrepancies between supply and demand by buying something cheaply and selling it again at as high a price as possible. The entrepreneur is a person who obtains and distributes resources at risk, thereby bringing the economy towards equilibrium (Murphy et al 2006). By the end of the 1700s, the concept of entrepreneurship had expanded to view the entrepreneur as a person who plans, supervises, organises or even owns factors of production. In the 1800s the distinction was made between those who supply funds and those who create profit (Coulter 2003).

In the 1900s, Knight saw it as the entrepreneur's function to carry the uncertainty within the economy on his shoulders. Knight distinguishes three types of uncertainty (Sarasvathy et al 2005):

- The first type of uncertainty occurs when different outcomes in the future exist and are known. Here the entrepreneur's role is to calculate probabilities and make decisions based on them. An example of this uncertainty would be to assemble a number of black and white marbles in a jar with a known distribution and ask someone, blindfolded, to pick out a ball and estimate the probability that it is black.
- The second type of uncertainty occurs when the future outcome exists but is not known in advance. An example of this uncertainty would be to assemble a number of black and white marbles in a jar without knowing the distribution and then ask someone, blindfolded, to pick out a ball and estimate the probability that it is black or white, respectively. After selecting a number of balls one forms a picture of the likelihood that the next ball is black.
- Knight calls the last type of uncertainty the true uncertainty. This occurs

when the future outcome does not exist and it is therefore not possible to know anything about it. The entrepreneur receives profits as compensation for handling the real uncertainty. An example here might be where a jar is filled with an unknown and ever changing bundle of things such as balls, cakes, sweets, insects and more, and then a person is asked to estimate the probability of picking out a black ball. No picture of probability can be formed.

However, it is the function that Schumpeter (1934) attaches to the entrepreneur that is often reflected in today's understanding of entrepreneurship. According to Schumpeter the entrepreneur bears no uncertainty about the economy – that is carried by the capitalist who allocates funds to the entrepreneur. Instead, the entrepreneur is an innovator who, by combining existing things, generates new opportunities and organisations in the economy: he or she is the main source of development in the economy. Schumpeter assumes that the starting point is an economy in equilibrium until an entrepreneur generates new opportunities by combining existing things, thereby creating a market imbalance. However, at the same time, the imbalance contributes to developing the economy. The new option can take the form of:

- the introduction of new products or quality thereof;
- the introduction of new production methods;
- the opening of new markets;
- the utilisation of new supply sources;
- the reorganisation of an industry.

Schumpeter assumes that new organisations will outperform existing organisations and create waves of change in the economy. He talks about this process as creative destruction: new projects and organisations are constantly being formed and others are shutting down. If an entrepreneur is successful, copycats imitate the entrepreneur and enter the market. As the market becomes saturated, a new equilibrium emerges in the economy. Of course one can raise objections against Schumpeterian theory, such as: is the new always better than the old? Why is uncertainty not related to the entrepreneur's actions? Nevertheless, there is no doubt that Schumpeter's views are relevant in view of the link between entrepreneurship, innovation and economic growth.

The social-psychological tradition

From the 1960s until the 1980s entrepreneurship was often defined from the perspective of a psychological mentality. McClelland's (1961) work *The*

Achieving Society kick-started these thoughts. This work presents the story of why some people concentrate on economic activity and are remarkably successful when others are not. In addition, it is a story about why some societies do better economically than others, despite the fact that they have a similar starting point. The need to achieve among the actors in a given society is identified as the key to the mystery. This need is linked to the entrepreneurial personality, which means that psychological explanations are gaining ground in entrepreneurship research. Specifically, psychological differences between entrepreneurs and non-entrepreneurs are of scientific interest (Carland 1984). One of the first studies to map the personal traits of successful entrepreneurs was by Hornaday and Bunker (1970). They pointed to many different entrepreneurial qualities, such as 'energetic participation in endeavour', 'confidence', 'desire to be your own boss' and 'need to accomplish' (Hornaday & Bunker 1970: 51).

After the 1980s, this literature seems to fade away, having been subject to criticism on three main fronts:

- Studying individual personality traits, such as the need to achieve, tends to ignore the influence that personal traits have on each other, and how environmental factors play a role in entrepreneurial behaviour.
- The psychological perspective has also led to such a wide range of traits and factors that the entrepreneur has been presented as an 'Everyman'.
- Finally, the studies did not make it possible to empirically identify the entrepreneur's personality in the crowd. In particular, Gartner's article: 'Who is the entrepreneur? Is the wrong question' (1988), has contributed to a showdown with the psychological way of thinking, at least in the sense of universal personality traits of entrepreneurs.

The psychological research route has, over the years, been supplemented by a sociological tradition where the emphasis is placed on relationships between people rather than on the individual. One can therefore talk about a social-psychological tradition concerned with man as an entrepreneurial player both individually and in groups (Aldrich 1999). The social-psychological tradition will be further elaborated in Chapter 2.

The emergence tradition

Newer theories have focused on understanding entrepreneurship as an organising process that leads to a particular output, namely the formation of a new organisation. What distinguishes entrepreneurs from non-entrepreneurs is not personality traits but the fact that entrepreneurs form new organisations (Gartner 1988). This idea was introduced in the theoretical field in the 1980s. Here, entrepreneurship is seen as an organisational phenomenon, entrepreneurship being 'synonymous with the behavioral act of new venture creation' (Pittaway 2003: 22).

By defining entrepreneurship as a process of organisational formation, entrepreneurship becomes synonymous with the building of new structures, because organisations are characterised by having a certain degree of formal policy, administrative structures and goals. There is, however, an important distinction between conventional organisation theory and the theory of entrepreneurship because the starting point for conventional organisational theory 'begins at the place where the emerging organisation ends' (Katz & Gartner 1988: 429). This means that entrepreneurship research focuses mainly on the process that leads to the creation of a new organisation, whilst organisation theory is mainly interested in what happens once the organisation has been created and developed.

From the beginning, this literature was largely behavioural in nature. This means that it has focused on the activities of the entrepreneur during the process of creating a new organisation. Carter et al (1996) reveal, for example, what activities 71 entrepreneurs are involved in during the start-up process.

The opportunity tradition

The emergence tradition has a competitor. We call the competitor 'the opportunity tradition'. Rather than defining entrepreneurship in terms of organisational formation, the opportunity tradition defines entrepreneurship as: 'discovery, evaluation and exploitation of opportunities to introduce new goods and services, ways of organising, markets, processes and raw materials' (Shane 2003: 4). Here, renewal or opportunity emergence is seen as the core of the entrepreneurial process and opening up to entrepreneurial activities may result in multiple outputs, including a new and independent organisation. Other possible outputs include entrepreneurship within the framework of existing businesses, voluntary organisations and public institutions.

Within the opportunity tradition the decisive factor is that entrepreneurship should be seen as something innovative. Entrepreneurial activities involve creativity and have the potential to change the existing economic market conditions. Eckhardt and Shane (2003) say that entrepreneurship involves the creation of new goals, new products or new means–end chains. It is not enough to optimise the existing targets, means or means–end chains – speaking about entrepreneurship, the creation or identification of new targets, means or means–end chains, is crucial. The focus is thus on the minority of organisations, either new or existing, which bring new products, processes, markets and reorganisations with them. This is based on opportunities that add something new to the world we already know. Opportunities are thus a key concept in the opportunity tradition. Eckhardt and Shane define opportunities as 'situations in which new goods, services, raw materials, markets and organising methods can be introduced through the formation of new means, ends, or means–ends relationship' (Eckhardt & Shane 2003: 336).

The book's starting point

Historically, the concept of entrepreneurship has been understood in a variety of ways. Many of these perceptions co-exist today and are still developing. This highlights the importance of positioning yourself within the range of perceptions, when writing a project or saying anything about entrepreneurship. The following section identifies and positions this book's perception of entrepreneurship.

A complementary approach

In the literature you will find many different ideas of how to understand the entrepreneurial process. Some believe that this process can be depicted as a phase or lifecycle sequence. This view holds that all entrepreneurial processes pass through the same stages and that these stages can be identified in advance. Some stage models deal with the organisation's overall lifecycle from the earliest starting point through to the end, for example, Kroeger (1974: 42) distinguishes between: 1) initiation, 2) development, 3) growth 4) maturity and 5) decline. Others zoom in on the earlier stages, when the idea is developed, the first concrete start-up steps are taken and the new organisation begins to take shape (Carter et al 1996; Davidsson 2006). The period before start-up is often called the 'gestation' or 'discovery' phase and the period just after launching, the 'early stage' phase. In some studies the entrepreneur is referred to as being 'nascent' in the period before the start and as the 'owner-manager' after starting up (Kelley et al 2016). The period before start up can be further divided into the time when the idea arises and is being explored ('potential entrepreneurs') and the later phase, taking concrete steps to start the business without it actually being launched ('nascent entrepreneurs'). In the literature on organisation start-up and development phases you will often find analogies to biological processes, where the distinction is between the organisation's inception, birth, childhood and adulthood. Despite similarities in many stage models and the common reference to biological processes, there is no universal agreement about the number of phases and their descriptions.

Today, the emergence and opportunity traditions represent two dominating perspectives in entrepreneurship research aiming to improve our understanding of the entrepreneurial process. They are often presented as competing perspectives. This book is based, however, on the idea that the two traditions can be viewed as complementary. The argument is that the entrepreneurial process in practice involves the emergence (discovery or creation) of opportunities, evaluation of opportunities and the organisation of opportunities. Opportunity emergence is concerned with the entrepreneur discovering or creating a business opportunity; for example, by combining something that already exists to a completely new or improved product. Opportunity evaluation focuses on the entrepreneur's assessment of the opportunity in terms of whether it is attractive to the market or not. Opportunity organising occurs when the entrepreneur tries to exploit the opportunity by implementing it, so that those in the market can see, understand and act upon it.

That the emergence and opportunity traditions can be seen as complementary approaches is also underlined by Bygrave and Hofer's definition of the entrepreneur: he or she is a person 'who perceives an opportunity and creates an organisation to pursue it' (Bygrave & Hofer 1991: 14). Or Shane's understanding of the core of entrepreneurship: 'Entrepreneurship is an activity that involves the discovery, evaluation and exploitation of opportunities to introduce new goods and services, ways of organising markets, processes and raw materials through organising efforts that previously had not existed' (Shane 2003: 4). The opportunity concept is central here, but note that there is also talk of 'organising efforts'.

Let's illustrate the complementarity of the two traditions with an example: the formation of a new student association. Student associations usually reflect a political position or a particular interest among a group of students, such as environmental issues or the relationship between developed and developing countries. A group of politically concerned students might believe they will have better opportunities to influence key decision-makers through their new association. A key issue for consideration here is whether there is 'room' for another association established in the traditional way or whether there is a need to organise themselves in an alternative way, such as through a virtual network. According to the 'emergence tradition' one can understand this case as a traditional process of collective organisation, whilst someone viewing this from the viewpoint of the 'opportunity tradition' would emphasise that this case constitutes a different and new opportunity

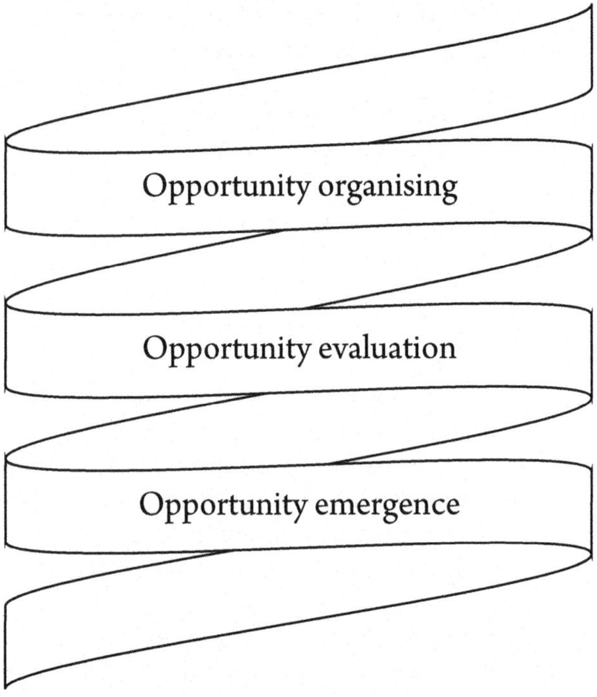

Figure 1.3 How entrepreneurship is construed in the context of this book

to perceive a student association. Both traditions thus add something to our understanding of a specific case.

Figure 1.3 illustrates this book's perception of entrepreneurship as a tripartite process involving the emergence, evaluation and organisation of opportunities. Both the emergence and opportunity traditions are involved. The figure is drawn as a spiral in order to emphasise that this book rejects the idea that the process is linear. The process is not one of clear and definable phases that naturally build on each other. Instead, it is often iterative, parallel and overlapping.

Chapters 3, 4 and 5 elaborate on the Figure 1.3. Chapter 3 focuses on opportunity emergence and thus its discovery or creation. Chapter 4 looks at opportunity evaluation and Chapter 5 on the exploitation of opportunities through organising. As nascent entrepreneurship and business start-up are very important in the entrepreneurship literature, Chapter 6 delves specifically into these topics, which can be related to the emergence tradition.

Central themes

The processes associated with emergence, evaluation and organisation of new opportunities are extremely complex. A multitude of different factors

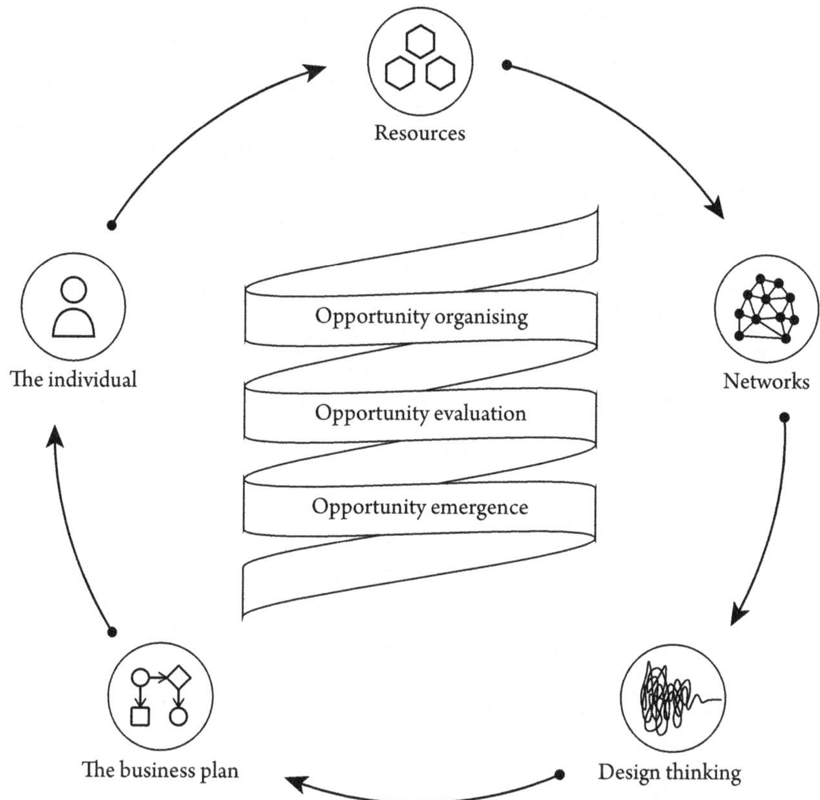

Figure 1.4 Core topics for entrepreneurship

come into play, such as environment, demography, the entrepreneur's previous experience and career, personality, self-understanding, strategic choices, etc. In particular, this book highlights five themes that influence the entrepreneurial process, or assist the entrepreneur in enabling the process. The themes are: 1) the individual, 2) resources, 3) network, 4) the business plan and 5) design thinking. They are illustrated in Figure 1.4.

Why are these issues important? The entrepreneurial individual plays a major role in the development of entrepreneurship. After all, it is an individual or a small group of individuals who initiate and implement the process. Furthermore, it is in the minds of individuals that imaginative and creative processes occur.

Resources are a necessary input in discovering or creating an opportunity and organising it. They are the materials that form the foundation for entrepreneurship. Resources can be broadly defined as human, social and financial resources.

Networking is also crucial. Despite the fact that entrepreneurship is, in many ways, a lonely journey, it must be emphasised that this process is also very much a network journey. The entrepreneur interacts constantly with others (bankers, potential customers, consultants, other entrepreneurs, etc.) and creates networks. These networks are absolutely crucial for him or her to gain access to the knowledge, resources, etc. that are essential for the development of entrepreneurship.

The business plan, understood as a written document, is not necessarily a part of all entrepreneurial processes, but some degree of planning is present in all of these processes. The business plan can also have different meanings. Sometimes it's important to create a basis for resource acquisition and evaluation of the entrepreneurial process. Other times the purpose is to support the entrepreneur in the planning process.

Design thinking is a unique problem-solving approach from which the entrepreneur can draw in order to create/discover, evaluate and organise opportunities. The approach is unlikely to be relevant for all entrepreneurs, but it holds great potential in relation to creatively finding good solutions to the complex challenges the entrepreneur typically meets on his or her journey, and to uncover something new that otherwise might not would have emerged.

Chapters 2, 7, 8, 9 and 10 deal with each of the five themes in greater depth, which is why they are only touched upon in a superficial manner here. So, as you read the book, you will not only gain a greater understanding of key activities in the entrepreneurial process, namely the emergence, evaluation and organisation of opportunities. You will also understand the key issues that affect these activities, or which can assist the entrepreneur in developing the entrepreneurial process.

The significance of context

So far we have talked about entrepreneurship as a phenomenon that takes place in a vacuum. We have not touched on how the entrepreneurial process is influenced by the unique context that surrounds it. A tendency to ignore the context is also found in entrepreneurship research. The focus tends to be on the flower (the new organisation) and the gardener (entrepreneur), whilst the garden (context) and its influence remains a mystery: it is a serious shortcoming (Hindle 2011).

The context within which entrepreneurship develops makes a difference because the context affects the type of network and resources that the entrepreneur has access to during the opportunity emergence, evaluation and organising processes. Similarly, different contexts play a part in affecting the entrepreneur's options. For example, there is agreement that contexts where norms and values encourage entrepreneurship also give rise to a higher level of entrepreneurial activity among its members (Gnyawali & Fogel 1994). Finally, disparate contexts confront the entrepreneur with different barriers and opportunities.

An entrepreneur within the context of a university may feel constrained by academic norms with their focus on contemplation and knowledge generation, rather than action and commercialisation. This can give rise to tensions in the entrepreneurial process. But the university context also gives the entrepreneur a lot of opportunities, for example in the form of unique knowledge that can be used to develop his or her opportunity. Last, but not least, entrepreneurs, when they break with their familiar contexts, may experience a feeling of loneliness if the context does not legitimise their entrepreneurial actions.

The importance of context has led us to design four special chapters in the book, which are often omitted from textbooks on entrepreneurship: namely a chapter on intrapreneurship (Chapter 11), a second chapter on social entrepreneurship (Chapter 12), a chapter on public entrepreneurship (Chapter 13) and a final chapter dealing with entrepreneurship policy (Chapter 14).

The international variation

Finally, this book has an international angle. Even though this book emphasises the universal concepts and ideas about entrepreneurship, international specifics are presented when regarded as relevant. After all, entrepreneurship develops within national, regional and local contexts and is influenced by the rules, norms and values that exist therein. Therefore there is great variation in entrepreneurial activity between countries.

Of course, legislation plays a role. In some countries and sectors, entrepreneurial activity is impeded or prohibited as a formal activity and often develops informally. This applies especially in communist and socialist countries where the state has a full or partial monopoly to organise economic activity. In all countries there are also rules for the creation of new firms and often there are also special rules for subsidies or preferential treatment for start-ups. Typically, entrepreneurs in the initial phase have access to concessional loans and cheap or free advice, fully or partially supported by national, regional and local authorities. The authorities can thus both inhibit and promote entrepreneurial activity, which obviously affects the entrepreneur's opportunities and incentives.

However, it's not just the formal laws and rules that play a role. Also important are the unwritten rules, i.e. culture-related norms and values in society. One example is the large variation from country to country in the perception of what activities women and men should undertake in public and economic life. Can women, for example, be presidents, ministers, police officers and generals? The answer varies enormously from country to country, and in many countries there has been a significant shift in these perceptions throughout history. Something similar applies to the role of the entrepreneur. In some countries it is considered acceptable for a woman to start and conduct business while in others it is controversial and is considered to be contrary to the accepted female role. This, of course, affects the proportion of female entrepreneurs in those countries. In most countries, the majority of entrepreneurs are men, but in some countries there are more women. In 2015, an extensive study of entrepreneurial conditions showed that in countries such as the Philippines, Indonesia, Thailand, Vietnam and Peru there were more female than male entrepreneurs, while in Tunisia and Egypt there are approximately three times more male than female entrepreneurs, and in Europe on average there are approximately twice as many male than female entrepreneurs (Kelley et al 2016).

Ready for departure

We hope that you now have a better understanding of why it is valuable to study entrepreneurship, what entrepreneurship is and how this book perceives the phenomenon. That was certainly the aim of this chapter. Now you are going on an exciting journey where you have the opportunity to immerse yourself, from both a practical and a theoretical angle, in the central issues of entrepreneurship. You know the itinerary, but before the final departure, we want to be absolutely sure that you pack your bag with the right concepts. Therefore we'll end this introduction with an overview of key concepts that are crucial for understanding the book:

- *entrepreneurship*: a broad concept that generally speaking can be defined as: emergence of new opportunities which are evaluated and exploited through organising;
- *the emergence tradition*: a tradition within entrepreneurship research that emphasises the creation of new organisational structures which function as a frame for an opportunity related to a specific market demand;

- *the opportunity tradition*: another tradition within entrepreneurship research that focuses on new opportunities as the core of entrepreneurship;
- *the entrepreneurial process*: the movement from discovering or creating an opportunity, to evaluation of the opportunity, to finally exploiting it through organising;
- *entrepreneur/intrapreneur*: the individual who initiates, strives for and organises entrepreneurship;
- *paradox*: a conflicting statement which will be introduced in the book as two conflicting theoretical perspectives;
- *perspective*: a theoretical approach which represents one of the two statements that pertain to the paradox;
- *opportunity*: an idea which is evaluated as capable of creating value for others;
- *opportunity emergence*: the process in which the opportunity emerges led by individuals who discover or create the opportunity;
- *opportunity evaluation*: the process in which the entrepreneur evaluates to what extent the idea represents an attractive opportunity;
- *opportunity organising*: the creation of some meaningful structures that support the realisation of the opportunity, for instance to collect resources, to coordinate activities and to involve others so that the wanted output can be obtained.

LITERATURE

Aldrich, H.E. (1999) *Organizations Evolving*, London: Sage.

Baumol, W.J. (1990) 'Entrepreneurship: Productive, unproductive and destructive', *Journal of Political Economy*, 98(5), 893–921.

Birch, D.L. (1979) *The Job Generation Process*, Cambridge, MA: MIT Program on Neighborhood and Regional Change.

Bolton, J.E. (1971) *Small Firms: Report of the Committee of Inquiry on Small Firms*, London: Her Majesty's Stationery Office.

Bygrave, W.D. & Hofer, C.W. (1991) 'Theorising about entrepreneurship', *Entrepreneurship Theory & Practice*, 16(2), 13–22.

Carland, J.W. (1984) 'Differentiating entrepreneurs from small business owners: A conceptualisation', *Academy of Management Review*, 9(2), 354–359.

Carter, N.M., Gartner, W.B. & Reynolds, P.D. (1996) 'Exploring start-up event sequences', *Journal of Business Venturing*, 11(3), 151–166.

Casson, M. (1982) *The Entrepreneur*, Totowa, NJ: Barnes & Noble Books.

Coulter, M. (2003) *Entrepreneurship in Action*, Upper Saddle River, NJ: Prentice Hall.

Davidsson, P. (2006) 'Nascent entrepreneurs, empirical studies and development', *Foundations and Trends in Entrepreneurship*, 2(1), 1–76.

Down, S. (2006) *Narratives of Enterprise: Crafting Entrepreneurial Self-identity in a Small Firm*, Cheltenham, UK and Northampton, MA, USA: Edward Elgar Publishing.

Eckhardt, J.T. & Shane, S. (2003) 'Opportunities and entrepreneurship', *Journal of Management*, 29(3), 333–349.

Gartner, W.B. (1988) 'Who is the entrepreneur? Is the wrong question', *American Journal of Small Business*, 12(4), 11–32.

Gartner, W.B. (2001) 'Is there an elephant in entrepreneurship? Blind assumptions in theory development', *Entrepreneurship Theory & Practice*, 25(4), 27–39.

Gnyawali, D.R. & Fogel, D.S. (1994) 'Environments for entrepreneurship development: Key dimensions and research implications', *Entrepreneurship Theory & Practice*, 18(4), 43–62.

Hindle, K. (2010) 'How community context affects entrepreneurial processes: A diagnostic framework', *Entrepreneurship & Regional Development*, 22(7), 599–647.

Hornaday, J.A. & Bunker, C.S. (1970) 'The nature of the entrepreneur', *Personnel Psychology*, 23(1), 47–54.

Katz, J. & Gartner, W.B. (1988) 'Properties of emerging organizations', *Academy of Management Journal*, 13(3), 429–441.

Kelley, D., Singer, S. & Herrington, M. (2016) *Global Entrepreneurship Monitor, 2010 Global Report*, GERA/Babson.

Kelley, D., Brush, C., Greene, P., Herrington, M., Ali, A. & Kew, P. (2015) Global Entrepreneurship: Women's Entrepreneurship, Special Report, GERA/Babson.

Kroeger, C.V. (1974) 'Managerial development in a small firm', *California Management Review*, 17(1), 41–47.

Landström, H. (1999) 'The roots of entrepreneurship research', *New England Journal of Entrepreneurship*, 2, 9–20.

McClelland, D.C. (1961) *The Achieving Society*, Princeton, NJ: D. Van Nostrand Company Ltd.

Murphy, R.J., Liao, J. & Welsch, H.P. (2006) 'A conceptual history of entrepreneurship thought', *Journal of Management History*, 12(1), 12–35.

Naffziger, D.W., Hornsby, J.S. & Kuratko, D.F. (1994) 'A proposed research model of entrepreneurial motivation', *Entrepreneurship Theory & Practice*, 18(3), 29–42.

Nordström, K. (2000) *Funky Business: Talent Makes Capital Dance*, London: Financial Times Management.

Pittaway, L. (2005) 'Philosophies in entrepreneurship: A focus on economic theories', *International Journal of Entrepreneurial Behaviour and Research*, 11(3), 201–221.

Sarasvathy, S., Dew, N., Velamuri, S.R. & Venkataraman, S. (2005) 'Three views of entrepreneurial opportunities', in Acs, Z.J. & Audretsch, D.B. (eds) *Handbook of Entrepreneurship Research*, New York: Springer, 141–160.

Saxe, G.J. (1872) *The Poems of John Godfrey Saxe*, Boston, MA: James R. Osgood and Co.

Schumpeter, J.A. (1934) *The Theory of Economic Development*, Cambridge, MA: Harvard University Press.

Shane, S. (2003) *A General Theory of Entrepreneurship: The Individual–Opportunity Nexus*, Cheltenham, UK and Northampton, MA, USA: Edward Elgar Publishing.

Shane, S., Locke, E.A. & Collins, C.J. (2003) 'Entrepreneurial motivation', *Human Resource Management Review*, 13, 257–279.

Steyaert, C. & Hjorth, D. (2003) *New Movements in Entrepreneurship*, Cheltenham, UK and Northampton, MA, USA: Edward Elgar Publishing.

2

Who is the entrepreneur?

Without a person who initiates and shapes the entrepreneurial process, no entrepreneurial processes exist. If new opportunities are to emerge, whether it's opportunities that lead to a new organisation or a radically different way of doing things within an existing organisation, they must be initiated and maintained by an individual or groups of individuals. The individual plays a particularly decisive role during the early start-up phase, when the new opportunity must stand up to testing. The new opportunity is dependent upon the individual, because at this stage no processes or activities have started running automatically. Only in the later stages of an opportunity's life cycle where it is organised, widely known and accepted, does the entrepreneurial individual play a less significant role: for example, key employees can take over important tasks and organisational factors in general are more dominant.

In other words, individuals or groups of individuals leave their distinct mark on the way that new opportunities emerge are evaluated and organised. Maybe these marks are even more important for entrepreneurial success than, say, the opportunities and the situation in a given industry or sector (Baum et al 2007). It is therefore crucial to understand the personality and qualities of the entrepreneur. Who is the individual who creates entrepreneurship? This particular question is much discussed in entrepreneurship. Can it be answered unequivocally? Is there something special within the entrepreneur that distinguishes him/her from others, or are all people potential entrepreneurs? Apparently, who the entrepreneur is remains a mystery, but let us see if we can get closer to the heart of the question.

Entrepreneurship in practice

It is time to learn from real life and meet with a French entrepreneur, Rémi. The story of Rémi is developed by Alain Fayolle. It is a fascinating story about wine, enthusiasm, need for independence, and much more, which provides us with great input to discuss the individual behind entrepreneurial endeavours.

CASE STUDY

A taste of the French wine business

(Devised by Alain Fayolle)

Rémi started a new business while studying at the EM Lyon Business School. In February 2008 he was interviewed about the start-up process. At that time he had been running the firm for over 10 years. We quote here extracts from his story as narrated by Rémi during this interview. His focus is mostly on his personal background, the emergence of the project, the decision-making process, and the very early stages of the start-up.

'I come from a technical background. I have a degree in industrial refrigeration and air conditioning engineering. I worked for three years at the American firm Carrier, the world leader in this sector. There I worked on major projects (the Channel Tunnel, Bibliothèque de France, etc.), which means that at the start of my career my job was mainly technical. Next, I went back to college in order to acquire some managerial skills and so joined the MBA programme at EM Lyon. During this programme, I met an entrepreneurship teacher during a business start-up course, and he sowed a seed that started germinating, which was: "Why not start a business?" At the time, the very idea of starting a firm was totally new to me, I had never even considered the possibility, and nobody in my family – parents, uncles, aunts or cousins – has ever created or owned a business. My mother and father are both civil servants, employed as teachers, needless to say that the world of business and entrepreneurship has never really been a conversational topic at home. However, during this course, I started contemplating the possibility of creating, developing and running a business. The more I thought about it, the more it appealed to me, as I saw in it an opportunity to satisfy my needs for self-development and fulfil personal objectives and ambitions, better than I ever could by working in a large firm. After asking myself the question over and again, I thought "Why not?" I'm not married, don't have any children and I don't have a lot of money. I had nothing to lose at the time. I did have a girlfriend of course, who I lost at the time, but it was not because of the start-up project, it was my fault: when you commit to starting a business, you engage in a time-consuming process, you see less of your friends, of your girlfriend, your family, you go out less, all the more since you have little money to spare and you concentrate on the project.

I was on my own at the beginning, and then a friend of mine joined the project, a friend from Alsace, who became my associate. In fact, there were supposed to be more partners originally, but several people were willing to support the start-up in the early stages without being financially involved, that is to say without investing money and taking shares in the capital. Even the staunch supporters of the project, the ones who wanted to commit financially, eventually stood down one after the other as time went by, and stopped attending important meetings, those during which important decisions needed to be taken. We had to rethink the project, the business plan, and the funding requirements. I dealt with it all without feeling too disheartened and held on to the project: you can't back down at the last minute, after more than a year's work. It's too late then to reconsider and update your CV to go job hunting.

CASE STUDY *(continued)*

More especially as, after coming back from England, I had begun a job search before quickly realizing that there was something incompatible between starting a new business and looking for a job. It seems impossible to do both at the same time. I experienced it without truly realizing this fact. At the time, I was sharing a flat with my girlfriend who was on the same MBA course at EM Lyon Business School, a year below me. There was everyday life, she was busy with her studies, and I was busy with my start-up project; and at the same time, I was undecided, I didn't really know what I wanted. My career summary looked good on paper, but I knew I would certainly need to go back to live in Paris, a prospect I did not relish. Yet I sent a couple of cover letters and got a couple of interviews. And it's true that when you step into one of these plush Parisian buildings where the recruitment consultant introduces you to the company's profile, you quickly realize that what they have to offer is potentially very interesting. The company is a large firm, with an international reputation, the job is particularly attractive and the salary is so much higher than what I could ever hope to earn by starting my own business (in my case, I spent a few months earning nothing). After the first interview, which goes well, you go back home and find it impossible to turn on the computer and resume work on some wacky business idea, you have no idea where it's going . . . so the computer stays off . . . and after a week or so, you turn it on, but you haven't made any progress . . . You do this two or three times, and that's it you can bury the project for good!

So I asked myself the question: "What shall I do?" There were things I knew I could always do later, and others that just cannot wait. Of course, you can always start a business at any time in

Figure 2.1 Turning a passion for French wine into a successful start-up: mission impossible?

CASE STUDY *(continued)*

your life, but there are moments when conditions are more favourable. And I felt that, in my case, all the conditions were met. I therefore made the decision to stop looking for a job, and to stop responding to the people I had met during interviews. From then on, I devoted myself totally to my start-up project.

This start-up project had no *a priori* reason for being. It was a project in wine, born out of my own interest and passion for it. At least, if it did not work out, I would have learned something about wine, which, for somebody like me, who loves cooking, can always be useful in everyday life. I am aware today that this is not the way you go about developing a business plan, but there was this thought, in the back of my mind, that if it did not work out straight away, it was so interesting that I would find the energy to turn it into something viable.
It is true that the wine sector is a tough one, where there is little money to make, which creates little value. The wine trade has existed in France for over 20 centuries, and people involved in the sector consider it in very traditional terms, be they involved in production, wine-making, or buying and selling. The wine sector also has regional particularities; you do not pull the same levers when you are in Burgundy, the Bordeaux region, Côtes du Rhône or Alsace. I immediately knew that understanding its specificities would be a very complex task. In order to better know the sector and understand its workings, I spent a year visiting the vineyards, tasting the wines, meeting people and giving the project time to mature. The initial idea, which I never put into practice, was to apply the Tupperware concept to wine selling: individuals organise sales parties at home where people can taste the wine, hosts get rewards, etc. The idea was to work with wine lovers and set up a network of knowledgeable customers who would organise home sales parties to sell carefully selected quality wines. But what works with plastic containers does not necessarily work with wine: the profit margin on plastic containers is high, whereas margins are low in the wine sector, so I quickly arrived at the conclusion that the initial idea was not viable. I rethought the original concept and opted for wine brokerage instead, which was in the end a rather conventional idea, especially when it came to implementation and distribution. By that time, I had come to realise that there were specific markets that could be commercially attractive, like hotel chains and restaurants. I had identified these targets because without a large sales force, it was out of the question to go and visit private people to sell them a couple of cases of wine at a time. It seemed more logical and efficient to target hotel and restaurant chains in order to negotiate with head office and then sell throughout their hotel and restaurant network. I also realised that this type of clientele used wholesalers dealing in all kinds of beverages: water, soft drinks, coffee, tea, wine, etc. But wine is not a product like any other, it is not water – even if it does contain some – it is not coffee, it is something that requires a specific kind of expertise! So I met with several hotel chain managers, who at least agreed to lend me their name so I could go and visit the local hotel managers. And this is how it all began! My first customers were chain-owned hotels, my very first customer was the Holiday Inn hotel chain.

At the beginning, I was on my own, I was working from a very old flat in Lyon. It was funny in a way: the staircase was a very narrow stone vaulted staircase, and I had to take the cases up

CASE STUDY *(continued)*

the stairs. The first few months, there were many of them, and after a while, there were more wine cases than there were personal things in the flat, I was no longer accommodating the business, it was the business which accommodated me, because there were even cases in the bath: they were everywhere! . . . '

Your immediate interpretation

What does the story tell you about the entrepreneurial individual? What is your initial impression? The following exercises can help you interpret the story.

- Make a list and discuss the personality traits revealed in the narrative. Who is Rémi?
- Rémi presents his stories for you and your fellow students. Your tutor asks you to give a brief statement of whether or not he can be defined as an entrepreneur. What are the arguments for and against? How do you define an entrepreneur?
- One of your fellow students emphasises that Rémi does not start up alone, but together with others. Does this tell you something about the entrepreneurial individual? Why do you think that entrepreneurs often start up in teams rather than alone?
- You have decided to start your own organisation, but you want to start it with others. What key issues would you consider in your efforts to put together the perfect start-up team? What characteristics, skills, networks, etc. should the other members of your start-up team possess?
- You meet one of your friends. She has already started two organisations. In discussing what makes an entrepreneurial person she claims that she was born to become an entrepreneur. What do you think about this argument?

Theories of entrepreneurship

As mentioned earlier, the number of entrepreneurs varies across countries, depending on, among other things, countries' unique economic, cultural and social situations. However, the individual level is also crucial for understanding the kind of people that generate, evaluate and organise new opportunities and thereby adopt the role of entrepreneurs. Theories, which have primarily been of a psychological nature, can give us some answers as to the characteristics of entrepreneurial individuals, but they point in different directions.

According to Korunka et al (2003) the development of theory about the entrepreneur as an individual can generally be considered in three phases. The first, 'optimistic' phase, particularly dominant in the 1960s and 1970s, essentially believes that entrepreneurs are born with a variety of traits that produce a universal and specific entrepreneurial personality that we can identify. By revealing this personality, it is possible to differentiate the entrepreneur from other individuals.

In the 1980s however, another, more critical phase of theoretical development arose. Here, the entrepreneur is seen as a much more complex phenomenon and it is not enough merely to look for personality traits. This allows the introduction of more dynamic and diverse theories, which among other things, focuses on the process and the interaction between individual and environment to explain the entrepreneur and entrepreneurship. It also opens up the possibility that individuals are not born as entrepreneurs, but are made into entrepreneurs. Anyone can evolve to become an entrepreneur over time. Whether individuals are motivated to try their hand at entrepreneurship will be the result of specific situations and experiences encountered during their lives.

A third and more recent phase, around 2000, focuses, once again on the individual's personality. However, rather than concentrating on identifying individual traits this research develops a more dynamic understanding of the entrepreneurial personality through the analysis of cognitive processes, intent, identity, etc.

In short, this chapter will introduce you to the paradox of whether entrepreneurs are:

Born or made?

Types of entrepreneurs

Before we plunge into the paradox it is important for you to remember that an entrepreneur is not simply an entrepreneur. We can distinguish between different types of entrepreneurs according to the various entrepreneurial opportunities and challenges they face. Here is a breakdown of entrepreneurs in six different groups, inspired by Ucbasaran et al (2001):

- 'Novice' entrepreneur (a person with no entrepreneurial experience).
- 'Habitual' entrepreneur (a person with previous entrepreneurial experience).

- 'Serial' entrepreneur (a person who is constantly establishing and selling organisations).
- 'Portfolio' entrepreneur (a person who owns several organisations simultaneously).
- 'Hybrid' entrepreneur (a person who is simultaneously self-employed and employed).
- 'Nascent' entrepreneur (a person who is in the process of considering the establishment of a new organisation – he or she can be either a 'novice', 'habitual', 'serial' or 'portfolio' entrepreneur). Nascent entrepreneurship, or the nascent entrepreneur, is thoroughly discussed in Chapter 6.
- 'Intrapreneur' (a person acting entrepreneurially within an existing organisation). This type of entrepreneurship is discussed, thoroughly, in Chapter 11.

Within the literature you will find many other interesting classifications of the entrepreneur, see Wickham (2006) for an overview. Now, let's get back to the paradox.

The entrepreneur is born

The 'entrepreneurs are born' perspective represents what we, earlier in this chapter, referred to as the optimistic phase. Despite the fact that psychology has played a crucial role in this phase, we begin with the economic trad-ition, which was reviewed in Chapter 1. This tradition considers the function performed by the entrepreneur, within the economy, to be crucial (Casson 2003), but doesn't delve into who the entrepreneur is as an individual and thus the important individual personality traits that are relevant to entrepreneurship. As Hébert and Link state: 'the entrepreneur has been a shadowy and elusive figure in the history of economic theory. Referred to often, but rarely ever studied or even carefully defined, the entrepreneur winds his way through economic history, producing results often attributed to faceless institutions or impersonal market structures' (Hébert & Link 1988: 11). Some economists, including Schumpeter (1934), stress the importance of the entrepreneur's character traits and personality. Overall, he sees the entrepreneur as a particularly innovative individual – 'A Great Man' who through creative destruction creates new waves of change in the economy. This distinguishes the entrepreneur from the 'ordinary' people who are more 'routine' in their activities. Entrepreneurial activity comes from special individuals who have the:

- desire to establish a private kingdom: 'First of all, there is the dream and the will to found a private kingdom, usually, though not necessarily, also a dynasty';

- will to conquer: 'Then there is the will to conquer: The impulse to fight, to prove oneself superior to others, to succeed for the sake, not of the fruits of success, but of success itself. From this aspect, economic action becomes akin to sport – there are financial races, or rather boxing-matches';
- joy of creating: 'Finally, there is the joy of creating, of getting things done, or simply of exercising one's energy and ingenuity' (Schumpeter 1934: 93–94).

The idea of the entrepreneur as a special individual has been continued in research focused on identifying the traits that make up the unique entrepreneurial personality. But can it really be true that one must be a special person to be an entrepreneur? Well, to discover or create opportunities, evaluate and pursue them through organising involves risk taking, the ability to find creative solutions, the need to perform, personal ambition and much more. They all sound like traits that are related to one's personality. One may wonder if there are certain people who are more likely to have these traits whilst certain other people prefer a more secure and conventional career path?

Character traits in the limelight

As mentioned in Chapter 1, entrepreneurship research from around 1960 up to 1980 focused on describing the entrepreneur as a person in possession of a particular set of traits (e.g. Hornaday & Aboud 1971; Hull et al 1980; Begley & Boyd 1987). In short, the entrepreneur is assumed to be a kind of 'describable species that one might find a picture of in a field guide, and the point of much entrepreneurship research has been to enumerate a set of characteristic describing this entity known as the entrepreneur' (Gartner 1988: 12). One of the aims of character trait research is to find out what differentiates the population of entrepreneurs from other groups in society. It would be quite rewarding if you could point out entrepreneurs in the crowd and support these unique entrepreneurs, so as to accelerate economic growth in society. The thinking behind trait research is that some people have certain attributes that make it more likely that they will find or create an opportunity and pursue it through organising. Personality traits are: 'constructs to explain regularities in people's behaviour, and help to explain why different people react differently to the same situation' (Llewellyn & Wilson 2003: 342), and research has focused on identifying individual or sets of traits, predicting entrepreneurial behaviour.

Over time, the range of character traits that have been identified as important to entrepreneurship is long. For example: apt to take risks, need to perform, independent, aggressive leader, self-efficacy, is action and goal oriented, innovative, intelligent, creative, tolerant of uncertainty and a desire to make money. These are enough to make you think that the entrepreneur is an extraordinary super-human – a hero or heroine. See Gartner (1988) for a more detailed overview of the key contributions to trait research. It should, however, be noted that discussions continue on whether the aforementioned characteristics are really stabile traits acquired at birth, or whether they are socialised and developed during life.

Some traits seem to have attracted more attention and spent more time in the limelight than others, such as risk-taking propensity, need for achievement, need for autonomy, self-efficacy, and internal locus of control; these are also known as Entrepreneurship's Big Five (Vecchio 2003). Thus, there are results showing that entrepreneurs exhibit a higher need to accomplish than others, they are more willing to assume risk; possess a greater need to be his/her own boss; believe they are able to control their surroundings rather than being led by them, and have a more developed faith in their own work-related powers and thus believe in their own abilities in relation to performing a given activity.

Since classic trait research assumes that the identified personality features are stable over time and that the entrepreneur has acquired these more or less at birth, we see this research as an example of a 'born entrepreneur' mind-set. Like in Hans Christian Andersen's story of the Ugly Duckling, it is origin and not growing up that decides who you are and what you become. 'Being born in a duck yard does not matter, if only you are hatched from a swan's egg'. The consequence is 'once an entrepreneur, always an entrepreneur, since an entrepreneur is a personality type, a state of being that doesn't go away' (Gartner 1988: 12).

Is it in the genes?

As a further development, of the discussion about entrepreneurs being 'born' with entrepreneurial traits, behavioural genetics has entered the field of entrepreneurship during the last decade (Nicolaou et al 2008). Behavioural genetics investigates genetic effects, often based on adaption or twin datasets.

Entrepreneurship research has often suggested that people with entrepreneurial parents exhibit a greater tendency to become involved in entrepreneurial activity in comparison with individuals whose parents are not entrepreneurial. But can this be explained genetically? According to Shane (2010), research indicates that certain gene combinations indirectly increase an individual's odds of ending up as an entrepreneur, although those gene combinations are still not identified. Thus, certain gene combinations might potentially influence an individual's personality traits, cognitive skills and environment selection, and through those impacts, the chances of individuals becoming entrepreneurs. For instance, individuals with a high level of activity, high intelligence and dyslexia have a greater tendency to become entrepreneurs, but we also know those characteristics are to some extent genetically determined. Also personal characteristics normally associated with entrepreneurs such as 'self-esteem, novelty seeking, risk-taking propensity, disagreeableness, extraversion, emotional stability, openness to experience and conscientiousness' (Shane 2010: 165) seem to be genetically determined to some extent.

However, individuals might also be genetically predisposed to search and select friends that are entrepreneurial, because they are attracted to such behaviour. In this way, even environmental effects, such as role model or social network effects involve some degree of genetic predisposition. Thus, parts of the trait, cognitive and environmental (e.g. social networks) effects are actually genetically predetermined.

Importantly, behavioural genetics is not only about genes; study of this field has actually changed the way we think about the environment. For instance, studies show that many environmental effects have a genetic component and that the effect of environment often depends on genes (Plomin et al 2008). This further implies that behavioural genetics does not eliminate the idea of the environment or socialisation at all. It is not gene determinism! It is combinations of genes rather that one gene that matters. It is combinations of genes in interaction with the environment that matters. Finally, one combination of genes can have several behavioural effects. Thus, one unspecified combination of genes might make an individual become a gambler, violent, or an entrepreneur, depending on their environmental stimuli (their parents, friends, etc.).

The entrepreneur is made

As we discussed in Chapter 1 the classic psychological literature – especially traits literature – has been subject to criticism. The subject area has been controversial since the late 1980s, which has given rise to what we referred to earlier as the critical phase in relation to answering the question: Who is the entrepreneur? As Gartner emphasises 'I believe the attempt to answer the question "Who is an entrepreneur?" which focuses on the traits and personality characteristics of entrepreneurs, will neither lead us to a definition of the entrepreneur nor help us to understand the phenomenon of entrepreneurship' (1988:12).

Focusing on upbringing and demography

One criticism of trait research that has been raised is how little it takes account of environmental factors. This has led to the idea that the entrepreneurial personality is shaped not only by birth but also that early childhood and demographic factors are important. Factors such as birth order, entrepreneurial parents, encouraging parents, work experience, education, gender, age, etc. are assumed to influence whether you become an entrepreneur (Hisrisch & Peters 2001); it is from such factors that the idea of becoming an entrepreneur has begun to sprout.

In terms of age, The Global Entrepreneurship Monitor Survey 2010 (www.gemconsortium.org, last accessed 16 August 2016) shows that worldwide the 25–34 year age group contains the highest percentage of people involved in the earlier phases of entrepreneurship, followed by the age groups 35–44 years and 45–54 years. Early stage entrepreneurial activity is less prevalent among 18–24-year-olds and least prevalent among 55–64-year-olds. When it comes to gender, the same study illustrates that in overall terms, women are less likely to be involved in entrepreneurship. There is, however, considerable variation in the proportion of female entrepreneurs across countries depending on the opportunities and normative, formal and cultural conditions which confront women in different countries (Klyver et al 2013). The female/male ratio is on average 0.96 in Africa whilst it is 0.46 in Europe. In Pakistan there is one female entrepreneur for every 18 male entrepreneurs, whilst there are five female entrepreneurs in Panama for every four male entrepreneurs. In Western Europe, women are primarily entrepreneurs in Austria and Switzerland where there are four female entrepreneurs for every five male entrepreneurs. This corresponds roughly to the proportion in the USA.

A wider picture of the entrepreneur

Born out of another critical response to trait research is the idea that one can explain the entrepreneur's person in a broader and more process-oriented context. Here, a series of components are seen as interacting with the entrepreneur to discover or create opportunities, evaluate and organise them. It views the entrepreneur as being formed by the interaction between the individual and a number of more environmental components. The interaction between the entrepreneur's market and life situation, network characteristics, type of organisation, access to resources, demography, etc. has a bearing on who will become entrepreneurs and who will not. You simply weave a broader and more dynamic theoretical framework than hitherto to capture what makes an entrepreneur and entrepreneurship.

In creating this framework we use contingency theories which have developed out of the idea that systems consist of various interacting components. Contingency theory implies that something is 'determined by/is contingent upon the situation'. Whether an individual becomes an entrepreneur or not, depends therefore on the situations and experiences that the individual encounters. Furthermore, the interaction between the various components makes the formation of very different entrepreneurial processes and entrepreneurs possible. Consequently, 'The process of starting a business is not a single well-worn route marched along again and again by identical entrepreneurs. New venture creation is a complex phenomenon: Entrepreneurs and their firms vary widely' (Gartner 1985: 697). So there is no single way in which an entrepreneur is created. One of the better-known contingency theories of entrepreneurship is Gartner's (1985) model depicted in a simplified version in Figure 2.2. The model shows how the entrepreneurial process is seen as a result of an interaction between four components (individual, organisation, environment and process).

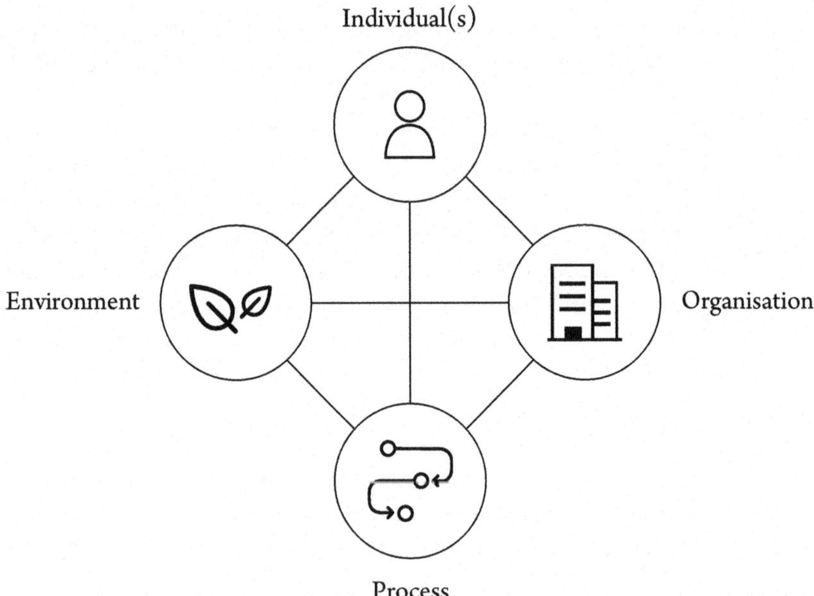

Source: Gartner (1985: 698).

Figure 2.2 Gartner's contingency model

Contingency theories provide us with a good overview of the mechanisms at play in entrepreneurship, but they tell us much less about the entrepreneur as a person. Instead, they focus on the interaction between certain structural or system components; factors external to the entrepreneur as subject (Jones & Spicer 2005).

The entrepreneur's cognitive processes

The critical phase has led to the point where entrepreneurs are no longer seen as a homogeneous group of individuals, and it has largely moved beyond the unilateral studies of traits and the idea that entrepreneurs are born (Baum et al 2007). At the same time, one cannot ignore the entrepreneur as a person in a field such as entrepreneurship, and scholars have, over time, gained a renewed interest in studying the entrepreneurial individual. So, in recent years we have seen the germination of an interesting research approach (the third phase of literature on the entrepreneur), which once again is more directly concerned with studying the entrepreneurial individual, focusing on, among other things, cognitive processes (Mitchell et al 2002). Cognition represents the study of how the mind and our thoughts are organised. It's about the entrepreneur's intellect rather than traits; how he or she understands and what he or she thinks about what is taking place in their environment and within themselves. It is the study of how the brain processes the impulses and the information that the entrepreneur receives from the environment. Therefore, although the entrepreneurial personality is the primary unit of analysis, there may also be an interactionist approach where both the individual and the environment play a role in creating entrepreneurs (Chell 2008). The cognitive approach can be used to understand why some individuals find or create opportunities and pursue them, while others do not; why some even choose to become entrepreneurs and others do not; whether entrepreneurs think differently from others, etc. (Mitchell et al 2004). Shaver and Scott (1991) take this approach in seeking knowledge about how the business world is represented in the cognitive processes of individuals, in both those who create new businesses and those who do not.

According to Shane (2003), the literature has specifically identified three cognitive characteristics that make entrepreneurs exploit opportunities:

- Entrepreneurs are more optimistic in their impulse processing than others. They therefore have a tendency to seize opportunities despite uncertainty about the outcome.
- Entrepreneurs have more willingness to generalise based on small

samples than others. They therefore have a tendency to take big decisions, despite the fact that they don't have much information available.

- Entrepreneurs use their intuition more than others. Entrepreneurs thus tend to refrain from collecting information as they possess an inner feeling or belief that exploiting a given opportunity is the right thing to do.

Identity and the entrepreneur

Another emerging branch of research is focused on understanding the entrepreneur as an individual through identity research (Down & Reveley 2004; Downing 2005; Stepherd & Haynie 2009; Hoang & Gimeno 2010). There are many different definitions of what an identity is. Some understand identity as a relatively stable core that individuals carry with them into the entrepreneurial process, and which guides the individual in the unknown situation (Sarasvathy & Dew 2005), while others increasingly see identity as a constantly changing socially constructed phenomenon. One definition focuses on how entrepreneurs make sense of themselves within their environment. Identity is defined as 'a person's sense of who he or she is in a setting' (Weick 1995: 461). According to this definition, a person's understanding of him-herself is constantly changing depending on who the person interacts with and in what contexts he or she participates. Identity thus takes the form of a continuous social process in which the entrepreneur is trying to create meaning and understanding of: who I am, what I do and what I experience. All this affects how the entrepreneurial process functions and entrepreneurs are created.

Similarly, an individual is assumed to have multiple identities. The entrepreneurial individual is not just an entrepreneur. He or she is perhaps also a parent, soccer player, student, half-day employee or pensioner. These other identities play a part in how individuals understand and perform the entrepreneurial identity. We cannot therefore always expect the individual to be fully dedicated to the entrepreneurial identity. It is also easy to find someone who is involved in the entrepreneurial process, but does not see themselves as an entrepreneur. For example, they see themselves primarily as an engineer, and the entrepreneurial process is only a tool for facilitating his or her identity as an engineer.

According to this research, all people can potentially develop an entrepreneurial self-understanding. Who it is that actually creates such an understanding depends on the social relationships the individual is involved in along with their existing self-image or desire for certain future identities. Because identity creation is taking place constantly and is a part of everyday life, this way of thinking breaks with the perception of entrepreneurship as an extraordinary hero-phenomenon.

The individual's process towards entrepreneurship

Before we finally resolve the paradox 'born or made', we will spend some time studying the process through which the individual goes in his or her journey toward entrepreneurship. As we will discuss, the process can be influenced by whether the entrepreneur sees themselves as a born or made entrepreneur. Figure 2.3, developed by Fayolle (2003), shows the individual's journey toward entrepreneurship as being divided into phases. If we are all potential entrepreneurs, the individual's process towards entrepreneurship is understood as being based on an indifference situation where individuals are not yet aware of entrepreneurship (Phase 1). However, an entrepreneurial awakening may occur, which stimulates the individual's interest and desire for entrepreneurship (Phase 2), which in turn can help individuals become motivated to engage in entrepreneurship and develop entrepreneurial intentions (Phase 3). This in turn can trigger the decision to act as an entrepreneur (Phase 4) from which, over time, arises one or another result of the operation (phase 5).

In some cases, the individual passes the entrepreneurial awakening stage very early in life. From childhood he or she dreams of becoming an entrepreneur and has therefore intended to pursue this career for a long time. At times, these types of people may say that they have always seen themselves as entrepreneurs, and they may even perceive themselves to have been born entrepreneurs.

Ajzen's 'theory of planned behaviour' also reflects the process of intention prior to action. The theory suggests that action presupposes a conscious intention to carry out the action. Intention is an indicator of how hard an individual will work to achieve something – for example entrepreneurship, and 'as a general rule, the stronger the intention to engagement in a behaviour, the more likely should be its performance' (Ajzen 1991: 181). It follows that entrepreneurial actions are not random or simply a result of social stimuli. They are also the result of an internal rational individual intention to perform an entrepreneurial act. Ajzen's theory gives us some tools to explain and predict entrepreneurial intention, as intention is referred to as the crystallization of three variables:

- perceived behavioural control: how difficult or simple the individual perceives the entrepreneurial project;

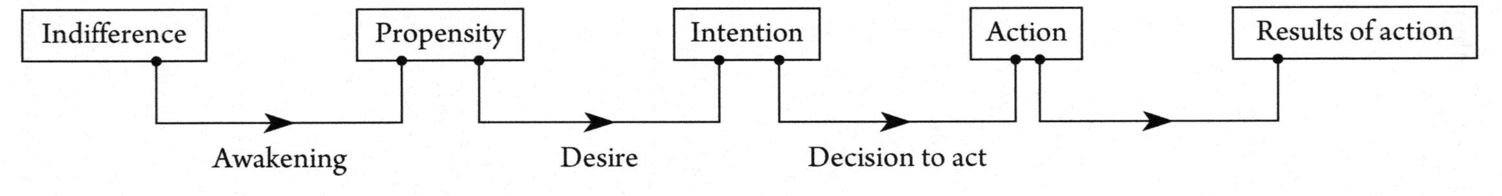

Source: Fayolle (2003), pp. 39.

Figure 2.3 Fayolle's individual process model

- subjective norms: the extent to which individuals perceive a social pressure to perform or not perform the entrepreneurial action;
- attitude towards the behaviour: the degree to which individuals will choose the entrepreneurial action, rather than another action – view of the action's favourability (Ajzen 1991: 183).

As a rule of thumb, the more the individual experiences behavioural control, the greater the respect awarded to the action by society, and the more the individual considers the act to be favourable, the stronger the individual's intentions to become a entrepreneur, which increases the individual's need to discover or create an opportunity.

Nevertheless, action sometimes precedes the individual's intention to journey toward entrepreneurship, for example, when an individual more or less randomly creates an opportunity he or she finds interesting and begins to develop it further, without really having a clear intention of becoming an entrepreneur. Shane concludes: 'People can and will discover entrepreneurial opportunities without actively searching for them' (Shane 2000: 451). New opportunities are discovered or created often as a result of our daily interaction with others in different contexts – that is, through externally oriented activities. The entrepreneurial opportunity can, over time, lead to the intention to become an entrepreneur, for example when the individual is curious to explore the possibilities of its potential, has no other career opportunities or is pushed into entrepreneurship by others who find the option attractive. Basically this is a more unconscious initiation of the entrepreneurial process, where the entrepreneurial awakening and intent forms over time in parallel with the individual beginning to act as an entrepreneur.

This type of entrepreneurship strongly underlines how we all have the potential to end up as entrepreneurs, although we may have no intention of doing so. Who will become entrepreneurs is difficult to predict. It depends on the circumstances, whom we meet, opportunity, chance, our needs, self-perception, and much more.

Entrepreneurs: born or made?

The entrepreneurial individual has lived a somewhat turbulent life, from a theoretical viewpoint. From being a shadowy figure to being regarded as the 'bee's knees' and subsequently being considered as a non-trendy area of research, the individual has again become interesting. Attempts to describe and identify universal and invariable facts concerning the entrepreneur's personality and character traits have not met with much success. Nevertheless

Table 2.1 The paradox: Born or made

	Born	Made
Who is the entrepreneur?	Special super-individuals	All are potential entrepreneurs
Perception of the entrepreneur	Stable over time – once an entrepreneur, always an entrepreneur	The entrepreneur is created through a process
Stimulation	Internal character features	External factors
Research focus	Character features attached to the entrepreneurial personality	The interacting individual and contextual factors that create individuals, cognitive processes and identity
Objectives	To be able to predict and point out the entrepreneur in the crowd	To understand the entrepreneur and how an entrepreneur is created

this research still, in many ways, seems to maintain many of the ideas of entrepreneurs as heroes who are more or less born for this profession. A contrary view is that entrepreneurship is not something you are; it is something one becomes. Life experiences, people you meet, one's self-perception, situations you get into, knowledge and experience you gain, etc. all combine to create entrepreneurs. Who will become an entrepreneur is not pre-determined and there are no general laws related to the personality that limit the number of us that can become entrepreneurs. We are all potential entrepreneurs. The 'born or made' paradox can be summarized as shown in Table 2.1.

The table shows how two perspectives have dominated research into the entrepreneurial individual. One perspective suggests that entrepreneurs are born. This means that entrepreneurs are special super-individuals who are born as entrepreneurs and remain entrepreneurs all their lives. It is primarily internal character traits that are assumed to determine entrepreneurial behaviour. Therefore, research has – at least in its classic form – primarily focused on the study of stable character traits associated with the entrepreneurial personality. The objective of this research is to be able to point out the special entrepreneurial person in the crowd.

Conversely, the other perspective that views entrepreneurs as made, emphasises that we are all potential entrepreneurs. The creation of entrepreneurs is a process in which primarily external factors play a role, which is underscored by the focus of this research. The research also includes reflections on cognitive and identity-related processes that are linked to the entrepreneurial individual, with the aim of understanding the individual, and how that individual, in interaction with external processes, is created.

A theoretical interpretation

Let us now return to the story about the French entrepreneur Rémi, attempting to understand the story from the 'born' and 'made' perspectives.

The born perspective

Through the lens of the born perspective, Rémi's story is about a man with certain inherited personal characteristics that do not fit into the role of corporate employment. He is born to be an entrepreneur, and therefore he skips a successful and promising career in a major world leading firm. The formal structures of the large organisation simply do not give him room to express who he is.

At first, the entrepreneurial personality trait influences Rémi unconsciously. Rémi has never considered the possibility of being an entrepreneur, yet, from unconscious processes his personality traits make him perform an entrepreneurial pattern of behaviour. This behaviour is especially triggered by meeting an entrepreneurship teacher when he joins an MBA programme. After this, the entrepreneurial traits have an all-consuming effect on Rémi as he becomes more and more aware of the fit between the entrepreneurial career option and his personality. Entrepreneurship can satisfy his distinctive personal needs.

Yet, when confronted with difficulties Rémi, during the start-up process, turns his attention towards the employment career option. He goes to job interviews. In the end, the entrepreneurial career option is, however, the winner. It underscores the born perspective's suggestion that once an entrepreneur, always an entrepreneur. Rémi does what he was born to do although he has some doubts.

Moving into the traits constituting Rémi's entrepreneurial personality, many of the traits from the born perspective can be associated with Rémi. Foremost, his story indicates that he holds a high need for autonomy. He leaves the corporate context to be free to accomplish personal goals of self-fulfilment rather than corporate goals. He is passionate about building a private kingdom to realise his personal lifestyle preferences. Also, Rémi's story shows a high level of risk-taking propensity. He enters the risky and hard-hitting French wine sector with an almost empty backpack in terms of sector-relevant knowledge, networks, experiences, etc. To comprehend the game of this wine sector, he travels around in the sector for a year. It indicates that Rémi holds a high internal locus of control. By actively gathering information on the wine sector, he perceives himself able to control the events of his entrepreneurial process as it unfolds within the boundaries of the sector. Moreover, he seems to believe that he is competent to create a new venture within this sector. It makes Rémi's story one about a high level of self-efficacy.

In this way, through the lens of the born perspective, we can conclude that Rémi is born with distinguishing entrepreneurial traits. They explain why Rémi enters entrepreneurship and the events of the new venture creation process.

The made perspective

The made perspective provides us with a very different understanding of what is going on in Rémi's story. Initially, Rémi does not hold any entrepreneurial intentions. He has not considered entrepreneurship as a potential career. After all, entrepreneurship has not been a part of his upbringing and he is working for a large company. It is from interactions with others and his contextual external circumstances that Rémi experiences an unanticipated entrepreneurial triggering. An entrepreneurship teacher evokes his interest in entrepreneurship with the question: 'Why not start a business?'

Thinking about new venture creation as a career option, Rémi seems to engage in a process of redefining himself and his career. Increasingly, entrepreneurship appeals to him, and eventually he seems to surrender to the entrepreneurial identity although he still finds his old career identity 'employee' tempting. Much indicates he is divided between the old identity 'employee' and the new identity 'entrepreneur'. In the end, it is reflection about his life situation that makes Rémi fully dedicated to entrepreneurship. Being young gives room for experimenting with starting a new venture. So far, he is not a father, husband, etc., and thus he does not have a complex set of identities and obligations that he needs to take into consideration.

As outlined by the made perspective, Rémi's process of new venture creation is formed in close interaction and collaboration with others (friend, different non-financial supporters, investors, actors within the wine sector, etc.). As an example, the original business idea, dealing with applying the Tupperware concept to wine selling, is transformed from the interactions. The new idea is to target hotel and restaurant chains. It is interesting to see how through the interactions Rémi constantly gains access to new resources, knowledge, networks, experiences, etc., and thus he opens a way into the French wine market. Without the interaction it is likely that Rémi would have run into a dead end street.

Individual cognitive processes also appear to play a role in Rémi's interactions with the environment. Being passionate about the entrepreneurial opportunity it looks like he has an inner feeling that starting a wine business is the right thing to do. Also, despite relatively little knowledge about the wine market, he is ready to take important decisions about the new venture project.

Thus, it is easy to find support for the made perspective. Rémi's story can be interpreted as a story about an entrepreneurial individual emerging from a wealth of interactions in which life situation, the market, age, others, identity and cognitive issues played a crucial role.

The Rémi case was developed by Alain Fayolle who sees new venture creation as a strategic and dynamic decision/action process triggered by a change in the individual's perceived instantaneous strategic configuration (Fayolle 2007). An individual's perceived instantaneous strategic configuration results from the combination of three sets of perceptions. The first one relates to the goals and objectives underpinning individuals' aspirations, the second concerns the individual's perceived resources and skills, and the third relates to the perceived opportunities and threats of the environment. The perceived instantaneous strategic configuration model amounts to applying a traditional strategic analysis process to new venture creation, led by an individual with bounded rationality. These changes in perception are what makes individuals go through various stages in their perception of new venture creation: indifference – propensity – action (Fayolle 2003). Moreover, Fayolle suggests in a private communication that it is valuable to draw on the commitment perspective to grasp what is going on in the case. Commitment can in his view be defined as:

> the moment when the individual starts devoting most of his time, energy, and financial, intellectual, relational and emotional resources to the start-up project. Once committed to the process, the individual no longer considers the possibility of turning back: the investments made would make opting far too difficult and would be experienced as a personal failure.

The commitment perspective is further elaborated in Fayolle et al (2011).

Testing the theory

Based on the above thoughts and discussions, you are ready to develop your own attempt to understand the entrepreneurial individual and the factors that create him or her. The following are suggestions for investigating the topic.

EXERCISES

1 **Interview with an entrepreneur.** Make a list of interview questions that seek to capture some of the most central debates about who the entrepreneur is and how he or she develops. Contact an entrepreneur, and interview him or her in order to test the theory presented in this chapter. Based on this, you can create your definition of who the entrepreneur is.

2 **Media images of the entrepreneur.** Search for newspaper articles that tell about successful entrepreneurs. Analyse the kinds of perceptions of the entrepreneurial individual that are presented in the media. Discuss how these images can influence how many and who are engaged in entrepreneurship in your country.

LITERATURE

Ajzen, I. (1991) 'The theory of planned behavior', *Organizational Behavior and Human Decision Processes*, 50, 179–211.

Baum, J.R., Frese, M., Baron, R. & Katz, J.A. (2007) 'Entrepreneurship as an arena of psychological study: An introduction', in Baum, J.R., Frese, M. & Baron, R. (eds), *The Psychology of Entrepreneurship*, Mahwah, NJ: Lawrence Erlbaum Associates, 1–18.

Begley, T.M. & Boyd, D.P. (1987) 'Psychological characteristics associated with performance in entrepreneurial firms and smaller businesses', *Journal of Business Venturing*, 2, 79–93.

Casson, M. (2003) *The Entrepreneur: An Economic Theory*, 2nd edn, Cheltenham, UK and Northampton, MA, USA: Edward Elgar Publishing.

Chell, E. (2008) *The Entrepreneurial Personality: A Social Construction*, 2nd edn, New York: Routledge.

Down, S. & Reveley, J. (2004) 'Generational encounters and the social formation of entrepreneurial identity: "young guns" and "old farts"', *Organization*, 11(2), 233–250.

Downing, S. (2005) 'The social construction of entrepreneurship: Narratives and dramatic processes in the co-production of organizations and identities', *Entrepreneurship Theory and Practice*, 29(2), 185–204.

Fayolle, A. (2003) 'Research and researchers at the heart of entrepreneurial situations, new movements', in Steyaert, C. & Hjorth, D. (eds), *New Movements in Entrepreneurship*, Cheltenham, UK and Northampton, MA, USA: Edward Elgar Publishing, 35–50.

Fayolle, A. (2007) *Entrepreneurship and New Value Creation. The Dynamic of the Entrepreneurial Process*, Cambridge: Cambridge University Press.

Fayolle, A., Basso, O. & Tornikoski, E. (2011) 'Entrepreneurial commitment and new venture creation: A conceptual exploration', in Hindle, K. & Klyver, K. (eds), *Handbook of New Venture Creation*, Cheltenham, UK and Northampton, MA, USA: Edward Elgar Publishing.

Gartner, W.B. (1985) 'Conceptual framework for describing the phenomenon of new venture creation', *The Academy of Management Review*, 10(4), 696–706.

Gartner, W.B. (1988) 'Who is the entrepreneur? Is the wrong question', *American Journal of Small Business*, 12(4), 11–32.

Hébert, R.F. & Link, A.N. (1988) *The Entrepreneur – Mainstream Views and Radical Critiques*, New York: Praeger Publishers.
Hisrisch, R.D. & Peters, M.P. (2001) *Entrepreneurship*, Boston, MA: McGraw-Hill.
Hoang, H. & Gimeno, J. (2010) 'Becoming a founder: How founder role identity affects entrepreneurial transition and persistence in founding', *Journal of Business Venturing*, 25(1), 41–53.
Hornaday, J.A. & Aboud, J. (1971) 'Characteristics of successful entrepreneurs', *Personnel Psychology*, 24, 141–153.
Hull, D., Bosley, J. & Udell, G. (1980) 'Reviewing the heffalump: Identifying potential entrepreneurs by personality characteristics', *Journal of Small Business Management*, 18(1), 11–18.
Jones, C. & Spicer, A. (2005) 'The sublime object of entrepreneurship', *Organization*, 12(2), 223–246.
Klyver, K., Nielsen, S. & Evald, M.R. (2013) 'Women's self-employment: An act of institutional (dis)integration? A multilevel, cross-country study', *Journal of Business Venturing*, 28(4), 474–488.
Korunka, C., Frank, H., Lueger, M. & Mugler, J. (2003) 'The entrepreneurial personality in the context of resources, environment, and the startup process – A configurational approach', *Entrepreneurship Theory and Practice*, 28(1), 23–42.
Llewellyn, D.J. & Wilson, K.M. (2003) 'The controversial role of personality traits in entrepreneurial psychology', *Education + Training*, 45(6), 341–345.
Mitchell, R.K., Busenitz, L., Lant, T., McDougall, P.P., Morse, E.A. & Smith, J.B. (2002) 'Toward a theory of entrepreneurial cognition: Rethinking the people side of entrepreneurship research', *Entrepreneurship Theory and Practice*, 27(2), 93–104.
Mitchell, R.K., Busenitz, L., Lant, T., McDougall, P.P., Morse, E.A. & Smith, J.B. (2004) 'The distinctive and inclusive domain of entrepreneurial cognition research', *Entrepreneurship Theory and Practice*, 28(6), 505–518.
Nicolaou, N., Shane, S., Cherkas, L., Hunkin, J. & Spector, T.D. (2008) 'Is the tendency to engage in entrepreneurship genetic?', *Management Science*, 54(1), 167–179.
Plomin, R., DeFries, J.C., McClearn, G.E. & McGuffin, P. (2008) *Behavioral Genetics*, New York: Worth Publishers.
Sarasvathy, S.D. & Dew, N. (2005) 'Entrepreneurial logics for a technology of foolishness', *Scandinavian Journal of Management*, 21, 385–406.
Schumpeter, J.A. (1934) *The Theory of Economic Development*, Cambridge, MA: Harvard University Press.
Shane, S. (2000) 'Prior knowledge and the discovery of entrepreneurial opportunities', *Organization Science*, 11(4), 448–469.
Shane, S. (2003) *A General Theory of Entrepreneurship: The Individual–Opportunity Nexus*, Cheltenham, UK and Northampton, MA, USA: Edward Elgar Publishing.
Shane, S. (2010) *Born Entrepreneurs, Born Leaders: How Your Genes Affect Your Work Life*, New York: Oxford University Press.
Shaver, K.G. & Scott, L.R. (1991) 'Person, process, choice: The psychology of new venture creation', *Entrepreneurship Theory and Practice*, 16(2), 23–45.
Stepherd, D. & Haynie, M.J. (2009) 'Birds of a feather don't always flock together: Identity management in entrepreneurship', *Journal of Business Venturing*, 24, 316–337.
Ucbasaran, D., Westhead, P. & Wright, M. (2001) 'The focus of entrepreneurial research: Contextual and process issues', *Entrepreneurship Theory and Practice*, 25(4), 57–80.
Vecchio, R.P. (2003) 'Entrepreneurship and leadership: Common trends and common threads', *Human Resource and Management Review*, 13(2), 303–327.
Weick, K.E. (1995) *Sensemaking in Organisations*, Thousand Oaks, CA: Sage.
Wickham, P.A. (2006) *Strategic Entrepreneurship*, Harlow: Pearson Education Limited.

Section 2

The entrepreneurial process

3

Emergence of opportunities

The entrepreneurial individual is crucial to understanding entrepreneurship, but many see the discovery or creation of opportunities as the core of entrepreneurial theory. An opportunity is an idea that is believed will create value for others. Without opportunities entrepreneurship cannot occur. Furthermore, many believe that a focus on opportunities is what makes the theory of entrepreneurship unique. But, what is an opportunity and where do opportunities come from? This is the theme of this chapter.

In order to discuss opportunities, we introduce another concept: the idea-concept. Ideas come before opportunities, but not all ideas grow and turn into opportunities. Some ideas remain at the idea level, because evaluation does not suggest that the idea can flourish and be realised. When we think of ideas and opportunities, it is therefore important to distinguish whether a market can be realised or not. If it is judged that a market cannot be realised the idea remains an idea. However, if it appears realistic that a market can be realised, the entrepreneur may take the initiative to develop the idea into an opportunity.

Entrepreneurship in practice

Now it is time to introduce a new real-life entrepreneurial story. This story is about one of the most successful and admired entrepreneurs in the world. It is the Starbucks case, which has been developed for this textbook by Saras Sarasvathy.

CASE STUDY

Serving the Starbucks coffee story

(Devised by Saras Sarasvathy)

In 2011, Starbucks Corporation owned and operated over 17,000 coffee shops and stores in 55 countries.

The first Starbucks store opened in Pike Place Market in Seattle in 1971. Inspired by another

CASE STUDY *(continued)*

gourmet coffee entrepreneur, Alfred Peet, three friends – English teacher Jerry Baldwin, history teacher Zev Siegl and writer Gordon Bowker – opened the shop to sell fine fresh-roasted coffee beans from around the world. Each founding partner invested a little over $1,000 and each also took out a bank loan of $5,000. The founders were fans of the American novel *Moby Dick* and named the store after the first mate on Captain Ahab's ship. In the early days, the founders purchased green coffee from Peet's and eventually began sourcing directly from coffee growers.

For about two decades bracketing the time the original Starbucks store was founded, coffee consumption in the US had been on a downward trend – declining from about three cups per capita per day in 1963 to two in the mid 1980s. Most people bought their undifferentiated mass-marketed coffee from grocery stores and had not even heard of speciality coffees from other countries. Also, in 1971, Seattle was facing a tough economic downturn called the Boeing Bust. Its largest employer, Boeing, had recently cut over 60,000 jobs and other industries were also in a slump. It is reported that a sign near the SeaTac airport read: 'Will the last person leaving Seattle turn out the lights?'

In this dismal economic climate and in the face of falling demand for coffee, Starbucks opened in the form of a narrow storefront in Pike Place Market. The founders of the little shop were not watching the trends, but wanting to fulfil their own desire for fine fresh-roasted coffee. Through frequent visits and conversations with Alfred Peet they had learned that imparting to their customers their own appreciation for good coffee involved educating them about its origins, aromas, flavours, preparation and different ways to enjoy it in their daily lives.

The current chairman, president and CEO of the company, Howard Schultz, was working for Hammarplast, a company that made everyday plastic products. In 1981, Schultz noticed that a little store in Seattle was buying increasingly large quantities of a rather simple plastic drip coffeemaker. He decided to investigate. Almost as soon as he got to know the founders and their passion for coffee, Schultz was drawn into becoming part of the enterprise. Here is how he describes what he felt on the plane flying back home from Seattle to New York after his first visit to Starbucks:

'I could feel the tug of Starbucks. There was something magic about it, a passion and authenticity I had never experienced in business. Maybe, just maybe, I could be part of that magic. Maybe I could help it grow. How would it feel like to build a business, as Jerry and Gordon were doing? How would it feel to own equity, not just collect a pay check? What could I bring to Starbucks that could make it even better than it was? The opportunities seemed as wide open as the land I was flying over'.

He joined the company a year later and a year after that visited Italy where he fell in love with the idea of a coffee-bar, the ambience, the romance and the notion of a place for conversation and community. But the original founders of Starbucks were not particularly enthralled about moving into the coffee-bar business. So Schultz started his own Il Giornale coffee-shops with investment from Ron Margolis, whom he calls 'the unlikeliest investor you could imagine'.

CASE STUDY *(continued)*

Margolis and Schultz were total strangers. But Schultz's wife knew Margolis and when she mentioned Schultz was in the process of starting a coffee-bar, Margolis expressed an interest in funding it. When Schultz met with Margolis, fully prepared with his business plan and eager to talk about financial projections, Margolis waved away the documents and only wanted to know about the details of Schultz's vision for the business. As Schultz describes it, 'The more I talked, the more enthusiastic I grew, until suddenly, Ron interrupted me, "How much do you need?" – and then proceeded to write a check for $100,000'.

He learned a lot in the process. He tried out several different features and offerings, many of which now form the core elements of the Starbucks experience, such as: the décor, the music, the Barista, the names for cup sizes on the menu, the ordering process and so on and so forth. Schultz made several changes in response to feedback, but also ignored feedback when he felt it might compromise the distinct identity he was trying to create. As he worked out the details in conjunction with customers, employees, investors and people in the community, he became increasingly convinced he wanted to purchase the original Starbucks company and wanted to name his growing chain the same.

When he sought to obtain financing to accomplish this, Schultz encountered every argument possible about why coffee could never be a growth industry. Here is the gist of his pitch to counter the arguments:

'What we proposed to do . . . was to reinvent a commodity. We would take something old and tired and common – coffee – and weave a sense of romance and community around it.

Figure 3.1 A Starbucks' cup ready for the coffee drinker

CASE STUDY *(continued)*

We would rediscover the mystique and charm that had swirled around coffee throughout the centuries. We would enchant customers with an atmosphere of sophistication and style and knowledge.

Nike is the only other company I know of that did something comparable. Sneakers were certainly a commodity – cheap and standard and practical and generally not very good. Nike's strategy was first to design world-class running shoes and then to create an atmosphere of top-flight athletic performance and witty irreverence around them. That spirit caught on so widely that it inspired myriads of non-athletes to lace up Nike shoes as well. Back in the 1970s, good sneakers cost $20 a pair. Who would have thought anyone would pay $140 for a pair of basketball shoes?'

In 1987, Schultz managed to raise enough funding from about 25 of over 240 people he talked to. Their investment enabled him to purchase the Starbucks brand. The rest is history, as they say.

Your immediate interpretation

The Starbucks story gives you an idea of the emergence of opportunities. How will you spontaneously interpret it? Here are some suggestions for what you might consider:

- You are going to write a letter to the editor of the local newspaper about the importance of opportunities. Why do you find them important? In light of the Starbucks story, how will you define an opportunity? Are both ideas and opportunities at play in the story and how?
- A reader asks: where do opportunities come from? With respect to the Starbucks story, how do you answer the reader's question? Another question posed by the reader is: who were the entrepreneurs who built Starbucks? What are they capable of doing which other people are not?
- Ask yourself: if Howard Schultz had not noticed the increase in sales of coffeemakers and gone to investigate, would he still have started Il Giornale or built some other highly successful company such as Starbucks? If yes, what would he have had to do differently?
- Think carefully: have you ever had an idea which you think has the potential of getting transformed into an opportunity? If your answer is yes – describe how you got the idea. And list three things you would do to transform it into an opportunity.

Theories of entrepreneurship

Theories of opportunities are generally about what the opportunities are, why, when and how they exist, what form they might take, and what role the entrepreneur plays in the process of their formation. Now we are going to take the bull by the horns and provide you with one or more perspectives on the nature of opportunities: it is not an easy task.

As in discussions about who the entrepreneur is, so there is also disagreement about what the opportunity is. Generally there are two perspectives on this issue. One emphasises that opportunities are around us all the time. They are just waiting for us to 'fall over' them – to discover them. On the other hand, the second perspective sees opportunities are something belonging to the future, which is *created* through the manner in which the individual acts and interacts with other people as well as his or her ability to reflect on these. Thus, opportunities do not exist independently of human activity and interference. This chapter introduces you to the two perspectives that form the paradox:

Discovered or created?

Opportunity versus idea

We began this chapter by noting that an opportunity is an idea that is evaluated as being able to create value for others and a market can be realized. The criteria for the evaluation are whether the idea is:

- anchored: bound to a product, a service or an experience that creates value for others;
- attractive: others are willing to pay for the value that represents the idea;
- at the right time and place: the environment is mature enough to receive the entrepreneur and his or her idea;
- capable of being done: the opportunity is practically feasible (Barringer & Ireland 2008).

The last point refers to the entrepreneur's possession of, or ability to acquire access to, the resources, expertise, legitimacy and knowledge required in order to make the idea of value to others. If the idea is evaluated as creating value for others (and not only for the entrepreneur him- or herself) to such an extent that others are willing to pay for the value, and it comes into existence at the right time and place, and it can be realised, the idea is considered to be a real opportunity. With that in mind, do you think that the diagram in Figure 3.2 is an image of an opportunity?

The figure illustrates how an opportunity is often differentiated from an ordinary idea – a thought. Ideas have the potential to become opportunities, but they do not meet the above criteria for an opportunity. You might have a really good idea, but all your competitors also have the same idea, and besides, the market may not be ready for your idea. As a result, the idea remains an idea, and it never turns into an opportunity. However, it is important to mention that it is often difficult to draw a clear dividing line between an idea and an opportunity. This is a fluid transition, which will also leave its mark on the discussions in this book.

The extent of intentions and capabilities

If one talks about opportunities, one should also discuss intentions. It doesn't really matter whether individuals have discovered or created opportunities if they do not intend to exploit them through organising. At the same time, one can argue that it is immaterial whether the individual has intentions to exploit an opportunity, if they have not discovered or created one, i.e. if they are not in possession of an opportunity.

This discussion was formally introduced by Bhave (1994), who identified two different paths to entrepreneurship. In the first path, the entrepreneurial process starts with the individual intending to start an organisation and then looking for an opportunity. In the second path, the entrepreneurial process begins with the individual, more or less randomly, discovering or creating an opportunity, after which the intention to exploit it develops. This way of thinking has already been touched upon in Chapter 2.

Bhave's (1994) deliberations identify that a society at any given time consists of a population where some have an intention to initiate entrepreneurship, some are in possession of an opportunity, some are in possession of both an opportunity and an intention, and some are in possession of either an opportunity or an intention. In 2004 the Danish team within the Global Entrepreneurship Monitor (GEM) (www.gemconsortium.org, last accessed 16 August 2016) collected data that points to the extent of opportunities and intentions within the Danish population. GEM is an international research project that aims to identify:

- correlations between a country's entrepreneurship activity and socio-economic growth;

Figure 3.2 Is this an opportunity?

Table 3.1 The extent to which opportunities and intentions are carried by Danes (percentage of the population)

		Opportunity		Opportunity
Intention	Yes	Yes		No
		Potential entrepreneurship 7 per cent		Waste of intention 3 per cent
Intention	No			
		Waste of opportunity 16 per cent		No entrepreneurship 74 per cent

Source: GEM Denmark (2004).

- how entrepreneurial activity varies across countries; and
- which national framework conditions encourage a country's entrepreneurial activities.

Over 60 countries have participated in GEM since the project began in the late 1990s. Data on entrepreneurship are collected annually in each of the participating countries. The most essential data collection is a population survey of a random sample of at least 2,000 adults. It is this data collected in 2004, to which we refer in Table 3.1 when determining the extent of opportunities and intentions in Denmark.

The table shows that approximately 74 per cent of the Danish population is completely uninvolved with entrepreneurship, while 7 per cent are in possession of an opportunity, which they intend to exploit; they are potential entrepreneurs. However, the two interesting categories are intention waste and opportunity waste: 3 per cent of the Danish population is located in the former category. These are people with the intention of starting an organisation, but who lack an opportunity to exploit. From a society's point of view this is a waste of intentions. In fact, about 30 per cent of Danes (3/(3 +7)), that intend to start an organisation are in need of a concrete opportunity.

The second interesting category is opportunity waste, where we find 16 per cent of the Danish population. People in this group are in possession of an opportunity, but they have no ambitions to exploit it through organising. A full 70 per cent of them (16/(7 +16)), have an opportunity that they do not intend to exploit. Again we can see a major waste from society's point of view. Thus, Table 3.1 clearly shows that the main loss in relation to Danish entrepreneurship is the lack of intention to exploit the opportunities that the Danes actually possess.

However, there is considerable international variation in both the extent of intentions and the extent of opportunities across countries. In the international GEM report of 2010 Kelley et al. (2011) show that the proportion of people who think there are good opportunities for starting a business in the area where they live varies greatly. They sketch out a pattern relative to the stage of economic development in countries. The less economically developed a country is, the greater the proportion of the population that believe there are good opportunities for starting a business. This immediately seems counter-intuitive – you would of course expect that there are more business opportunities in countries that are economically developed. However, according to Kelley et al (2011) this arises because the population in countries with different stages of development have different types of businesses in mind. In the less developed countries, such as Uganda, many of the business opportunities envisaged are necessity driven rather than opportunity driven, which is being further discussed in chapter 6. People start businesses because they have no other sources of income. It also means these necessity-based businesses are often less innovative and without growth potential.

One can therefore conclude that the waste of intention and waste of opportunity will vary across countries according to their economic development stage. But it is likely to be an important issue around the world.

Types of opportunities

In discussions about what an opportunity is and how it arises, two theorists are frequently referred to: Schumpeter (1934) and Kirzner (1973). As mentioned in Chapter 1, the core of Schumpeterian theory is that opportunities will emerge through new combinations of existing resources. They are also characterised by the fact that they break with the existing perceptions and ways of doing things. A fun example of how existing knowledge can be combined in producing something new is the story of an industrial designer who in 2000 took out a patent for a new type of bulletproof vest. The vest is based on the knowledge and study of insects. Some insects are soft on the inside, but have a robust and animated skeleton on the outside. The vest was designed according to those principles and thus broke with the existing construction of bulletproof vests. The industrial designer got the idea for the vest when he saw a programme on insects on the Discovery Channel. Therefore, by combining the existing knowledge of bulletproof vests with the knowledge of insects, the designer created a whole new, more flexible and comfortable vest.

On the other hand, Kirznerian opportunities are characterised by the entrepreneur's use of existing market information to see whether there are 'holes' in the market in terms of resources that can be used more efficiently than they are currently. In other words: is there potential value in the market that has not yet been optimally used by others? Here, the entrepreneur focuses on optimising and making the existing market effective. For example, the establishment of yet another hair salon on yet another street corner can be an example of a Kirznerian opportunity if the salon fills a potential market that has not yet been exploited. Figure 3.3 provides a simplified illustration of the differences between Schumpeterian and Kirznerian opportunities.

Figure 3.3 further elaborates the difference between the two types of opportunities from a market perspective. Schumpeterian opportunities can be understood as a violation of the existing balance that exists in markets, because they break with existing ways of doing things. It follows that an opportunity in the Schumpeterian sense need not occur because the existing market has a need for the new opportunity. The opportunity arises because existing knowledge is recombined, creating development in the light of the known market. In some cases, the new opportunity, as mentioned in Chapter 1, even reorganises entire industries.

Kirznerian opportunities, however, can be illustrated as a compensation for disequilibrium and are instrumental in creating a balance in the markets. Often, the equilibrium in markets occurs when unmet needs are suddenly covered by new opportunities. For example, an entrepreneur may discover how a hitherto very costly product can be made cheaper or faster. Therefore, the Kirznerian opportunity will not be innovative in the same manner as a Schumpeterian opportunity. It is instead helping to provide equilibrium in the markets.

We can conclude that Kirznerian and Schumpeterian opportunities play different roles in the market. However, they can also be seen as complementary approaches to opportunities. While Schumpeterian opportunities create imbalance in the market, Kirznerian opportunities bring the market back into equilibrium. Therefore, Figure 3.4 is drawn as a ring.

Figure 3.3 Schumpeterian versus Kirznerian opportunity

Discovering opportunities

Now we're going to look at the process that leads to a new opportunity. The Kirznerian opportunity can be said to be objective in nature. It is simply a part of our environment (profit gaps in the market) just waiting to be discovered. The concept of objectivity refers to the fact that the opportunity exists independently of human intervention, time and place. It follows that we can take it for granted that opportunities exist as part of our world despite the fact that we are not always aware of them. Shane and Venkataraman put it that: '. . . the opportunities themselves are objective phenomenon that are not known to all parties at all times. For example, the discovery of the telephone created new opportunities for communication, whether or not people discovered those opportunities' (Shane & Venkataraman 2000: 220).

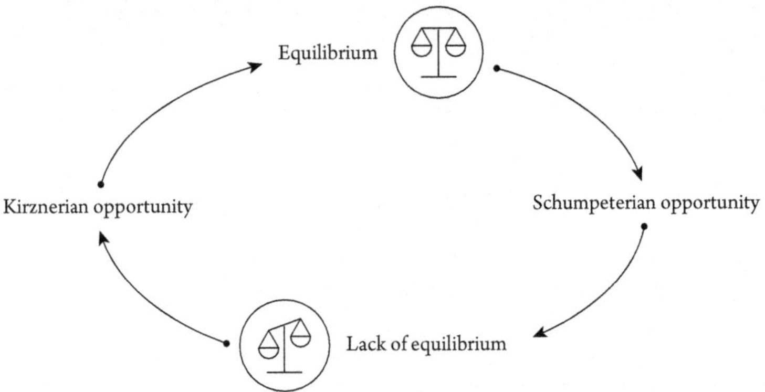

Figure 3.4 Two perceptions of opportunities

However, if opportunities are objective, why don't we all 'fall over' them? Why do only some individuals in our society spot the opportunities? The answer to this question is multi-faceted. Some entrepreneurs proactively seek opportunities. However, many opportunities emerge as a result of the entrepreneur discovering an opportunity without consciously seeking it. Kirzner introduces the concept of 'alertness' to capture this type of discovery. The term refers to: 'the ability to notice, without search, opportunities that have hitherto been overlooked' (Kirzner 1979: 48). We might say that 'alertness' refers to a kind of built-in alarm system within the entrepreneur that responds to unforeseen opportunities that he or she then turns his or her attention to more or less unconsciously and involuntarily. This entrepreneur discovers new opportunities without actively searching for them.

However, if we continue with the discussion about 'alertness' the question remains as to whether all people have a constant preparedness for opportunities, or whether some people are more likely to discover opportunities than others. In this context Shane and Venkataraman state that: 'recognition of entrepreneurial opportunities is a subjective process' (Shane & Venkataraman 2000: 220). This means that although the opportunity is objective, the discovery of the opportunity is linked to the individual. For example, the individual's information and experience in a particular field will, in most cases, lead to a greater degree of awareness of solutions and new ways of tackling challenges. Shane (2000) examines this by allowing a group of entrepreneurs with diverse backgrounds to see the same technology. They arrived at very different ways of looking at the technology as a potential opportunity, depending on the information and experience they possessed.

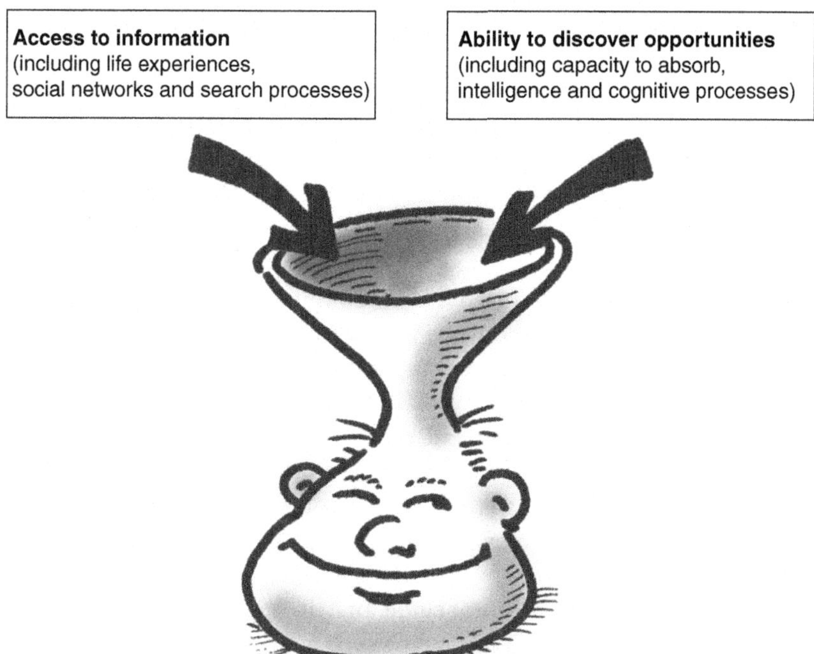

Source: Inspired by Shane (2003).

Figure 3.5 The individual and opportunity discovery

Figure 3.5 illustrates the opportunity discovery process of the individual.

The figure emphasises that access to information is important to opportunity discovery, and explains that such access will depend on our life experience, social networks and our efforts to seek opportunities. Research shows that the more people seek out opportunities, the more likely it is that they discover an opportunity. Additionally, the figure indicates that our ability to discover opportunities depends on our absorptive capacity (i.e., our ability to interpret information in a useful manner, for example, to see solutions to the problems we face), intelligence and cognitive processes. The latter refers to the fact that we all have a different cognitive set-up, which according to Chapter 2 refers to how the entrepreneur understands and thinks about what is taking place in his/her environment and within him-/herself. The perception of opportunities will then be different between entrepreneurs, depending on how his or her brain works. Entrepreneurs typically see an opportunity more optimistically than others and act faster on the opportunity than others despite the lack of information because they possess an inner belief that the opportunity has potential.

Creating opportunities

If you believe that opportunities are not objective phenomena in our surroundings, there's nothing to discover: many share this belief. Opportunities are not 'concrete realities waiting to be noticed, discovered, or observed by entrepreneurs' (Gartner et al 2003: 104). Instead, opportunities are something created by humans: 'opportunities and markets have to be invented, fabricated, constructed, made' (Sarasvathy 2008: 181). Without human intervention, there would be no opportunities. They talk about opportunities as subjective realities. As we see it, Schumpeterian opportunities are examples of the fact that human action is pivotal to the creation of opportunities. They are not based on existing information on markets, prices, consumer preferences, etc. Instead, what is central is the human ability to act creatively, by creating new combinations, where creativity refers to the ability to think innovative thoughts. In addition, this perspective suggests that the interaction between people plays a role in the creation of opportunities.

We can therefore conclude that if opportunities are not objective phenomena, they can instead be seen as social constructs, which are created in everyday life through entrepreneurs' interaction with others, their contexts and themselves. On this subject, Fletcher says: 'entrepreneurial activities, features, and characteristics are not "objects" given a fixed or static ontological status as they come into being. Instead, they are dynamic and constantly emerging, being realized, shaped and constructed through social processes' (Fletcher 2003: 127). Instead of seeing opportunities as objective truths that are present at all times and potentially visible to all, they are an everyday phenomenon. 'We need to recognize that the entrepreneurial activities of everyday life have a great capacity to move us in new and unexpected directions' (Boutaiba 2004: 24). Figure 3.6 is an illustration of how opportunities are created in the interaction between the entrepreneur, other people and their contexts in daily life.

Often our daily interaction leads to the reproduction of things that already exist. Humans can to a great extent be controlled by routine. But sometimes something new occurs, such as a new opportunity. Figure 3.6 shows, indirectly, how opportunity creation is not merely a matter of discovering an optimal opportunity. Because opportunity creation is based on daily interactions, the key point instead is: what occurs here and now? What can be done? What makes sense in light of the current situation? Is it possible? In other words opportunity creation is very much a pragmatic part of everyday life.

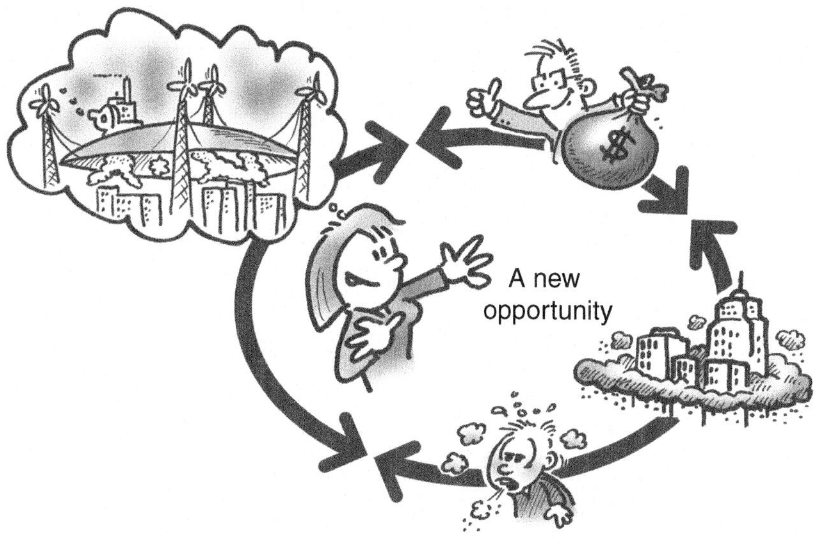

Figure 3.6 A model of opportunity creation

Listen, for example, to the story of how the opportunity linked to eBay was born. The entrepreneur behind eBay says:

> So people often say to me – 'when you built the system, you must have known that making it self-sustainable was the only way eBay could grow to serve 40 million users a day'. Well . . . nope. I made the system self-sustaining for one reason: Back when I launched eBay on Labor Day 1995, eBay was not my business – it was my hobby. I had to build a system that was self-sustaining . . . Because I had a real job to go to every morning, I was working as a software engineer from 10 to 7, and I wanted to have a life on the weekends. So I built a system that could keep working – catching complaints and capturing feedback – even when Pam and I were out mountain-biking, and the only one home was our cat. (Sarasvathy 2008: 189)

The story is a good example of how opportunity can arise as a result of everyday interactions. The entrepreneur is trying to create an opportunity that can be achieved in light of the other people he interacts with (Pam) and his context (his work). At the beginning he did not know that the opportunity would end up with eBay, as we know it today. He started only in a small way, to create an opportunity, and he took his starting point in everyday challenges.

Last but not least, it follows from the above that opportunities are constantly evolving. Opportunities change constantly as a result of the interaction.

Table 3.2 The paradox: Discovered or created

	Discovered	Created
Opportunity character	Objectively given unit in the environment	Dependent on the interactions of the individual
Opportunity emergence	Involves discovery	Involves creation
Opportunity source	The individual who is attentive towards existing market information	The individual who creates by means of his or her creativity
Opportunity status	The opportunity is stable	The opportunity is dynamic
Opportunity type	Kirznerian hole in the market	Schumpeterian market ruption

Opportunity creation is a process where the entrepreneur does not necessarily determine the development. The entrepreneur is just one of many actors who have influence on the process.

Opportunities: discovered or created?

The focus of this chapter has been a review of two perspectives on opportunities. One perspective argues that opportunities are discovered, while the second perspective sees opportunities as being created. Table 3.2 summarises the two perspectives that make up the paradox: discovered or created.

As shown in Table 3.2, the discovery perspective views opportunities as given objects in the environment. Their formation involves the individual's discovery of 'holes' in the market in the form of untapped resources. This makes clear that the source of opportunity is the individual's awareness of current market information. It is assumed that the opportunity discovered remains the same over time – it is stable. In terms of type, this form of opportunity is Kirznerian.

On the other hand, the creation perspective views opportunities as being closely linked to the individual's actions. The individual is again rooted in a social context, which is why he or she interacts with others and the environment in general. All of this contributes to the creation of opportunities and emphasises that the process of emergence requires the intervention of a creative individual. Since the process that creates opportunities is a result of interacting elements (such as the entrepreneur him-/herself, other individuals and their contexts), the opportunity is constantly changing – it is dynamic. This perspective refers partly to Schumpeter's thoughts on the opportunities as new creative combinations of the existing order.

If you think it makes no sense to see opportunities as being either created or discovered, you can choose to take the same stance as Sarasvathy et al (2002). They stress that some opportunities 'lie buried in the soil waiting to be dug out by the alert individual. Yet, others require several stakeholders, including founding entrepreneurs to act effectually to "create" them (or nurture them into being) in a dynamic and interactive process of contingency, design and negotiation' (Sarasvathy et al 2002: 2). Opportunities are thus not necessarily a question of 'either/or'. There are perhaps both opportunities requiring discovery and opportunities requiring creation.

A theoretical interpretation

There are many interpretations of one story. What follows are two different interpretations of the Starbucks story that began this chapter, in light of the discovery and creation perspectives.

The discovery perspective

Viewed through the discovery perspective the Starbucks story is basically about an existing and available market opportunity which, yet, has not been discovered – it is untouched. Selling fresh-roasted quality coffee represents some unexploited value, a 'hole' in the market. The three original founders of Starbucks seem to have spotted this 'hole' more by luck than judgement. They just follow their dream. Yet, it can be argued that the CEO of a company selling plastic products, Howard Schultz, represents the alert Kirznerian entrepreneur of the Starbucks story. His alert capabilities make him constantly scan the market for opportunities. Being attuned to changes in the market, he discovers that a small store in Seattle is buying an increasingly number of plastic drip coffeemakers.

The alertness of Schulz seems to unfold rather unconsciously. After all, he is not actively searching for opportunities, and it is only after meeting the original Starbucks trio that he begins to dream of building a new organisation. He wonders: 'How would it feel to own equity, not just collect a pay check?' It is especially Schulz's professional experiences, knowledge and access to information on the plastic product market combined with competences to interpret this information and turn it into a valuable opportunity that makes him discover the Starbucks opportunity. In this manner, he spots what others did not spot.

Although the three founders have done some of the work in terms of formulating the opportunity, Schulz does not just imitate what they are doing.

Based on further market analysis of the special roasted coffee business and the idea that coffee is not just a hot and dark beverage – it is an entire ritual – Schulz digs deeper into the opportunity 'hole'. Especially, inspired by Italian coffee-bars he finds inspiration to a large-scale development of the opportunity. In this way, Schulz extends the original Starbucks opportunity and opens up for the opportunity to grow to a massive international success despite many critics argue that coffee cannot be a growth industry.

The creation perspective

It is also possible to perceive the Starbucks case through the creation perspective. Then it is a story about the Starbucks opportunity as emerging from a process of creation, imagination and social interaction. After all, there are no trends in the market – at the point in time of the establishment of the first Starbucks shop – which suggest that opening such a shop will be a success. On the contrary, the market shows no need for fine coffee, thus, there is no opportunity to discover.

Rather than taking departure in the existent market, the three founders invent the Starbucks opportunity using their creativity, imagination, own vision and taste. It shows that the opportunity is indeed a result of subjective processes. Since there are no market trends to watch and they hold little professional knowledge of fine-roasted coffee, the trio very much interact with an experienced gourmet coffee entrepreneur, Alfred Peet, to form the opportunity. In this way, the opportunity is from the beginning emerging from social interaction.

Yet, the creation perspective is particularly apparent from Howard Schulz's activities. His is innovating the original Starbucks opportunity through additional creative thinking and social interaction. Combining the original concept with a wealth of experiences, ideas, etc. emerging from his visits to Italy, and everyday interactions with investors, customers, employees, own imagination of future needs, etc., Schulz reinvents coffee as a commodity. The process reflects that opportunity creation is a dynamic and continuously evolving process of social interaction. Opportunities are not fixed or permanent.

Schulz's innovative efforts turn a coffee industry, focused on mass-marketed coffee from grocery stores, upside down. He builds a completely new and unique culture around coffee, appealing to millions of people around the globe. Transforming an industry as we knew it, Schulz is a Schumpeterian entrepreneur who carries out creative destruction.

Above, you find two interpretations of the Starbucks start-up process based on the perspectives: discovered or created. Yet, the author behind the Starbucks case, Saras Sarasvathy, suggests a third interpretation derived from the effectuation perspective. In this book, you learn about effectuation theory in Chapter 5. This perspective puts forward that idea that the emergence of opportunities is not a matter of either discovery or creation. Saras explains in a private communication:

> Both discovery and creation processes go into transforming ideas into opportunities. If the original founders had not acted on their personal passion for better coffee and the inspiration they found from Alfred Peet, Howard Schultz may have had nothing to 'discover', at least not in the speciality coffee business. Yet, if Schultz had not been 'alert' to the increased sale of coffee machines and followed up with an investigation, his desire for becoming an entrepreneur and his ambition to achieve great success may not have been given an outlet for action. Also, even after he 'discovered' Starbucks, he had to do a lot of 'creation' to get it to be the opportunity it is today. Everything he did in building and growing Il Giornale involved discovery (about the tastes and preferences and pains and prejudices of all his stakeholders including customers, suppliers, employees and investors) as well as large amounts of co-creation – these stakeholders actively participated in forming the identity of the company that is embodied in its brand and consists in its main asset.

Sarasvathy furthermore outlines that whereas new opportunities emerge from unique mixtures of discovery and creation, the action of the entrepreneur is always effectuated action. Sarasvathy explains it this way: effectuated action involves entrepreneurs' interactions 'with other people and with the objective environment around them in ways that end up transforming the people they interact with into stakeholders who in turn reshape and co-create the environments around them' (Sarasvathy et al 2008).

Testing the theory

It's time for you to get back on track. Make sure you keep the above theories and discussions in mind when you are out in the field carrying out your own tests on opportunities and their emergence.

? EXERCISES

1 **Study of technological progress and opportunities.** Search the Internet. Make a list of three major technological advances that have occurred since you began your education. Describe two opportunities that have emerged in the wake of these advances. Can you come up with additional opportunities that have arisen as a result of these advances, but have not, as yet, been exploited?

2 **New case study.** Find an article – any newspaper article or a magazine article – about an entrepreneur. If this is not possible then interview an entrepreneur you know. Analyse how the entrepreneur's opportunity emerged, making reference to the above theories and discussions.
3 **Draw your opportunity library.** It appears from this chapter that your identification of new opportunities depends, among other things, on the information that you already possess. Information may be a result of your life experience, education, your spare time, your hobbies or socializing with friends, classmates, family, etc. Take a piece of paper. Draw your brain. Imagine your brain as a library with a lot of books that contain the information that you possess. Now type the names of the books: are they about gardening, football or arithmetic? Now assess the combination of the library's books and determine what opportunities you have the potential to discover or create.

LITERATURE

Barringer, B.R. & Ireland, R.D. (2008) *Entrepreneurship: Successfully Launching New Ventures*, Upper Saddle River, NJ: Prentice Hall.

Bhave, M.P. (1994) 'A process model of new venture creation', *Journal of Business Venturing*, 9, 223–242.

Boutaiba, S. (2004) 'A moment in time', in Hjorth, D. & Steyaert, C. (eds) *New Movements in Entrepreneurship*, Cheltenham, UK and Northampton, MA, USA: Edward Elgar Publishing, 22–57.

Fletcher, D.E. (2003) 'Framing organisational emergence: Discourse, identity, and relationship', in Hjorth, D. & Steyaert, C. (eds) *New Movements in Entrepreneurship*, Cheltenham, UK and Northampton, MA, USA: Edward Elgar Publishing, 9–46.

Gartner, W.B., Carter, N.M. & Hills, G.E. (2003) 'The language of opportunity' in Hjorth, D. & Steyaert, C. (eds) *New Movements in Entrepreneurship*, Cheltenham, UK and Northampton, MA, USA: Edward Elgar Publishing, 103–125.

Kelley, D., Bosma, N. & Amoros, J.E. (2011) *Global Entrepreneurship Monitor – 2010 Global Report*, GERA/Babson College.

Kirzner, I. (1973) *Competition and Entrepreneurship*, Chicago, IL: University of Chicago Press.

Kirzner, I. (1979) *Perception, Opportunity, and Profit*, Chicago, IL: University of Chicago Press.

Sarasvathy, S.D. (2008) *Effectuation: Elements of Entrepreneurial Expertise*, Cheltenham, UK and Northampton, MA, USA: Edward Elgar Publishing.

Sarasvathy, S.D., Dew, N., Velamuri, S.R. & Venkataraman, S. (2002) 'A testable typology of entrepreneurial opportunity: Extensions of Shane & Venkataraman (2000)', working paper, University of Maryland and University of Virginia.

Sarasvathy, S.D., Dew, N., Read, S. & Wiltbank, R. (2008) 'Designing organizations that design environments: Lessons from entrepreneurial expertise', *Organization Studies*, 29(3), 331–350.

Schumpeter, J.A. (1934) *The Theory of Economic Development*, Cambridge, MA: Harvard University Press.

Shane, S. (2000) 'Prior knowledge and the discovery of entrepreneurial opportunities', *Organization Science*, 11(4), 448–469.

Shane, S. (2003) *A General Theory of Entrepreneurship: The Individual-Opportunity Nexus*, Cheltenham, UK and Northampton, MA, USA: Edward Elgar Publishing.

Shane, S. & Venkataraman, S. (2000) 'The promise of entrepreneurship as a field of research', *Academy of Management Review*, 25(1), 217–226.

4

Evaluation of opportunities

Opportunity evaluation is a key theme in entrepreneurship. An entrepreneur cannot simply expect that the opportunity and the organisational effort he or she plans to make in order to exploit it will be viewed by the market as attractive and in the right place at the right time. It is not certain that the market can and will fulfil the value that the opportunity and its organisational implementation represents. The opportunity may simply prove to be unprofitable. Therefore, the entrepreneurial process involves the evaluation of each opportunity, whereby the entrepreneur seeks to determine whether the idea that he or she intends to pursue, creates value in the eyes of the market and can thus be considered as a real, strong and feasible option. You could say, 'evaluation is the key to differentiate an idea from an opportunity' (Keh et al 2002: 126). Entrepreneurs normally have no difficulty in generating new ideas, but far from all ideas are actually opportunities, and it is often particularly interesting for the entrepreneur to assess whether the idea represents an economically viable option, at least in the long term.

As mentioned in Chapter 3, it can often be difficult, conceptually, to determine whether you are dealing with an idea or an opportunity. The transition from an idea to an opportunity is a broad and grey area. Therefore, there may be many situations where you think that the wrong term is being used. For example, some may argue that this chapter should be called 'evaluation of ideas' and not 'evaluation of opportunities'. It is therefore important to read the chapter flexibly with regard to the concepts of 'opportunity' and 'idea' and just remember that evaluation is the very process where the entrepreneur seeks to assess whether the idea represents an opportunity or not.

Entrepreneurship in practice

Now, let's move into the Danish fashion scene and meet an entrepreneur who has greatly helped to define that scene. The entrepreneur's name is Naja Munthe and the organisation called Munthe plus Simonsen. Here is the story of the organisation's start-up. In particular, note how Naja and her partner Karen evaluate the potential of their idea, both initially and during the process. How do they find out whether it is viable and represents a real entrepreneurial opportunity that creates attractive value to others?

CASE STUDY

'The sky is the limit'

(Devised by the authors)

Naja and Karen had a very successful start to their entrepreneurial journey. Their clothing line was a tremendous success, more or less from the beginning. Customers wanted the luxury bohemian style Naja and Karen delivered. Naja said: 'We rode on a wave of success, where, basically, we couldn't do anything wrong . . . Karen was always saying: "The sky is the limit" and I thought that was kind of cool, because then there were no limits. It became our motto'. However, the outward tempestuous journey filled with success turned and moved in a more sombre and negative direction in 2006. Munthe plus Simonsen was threatened with bankruptcy and went into administration. Had Naja and Karen's idea not, after all, had what it takes to survive in the market?

Figure 4.1 Naja Munthe and Karen Simonsen

CASE STUDY *(continued)*

Next stop the big city

Naja and Karen met each other in the 1990s as students at the Design School in Kolding (Denmark's seventh largest town), where they quickly became friends and worked closely together. After graduation, neither of them had any specific career plans. One cold winter day in 1994 Karen, who had found herself a boyfriend in Copenhagen (the capital of Denmark) asked: 'Shall we go to Copenhagen and start a company?' Naja nodded yes, although she also points out: 'It was not very prudent. We did not have definite and finely-honed plans for what we should do'. They formally established a business but it was not based on a clear idea. Instead, they filled their time with whatever jobs they got offered: 'We started basically from one end and offered our services for all kinds of things'. The two girls worked as TV presenters, stylists, writers, lecturers and much more.

Themselves as customer

In parallel with undertaking these jobs, Naja and Karen put together their first clothing collection in 1995 without any careful thought as to the potential customer group: 'When we designed our very first collection, we didn't think about who our end customer was. For very many years, we used ourselves as a target group. We only thought about what we liked'.

Therefore, it is not surprising that Naja and Karen tried to sell their first collection by calling their favourite, nationally renowned shop, Norgaard, in central Copenhagen. However, it was necessary to call several times since the store's staff did not seem particularly interested in what the two young designers had to offer. Eventually the staff became tired of their many calls, and gave them a minute to present their clothes, but they were not to expect anything to come from it. The proprietor of the store ended up buying their entire collection. That experience taught Naja: 'Never take no for an answer. You have to go on and on. One thing you can be confident of, out there in the real world is that there are a lot of doors that are closed'.

A couple of dressmakers?

The two young girls experienced many difficulties in opening the doors. The Danish fashion industry was at this point in its own fledgling start-up phase, and Naja and Karen met the challenge of helping to create and shape the industry as a whole. They had no one to lean on. There were no role models or precedents to guide them. With no guide, they were left to find their first supplier through the yellow pages, which ended up with them accidentally hiring a cushion factory to sew their first collection. 'When we opened the door to the factory we were greeted by a sight we had not imagined. They made plastic cushions for homes, and the last thing they knew about was making clothes'. It was not easy to attract media attention in an attempt to market the collection either. Naja says: 'Also in relation to the media, which is how you make a living these days, it was extremely difficult to get any attention, particularly as a designer. We were just seen as a couple of blond dressmakers who sat around stitching together dresses for ourselves'.

As a result of their enormous drive and fighting spirit Naja and Karen did, after all, manage to push through the barriers. They knew how to draw attention to themselves and their products

CASE STUDY *(continued)*

through a lifestyle where only the best is good enough, and through promotion of their own expression rather than a commercial expression. 'We made it a point of honour not to be commercial . . . We were not focused on an end-user, or whether things were economically viable'. So when Magasin (a major Danish department store) approached them with a desire to promote their products, they said no. Magasin is too commercial.

In the early years, their lifestyle and 'only the sky is the limit' philosophy led to Naja and Karen buying a lot of expensive furniture, renting 1,600 m^2 of office space, opening stores and setting up showrooms in the heart of the most dominant fashion cities and hiring expensive models. For example, they hired Cindy Crawford for one of their campaigns. These activities were successful in marketing terms. They received a lot of positive feedback in the form of high earnings and various Danish prizes such as the branding award of the year, and Naja was awarded the prize for being the year's Danish businesswoman. However, the success would unfortunately end.

Suspension of payments

'If you are employed as a checkout assistant at a supermarket and drink champagne every night, at some point in time your income will not be quite in proportion with your consumption. The same thing happened to us'. In 2006, Naja and Karen were staring bankruptcy in the face and subjected to a suspension of payments. According to Naja, there are several explanations for things going wrong, such as poor business insight, lack of counselling, evaluation of the market, and a number of stupid errors. An example of the latter is that they forgot to cater for an expense of 1 million Danish kroner (approximately US$200,000) in postage for sending out a Cindy Crawford catalogue.

Naja and Karen used the suspension of payments crisis as a timeout to think about how to create a more robust business structure with a balance between revenues and expenditures. After receiving a capital injection they rolled up their sleeves and cut back in every imaginable area of the organisation. 'We shut that one down, we have to dismiss them, we make savings here, we cancel this showroom. Can we afford this? Yes, but only 50 per cent'. Naja and Karen began to think more economically, commercially and strategically about how they could optimise the organisation through 'lean business'. 'There was clearly a greater focus now on earnings and managing an economically viable business . . . There was also greater emphasis on not being so egocentric in our expression. We were still faithful to what we are, but we also thought about others . . . thinking commercially and about the end-user'. Nevertheless, they still didn't undertake any formal market research to understand who the customers were. Information about core clients was picked up, for example, through distributors, employees and vendors. These same stakeholders were also involved in redefining Munthe plus Simonsen's design line.

Last but not least, Naja and Karen began using the franchise organisational model, rather than owning shops. In this way they spread the risk and involved people with local business knowledge about who buys their products, where and why.

CASE STUDY *(continued)*

Postscript of a divorce

In 2009, Naja and Karen chose to end the long marriage between them within the fashion industry. Karen was bought out by Naja (still using the company name Munthe plus Simonsen) and started up for herself. Naja faced the challenge of continuing one of the most influential design brands in the Danish fashion industry and she now sets – especially in light of the financial crisis – business acumen and market rules high on the agenda rather than the champagne approach guided primarily by personal preferences. Naja and Karen both seem to have found a way forward after the divorce, but they've also learned a lot from Munthe plus Simonsen's very turbulent and challenging journey.

Your immediate interpretation

Now it's your turn to get involved. Think about the Munthe plus Simonsen story and give your interpretation of how Naja and Karen evaluated whether their idea was valuable in light of the market and hence whether the idea represented a real opportunity. Below are some prompts for reflection, which can help you interpret the story:

- A well-known newspaper gives you the task of writing an article on how Naja and Karen evaluated whether their idea represented a profitable opportunity. What would you focus on? Did they evaluate the idea at all? If yes, what characterises the evaluation process?
- Your description is so convincing that Naja and Karen immediately appoint you as their personal adviser. What recommendations do you give them as to how they can streamline their evaluation of an idea in the future? Undertake the task as follows. First list two or three positive aspects of the way they have so far evaluated opportunities. Then list two or three negative features associated with their evaluation process. Finally, give your opinions on how they can turn the negative aspects into something positive and improve their evaluation processes in the future.
- One day Naja comes past your office. She is considering conducting a market analysis of core customers and competitors. The analysis must support an assessment of the feasibility of a particular idea, including how that idea can be adapted, modified, etc., so it better reflects market conditions. Provide suggestions as to what evaluation-related advantages and disadvantages may be associated with performing such an analysis.

Theories of entrepreneurship

As you read the literature on entrepreneurship, you will quickly discover that opportunity emergence and organising are two key issues. Discussions about opportunity evaluation are less noticeable. 'Little is known about how entrepreneurs actually evaluate opportunities' (Keh et al 2002: 125). That we know no more about this subject is a mystery when you consider how central it is to the entrepreneurial process. After all, the evaluation tells the entrepreneur whether he or she can expect the idea to become an economically viable opportunity, or what the entrepreneur must do to achieve it. Finally, the evaluation is in many ways a bridge between the emergence and organising of opportunities since it tells the entrepreneur whether it makes sense to use resources to pursue this opportunity by organising activities.

Based on the existing literature about how opportunities are evaluated in the entrepreneurial process, we will highlight two perspectives on opportunity evaluation, which make up this chapter's paradox: instrumental or legitimate.

The first and most familiar perspective emphasises how opportunity evaluation is a means to achieve a particular result or goal. Different formal business administration techniques and methods are needed to assess the extent to which it is possible to achieve the goal. As mentioned, the goal is often to create a profitable organisation that can survive in the market. Thus, evaluation is perceived to be an instrumental and decisive action. The evaluation process is characterised by the entrepreneur systematically pursuing specific and predefined rules of analysis.

Conversely, we find the 'legitimacy perspective', which emphasises that the creation of legitimacy is essential for the evaluation of options. According to this perspective, the entrepreneur's success depends on whether he or she can get others (including the entrepreneur's organisation) to accept the opportunity as being valuable and attractive. If successful, the entrepreneur may rightly judge that the idea represents an opportunity. The entrepreneur will evaluate this opportunity positively.

When a new idea occurs, its legitimacy is typically low because it is unknown. This is known in the scientific literature on the topic as 'liability of newness'. Therefore, the entrepreneur's challenge is to find market players that will support the idea with, among other things, resources. This requires legitimacy – that others accept it as a valid opportunity in a market context. Without legitimacy, the idea could not be considered a real opportunity, because it cannot be realised. The legitimisation process is fundamentally a social process in which the entrepreneur, through interaction with the market, achieves an impression of whether the idea represents an opportunity or not. Systematic analysis is not employed and social interaction determines how the evaluation process unfolds and its outcome. Rather than a formal evaluation process with a specific start and end point, it is more one of continuous evaluation, which takes place as a natural part of everyday entrepreneurial processes, and which the entrepreneur makes more or less unconsciously or strategically.

The paradox that will be explored in this chapter on opportunity evaluation, is therefore whether the evaluation is:

Instrumental or legitimate?

What is evaluation?

Traditionally, evaluation is defined as 'the systematic determination of merit, worth, and significance of something or someone using criteria against a set of standards' (Hindle 2010: 108). Generally, evaluation can take many forms (classical evaluation, impact evaluation, user evaluation, etc.). An example of a well-known evaluation tool is cost–benefit analysis, where the effects are evaluated in light of the costs. We often associate evaluation with a retrospective and systematic assessment of performance and processes that have been associated with a given activity; for example, evaluation of a government initiative that has run over a period of years. Has the initiative been accomplished in accordance with the set targets in terms of the direct and indirect resource consumption? So, evaluations are often carried out in connection with something that has already been undertaken. Moreover, the activity being evaluated needs clearly established goals. However, the reasons for undertaking an evaluation vary greatly and may be for the purpose of control, documentation, legitimation, strategic manoeuvre or learning.

The process of evaluating entrepreneurial opportunities differs in significant ways from the typical evaluation process. The evaluation aims to determine whether the concept represents a future attractive option in a market that may not even exist yet and this makes the idea's evaluation and development difficult to predict. Within entrepreneurship we are therefore faced with a challenging, forward-looking evaluation (ex-ante), not a retrospective evaluation (ex-post). It's about visualising and predicting the future to determine whether the idea can form the basis for a profitable and sustainable organisation. 'The entrepreneur must forecast future prices and goods and resources and use intuitive judgement to gauge market potential' (Keh et al 2002: 130), and he or she has limited access to information on past performance, such as the development in sales figures.

In entrepreneurship, the purpose of evaluation is not to verify or substantiate something that has already happened, but to assess the future potential of an idea. This makes the evaluation process more uncertain, complex and risky. The decision to implement an opportunity is made in a situation where the entrepreneur does not know the future conditions (uncertainty) and he or she must take into account many factors (complexity). Uncertainty is closely associated with risk. The entrepreneur's perception of risk associated with an entrepreneurial project is therefore an important element in the evaluation process. If he or she determines that the risk is low, the probability of the project's realisation will be high and vice-versa.

This shows that the assessment of whether an idea is valuable for others and feasible is, in essence, a cognitive and emotional process, meaning that it takes place in the minds of the entrepreneur (Grichnik et al 2010). The entrepreneur may seek other people's advice to support the process or utilise various tools, but ultimately it is his or her decision. Since cognition varies from person to person, two people with the same idea and in the same situation may very well end up taking different decisions. One may be more optimistic and willing to take a risk than the other and therefore seek to pursue an opportunity from which the other refrains.

Finally, the entrepreneurial evaluation characterised by the need for, and extent of, the necessary evaluation activities vary according to the idea's complexity and unique circumstances. Consequently there are more questions to answer when evaluating an idea for 'new high-tech equipment for offshore structures' than the idea of 'a home delivery service for breakfast rolls and bread'.

The instrumental evaluation

The instrumental perspective is the most widespread in the literature (textbooks, research articles, reports, etc.) on the evaluation of opportunities. Perhaps this is because the perspective, in a situation filled with uncertainty and risk, provides the entrepreneur with some clear and simple guidance on how he or she can evaluate and even predict whether an idea is or may become profitable. Basically, the instrumental perspective consists of a series of tools and guidelines to gather information that can support the evaluation process. The tools and guidelines are rational and analytical in nature. By applying these, the entrepreneur, expects to gain insight into whether the idea represents a real present/future opportunity or not, including whether the opportunity is attractive to the entrepreneur him-/herself given his/her unique expertise, resources and circumstances (Haynie et al 2009). In other words, the instrumental perspective seeks to give the entrepreneur control over the evaluation process with the entrepreneur's own situation as a starting point. Such an evaluation is believed to enable the entrepreneur to assess in advance whether he or she can achieve his/her goals before the actual organising of the opportunity is begun. It reflects how evaluation according to the instrumental perspective is something that happens before the actual entrepreneurial activity and the decision to exploit the opportunity: well before the entrepreneur seriously commits to involving other actors (such as investors), arranges access to resources (such as capital) and establishes technology (such as machinery). Haynie et al write: 'Evaluations of opportunity attractiveness – that is, the potential of the opportunity to generate competitive advantages and entrepreneurial returns to the firm – likely proceed and are separate from the decision to exploit' (Haynie et al 2009: 338).

The instrumental collection of evidence to underpin the evaluation takes place as an analytical process where the entrepreneur is recommended to divide the evaluation into areas. There is no consensus on which areas are key, but a good proposal comes from Barringer and Ireland (2010). They suggest that the entrepreneur should specifically focus on four areas:

- product/service;
- the market/industry;
- organisation;
- financing.

The evaluation's main interests are therefore: are customers interested in the entrepreneur's product/service? Is there room in the market for such a product/service in light of competitors, market trends, etc.? How must the entrepreneur organise him-/herself to reach customers? What financial resources are necessary to realise the idea? Of these areas, some researchers consider evaluation of the market/industry as particularly important: 'Unquestionably, the analysis of the industry and market in which the business will operate is the most important analysis of the entire feasibility study. Without customers – without an industry and market that are receptive to the business concept – there is no business' (Allen 2006: 90).

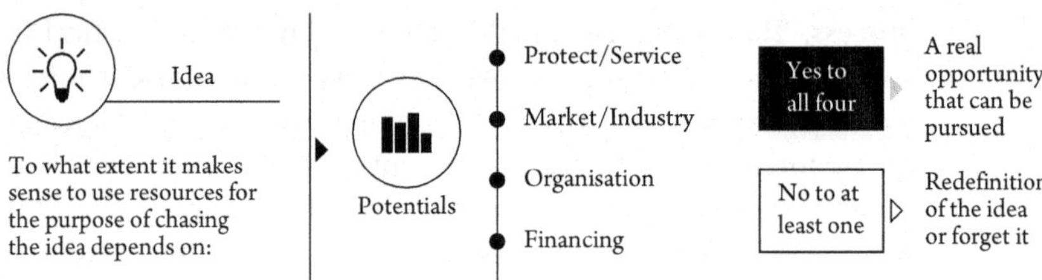

Source: Inspired by Barringer & Ireland (2010).

Figure 4.2 A procedural model of opportunity evaluation

Typically, the evaluation will follow certain pre-defined phases. Based on Barringer and Ireland's key areas above, a procedural model might look as depicted in Figure 4.2.

The model shows how the entrepreneur can assess whether he/she ought to pursue the idea further, through analysis of the four areas of 'product/service', 'market/industry', 'organisation' and 'funding'. In support of the analysis of each area the literature often refers to traditional management theories. For example, in connection with analysis of the market/industry, tools such as 'SWOT analysis' (Pahl & Richter 2007) and Porter's 'Five Forces Model' (Porter 2008) are often referred to.

As mentioned, there is no universal agreement on these areas. Some researchers, such as Hindle et al (2007) and Allen (2006), specifically emphasise the importance of evaluating the human factor, i.e. the attributes and skills of the entrepreneur or entrepreneurial team. This is also included in Barringer and Ireland's (2010) organisational dimension. For example, an engineer may be an excellent engineer and inventor, but incompetent as a salesperson and manager. Many investors, especially venture capitalists and business angels who invest in risky projects with high news value, place great emphasis on evaluation of the human factor when contemplating whether to invest in the new opportunity or not.

Evaluation is thus undertaken by considering both external factors, such as the market and internal factors such as the human factor. Together, the structures and processes of these external and internal factors create a picture of whether the entrepreneur's idea can result in a product, process or service that creates value for others and is thus feasible.

One way of getting an overall picture of the idea's chances of being realised is the business plan, which will be discussed in detail in Chapter 9. It is considered by many researchers within the instrumental perspective as the key to entrepreneurial success: 'Some entrepreneurs are impatient and do not want to spend the time it takes to write a business plan. This approach is usually a mistake. Writing a business plan forces an entrepreneur to think carefully about all the aspects of a business venture. It also helps a new venture to establish a set of milestones that can be used to guide the early phases of the business rollout' (Barringer & Ireland 2010: 49).

Evaluation of opportunities with great potential

Opportunities differ in scope and potential. Some are small and local, others large and global. Some result from a new organisation being created, others unfold within an existing organisation. But how does one evaluate the potential of a specific opportunity in advance? What criteria can be used to identify opportunities with great potential, and find the tools that enable systematic evaluation ex-ante?

Wickham (2004) emphasises three key criteria for evaluating opportunities. He refers to the importance of assessing the possibilities of its potential in light of the 'scale', 'scope' and 'span'. The first refers to the opportunity's size and 'scope' to the value that it provides in the short and long term. 'Span' refers to the opportunity's durability over time – is it a one-hit wonder or does it have lasting potential? A successful opportunity may well be a flash in the pan, as long as its 'scale' is great. As an example, Lance Armstrong launched a yellow rubber wristband with the inscription 'Live Strong' during the Tour de France in 2004. The goal of the bracelet was to raise money for cancer research, and in general to make the world more aware of the disease and the importance of living life fully while you have it. The bracelet was a huge sales success and created a fashion the world over. But as the Tour de France 'yellow fever' died down, so did the bracelet's popularity.

Hindle et al (2007) base their model on slightly different criteria. A particular feature of this evaluation model is that it takes place on three levels. First the idea is assessed as to its viability, then its development potential and finally, whether it can be implemented. For each of these levels five dimensions, similar to Barringer and Ireland's four dimensions, namely product, market, industry, people and money, are evaluated. The model is developed based on two PhD dissertations on opportunity evaluation. Accuracy in evaluations of a large number of innovative ideas based on the model has, through testing, proved to be high and it is believed therefore to provide a clear identification of the idea's potential. The model should not be regarded as a kind of oracle as it rests on evaluation of different areas that are highly subjective. What it does provide is primarily a systematic evaluation process. In addition, it

THE VIQ FRAMEWORK	Module I Idea Assessment	Module II Idea Enhancement	Module III Venture Implementation
Product	Innovation IP Protection	Value Proposition	Development Operations
Market	Market receptiveness	Target market Dynamics	Distribution Communications
Industry	Industry attractiveness	Sustainable com- petitive advantage	Competitor Map
People	Personal aspirations Connectedness	Abillity to execute	Milestones Risks
Money	Revenue Model Margins & Cash cycle	Break-even, Turning cash	Financial plan Investment offering

Source: Hindle et al (2007).

Figure 4.3 The VIQ model

constitutes the starting point for dialogue, for example between investor and entrepreneur, between consultant and entrepreneur, and between students themselves if they are asked to assess whether a particular idea is a possible opportunity.

Figure 4.3 shows the model, which consists of five dimensions and three levels of evaluation. The model is called the Venture Intelligence Quotient (VIQ).

Level 1 (Idea Assessment), indicated on the left-hand side of the model, covers the evaluation of whether the idea, which constitutes the foundation for the entrepreneurial process, is worth pursuing. The second level (Idea Enhancement) focuses on strengthening the idea. Can the elements that constitute a successful opportunity be developed based on the idea? In other words, the idea's potential is identified and understood. The third level (Venture Implementation) deals with the effective implementation of the idea. This section provides suggestions as to how the entrepreneur can actually build a new organisation based on the idea. This covers the last part of the VIQ tool, issues that this textbook focuses on in Chapter 5.

As previously mentioned, the five dimensions of the model are:

- product = the essence of the idea, which may be a product, service, experience or process;

- market = the group of clients and organisations who are interested in the idea and have the resources to acquire the product or service that the idea represents;
- industry = organisations offering the same or substitute products, services, experiences or processes;
- people = the entrepreneur/the entrepreneurial team;
- Money = the financial dimension.

Evaluation through the creation of legitimacy

Evaluation is not, however, always an instrumental process of evaluation with the areas defined in advance of actual entrepreneurial activity. Furthermore, it is not always the case that evaluation is a systematic, time-limited and analytic process geared to a particular objective and based on certain specific tools to downplay the complexity of the situation. Some entrepreneurs simply don't use such logic to evaluate their ideas; or they combine this logic with other evaluation methods. Some reasons may be that few ideas are so 'ready' that it is possible to test them here and now, through an instrumental evaluation process. In addition, the entrepreneur may not have 'time' to sit down and carry out a detailed instrumental evaluation, because the idea must be exploited here and now or else its potential opportunities dwindle, e.g. other competing actors may seize the opportunity before the entrepreneur. Finally, one can also, in light of the complexity and risk surrounding entrepreneurial evaluations, easily put a big question mark over whether it is possible to predict which ideas represent successful opportunities in the future. This is especially true when the entrepreneur has a very innovative business idea, such as Skype, which gives rise to considerable evaluation challenges in all directions. Maybe entrepreneurs instead of evaluating instrumentally simply have to act and create legitimacy for themselves and their processes.

As an alternative to the instrumental perspective, evaluation can also be seen as an integral part of everyday entrepreneurial processes. Only by acting on the idea, confronting others with the idea and testing its attractive aspects, negative aspects, capacity development, etc. in a social context, is it possible to get an understanding of whether the idea represents an opportunity. Here, the evaluation focuses on whether the idea is attractive to others rather than just the entrepreneur, or how the idea could be modified so that it is attractive to others. The latter says that there may be a need to continually reassess the idea depending on the feedback that the entrepreneur receives from the environment. All this underlines the legitimacy of the perspective. Instrumentation models may incorporate an assessment of legitimacy, but the basic mindset is totally different from the legitimacy perspective.

What is legitimacy? In short, something is legitimate if it complies with the norms, values, beliefs, practices and procedures that are accepted by a particular social group (Johnson et al 2006). According to a famous definition, legitimacy is 'a generalized perception or assumption that the action of an entity is desirable, proper, appropriate, within some socially constructed system of norms, values, beliefs and definitions' (Suchman 1995: 574).

It follows that the entrepreneur's idea can be considered a legitimate option when the economic, social and political surroundings accept its existence as a valid part of the market. According to this approach, the environment plays an important role in determining when there is 'room' for a given entrepreneurial process, and when not. This is especially evident when a new type of organisation or a new industry is evolving; 'Organization populations emerge when the goods and services they provide are seen as legitimate and desirable by the host society' (Reynolds 1991: 57). Therefore we can say 'certain kinds of organizations simply cannot be founded before their time' (Aldrich 1999: 75). As previously indicated, the more innovative and 'new' the entrepreneur's idea, the more problems he or she can expect in convincing others of the idea's relevance and legitimacy, as the environment may have difficulty understanding the idea, and what to do with it. Aldrich and Fiol put it thus: 'The first organization of its kind faces a different set of challenges than the one which simply carries on the tradition pioneered by many predecessors' (Aldrich & Fiol 1994: 663). As a consequence the 'new' entrepreneur simply lacks the acquaintance and confidence of others, which are critical for them to become engaged in the emerging opportunity. Another consequence of being an innovative entrepreneur in an emerging market is that he or she lacks role models to lean on. Role models are seen as critical to entrepreneurial success.

Without the necessary legitimacy, the entrepreneur will have difficulty in raising the necessary capital, recruiting employees, getting customers etc. 'Among the many problems facing innovative entrepreneurs, their relative lack of legitimacy is especially critical' (Aldrich & Fiol 1994: 645). An empirical study of a large number of organisations in their early years confirms that the ability to survive depends on the ability to achieve legitimacy (Delmar & Shane 2004).

Legitimacy cannot be obtained and evaluated from behind a desk and through symbolic actions and planning. It is primarily through action and interaction with other actors, not least the other market players that the entrepreneur can determine whether others perceive the opportunity to be legitimate. To emphasise the point Quinn (2004) recounts a story about how he and a group of colleagues invited a consultant to assist them in finding their core competency as a foundation for an entrepreneurial project. The consultant asked them to write a list of their views on their core competencies. They were then told to throw away the final list, as it was not usable. Instead, they were advised to email friends and business partners to get them to identify their core competencies. The moral is that our 'best' self is when we create value in the eyes of others and not our own eyes. Our best self is the self that is legitimate in the eyes of others, and this we can only find by interacting with others. As Quinn writes, 'Reading what these people have written, I felt approved and received' (Quinn 2004: 128).

Legitimacy as a process

Johnson et al (2006) indicate the process by which new objects – such as a new idea – gain legitimacy and are thus evaluated as a real possibility. The process consists of four phases: 1) innovation, 2) local validation, 3) diffusion and 4) general validation. The first phase covers the creation of the idea. The next phase is characterised by local stakeholders who must be convinced that the new opportunity is possible to relate to and makes sense in the context of existing norms, values, procedures, etc. Once accepted in the local environment – or other close relationship-based contexts – the new opportunity can start to spread into other contexts. 'As the new object spreads, its adoption in new situations often needs less explicit justification than it may have needed in the first local context' (Johnson et al 2006: 60). As a result of the spread, the new object will, over time, become more widely accepted as a natural part of the environment. The legitimacy process can thus be seen as ripples that spread across the water and eventually disappear completely and become an integral part of a larger sea. The spread is dependent on social interaction and acceptance, which controls the progress of the process.

Strategies for building legitimacy

As previously mentioned, evaluation according to the legitimacy perspective take place more or less consciously from the entrepreneur's side. Here we indicate various deliberate actions that the entrepreneur may make to convince the environment of legitimacy in terms of the idea's relevance. For example, the entrepreneur may imitate other organisations that have already been accepted into the environment, or may seek to obtain official certificates to emphasise that the idea actually makes sense in light of the existing (Shane 2003). Furthermore, it may be appropriate for entrepreneurs to cooperate with others to gain legitimacy in society, for example through a new trade organisation or a new network, rather than seeking legitimacy separately. Another strategy for building legitimacy is to focus on creating trust among key stakeholders that will provide the entrepreneur with access to knowledge, resources, etc. Trust is important because it is fundamental to all types of interaction between people. The entrepreneur has various opportunities to build trust. For example, he or she can convince others that the option makes sense, by acting 'as if' the opportunity was already a successful reality. 'Founders who can behave "as if" the activity were a reality – producing and directing great theatre, as it were – may convince others of the tangible reality of the new activity' (Aldrich & Fiol 1994: 651).

Many other approaches can be used to promote legitimacy, including practical/symbolic actions such as producing a business card, letterhead and a website. Legitimacy can also be obtained by the entrepreneur drawing on people who have high legitimacy within a particular business area, for example by using a mentor or by putting together a management or advisory board. Finally, contact with an existing organisation that has legitimacy can provide a route to greater legitimacy. If an entrepreneur can write 'trusted by' a well-known organisation on the business card, it helps to overcome his or her 'liability of newness'.

According to the legitimacy perspective the entrepreneur rarely pursues a practical strategy in relation to creating legitimacy. Instead, the process of legitimacy tends to be experimental and exploratory, with the entrepreneur, through his or her daily actions in the market, looking out for signals that tell him or her if the idea is perceived as legitimate. Metaphorically, the entrepreneur carries their idea under their arm and goes into the field to test it by trying to convince others of its merits, so as to evaluate the idea's degree of legitimacy – is it worth pursuing further? Through his or her attempts to convince others of the idea's virtues the entrepreneur receives various forms of feedback that tell him or her if the idea is the basis for a realistic opportunity. Feedback can take the form of resources, knowledge, new opportunities, barriers, etc., which of course can actually serve as physical inputs for shaping the idea into an opportunity, and later an organisation. However, feedback also has symbolic value as it tells the entrepreneur whether others perceive his or her opportunity as legitimate. This leads to a clarification of whether the entrepreneur's idea makes sense, and thus whether it is appropriate to pursue it further as an option.

So the idea is evaluated according to the legitimacy perspective through exploration and experimental activities and social interactions rather than through the utilisation of systematic and analytical tools prior to the actual entrepreneurial process. Evaluation takes place in the process and it is also here that the criteria for what should be evaluated are created. As a result, evaluation becomes a progressive and procedural journey where the entrepreneur, over time, creates an assessment of the idea as a potential opportunity.

Different types of entrepreneurs experience different challenges in relation to the creation of legitimacy. For the engineer, who has created a physical prototype of his or her idea, it is often relatively easy to create legitimacy around it, as market participants have something concrete to relate to. Conversely, someone who intends to sell a consulting service or a cultural performance is faced with the challenge of creating legitimacy on a more intangible product, which essentially is the person him-/herself.

Evaluation: instrumental or legitimate?

You have now been presented with two different perspectives on the evaluation of opportunities; namely the instrumental perspective, and the legitimacy perspective. These are summarised in Table 4.1.

As the table shows, the instrumental perspective views evaluation as a means for achieving a particular goal. The goal indicates directions for action so that it can be determined how and whether the idea can become a viable opportunity. Evaluation criteria are defined prior to the actual evaluation process and the evaluation itself is limited in time by a specific start and end point. The criteria often emerge from different analytical frameworks such as the VIQ tool or the business plan. These frameworks often indicate a linear, rational and systematic chain of analytical evaluation activities that

Table 4.1 The paradox: Instrumental or legitimate

	Instrumental	Legitimate
Evaluation perception	Tool to achieve a certain objective	Legitimacy creation
Evaluation objective	To state the direction for action	To convince the actors of the market of the idea
Evaluation criteria	They should be formulated before the process	They emerge during the entrepreneurial process
Evaluation process	Rational, systematic and analytic	Social, interactive, experimental and exploring
Evaluation character	Evaluation and entrepreneurial action are two separate activities	Evaluation and entrepreneurial action are two inseparable activities

the entrepreneur must undertake to achieve the goal. Finally, the instrumental perspective often looks upon evaluation and actual entrepreneurial action as two separate activities. First evaluation and then action based on the evaluation's recommendations.

In contrast, the legitimacy perspective emphasises that legitimacy building is the focal point of the evaluation process, which takes place on a continuous basis and aims to convince market participants of the idea's excellence and potential. Here, the criteria for evaluation are not determined in advance, but in the legitimation process, where interaction with the market will gradually signal what criteria are relevant: the evaluation process is social, interactive, experimental and exploratory. By presenting the social environment with the idea, the entrepreneur has the opportunity to build trust, acceptance and understanding, which will often end up in a continuous reassessment, adjustment, alteration, etc. of the idea, depending on the feedback that the entrepreneur receives from others. The entrepreneur takes the idea into the market and tests it. This highlights how, according to the legitimacy perspective, the evaluation process and the entrepreneurial act are two inseparable processes.

A theoretical interpretation

In light of the above theory, we now offer our interpretation of the Munthe plus Simonsen story with which we started the chapter; firstly through the lens of the instrumental perspective, and then according to the legitimacy perspective.

The instrumental perspective

At first glance, it may be difficult to understand the story of Munthe plus Simonsen from the instrumental perspective. At the start of the entrepreneurial process Naja and Karen had no definite idea or specific target that they aimed to achieve through rational and analytical processes – quite the contrary. However, looking at the story over time, it seems that Naja and Karen became increasingly focused, goal-oriented and concerned with planning in terms of their activities. In particular, the suspension of payments caused them to stop, analyse and systematically evaluate what they could do to create a clothing line and business model that the market would find attractive. Evaluation was an exploratory and experimental process for them, which resulted in Naja and Karen clarifying their goal and, through analysis of the budget, identifying the financial cuts that were necessary to achieve that goal. In other words, they really cut the business down to the bone through a systematic financial evaluation. The goal then was to create a mature and economically viable organisation, and they knew that they must continually look at how they could optimise the business and what economic consequences were associated with which activities. It was no longer enough for them that they were making great clothes – it also had to be a profitable business.

After starting out refusing to be a commercial organisation Naja and Karen began to think commercially and analytically. In part, the focus moved away from what they liked and their own lifestyle by, for example, thinking about who the end-user was and why they should buy their clothes. As part of the more commercial orientation, Naja and Karen effectively made a rational analysis of the client group and therefore an analysis of the product's potential in light of the market: enabling them to integrate the market's needs and desires in their designs. This was achieved by including distributors, employees, vendors, etc. in the evaluation of the Munthe plus Simonsen target group, and in the redefinition of the organisation's design line. Last but not least, Naja and Karen sought to create a more stable and profitable situation through franchising. This may indicate that a form of organisational assessment took place.

In other words it is clear that the suspension of payments gave rise to a more instrumental approach to evaluation, with goals being set prior to the evaluation process, and systematic analysis tools being put into service.

The legitimacy perspective

Taking the opposite view, the early part of the Munthe plus Simonsen story provides plenty of evidence of the legitimacy perspective. It is a tale of two young girls who encounter great difficulty in convincing the world that they have an attractive product and in generally achieving legitimacy as entrepreneurs. In particular, the fact that Naja and Karen started up within an industry that was not yet in itself an accepted part of the market, created legitimacy challenges for the young entrepreneurs. They were not just trying to convince the outside world about their own collection, but also about the value of a whole new industry. As a result, the media, sales channels, etc. initially rejected them, and they had no role models to lean on.

However, their organisation spread like ripples on the water and became increasingly viewed as legitimate, primarily because Naja and Karen appeared to have a good insight into how to create positive awareness and credibility in the fashion world. This is evident in that they first and foremost pushed their way through to Norgaard, a respected retailer in central Copenhagen. Since this particular sales channel itself enjoys widespread social acceptance in the fashion world, others easily accepted their collection as attractive. Naja and Karen opened the door to the sales channel by daring to explore, being persistent, not taking 'no for an answer' and by showing off their products. Drive, persistence and interaction with the 'right' people are hallmarks of Naja and Karen's creation of legitimacy.

Another interesting way that Naja and Karen entered the market through the creation of legitimacy was by acting 'as if' they had a very precious product, which was already widely accepted in the fashion industry. They acted 'as if' and made symbolic gestures that gave them a successful and prestigious image and status in the fashion industry, such as hiring famous supermodels, setting up in expensive office buildings with exclusive furniture and establishing shops and showrooms in key fashion cities from an early stage of the entrepreneurial process. Through these actions Naja and Karen also stand out from the crowd, which is very advantageous in an industry like the fashion industry. It is obvious that the evaluation process at the beginning is very much an integral part of the entrepreneurial process. This is expressed by virtue of the fact that Naja and Karen did not seem to use legitimacy as a deliberate strategy. In fact, from an early stage they made it a point of honour not to relate their designs to the market or to bother about what others thought of them and their collection.

Naja and Karen's exploratory and experimental approach to opportunity evaluation led, at the beginning of the story, to positive feedback from the market, which was carried through in the way that they apparently hit an upward market trend with their clothes. Important feedback also came in the form of growing earnings, and prices, both of which can be construed as official certificates creating additional legitimacy around Munthe plus Simonsen. Naja and Karen certainly got that right. They created an attractive option, which emerged at a time when the bohemian style was popular. In fact there is strong evidence that Naja and Karen's actions and the example they set not only created legitimacy for their own organisation, but also contributed to the growing legitimacy of the Danish fashion scene as a whole.

Unfortunately, however, legitimacy is not something you have in perpetuity once it is acquired. You can also lose legitimacy, as the late stages of the Munthe plus Simonsen story reveals. The fact that the organisation was subject to a suspension of payments makes it clear that Naja and Karen did not have legitimacy in everyone's eyes. They understood the rules of legitimacy in the fashion industry at an image and collection level, but they had not understood in detail how business legitimacy is created, despite having won awards such as businesswomen of the year. In view of that, the restructuring of their business can be seen as an exercise in repairing some of the legitimacy that they have lost in the business world as a consequence of the suspension of payments.

Testing the theory

The interpretations, thoughts and discussions throughout this chapter have prepared you for developing your own tests for understanding opportunity evaluation. Here are some exercises that you can start with.

EXERCISES

1 **Conceptualising evaluation.** First, undertake a brainstorming exercise that results in you writing down all the words that you associate with evaluation. Then organise the words into some broad definitions of what evaluation is. Finally determine whether your definitions of evaluation reflect the instrumental perspective, legitimacy perspective, or a combination of the two.

2 **Consultant.** As you know, Munthe plus Simonsen has had a stormy voyage. Imagine that Naja and Karen contact you wanting to hire you as a consultant. They ask specifically for an analysis of the following:

   1. What are the two most beneficial things that they have done in terms of evaluation?
   2. What are the two most negative things they have done?
   3. What could they have done to turn the negative things into something advantageous?

3 **Write your own review narrative.** Start with a business idea (either an idea you already have or a new thought). Turn on your computer and write a narrative about how you would evaluate the idea. You have 10 minutes to write your narrative. Working in pairs, read your narratives to each other. Analyse together, whether the narratives provide evidence that you would make an evaluation from the instrumental perspective, legitimacy perspective, or a combination of the two.

LITERATURE

Aldrich, H.E. (1999) *Organizations Evolving*, London: Sage.

Aldrich, H. & Fiol, M.C. (1994) 'Fools rush in? The institutional context of industry creation', *The Academy of Management Review*, 19(4), 645–670.

Allen, K.R. (2006) *Launching New Ventures: An Entrepreneurial Approach*, Boston, MA: Houghton Mifflin Company.

Barringer, B.R. & Ireland, R.D. (2010) *Entrepreneurship: Successfully Launching New Ventures*, Upper Saddle River, NJ: Prentice Hall.

Delmar, F. & Shane, S. (2004) 'Legitimating first: Organizing activities and the survival of new ventures', *Journal of Business Venturing*, 19, 385–410.

Grichnik, D., Smeja, A. & Welpe, I. (2010) 'The importance of being emotional: How do emotions affect entrepreneurial opportunity evaluation and exploitation?', *Journal of Economic Behavior & Organisation*, 76, 15–29.

Haynie, M.J., Stepherd, D.A. & McMullen, J.S. (2009) 'An opportunity for me? The role of resources in opportunity evaluation decisions', *Journal of Management Studies*, 46(3), 337–361.

Hindle, K. (2010) 'Skillful dreaming: Testing a general model of entrepreneurial process with a specific narrative of venture creation', *Entrepreneurial Narrative Theory Ethnomethodology & Reflexivity*, 1, 97–137.

Hindle, K., Mainprize, B. & Dorofeeva, N. (2007) *Venture Intelligence: How Smart Investors and Entrepreneurs Evaluate New Ventures*, Melbourne: Learnfast Press.

Johnson, C., Dow, T.J. & Ridgeway, C.L. (2006) 'Legitimacy as a social process', *Annual Review of Sociology*, 32, 53–78.

Keh, H.T., Foo, M.D. & Lim, B.C. (2002) 'Opportunity evaluation under risky conditions: The cognitive processes of entrepreneurs', *Entrepreneurship Theory and Practice*, 27(2), 125–148.

Pahl, N. and Richter, A. (2007) *SWOT Analysis – Idea, Methodology and a Practical Approach*, Santa Cruz, CA: GRIN Publishing.

Porter, M.E. (2008) 'The five competitive forces that shape strategy', *Harvard Business Review*, January, 86–104.

Quinn, R.E. (2004) *Building the Bridge as You Walk on It: A Guide for Leading Change*, San Francisco, CA: Jossey-Bass.

Reynolds, P.D. (1991) 'Sociology and entrepreneurship: Concepts and contributions', *Entrepreneurship Theory and Practice*, 16(2), 47–70.

Shane, S. (2003) *A General Theory of Entrepreneurship: The Individual–Opportunity Nexus*, Cheltenham, UK and Northampton, MA, USA: Edward Elgar Publishing.

Suchman, M. (1995) 'Managing legitimacy: Strategic and institutional approaches', *Academy of Management Review*, 20(3), 571–610.

Wickham, P.A. (2004) *Strategic Entrepreneurship*, Harlow: Pearson Education Limited.

5

Organisation of opportunities

It is now time to exploit the opportunity; this requires organising ability. Organising is essentially about developing some meaningful practice, structures and systems that we call organisations. The process itself involves the coordination of elements such as people, resources, strategies, competition, technologies, etc., and it evolves in a complex milieu of interacting individuals. The process of getting organised is seen as a tool to realise the opportunity and take it to the market through the formation of new independent organisations or organisational units within existing organisations (Allen 2006). One can also envisage the entrepreneur taking his or her opportunity to market through the purchase of a franchise unit or by selling the opportunity to an existing organisation. In this chapter we will, however, concentrate on what the organising of opportunities through new organisational formation involves.

Entrepreneurship in practice

Before we go into a lengthy theoretical explanation of how opportunities can be exploited through the organisation, it is time, once again, to meet an entrepreneur. His name is Claus Meyer and is a well-known chef from Denmark. Just listen to his story about how he organised his entrepreneurial activities, including an established restaurant Noma, which in 2010 and again in 2011 was named the world's best restaurant by *Restaurant Magazine*. In parallel with organising the process he went from being a university student to a successful serial entrepreneur.

CASE STUDY

A famous chef, 'It just happened'

(Devised by the authors)

'I've never wanted a big company. I wanted great successes, but not many employees, high turnover or seven or eight companies, which it probably is right now. It's something that just happened. I've never worked with plans. Until a few years ago I didn't work with budgets, and the idea of having a board is only four years old. We never took bank loans. I've only done that once and it was not a success . . . So we started in the easiest way'. This is how Claus describes his approach to entrepreneurship. In 2010, the Meyer Group (including subsidiaries) consisted of a number of food companies that together employed more than 300 people.

Claus grew up in the Danish 'food culture' of the 1960s and 70s: a time characterised by many women leaving the kitchen in favour of paid labour. Danish households were filled to the brim with frozen vegetables, minced meat, frying margarine and other foods that made life easier and kept costs down – often at the expense of food quality and the consumer's experience. At the beginning, Claus had no special interest in food, but as a young man he found himself in the house of a famous chef in southern France. The experience founded a mission for life within him. He would transform and improve the Danish/Nordic food culture: put the experience, the soul, the quality and sincerity back into the food, but how? Claus had no plan as to how he might realise his mission.

Others might have undertaken training as a chef, but not Claus. Instead, he enrolled on a course as a student at Copenhagen Business School, and consequently Denmark's most famous chef never trained as a chef. At the business school he took a business administration degree, specialising in starting and developing businesses. Claus chose this approach because, to a great extent, he already saw entrepreneurship as a future career path: both his father and grandfather having been self-employed.

As a 20-year-old young man Claus started his first entrepreneurial project: 'take away food' from his two-room studio apartment in Copenhagen. He delivered the food on his Raleigh bicycle. Later he talked the business school's rector into letting him take over the school canteen. It was the beginning of a long entrepreneurial journey: many organisational projects have been set up in the years since (The Chocolate Company, Meyer and Tingstrøm staff restaurants, corporate 'pampering' outings/team building, fruit breeding, Noma, Meyer's Deli, etc.). Figure 5.1 provides an overview of the Meyer Group organisations in 2008.

The mission comes into focus

'I had the best idea of my life about four years ago: it synchronised the last 15 years of my life. I didn't want to go into the restaurant business, but I got an offer . . . a nice place . . . an old warehouse in Christianshavn. My idea was to build a Nordic gourmet restaurant'. Colleagues laughed. Nordic food is not 'fine' – not worthy of a gourmet restaurant. The restaurant would be ridiculed as the 'whale-restaurant'. Nevertheless, Claus established the restaurant, Noma,

CASE STUDY *(continued)*

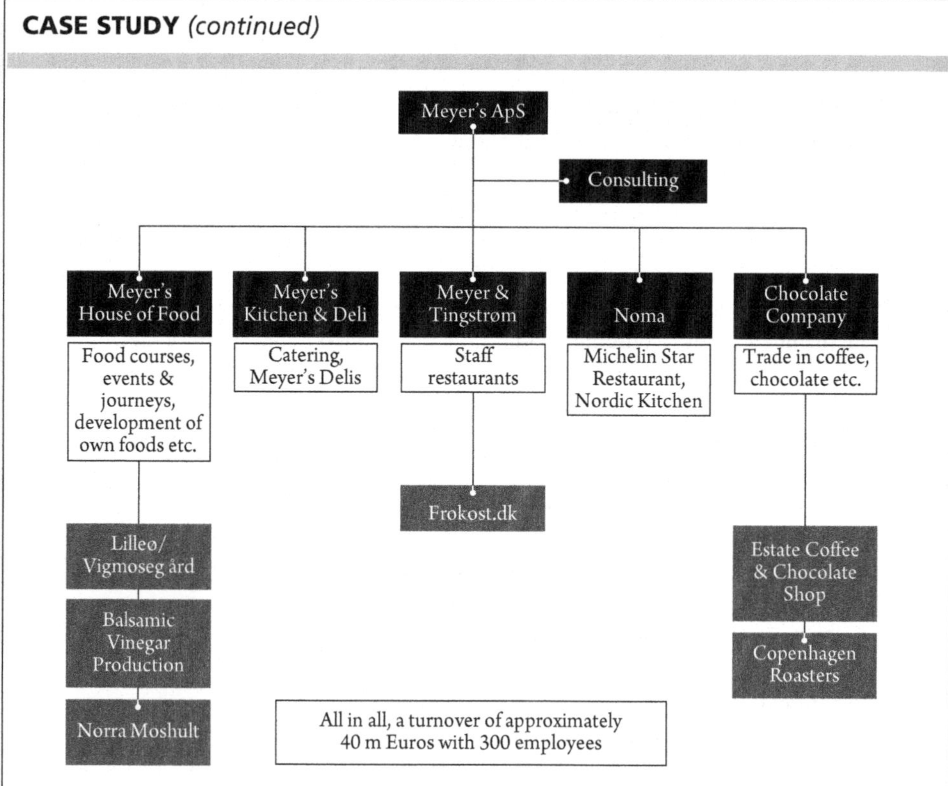

Figure 5.1 Organisation diagram: The Meyer group

with his partner René Redzepi, who has experience in the gourmet business. They cultivated the unique history, taste and origin of Nordic cuisine. Nobody had thought of it before. Thai, French and Indian cuisine, we all know, but what is Nordic cuisine? Neither of the two entrepreneurs had dreams of creating great economic success: it was about something bigger. As with Claus' mission in life their real success criterion was to define the Nordic kitchen and create a common mission among Nordic farmers, small and large businesses, citizens, politicians, etc. to promote Nordic food of high quality. It all led to a huge success. In 2008, Noma was awarded two Michelin stars and, as mentioned, it was named the world's best restaurant in 2010 and 2011.

A Nordic movement

The establishment of Noma was essentially a process involving a lot of different people, first and foremost partner René Redzepi. Claus' role was primarily to support René based on his experience as an entrepreneur: 'I supported him and helped with finance, building the website, recruiting staff, creating the first menus, chose the graphic designer, took care of the contractual relationships with the owners of the premises, but probably most important,

CASE STUDY *(continued)*

I brought together all of the Nordic food-intelligence . . . Ministers from Norway and Denmark, etc. even people from the Nordic food industry . . . to discuss how everyone could share our vision'. Claus simply chose to invite ministers, top officials from the Nordic food industry, journalists and famous chefs for a symposium to articulate the idea of Nordic cuisine. The participating chefs were set the task of defining a manifesto for the new Nordic cuisine, formulated as 10 commandments.

The manifesto would be launching a whole new movement – a movement with many different members (cooks, consumers, politicians and business people from all the Scandinavian countries). The movement came together to promote Nordic food culture based on the manifesto's words. The Nordic Ministers for Food were also part of the movement, launching a 'New Nordic Food Programme' based on the manifesto. This programme allocates funds to organisations and individual people who develop, produce or market products in accordance with the manifesto.

So, a restaurant and the concept on which it was founded has become a Nordic movement. Through the movement, Claus fulfilled his mission of creating a platform for a Danish/Nordic food culture. One that is not all about frozen vegetables, minced meat and frying margarine, but a food culture that promotes the uniqueness, the origin and quality of Nordic cuisine.

Dancing around

Reflecting on the creation of his entrepreneurial ventures, Claus relates how he cooks to how he creates organisations: 'There are many similarities. The way I love to cook is without a recipe or a definite plan. I love to go somewhere, for example, Hungary, and see which vegetables are in the garden; what meat is available and what's in the fridge. Then I dance a little, thinking about what I can do and what I know. On the way I interact a little with the surroundings – and that's also how I do business. I listen to people; I talk to my employees. If I have a dishwasher who is good with flowers, I would be stupid if I didn't ask him to arrange the flowers. If I meet someone who wants to build a dairy and it could be bigger and better if we did it together, then I would be attracted. So I build businesses in the same way that I cook: I dance around, see what happens and try to feel the energy'.

Similar thoughts are expressed in an interview with the *CBS Observer* in 2008. Claus Meyer explained: 'I've never made many plans. My plan has been to be open to the outside world, so you can't just rush past the opportunities that present themselves. I think this has been good for my dream because I have always been open to new paths, but it has not necessarily been good for the individual companies. Growth comes from planning and financing. I have not planned and I have not taken loans and this means that everything has gone very slowly. If I had done things differently, I could probably have experienced much faster growth'.

However, the larger the Meyer group became, the more Claus experienced a need to professionalise and structure its organisation. He set up a professional board, but mostly it functions as a provider of inspiration. He likes to retain control himself. 'The board supports me

CASE STUDY *(continued)*

in having a well organised company with the right skills in the right positions relative to what we want to do. Who should be the leader? . . . I do not know much about building large organisations. I didn't want to have a big organisation, but now I have one . . . I hope that I am a good priest and a visionary person and that all employees want to follow my footsteps. But I'm not the classic leader'. The board often advises Claus to think more about making money, but he has a larger vision of his entrepreneurial activities than financial goals.

Your immediate interpretation

How do you understand the organising process that Claus talks of? Here are some questions that may help you to reflect on the story in terms of organising:

- You are a stand-in teacher in an eighth grade class (15-year-olds) at a state school. Based on Claus' story, your task is to explain to the class what an organisation is and how organisations are created. What do you tell the class?
- You draw a timeline on the blackboard that gives the class an overview of Claus' progress. You get a reaction. One of the boys in the class asks you: 'When do you know that the entrepreneurial process has led to the establishment of a new organisation?' What is your answer?
- A girl in class is also curious. She asks: 'Why do you think that Claus didn't start by establishing Noma, which is really the opportunity that truly realises his mission in life?' Do you have a good answer?

Theories of entrepreneurship

As you know, organising opportunities is the subject of this chapter. The literature offers many different interpretations of what organising involves. Some believe that the organising process is a conscious, deliberate process that plans for and aims to achieve a predetermined and predictable goal – a successful organisation. In this way the entrepreneur is seen as a kind of rational architect who organises the process and the opportunity optimally through planning. This interpretation seems to be widespread in society, among politicians, educators, consultants, banks, etc., and it reflects what we would call a planning perspective of organising.

However, the literature also contains an alternative view of the organising process, which we call the improvisation perspective of organising. This perspective emphasises that in many cases the entrepreneur starts out with no clear goal as to what organisation he or she wants to create, and even if the entrepreneur starts out with a clear goal, this can change because the future, environment, etc. are not predictable but are changing and insecure. The latter becomes particularly clear if you think about how the entrepreneur often finds him- or herself in an organisational situation where the parameters of the opportunity, such as market demand structure, customer group, prices, competition, etc., are not yet known, because entrepreneurship is fundamentally about creating something new – creating the future (Shane 2003). The improvisation perspective argues that since there is so much uncertainty associated with entrepreneurship, planning makes less sense. Instead, the entrepreneurial process is, in practice, characterised by entrepreneurs feeling their way forward, constantly reconsidering their environment, asking others for advice and finding resources along the way, which constantly opens up new opportunities and goals. It's basically about improvisation. Only through many and unpredictable small steps is a new organisation realised. Together, the planning and improvisation perspectives represent a paradox:

Planning or improvising?

What is an organisation?

In organisation theory, it is often assumed that the organisation is something that already exists. However, the focal point of entrepreneurship is the organisation-in-creation, and hence the emergent organisational processes that lead to a new organisation being created (Katz & Gartner 1988: Gartner et al 1992). Nevertheless to understand what the organisation process involves, it is first and foremost worth looking at what characterises an organisation. An organisation is, in itself, an incredibly broad and ambiguous concept, and numerous perspectives are used to define an organisation (March & Simon 1958). This perhaps is because organisations are in many ways obscure entities, processes and structures that we take more or less for granted as they are around us all the time, and shape us as we shape them. Some of the perspectives of an organisation place weight on the organisation's formal structures, common rules, administrative procedures, frameworks and goals. Others focus on the more informal, process-oriented, interactive, social and human dimensions in their definition of an organisation (Morgan 1997). As an example of the latter, Weick (1995) offers an interesting suggestion for the individual and social cognitive sense-making processes that lead to a new organisation being created. Katz and Gartner (1988) refer to McKelvey's (1980) definition of an organisation that provides both structural and process-oriented dimensions. An organisation is a 'myopically purposeful [boundary-maintaining] activity system containing one or more conditionally autonomous myopically purposeful subsystems having input-output resource ratios fostering survival in environments imposing particular constraints' (Katz & Gartner 1988: 430).

Formal organisations are relatively easy to identify whereas informal organisations can be much more imperceptible.

Berger and Kellner offer a different definition of an organisation: 'Every human organization is, as it were, a crystallization of meanings, or, to vary the image, a crystallization of meanings in objective form' (Berger & Kellner 1981: 31). Organisations are thus organised communities consisting of actors, resources, knowledge, etc., where the glue that holds it all together is commonly held and generally accepted opinions and perceptions among stakeholders about why they appear as objective structures, systems, norms and logics. These control the stakeholders' opinions and actions whilst also being shaped by them.

One can also argue that organisations are basically about a kind of group formation where individuals are not just random people who gathered on a pedestrian street. On the contrary, the individuals interact in the organisation to achieve a common goal:

> At first a primitive organization emerges from cooperation between individuals who wish to pool their efforts to achieve a common goal, such as bringing a new product to market. This primitive organization has not got a structure in the technical sense of the term because cooperative effort is more a result of individual motivation than it is an organizational achievement. However if the primitive organization is going to survive beyond its initial project it will develop an elaborated social structure and become an organization in the usual sense of the world. (Hatch 1997: 177)

In the process of moving from a primitive to an elaborated organisation, individuals come together through a series of processes that establishes:

- more formalisation: framed by some common rules and physical limits;
- more complexity: underlines the need for administrative functions, linking activities;
- clarification of objectives: aimed at a specific overall goal.

Organisations can therefore be said to be a framework for any kind of concerted social and human action. However, because starting a new organisation involves basically only one, or a few entrepreneurs, you might not immediately think about social unity. Nevertheless, parallel to the organising of the entrepreneur's opportunity (designing a logo, pooling resources, exchanges with clients, etc.), the entrepreneurial opportunity develops from being attached to the entrepreneur to becoming an accepted social organisation, which also involves other actors in addition to the entrepreneur. The involvement of other actors can be seen as a prerequisite for entrepreneurial organisation. 'People construct organisations to accomplish things they cannot do on their own' (Aldrich 1999: 75). The many actors involved require further formalisation, direction, and thus structure. The starting up of a new organisation thus takes shape through a lot of different actors' interactions. The more actors involved in the process, the more complex it becomes and the greater the demands for the organisation-in-creation to be formalised in relation to objectives and administrative processes.

What does organising involve?

We see organising as a process that is about creating a new organisation over time. Inspired by Fayolle (2003), we have divided the development of a new organisation into five phases. The phases cover getting an idea, evaluating and shaping it into a real opportunity, conceptualising the opportunity of an entrepreneurial project so that it can be exploited by making the opportunity of a new emergent organisation actually happen, which in turn and over time becomes increasingly stable in its design. This chapter focuses mainly on the fourth phase. The last phase is outside this book's sphere of interest. As we established in Chapter 1, this book divides the entrepreneurial process into three phases, namely: 1) opportunity creation, 2) opportunity evaluation and 3) opportunity organisation. This classification is generally in line with Fayolle's thoughts. Figure 5.2 illustrates the five phases mentioned.

As the five stages are described here, the entrepreneurial process appears as a linear and progressive process. However, Fayolle's point about the phases

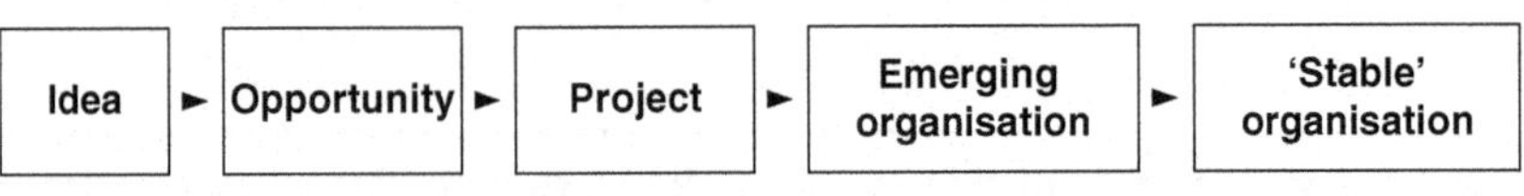

Source: Fayolle (2003: 41).

Figure 5.2 The development of a new organisation

is to show that there may be feedback from later phases to earlier ones. Furthermore, the development phases do not necessarily occur in that order. For example, some entrepreneurs will establish a formal organisation before they have evaluated whether the idea represents a real opportunity. Finally, the process may stop at a certain stage without a new organisation ever being formed.

As such, Fayolle's phase model shows that the organisation does not consist merely of a single step – going from a situation 'without organisation' to a situation 'with a new organisation'. On the contrary, one can talk about a series of fluid organisational steps on the way towards a new independent organisation or organisational unit within an existing organisation. Since there is a smooth transition from the 'without organisation' to the 'with a new organisation' situation, it is difficult, in practice, to determine when the organisation is formed. Is it when the external funding is secured? When the first bill is paid? After the first sale takes place? When the organisation is formally registered with the authorities?

Whilst Fayolle's model provides an overarching vision of how we can understand the organisation in terms of the entrepreneurial process as a whole, Figure 5.3 shows some elements of the organisational efforts the entrepreneur must make to realise his or her opportunity in the market.

The figure illustrates that the organisation requires resources in terms of raw materials, capital, human and social resources, information, knowledge, customers, etc. Chapter 7 examines the resource challenge in more detail.

Acquisition of resources requires the entrepreneur to act and interact with the environment, since it is rare that he or she already possesses the necessary

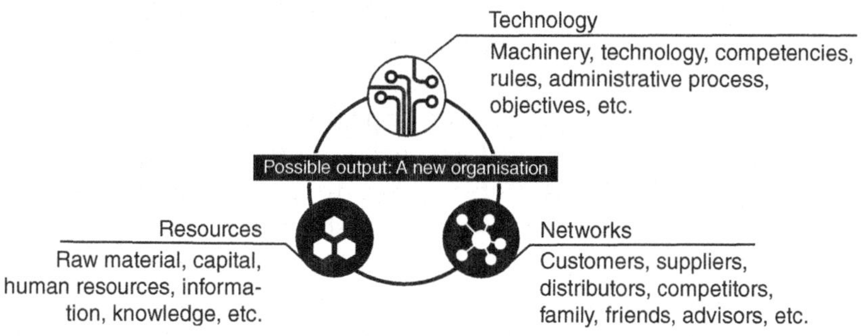

Source: Inspired by Jones (2007).

Figure 5.3 The organising components

resources. This makes the formation and development of networks a critical factor. As Aldrich said: 'All nascent entrepreneurs draw upon their existing social networks and construct new ones in the process of obtaining knowledge and resources for their organizations' (Aldrich 1999: 81). Relevant actors in these networks include customers, shareholders, suppliers, distributors, competitors, advisors, family, friends, etc. The network challenge is set out in Chapter 8.

A third important factor in the formation of an organisation is the establishment of technology, in a broad sense, so that inputs can be transformed into products and services with the use of resources. Technology refers to machinery, buildings, control systems, etc.

In the final organisation these three components are in place; a resource base, a technology and a network are all established. In the early phase, the task for the entrepreneur is to establish these conditions: to accumulate resources, to establish the technology, to develop the network – definitely not an easy task. There are a multitude of diverse activities to be deployed simultaneously. As an illustration of the complexity, Aldrich (1999) refers to a US study that points to 17 key activities as being relevant in the entrepreneurial process. The activities are shown in Figure 5.4. The list should not be taken to mean that all entrepreneurs carry out all listed activities. Every organisation is unique, or in other words, organising is not a generic route, to be marched again and again by the same entrepreneurs (Gartner 1985). Instead the processes vary 'vastly in their characteristics as do the entrepreneurs who create them' (Bhave 1994: 224).

The activities that are most representative of the individual entrepreneur can be closely linked with the country in which a business is started. Data from the World Bank, an international bank which provides financial support to developing countries around the world, shows that there is a big difference in how easy it is to start a business (World Bank, www.doingbusiness.org, last accessed 20 December 2016). Depending on how business-friendly the regulations are in a country, it may be easier or harder for an entrepreneur to start up. Ease of start-up is, is measured, among other ways, by comparing different countries' procedures (number of procedures to complete before starting), time (number of days to wait before acceptance to start), cost (percentage of the gross national income per capita) and minimum capital (minimum capital requirement) to open a new business. For example, according to the *Doing Business 2010* report, Australia ranked third on the first sub-index 'Starting a business' behind only New Zealand and Canada. In Australia there are two procedures required to start a business, which take on average two days to complete. Further the offi-

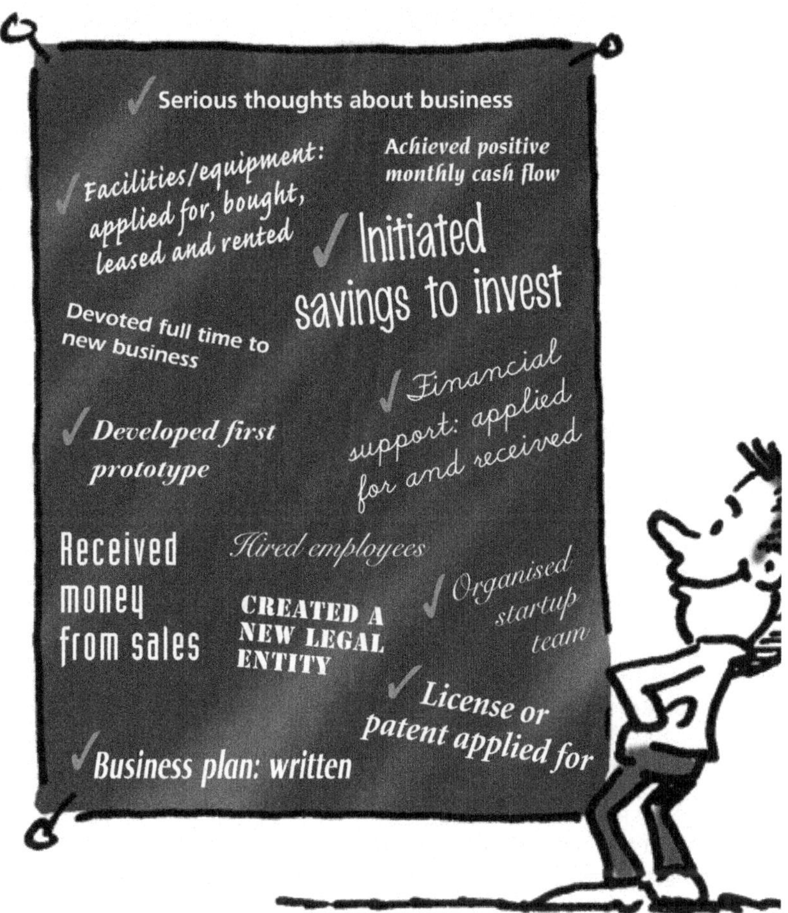

Source: Inspired by Aldrich (1999).

Figure 5.4 Crucial activities in the start-up process

cial cost is 0.8 per cent of the gross national income per capita, and there is no minimum capital requirement. By contrast, in Guinea-Bissau, which ranked among the worst (183rd out of 183) on this same sub-index, there are 16 procedures required to start a business taking 213 days to complete. The official cost is 323.0 per cent of the gross national income per capita, and a minimum capital investment of 1006.6 per cent of the gross national income per capita is required (World Bank, *Doing Business 2010* report).

Organising is not always a success

Organising does not always lead to the establishment of a new organisation. Often the entrepreneur chooses to abort the process. The GEM survey results from 2010 show that there is a diminishing participation during the entrepreneurial process, from having the intention to start a new organisation to actually starting up or already having established a new organisation. The study shows for example that in the United States, whilst 7.7 per cent of Americans intend to start-up, only 4.8 per cent have taken concrete steps to do so and only 2.8 per cent actually runs a fledgling (less than three-and-a-half years old) organisation (Kelley et al 2011). The same fall-off pattern is also found in other countries such as Denmark, Germany, Sweden and the United Kingdom, although there are variations in the number of respondents who have the intention of starting up, have taken concrete steps or are already running a start-up.

The figure obviously raises the question: why is there so much failure in the entrepreneurial process? Overall, Brush and Manolova (2004) point to various barriers such as weak knowledge, opportunity identification, product/service development and the ability to develop systems and structures. In addition, problems of legitimacy occur, barriers in relation to creating relevant networks and the ability to identify and develop an attractive resource base. Finally it is pointed out that risk can be a key issue. So that we can get a closer look into the reasons why entrepreneurial organising ends, it makes sense to distinguish between the processes that, according to Fayolle's (2003) model – see Figure 5.2 – lead to a 'stable organisation' and the processes arising once such an organisation is established. The barriers, which the entrepreneur specifically meets in the process towards a 'stable' organisation are, according to Brush and Manolova (2004), divided into two main categories: personal challenge (getting suitable health insurance, balancing time and lack of mentors) and social challenges (being taken seriously and receiving support) (Brush & Manolova 2004: 280).

When considering perceived barriers associated with the post-establishment period, it is crucial, according to Levie et al (2011) to note that organisational efforts are not only terminated for negative reasons or venture failure, such as bankruptcy. Often an organisation is closed down on the basis of more voluntary and positive considerations. Maybe it was not the intention, from the beginning, that the organisation should persist for a longer period than to exploit temporary market opportunities or achieve a desired sale. Alternatively the organisation may be closed down because the entrepreneur simply gets a better job offer, or it no longer meets the entrepreneur's needs when he or she is looking for new challenges. In a GEM study Bosma et al (2008) focused on why entrepreneurs within the past 12 months had closed down an organisation. Here the results show that about one-third of organisations have actually been continued in a different form or with other owners.

Note: Potential entrepreneurs: percentage of those aged 18–64 who expect to start a business within three years.
Nascent entrepreneurs: Percentage of those aged 18–64 who are currently involved in setting up a business they will own or co-own.
New organisation: Percentage of those aged 18–64 who are currently an owner-manager of a new business (max 42 months old).

Source: Kelley et al (2011).

Figure 5.5 The diminishing participation during the entrepreneurial process in the USA (% of population)

The change should thus be recorded as a continuation rather than an exit. In a discussion of failure, Levie et al (2011) refer to studies showing that as little as 4–5 per cent of the businesses close due to legal bankruptcy or insolvency. Other reasons included a resale, voluntary closure, illness, retirement, etc.

Seen in this light, Wickham's (2004) point about the importance of understanding success and failure as being subjectively determined also makes sense. This means the entrepreneur's experiences of success or lack thereof in the entrepreneurial process must be seen in light of the entrepreneur's expectations, motives and objectives. If these are not met, the entrepreneur will probably consider the process to be a failure. For example, if an entrepreneur's objective is to improve the balance between work and family life, then success is when this balance is realised. Another entrepreneur may be more motivated by economic growth. For him or her the key to success is not the creation of a 'balanced life', but the making of profits.

Organising can be planned

Now it is time to look more specifically at how the organising process might proceed by looking deeper into the two perspectives that we introduced earlier: the planning and improvisation perspectives. Let's start with the former.

The planning perspective in entrepreneurship has its roots in classical management theory where manufacturing organisations are seen as entities, created by the manager to achieve predefined goals. The manager builds and operates the organisational machine using tools such as rational analysis and planning (Hatch 1997). Thus, the perspective suggests that the organising is intentional, rational and considered, and the process of organising can be driven by analysis (competitor analysis, customer analysis, etc.) and planning. Finally it can be steered towards a specific goal. So, the perspective assumes that the entrepreneur has a clear picture of the goal (the organisation) that he or she wants to achieve, right from the start.

Sarasvathy (2008) talks of the planning perspective's vision of the organisation as a causal process in which the entrepreneur has to ask him-/herself the question: 'What must I do to achieve the desired goal – a successful organisation?' The challenge for the entrepreneur is now to choose the optimal strategies, resources, networks, etc., that enable them to achieve the best possible result. Through analysis, rational and objective decision-making (where they seek to maximise benefits and minimise the drawbacks), they are able to make those choices and produce a plan, which they predict will result in goal achievement. The entrepreneur focuses on the dimensions of the organisational process, which they believe to be predictive and enable them to control the course of events (Sarasvathy 2001).

It is assumed that the entrepreneur has almost complete information, clear preferences, and an available adequate resource base, and that the entrepreneur makes a plan with set steps for the entire organisation from the beginning. He or she plans before taking action. This last point highlights how the entrepreneur, in preparing the organising process is separated from the activities and challenges along with the risks associated with organising. That planning can be separated from the action, also points to the presupposition that the environment is more or less stable and transparent. The reason is that the planned process is expected to be relevant, in terms of the environment, at the time of implementation. Consequently, the planning perspective only makes sense if we assume that the future – or at least important aspects of the future – is predictable, that the entrepreneur's goals and preferences are clear, and that the environment is independent of the entrepreneur's actions. The logic behind this causal thinking is that to the extent the entrepreneur can predict the future, he or she is also able to control the future and thereby reduce the uncertainty and risk associated with organising (Sarasvathy 2008).

To illustrate the planning perspective Sarasvathy (2008) describes a cook creating a meal. Rationally, the chef starts by choosing the menu, which he or she will prepare. Then, the cook finds a recipe that he or she can follow in preparing the food. The next step is purchasing the ingredients that the recipe suggests, and then the meal can be created. The process 'starts with selecting a menu as a goal and finding effective ways to achieve the goal' (Sarasvathy 2008: 74). Figure 5.6 illustrates this process.

The recipes which the entrepreneur can use to create a new organisation are many. The literature recommends that first and foremost the entrepreneur answer questions such as: what is the goal, vision and mission of the organisation? How will the entrepreneur organise and manage the organisation, including issues such as number of employees, organisational procedures, management style, organisational structure, etc.? How can the entrepreneur achieve organisational 'lift-off' in terms of strategy, marketing, growth, internationalization, etc.? The answers can be built into the business plan model, which is discussed in Chapter 9.

Organising is all about improvisation

Entrepreneurs are, however, rarely faced with predictable environments and they have by no means complete information about the future, clear preferences about goals or unlimited resources, which the planning perspective seems to assume. The organising process is simply too complex and unclear, and it will only show its true nature through the entrepreneur's actual activities and struggles to understand the goal, gain access to and control over resources, establishing an organisation, etc., and even then the nature and direction of the organising process will take new forms. These thoughts are captured by the improvisation perspective on organising.

This perspective emphasises first and foremost that the entrepreneur cannot, in advance, articulate a clear goal of the organisation or a plan for achieving his or her objective. Instead, an entrepreneur needs to give up control and build on the often-limited resources that he or she has available right now. The entrepreneur must look to the present situation and current opportunities and find new directions along the way to transform this opportunity into a new independent organisation or organisational unit within an existing organisation. The perspective is based on the idea that a bird in the hand is worth more than two in the bush (Sarasvathy 2008). In other words, make use of what you have when organising instead of starting with the ultimate goal. The entrepreneur's starting point should be based on what is sure and not on a dream of achieving a Bill Gates level of success that he or she may never achieve.

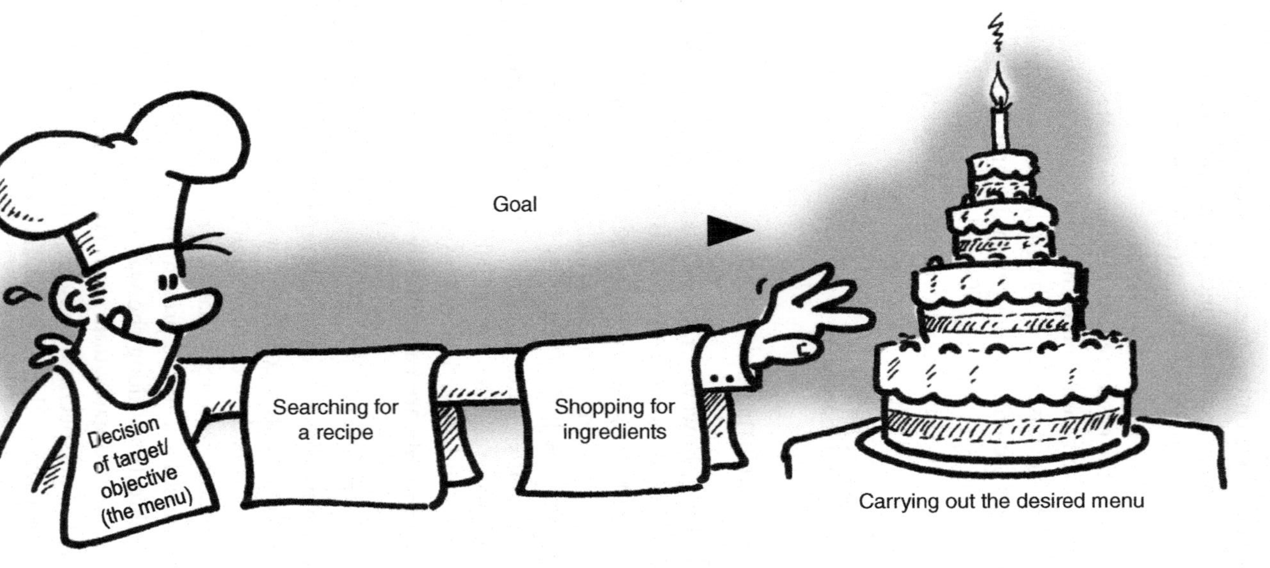

Source: Inspired by Sarasvathy (2008).

Figure 5.6 The planning perspective

Sarasvathy (2008) uses the term 'effectuation' to capture the logic behind the improvisation perspective's approach to organising. According to the effectuation-mind the organising is characterised by the entrepreneur asking him-/herself: 'What effects can I achieve with the resources I have?' Thus: 'What do I do right here?' Whereas the entrepreneur's challenge in the planning perspective was to choose the most optimal strategies, the entrepreneur's challenge when entering an improvised scene is to create the organisation through the exploration of possible combinations and modifications of the available means. It requires an open approach to organising, where the entrepreneur involves others because it is through interaction with others that he or she can gain access to new resources, which can help to create larger and more valuable organisations. To a great extent, the involvement of others generates a dynamic organisation because the entrepreneur must at all times behave flexibly, creatively and experimentally with the varying inputs that interaction with others give rise to. The organisation may end up with several different outcomes that cannot be predicted in advance.

Sarasvathy (2008) illustrates the effectuation perspective by once again relating organising to the preparation of a meal. The cook begins the improvisation process by looking in kitchen cupboards to find out which raw materials, ingredients and tools he or she has available. Then the cook designs possible meals that can be created from the ingredients found. It is a process characterised by improvisation, where the cook has to feel his or her way and try out different combinations. Actually, the meal is often developed in parallel with the cook preparing it. The cook 'starts with a given kitchen, and designs possible, sometimes unintended, even entirely original meals with its contents' (Sarasvathy 2008: 74). The process may thus end up in vastly different meals that you could not have predicted in advance. It is the many small steps involved in looking into the cupboard and trying out the available resources that creates the menu. The result of this process can only be seen in retrospect – when you look back and see what actually happened. Figure 5.7 illustrates this process.

Sarasvathy (2008) elaborates on how the organising process evolves in light of the improvisation perspective. Improvisation is often connected with a random process, but as illustrated in Figure 5.8, it is nevertheless possible to identify features that characterise improvisation. Sarasvathy (2008) argues that entrepreneurs typically have three resources available as they enter the organising process, namely, insight into: 1) 'Who I am' 2) 'What I know' and 3) 'Whom I know'. From these resources the entrepreneur assesses what possible actions he or she can implement, which the entrepreneur often only becomes

Source: Inspired by Sarasvathy (2008).

Figure 5.7 The improvising perspective

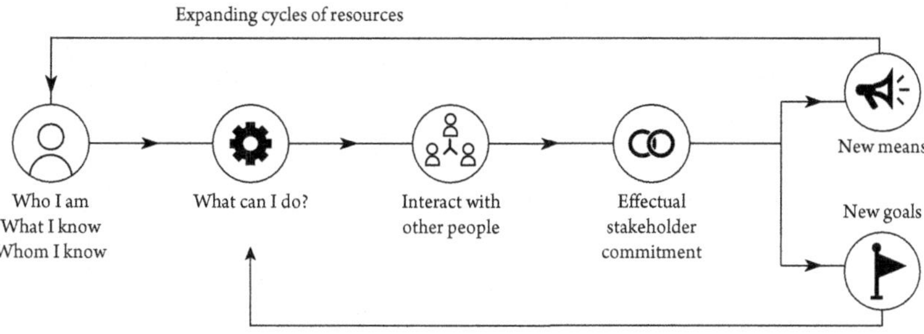

Source: Sarasvathy (2008: 101).

Figure 5.8 Clarification of the improvising perspective

aware of through interaction with others. Sometimes the interactions lead to these others becoming attached to the emerging organisation, such as in the role of investor, advisor, partner, customer, etc. The many new actors who are involved in the entrepreneurial process also means that new means and thus resources and objectives become part of the entrepreneurial process and that opens new potential avenues for activities on the part of the entrepreneur.

Organising: planning or improvisation?

The paradox in this chapter is whether the organising progresses as a planned process, or whether the organisation is more improvisational in character. Table 5.1 summarises the core of the paradox.

In the planning perspective, the goal is therefore determined in advance and the key issue for the entrepreneur is: 'What can I do to achieve the desired goal?' It is assumed that the entrepreneur through rational decision-making, analysis, control, generic recipes and planning can shape the organisation towards the desired goal. Process predictability is high, since it is assumed that the environment is fairly stable and transparent, the entrepreneur's preferences are clear, and the goal is given.

On the other hand, the focal point of the improvising perspective is that resources are limited, so the entrepreneur's starting point must be based on the question 'What can I achieve with the resources I have?' What kind of organisation can he or she create? By being open in the organising, focused on 'here and now', feeling one's way and interacting with other players, the entrepreneur forms an organisation based on the means that he or she has available and additional resources that are gradually added to the organisation as a result of the entrepreneur's involvement with others. The predictability of the

Table 5.1 The paradox: Planning or improvisation

	Planning	Improvising
Starting point	The target is given	The means are given
Crucial question	'What can I do in order to achieve the desired effect?'	'What can I do with these means?'
The role of the entrepreneur	A rational architect	An improvising creator and social agent
Crucial activities	Analysis, planning	Small steps, interaction
Predictability of output	High	Low

organising process is low as it is available resources, the participating actors, the many small steps and social interactions that shape the organisation.

Sarasvathy's thoughts on improvisation dominate this chapter, and it is important to conclude by mentioning that she does not see planning and improvisation as 'either-or'. According to her, elements of both planning and improvisation can be identified in any organisation. However, Sarasvathy (2001) assumes improvisation processes to be more frequent and useful in understanding the uncertain, risky and unpredictable conditions that are often the hallmark of entrepreneurial situations.

A theoretical interpretation

And so back to the chapter's beginning, where you met Claus Meyer and heard his organising story. We will now offer an interpretation of the story firstly from a planning perspective and then we'll shift the focus to the improvising perspective.

The planning perspective

A planning-based interpretation of Claus' story is in many ways difficult, because the story is simply better aligned with the improvising perspective. However, on closer inspection planning and calculation are also present in the story.

Firstly, Claus has a long-term mission and therefore a goal. It is within this framework that he improvises. There are then certain business types and areas that he will not get involved with because they are inconsistent with the mission. This indicates that Claus is partly rational in his organising and that this is somewhat controlled by the question: 'What can I do to achieve the desired effect?' For example, in Noma, one can say that Claus identifies an appropriate business partner who has knowledge of haute cuisine and experience in the gourmet industry to achieve his initially established objective. Together they create an output that fulfils that goal.

The story also raises the question of whether Claus perhaps plays (at least in part) on his image and brand as 'missionary', which is, so to speak, above mundane calculation and goal-oriented behaviour. It is certainly a fact that at one point in time he chose to study at Business School, specializing in starting and developing businesses, where he must have heard a lot about the rational models, economic management and the like. This education must have given him the business acumen and analytical tools that can be used selectively to create new organisations. Of course, he says: 'I've never worked with plans', but it can be understood in the sense that he has not produced actual business plans before starting-up. However, he has obviously thought strategically and thoroughly considered the steps he takes.

Finally it is worth noticing that Claus at some point chooses to make use of a professional board. The board support him in developing a structured and focused organisation: 'The board supports me in having a well organised company with the right skills in the right positions relative to what we want to do'. He is probably aware that traditional, rational organisational leadership is not his strong point, and to compensate for this he will establish a board that can rein in his desire for improvisation. This decision also indicates that Claus thinks and plans rationally in his organising activities.

The improvising perspective

Although there are elements of planning in the story, we can't ignore that it is predominantly told in the spirit of the improvising perspective. Claus' approach to entrepreneurship is oriented towards improvisation. In many ways he keeps away from planning or at least he tries to minimise that side of things.

The improvising perspective is demonstrated by the fact that Claus from the outset had no clear intention of where he wanted to go with his organising activities. Instead, his starting point was the means that he had with him right from the time when he started his student business. A key motto seems to have been: 'we started in the easiest way'. In this way he has, step-by-step, created a complex of food-based companies with a focus on quality. So, we are also talking about an organising process that had no predefined goal or strategy. Based on a lot of small actions and interactions an output that no one could predict was created, along with some results that were never sought after. As Claus says: 'I've never wanted a big company', but all the same he ended up with one. Claus is aware of the unpredictable nature of organising. For example, as he says about the Nordic cuisine: 'How the new Nordic movement will end up is not something I can explain. We will know that in about 10–20 years'.

Claus' story clearly illustrates that he has a social and interactive personality and how, by involving others, being close to them and getting them to feel a connection with his organising activities, Claus constantly creates new things. As he says: 'Better to win a small victory with the people you love than reaching for a distant goal'. Claus seems to be an expert at mobilising resources, through interaction with others, for the organisations he has helped to develop. But Claus also understands the need to involve other stakeholders in a broader sense. This shows in the story of the symposium he organised of ministers, CEOs and the like.

However, the improvisation perspective is probably best illustrated by how Claus compares the entrepreneurial organising process to cooking. He says he dances about the food, and he draws on the resources available to him when he cooks. He lives, so to speak, in accordance with Sarasvathy's (2008) theory of entrepreneurship as an improvisational process, focusing on the means available.

Finally, one can ask: 'Why didn't Claus start with establishing Noma, which is really the opportunity that truly realises his mission in life?' This can also be explained using the improvisation perspective. At the beginning Claus hardly had the necessary skills and resources to start Noma. He had yet to gain legitimacy as an entrepreneur in his environment, sufficient experience or cooking skills, and above all, he had not met the people who have contributed to the opportunity creation. A lot of small steps had to be taken before Claus was ready to realise his mission.

Testing the theory

Think of what you have learned in the chapter and try to review some of the exercises below. This will help you gain an increased understanding of organising for entrepreneurship.

? EXERCISES

1 **Put yourself in focus.** Think back to the process that you went through when you had to choose your course of study. Draw a picture of the process and reflect on whether planning perspective, improvising perspective or a combination thereof, can best explain the process.
2 **Elevator pitch.** Identify two or three advantages and disadvantages of the planning and improvising perspectives respectively, as seen from the entrepreneur's point of view. Next write out an elevator pitch (see Chapter 1), where you first 'sell' the improvising perspective and then the planning perspective to an audience.
3 **'Both-and' exercise.** Sarasvathy (2008) believes that elements of improvisation and planning can both be found in the entrepreneurial organising process. Start by choosing a case (possibly one of the cases that are presented in this book) and analyse the case study in light of the two perspectives. Can both perspectives be identified?

LITERATURE

Aldrich, H.E. (1999) *Organizations Evolving,* London: Sage.

Allen, K.R. (2006) *Launching New Ventures: An Entrepreneurial Approach,* Boston, MA: Houghton Mifflin Company.

Berger, P.L. and Kellner, H. (1981) *Sociology Reinterpreted: An Essay on Methods and Vocation,* New York: Doubleday Anchor.

Bhave, M.P. (1994) 'A process model of new venture creation', *Journal of Business Venturing,* 9, 223–242.

Bosma, N., Acs, Z., Autio, E., Conduras, A. & Levie, J. (2008) *Global Entrepreneurship Monitor 2008 Executive Report,* London: Global Entrepreneurship Monitor Association.

Brush, C.G. & Manolova, T.S. (2004) 'Start-up problems', in Gartner, W.B., Shaver, K.G., Carter, N.M. & Reynolds, P.D. (eds), *Handbook of Entrepreneurial Dynamics – The Process of Business Creation,* Thousand Oaks, CA: Sage, 273–285.

Fayolle, A. (2003) 'Research and researchers at the heart of entrepreneurial situations', in Steyaert, C. & Hjorth, D. (eds) *New Movements in Entrepreneurship,* Cheltenham, UK and Northampton, MA, USA: Edward Elgar Publishing, 35–50.

Gartner, W.B. (1985) 'A conceptual framework for describing the phenomenon of new venture creation', *Academy of Management Review,* 10(4), 696–706.

Gartner, W.B., Bird, B.J. & Starr, J.A. (1992) 'Acting as if. Differentiating entrepreneurial from organizational behavior', *Entrepreneurship Theory and Practice,* 16(3), 13–31.

Hatch, M.J. (1997) *Organization Theory,* Oxford: Oxford University Press.

Headd, B. (2003) 'Redefining business success: Distinguishing between closure and failure', *Small Business Economics,* 21(1), 51–61.

Jones, G.R. (2007) *Organizational Theory, Design, and Change,* Upper Saddle River, NJ: Prentice Hall.

Katz, J. & Gartner, W.B. (1988) 'Properties of emerging organizations', *Academy of Management Review,* 13(3), 429–441.

Kelley, D., Bosma, N. & Amoros, J.E. (2011) *Global Entrepreneurship Monitor, 2010 Global Report,* GERA (www.gemconsortium.org, last accessed 20 December 2016).

Levie, J., Don, G. & Leleux, B. (2011) 'The new venture mortality myth', in Hindle, K. & Klyver, K. (eds), *Handbook of Research on New Venture Creation,* Cheltenham, UK and Northampton, MA, USA: Edward Elgar Publishing, 194–215.

March, J.G. & Simon, H.A. (1958) *Organizations,* New York/London/Sydney: John Wiley and Sons.

McKelvey, B. (1980) *Organizational Systematics,* Berkeley, CA: University of California Press.

Morgan, G. (1997) *Images of Organization*, 2nd edn, Thousand Oaks, CA/London/New Delhi: Sage Publications.
Sarasvathy, S.D. (2001) 'Causation and effectuation: Toward a theoretical shift from economic inevitability to entrepreneurial contingency', *Academy of Management Review*, 26(2), 243–263.
Sarasvathy, S.D. (2008) *Effectuation: Elements of Entrepreneurial Expertise*, Cheltenham, UK and Northampton, MA, USA: Edward Elgar Publishing.
Shane, S. (2003) *A General Theory of Entrepreneurship: The Individual–Opportunity Nexus*, Cheltenham, UK and Northampton, MA, USA: Edward Elgar Publishing.
Weick, K.E. (1995) *Sensemaking in Organizations*, Thousand Oaks, CA: Sage Publications.
Wickham, P.A. (2004) *Strategic Entrepreneurship*, Boston, MA: Pearson Education.

6

Nascent entrepreneurship

As you have probably already sensed, there are many different ways of understanding what entrepreneurship is, and each of these understandings has their own purpose and existence. Without suggesting, in any way, that one understanding is more correct than any other, entrepreneurship is most frequently understood in terms of business start-up. This understanding is closely associated with nascent entrepreneurship, or 'nascent entrepreneurs'. Whilst the focus on start-up concerns the actual occurrence of 'business start-ups', nascent entrepreneurship focuses on the process leading up to the start up of a business. Nascent entrepreneurship is thus about the discussions and activities that take place as individuals go through the process from first having the intention to start a business, through to achieving the start-up. In other words, everything that precedes the business start-up.

What are these considerations that people go through from the first spawning of the idea through to starting the realised business? How do they dare to try? What drives them? What resources do they need, and are they available? Do they know enough about how to run a business? How do they get started? Is there a formula, an order or a checklist that one can sensibly follow? These are questions that nascent entrepreneurship and this chapter deal with.

Entrepreneurship in practice

Before we get started with the various theories and models that have been developed within research to understand nascent entrepreneurship, we present an interesting story from Uganda about the starting of a soap company – a start-up where strong individuals were involved, but also where a strong collective or community plays a crucial role.

CASE STUDY

ADAM: community entrepreneurship

(**Devised by Benson Honig**)

Pearl had an important decision to make, but worried she was out of her depth this time. James was standing before her insisting that the only way forward for their rural co-op to succeed was to purchase a motorcycle for transportation of their soap products – but she simply had no idea what kinds of expenses she would have to anticipate. How much would petrol and oil cost? What about spare parts? What would happen if the motorcycle broke down?

ADAM, their soap-making co-op, began 18 months ago, when one of their former village members – Sam – returned from Kampala, having finished university and successfully running his own tourism and consulting firm. The village – Baakijjulula, in the Mityana district of Uganda – was about an hour-and-a-half taxi ride from the urban capital Kampala, but seemed to be a century apart in many other ways. Only dirt roads led to the village. There was no running water and almost all of the houses in the village lacked electricity. Most people survived by basic subsistence farming and a little poultry raising: one of their biggest challenges was to pay the small costs of school fees, uniforms, and other basic educational needs of the community's children. HIV was rampant, and there were many grandmothers raising their grandchildren by themselves. There were few if any opportunities to work or enter the labour market – as there were no factories or service businesses nearby. The barter economy tended to be the norm – people traded what they had, such as the odd chicken – for special services such as midwifery or simple mechanics.

Pearl takes up the story: 'When Sam came to visit, after nearly 10 years of "city living", he brought along a young "*muzungu*" (white person, in Swahili), a female college student named June, from the United States. Together, they assembled the entire village for a community meeting. Sam knew how poor the community was – he was one of the very few lucky ones to escape and earn a real education in Kampala. Most of the other boys were virtually illiterate, and just "hung about" in the roadway when they weren't helping out with their home gardening chores. Sam and June asked everyone to share with each other, what they thought was wrong with Baakijjulula. The meeting lasted all night. People complained about everything. Of course, the men did most of the talking, as they often did – they took over the meeting. Health issues (the nearest clinic was a long bus ride away), no running water or electricity, no money for school fees, leaking roofs in the rainy season, no opportunity for work, poverty, the list of grievances went on and on. After hearing about all the problems, Sam and June made a suggestion. They asked us to write down on a piece of paper all the things we spent money on for the next month . . . every Ugandan cent. They indicated they would return for another community meeting in a month's time.

The next time Sam and June visited, we were ready. Everyone handed in their forms, and June tallied up the numbers. Farming items and school fees led the list, followed by something

CASE STUDY *(continued)*

that surprised all of us – the third most common item of expense on everyone's budget was soap. That's when we had this great idea – what if we started a soap-making factory in our own village? We could sell soap to our rural neighbours – because like us – they must also be purchasing soap products. Would it be possible?

June stayed in the village for the following month, to help us organise what they called a "cooperative". It was complicated work. We had to organise a leadership body, a set of rules, collect small investment money – the list of things we had to do seemed endless. While we were organising with June, Sam went to the university in search of soap-making capabilities. The following month, he returned with Thomas, a soap-making expert from Kampala. By that time, June had organised us into a fully functioning cooperative, with a leadership and a clear set of rules regarding how money would be earned, and how it would be shared. Thirty people joined our co-op. We called our co-op "ADAM".

When Thomas arrived, we set to work learning the secrets of soap manufacturing. It wasn't easy. Many people didn't trust Thomas, and kept challenging him regarding the exact recipe and techniques involved. It took more than a month of dedicated training for us to learn how to make the concentrated liquid soap – but when we were done – we were so proud! We had made very attractive yellow and green liquid soap, which we bottled in leftover plastic containers. A visiting professor, Dr. Benson Honig, arranged to have a logo and labels designed for us in Canada. We began selling to all our neighbours, and for the first time ever we generated our own employment opportunities.

Of course, not everything went smoothly. Transportation was a serious problem. We had to rely on local "*matatus*" (shared rural taxis) to go in and out of Kampala for our raw materials. One of the most important ingredients – palm oil – had to be directly imported from Congo, by sending someone off to the border with gallon jugs on a two-day rural bus ride. We always worried that our procurers would have difficulty crossing the borders, and obtaining the critical ingredients. Even worse, it seemed that the women wound up doing all of the work, and the men made all the decisions and took all the money. Two events recently happened that shook the very foundations of the co-op. First, one of the men responsible for purchasing the raw material from Kampala claimed that all our working capital was "stolen" from him by a middleman. We had no way to verify what took place, but it almost bankrupted us. Next, one of the married men was caught womanising with one of the young unmarried women working at the co-op. For that offence, he was "run out of town" and can no longer show his face in our village. One thing led to another, and when we were nearly insolvent, the women got together. ENOUGH!! We said. How come we do all the work, and you men take all the money? In any case, you wind up squandering our profits or mismanaging the co-op. We women got together, and with June's help, we took over financial and managerial control of the co-op. Because I had two years of secondary school, I became the bookkeeper and day-to-day co-op manager. With careful control, we began, for the first time, making and distributing co-op profits to our membership.

And now, James, one of our delivery boys, was standing before me, asking about purchasing

CASE STUDY *(continued)*

a motorcycle for the co-op that would cost at least US$1500 – about five months of our total revenue! He claimed that we were losing both money and time when we sent our product on the bus to other small towns. He assured us that we would make up that lost time and money by not having to send someone to Kampala by bus each week to buy raw materials. But, there were many unanswered questions. How much would insurance and maintenance cost us? What if the motorcycle was in an accident or was stolen? Who would take care of it? As I pondered all these questions, I knew we had only $850 in cash deposits, and another $600 invested in product. I also knew that we were losing a lot of time due to material shortages. There were times that we shut the factory down for two days while we waited for supplies. Our transportation costs – for both sales and ingredients – accounted for almost 20 per cent of our overall costs. But a motorcycle – I just had no idea of how to make this decision'.

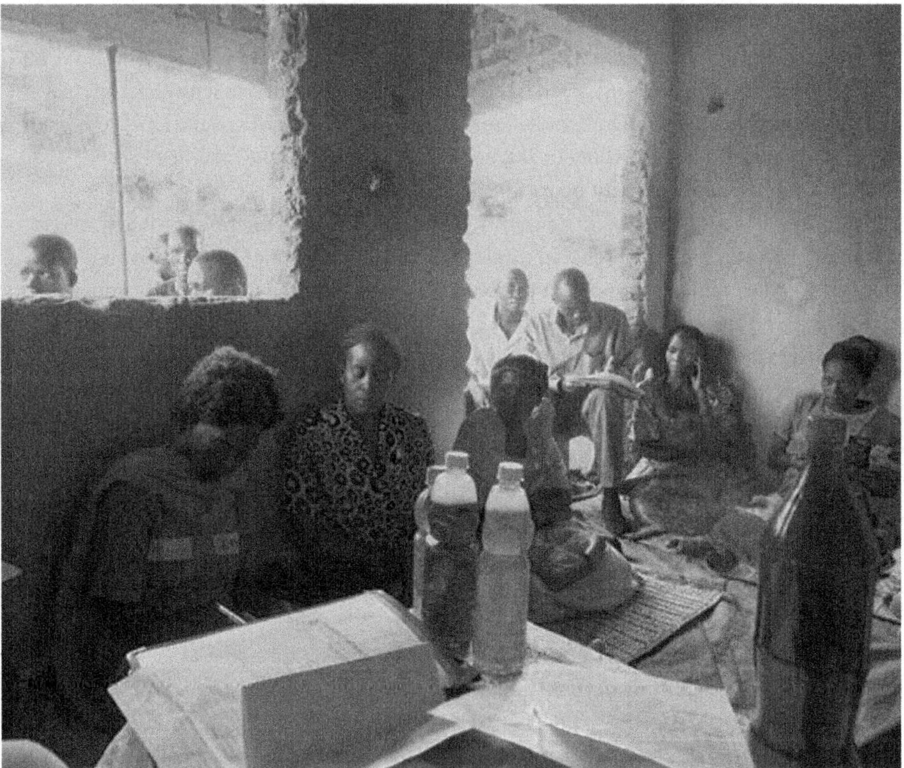

Source: Benson Honig.

Figure 6.1 The women in charge of ADAM, a soap-making co-op

Your immediate interpretation

What does the ADAM story tell you about the problems and challenges 'nascent entrepreneurs' experience during the start-up process? What is your immediate interpretation of the story? The following questions and exercises may help you along the way:

- Where did the idea for ADAM come from? How would you interpret opportunity emergence from a discovery perspective and a creation perspective?
- Who is (are), in fact, the entrepreneur(s) in the story? What different roles do Pearl, Sam, June and Benson play? Who do you think is most important?
- Pearl says that 'the list of things we had to do seemed endless'. What kind of activities would this include, and how could they be organised? To what extent would a business plan help with organising things?
- When you look at the situation Pearl is in, what do you think she should do? Should she buy the motorcycle or not? And what things should she consider when she tries to make the decision?

Theories of nascent entrepreneurship

There can be many different grounds for, and reasons why, individuals choose to start a business. Some want a different and more interesting working life, some want more family time, some want to earn money, some just want to try something new, some have been fired, and yes, some may not have many other options. Of course, it is often a combination of reasons that best captures why some choose to start a business, but it is also a matter of perspective. In this respect, we can basically talk about two main perspectives that attempt to explain the motivation to start a business.

One perspective focuses on people being drawn to attractive business opportunities, working conditions and circumstances in which they choose to change career tracks and test themselves as an entrepreneur or as self-employed. Here then, one is drawn to an attractive career path and the choice to become independent is a definite strategic choice. The second perspective focuses on being pushed into a career change because one does not really have other options – here we are talking about a survival strategy, for example, when someone is unemployed and has not been successful in finding work, but is desperate to get an income to pay rent and support themselves and their family. A decision to start a business from this perspective is much less strategic and more of a necessary choice forced by circumstances. This chapter therefore introduces you to the paradox:

Necessity or opportunity?

Entrepreneurship, self-employment and nascent entrepreneurship

There are a variety of theories and models that try, in various ways, to explain why some choose to start businesses whilst others choose alternative career paths. In the career literature – which has a broad focus on different career types and not just self-employment as a career choice – there are two main types of explanatory models. One could be called the 'person–job fit' model, which focuses on the idea that people will eventually find a career that is an appropriate fit between their desires, ambitions and abilities, and what a given career offers and demands (Holland 1997). Here we are talking about a rational perspective, illustrated by the fact that the individual optimises his or her fit throughout his or her career by continuous alignment of personal interests and career characteristics. The theory is normative as it seeks to explain how individuals should optimise their career choice.

The second perspective is descriptive as opposed to normative, and instead focuses on how career decisions are made, and not least what affects such decisions (Sauermann 2005). Here the focus is therefore on the various factors that influence individuals' career decisions, and how they process the input in order to ultimately make decisions. This is a behavioural perspective that does not focus on providing a guide to how such decisions should be taken, as is the case with the 'person–job fit' perspective.

It is the behavioural perspective that is dominant within the nascent entrepreneurship literature. We have tried to group the different types of impacts that affect individuals' choice of business start-up (Figure 6.2).

There are three main types of impact: institutional factors (or environmental factors), 'life events' and individual factors. These will, individually and collectively, affect nascent entrepreneurship, including both the decision to launch start-ups as well as the final result. And this influence will occur either via opportunity-based motivation, necessity-based motivation, or a combination thereof. When factors bring influence to bear via opportunity-based motivation, the impact is often through influence on 'perceived behavioural control', 'subjective norms' and 'attitude towards the behaviour', as

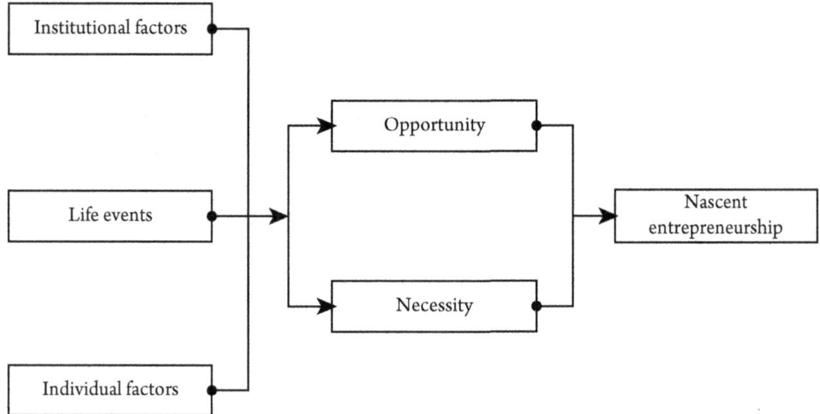

Figure 6.2 Influence of nascent entrepreneurship

we mentioned previously in Chapter 2. In the following, we review the three factors (institutional factors, life events and individual factors) that influence nascent entrepreneurship.

Institutional factors influencing nascent entrepreneurship

There are a wide range of environmental factors that affect the degree to which individuals consider starting a business, as well as whether their deliberations end with a successful start-up (Bruton et al 2010). These environmental factors are also called institutions. Institutions are socially created structures that shape individuals' 'interpretation' and 'sense-making' of what they are experiencing, and thus affect their subsequent choices and behaviour. Institutions are divided into two main types. There are formal institutions such as the judiciary and ministries that operate through regulation, laws and instructions, and then there are informal institutions such as culture, social norms, rules, etc.

Institutions help to create the framework for nascent entrepreneurship and thereby to influence the attractiveness of self-employment for the individual. For example, a country can affect individuals' inclination to start businesses by easing the administrative burdens associated with company operations, various tax benefits, security of private property, creating a credible financial system and in general building a society where it is attractive to become self-employed. However, a series of informal structures is also crucial – for example, cultural features that award high status for being self-employed. In addition, a number of studies show that both culture and religion are very important in attracting people to an entrepreneurial career. For example, cultures with a high degree of individualism coupled with the Protestant religion are often associated with high entrepreneurial activity.

The various institutions do not necessarily have the same effect on every individual. Each person reacts individually within institutions. Some are more sensitive to cultural influences than others, and some will even 'swim against the tide'. However, there is a tendency for institutions to standardise behaviour within a population: a process known as isomorphism (DiMaggio & Powell 1983), for example, greater corruption in a country where corruption is widely accepted, than in a country where corruption is considered contemptuous.

Individual factors influencing nascent entrepreneurship

Besides institutional factors there are also a number of individual factors that matter. In previous chapters, we have already discussed the meaning of financial, human and social resources that affect the behaviour of entrepreneurs. However, there are many other individual factors.

One of the most significant, which has been the subject of much research, is gender. Research shows that women and men are equally likely to start a business, but for different reasons and with different results (Klyver et al 2013). The discussions about the difference between male and female entrepreneurship must, of course, be seen in close interaction with discussions on gender equality in the labour market.

Research shows that women, more often than men, start businesses as a result of being motivated to achieve a different family and work balance. They are often less growth oriented in the traditional profit-oriented sense. The research also indicates that women experience discrimination in access to capital, although the results are not conclusive and there are heated discussions on this point. There are also indications that women experience disadvantages due to less effective social networks, caused among other things by interrupted careers related to children.

Some of the findings on gender equality are paradoxical. Among industrialised countries, there are, of course, different degrees of equality. In industrialised countries with the highest degree of equality we find the biggest difference in the start-up rate among men and women. This is due to the benefits associated with actions to promote equality, primarily available for employees but not for the self-employed. As a result, female entrepreneurs experience specific handicaps if they choose to become self-employed, rather than if they choose a career as an employee where equality benefits are available.

There are also a number of psychological traits often associated with entrepreneurs. They have high confidence, are extroverts, optimistic, risk-takers, etc. Their preferences for their working life are often associated with a desire for self-fulfilment, autonomy and freedom, and to a much lesser degree (than is often believed) a desire for high monetary rewards. These psychological themes have already been discussed in Chapter 2.

An individual factor that we have not, however, discussed already is that of opportunity costs. When a person has a good education, a good social network, extensive experience and so on – in short, when a person has high human and social capital – that person has a better chance of starting a business successfully. They can use their access to the resources and they can use their knowledge to ensure they start a business with an idea, and develop it in a way that creates competitive advantages and thereby ensures survival and profits. This point is pretty much agreed upon. However, there's a problem when you use these explanations to understand why some people start companies when others do not, because the social network and experience can also be used to get good-quality jobs as an employee. So it seems the different resources affect several different career opportunities. We therefore speak of an opportunity cost. Opportunity costs associated with starting a business are related to when one rejects other alternatives such as the offer of a job and the value lost by rejecting that job or other alternatives.

The literature on nascent entrepreneurship focuses a lot on individual factors, and this is probably, in part, because entrepreneurship research has always, to a certain extent been concerned with the cult of the individual – the entrepreneur as a hero. However, many companies are started not by individuals, but by groups of individuals – by teams. In a study of American start-ups, it turned out that 52 per cent of all businesses were started by a team rather than by a single individual. Of these, the vast majority were teams of two people (74 per cent), but there were also teams of several people, and in some cases even more than five people (Ruef et al 2003). The composition of the teams will depend on a variety of mechanisms, including:

- homophily (people are equal with regard to 'ascriptive characteristics' such as gender, age, ethnic background);
- functionality (people have different skills, knowledge and experience, and personal traits);

- networks (people already know each other);
- geography (people living in the same area).

The composition of a team is highly crucial for future success. One must, on the one hand, put together a team with some diversity to allow members to complement and reinforce one another – and this diversity relates to both personality traits and the knowledge and experience that the members bring. On the other hand, one must also be sufficiently in agreement as to how the company should be run so as to avoid too much of the team's energy being devoted to internal disagreements and conflicts. It is a difficult but essential balance. It is often said that venture capitalists focus more on the composition of the team than on the business idea when they make their investments. There is also strong evidence to suggest that the various formations of the teams are important for survival and performance, but also that it depends on the situation, including industries, the degree of innovation and the company's lifecycle, etc.

Life events influencing nascent entrepreneurship

Apart from the institutional and individual factors already mentioned, there are also factors related to specific events or people's lives that affect whether they choose to start a business or not, and whether they will be successful with it. There are two types of explanation. One type of explanation relates to the pattern of life over time, from childhood through adulthood and old age. This explanation is the lifecycle explanation. In contrast to the lifecycle explanation there are explanations focusing on individual events and events that affect the decision of whether or not to start a business: we might call them event explanations. These two types of explanation are clarified below.

Lifecycle

There are periods in a person's life where one is more likely to take the plunge into entrepreneurship than others. Life stage theory is a theory that attempts to explain these differences. The focus is on different transitions in the lives of individuals which follow a relatively well-defined pattern and where one transition affects the next. Key transitions include, among others, from being a student to graduation, single to being married, from couples to becoming parents, from married to being divorced, from being a student to becoming an employee, and from being an employee to retiring (Figure 6.3). In this chapter, we are particularly interested in how these different transitions affect the decision to become self-employed.

Figure 6.3 Lifecycles and nascent entrepreneurship

There are two key mechanisms in the pattern and the tendency to start a business over time. One mechanism is the resource accumulation that occurs over time as people get older and acquire knowledge, experience and networks. This accumulation increases the tendency to start a business. The second mechanism is risk willingness, which is often assumed to decrease with age. Young people often have less responsibility and often only for themselves, but as they become adults they will have added responsibility for others, and this will reduce their risk willingness. When you are nearing retirement, there is often more to lose than to win, and this will also reduce risk willingness. The two conflicting mechanisms have been empirically shown to mean that the probability of start-ups increases as people get older, peaking in their middle 30s, and then decreasing towards retirement age.

In several countries, there is a displacement of these lifecycle effects. More and more older people – and even the retired – have started a business the past decade. This has meant that the curve flattens out and becomes more widespread in the later part of their lives. This concept has been referred to as senior entrepreneurship. There can be several reasons for this trend, which often include decreasing pension and an increasing desire among older people to continue working.

Events

Life stages are one thing, but there are also many unique things that occur throughout life. We all know of situations or events, either in our own life or in that of others, where these events have had a crucial effect on life: situations where life takes a turn because of a single event.

Our lives can be divided into working life and social/family sphere, or privacy, if you will. These spheres are connected and closely related – what happens in one sphere affects what happens in another sphere. Therefore, one can also find an explanation for why some people start a business in different life situations associated with the two social spheres.

In entrepreneurship, research focuses on a variety of such events – for example, divorce or children moving from home. These events can affect people's career choices because they free up some resources, cause changes in risk willingness, create necessity, or simply create a desire to try something new. For example, there are many examples of how being suddenly fired from a job gets people to try to achieve their old dream of becoming an entrepreneur. If they had not been fired, they would certainly never have had the impetus to get started: the dismissal provided the necessary impetus. However, we also see the opposite happening, where someone who is self-employed is offered an attractive job and closes the business in order to become an employee. The focus here is not the stage of life, but the event itself.

Hybrid entrepreneurship and freelancers

Although we are talking about employees and entrepreneurs as two mutually exclusive alternatives, it is actually very common that one is both at the same time. This is called 'hybrid entrepreneurship' – when people are, simultaneously, both employed and self-employed. Reducing the risk and opportunity costs is often why some choose a hybrid approach to starting a business. One frequently sees a hobby develop into a business that starts out small and gradually grows larger. This is a small, intentional process. The individual may already have a job and the company starts up quietly while they fit it in alongside their full-time job. When they are in a better position to determine whether the company can be successful, or when they simply cannot handle both tasks in parallel, they leave the job; thus, they have reduced the risks involved. Of course, there are also people who are more permanently hybrid entrepreneurs – for example, if they are running a business as a recreational interest. We have seen examples of people who import wine in their spare time or start microbreweries.

Moreover, some people find themselves in a grey area where freelancers are formally self-employed but are actually in a form of employment through a contractual relationship with a particular company. Another example is Uber, where taxi drivers find themselves in a grey area between self-employment and an employment relationship. The upheaval in labour market conditions and technologies that have occurred in industrialised countries in recent times suggests that in the future an increasing number will be hybrid entrepreneurs or pushed into a looser employment relationship in a formal contractual sense.

The start-up process

So, how does the entrepreneur get from the idea and intention to start a business to running a successful business? There are different approaches to describe this process, and the emphasis in the entrepreneurship literature has naturally tended to be on the start-up stage, and less on the stages following the establishment of the undertaking.

Basically, these different approaches can be found in what we call the business lifecycle models and process models. We describe each of them below.

We talked earlier in the chapter about lifecycle models describing individuals' stages through life. In business cycle models we use an analogy that explains these models as organisms. Bhidé (2000: 244) describes the analogy as follows: 'The lifecycle approach posits that just as humans pass through similar stages of physiological and psychological development from infancy to adulthood, so businesses evolve in predictable ways and encounter similar problems in their growth'.

The models are based on a number of assumptions. Firstly, a company goes through a number of identifiable phases. The sequence of these phases is predetermined and predictable, and companies evolve from a primitive stage to a more advanced stage over time (Levie & Lichtenstein, 2010).

Each stage is characterised by some special challenges that entrepreneurs face and must solve. The solution to a challenge in one stage is associated with a challenge in the next phase. The most famous business lifecycle model is Greiner's (1972). He differentiates between five stages with associated challenges:

- growth through creativity (challenge: crisis of leadership);
- growth through direction (challenge: crisis of autonomy);
- growth through delegation (challenge: crisis of control);
- growth through coordination (challenge: crisis of red tape);
- growth through collaboration (challenge: not defined).

These models provide good sense at an intuitive level and therefore have high face validity. Consequently, they are also popular models and are often used. However, they have also received considerable criticism. The fact that different authors have proposed different stages and how many stages there actually are, is in contrast with the idea that stages are predetermined and predictable. It has not been possible to validate the models empirically.

In response, other models have been developed that are better described as process models. These models assume no predetermined and predictable pattern in the development of companies. Instead, they see development more as an iterative process between creation and discovery, evaluation and organisation of opportunities, where feedback processes, adaptation and complexity play a much larger role. Examples of these models are the effectuation model, Levie and Lichtenstein's (2010) dynamic state model, and Shane's (2003) model of the entrepreneurial process.

In an attempt to conceptualise what characterises companies during their formation, in the very early stages before or right after the company was created Katz and Gartner (1988) identified four attributes: intent, resources, boundary and exchange. For each characteristic we can connect a variety of activities. For example, intention is connected to entrepreneurs advertising the business or participating in networks for entrepreneurs. Resources are connected to the entrepreneur obtaining funding through banks, business angels or venture capitalists. Boundary is associated with activities such as becoming registered for tax and obtaining other approvals. Last but not least, exchange is connected with the acquisition of telephone, email, address, etc.

Later empirical research has shown that different entrepreneurs implement these various gestation activities in a very different order and at a very different pace. It has been quite difficult to find a system and pattern to the order in which entrepreneurs implement the various activities, and many have concluded that it is completely individual. This has also contributed to the criticism of the previously described business lifecycle models. Nonetheless, one study has, to a certain extent, been able to create a pattern in activities that shows promise, but still requires validation through other future studies. In an Australian study, Gordon (2012) found empirical evidence that activities relating to exploration are dominant in the early start-up phase, and this is slowly taken over by activities dominated by exploitation.

Studies of the total time periods associated with business start-up have also shown that the start-up process will vary in length. Some react quickly and start in the same year, while others are underway for years. Somewhat surprisingly, this was found in one of the first studies of the start-up process (Carter et al 1996). Whilst some started and some gave up, there was a considerable (surprisingly large) proportion that were 'still trying'. One-and-a-half years after they were first contacted and had indicated they were in the process of starting a business, about a third reported that they were still about to start a business, whilst 48 per cent had started and 20 per cent had given up. This indicates something about the length of the start-up process and about persistence. The entrepreneurs had not given up, but had not started: many remain in this category, perhaps because it keeps their dream alive despite not having made much progress.

Necessity perspective of nascent entrepreneurship

There are different perspectives that can explain why some people start businesses and others do not. In earlier years, entrepreneurship research distinguished between push and pull factors. Amit and Muller (1995: 64) distinguish thus between the two factors:

> 'Push' entrepreneurs are those whose dissatisfaction with their positions, for reasons unrelated to their entrepreneurial characteristics, pushes them to start a venture. 'Pull' entrepreneurs are those who are lured by their new venture idea and initiate venture activity because of the attractiveness of the business idea and its personal implications.

Since then, this distinction has been frequently replaced by a difference between necessity or opportunity-based motivation, mainly driven by Global Entrepreneurship Monitor project (GEM), which over the years has tried to measure whether start-ups are subject to a pull motive (opportunity) or a push motive (necessity).

There is great variation in the proportion of individuals in a country that are respectively pulled or pushed into entrepreneurship. Not surprisingly, people in Africa who start businesses are far more pushed into it compared with, for example, people in Europe and North America. Of course, there are also major differences in the different parts of the world. GEM's measurement of this is an attempt to categorise and measure this objectively.

Sensibly, this measurement disregards the fact that there are different degrees of necessity, and that what necessity is can be perceived quite differently from continent to continent. For some people necessity refers to basic needs (such as food), while for others it refers to other much more sophisticated needs (for example, self-realisation). Furthermore, necessity has often been associated with economic necessity, whilst moral, religious or cultural necessity have not been discussed – but perhaps should be? GEM has, perhaps problematically, treated necessity and opportunity as different types of motivation, and as something that is relatively objective. However, the distinction can also be seen as being different perspectives, and thus a paradox arises. It depends on the eye of the beholder.

Most start-ups contain both an opportunity and a necessity element, and so the concepts can also be seen as perspectives rather than types of motivation.

From the necessity perspective, entrepreneurship is not a free choice but a necessary choice, which is, to some extent, determined by the environment or by events in that environment. Necessity can have different degrees ranging from being a matter of survival, to being a need to improve relative living conditions. The necessity perspective often refers to an unsustainable economic situation, because of redundancy, divorce etc. Dismissal, in itself, will not necessarily immediately push people into entrepreneurship, but prolonged unemployment may. As the possibility of assistance in the form of unemployment benefits or public services disappear, and as any savings are depleted, the pressure to do something increases, and one possibility could be to take the plunge and become an entrepreneur.

The view from this perspective is that the person is involuntarily forced into self-employment by external circumstances that are out of their own control. It is not necessarily a last resort, but it is a resort among few other unattractive alternatives.

Opportunity perspective of nascent entrepreneurship

The second perspective – opportunity perspective – takes a different view, looking at entrepreneurship as an active and conscious choice amongst several other attractive options. Here the individual is drawn into entrepreneurship because it is attractive, and in order to exploit a business opportunity.

There may be several reasons for people positively choosing to become an entrepreneur. Some of the most often discussed are (Carter et al 2003):

- independence;
- material incentives;
- social approval and status;
- fulfilment of personal values or norms;
- self-realisation.

Contrary to the general assumption, material and financial motives are rarely the primary driving force; instead it is the desire for independence and self-realisation. Research also shows that, on average, when taking into account their abilities, skills and knowledge, people do not earn more as entrepreneurs than they would as an employee. On the other hand, there is a greater disparity of earnings among entrepreneurs, and therefore we see entrepreneurs who are richer than average. However, these are few and far between – most earn less than they would as employees.

Table 6.1 The paradox: Necessity or opportunity

	Necessity	Opportunity
Basis of action	Environmentally determined	Deliberate, strategic choice
Motive force	Push	Pull
Motivation	Survival/Better living conditions	Exploit a possibility (self-realisation)
Career possibility	The only choice (last)	One among several
Potential	Low	High

All things considered we can say that the opportunity perspective sees entrepreneurship as a conscious choice by people who really have many other options. They are attracted to the opportunity to test themselves or their idea.

Nascent entrepreneurship: necessity based or opportunity based?

We have now come to the paradox that, in this chapter, is concerned with business start-ups being based on opportunity or necessity. Table 6.1 sums up the differences between the two perspectives.

Starting a business from a necessity perspective is context determined rather than being the result of a deliberate strategic choice. Individuals are pushed into entrepreneurship to survive or to improve an otherwise relative standard of living. We speak of it only as being the last alternative. The 'burning platform' can, of course, be seen in both absolute and relative terms, and there can be big differences in how it is interpreted in developing and industrialised countries, just as poverty is perceived differently from country to country. Often, but not always, companies initiated out of necessity have less growth potential, because there are fewer resources for developing the business model and the company.

Conversely, according to the opportunity perspective, start-ups are seen as an optimistic view of individuals' freedom of action and as a deliberate and strategic choice. It is therefore a question of individuals who are trying, to some extent, to optimise their life values through their career choice. They are driven by an attractive option that they want to exploit, and which draws them into entrepreneurship. They strive for the realisation of dreams. This option is just one among other possibilities, including, for example, good opportunities as an employee of a private or public organisation. Opportunity-based start-ups often have a much greater chance of establishing firms with growth potential, because the business opportunities are more often unique.

A theoretical interpretation

The necessity perspective

The necessity perspective is perhaps the most intuitive perspective to take in this case. People in Baakijjulula are poor, have no electricity or running water, there are very few job opportunities, and the quality of health is low among the population. They 'survived by basic subsistence farming and a little poultry raising'. Therefore, one can see the start of ADAM from a necessity perspective where community members were pushed into entrepreneurship to survive, or at least to create better living conditions. It is a necessity and there are not many other options. The special feature is, however, that the start-up is exceptionally difficult because there are very few, or almost no resources available to get the business started. So in this respect the business start-up was not an easy or natural way to raise living standards in general, otherwise they would probably have started several businesses already. One can easily imagine that many would have liked to start a business earlier if it would increase their standard of living, but many have been locked into their current situation.

One of the interesting aspects in the case study is that the community members were not individually able to mobilise the necessary financial and knowledge resources to start the soap factory, but by pooling limited resources in a co-op it was possible. It was a collective effort that enabled it – an effort, which was in fact initiated by an outside view provided by Sam who had been raised in the village. So, the push into entrepreneurship was maybe a little different than described earlier in this chapter, as it was not pressure felt by individuals, but rather a collective sense of pressure.

The very idea creation and development of the business was also a collective process. They could not individually discover the idea. It required a collective process and, not least, external intervention by Sam, June and Benson.

The opportunity perspective

The case can also be interpreted from an opportunity perspective. An old adage says that 'necessity is the mother of invention'. Looking at this case from an opportunity perspective, we can see that the very problems experienced by the residents of the village present opportunities for them to exploit in terms of businesses in their region and their rural environment. Opportunities must first be recognised. Large firms often overlook the needs of the rural poor. At 'the bottom of the pyramid' the number of units sold is typically smaller and may go unnoticed – although profit margins can be somewhat larger. Locally sourced solutions often represent an important opportunity that the rural poor are often knowledgeable enough to exploit. In this case, by examining how they typically spend their money, they were in a position to identify a good manufacturing opportunity. By using local labour, some locally sourced ingredients, recycled packaging, and by leveraging their local expertise and connections, they were in an excellent position to exploit the soap-making initiative. As always, the 'trick' is to identify an opportunity not already identified by everyone else. In the case of the soap-making project, there was considerable knowledge necessary to produce the product – something to which their neighbours did not have access. Furthermore, the co-op project necessitated an array of labour – not only to make the soap, but also to obtain the ingredients, and develop and market the products. Each of these elements of the supply chain provided yet more opportunities to exploit and develop sustained competitive advantage (SCA) – the most critical ingredient to any ongoing enterprise.

Testing the theory

Now think about what you've read and learned in the chapter. Maybe you would like to know more about why some people start a business but others do not, and about which activities and processes they go through when they are trying to start. To help you on your way, try going through the following exercises.

? EXERCISES

1 **Contact your local business organisation.** Many countries and regions have a number of offers, provided by the local business organisation, that are open to people who are considering starting a business. It may be free advice or courses. Find the organisation closest to you and investigate what offers are available to you – either via the Internet or through direct contact. Next, consider whether you want to participate in one of the offered activities or other opportunities.

2 **Analyse your country or a country around you.** Visit the Global Entrepreneurship Research Association's website (http://www.gemconsortium.org/data/key-indicators, last accessed 28 December 2016). Try to generate some different tables and graphs to understand nascent entrepreneurship in the country you are analysing. Maybe try to compare it with other countries. Based on this, write a little blog and upload it to one of the social media you are using and engage in a dialogue with the responses it generates.

3 **Your life.** Think about your life both in the past and the future. Of course you won't know what the future will bring, but maybe you have some hopes about what will happen and take place in the forthcoming different decades. Think about it and note it down on a timeline. Then try to judge when you think it is most probable – if at all likely – that you will start a business. Also, try to think about not just when it is most likely, but also when it would be most prudent. Life

will take many unexpected twists and turns in the future, so try to save the memo and look at it again many years from now.

LITERATURE

Amit, R. & Muller, E. (1995) '"Push" and "pull" entrepreneurship', *Journal of Small Business and Entrepreneurship*, 12(4), 64–80.

Bhidé, A. (2000) *The Origin and Evolution of New Businesses*, New York: Oxford University Press.

Bruton, G.D., Ahlstrom, D. & Li, H. (2010) 'Institutional theory and entrepreneurship: Where are we now and where do we need to move in the future?', *Entrepreneurship Theory & Practice*, 34(3), 421–440.

Carter, N.M., Gartner, W.B. & Reynolds, P.D. (1996) 'Exploring start-up event sequences', *Journal of Business Venturing*, 11(3), 151–166.

Carter, N.M., Gartner, W.B., Shaver, K.G. & Gatewood, E.J. (2003) 'The career reasons of nascent entrepreneurs', *Journal of Business Venturing*, 18(1), 13–39.

DiMaggio, P.J. & Powell, W.W. (1983) 'The iron cage revisited: Institutional isomorphism and collective rationality in organizational fields', *American Sociological Review*, 48(2), 147–160.

Gordon, S.R. (2012) 'Dimensions of the venture creation process: Amount, dynamics, and sequences of action in nascent entrepreneurship', PhD thesis, Queensland University of Technology.

Greiner, L.E. (1972) 'Evolution and revolution as organizations grow', *Harvard Business Review*, 50(4), 37–46.

Holland, J.L. (1997) *Making Vocational Choices: A Theory of Vocational Personalities and Work Environments*, 3rd edn, Odessa, FL: Psychological Assessment Resources.

Katz, J. & Gartner, W.B. (1988) 'Properties of emerging organizations', *Academy of Management Review*, 13(3), 429–441.

Klyver, K., Nielsen, S. & Evald, M.R. (2013) 'Women's self-employment: An act of institutional (dis)integration? A multilevel, cross-country study', *Journal of Business Venturing*, 28(4), 474–488.

Levie, J.D. & Lichtenstein, B.B. (2010) 'A terminal assessment of stages theory: Introducing a dynamic states approach to entrepreneurship', *Entrepreneurship Theory and Practice*, 34(2), 317–350.

Ruef, M., Aldrich, H.E. & Carter, N.M. (2003) 'The structure of founding teams: Homophily, strong ties, and isolation among U.S. entrepreneurs', *American Sociological Review*, 68(2), 195–222.

Sauermann, H. (2005) 'Vocational choice: A decision-making perspective', *Journal of Vocational Behavior*, 66(2), 273–303.

Shane, S. (2003) *A General Theory of Entrepreneurship. The Individual–Opportunity Nexus*, Cheltenham, UK and Northampton, MA, USA: Edward Elgar Publishing.

Section 3

The entrepreneurial content

7

Resources

In order to carry out the entrepreneurial process, it is necessary to have access to a variety of resources (Alvarez & Busenitz 2001). The entrepreneur needs money, knowledge, materials, energy, enthusiasm, motivation, staff, help from friends and family, etc. The list of resources that may be necessary to implement an entrepreneurial process is virtually inexhaustible, but the necessary resources and the combination thereof are dependent, in each case, on the situation. We will go, in detail, into how all these different types of resources can be categorised.

Many have argued that the acquisition of resources is among the major factors that distinguish traditional management behaviour from entrepreneurial behaviour. As managers operate within an already established business context, they usually have access to the necessary resources. Their behaviour is then characterised by attempts to streamline and optimise the use of these resources. In contrast, entrepreneurs often have no, or very few, resources. However, instead of accepting these resource constraints entrepreneurs are characterised by their ability to exploit opportunities regardless of their access to resources. As Stevenson and Jarillo put it: 'entrepreneurship is a process by which individuals . . . pursue opportunities without regard to the resources they currently control' (Stevenson & Jarillo 1990: 23). Accordingly, entrepreneurs act in spite of the fact that they may, here and now, lack essential resources. So, whilst managers act with what they have, entrepreneurs act in spite of what they have. In this chapter we will introduce you to the entrepreneur's identification and use of resources.

Entrepreneurship in practice

We start this chapter with a story of entrepreneurship and resources. It's a story about the organisation Logopaint (Logopaint has now been renamed AMAYSE; www.amayse.com, accessed 24 January 2017), which was founded in 1997. In 2007 the organisation had a turnover of nearly US$2.6 million. In 2011, Logopaint had approximately 25 employees and sales offices in several places around the world.

CASE STUDY

The idea of 3D carpets

(Devised by the authors)

Logopaint supports itself by optimising advertising and sponsorship in sport. They even state on their website: 'The company's general goal was and still is to optimize advertising in sports and sponsoring'. They want to be the best in their niche and they are trying to achieve this through increased product value, delivery, experience and professionalism. They try to differentiate themselves primarily by taking responsibility for their products from start to finish. 'We want to make it easy and efficient to work with us. We take responsibility for our products, and ensure quality before, during and after delivery, so the client experiences that we see our products through to the end'.

The organisation mainly provides two different products for sports: 3D carpets and 3D barrier boards, which today are found in more than 50 countries worldwide and used in more than 500 football clubs, including Bayern München, Juventus and FC Barcelona, and are bought by customers such as Coca-Cola, Toyota, etc. The products are used for many different sporting events such as football, handball, volleyball, auto racing, basketball and ice hockey. The most unique product is the first of these products – 3D carpets (Figure 7.1 shows an example: they are located – rolled out – just behind the goal line next to the goal on a football field). Through the use of specially developed computer software, the writing on the carpets appears to stand up when seen from a camera angle without this actually being the case, providing companies with more effective branding and advertising of their services in connection with various sporting events.

Figure 7.1 Logopaint's 3D carpets

CASE STUDY *(continued)*

There are several different stories about how the idea for 3D carpets arose and nobody knows, several years after they were first launched, which story is actually right – it may well be a combination of parts of several versions. One story focuses on the notion that the idea occurred more or less by chance, when one of the characters from the start-up team was standing on the top of a ladder and noticed that the font on carpets is perceived and looks different from different angles, especially at heights. 'It's almost as if the writing sometimes stands up' was the realisation at that time.

This surprise made the team look more systematically at how writing on carpets (i.e. parallel to the ground) looks from different angles. Several of the start-up team had an educational and experiential background of working with computer science and mathematics at a high level. This knowledge was crucial for development. They ultimately developed a formula that will calculate what different fonts look like from different angles. Their idea was that the formula could be used to streamline advertising, branding and sponsorship in sport. By laying carpets in different places in a stadium (for example, behind the goals in soccer, as shown in Figure 7.1), they could calculate how the writing should be designed in relation to the cameras in a stadium, so that when viewed on television the writing appeared vertical from the viewer's perspective.

The opportunity had quite significant advantages in terms of what was permitted in football stadiums at the time. There are, for example rules on how close signs, barrier boards and the like may be to the touchline for the safety of the players. With these carpets the safety distance is no longer a limitation. Sports people can just run over the carpets. It is suddenly possible for the various stadia to have an extra row of barrier boards beyond the one or two rows of boards that most major stadiums have. Furthermore, and perhaps most importantly, the new row of boards is in far the best place, since it is located exactly behind the goal line. The potential is huge; they know that. But how big? And how can they ensure that no other competitors quickly imitate their products? These are some of the thoughts that the team discuss assiduously in the start-up process.

Patenting: arguments for and against

Even during the development of the idea they realised that the safest way to avoid imitation by competitors was to patent the idea. But the cost – both in terms of money and time – is enormous when applying for a patent and then you are not even sure of getting the patent when you apply for it. Neither can you just apply for a single patent that is valid worldwide. Different countries and different continents have their own patenting systems. It is therefore quite costly if you want a patent covering most of the world.

The application for patents is particularly expensive for the start-up team, as they find it necessary to buy in assistance. No one in their family or circle of friends had sufficient knowledge or experience of applying for patents. Therefore, they contacted various lawyers, specialists and patent agents specialising in patent applications, and these are very expensive.

CASE STUDY *(continued)*

Economically they were faced with a dilemma. On the one hand, they believed in the idea and the importance of the patent. This spoke in favour of applying for patents in as many parts of the world as possible. On the other hand they didn't have the financial resources required to apply for patents worldwide or even in several countries. They therefore needed to raise more funds if they were to go through with making a broad patent application. This constituted a significantly greater risk if it all went wrong. If they failed to get a patent on the idea, or if the idea simply had no value on the market, all the funds would be wasted and the entrepreneurs would suffer an economic blow. At the same time they ran a risk in applying for a patent in the sense that it would take much longer before they were ready to enter the market. In that time, potential competitors may be able to catch up with them or find other attractive technical solutions.

A golden middle way

Logopaint's start-up team chose a middle ground and took out a patent in many countries, but with important exceptions. They did not patent in China, Japan, Portugal, Eastern Europe, the Gulf countries and others. Their criteria for selection of countries was first and foremost that the country had a known and conspicuous football league, and next that the patent system in that country was not a complete jungle. They encountered many different problems in the process, especially in legal battles with a South African company that had a similar, but not identical, patent already. Along the way, many of these legal problems were solved with licence agreements, but in 2008 Logopaint acquired the South African firm, including their patent rights.

Despite the fact that Logopaint does not have patents in all countries, they are market leaders in all the markets where they operate. In the countries where they have a patent, they have 100 per cent market share, whilst they are content with about 80 per cent of the market where they have no patent. At Logopaint they have often discussed the significance of these patents. On this subject, Logopaints business development director says: 'We would not have been in the position we are in today if we did not have our patents – they gave us access to the market'.

Your immediate interpretation

What does the story tell you about resources? How would you immediately interpret it? The following exercises can help you form an understanding of the story:

- You are the keynote speaker at a conference. The topic is entrepreneurship and resources. Start with the Logopaint story and explain to the audience which resources are important to the story and the ways in which resources play a role in the entrepreneurial process.

- Your speech gives rise to a discussion about how to categorise the type of resources that are at stake in the story. What categories do you think are relevant?
- When you get home from the conference, you can't stop thinking about the day's discussions. You think generally about the resources that you believe are critical for starting a new independent organisation. Make a list of these resources.
- You meet one of your friends who has already started an independent organisation. In discussing the importance of resources for entrepreneurs he claims that it is always the idea that is crucial for the entrepreneur's success. If the idea is good, it's easy to attract the necessary resources. What do you think about this argument?

Theories of entrepreneurship

The Logopaint story is a good illustration of how entrepreneurs are constantly being confronted with resource issues. They constantly find themselves in situations where they must weigh up whether it is better to continue working with the resources they have readily available at any given time or alternatively spend their time and limited resources obtaining or developing new and greater resources to pursue their potential. In other words, should the entrepreneur focus on exploiting existing resources or on exploring new resources in the entrepreneurial process?

Balancing takes place in an uncertain context in the sense that decisions about resources must be made before knowing anything about the profits that can be achieved by exploring new resources and/or exploiting existing resources (Shane 2003). How entrepreneurial resource decisions are made are often based on the entrepreneur's expectations about the future.

By exploiting existing resources, the entrepreneur focuses on the effective implementation of his or her existing resource base to evaluate and organise the opportunity. The advantage is that the entrepreneur has control over his or her resources, and thus the risk associated with resource utilisation is relatively low. The disadvantage may be that focusing on existing resources limits the development potential because the existing resources set the framework determining what is possible. Conversely, the entrepreneur chooses to explore new resources. Here, the benefit is that new resources and combinations of resources can be a catalyst for creative development of the opportunity. The problem attached to this perspective is, among other things, that the entrepreneur does not possess the same control over resources. So, this chapter deals with the choice between exploiting existing resources and explore new resources, and thus the paradox:

Exploit or explore?

From a market to a resource focus

Before we elaborate on the paradox, we will need to define what we mean by a resource, but first a little history. Theories about resources and their importance originate within the 'strategy' literature, which made a breakthrough in the mid 1980s and early 1990s, although Penrose's (1959) ground-breaking book *The Theory of the Growth of the Firm* had introduced the discussion much earlier. The discussion in the strategy literature focuses on how organisations create long-term competitive advantage. Although the debate has, of course, many different shades, it is primarily divided into two types of argument: the 'inside-out argument' and the 'outside-in argument'. The latter argument maintains that creating sustained competitive advantage comes through better positioning in the market and differentiation from your competitors. On the other hand, the inside-out argument claims that sustained competitive advantage is best established within the organisation through its unique combination of resources. The outside-in argument takes the market as its starting point and then looks into the organisation (hence, outside-in), whilst the inside-out argument is concerned firstly with the organisation's internal resources and then looks at the market (hence, inside-out). The discussion is therefore about whether sustained competitive advantage is created outside the organisation, in the market, or within the organisation, through its resources and capabilities.

However, it is important to bear in mind that everyone agrees that both outside-in positioning and possession of unique resource combinations are crucial for obtaining competitive advantage. The disagreement lies in whether one should choose to focus on the unique resource combination in the long term, and adjust in the short term through market positioning, or whether market positioning is decisive in the long term, and that the necessary resources and capabilities must be acquired in the short term.

Within the entrepreneurship literature it is the inside-out argument that is particularly inspiring when resources are discussed. The argument also typically compares with resource theory, which we review next.

Resource theory

According to resource theory the best means by which both entrepreneurs and existing organisations gain sustained competitive advantage is through control of valuable resources. Although resource theory was originally developed with larger established organisations in mind (Wernerfelt 1984), it has also had great influence on entrepreneurship theory. Larger established organisations may have ownership of more resources compared to independent entrepreneurs, but what resources the entrepreneur directly owns may be less important than what resources he or she has control over (or has the opportunity to gain control over) (Stevenson & Jarillo 1990). It is therefore immaterial whether someone else owns a given resource that is needed by the entrepreneur as long as he or she has control over it and determines how it is put into use in pursuing the opportunity. Despite resource theory's frequent references to the established organisation, we will hereafter only focus on the entrepreneur.

Additionally, resource theory is built on two basic assumptions. First is the assumption that the actors in an industry are heterogeneous and therefore have unequal control over strategic resources (Barney 1991). They simply do not have access to, and control over, the same resources. The second assumption is that resources are not perfectly transferrable between actors (Barney 1991). This means that resources are not readily passed from one entrepreneur to another because the value of resources depends on the holder and the holder's ability to exploit them.

Based on these assumptions, it is Barney's (1991) view that entrepreneurs achieve sustained competitive advantage by having access to and control over resources that are both heterogeneous and immobile – more on this later.

The resource concept

Before we start discussing what characterises valuable resources in relation to creating competitive advantage, we should discuss what we really mean by a resource. There are many different definitions of what a resource is, but generally within resource theory, resources have a broad definition. Wernerfelt defines a resource as follows: 'By a resource is meant anything which could be thought of as a strength or weakness of a given firm. More formally, a firm's resources at a given time could be defined as those (tangible and intangible) assets which are tied semi permanently to the firm' (Wernerfelt 1984: 172).

A similar focus to define resources as anything that helps entrepreneurs to perform is seen in Barney's definition: 'firm resources include all assets, capabilities, organizational processes, firm attributes, information, knowledge, etc. controlled by a firm that enable the firm to conceive of and implement strategies that improve its efficiency and effectiveness' (Barney 1991: 101). The resource concept thus covers an infinite number of resources that share the fact that they support entrepreneurs in pursuing opportunities through organising.

Valuable resources

The next question then concerns what makes a resource valuable. Barney (1991) writes that resources are heterogeneous and immobile in order to create sustainable competitive advantage. Wernerfelt says that valuable resources are to keep competitors at bay: 'What a firm wants is to create a situation where its own resource position directly or indirectly makes it more difficult for others to catch up' (Wernerfelt 1984: 173). Here he introduces the concept of 'resource position', which is crucial. An entrepreneur's resource position is formed by the combination of resources over which they have control. Access to, and control over new resources, naturally changes the resource position.

However, access to and control over new resources that immediately seem to strengthen the resource position is not sufficient to ensure that a resource is attractive. The resources that are attractive are those that can help to create a barrier relative to a competitor's resource position. A barrier, in other words, to keep current and future competitors out of the game. On this matter, Wernerfelt writes:

> The general attractiveness of a resource, understood as its capacity to support a resource position barrier, is only a necessary, not a sufficient, condition for a given firm to be interested in it. If everyone goes for the potentially attractive resources and only a few can 'win' in each, firms will lose unless they pick their fights well. So firms need to find those resources which can sustain a resource position barrier, but in which no one currently has one, and where they have a good chance of being among the few who succeed in building one. (Wernerfelt 1984: 174 175)

Barney (1991) has developed some criteria that can be used to assess whether a resource contributes to such a barrier. On these criteria he writes:

> a firm resource must have four attributes: (a) it must be valuable, in the sense that it exploits opportunities and/or neutralizes threats in the firm's environment, (b)

Table 7.1 Evaluation of resources

Characteristics of the resource position				Competitive consequences	
Valuable	Rare	Non-imitable	Non-substitutable	Competition	Economic performance
No	–	–	–	Disadvantage	Below average
Yes	No	–	–	Competitive equality	Normal
Yes	Yes	No	–	Temporary advantage	Above average
Yes	Yes	Yes	No	Temporary advantage	Above average
Yes	Yes	Yes	Yes	Sustained advantage	Highest

Source: Inspired by Barney (1991).

> it must be rare among a firm's current and potential competition, (c) it must be imperfectly imitable and (d) there cannot be strategically equivalent substitutes for this resource that are valuable but neither rare or imperfectly imitable. (Barney 1991: 105–106)

Applying these criteria, one can build the model shown in Table 7.1. The table can be used to compare an entrepreneur's resource position with its competitive implications. So, whilst its primary function is to evaluate the combination of the entrepreneur's resources, it can also be used to assess the value of a single resource.

When the resource position is not valuable, the model predicts that the entrepreneur will be at a competitive disadvantage, perform below average and thus eventually be forced to close down. When the resource position is valuable, but not rare, competitive equality and a normal performance are achieved. The entrepreneur can achieve a better situation with temporary competitive advantage, where his or her performance is above average in two different ways, i.e. when the resource position is valuable and rare but can be imitated, or when the resource position is valuable, rare, non-imitable but not substitutable. Last, but not least, achievement of sustained competitive advantage and the potential for peak economic performance arises when the resource position is valuable, rare and cannot be imitated or substituted.

A three-way split of resources

We have now discussed resource theory and what is needed for resources to be valuable and capable of providing entrepreneurs with sustained competitive advantage by creating a barrier through resource positioning. We have also defined what a resource is, but so far we have worked with resources in broad terms. We will now try to remedy this. We will not restrict the definition, but on the other hand we will divide the resources into a number of different categories.

There are numerous ways in which we may categorise resources. One way might be to divide resources into hardware (start-up capital, machinery, buildings etc.) and software (knowledge, social relations, rumour, reputation etc.). On occasions we can also distinguish between natural resources and intangible resources. This has historically been the case in economic theory with its emphasis on physical capital and labour, although in more recent times sociologists have also indicated the importance of other resources. Here, inspired by Coleman (1988), we categorise resources under the following headings:

- financial resources;
- human resources;
- social resources.

Somewhat simplified, financial resources refer to the money that the entrepreneur has in his or her pocket, whether borrowed or their own. Human resources refer to the knowledge and skills that the entrepreneur (or team of entrepreneurs) possesses. Social resources are the benefits the entrepreneur enjoys through the use of personal contacts and acquaintances.

In discussing the tripartite categorisation it should be mentioned that the concept of 'capital' is often used synonymously with resources in the literature. Thus, some talk about financial capital (financial resources), human capital (human resources) and social capital (social resources). This terminology follows a supply logic where the supply is understood to be the resources that a person owns or has temporary control over (Stevenson & Jarillo 1990). Financial capital is a term that refers to the supply of financial resources at an entrepreneur's disposal. Similarly, human capital is a concept for the supply of human resources that an entrepreneur has available. Finally, social capital is a term for the supply of resources that the entrepreneur has available through his or her contacts. In this book we use the concept of resource rather than the concept of capital. Table 7.2 provides some specific examples of financial, human and social resources.

Financial resources

Although there are many different types of financial resources, it makes sense, in terms of this book's objective, to work with two main types: equity

Table 7.2 Three categories of resources

	Financial resources	Human resources	Social resources
Explanation	Capital supplied by the owners or external players	Intangible resources such as knowledge and experience	Resources provided by the entrepreneur's personal contacts
Examples	Equity capital (own money) Debt capital (borrowed money)	Education and training Experiences (business, start-up, managerial experience . . .) Engagement, motivation and enterprise	Entrepreneurial role models A large network Diverse networks Supportive circle of friends

and debt. Equity is the financial resources made available by the owners of an organisation with the expectation of a say in decisions and future returns. Supply of equity can either be via owners' deposits of cash or other assets, or by the owners retaining a portion of the profits of the organisation. Debt capital is the capital not provided by the organisation's owners such as mortgages, bank loans, supplier credits, etc. Debt capital is often divided into what can be described as short-term debt and long-term debt.

Human resources

The list of examples of human resources is almost endless (Becker 1993). We will therefore only concern ourselves with a few. A human resource is inherent within people. Formal education may enable individuals to be more able to recognize opportunities and implement entrepreneurial processes, whilst more focused training – such as entrepreneurship training – should hopefully contribute positively to the entrepreneurial process. Experience also seems to play a significant role, although one can speak of many types of experience. The requisite experience is, of course, dependent upon the type of entrepreneurial process that you have to deal with as an entrepreneur. Typically, relevant work experience and previous start-up and managerial experience are types of experience that are essential to the successful implementation of entrepreneurial processes. Cognitive psychologists have also identified a wide range of cognitive abilities that seem to affect the entrepreneurial process positively and which can be regarded as human resources. Several of these we have already pointed out in Chapter 2.

Social resources

Social resources are somewhat different from the other two. Firstly, it is not a resource that a single person can possess in the way that they might with both financial and human resources. Social resources are something created in the interaction between people (Coleman 1988). They belong to the relationship between these people, but not the individual. In this way, social resources are something that entrepreneurs and intrapreneurs have access to through their personal relationships. Chapter 8 elaborates on examples of social resources and how they can be provided.

Differences and connections between resource categories

The interesting thing about the above tripartite division is not so much the division in itself, but the basic differences between the three types of resources. Some of the resources are reduced when used, while others actually multiply with increased use. For example, financial resources are reduced when they are used. Money can only be used once – unfortunately. However, it's not necessarily true for human and social resources. When the entrepreneur uses the knowledge gained from education, there is also a revitalization of knowledge that takes place, because it is being reproduced and possibly strengthened. It is commonly accepted that new knowledge is created when existing knowledge is brought into play in new contexts. For example, educational knowledge can contribute to the creation of new knowledge, and through its use, the human resource increases. This is often the case with social resources as well. When one interacts with the environment and one's personal contacts in an effort to provide valuable resources to implement the entrepreneurial process, that generates new knowledge in the relationship, which can be used later. Pushed to its logical extreme, one could say that people who never talk to anyone and don't know anyone will have difficulty getting hold of resources in their environment in comparison with individuals who frequently interact with their environment. One can therefore again conclude that the increased use of social resources may contribute to the further development of the resource.

The last thing we need to discuss about the tripartite division is the relationship between the three types of resources. It is interesting that the various resources can be transformed from one type to another (Bourdieu 1986). Social resources are often seen as the resource type that activates the other two (Burt 1992). For example, it is possible to use one's personal networks (social capital) to recruit new qualified employees (human resources) or to obtain financial resources. There are actually several studies that suggest that personal contacts, including friends and family, are by far the leading

Table 7.3 International variations in financial, human and social capital

	US	Brazil	Sweden	China	Ghana	India
GDP per capita 2010 (2008 US Dollars)*	46,653	10,847	36,139	7,206	1,533	3,354
Mean years of schooling of adults**	12.4	7.2	11.6	7.5	7.1	4.4
Most people can be trusted**	39.3 %	9.4 %	68.0 %	52.3 %	8.5 %	23.3 %

Note: * World Bank: Human Development Index (http://hdr.undp.org/en/content/human-development-index-hdim last accessed 20 December 2016).
** World Value Survey (http://www.worldvaluessurvey.org/, last accessed 20 December 2016).

investor in the entrepreneur's start-up processes. However, there are many other ways in which the three types can interact. You can buy advice on marketing (human resources), through use of your financial resources. Or you can use your knowledge of business plans (human resources) to convince a banker that you need more credit (financial resources).

International differences

It's no great surprise that there are large international differences in the average supply of resources available to individuals worldwide. Table 7.3 provides an insight into these differences. As a measure of financial capital, the table shows how GDP per capita varies from US$3,354 in India to US$46,653 in the USA in 2010. There are thus significant differences in average wealth. One way to measure differences in human capital is the average schooling of a country's population. Here again, the table shows great variation, whilst the US population goes to school for an average of 12.4 years, the average in India is just 4.4 years. Last but not least, the proportion of the population in a country that considers that people can be trusted is used as a measure of social capital. Here, Sweden ranks highest with 68 per cent of people believing that one can trust people, whilst Brazil and Ghana are at the bottom with only about 9 per cent believing that most people can be trusted. These indicators clearly suggest large international variation in financial, human and social capital. Furthermore, it should be noted that within each national context there can also be variations depending on the political, social and historical fabric of society.

Resource exploitation

Now back to the paradox. As mentioned earlier, the entrepreneur is faced with a dilemma in relation to identification and use of resources. The entrepreneur will assess whether he or she must continue working with and leveraging the existing resources that they have available or whether they must use their often limited resources to explore new resources. We are talking here about the paradox: resource exploitation versus resource exploration.

According to March, exploitation activities cover: 'efficiency, selection, implementation, execution' (March 1991: 71). This means that the entrepreneur uses the existing resource position through rational and systematic consideration of how he or she can most effectively select and deploy those resources so that they best support the opportunity.

Thus, resource identification and use is about strengthening an already given direction (Van de Ven et al 1999). This underlines the assumption that the entrepreneur has, in advance, a picture of the direction in which he or she will move. The entrepreneur, in other words, has a clearly defined goal for the resource use. The challenge is to maximise efficient use of existing resources to achieve the goal. Further, the perspective assumes that the entrepreneur knows, in advance, the value of a resource in terms of the entrepreneurial process. Resources are objective entities. They are what they appear to be. From the outset, the entrepreneur can point out which resources he or she must identify and use in order to realise the goal.

Given that the starting point is the optimisation of existing resources, the entrepreneur is presumed to have management and control of resource use in the entrepreneurial process: it reduces the complexity and risk associated with the process. On the other hand, the entrepreneur, as mentioned earlier, cannot be expected to move the opportunity in radically new and unexpected directions, as using existing resources limits the opportunity and its realisation. The resource exploitation perspective thus leads to a relatively stable and linear entrepreneurial process.

As the exploitation perspective in many ways excludes the identification and application of radically new resources and resource combinations and hence new ways to exploit opportunities, it reflects a short-term approach to resources. The reason is that the entrepreneur focuses on how he or she can improve in the light of the current resource position. This involves not thinking about how he or she can keep up with the continuous processes of change in future markets, where products, services and processes constantly become out-dated and/or obsolete and must make room for the new, which requires exploration.

Resource exploration

Usually the entrepreneur does not control, from the start of the entrepreneurial process, all the resources required to realise the opportunity. 'For most new ventures, an optimal set of organizational resources is not developed instantly but rather evolves, and changes over a period of weeks, months, and years' (Lichtenstein & Brush 2001: 41). The entrepreneur experiences resource constraints. Similarly, the entrepreneurial process is often dynamic and characterised by risk and complexity so the entrepreneur cannot easily assume that the existing resources are sufficient, or that he or she can predict in advance the value of resources in terms of the entrepreneurial process. In other words, resources cannot be taken for granted. For these reasons, the entrepreneur starting from a position of limited resources must explore and perhaps even create new resources.

According to March, exploration activities include 'search, variation, risk taking, experimentation, play, flexibility, discovery, innovation' (March 1991: 71). Unlike the exploitation perspective, exploration is about expansion, flexibility, experimentation and expression, which may lead to the creation or discovery of new opportunities and countless new ways of evaluating and organising. Here the entrepreneur is not limited and focused on the existing resource position and its optimisation. Instead through play, proactive and open interaction with the environment, the entrepreneur attempts to create resources that can lead him or her in exciting new directions in terms of the developing entrepreneurial process. This is resource behaviour, where new boundaries are constantly tested.

That new boundaries are being constantly tested, naturally also means a more risky and unpredictable entrepreneurial process. The entrepreneur simply cannot predict how he or she will end up. Unpredictable resource identification and usage, as previously mentioned, makes it difficult for the entrepreneur to establish control over the entrepreneurial process. Especially because the entrepreneur must acquire resources, before the actual value of the opportunity is known it is in the interaction with the environment that the value of the resource is created. This means that the value is a result of how the entrepreneur actually utilises the resource in the entrepreneurial process.

The exploration perspective reveals a dynamic approach to the identification and use of resources. There is also a forward-looking and long-term perspective. The reason is that an exploratory entrepreneur is continually open to unexpected resources that can lead to radically new opportunities or ways to exploit them. In this way the entrepreneur is also better equipped to survive in the longer term with the future's markets requirement for continual change.

Sarasvathy's (2008) model presented in Chapter 5 gives an idea of how the entrepreneurial process can be seen as having a starting point in the use of limited resources ('Who I am', 'What I know' and 'Whom I know'). However, it is through interaction and exploration of the environment in the entrepreneurial process that entrepreneurs gain control over resources beyond immediate verification. Through exploration, new resources are constantly added that support the entrepreneurial process by being transformed into opportunities and organisations. Sarasvathy's (2008) theory can thus be seen primarily as an example of the exploration perspective's representation of the resource issue, despite the theory also having elements of resource exploitation.

A similar logic is found in Baker and Nelson's (2005) bricolage approach to resources. Overall, the bricolage concept refers to resource exploitation logic, because it is fundamentally about 'making do with what is at hand'. Nevertheless, the bricolage concept certainly contains elements of resource exploration, since the point is precisely that entrepreneurs are exploring and creating new resources through 'applying combinations of the resources at hand to new problems and opportunities' (Baker & Nelson 2005: 333). Here, the entrepreneur defies the environment and his or her own resource limitations and will sometimes get successful organisations to grow apparently from more or less nothing.

Resources: exploit or explore?

We have, above, discussed two different perspectives on how entrepreneurs can relate to resource identification and use. The discussion is summarised in Table 7.4.

The exploitation perspective thus argues that the entrepreneur should make effective use of existing resources that are available, whilst the exploration perspective holds that the entrepreneur should seek new resources based on the limited resources that he or she typically controls. The focus of the exploitation perspective is to 'improve effectiveness of your current situation', and this perspective is very much about stability and the short term. The exploration perspective is more about the entrepreneur continually 'moving on' by interacting with the environment and creating new resources and resource

Table 7.4 The paradox: Exploit or explore

	Exploit	Explore
Resources	Existing resources	New resources
The entrepreneur's role	To use existing resources efficiently	To find and gain control of the new resources
Focus	To improve efficiency	To move
Changeability	Stability	Dynamics
Perspective	Short term	Long term

combinations. It is therefore directed towards something more long term and represents a more dynamic approach to resources in entrepreneurship.

However, it is important to emphasise that entrepreneurs in practice can benefit from both perspectives. As March (1991) argues, the discussion about exploitation and exploration is not a question of 'either-or' but rather a question of balance. March writes: 'maintaining an appropriate balance between exploration and exploitation is a primary factor in system survival and prosperity' (March 1991: 71).

A theoretical interpretation

Below are two different interpretations of the Logopaint story that started the chapter. In the interpretations the story is related to the above theory and interpreted from each of paradox perspectives.

The exploiting perspective

If you choose to look at the Logopaint story from an exploitation perspective, the focus will primarily be on how Logopaint attempted to optimise the use of their existing resources. The story is about the schism between financial resources and the application for patents. The first question that arises is what type of resources a patent represents. Is this an example of a monopolised human resource or a 'tied' financial resource base? The immediate impression is that a patent is closest to what we refer to as a human resource. The patent begins as knowledge in the form of the formula being developed. Later it becomes a patent, but the patent is really just a temporary monopolisation of the knowledge inherent in Logopaint's entrepreneurs from the outset. In terms of the exploitation perspective the patent therefore represents a crystallisation of existing resources, which were owned by the Logopaint entrepreneurs from the beginning of the entrepreneurial process.

Furthermore, from the exploitation perspective, the purpose of the loan capital appears to be for the optimisation of existing resources through patenting and not the development of new resources. The act of applying for the patent is, in itself, an indication of wanting to optimise what one already possesses and is good at. The Logopaint story focuses on improving the existing situation and provides no indication that the firm was attempting to 'move on' by simultaneously creating resources with which to create new opportunities that could create competitive advantage in the long term in respect of future markets.

When the story is interpreted from an exploitation perspective, we can also argue that despite the fact that Logopaint obtained new capital to fund patent applications, they still felt that they were only working with those resources over which they had considerable control. Firstly, they sought patents only when they believed that the probability of success was greatest. They did not apply for patents in markets where they believed that the risk of their patent application failing was great. Thus, the financial resources used were under reasonable control. Secondly, they used the loan carefully without taking too great a risk that this capital might suddenly take control of them, for instance through loan conditions. One can thus argue that Logopaint primarily optimised the resources they controlled. They restricted themselves to applying for patents with the money they could control, despite the fact that some of this money was borrowed.

The exploring perspective

Logopaint's story can also be interpreted completely differently, i.e. from an exploration perspective. As is often the case in entrepreneurship, Logopaint had, at the start, basically no control over all the resources necessary to realise their potential. They were, in other words, left to explore the environment in order to generate additional financial resources. In connection with the exploration, the company focused on finding and increasing control over as many new resources as humanly possible. It can easily be imagined that Logopaint had, in some way a risk profile that prevented them from borrowing certain types of capital. It is very likely, but the story may still be interpreted to mean that they wanted patent protection in as many markets as possible.

Logopaint's limitations are primarily set by their ability to obtain the financial resources required to design and process patent applications. So when they chose not to apply for a patent in the Chinese market for instance, it was largely because they simply could not fund the application. It is not because they chose to limit themselves and stick to the resources they already had control over. So, it's the various markets, their risk profile and the associated potential capital that sets limits on the number of patent applications. In other words, Logopaint's strategy was to obtain as many patents as it was possible to borrow the money to fund applications for. By gaining many patents they could then explore opportunities in a larger geographical area, thereby opening the door to more new opportunities. This allowed them to move developmentally and create competitive advantage in the long term.

The story's conclusion underlines how, as mentioned in the exploration perspective, resource value cannot always be predicted in advance. Logopaint is, in any case, doubtful as to whether the acquired patents create the value intended, as the company also ended up with a large market share in those markets where they have not acquired a patent for their product.

Testing the theory

Based on the above thoughts and discussions, you are ready to develop your own tests to understand resources and how they are part of the entrepreneurial process. The following are suggestions for exercises.

EXERCISES

1 **Interview an entrepreneur.** Make a list of interview questions that seek to capture some of the central debates on the role of resources in entrepreneurship. Contact an entrepreneur, and interview him or her in order to test the theory presented in this chapter.

2 **The resource utilisation.** Which innovative ideas can you come up with, to start leveraging your existing resources? Make a list of your existing resources, providing an overview divided into financial, human and social resources. Now try to combine these resources to come up with innovative business ideas that can facilitate an entrepreneurial process.

3 **Give advice to a friend.** One of your friends who is a trained electrician, and has always had a passion for design, tells you that he is working on an opportunity. He intends to design upmarket and expensive lighting. You have confidence that he has the skill to put the electronics, light and design together with the ability to make it special. Then he asks you for financial advice. He has saved US$50,000, and is willing to put up more. But, on its own, the US$50,000 is not enough. What should he do? What options does he have? And what is important to consider?

LITERATURE

Alvarez, S.A. & Busenitz, L.W. (2001) 'The entrepreneurship of resource-based theory', *Journal of Management*, 27, 755–775.

Baker, T. & Nelson, R.E. (2005) 'Creating something from nothing: Resource construction through entrepreneurial bricolage', *Administrative Science Quarterly*, 50, 329–366.

Barney, J.B. (1991) 'Firm resources and sustained competitive advantage', *Journal of Management*, 17(1), 99–120.

Becker, G.S. (1993) *Human Capital: A Theoretical and Empirical Analysis, with Special Reference to Education*, Chicago, IL: University of Chicago Press.

Bourdieu, P. (1986) 'The forms of capital', in Richardson, J.G. (ed.), *Handbook of Theory and Research for the Sociology of Education*, New York: Greenwood, 241–258.

Burt, R.S. (1992) *Structural Holes – The Social Structure of Competition*, London: Harvard University Press.

Coleman, J.S. (1988) 'Social capital in the creation of human capital', *American Journal of Sociology*, 94, 95–120.

Lichtenstein, B.M.B. & Brush, C.G. (2001) 'How do "resource bundles" develop and change in new ventures? A dynamic model and longitudinal exploration', *Entrepreneurship Theory and Practice*, 25(3), 37–59.

March, J.G. (1991) 'Exploration and exploitation in organisational learning', *Organization Science*, 2, 71–87.

Penrose, E.T. (1959) *The Theory of the Growth of the Firm*, New York: John Wiley.

Priem, R.L. & Butler, J.E. (2001) 'Is the resource-based "view" a useful perspective for strategic management research?', *Academy of Management Review*, 26(1), 22–40.

Sarasvathy, S.D. (2008) *Effectuation: Elements of Entrepreneurial Expertise*, Cheltenham, UK and Northampton, MA, USA: Edward Elgar Publishing.

Shane, S. (2003) *A General Theory of Entrepreneurship: The Individual–Opportunity Nexus*, Cheltenham, UK and Northampton, MA, USA: Edward Elgar Publishing.

Stevenson, H.H. & Jarillo, J.C. (1990) 'A paradigm of entrepreneurship: Entrepreneurial management', *Strategic Management Journal*, 11, 17–27.

Van de Ven, A.H., Polley, D., Garud, R. & Venkataraman, S. (1999) *The Innovation Journey*, Oxford: Oxford University Press.

Wernerfelt, B. (1984) 'A resource-based view of the firm', *Strategic Management Journal*, 5, 171–180.

8

Networks

An entrepreneur without a network is like an angler without a fishing rod. In order to be successful, the entrepreneurial process requires the involvement of more than just the entrepreneur. Entrepreneurs involve a number of different people through the entrepreneurial process. These may be people closely connected to the organisation, including customers, suppliers, investors, auditors, etc. However, it might also include people who have a less visible, but equally crucial role in the entrepreneur's success. Here we might consider the significance of receiving free help and advice from experienced friends and family members along with the importance of emotional support and having the right 'backing on the home front'.

So, the social environment, of which they are a part, including the network they possess, influences entrepreneurs. Entrepreneurial decisions are made not in a vacuum, but rather in social contexts. In a ground-breaking article, Aldrich and Zimmer wrote: 'The approach we take, by contrast, focuses on entrepreneurship as embedded in a social context, channelled and facilitated or constrained and inhibited by people's position in social network' (Aldrich & Zimmer 1986: 4).

Entrepreneurship in practice

The music industry is loaded with entrepreneurship, networking and shifting careers. We now introduce you to a story about an entrepreneur who out of his interest in hip hop music engaged in a number of entrepreneurial activities in collaboration with other people.

CASE STUDY

A hip hop entrepreneur

(Devised by the authors)

'I'm a pornstar baby baby baby pornstar . . . ' So sings an entrepreneur and musician who over many years made his way from being an underground hip hopper to a commercial and successful dance musician, primarily within the Danish market. It is the story of Mike Simonsen, who along with the two well-known and respected DJs, producer Ronnie NME Veiler and producer Kenn 'The Killer' started the dance group Cargo. Cargo's best-known hit is probably 'Pornstar'. It is important here to bear in mind that it's the story of Mike we are putting the spotlight on and not the group Cargo.

Mike, an otherwise ordinary boy, comes from a small provincial town in Denmark. During his early teenage years he became interested in hip hop music and the underground culture associated with it. At that time, hip hop was an underground culture in Europe that had not been noticed by the vast majority of European teens. It was a long time before hip hop groups like the Beastie Boys and Run-DMC in the late 1980s made their way into the European charts. The entire European wave was initiated by, among other things, two films called *Beat Street* and *Breaking*.

Before hip hop's commercial breakthrough, there was a small crowd of young Europeans who were heavily inspired by American hip hop culture. They made hip hop music, 'scratching' turntables and painting illegal graffiti at night in their local areas. Many of them were dedicated, living and breathing hip hop. To a great extent we are talking about an underground culture where very few are involved, but where those involved all know each other. Many of the early hip hoppers then became DJs in the discos and nightclubs across the country. Over time the hip-hop culture grew much larger and more precisely in the footsteps of commercial successes like the Beastie Boys and Run-DMC.

Then it got serious

As Mike got older, it became clear to him that he wanted to be something 'in music'. He tried many different things throughout his youth, but everything can be related back to his dedication and passion for hip hop culture. At 22 years of age, he and a good friend and hip hop/DJ colleague started their own studio. It was a dream come true to be able to sit in his own studio, but at the same time they also had an ambition to get a record deal and put their hip hop music on the air. It was difficult, but they fought hard for several years with studio costs being funded through various ad hoc jobs such as production of radio commercials and various DJ jobs.

At some point they realised that they were stuck and not really moving forward, so they decided to close the studio and go their separate ways. They wanted new adventures and to explore other opportunities to break through. At this point Mike's ambitions had changed. From his earlier self-perception as a hip-hopper, he now had a wider view of himself as an

CASE STUDY *(continued)*

artist and rapper. This meant that he had become more open to other music styles and the commercial part of the music industry. Mike's ambition was now to become a successful musician without breaking the connection to his past and hip hop.

An opportunity is created

A few months before Mike and his partner closed their studio, Mike contacted two former acquaintances from the early hip hop period – Ronnie NME Veil and Kenn 'The Killer'. Both Ronnie and Kenn were by then recognised and respected DJs and producers who had long had commercial success on the Danish scene. Mike had not been in contact with Ronnie or Kenn for many years, but he remembered them from the earlier hip hop days and they also remembered Mike.

Mike wanted them to do a remix of Mike and his partner's latest attempt at a breakthrough – a song called 'What's the Matter in Paradise?' If they could get these famous people to remix their number, it would be easier to break through, but it never materialised, so they decided to close the studio and give up the song.

Instead, Ronnie and Kenn got Mike to rap for a number they were about to record. As often happens when talents meet by chance, there is creativity: in this instance a track called 'The Horn', a dance number in keeping with 1990s dance music. They decided to call the group Cargo. It was relatively easy for them to get the single 'The Horn' published by Scandinavian Records, mainly because of the reputations of Ronnie and Kenn. Nevertheless, the record company stipulated that their next single must be a big hit if they were to continue to release Cargo's records. Cargo's second single, to be called 'Loaded with Power', had to reach the top five in the 'dance chart'.

New strategy

As a reaction to the record company's requirements the team changed their strategy. They were all DJs with a relatively large network of colleagues. They also knew that the dance chart acts as a guide to many of the decisions that record companies make. The dance chart is a list of the dance hits that DJs across the country consider to be most successful on a weekly basis. So, it is the DJs – with all their semi-secret and non-commercial releases – who decide what is in the dance chart. So, the dance chart is not like other charts, which reflect the singles with the highest commercial sales. Of course those sales may be the result of the dance chart's weekly list. The different DJs' votes are weighted according to how many people are on the dance floor when each song is played. This means that the DJs who play at the major venues have tremendous power over which songs will be voted for.

The three musicians in Cargo burned about 20 CDs with their new track 'Loaded with Power' and sent the CDs to the most powerful of their DJ colleagues encouraging them to vote the number into the dance chart. The following week they entered the top 10, and the following week were in the top two. The single was later Grammy-nominated.

With the single 'Loaded with Power' placed in the dance chart Cargo got a record contract for an entire album. The album entitled *The Movie* sold 2,500 copies.

CASE STUDY *(continued)*

An opportunity is organised

However, this was not enough for Mike and Cargo. They did not think they had made enough of the musical material. Most of all, they were annoyed that the record company had not prioritised them in budgetary terms compared to other emerging groups. The commercial success was not satisfactory although, in the wake of the release, the group undertook an extended tour, primarily consisting of club venues.

At one point, the director of record company, who obviously has an impact on the prioritisation of new emerging groups, was replaced. The new director happened by chance to hear his young daughter singing 'I'm a pornstar pornstar baby baby . . . ' – the most famous song from the album *The Movie*.

The director asked his daughter who she was listening to and of course she told him it was Cargo. According to Mike this event was decisive in the Director's decision to change the company's strategy and priorities for Cargo. Among other things Cargo were provided with a completely different and larger budget. At the same time the first album was re-launched, but now with a new cover and a new female front person. Everything else remained exactly as before although the new album was called *The Movie Goes Party*. Among other things, the larger advertising budget meant that commercials for the new album appeared on one of the largest national TV stations.

The new album debuted at number 13 in the Danish list of best selling records. The following week they were in sixth place and in the third week in seventh place. In all, the record spent six weeks in the top 20 of most sold albums and went gold platinum (25,000 records sold) within a month.

Figure 8.1 The dance group Cargo

CASE STUDY *(continued)*

A new chapter

After several years Cargo disbanded. Mike lived for a time doing different jobs including an apprenticeship as a graphic designer and then operating his own small advertising agency, whilst enjoying his DJ job at the weekends. At times he was also a professional DJ and had no other income. By chance and in connection with a DJ job he met Aba – a younger man with an interest and musical skills in dance music. They got together as a group called AbaSimonsen and had great success with remixes and their own numbers in the Danish market. After a couple of years, having had big domestic success, they split up and, while Steffen Aba is still very active on the dance and house music scene, Mike mostly keeps in touch with the industry these days through occasional DJ jobs. Aba seems to be among the new rising stars. Working mainly as a producer he has received three nominations for 'best remix' and received gold and platinum discs for his involvement in the hit 'Chuck Norris'. A new generation is emerging.

Your immediate interpretation

What does the story of Mike and Cargo tell you about the importance of networking? What is your initial interpretation of the story? The following exercises can help you to form an understanding:

- Do networks play a role in the story? Make a list of the meanings attributed to network and 'networking' as expressed in the story. Discuss these meanings.
- How has Mike created his network? How has he used his network, and is there is a pattern in how he uses it?
- What does Mike's network look like? Does his network include many or just a few people? Are the people in his network similar or different? What other factors can be gainfully used to describe Mike's network?
- You have decided to start your own organisation and want to make sure that you get the most out of your network. What would you take into account in your attempts to 'network' and in creating the perfect network of contacts? Who should your network contain and how will you get in contact with them?
- You meet one of your friends. She is a successful entrepreneur. In discussing the importance of networking for entrepreneurs she declares that she was quite conscious and calculating in her use of networks, and that explains her success. What do you think of this argument?

Theories of entrepreneurship

The story we have just presented has many links to this chapter's topic, namely the theory of entrepreneurship and networking. The theory concerns how networks affect the entrepreneur's decisions and behaviour. However, that's about as far as any agreement on the subject goes because there is considerable disagreement about the importance of networking and the way entrepreneurs should network. In terms of these disagreements we can identify two fundamentally different perspectives on the significance of networks and how to approach networking. The two perspectives are reflected in the paradox: rational or embedded? One perspective discusses whether entrepreneurs can regard the network as a rational tool for deliberate and calculated use in order to succeed in their efforts to discover or create, evaluate and organise. This focuses on how networks can be changed and optimised depending on what resources the entrepreneur needs. The second perspective sees the network as a result of the entrepreneur's past. Networks are thus a consequence of the life that is led, and are thus something within which people are deeply embedded. The individual therefore has little possibility to manage and use the network efficiently. In other words, networks comprise uncontrollable conditions that the entrepreneur cannot change at will. Put another way, this chapter deals with the paradox of whether a network is a rational tool or a set of uncontrollable conditions within which the entrepreneur is embedded. In short, the paradox is:

Rational or embedded?

Theory of entrepreneurship and networks

Theory of entrepreneurship and networks builds on and is a source of traditional social network theory. The traditional theory, originally developed in sociology, has since spread to several social science disciplines, including organisational and entrepreneurship theory. The central argument of social network theory is that the network influences individuals' behaviour. Lin (2001) mentions four main ways in which networks influence individuals' behaviour. Networks can help to:

- provide people with information that can be applied to the situations they face;
- influence other people in the network; network relations have, so to speak, influence on the decisions and actions made;

- create social legitimacy for people within a network structure; people can then effectively gain access to resources through other individuals in the network vouching for them;
- develop and enhance personal identities; individuals can strengthen their identity by interacting with others who wish to maintain their identity.

The theory of entrepreneurship and networks has primarily focused on the resources that can be provided through the network. Hoang and Antončič write:

> Interpersonal and interorganizational relationships are viewed as the media through which actors gain access to a variety of resources held by other actors. With the exception of work on the role of networks to access capital ... most research has focused on the entrepreneur's access to intangible resources ... A key benefit of networks for the entrepreneurial process is the access they provide to information and advice. (Hoang & Antončič 2003: 169)

The resources that can be mobilised through social networks are often referred to as social capital. Social capital refers to the means and resources, the entrepreneur enjoys through using his or her personal contacts and acquaintances.

Although social network theory has a long history, the interest in networking within entrepreneurship is somewhat newer. The first contribution dates back to Birley (1985), Aldrich and Zimmer (1986) and Johannisson (1988). These contributions can be seen as a backlash against the research characterised by, among others, the psychological tradition in which the entrepreneur was treated as an individual without regard for the environment within which the individual existed. On the contrary, as mentioned, the theory of entrepreneurship and networks considers an entrepreneurial network to be a medium through which the entrepreneur may gain access to different resources. In this way, the individual and the individual's environment function simultaneously in the theory of entrepreneurship and networking. In fact, the network's role is not only related to the start of a new organisation but is valid throughout the entire lifecycle of the organisation (Hoang & Antončič 2003).

The heterogeneity argument

However, before we address the paradox, we must look more closely at different types of network arguments that characterise both sides of the paradox. For although there is consensus that networks play a crucial role for entrepreneurs, there is disagreement about what a good and efficient network looks like. The dissimilarity – or heterogeneity – argument suggests that differences among individuals in the entrepreneur's network and weak relationships between these are the most efficient network. This should be seen in relation to the argument for uniformity or the homogeneity argument, where it is argued that networks consisting of uniform (homogeneous) and strongly associated persons are most effective. This argument is presented in the following section on homogeneity.

The foundation of the argument for heterogeneity is that entrepreneurs obtain optimal access to valuable market information that they can apply through the entrepreneurial process by having networks that consist of diverse individuals with regard to their attitudes, values, jobs, experiences, skills, etc. Through these differences among the people of the network, the entrepreneur becomes, so to speak, the centre and bridge for information and increases the possibility of discovering or creating, evaluating and organising new opportunities.

The argument takes place at two different levels:

1. The relational level, which focuses on the relationship between the individual entrepreneur and his/her contacts. The relational level is illustrated in Figure 8.2 by the dotted box between the entrepreneur and his/her colleague.
2. In contrast, the network level includes all contacts the entrepreneur has in his/her entire network. The network level is illustrated in Figure 8.2 by the box around the entrepreneur's total network. Overall, Figure 8.2 illustrates the heterogeneity argument.

The relational level

At the relational level the heterogeneity argument is strongly inspired by – if one cannot actually say it comes from – Granovetter's ground-breaking article of 1973 on the strength of weak relationships. Granovetter defines the strength of relationships as follows: 'the strength of a tie is a (probably linear) combination of the amount of time, the emotional intensity, the intimacy (mutual confiding), and the reciprocal services which characterize the tie' (Granovetter 1973: 1361). So, the less emotional attachment, trust and reciprocity between an entrepreneur and his or her contact, the weaker the relationship. In Figure 8.2 a weak relationship is indicated by the dashed arrows between the entrepreneur and the entrepreneur's contacts (friend, customer, family member or colleague).

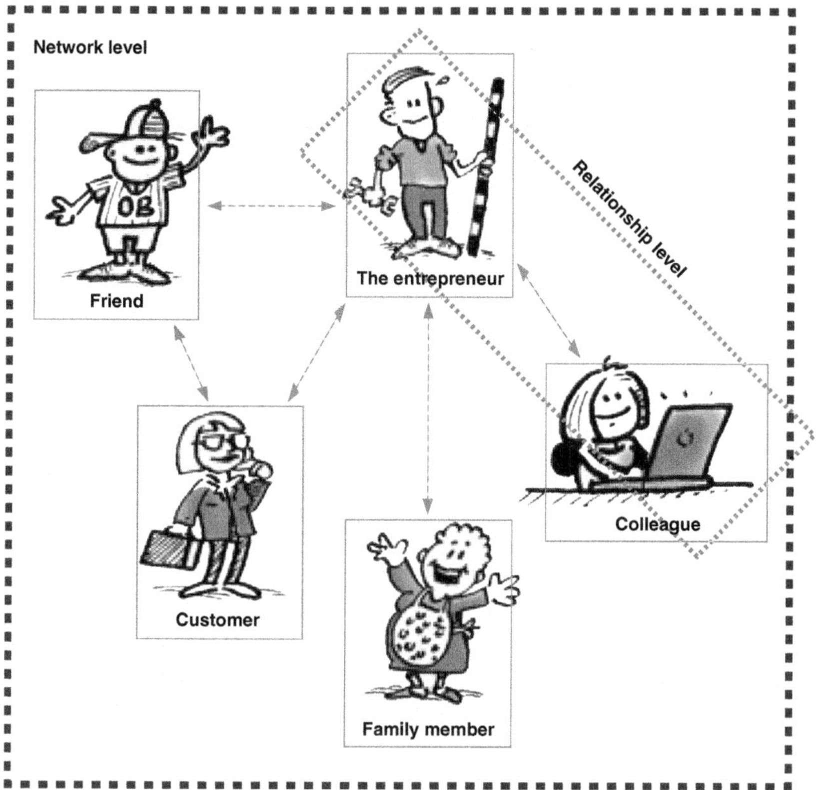

Figure 8.2 Weak relations and a heterogeneous network

Granovetter argues that the strength of the relationship affects the nature and value of the information that the entrepreneur gets from his/her contacts. According to him, one is more inclined to receive valuable information from the weak relationships because these relationships generally behave in other social networks than the entrepreneur him-/herself and therefore possess different information. He thus believes that entrepreneurs with many relatively weak links and relatively few strong relationships have better access to valuable information and better ability to disseminate information about their options than entrepreneurs with relatively few weak relationships and relatively many strong relationships.

The network level

Burt (1992) backs up Granovetter's argument for weak relationships. He argues that the typical drawback of strong relationships is that they are often strongly related to each other and thus possess the same information. In this way having many strong relationships is unimportant because, through using the existing network, you already have access to the information that these contacts possess. Information one can receive from a strongly related contact can surely also be gained from other strongly related contacts in the network. For example, it is not necessary or more rewarding to have two uncles with experience in the consulting industry, if it is this area of business in which you want to become established. The advice offered by each of the two uncles is unlikely to differ significantly from the other, and the advice from one uncle and the contact with him will usually be enough.

At the same time, Burt (1992) raises the argument for the heterogeneity of the network level, where the entrepreneur's total network, meaning all the entrepreneur's contacts, is brought into focus. In this context, Burt talks of the importance of structural holes in the overall network and the opportunity for entrepreneurs to serve as a bridge between different parts of the overall network. Structural holes in a network occur when some individuals in the entrepreneur's network are not interconnected – do not know each other. The more people who do not know each other, the more structural holes there are in the entrepreneur's network. When there are some people who do not know each other, there will be people in the network who become key figures and build bridges between different parts of the overall network. They get access to what Burt calls non-redundant information, which is crucial in order to discover or create, evaluate and organise opportunities, i.e. information that no other contacts in the network possess. Figure 8.2 shows a network with a structural hole between the entrepreneur's family members, customers and friends and colleagues.

The homogeneity argument

The argument about homogeneity is almost the opposite of the heterogeneity argument. Here it is argued that dense networks are the best, where as many people as possible in the network know each other, and where the relationship between the entrepreneur and these people is strong. Weak contacts and heterogeneous networks consisting of many bridges therefore play no role in this argument. How can that be?

The starting point for disagreement between the homogeneity and heterogeneity arguments is basically what kinds of resources are considered to be important. The heterogeneity argument focuses on information and specifically market information primarily related to discovering or creating, evaluating and organising capabilities. The homogeneity argument, however, focuses on resources, such as emotional support, sensitive market

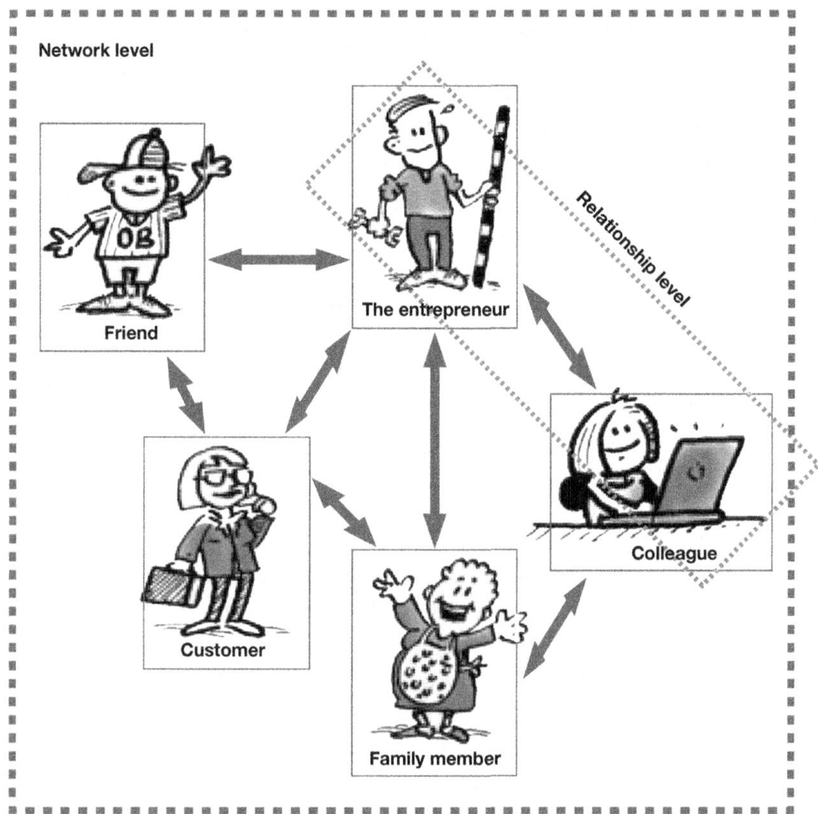

Figure 8.3 Strong relationships and a homogeneous network

information and access to financial resources. From this perspective it is therefore about gaining access to the type of resources that are exchanged only if both parties trust each other, spend much time together, have an emotional attachment to each other and where reciprocity exists between the two parties: Granovetter's definition of what creates a strong relationship. The homogeneity argument is strongly inspired by Coleman's (1988) work on the relationship between social and human capital. As is the case with the heterogeneity argument the homogeneity argument may also be explained on a relational level and network level (see Figure 8.3).

The relational level

On the relational level, the homogeneity argument's point is that the entrepreneur needs contacts that he or she has strong and close relations with. In such strong relationships, trust and mutual commitment between the contacts are often established, increasing the likelihood that the entrepreneur will receive the necessary emotional support required under the otherwise sometimes chaotic and complex entrepreneurial process. People who are not close to the entrepreneur will probably not spend their time and energy on emotional support. The same applies to the resource-sensitive market information. There is information, e.g. about markets, that people only share with people they trust. Moreover, very sensitive market information, such as information on conflicts or research efforts in another organisation, can be crucial to successfully discover or create, evaluate and organise opportunities.

Regarding access to financial capital the homogeneity argument may also be used. Bygrave et al (2003) surveyed the relationship between entrepreneurs and their private investors across 29 countries. They found that 40 per cent of entrepreneurs' investors were close family members and a further 8 per cent were other family relations. Only 8 per cent of the entrepreneurs who received private investment obtained capital from a stranger. These results aroused great interest when they were published. Focus was directed away from the earlier primary concern about the availability of venture capital, which can be described as professional and risk capital as too many entrepreneurs may find it almost unattainable – impossible to get into their hands. The bold arrows between the entrepreneur and the entrepreneur's contacts (friend, customer, family member or colleague) in Figure 8.3 indicate a strong relationship.

The network level

At the network level there is also an argument for homogeneity. In their cutting-edge article of 1986 Aldrich and Zimmer wrote that entrepreneurs embedded in dense networks, where many people in the network know each other, are more likely – based on mutual trust – to increase the collective power to act. When individuals are strongly associated in a dense network there is an increase in the likelihood that they will act as a whole and with a common goal in mind. Such collective action can be crucial for the implementation of the entrepreneurial process.

People in dense networks are also generally more uniform in relation to attitudes, values, jobs, experiences, skills, etc. than the people in a network where few know each other. Therefore, one can imagine that the entrepreneur's contacts share the same passion for a particular hobby, which means that they know each other on a personal level. Because of the personal dimension of the network and the shared interests, the provision of emotional support and exchange of sensitive market information are also more likely in dense networks than in less dense networks. The box around the entire network in Figure 8.3 indicates the network level.

Effective networking is situation dependent

We have now discussed two opposing arguments about what an effective network should look like when the entrepreneur battles his or her way through the entrepreneurial process, namely the heterogeneity argument and the homogeneity argument.

Immediately, both arguments appear to hold water: there is sense in them both. Both arguments also seem to hold true empirically. Various studies have, each in their own way, supported the heterogeneity and the homogeneity arguments. The explanation for these opposing arguments, making sense individually and being empirically supported, lies in the fact that social networks are dynamic (Larson & Starr 1993). Entrepreneurs meet and confront various challenges throughout the entrepreneurial process, and each of these requires access to different resources. Some resources are acquired most effectively through diverse social networks with many structural holes and weak relationships with people, while other resources are procured through dense networks where there are strong relationships between the characters.

The effective network therefore depends on the situation the entrepreneur is in. The challenges determine which resources are in demand, and hence which network the entrepreneur should aim for. Lin (2001) expresses this synthesis between the heterogeneity argument and homogeneity argument as follows: 'For preserving or maintaining resources (i.e. expressive actions), denser networks may have a relative advantage . . . On the other hand, searching for and obtaining resources not presently possessed (e.g., instrumental actions), such as looking for a job or a better job, accessing and extending bridges in the network should be more useful' (Lin 2001: 27).

There are several different models, primarily lifecycle models, that attempt to describe how the entrepreneur's network evolves with the advancement of the entrepreneurial process. In the very early stage when the entrepreneur is looking for an opportunity, the entrepreneur needs non-redundant market information to either create or discover a new opportunity. Therefore, the entrepreneur is interested in a network consisting of many diverse people, a network with many structural holes, and where the entrepreneur has weak relationships with people (Klyver & Hindle 2007). When the entrepreneur

Figure 8.4
Heterogeneous and homogeneous networks across the lifecycle of an organisation

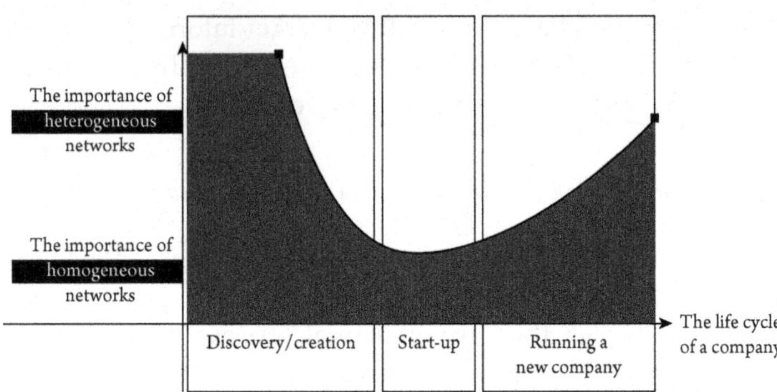

Source: Klyver & Hindle (2007: 26).

has identified an opportunity and is about to start the organisation, completely different resources are suddenly needed. During this stage there is a demand for advice and support to help with taking the final decision to start and also perhaps a need for capital injection. Therefore the aim is to utilise a closer network consisting of many strong relationships, including many family members (Evald et al 2006).

After the organisation has started, and the enterprise moves forward, some of the people in the network are replaced. In this phase it is essential for the entrepreneur to become established in the market, and the entrepreneur therefore needs access to market information again. Therefore the network will once again switch to a network consisting of many diverse people, a network with structural holes and a network with more weak relationships to, among other things, new contacts (Evald et al 2006).

So, we can see that the network changes throughout the entrepreneurial process and these changes can be attributed to the problems that confront the entrepreneur, and thus the resources that the entrepreneur needs. Figure 8.4 illustrates this graphically.

However, the efficiency of the network depends not only on the company's lifecycle, but on a number of other factors such as industry, gender, culture, etc. Klyver et al (2008) discuss whether the network should be understood as just universal and generic regardless of context, or whether the network should be understood in close interaction with the context. They show how the network plays a different role for entrepreneurs in 20 different European countries. A number of studies centred around Howard Aldrich's work have also tried to find similarities and differences between the way entrepreneurs use and apply their network. Concluding a review of these studies, Dodd and Patra (2002) wrote 'in summary, the results from this series of linked (although not methodologically identical) studies indicate some homogeneity, suggesting a degree of generic universal entrepreneurial behaviour, and some heterogeneity, highlighting the importance of cultural differences' (Dodd & Patra 2002: 119).

Research also suggests that not only the structure of the network matters, but also the entrepreneur's ability and motivation to engage in networking behaviour (Baron & Markman 2003). Entrepreneurs have various degrees of social skills and various degrees of comfort in interacting with other individuals, which influence what they can gain from their social networks. Thus, entrepreneurs with similar social networks might receive different network benefits depending on their individual social skills and motivation to interact with the people in the network.

So, the conclusion must be that although the network is important for entrepreneurs in all contexts and cultures, there are crucial differences in how networks are used and how networks operate.

Networks seen as a rational tool

So far we have discussed two different types of networks, heterogeneous and homogeneous, each of which have their merits depending on the various challenges the entrepreneur encounters during the entrepreneurial process. But what we have not dealt with is whether entrepreneurs use and apply their network in a rational and calculated manner or whether the network is more akin to something that controls and limits the entrepreneur's opportunities. This is the paradox about whether the network is a rational tool, or whether entrepreneurs are (for better or for worse) embedded in their network.

From a rational perspective, the entrepreneur is considered to be a goal-oriented actor who chooses his or her characters in the network based on who is expected to contribute the best and most important resources in relation to the implementation of the entrepreneurial process. It is a simple case of rational and arithmetical calculation to decide on who it pays to get involved with. The characters in the entrepreneur's network are thus 'supporters' who will each bring resources into the process such as councils, funding, or more intangible resources like legitimacy.

According to the rational perspective, the relationship between entrepreneurs and the people involved will often be concrete (i.e. supportive), emotionally neutral, quasi-contractual and short-sighted. People are selected with care, but are also carefully dropped again once they no longer support the process in the best possible way.

The rational perspective of networks is widespread among researchers, politicians, consultants and entrepreneurs. Networking events are an entirely natural thing today and networking has become a natural part of many other events. There are a number of speakers and consultants who focus on the importance of networking. Stephanie Speisman (Speisman 2011) is a coach and has, among other things, formulated 10 popular tips for successful business networking. Her advice largely reflects a rational approach to networking, although some of it more than other parts. Among the most rational pieces of advice in terms of assumptions are the following:

- Ask yourself what your goals are in participating in networking meetings so that you will pick groups that will help you get what you are looking for.
- Have a clear understanding of what you do and why, for whom, and what makes the way you are doing it special or different from others doing the same thing. In order to get referrals, you must first have a clear understanding of what you do that you can easily articulate to others.
- Be able to articulate what you are looking for and how others may help you. Too often, people in conversations ask, 'How may I help you?' and no immediate answer comes to mind.

Speisman's advice reflects an intention to utilise the network's potential in the most efficient way, at the same time considering the network to be something that can be controlled through planning and careful organisation.

Keith Ferrazzi (http://www.keithferrazzi.com, last accessed 14 August 2016) is among the best-known of the networking consultants and advisors. His motto is 'Business is human. Relationships power growth'. He believes that success is self-determined, but that it can only be achieved through the help of others. In his popular book *Never Eat Alone: And Other Secrets to Success, One Relationship at a Time* he outlines how personal networking should be undertaken in order to achieve success (Ferrazzi 2005). Among his three most famous pieces of advice are:

- Don't keep score: it's never simply about getting what you want. It's about getting what you want and making sure that the people who are important to you get what they want, too.
- 'Ping' constantly: the ins and outs of reaching out to those in your circle of contacts all the time – not just when you need something.

- Never eat alone: the dynamics of status are the same whether you're working at a corporation or attending a society event – 'invisibility' is a fate worse than failure.

Ferrazzi's understanding of networks is another illustration of a rational approach to social networks and an example of networks being considered and treated as an adjustable tool.

Embedded in networks

As we have already mentioned, there is also a different perspective, namely the embedded perspective. The embedded perspective goes one step further in terms of social embeddedness and the socialisation of human behaviour. The rational perspective recognises the influence of the social surroundings, but retains a belief that people govern themselves and determine what these social surroundings look like. This is not the case with the embedded perspective. The embedded perspective goes one step further in terms of social embeddedness and socialisation and is more sceptical about the ability of people and entrepreneurs to be rational and calculating in selecting the network that suits them.

Whereas the rational perspective focuses on the entrepreneur's opportunity to choose, the embedded perspective focuses on the network being something that is carried forward from the past. Networks are bounded by history – they are a result of the life you have led and the people you've met and interacted with. According to this perspective, the entrepreneur cannot actively select a network in relation to the problems he or she faces without there being consequences. Rather than being something that can be chosen or not chosen, the network is given from the past. For example, for many entrepreneurs there is a need to discuss with and involve their spouse in the crucial decisions to be made during the entrepreneurial process. Many of these decisions can also have a decisive influence on future family life, including for example, economy, leisure and working hours. These entrepreneurial decisions cannot be considered and taken in isolation. Thus, the spouse, whether supportive or not of the entrepreneurial process, becomes involved and has a decisive influence in many cases.

In the embedded perspective, networking is regarded as something that is created and maintained through all life's activities, and it cannot be identified and isolated in relation to specific challenges such as the start-up of an organisation. Social networking is something that is created holistically through the activities a person performs. Similarly, a network is the result of a person's past activities. A person's network is a result of the life that is led, and thus there are some who have large, diverse networks. Others, however, have less and dense, homogeneous networks: not because they have chosen it, but because the life they have led has resulted in it.

The embedded perspective and the rational perspective hold different views as to the nature of relationships. In the rational perspective, relationships were described as being specific (i.e. supportive), emotionally neutral, quasi-contractual and short-term. The embedded perspective describes relationships as broader (both supportive and obstructionist), emotional, trusting, mutually binding and long term.

The embedded perspective is somewhat more sceptical in relation to the network's positive impact on the entrepreneurial process. That it may be the case is not rejected – not at all – but it stresses that the network can also act as a barrier to entrepreneurs' progress through the entrepreneurial process. Aldrich and Zimmer wrote the following in their famous article: 'The embedded nature of social behaviour refers to the way in which action is constrained or facilitated because of its social context' (Aldrich & Zimmer 1986: 4).

The consequence of devoting oneself to the embedded perspective is that you can no longer consider the network as a tool to be used in isolation in relation to specific activities. Networking is, however, something that is embedded and brings some structure that defines and constrains the opportunities you have to network. The network becomes something that controls us rather than being something that we control and therefore we can say that for better or for worse entrepreneurs are embedded in their network.

Network: rational or embedded?

We have now discussed the two different perspectives on the nature of entrepreneurial networks. They are illustrated in Table 8.1.

The rational perspective describes the entrepreneur as a focused and rational actor who considers the network as a tool. The relationship between the entrepreneur and the people in his/her network are concrete, emotionally neutral, quasi-contractual and short term. Research within this perspective seeks to identify and determine what the most effective network for entrepreneurs looks like. The rational perspective gives low priority to the social context compared to the embedded perspective. The main criticism of the rational perspective from the view of the embedded perspective is that the

Table 8.1 The paradox: Rational or embedded

	Rational	Embedded
View of the entrepreneur	Goal-oriented, rational player	A socially embedded player
View of the networks	A rational tool	Ungovernable condition
View of the relation	Concrete, emotionally neutral, contract like and short term	Diffuse, emotional, trusting, reciprocally binding and long term
Focus	Effective networks	The facilitating and restricting qualities of the network
The importance of social contexts	Low	High

entrepreneur is under-socialised. This means that the social context is not given sufficient importance in describing the entrepreneur's actions. In contrast, the entrepreneur is seen as having more power over his/her own behaviour and decisions, than may actually be realistic.

While the rational perspective can be criticised for being under-socialised, the embedded perspective is criticised for the opposite, namely being over-socialised. This means that the embedded perspective does not give adequate consideration to the entrepreneur's own actions, but primarily focuses on how decisions are externally determined by the social context. One can therefore say that the embedded perspective places a higher priority on importance of the social context.

Over-socialisation means that the embedded perspective considers the entrepreneur as a socially embedded person who, with his/her network, has to deal with uncontrollable circumstances. The relationships between the entrepreneur and the people in the network are broad, emotional, trusting, mutually binding and long term. The role of research is, according to the embedded perspective, to clarify how the network promotes and/or limits entrepreneurs.

A theoretical interpretation

Below are two different interpretations of Mike's story that began this chapter. In the interpretations, the story is linked to the theory and focuses on the paradox: rational or embedded?

The rational perspective

If you choose a rational interpretation of Mike's story, the focus will be on how Mike consciously, rationally and in a calculative manner uses his network in his efforts to become a successful musician. These are many facets to deal with. Firstly, one can argue that Mike and his partner in the music studio chose each other as partners, hoping to obtain various benefits. Initially it may have been to reduce or further share the economic costs and risks. However, another advantage that may have played a crucial role was that they possess different skills and thus collectively offered a better product. 'Together' they believed that they were something special. Therefore, they both have some clear advantages and motives for joining forces with each other. They choose each other, but as time goes by they each eventually recognise that they have not quite reached the point where they wanted to be and they begin to doubt whether the team and the partnership is right for them. They therefore unanimously chose to go their separate ways. We might say that here they have taken a conscious decision to 'drop' each other.

Another situation that illustrates the rational network approach is the way Mike initially selects Ronnie and Kenn to remix their 'What's the Matter in Paradise?', and subsequently how Ronnie and Kenn want Mike to rap on their number 'The Horn'. They had probably discussed which of their contacts would best help them with this rap. They had screened the market for rappers and contacted those that they think can best give them what they need.

However, the situation where we can see the most rational behaviour is the way in which Cargo as a group used their network to secure a record deal. They had a product/album, but were only guaranteed a recording contract if their second single was a great success. So, they deliberately changed their strategy and in a calculated and intelligent way they used their network to legitimise and promote their product. By getting the single 'Loaded with Power' into the 'dance chart' through their network of Danish DJs they convinced a record label of the group's value, and they got a contract for an entire album. Here we are talking about a decidedly instrumental approach to the network where the network was used to achieve the objectives that the entrepreneurs had in mind.

The embedded perspective

Mike's story can, however, also be understood completely differently, namely from an embedded perspective, which focuses on networks as uncontrollable conditions. It may well be that in some situations he has deliberately used his network to promote his own interests, but overall the network that he uses is the result of his life. The contacts that he uses during the course of his career are, for the most part, contacts or people he got to know many years back in his early hip hop period. These are the people he has created relationships with, without having, at that time, any kind of calculative intentions. For this reason, these contacts proved to be decisive many years in later life. The common past, and the confidence built up in its wake, means that those people later in life have a soft spot for each other. Therefore, they want to help each other – not to get something in return, or because they owe each other anything, but rather to celebrate the relationship and the past.

Mike had not seen many of the people that had been around him in the earlier hip hop period for many years. When he met them, it was about hip hop and love of the underground culture. At that time, no one thought about whom it might be prudent to know in the future if you wanted to make a record. In any case, if some had thought so, it would have probably been impossible to predict who ended up in powerful positions. One can therefore say that the network that turned out to be conducive to Mike's music career was created under a completely different agenda, and with completely different intentions.

Perhaps one can't exactly say that Mike's network has limited his career, as the story has unfolded here in this chapter, but maybe one can say that Mike's past life, and the network that resulted from it, set and defined the limits and possibilities for him as a dance musician. We might ask whether he would have had the same success with the same talent but without a past as a hip-hopper.

Testing the theory

Based on the above thoughts and discussions, you are ready to develop your own attempts to understand the entrepreneurial network and how it influences the entrepreneurial process. The following are suggestions for investigating the topic.

? EXERCISES

1 **Interview an entrepreneur.** Make a list of interview questions that seek to capture some of the most important discussions about how networks work. Contact an entrepreneur, and interview him or her in order to test the theory presented in this chapter on entrepreneurial networks. Based on this, express your opinion on this paradox: rational or embedded?

2 **The film *The Social Network*.** Watch the movie *The Social Network*, a film about the start-up

process of Facebook. What is the network view portrayed in the film? Is it consistent with a rational or an embedded view on social networks? How would the story have been if social networking was not part of it?

3 **Keith Ferrazzi.** Go to http://www.keithferrazzi.com. Study the various pieces of advice Ferrazzi gives about networking and assess how similar advice would sound from an embedded perspective. What do you think of Ferrazzi's advice? Does it make sense and will it promote entrepreneurial performance?

4 **Describe your own network.** What does your network look like? Is it small, large, heterogeneous, homogeneous, etc.? How many relationships from your childhood, youth, adulthood, etc.? How strongly attached are you? Do the people in your network know each other? Why do you think your network looks the way it does?

LITERATURE

Aldrich, H.E. & Zimmer, C. (1986) 'Entrepreneurship through social networks', in Sexton, D.L. & Smilor, R.W. (eds), *The Art and Science of Entrepreneurship*, New York: Ballinger, 3–23.

Baron, R.A. & Markman, G.D. (2003) 'Beyond social capital: The role of entrepreneurs' social competence in their financial success', *Journal of Business Venturing*, 18(1), 41–60.

Birley, S. (1985) 'The role of networks in the entrepreneurial process', *Journal of Business Venturing*, 1, 107–117.

Burt, R.S. (1992) *Structural Holes – The Social Structure of Competition*, London: Harvard University Press.

Bygrave, W.D., Hay, M. & Reynolds, P.D. (2003) 'Executive forum: A study of informal investing in 29 nations composing the Global Entrepreneurship Monitor', *Venture Capital*, 5, 101–116.

Coleman, J.S. (1988) 'Social capital in the creation of human capital', *American Journal of Sociology*, 94, 95–120.

Dodd, S.D. and Patra, E. (2002) 'National differences in entrepreneurial networking', *Entrepreneurship and Regional Development*, 14(2), 117–134.

Evald, M.R., Klyver, K. & Svendsen, S.G. (2006) 'The changing importance of the strength of ties throughout the entrepreneurial process', *Journal of Enterprising Culture*, 14, 1–26.

Ferrazzi, K. and Raz, T. (2005) *Never Eat Alone: And Other Secrets to Success, One Relationship at a Time*, New York: Currency Doubleday.

Granovetter, M.S. (1973) 'The strength of weak ties', *American Journal of Sociology*, 78, 1360–1380.

Hoang, H. & Antončič, B. (2003) 'Network-based research in entrepreneurship – A critical review', *Journal of Business Venturing*, 18, 165–187.

Johannisson, B. (1988) 'Business formation – A network approach', *Scandinavian Journal of Management*, 4, 83–99.

Klyver, K. & Hindle, K. (2007) 'The role of social networks at different stages of business formation', *Small Enterprise Research*, 15, 22–38.

Larson, A. & Starr, J.A. (1993) 'A network model of organisation formation', *Entrepreneurship Theory & Practice*, 17, 5–15.

Lin, N. (2001) *Social Capital – A Theory of Social Structure and Action*, New York: Cambridge University Press.

Speisman, S. (2011) '10 tips for successful business networking', available at www.businessknowhow.com/tips/networking.htm (last accessed 20 December 2016).

9

The business plan

Many entrepreneurs need a business plan, and many have also made one. However, there are also entrepreneurs who have prepared a business plan without actually needing it, and without actively making use of it. The business plan has become the major focal point of many textbooks and courses on entrepreneurship, with its importance being drummed into the heads of entrepreneurs. There is, however, much to suggest that the business plan's role and significance is more complicated than it may appear.

The business plan may have an important role in the planning of the entrepreneurial process, both internally in relation to the entrepreneur him-/herself and externally in relation to third parties such as investors. However, the business plan also plays other important roles that are more symbolic and provide legitimation in relation to the environment. At the same time there are some who argue that the business plan may in fact impede the entrepreneur's creativity. You will be introduced to these topics and issues in this chapter.

Entrepreneurship in practice

Here's a case study written by Thomas Cooney and Anita Van Gils about Michael, who in 2010 started Mobitrix – a medical software business – and about how Michael employed his business plan in the process.

CASE STUDY

Mobitrix: a start-up company in the medical software industry

(Devised by Thomas Cooney and Anita Van Gils)

On a sunny Sunday afternoon in May 2011, Michael was sitting in the garden of his home. His thoughts would occasionally stray to the challenges that faced his business and to the major decisions that must be taken in the weeks ahead. He had established a business plan for

CASE STUDY *(continued)*

Mobitrix nine months previously, but the current business situation looked completely different. He could not help wondering how he should proceed with his business idea and with his plan!

Before starting his own business, Michael had been working for more than 10 years with different software companies in the medical sector. As a product manager, he was primarily responsible for the interface between the needs of the company's clients and the development of appropriate technical software solutions to meet those needs. This meant that both he and the software entrepreneurs frequently had to be imaginative to work around the distinctive challenges that each job would bring. In addition to this role, Michael also monitored the implementation of the different projects in the hospital setting. It was during the time that he spent on these projects in medical labs that Michael spotted several opportunities for product development.

One of these opportunities arose from concerns for patient safety. Medical caretakers are responsible for providing the correct medication to the patients (specifically with regards to blood transfusion), but many stories exist of errors that could have been prevented if the carer had access to correct and up-to-date information through the right software solution. Because Michael was very Apple-minded, and generally a first-mover in trying out Steve Jobs' newest creations, he had been considering how the iPhone, iPod and iPad could add value in creating mobile solutions for the health care business for some time. He pitched his idea to his bosses, but they did not see how these opportunities could fit in with their current portfolio of software products. Michael became increasingly frustrated with the lack of innovativeness in the companies' activities and plans, until eventually he woke up one night in a hotel room and started writing the first pages of a plan to start his own business as the many different possibilities and ideas rushed through his mind.

Mobitrix, a one-person business activity, was established in September 2010. Educated as a medical laboratory technologist with a Masters in Biomedical Technology, Michael soon realised that his business experience was very limited. As he had close contacts with entrepreneurship teachers at the School of Business and Economics at Maastricht University, he evaluated the possibility of collaborating with students on the development of a business plan. Bart, a medical engineering graduate taking a Masters in International Business in Entrepreneurship and Small Business Management, welcomed the opportunity to combine his medical and business expertise, and so began supporting Michael in researching and writing a business plan. For Michael, the development of a business plan helped him to put fine detail to his ideas and to evaluate the viability of the many possible market entry options that lay before him. He first had to decide on a business model: would he deliver his products to medical equipment companies, medical software companies or to the hospitals themselves? He felt that the programming of the software would need to be outsourced, so selection criteria for suppliers had to be established. Michael and Bart discussed financial projections extensively, made an initial projection of the break-even point and decided that no external investment was needed at that time as the money required for the software development could be covered

CASE STUDY *(continued)*

from Michael's own funds. Finally, they decided on a first important goal – they aimed at presenting Mobitrix's first product concept at the Medica Exhibition (the world's largest medical technology exhibition) which was to be held in Dusseldorf in November 2010.

During those first months of activities, many unexpected issues arose that required Michael's immediate attention. For example, while planning the first software developments, Michael accidentally discovered a scanning accessory that was developed for iPhone and iPod Touch, and which would perfectly fit the hardware requirements needed for the development of an application (app) that could solve the patient safety problems. Michael believed that putting barcodes on blood bags, medicines and on each patient's hospital wristband, and then scanning those barcodes with the mobile device, would almost certainly decrease the number of medical errors currently occurring. After carefully writing the software specifications and the functional design, Michael outsourced this first software development project to a company in Sri Lanka. Although the cooperation went smoothly, the development time was much longer than was planned.

Eventually, Michael and Bart managed to have their first app completed before the Medica Exhibition. While the final users for this app would be hospital personnel, Michael and Bart decided that the best strategy was to target their product for sale to medical equipment manufacturers and software companies. Initial reactions at the exhibition were very good, both from their targeted client segment and from end users. Mobitrix received visitors from very diverse and sometimes very large companies (including Philips Healthcare, GE Healthcare, Tieto, Panasonic, etc.), and Michael and Bart were usually asked highly focused questions. A later analysis of their interactions at the Exhibition showed that the leads generated consisted of 43 per cent of C-level functions (CEO, CTO, CFO), of which 70 per cent indicated an interest in

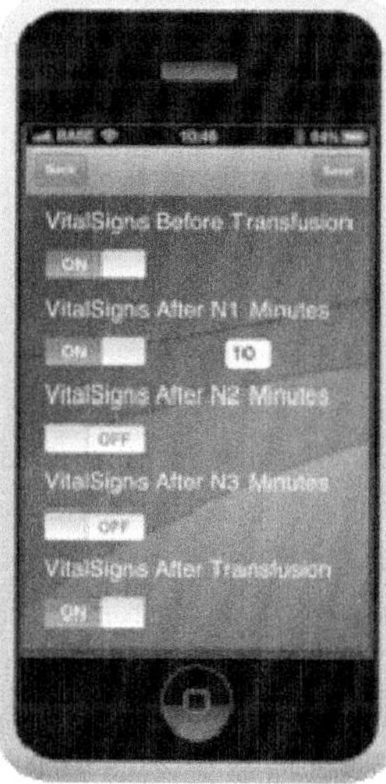

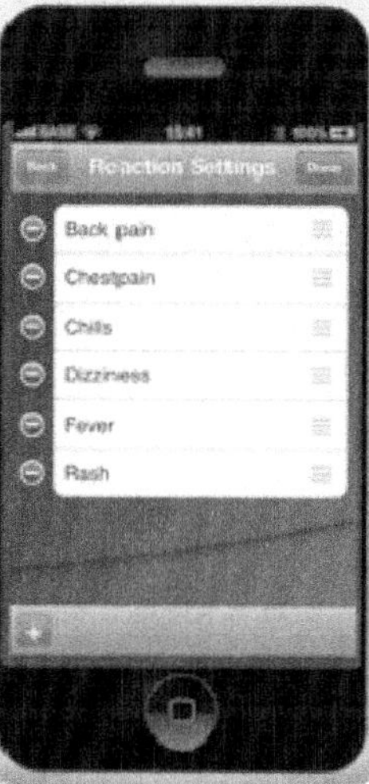

Figure 9.1 Delivering health care through an iPhone

CASE STUDY *(continued)*

having apps developed for them. Michael collected more than 100 business cards from people that showed significant interest, and secured at least five serious leads from medical and software companies that needed to be followed up. Moreover, shortly afterwards, the first app that they had produced was accepted by Apple's app store. Although the selling price of this app was just 3.99 Euros, for the owner it was a pilot project to test if he could manage the whole process. Meanwhile, a new software app for bedside registration was also in development in India, and this project would use the first app that they had produced.

In the months following the Medica Exhibition, Michael contacted all of the people that had shown interest at the exhibition, and he completed several interesting meetings. For example, one contact was with an Italian technology company that produces smart blood refrigerators. As their product covered the whole process from lab to nurse, but lacked the additional bedside registration, Mobitrix's software seemed to be a perfect fit. A second promising contact was with a Swedish company that produces haematology cell imaging solutions. Yet another contact was with a hospital ICT manager who saw the demo app and was surprised by the quality and speed of the barcode recognition. These people were interested in getting access to the improved barcode recognition functionality in their apps. Despite these meetings, no cooperation agreements could be developed. Several companies indicated a preference to postpone their investments in mobile solutions until the summer of 2011. For the software companies the major problem related to the integration of the proposed apps with existing systems.

Although Michael realised that starting up a venture is a bumpy ride with many highs and lows, the existing lack of follow-up projects really made him doubt the viability of his general business idea. However, as he was positive that the opportunity was recognised by the medical personnel, he persisted in pitching his idea. But instead of targeting his products at medical equipment or software companies, he started making appointments with doctors in hospitals to demonstrate his mobile solutions. These visits persuaded him yet again about the potential of the product, as doctors were very enthusiastic about the viability of his idea, and even offered suggestions for other apps that needed to be developed. Michael then convinced a team of doctors in a Belgian hospital of the added value of his product, and they decided to start a pilot project with him. Michael realised that this was an important breakthrough, as it created a reference project that would also increase his credibility with other clients. Unfortunately, the implementation of the project could not begin until he convinced the IT personnel and the management team of the value he could add to the processes in their hospital. Therefore, he needed to carefully prepare a presentation for this group, as they would probably use different decision-making criteria from the doctors.

But there are other issues that cause Michael to reflect on the actions that he has taken in recent months. The medical team in the pilot hospital has indicated that they are unable to do business with a one-person company, as service must be guaranteed even when an entrepreneur becomes sick or has an accident. For reasons such as this, Michael has been contemplating the benefits of partnering with a larger company. Should he then update his business

CASE STUDY *(continued)*

plan in order to prospect for these partners? In his initial version of the plan, the first sales were estimated to be realised in December 2010, while five months later, the venture really was still in the pre-sales state. Besides, in the plan, much more software development had been planned, but this was postponed, given the longer development time of the first two projects. As he expected to start with the first pilot project, it could also be the ideal moment to find some external financing. He definitely needed a change to his business plan for such a purpose. However, he wondered how he could write a business plan which on the one hand was sharp, goal-oriented and convincing to potential partners and, on the other hand, sufficiently flexible to absorb surprises and take advantage of new opportunities.

Your immediate interpretation

What does the story tell you about Mobitrix and the importance of business plans? How do you immediately interpret the story's twists? The following exercises can help you interpret the story:

- How does Michael use the business plan during Mobitrix's start-up period? What purpose does it serve? Do you get the feeling that he places a high priority on a written business plan?
- Does he have a written plan, or is it more about loose ideas and thoughts that are not necessarily written down? Do you think it is important that the business plan is written down and specific rather than being just at the idea and thought level?
- You have decided to start your own organisation, and you have been advised to write a business plan before you start up. What should such a plan include, how long should it be and how should it be developed?
- You meet one of your old friends from school. She has just graduated with an MSc in International Business. She is now considering starting her own organisation, where she and her partner will advise small businesses who want to start exporting to China. During their studies, both your old friend and her partner have devoted a lot of time and effort to China. They have been on several trips, have undertaken a semester's internship in China and have written their thesis on the subject of exporting to China. They claim they have a very good knowledge of the subject and that they also have the necessary contacts to make a start. They therefore believe that it is a waste of time to write a business plan. What do you think?

Theories of entrepreneurship

The Mobitrix story is closely related to the main topic of this chapter, i.e. the business plan. In many ways the story discusses business plans and how the entrepreneur describes and communicates his or her recognition of and plans (both ex-ante and ex-post) related to, the generation, evaluation and organisation of a new opportunity. This represents description, in a structured form, of the entrepreneur's insights and plans in relation to Chapter 3 on the emergence of opportunities, Chapter 4 on the evaluation of opportunities and Chapter 5 on the organising of opportunities.

There are many definitions of what constitutes a business plan. On their website, the US Small Business Administration defines a business plan as follows: 'A business plan precisely defines your business, identifies your goals and serves as your firm's resume. Its basic components include a current and pro forma balance sheet, an income statement and a cash flow analysis. It helps you allocate resources properly, handle unforeseen complications, and make the right decisions' (www.sba.gov, last accessed 20 December 2016).

Those who promote the importance of a business plan are often supporters of the planning perspective as opposed to the improvisation perspective (as discussed in Chapter 5). They believe that organisational processes can be controlled and see the business plan as an important management tool for implementing the entrepreneurial process as painlessly as possible. Conversely, there are others who view the business plan more sceptically; namely as a curb on creativity. They argue that entrepreneurs are pressured into a certain mind-set through the business plan's structure, and that their otherwise crucial creativity is reduced. The paradox in this chapter is therefore whether the business plan is a:

Management tool or creativity curb?

The business plan: context, content and process

Before discussing the paradox further, we will concentrate on some other fundamental factors that relate to the business plan. The discussion about the business plan is often equated with the concept of planning. 'The plan' is the content or output of a 'planning process', called 'planning'. Planning takes place within certain limits and conditions as 'context'. This separation is illustrated in Figure 9.2 (De Wit & Meyer 1998).

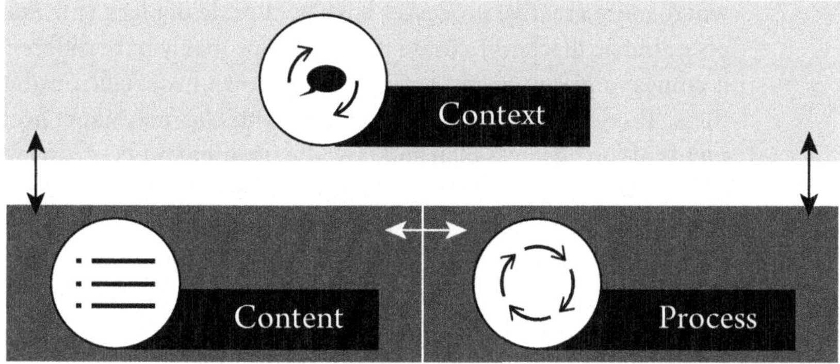

Source: Inspired by De Wit & Meyer (1998).

Figure 9.2 The plan context, content and process

As the figure illustrates, the three dimensions are connected and influence each other. One can therefore imagine that in some industries (contexts) the requirement for the business plan and the planning process is greater than in other industries. Honig and Karlsson (2004) found, for example, that entrepreneurs in the production sector are more likely to produce a business plan than entrepreneurs in other industries. They explain that the tendency arises because production-based industry has a planning approach. New entrepreneurs are therefore more willing to produce a plan and imitate the tradition in order to achieve legitimacy and gain the understanding of the other actors and stakeholders.

One can also imagine that the need for, and relevance of, a business plan varies according to the degree of uncertainty in the actual idea and the context within which it occurs. The need is probably limited in very simple and traditional small businesses such as shops and craft businesses where the uncertainty is relatively low. Likewise, the planning approach is of limited relevance and value in connection with business ideas that are radically innovative, such as Skype and Google (Sarasvathy 2008).

One may also imagine that having a need for a high level of venture capital (context) will impose different demands on the business plan's content than if the entrepreneur can personally finance his or her organisation's start-up. Here, additional detailed information on financial matters will be required. Alternatively, one may envisage that people with different backgrounds (contexts) have different needs for business plans. For example, some individuals have an education where planning plays a major role (for example, engineers, business economists or production planners), whilst others have an education where more creative processes have held pride of place (for example, designers or music teachers). These people will probably have different needs when it comes to planning and writing things down in specific business plan structures. There is a myriad of different contexts that may affect both the requirements of the business plan and how the planning process can take place.

However, the process can also affect the content, and the content can influence the process. One could, for instance, imagine that a particular way of doing things will lead to restrictions in the content itself. If, from the outset, the entrepreneur decides to ignore recommendations from an advisor, to involve various key stakeholders in the planning process – including actors, local communities, financial advisers, family members – one can easily imagine that some of the critical comments they have regarding the project will be completely ignored and will not appear on the final written plan (content).

One can also imagine that if the entrepreneur takes a predefined table of contents as the starting point for his or her business plan, it will influence the process because using an index as a starting point can in itself lead to a structured analytical approach (process).

Written document or thought process

It has often been discussed whether it is the business plan as a written document that is crucial or whether it is the thought and planning process that is essential. Shane tries to capture the discussion this way: 'The entrepreneur formulates a plan, in mental or written form, for the organizing process . . . the planning then leads to organizing activities' (Shane 2003: 221).

The arguments for the plan as a written document are that the entrepreneur obtains clarity on the decisions to be taken in relation to the supply of products, on which markets to become involved with and what constitutes the organisation's competitive advantage. Additionally, the plan as a written document can be important in relation to communication with an external third party such as banks, investors, customers or suppliers. Furthermore, the written document also plays a role in terms of internal communication and reflection. The business plan can be used in communicating with new employees – as a foundation in the socialisation of desired behaviour, and communication of organisational goals – but the plan may also, in other ways, contribute to the maintenance and possible strengthening of the entrepreneur's motivation. Baker et al (1993) cite three main reasons for the written business plan being better than the informal, unwritten thought process for small businesses:

1. The written plan ensures critical thinking.
2. It can be used in both internal and external communication.
3. It can serve as internal control of company development.

They found this third feature of the plan to be the most important function for most small businesses.

However, there are also people who argue that the very act of writing down the plan is often unnecessary and that the important thing is the right thought process. It's the process of thinking that provides clarity regarding the organisation's objectives and how they can be fulfilled. Ultimately, it is the process that provides motivation, not the written plan. Market conditions, technological possibilities, regulatory and numerous other factors related to the organisation's environment change so fast today that the written business plan becomes out-dated almost before it is finished. Therefore, continual rethinking is crucial.

However, there is a further argument against the written business plan, an argument that specifically applies during the start-up of an organisation. People about to exploit an opportunity are often short of time and resources. For them it's about getting the opportunity realised through the organisation as soon as possible, so that cash flow is initiated and the organisation can begin to earn money and pay wages. The longer the process takes, the greater the financial risk run by the entrepreneur, and the greater funding required for the start-up. They are, therefore, busier with getting the organisation started up and entirely operational rather than sitting around devising long-term strategic plans. David Madié, co-founder of Start-up Company and later Growth Company, which has offices in both Copenhagen and New York, has previously stated:

> Proponents of writing a business plan will reply, that it never can be detrimental to have a good plan. But actually, it can. The big problem with the business plan is all the time spent on it – maybe 100 hours or more, leading to several weeks of work . . . The worst is not the time and energy spent on writing worthless business plans. The worst thing is, what the time could otherwise be spent more wisely on tasks, which could increase its chance of survival, growth and ability to obtain financing from either banks or investors. (Madié 2007: 34–35; translated into English from Madié's original Danish text)

There is thus a lively debate about whether it's the plan in written form or the thought process that is decisive for completion of the entrepreneurial process. A debate where there are rational arguments on both sides. It's not all entrepreneurs who write a business plan. In Shuman et al's (1985) study of Inc. 500 companies, they concluded that 49 per cent of the companies developed a business plan during their start-up process. Delmar and Shane (2003) concluded that 40 per cent of the Swedish companies they studied had a written business plan.

These studies show that the preparation of a business plan is widespread, but it may be even larger than the percentages show, because the definition of a business plan is unclear. As a rule one tends to think of a fully developed business plan with detailed product descriptions, budgets and market analysis, typically a document of 10–20 pages. However, there may also be a more concise document, often called a concept statement, which primarily and succinctly describes the likely demand from future customers and the value proposition associated with the new product or service (Barringer & Ireland 2008). In addition, a PowerPoint presentation or other visual material has a similar effect for the entrepreneur and business development as a written format. Business plans may therefore have different formats that may be relevant at different stages of venture development, or in relation to various stakeholder groups.

Planning

Before jumping into the discussion of the business plan's content and its associated paradox, we will briefly discuss some issues about the close relationship between planning as a process and the business plan as output. There will therefore, as previously indicated, be parallels in this section to the discussions that you dealt with in Chapter 5 on the organisation of opportunities.

During a planning process, there are some critical factors that one should be aware of in connection with the development of a business plan. These factors are critical to ensuring that the business plan will work as intended. Kuratko and Hodgetts (2004) combine these factors into four main factors:

- Goals must be realistic.
- The plan must provide commitment and dedication.
- The plan must include milestones.
- The plan must be flexible.

It is crucial that the targets set are realistic both externally with stakeholders, including, for example, potential investors or lenders, and internally in relation to their own motivation. If the targets are unrealistic and not adequately thought through, it is difficult to attract investors or lenders. At the same time it is difficult to maintain the motivation to get through the entrepreneurial process when one can see that the goals are unrealistic and unattainable. It is also important that the plan contains some milestones by which various activities must be completed and show how these activities are interrelated. This makes it possible to check whether one is in step with the timing of the plan and thus on track. Last but not least, it is crucial that the plan is flexible. This may be a little inconsistent with the planning milestones. To implement the entrepreneurial process is a relatively complex, difficult and unpredictable process and it may therefore be important to create room for changes along the way.

One way the complexity and unpredictability can be overcome, especially in the first part of the 'planning' process, is by making use of the Business Model Canvas. The method is seen by many as an adjunct to writing a more complete-reflected business plan and is often considered to be a tool to understand and reflect on the business model that can support the implementation of the idea.

Since 2010, when Alexander Osterwalder and Yves Pigneur published the book Business Model Generation the Business Model Canvas has been used by many as the basis of the method by which they have written their business plan. The model focuses sharply on how they can earn money, and thus helps existing businesses and entrepreneurs to better understand what it is that makes their business unique. This is especially interesting for investors or top management, in order to better assess whether the new business areas or entrepreneurs in which they invest can actually generate income. No idea is better than the business that is built up around it, and therefore understanding of business models, and the ability to put the right pieces together in reality, are at least as important as the product itself or the solution that has been devised. Popularly, it is said: 'Innovation without understanding of business models is as big a risk as investing heavily in the development of sports talent without simultaneously investing in training facilities, coaches and travel to important tournaments'.

The hallmark of the Business Model Canvas is that the method includes a number of building blocks that influence each other. The building blocks can be broadly classified into two main components. The first main element focuses on customers and sales, and the other main element puts the spotlight on the company to provide the solution and customer value. These two, in combination, determine whether an entrepreneur has an opportunity that can be exploited and organized or not, and how this can be done.

The building blocks of the Business Model Canvas in relation to customers and sales are:

1. Value propositions: The products and services a company offers to meet customer needs. Here the key question is, 'What do you sell?'
2. Customer segments: In order to build an effective business model one must determine who the customers are. The question 'Who buys the product/service?' is the focus here.
3. Revenue streams: The possible sources of income. So the central question for consideration is, 'How will money be earned?' After putting the spotlight on the possible sources of income, it is also a good idea to discuss the pricing model behind the product or service. This then leads to a supplementary question about how the price of the product/service is to be determined.
4. Channels: Indicate distribution and communication channels needed to reach the customers. Therefore, the important question is, 'How will customers find the product/service?'
5. Customer relationship: The relationship with the customer – thus, the relationship with the customer must be discussed and clarified.

The building blocks of the Business Model Canvas in relation to the business are:

6. Key activities: The most important key activities to be carried out in the company to create value for customers. Important here, is being able to answer, unequivocally, the question, 'What does the company do?'
7. Key resources: The resources necessary to create value for the customer. To this end, the key question is often, 'What does the company consist of?'
8. Partners: Which partners and suppliers will be affiliated with the company. The question here is, 'With whom shall the company work in order to deliver the activities that will ultimately deliver the desired customer value?'
9. Cost structure: What costs are involved, i.e., the central question is, 'What is the business's cost structure?'

Together, these nine elements constitute a business model and will be the basic building blocks of every good business. How a good business model is achieved depends on how the individual building blocks are put together. The advantages of the Business Model Canvas is that it creates an overview, showing how the different building blocks influence each other and why they are dependent on each other, and not least, it provides a team of entrepreneurs with a common frame of reference so that a common understanding of what the business is about can be obtained. The achievement of a common language and a common understanding may not only be crucial for internal communications but also externally.

The plan's content

A plethora of advice exists on what a business plan should contain. Often these suggestions are shown as the table of contents proposed in the business plan. However, despite these numerous proposals for the content of the business plan, which are almost presented as universal, the only credible universal advice is that the business plan must be adapted to the opportunity, the situation and the target audience of the plan. Of course, how different types of opportunities are best described in a business plan will vary. The situation concerning the opportunity also has great influence on how the business plan should fit together. For example, one might imagine that entrepreneurs with ambitions towards export and growth would have to structure their business differently from an entrepreneur who simply wants to establish him- or herself locally. Finally it is natural that different audiences (be they bankers, investors, customers, suppliers, accountants, etc.) will have different requirements for the information in the business plan.

That said, Table 9.1 illustrates three examples of what the contents of a business plan might look like.

The three different proposals should be considered as separate suggestions for solving the same problem. There is nothing that speaks more for one

Table 9.1 Three examples of the contents of a business plan

Kuratko & Hodgetts (2004)	Schilit (1987)	Business plan journal
Executive summary	Executive summary	Executive summary
Business description	Background and purpose	Company analysis
Marketing	Objectives	Industry analysis
Operations	Market analysis	Customer analysis
Management	Development and production	Competitive analysis
Financial	Marketing	Marketing plan
Critical risks	Financial plans	Operations plan
Harvest strategy	Organisation and management	Management team
Milestone schedule	Ownership	Financial plan
	Critical risks and problems	Appendix
	Summary and conclusion	

than for another, unless the possibility of the situation and target group of the business plan is taken into account. Furthermore, there is some overlap between the three proposals, all of which have sections on management, finance and market conditions.

As you can see, there are many different views on what the contents of the business plan should be. The essential thing in determining a given plan is to think through what type of information is crucial in the specific situation. Below is some advice that may be helpful in the preparation of the plan. The recommendations are some of the proposals Kuratko and Hodgetts (2004) come up with. The business plan should:

- not be too long;
- be oriented toward the future;
- avoid exaggerations;
- clarify critical risk factors;
- identify the target group;
- be written professionally (in the third person);
- catch the reader's attention and interest.

The business plan as a management tool

Now we will deal with the paradox and discuss the two seemingly opposite perspectives. One perspective sees the business plan as a management tool and the other sees the business plan as a curb on creativity. We begin by discussing the business plan as a management tool.

This view of the business plan is by far the most commonly held and follows a rational logic, where the business plan is seen as a means to manage and plan for an organisation's future. Wickham (2004) describes the business plan as a entrepreneurial tool targeted to exploit opportunities, and Delmar and Shane argue:

> Business planning helps firm founders to undertake venture development activities because planning facilitates goal attainment in many domains of human actions . . . Specifically, we argue that planning helps firm founders to make decisions more quickly than with trial-and-error learning; and to turn abstract goals into concrete operational activities more efficiently. (Delmar & Shane 2003: 1166)

According to Delmar and Shane (2003), the use of business plans has three major advantages:

1. First, the business plan and planning process can be used to make decision-making faster by identifying missing information before the (financial) resources are tied up.
2. Second, the business plan is a tool for managing supply and demand of resources in such a way as to avoid bottlenecks.
3. And finally, the business plan is a way to identify the activities that must be initiated to achieve the targets set within the timeframe.

Schilit (1987) also sees the business plan as a management tool:

> What is a business plan? Essentially, it is a vehicle to: 1) Assess the current and future state of an organization and its environment; 2) Delineate long-range and short-range objectives based on this assessment; and 3) Develop appropriate action guidelines to achieve these objectives. It is clearly the result of diligent market research and sound financial projections. (Schilit 1987: 13)

When one looks at the business plan as a management tool, it can be traced back to a conviction that the future can be predicted. March (1997) speaks of some pre-conditions that must be present before planning, in its perfectly rational sense, can be undertaken:

- knowledge of alternatives;
- knowledge of consequences;
- a consistent preference ordering;
- a decision rule.

When the business plan is seen as a management tool, it is built on the assumption that the entrepreneur is familiar with the various future alternatives, such as the ways in which he or she imagines that the market can develop, and also that he or she is able to realise the consequences of the alternatives. What does it mean for the entrepreneur if the market develops according to the different alternatives? And subsequently over time, the entrepreneur maintains a consistent set of preferences for these alternatives and thus makes a rational choice. Although some are very critical of these assumptions, proponents of the business plan as a management tool are often convinced that although the assumptions are only valid to a certain degree, it always makes sense to try to steer their way through the entrepreneurial process rather than wandering indecisively and unwittingly through the process.

Proponents of the business plan as a management tool are not necessarily immoveable in their belief in the above assumptions. They just lean more towards management than towards random behaviour. Many of them are actually critical of the approach in relation to the previously mentioned preconditions set out by March (1997). Proponents of the business plan often admit to bounded rationality (Simon 1947), where people and therefore entrepreneurs are considered as individuals who are unable to collect and process full information to predict and control their future completely rationally. People and entrepreneurs try to act rationally, but their behaviour remains rationally bounded, partly because they cannot grasp all the information present, and partly because they cannot analyse and treat it sufficiently rationally. Proponents of the business plan also recognise that it is not possible to determine the consequences of various options completely. Finally, they recognise that people, and therefore entrepreneurs, do not have consistent preferences over time. What an entrepreneur wants at a specific time can easily change later on.

Proponents of the business plan as a management tool are not naive in relation to the assumptions on which they base their beliefs. They are aware that people can only act with bounded rationality, but they still recognise the importance of planning and the importance of the business plan in managing this process.

The business plan as a creativity curb

There are empirical studies showing that planning has no positive impact on entrepreneurs' performance. Honig and Karlsson write: 'We found that those who wrote business plans were no more likely to persist in nascent activity as compared to non-planners' (Honig & Karlsson 2004: 43). These studies have led to discussion of other logics of human behaviour. The logic that characterises the planning approach and vision in the business plan as a management tool is what might be called the logic of consequentiality (March & Olsen 1989). It's about predicting and prioritising based on the entrepreneur's preferences compared to the alternatives with the most profitable consequences in the future. However, there are indications that other logics can also be in play.

It is possible that some entrepreneurs are using previous experience (experience based logic). They simply use the experience they have in the past to carry out the entrepreneurial process anew. Here, one can envisage that the knowledge from experience that comes into play is, in many ways, intangible and hard to describe. Nevertheless, it can still be of critical value to the entrepreneur. Several empirical studies show that entrepreneurs, who have previous start-up experience, are more likely to succeed than entrepreneurs who start an organisation for the first time. It could be that the effectiveness of experience-based logic can match the benefits of the logic of consequentiality.

One can also imagine that some entrepreneurs simply mimic what other entrepreneurs have done in the hope that this behaviour will again prove to be effective. Or they do it because it is expected from their environment. Honig and Karlsson write specifically about these environmental expectations, which almost force entrepreneurs into a planning approach:

> It appears that new organizations do not write business plans to improve performance, rather, they do so in order to conform to institutionalized rules and to mimic the behavior of others . . . In sum, we propose that new organizations plan because they are reacting to how they are expected to plan, because they imitate other successful organizations in their fields that plan, or because they are told to plan. (Honig & Karlsson 2004: 43)

There are then many things that speak against the benefits of the business plan as a management tool, but we have still not discussed the greatest of them all. We have considered some reasons for writing a business plan and some of the logic that drives entrepreneurs, but we have retained a degree of optimism in the business plan. Even if the plan is seen as something that one writes in order to satisfy demands from the environment, the plan plays an important role in the entrepreneurial process.

However, some people think that the business plan has an inhibiting effect on the entrepreneur's creativity. They argue that when entrepreneurs start working with business plans, they are squeezed into a structured and logical form of thinking that spoils creativity. It is strategic thinking that is important in the planning process, and this requires a much higher degree of creativity than the logics of consequentiality and rationality.

Successful planning requires that the entrepreneur thinks 'out of the box' and breaks with the existing dominant paradigms in the market. It requires creativity and lateral thinking (De Bono 1992), and creativity and structure do not go together. Creativity is therefore spoiled if you begin to work with business plans, which deliberately structure the process. The famous painter Picasso once wrote: 'Every act of creation is first of all an act of destruction'. This quote illustrates the importance of breaking with the existing dominant paradigms for creating new opportunities rather than filling some existing structures, which is what planning is fundamentally about. Another quote by Kierkegaard also illustrates the importance of creativity and a break with the existing: 'He who follows in the footsteps of others, never gets in front'.

Opponents of viewing the business plan as a management tool are opponents precisely because they prioritise creativity over the logic of consequentiality in the entrepreneurial process. It is not because they ignore and fail to appreciate logic and rationality. They just think that creativity is more important. They see entrepreneurship as art, where opportunities are, to a greater extent, generated and utilised as a result of a creative and intuitive process than as a logical and rational process. Ohmae, one of Japan's best-known writers in strategic thinking, writes:

> My message, as you will have guessed by now, is that successful business strategies result not from rigorous analysis but from a particular state of mind. In what I call the mind of the strategist, insight and a consequent drive for achievement, often amounting to a sense of mission, fuel a thought process which is basically creative and intuitive rather than rational. (Ohmae 1982)

Business plan: management tool or creativity curb?

We have now discussed the business plan context, content and process and additionally we have discussed a paradox about the role of business plan for the entrepreneur, i.e. the business plan as a management tool or the business plan as a curb on creativity. The discussion is summarised in Table 9.2.

The first perspective, i.e. the business plan as a management tool, sees the business plan as a means to plan the entrepreneurial process. Here, the logic of consequentiality is followed, which gives logic priority over creativity in its importance for business development. The focus is on consistency in the analysis undertaken and the recommendations proposed and planning is thus considered as a science.

Table 9.2 The paradox: A management tool or creativity curb

	Management tool	Creativity curb
What is the business plan?	Tool for planning	Creativity curb
Logic	Logic of consequentiality	Other types of logic (experience logic; imitation logic)
The importance of business development	Rationality over creativity	Creativity over rationality
Focus	Consistency	Break with the existing
Metaphor	Science	Art

The second perspective, on the other hand, sees the business plan as a curb on creativity and thus on the entrepreneur's ability to complete the entrepreneurial process. It argues that planning is often based on other logics, and there may be other reasons to write a business plan rather than following a traditional logic of consequentiality. Here creativity has priority over logic. It's about breaking with the existing and thinking laterally about how players in the markets already think. It's about thinking 'out of the box'. Therefore, planning is considered to be more of an art than a science, and a business plan is considered more of a hindrance than a help in implementing the entrepreneurial process.

A theoretical interpretation

Below are two different interpretations of the Mobitrix story, which began this chapter. In the interpretations the story is linked to the theory above.

The management tool perspective

The immediate interpretation of the Mobitrix case study can easily follow the management tool perspective where the business plan is considered as a means to manage and plan the evaluation and organisation process of the business opportunity. Although Michael acknowledges that many things did not evolve as he expected, one could, according to the management tool perspective, easily imagine that the whole thing would have been even worse without planning and the scheduling process.

Firstly, there is nothing in the management tool perspective that doesn't accept that a business can be flexible – just as Michael also finally realises at the end of the case study. Various unforeseen events can change the premises of a business plan that will then require the plan's adjustment. It is quite common in relation to the management tool perspective to accept continuous adjustments to the plan in accordance with the development of the business opportunity.

In this way the case study provides a good illustration of how the process and the plan may affect each other. Additionally the case study shows how the context in terms of different audiences and purposes for the business plan will require different content within the plan. The latter is clearly illustrated when Michael is considering updating the plan to attract potential new partners.

Secondly, one can say that because the real business situation does not develop according to the business plan, this is not an argument against trying to control what can be controlled. It may be poor planning or poor execution of the plan's activities that explains why the plan and reality are not identical. It may also be that things would have turned out even worse without the plan. The plan has, after all, given Michael some milestones to aim for in trying to develop a sustainable business. The plan has ensured consistency and targeted behaviours.

The creativity curb perspective

In the creativity curb perspective it is understood as fact that the business plan and business opportunity do not develop in line with each other; quite different from the management tool perspective. Here we will consider this fact just as a sign that the business plan lacked the ability to predict the future and give the entrepreneur the necessary input on goals and actions.

The business plan that Michael prepared in the early stages of business start-up is now nine months old and totally out of touch with how things look in reality. Many unexpected things occurred along the way that Michael had not anticipated, including the scanning accessory developed for iPhone and iPod Touch and a longer development time in Sri Lanka than expected.

According to the creativity curb perspective, these unexpected events mean that much time and resource is used to predict an unpredictable future. This time and these resources could have been used far more productively to develop the product or contact different types of stakeholders, including investors, suppliers and not least potential customers. One could also easily imagine that the plan has given Michael a picture of reality and the future, which later becomes difficult to deviate from – even when it turns out that the picture described in the business plan does not hold true.

The case outlines Michael's frustrations over the plan's inadequacy in predicting the future more than the pleasure of the positive developments that have taken place. Disappointment over the lack of interest for follow-up at the Medica exhibition in Düsseldorf clearly shows how the energy is channelled in a negative direction when the plan does not hold true – energy that could probably be used more creatively to think in new and different paths about how the business could be developed.

There are also several situations in the case study which suggested that various unexpected events are crucial for changes in the business opportunity. It is in this way that a creative response to unforeseen events contributes to the development of business opportunities rather than a long-term plan.

Testing the theory

Based on the above thoughts and discussions you are ready to develop your own attempt to understand the business plan's impact on the entrepreneurial process. The following are suggestions for investigating the topic.

EXERCISES

1 **Interview an entrepreneur.** Create an interview guide with interview questions that contains two main parts. The first part focuses on the overall benefits entrepreneurs may experience in connection with the use of business plans. The second part contains the disadvantages and problems that an entrepreneur may face with the use of business plans. Then contact an entrepreneur, and interview him or her in order to test the theory presented in this chapter on business plans. Based on this, create your opinion on this paradox: a management tool or creativity curb?

2 **Interview a banker/investor.** Do you know a banker or others who deal with investments in new business opportunities on a daily basis? Interview them about how they evaluate a business plan, what information they want and how they want it designed.

3 **The perception in the media.** Go to a library and find a database of print media. Search the term 'business plan'. You can choose to make your search broad or narrow, either by choosing a short or long period of time, or by choosing that the term 'business plan' should be included in the headline of the article or not. Read and then analyse the articles, and sort them according to their view of the business plan. Based on your analysis draw a conclusion about how the general view of business plans are in your country. Does it tend to view the business plan as a management tool or as a curb on creativity?

4 **Create an outline for a business plan.** Do you have a small idea that you are fiddling around with? If so, then search your social network to see if you know someone who is thinking of starting his or her own organisation. Next, try to make a more detailed outline of what a business plan for this opportunity should contain and to whom it should be addressed. You can then, when the outline is finished, continue working and write a complete business plan.

LITERATURE

Baker, W.H., Addams, H.L. & Davis, B. (1993) 'Business planning in successful small firms', *Long Range Planning*, 26(6), 82–88.

Barringer, B.R. & Ireland, R.D. (2008) *Entrepreneurship: Successfully Launching New Ventures*, Boston, MA: Pearson/Prentice Hall.

Business Plan Journal, www.businessplanjournal.com (last accessed 20 December 2016).

De Bono, E. (1992) *Using the Power of Lateral Thinking to Create New Ideas*, London: Harper Collins.

De Wit, B. & Meyer, R. (1998) *Strategy – Process, Content, Context*, London: Thomson.

Delmar, F. & Shane, S. (2003) 'Does business planning facilitate the development of new ventures?', *Strategic Management Journal*, 24, 1165–1185.

Honig, B. & Karlsson, T. (2004) 'Institutional forces and the written business plan', *Journal of Management*, 30, 29–48.

Kuratko, D.F. & Hodgetts, R.M. (2004) *Entrepreneurship – Theory, Process, Practice*, Mason, OH: Thomson.

Madié, D. (2007) 'Farvel til forretningsplanen! Start af virksomhed kræver handling', *Iværksætteren*, 7, 34–36.

March, J.G. (1997) 'Understanding how decisions happen in Organizations', in Shapira, Z. (ed.), *Organizational Decision Making,* Cambridge: Cambridge University Press, 9–32.
March, J.G. & Olsen, J.P. (1989) *Rediscovering Institutions: The Organizational Basis of Politics,* New York: Free Press/Macmillan.
Maurya, A. (2012) Running Lean, 2nd edn, Sebastopol, CA: O'Reilly Media, Inc.
Ohmae, K. (1982) *The Mind of the Strategist: The Art of Japanese Business,* New York: McGraw-Hill.
Osterwalder, A. & Pigneur, Y. (2010) *Business Model Generation – A Handbook for Visionaries, Game Changers and Challengers,* Hoboken, NJ: John Wiley and Sons, Inc.
Sarasvathy, S.D. (2008) *Effectuation: Elements of Entrepreneurial Expertise,* Cheltenham, UK and Northampton, MA, USA: Edward Elgar Publishing.
Schilit, W.K. (1987) 'How to write a winning business plan', *Business Horizon,* September–October, 13–22.
Shane, S. (2003) *A General Theory of Entrepreneurship: The Individual–Opportunity Nexus,* Cheltenham, UK and Northampton, MA, USA: Edward Elgar Publishing.
Shuman, J.C., Shaw, J.J. & Sussmann, G. (1985) 'Strategic planning in smaller rapid growth companies', *Long Range Planning,* 18(6), 48–53.
Simon, H.A. (1947) *Administrative Behavior,* New York: The Free Press.
Wickham, P.A. (2004) *Strategic Entrepreneurship,* London: Prentice Hall.

10

Design thinking

Design thinking is a unique creative approach to launching and developing entrepreneurial processes. One might say that it provokes new ways of thinking and offers exciting methods and processes that act as a springboard for manoeuvring and creating the complex and unfamiliar. It is not necessarily an approach that makes sense for all entrepreneurs to start using, but it's definitely worth knowing its possibilities. There are two particular reasons why design is relevant to entrepreneurship. First of all because it offers a way of thinking that makes entrepreneurs able to address complex entrepreneurial issues in new ways. Secondly, entrepreneurs gain access to design methods and processes that can enable entrepreneurial opportunities to be discovered/created that otherwise would not have emerged.

You should bear in mind that in this chapter we present design thinking primarily as a way of solving problems. In the problem-solving process the design thinker is empathetic, collaborative, visual, creative, 'tries things out' and is exploring new knowledge while existing knowledge is being utilised. Designers are known to reshape tumultuous and dilemma-filled problems into opportunities. The core of this chapter is how the entrepreneur can address entrepreneurial problems in the same way that a designer tackles problems in the design process.

Entrepreneurship in practice

CASE STUDY

Kicked out of the comfort zone

(**Devised by Birgitte Norlyk**)

'Designandelen' (in English: 'Design Co-op') is a regional design-driven innovation platform that was born in the midst of a crisis in 2010 when the market was not functioning ideally. This

CASE STUDY *(continued)*

public enterprise, with its focus on generating entrepreneurship, innovation and growth, was regarded as a particularly important and challenging counterpoint to the economic crisis. A multitude of different industries and companies went through various design-enabled innovation processes during the platform's three-year lifespan. Here are just two examples. The first concerns a supplier of christening gifts and children's jewellery who developed a well-known and sought-after brand. Before its meeting with Designandelen the company was more or less unknown to end users. The second example concerns an entrepreneur who developed a patented apparatus that can move almost any type of bed, and is particularly useful for hospitals. There are many other examples that support one of Designandelen's core messages: design is for everyone.

The purpose of Designandelen is the building of a two-tier design market where creative design entrepreneurs, deliver to the larger public and private sector organisations that require design services. Synergy generated through the meeting of these actors is utilised with a view to increasing the use of design and design thinking in larger organisations, and hereby helps them to innovate and grow. At the same time, small design entrepreneurs are strengthened and become professionalised. The latter is done largely by helping them put together interdisciplinary teams so that they can form informal consortia capable of undertaking more extensive projects for large design-hungry organisations. Hence the name Designandelen, which is inspired by the cooperative movement principles that enable the small to become large in the market.

Spreadsheets in suits

The small design entrepreneurs in contact with Designandelen come from a variety of professional backgrounds, such as fashion and textiles, industrial design, jewellery and metal design, crafts, graphic design, form design, as well as event and performance designers. Many have irregular part-time or freelance work. Of course, their budding businesses and entrepreneurial processes are quite different, but there is a tendency for crossover to occur between the processes. Their background makes them love the early creative stages of the entrepreneurial process in which new ideas, services and concepts are created, and they tend to constantly pursue new ideas. The organising of ideas, defining and focusing them to become market opportunities and transforming them into growth opportunities, increased revenue and new businesses do not seem to be the primary interests and motivations for design entrepreneurs. Therefore, Designandelen helps them with these more business development processes.

The design entrepreneurs experience great difficulties with thinking in terms of business economics, with its emphasis on the market and customers. For them, it's all about the development of their personal creativity. On the one hand, the designers feel that their identity, values and dreams are threatened by entrepreneurs, whilst on the other hand, they understand that change and a new definition of their own values and competencies are required in order to realise their dreams of living from design, and of translating design ideas into a concrete reality.

Many of them describe the starting up of a business as a form of violence against their

CASE STUDY *(continued)*

person. For them, starting and growing their own business is a move away from a safe and familiar place (the designer's workshop) towards a new and potentially dangerous place (entrepreneurship): 'I really needed a kick in the rear', 'I had to be forced out of the workshop'. The design entrepreneurs know that right now they are playing in their own creative field, and that it is time to work with other actors and the market, but it's not easy. Entrepreneurship is also something that gives rise to a split in the designer's identity, which is based on a set of values focusing on innovation and creativity. The design entrepreneurs describe the design process as working with a future yet unknown: 'As a designer one makes things that do not yet exist'. Another designer describes the purpose of his designs as being to create novel 'eye candy'. Being a designer is described with words like imagination, wonder, play, poetry, thought, etc. They talk about the importance of 'being in their work' and one designer said that in her former profession she had a feeling that 'something was missing – THE POWER TO CREATE!'

The design entrepreneurs typically experience a division between designer identity and business identity. Reason and emotion are constantly fighting about the right decision. The business side does not have the same appeal as design since 'by nature I can forget the things I can't be bothered about', 'budgeting, cash flow, business plans . . . are not insanely interesting . . . but thinking about it now does lead to fewer problems later'. On the whole, many design entrepreneurs sense a loss of freedom by being placed in the boxes and stereotypes that they believe are represented by business economic thinking: 'Seller? No, damn it! Sellers are untrustworthy, overly smart and have no understanding of aesthetic and design value', 'Smarmy used car salesmen'. Representatives of accountancy and finance are described as 'hardcore business guys' and 'spreadsheets in suits'; 'I'm afraid to be put in boxes'. However, throughout the courses organised by Designandelen, many design entrepreneurs experienced a gradual recognition of the need to know the essential rules of the financial system: VAT, tax deductions, etc.

No quick fixes

If we move our attention to Designandelen's work with the larger, more established organisations, we see, in many ways, the opposite challenges and opportunities. Here, Designandelen's work is concerned much more with opening up the existing organisations' structures and routines, so there is room for the provocative thinking that design processes and methodologies bring into play. A multitude of different public and private organisations are in contact with Designandelen: SMEs, larger business giants and public organisations. Some of these are supported in using design to differentiate themselves from competitors, others to innovate, develop new strategy, branding and for visual identity development, better information flow, user experience and involvement and enhanced customer experience. As previously mentioned, the central purpose is largely to match the larger organisations with interdisciplinary creative teams of design entrepreneurs, and to constructively challenge the business logics and routines of the organisations. These are not quick fixes, but lengthy processes: conversion

CASE STUDY *(continued)*

processes over time that in many cases eventually end up in eye-opening discoveries about what design can do for the more established organisations.

In Designandelen's work for the larger organisations, design entrepreneurs use a host of different design methods to open up and develop the existing organisations, such as the user journeys, personas, prototyping, ethnographic observations. Users are greatly involved in various co-creation processes. One example is a manufacturer of trucks and snow-clearing machines, which established a new mind-set through design work. The company now sells safety on the roads instead of various machines, and it is a mind-set that permeates everything the company does and when it thinks strategically. A specialist in lighting for large rooms/spaces went from working from assumptions about what customers and users wanted, to working and innovating on the basis of an informed and thorough understanding of the customers. Getting involved with the small creative design entrepreneurs is challenging for many of the more established organisations. The director of a large room/space lighting firm points to this: 'The question is whether we should just continue grinding along in the same old way, or try to be better . . . It was perhaps a little more extensive than we had just expected, but it was worth it! However, it was – and it is still – hard, for there is a lot of work in it'. He gave the designers access to his business and permission to make customer inquiries. The designers conducted workshops with employees and much more, and the company is now working even more with the new opportunities, design thinking and methods.

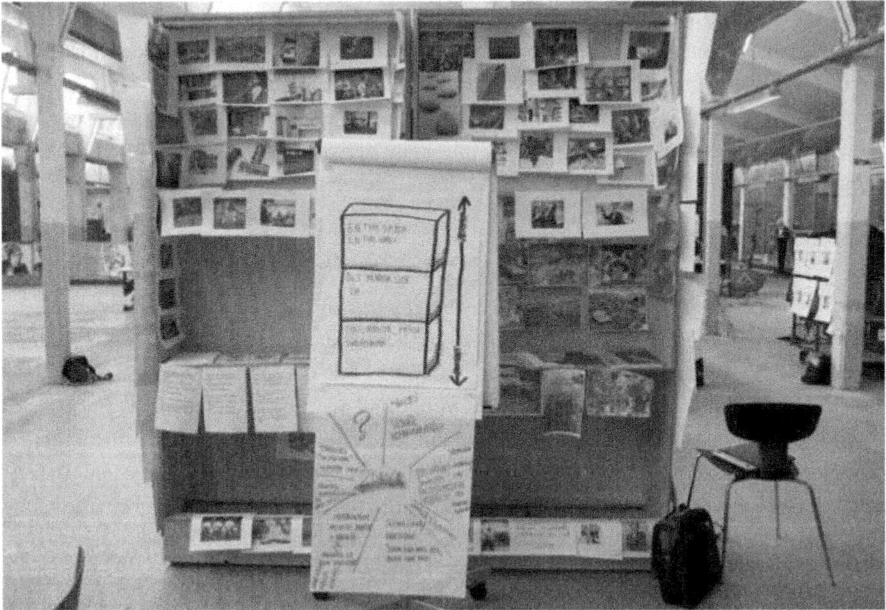

Figure 10.1 Drawings and images from a design thinking process

Your immediate interpretation

The following small exercises should allow you to begin your interpretation of what is happening in the case. What is happening when we talk about the intersection between design thinking and entrepreneurship? As in previous chapters, we will then give you some theoretical tools to understand the deeper layers of the case:

- Imagine that you are providing an entrepreneurship course 'The Road to Company Growth'. The participants are nascent design entrepreneurs who have not yet had their first customer. How would you design this course? What should be the main content? What teaching method should you use?
- After reading the case, it is clear to you that there are many barriers at the intersection between design and business creation. Identify at least three barriers and write them down.
- You are the Finance Minister. You are considering the allocation of a larger amount of the state budget for the development of design entrepreneurship. For which initiatives would it be appropriate to allocate funds and how should they proceed?

Theories of entrepreneurship

In terms of theoretical literature, the area with which we are concerned constitutes the intersection of entrepreneurship and design thinking, which is not a well-established branch of the entrepreneurship literature, but is still in its infancy.

On the other hand, there is a relatively large and undoubtedly growing literature on how existing companies can make use of design and design thinking in order to, for example, strengthen their innovation and competitiveness. Design thinking is touted as a new and exciting paradigm for business (Dorst 2011). On the whole, design thinking is increasingly portrayed as a kind of 'wonder pill' to assist in solving all sorts of complex problems, including helping to build economic growth, sustainability, increased prosperity, enhanced quality of life, etc. At any rate, a large number of reports around the world seem to support the idea that design creates great value at various levels and on numerous fronts. *The Design Economy Report* (2015) by the UK's Design Council shows, for example, that in terms of the total gross value added in the UK, the design economy generated 7.2 per cent thereof and design generated 7.3 per cent of total UK exports in 2013.

The coupling between the two literatures on entrepreneurship and design thinking is very interesting and a central paradox arises. The paradox consists of two perspectives: entrepreneurial thinking versus design thinking. This chapter differs slightly from the previous chapters for two reasons. First and foremost is that one of the paradox perspectives is called the same as the title of the chapter. Secondly, we choose, in this chapter, to let our understanding of entrepreneurial thinking be inspired by a specific definition of entrepreneurship – namely Shane and Venkataraman's (2000) classic definition. That is to say, in this chapter we take entrepreneurial thinking to be a discovery-driven way of thinking and acting entrepreneurially. On the other hand, we present design thinking as an iterative-driven way of thinking and acting, which among other things involves a close interaction between the discovery and creation processes. Now we can see the paradox emerge, which you will understand so much better when you have read the chapter. This chapter's paradox is:

Entrepreneurial thinking or design thinking?

Three views of design thinking?

The concept of 'design thinking' was first described in Rowe's book *Design Thinking* in 1987. Since then, the popularity of the concept has almost exploded, both in theory and in practice. Design is one thing, and design thinking is something else. Design thinking is about the way designers think (and act), which is increasingly seen as being relevant to more or less all disciplines, government agencies, private companies, entrepreneurs and others who work with complex problem-solving and innovation. However, to understand what design thinking is, you first have to consider design as a concept; and design is a really difficult concept to define. Just like fruit juice that has been increasingly diluted, the design concept of today has been diluted and become fragmented. Design can, for example, be a shaping craft, industrial design, strategic design, product design, communication design, interaction design, engineering design, graphic design, service design, fashion, design icons, etc. Design can be an activity limited in time and space, and it can be a whole process, a name for a profession or industry, as well as referring to an output. Traditionally, design has been about making products beautiful, practical and smart, but today design is so much more. One can distinguish between 'a design', i.e. a designed chair, lamp, etc. and 'to design'. To design is a process where you think and solve problems as a designer, and this leads to the concept of design thinking. Table 10.1 presents three views of design thinking, which are described below.

Table 10.1 Three views of design thinking

	The designer	The discipline	Organisational resource
Focus	The designer's way of thinking and working	Design as a theoretical discipline that is relevant to many other fields	Organisations in need of innovation, differentiation, etc.
Purpose	Understanding how designers solve problems	Present approaches to working with wicked problems	Innovation, strategy-making, organisational transformation
Starting point	Design problems are complex and problems and solutions co-evolve	Design problems are wicked problems	Organisational problems are design problems
Key contributions	Schön (1983); Cross (2006)	Simon (1969); Buchanan (1992)	Dunne and Martin (2006); Brown (2009); Verganti (2009)

Source: Inspired by Kimbell (2011).

The designer

The first view is based on the designer, and how he or she works with ill-structured problem solving, as well as their cognitive style within this process. Schön (1983) makes a classic contribution in this regard, where the core of designers' practice is reflection-in-action. Cross (2006) is another key example.

The discipline

However, design thinking can also be seen as a more general theoretical discipline, a branch of knowledge. For example, Simon (1969) presents his science of design, which focuses on the creation of new artefacts. An artefact covers anything human-made, as opposed to anything created by nature. However, an artefact can also be something natural that humankind has influenced, such as a trained dog. Simon points out that we are all potentially designers: 'Everyone designs who devises courses of actions aimed at changing existing situations into preferred ones' (p. 111). Buchanan (1992) is another example of a more general theory of design thinking. He introduces a popular concept, namely 'wicked problems'. Wicked problems are hard to work out, in contrast to problems that can be relatively easily tamed and thus solved. Wicked problems have something contradictory and paradoxical built into them, which is why they cannot be defined up-front. Instead, the problem constantly changes face whilst one is trying to solve it. Design thinking's task is to find/create good solutions to wicked problems.

Organisational resource

Last but not least, design thinking can be seen as an organisational resource. Here design thinking is typically related directly to challenges in businesses, such as innovation. As an example, design thinking here is defined as 'a discipline that uses the designer's sensibility and methods to match people's needs with what is technologically feasible and what a viable business strategy can convert into customer value and market opportunity' (Brown 2009: 2). Some contributions within this understanding are criticised for being stretched too far in order to make design 'palatable' for business and other practitioners, by explaining the design process in too simple and linear a fashion, or toning down design for a creative toolbox. Whilst contributions in the first two columns of Table 10.1 explain design thinking in design terms, this last approach increasingly tends to mould the concept into an analytical business understanding.

This third and very business-assimilated approach to design thinking is driven by the example of IDEO, an international design and consultancy (www.ideo.com, last accessed 29 December 2016), focusing on leaders, entrepreneurs and other practitioners in the design world. Within this design thinking literature you will find many references to the theories, models and concepts that the business audience is already familiar with, such as references to Michael Porter's work (e.g. in Borja de Mozota 1998). Finally, this part of the design thinking literature is geared more towards, and developed by practice compared with the more classic design thinking literature of which columns 1 and 2 in Table 10.1 are examples (Johansson-Sköldberg et al 2013).

But why is there a need to use design thinking as an organisational resource? According to Martin (2009) it is because it is dangerous to base business on only an exploitation or exploration logic. Exploitation covers firms seeking to maximise profits by exploiting, perfecting and managing existing knowledge and ideas. Redefining, efficiency, selection, execution and implementation are key elements. Exploration, on the other hand, is related to the company focusing on searching for new ideas and knowledge, to invent new business. Experimentation, play, flexibility, discovery, risk-taking and innovation are key elements here (March 1991). Exploration alone will often leave the company vulnerable and unstable. It may be difficult to consolidate the company and acquire resources to invest in new explorative activities: 'The business that creates value only through exploitation will exhaust itself in due course. It can't keep exploiting the same piece of knowledge forever' (Martin 2009: 19). Companies tend to become 'trapped' in one of the two logics. Herein lies the root of the problem. Although various types of problems require different degrees of exploration and exploitation in order to solve them, there is a broad consensus that problem-solving generally requires a mix of the two. In the general business literature the problems relating to the interaction and balance between exploitation and exploration are described as ambidexterity (O'Reilly & Tushman 2013). Design thinking provides an idea of how businesses can utilise both logics, thus creating a better balance between exploitation and exploration.

The design thinking process

Hopefully you are now keen to gain more knowledge of what design thinking is, and how the design thinking process operates in reality? There is no universal answer to these questions, but below we try to highlight some typical features associated with the process.

In the design thinking process there are constant movements between exploitative and explorative thinking and action. Additionally, the central nerve in the process is the continuous interaction between the past, present and future. There are many design thinking process models that illustrate the complex iterative nature of repeated cyclical movements between exploitative and explorative, present, past and future. However, it is clear that it is extremely difficult to create models and thus the framework for such a creative phenomenon as design thinking without this framework becoming a deterrent. Simon (1969) describes the design thinking process as consisting of seven sub-processes: define, research, ideate, prototype, choose, implement and learn. A similar process model is proposed by the Hasso Plattner Institute of Design at Stanford University (dschool.stanford.edu, last accessed 29 December 2016). Brown (2009) indicates a process consisting of three sub-processes: inspiration, ideation and implementation. Dunne and Martin (2006) and Liedtka and Ogilvie (2011) offer other process models. Figure 10.2 is this book's example of a model in which we have tried to illustrate the basic logics and sub-processes that help the design thinking process unfold. The shading illustrates how the entire figure is twisted into a network of co-creation processes and shows that co-creation is central to understanding design thinking, independent of the 'stage' of the process in which the design thinker happens to be.

In the following, we take you on a journey where we delve, in greater detail, into the model's movements and four closely related sub-processes.

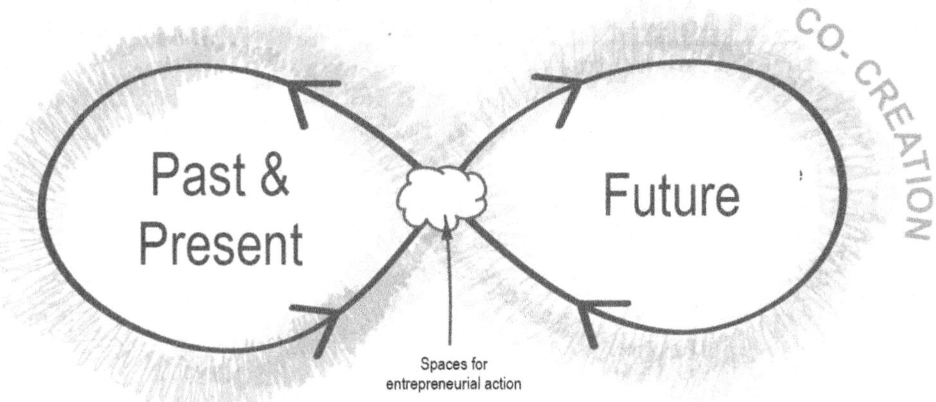

Sources: Inspired by Liedtka & Ogilvie (2011) and Nielsen et al (2016).

Figure 10.2 The design thinking process

Discover the present: 'What is?'

The design thinking process can begin anywhere in the figure above. However, it will often start out with the discovery of 'What is?', i.e. the past and present of the problem area one seeks to solve. The problem area is discovered in its entirety and in depth. The design thinker goes behind the problem, takes hold of its deeper layers that have been forgotten up to now and looks into the complexity, paradoxes, limits, players, history and relation to other problem areas. The design thinker looks at almost everything when first approaching the problem area, since he or she does not yet know what is not worth understanding. A crucial part of the design thinker's discovery of 'What is?' is listening and empathic understanding of the users and other stakeholders for whom he or she is designing something. What are their needs, 'pains', values, history, opinions, etc. and why they are as they are? What do these people do, what do they not do, and why? It is said that design is human centred. To understand those for whom one is designing first of all requires empathy, the ability to put oneself in these people's shoes and see the reality through their eyes rather than one's own. Design methods that can help along the way include various methods of data collection and problem identification methods, e.g. ethnographic interviews and observation methods, techniques from anthropology, cultural probes and journey mapping and personas. Typically the design thinker finds, through his or her discovery of 'What is?' that problems are rarely what they initially think they are. The 'What is?' processes enable the problem area to be seen in a new light.

Envisioning the future: 'What if?'

All the new insights obtained through the 'What is?' process are a sort of food for the further design process. Through creative, divergent and future-oriented 'What if?' processes this food is flipped, challenged, disturbed, provoked and then combined in different ways. For example, constraints are actively used to provoke the designer into thinking outside the box about the problem area and its solutions. Designers even draw imaginative constraints for themselves, so that they can become even more creative in the 'What if?' process. The idea behind the 'What if?' processes is to open up a wealth of different pictures of possibilities and solutions. In general, 'What if?' processes constitute a large part of the design process, which means that to a great extent the design process is not about homing in on a solution. New impulses, input from others, provocation and contrivance take this continuous process in new directions. The design thinker likes to remain in the divergent 'What if?' for a long period and will often return to it to ensure that new and surprising ideas and thoughts emerge. Typically, the 'What if?' processes involve different brainstorming techniques and related methods of provocation, e.g. constraints, analogies and random stimulation methods are used to create many alternative images of the future potential for solutions and opportunities.

To really ensure that things are turned upside down and recreated in new ways, design thinking time and resources are often invested to include users, other stakeholders, experts, etc. in the 'What if?' process. There will thus be a co-creation process, which may have the advantage of being interdisciplinary. The logic is that something larger always occurs in a group, and the interaction and interdisciplinarity provide much interesting knowledge, surprises and contradictions, whilst it will still be possible to stop along the way and make adjustments if the new idea does not create value, is not relevant to the user and other stakeholders, or for other reasons is simply not implementable. The latter emphasises the close interrelatedness between the 'What if?', 'What wows?' and 'What works?' processes.

Select futures: 'What wows?'

Whilst undertaking the divergent 'What if?' processes the design thinker employs an experimental logic that can be summarised as 'fail fast, fail cheap, and move on'. To ensure relevance, it is essential to gain insight into whether the many new ideas about the emerging solutions and opportunities meet the users' and other stakeholders' needs. That is also why the design thinker engages in dialogue and co-creation with others. The goal is to get a picture of what could have a future in the real world, 'What wows?', or to find out how the solution can be developed, adjusted and modified so as to have the potential to cover the needs. It is thus, so to speak, through close interaction and various feedback mechanisms that the many created images of future solutions and opportunities are evaluated.

The design thinker gathers feedback from the market by using different idea evaluation methods, and assorted idea selection methods to select what wows. One often talks in this respect of the 'What wows?' process being very much a prototype-driven process. A prototype is an early draft, example or model that, in physical form, conveys ideas, concepts, products, services, etc. By continually gathering design process knowledge and ideas into a prototype and bringing it quickly to the market, or alternatively making it the focal point for dialogue, the design thinker receives enriched feedback. The assumption is that physical forms are simply easier to relate to. The feedback may lead to new prototypes, understanding of 'What is?' or 'What if?', which in turn will move the design thinker back into the design process. By iteratively moving back and forth between the exploration of 'What is?', envisioning future alternatives 'What if?', testing and selecting 'What wows?', as well as continuous further tests and experiments with 'What works?' (see below), new and exciting understandings of the area in which the entrepreneur can act, gradually become apparent.

Test futures: 'What works?'

The activities undertaken by the design thinker in 'What works?' is closely associated with the 'What wows?' processes. It is through testing and acting in the market that he or she can find out what works. Different learning launching processes can be used to create understanding of what works. According to Brown (2009) a guide to what will work is whether the project is feasible (possible to implement in the foreseeable future), viable (a likely part of a business model) and desirable (wanted by, and meaningful for, other people).

Design thinking methods

We hope that you have gained the impression that design thinking offers the entrepreneur numerous concrete and new methods that can support him or her in the entrepreneurial process. Design is known for its large toolbox that contains a wealth of different methods that support work with wicked problems. You can Google your way to several of these methods and again, you can go to the Hasso Plattner Institute of Design at Stanford University's website (www.dschool.stanford.edu). The Institute provides you with a clear and free starting point for many of its methods. In searching for design methods you should be aware that the methods do not represent a complete package. On the contrary, they should be individualised and redesigned. You must get them to work for you. Customise the methods to suit the design thinking process you are in. It is possible that the same method may be appropriate for use in several versions, and also for supporting various parts of the design process. For example, the same method can be used to support 'What if?' processes, and in another variation, the method can be used to discover 'What is?' Figure 10.3 illustrates some key design methods.

In general, there are two meta-methods, which are annexed to the design thinking process.The first meta-method can be named 'thinking with the hands'. The designer uses it to produce ideas, concepts, things, etc. tangible through visualisation, mock-ups and prototype construction. Co-creation is the second continuous meta-method, more fundamentally concerned with discovery, creation, evaluation and launching the new product or idea through creative and social interaction processes engaging the users, suppliers, manufacturers, experts and other stakeholders in the design thinking process. Co-creation allows for the future scenarios of the design thinker, users and stakeholders, to meld together and become real opportunities.

Entrepreneurial thinking

There are many views as to what constitutes entrepreneurial thinking. However, as mentioned earlier in this chapter our understanding of entrepreneurial thinking has been inspired by a specific definition of entrepreneurship, namely Shane and Venkataraman's (2000) classic definition. That is to say, in this chapter we take entrepreneurial thinking to be a discovery-driven way of thinking and acting entrepreneurially, which you can also read about in Chapter 3. At the core are the discovery, evaluation and exploitation of existing opportunities. There are two fundamental prerequisites for entrepreneurship, according to this understanding: lucrative opportunities and enterprising individuals. Entrepreneurial opportunities are defined as 'those situations in which new goods, services, raw materials, and organising methods can be sold at greater than their cost of production' (Casson 1982 in Shane & Venkataraman 2000: 220). As mentioned in Chapter 3, it is the entrepreneur's more or less unconscious alertness that makes him or her able to recognise the opportunities for entrepreneurial profit. The opportunity

Figure 10.3 Visualisation of different design methods

is something that the market holds, and that exists independently of the entrepreneur.

It is interesting that in addition to explaining when, why and how new opportunities emerge and are discovered, Shane and Venkataraman (2000) emphasise that it is essential to understand why, when and how different modes of action are used to exploit opportunities. To qualify as an entrepreneur, it is not enough to simply discover a lucrative opportunity. The opportunity must also be organised and transformed into market value and entrepreneurial profit, which Shane (2003) builds on in his book *A General Theory of Entrepreneurship*. This book describes, among other things, how entrepreneurs evaluate opportunities, collect resources and organise themselves, form strategies, plan and develop competitive advantages, protect themselves against competitors using the network and select employees, juggle with costs, etc. in order to exploit entrepreneurial opportunities through various exploitation modes and with reference to market mechanisms and institutional context. For example, it highlights four specific exploitation modes: independent start-up, spin-off, acquisition/licensing and corporate venturing.

Therefore, in addition to acting on the discovery of new opportunities, dealing with entrepreneurial thinking is just as much about how the new opportunity is made use of and converted into market value. This is made difficult by the fact that the conversion of the new is linked to great uncertainty and incomplete information. For example, it is only after having exhausted the possibilities that the entrepreneur can be sure that his or her guesses about the product service are correct. Does it work? Can it be produced? And what about the market? Is there a demand? What price will customers pay? Can it be sold in large enough quantities? What about the competition? Will it all end up producing entrepreneurial profit? Shane (2003) suggests, among other things, that in order to deal with the uncertain situation, the entrepreneur may develop different strategies, such as growth from small scale, entry by acquisition, focus strategy and forming alliances.

Design thinking

Design thinking represents a conscious approach to entrepreneurship in the sense that using relatively concrete and systematic processes and methods, the entrepreneur can proactively apply design thinking to shape new opportunities and the entrepreneurial process as such. That said, it must also be emphasised that design thinking cannot stand alone. Rather, it is a phenomenon that can assist entrepreneurship. There are many factors independent of design thinking that are crucial to how the entrepreneurial process will proceed, such as the individual's entrepreneurial traits, resources and networks, or stakeholder resources and motivation. Unique characteristics of the market and society, of which the entrepreneur is a part, or wants to create, can also be essential.

According to design thinking, breaks for new entrepreneurial opportunities occur through a complex and iterative interaction between processes, where the past and the present are detected and reframed, ideas for the future are created, and different solutions and opportunity spaces are selected, tested and experimented with, which together provide a picture of the solutions – and possibilities for an opening that the entrepreneur may act on in the future. This means new entrepreneurial opportunities are 'designed' through frequent and creative movement between the past, present and future, which involves exploitation as exploration and discovery as creation. The movement occurs in close interaction and co-creation with users, stakeholders and other relevant actors, and the entrepreneur has different design methods to lean on and make use of throughout the process. The design thinker's large toolbox, which includes 'thinking with your hands', assists the entrepreneur in moving cyclically between sub-processes, discovering the present, envisioning the future and selecting and testing futures.

Because of design thinking's iterative logic, evaluation and exploitation of opportunities are difficult to separate from their discovery/creation. The entire entrepreneurial process's elements are closely associated. The entrepreneur will be continuously inspired and will keep receiving new inputs, which means the entrepreneur continuously discovers and establishes new possibilities, which must be addressed in terms of with whom and how they can be realised. The entrepreneurial process is a continuous process of redesigning, but the key is that the process's focal point is empathy, because it is people centred. The focus is on how the entrepreneur covers user and stakeholder needs, including needs they might not even immediately know they have. As such, there is nothing new in that it is important to understand the user's needs, but the design thinking entrepreneur dives into and around the user's reality. For him or her, the user is not a segment, but a person with leisure time, feelings, values, beliefs that are embedded in some unique institutions and relationships that are constantly evolving. That design thinking is people centred means that the entrepreneur has focused on creating human value. Throughout the entrepreneurial process, from start to finish, the entrepreneur tests what value each new offering has for the users and other stakeholders.

The frequent tests are typically driven by rapid and experimental prototyping, which provides good opportunities for effective feedback, flexible adjustment and further development and creative reframing of the problem and solution. The design thinking entrepreneur quickly enters 'the real world', observing, understanding, listening to and co-creating with others. The close interaction between the entrepreneur, users and other stakeholders ensures the relevance of the new product/service/idea. The entrepreneur is less concerned with him- or herself, and he or she does not see it as a core mission to convince others about how wonderful the item is. Instead, the entrepreneur, right from the outset, co-creates and adjusts the new brand with them, as he or she designs something.

Co-creation is central to the entrepreneurial design thinker. Design thinking can generally be seen as the solving of entrepreneurial problems and entrepreneurial processes through a social co-creation process. Entrepreneurial ideas, concepts, services, opportunities, business models and organisations thus become more commonly produced solutions, where users, stakeholders, and possibly others, come to feel a sense of ownership and acceptance of the new idea before it is implemented, which may be assumed to reduce the entrepreneurial risks.

Although current needs, for example, user needs, will have a major role to play in the entrepreneurial design thinking process, design thinking is also, to a great extent, orientated towards the future, and it is significant that the future is seen in terms of multiple phenomena. At any rate, the design thinking process produces a multitude of different images of possible future entrepreneurial activities, through, amongst other things, the active use of provocations and constraints. These fire up the entrepreneur's imagination, and get him or her to think about problems, solutions and opportunities in entirely new ways. Constraints are not something that the entrepreneur should try to avoid or eliminate. They are the route to good and often radical solutions and possibilities that the entrepreneur would not otherwise have found/created.

Finally, one can argue that the design thinking entrepreneur will tend to focus on the front end of the entrepreneurial process where the new idea emerges and circulates for a relatively long period. According to Sanders and Stappers (2008), the focal point for design is the fuzzy front end, where new ideas and concepts are created and converted into prototypes, products and various other benefits and services that create human value. The designer is not usually trained in the back end, i.e. in seeing the commercial value of the new idea, its implementation and the exploitation of opportunities in the light of the market, so this is probably why it is afforded a lower priority.

After you've digested the above, you might think that the design thinking perspective is reminiscent of an entrepreneurship theory with which you were presented in Chapter 5: effectuation theory. The similarity between the above and effectuation theory is not so strange. Effectuation theory is, in fact, largely inspired by Herbert Simon's (1969) thoughts, as Saras Sarasvathy, the woman behind effectuation theory, was originally one of Herbert Simon's doctoral students. Sarasvathy et al (2008) see entrepreneurs as designers of new artefacts, where the artefacts are, for example, new organisations, institutions and markets. As we mentioned earlier in this chapter, Herbert Simon is one of the classic design theorists. Effectuation theory testifies that entrepreneurship and design thinking have much in common. The similarities have, for example, led Boland et al (2008) to refer to the entrepreneur as a designing manager, Kortzfleisch et al (2013) to create the concept of entrepreneurial design thinking, and Nielsen and Christensen (2014) to emphasise what the traditionally based design management literature can learn from entrepreneurship.

Entrepreneurship: entrepreneurial thinking or design thinking?

As you may recall, this chapter's paradox concerns entrepreneurial thinking versus design thinking. Design forms its own creative way of thinking, acting and tackling entrepreneurial problems, which in one sense is contrary to the dominant discovery-driven approach in entrepreneurship. The paradox is summarised in Table 10.2.

Whilst entrepreneurial thinking represents a classic approach to entrepreneurship, the design thinking entrepreneur offers a new approach to thinking, acting and addressing problems in the unfolding of the entrepreneurial process. In entrepreneurial thinking, opportunities emanate from the entrepreneur being alert to and discovering failures of the present and the past, what has already happened, and exploiting these failures. Design thinking

Table 10.2 The paradox: Entrepreneurial thinking or design thinking

	Entrepreneurial thinking	Design thinking
Main orientation	Exploitation of past and present	Exploitation and exploration of past, present and future
Driving forces	Discovery driven	Driven by the interplay between discovery and creation, empathy, rapid prototyping and co-creation
Approach	Unconscious alertness	More conscious
Who	The individual	Socially constructed
Assumption of the entrepreneurial process	Linear	Iterative
Future orientation	Low	High and multiple
Output	Entrepreneurial value	Human value
Key focus	The back end	The front end
Constraints	Have to be eliminated	A way forward

tells a different story about new opportunities, which involves an iterative interplay between exploiting and exploring, discovering and creating, past, present and future through, e.g., empathy, rapid prototyping and co-creation. Certainly, entrepreneurial design thinkers often start with 'What is?', but the purpose is not to identify gaps and opportunities for streamlining the existing through the use of existing knowledge; the aim is rather to see things in new ways and to reframe the problem. This, in turn, promotes thinking outside the box and the creation of something new. Since the concept of alertness from entrepreneurial thinking is associated with unconscious action, and design thinking represents a more conscious approach to the emergence of something new, then there is, here, a difference between entrepreneurial thinking and design thinking.

Another thing is that entrepreneurial thinking is concerned with the entrepreneur as an individual. It is the individual who spots the opportunity, and it is an individual who exploits it. However, design thinking does better in solving entrepreneurial problems and entrepreneurship as a social co-creation process. A further important point is that opportunity emergence in design thinking is hard to separate from the processes of opportunity discovery/creation, evaluation and exploitation – the opposite of entrepreneurial thinking, which is based more on a linear logic. First we discover the opportunity, then evaluate it, and eventually it will be utilised. Furthermore, design thinking is very much orientated towards the future, and that future is a multiple concept. Design thinking brings speculative futures into the entrepreneurial process. Entrepreneurial thinking is evidence of a more controlled approach to the future as one is always aware that entrepreneurial opportunities are dependent on the earning of profit. Therefore, the only future images that come into play are those that link to the entrepreneur's current expectations about the market, such as prices, competitive strength, cost, resources, and so on. The future horizon is thus shorter, more limited and fixed than it is in design thinking, where, for example, fiction is used as a future method. Constraints are something to be eliminated in entrepreneurial thinking, as they can stand in the way of the entrepreneurial profit creation. However, for the entrepreneurial design thinker constraints are a positive element.

The two perspectives differ further, in that the design thinker takes an empathic and people-centred approach to the entrepreneurial process. The focus is on creating human value. At the start, less interest is placed on whether the entrepreneur achieves his or her goals and the creation of entrepreneurial value, which is central to entrepreneurial thinking. Last but not least, entrepreneurial thinking focuses more on the exploitation and execution of new opportunities in comparison with design thinking. Once the opportunity is detected, the entrepreneurial thinker moves forward quite quickly in terms of creating a business out of the opportunity. This brings into play what we have called the back end of the entrepreneurial process, where the opportunity is exploited quickly. The design thinking entrepreneur will increasingly focus on the front end of the entrepreneurial process. Therefore, an entrepreneurial thinker might fear that a design thinking entrepreneur fails to get beyond the creative reframing processes and is thus faced with some form of barrier to moving forward with the execution of the project.

A theoretical interpretation

Back at the beginning, you were presented with a case. It is now time to provide an interpretation of the case in light of the paradox and its two perspectives.

The entrepreneurial thinking perspective

In line with entrepreneurial thinking, Designandelen constructs a two-sided market of supply and demand, sellers and buyers to strengthen smaller design entrepreneurs and introducing design thinking to larger, established organisations. What makes this two-sided market work together is the existence of objective opportunities, namely the problem spaces of the larger organisations. These are objectives within which small design entrepreneurs see potential opportunities for creating entrepreneurial profit, and why it makes any sense for entrepreneurs to be part of the design cooperative project. It also emphasises the entrepreneur's degree of future orientation. Their thinking concerns orders and profit in the here and now, not the future. Entrepreneurs' objective in getting hold of the opportunity is to create value for themselves as entrepreneurs by capitalising on the opportunity. By having the small design entrepreneurs solve the tasks of the larger organisations, the market, as a whole, is optimised and more efficient than it was before the design entrepreneurs spotted the opportunity.

The Designandelen project plays the role of one who first discovers the opportunities and makes these existing options clearer for the smaller entrepreneurs. But the project's role does not stop there, for the opportunities have a character that prevents the design entrepreneurs from immediately seizing them. Designandelen helps entrepreneurs to eliminate this constraint. Designandelen puts together entrepreneurs within interdisciplinary consortia so they become large enough to effectively bid on and undertake jobs. Here we are talking about an exercise that helps to streamline the existing market. Finally, since business start-ups appear to be something of a secondary concern for businesses that are primarily focused on their creative professionalism, Designandelen puts significant effort into improving the back end of the entrepreneurs' processes.

The design thinking perspective

Viewing the case study through a design thinking filter, the starting point for the story is that the larger established organisations cannot continue doing what they do and operating in the same vein as they always have; and it is because the organisations themselves have come to realise this that they get involved with Designandelen. They have a good sense of where the real problems lie, but there is a need to push things in new ways, and deeper, in order to understand why they have a problem and whether there are some hidden opportunities to create new thinking and innovation. Designandelen brings together design entrepreneurs for these tasks and in multidisciplinary teams, in order to ensure as much diverse disruption as possible within the established organisations. These entrepreneurs with their 'fuzzy brains' are trained to be creative first movers, to see the new, to create opportunities and innovation. They dare to turn things upside down, and this they do by treating the larger organisation's problems as wicked problems, which they often also are, and by starting out with gaining an in-depth understanding of the organisation's problems and their users and stakeholders.

Design entrepreneurs begin their iterative processes and actively use their toolbox to understand the larger organisation's problem areas, users, stakeholders, reframe the whole effort and create numerous pictures of the established organisation's forward-looking solutions and opportunities, test them regularly and pick out some promising examples for further consideration. It is a long process. The larger organisation's eyes must be opened to what design thinking can do for them and Designandelen has to assist the design entrepreneurs in opening the larger organisation's eyes. Large organisations will tend to be impatient, and have difficulty with spending so much time in the fuzzy front end, without being able to see the actual market value it will deliver. For some it is also challenging to engage their users, customers, suppliers, etc. in new ways. When they experience constraints, the larger organisations get the urge to withdraw from Designandelen and from cooperation with entrepreneurs. However, it is precisely these constraints that provide design entrepreneurs with something exciting to work on. It is a dilemma. Over time many of the larger organisations move and change themselves in different ways, but all in a direction where there is a better interaction and balance between exploitative and exploratory processes.

Testing the theory

Following on from the thoughts and discussions that you have become acquainted with throughout the chapter, it is now time for you to develop your own tests. The goal of these tests is to strengthen your understanding of how design thinking can support, and may even be the enabling aspect of the entrepreneurial process.

EXERCISES

1 **First, a little warming up exercise.** Imagine that a group of Lauras landed a spaceship on Earth. They do not speak any earthly language. Using sketches, photographs, objects, etc. you should now explain to the group of Lauras how design thinking could assist the development of the entrepreneurial process.

2 **Now try your hand at the design thinking process.** After studying your fellow students your observations lead you to the following question about a new way of drinking coffee 'on the go': how can one design new ways to drink coffee while on the road? You will design a solution. 1) Interview a fellow student: what is meaningful to him or her in relation to drinking coffee 'on the go'? What are their needs, troubles, desires, and why are they as they are? 2) Do three sketches of radical solutions that meet your fellow students' needs. One of these solutions must be the most ridiculous solution you can possibly think of. 3) Share your solutions with others to obtain feedback. 4) Reflect and sketch a new option. 5) Build a prototype of the solution. 5) Share your prototype with others to gather more feedback. 6) Reflect and sketch a new option.

3 **Now, select a problem area yourself for which you want to find a good solution.** Go through the same process as described above.

LITERATURE

Boland, R.J., Collopy, F., Lyytinen, K. & Yoo, Y. (2008) 'Managing as designing: Lessons for organizational leaders from the design practice of Frank O. Gehry', *Design Issues*, 24(1), 10–25.

Borja de Mozota, B. (1998), 'Structuring strategic design management: Michael Porter's value chain', *Design Management Journal*, 9(2), 26–31.

Brown, T. (2009) *Change by Design: How Design Thinking Transforms Organizations and Inspires Innovation*, New York: HarperCollins.

Buchanan, R. (1992) 'Wicked problems in design thinking', *Design Issues*, 8(2), 5–21.

Casson, M. (1982) *The Entrepreneur*, Totowa, NJ: Barnes & Noble Books.

Cross, N. (2006) *Designerly Ways of Knowing*, Berlin: Springer.

Design Council (2015) *The Design Economy Report*, London: Design Council.

Dorst, K. (2011) 'The core of "design thinking" and its application', *Design Studies*, 32(6), 521–532.

Dunne, D. & Martin, R. (2006) 'Design thinking and how it will change management education: An interview and discussion', *Academy of Management Learning and Education*, 5(4), 512–523.

Johansson-Sköldberg, U., Woodilla, J. & Cetinkaya, M. (2013) 'Design thinking: Past, present and possible futures', *Creativity and Innovation Management*, 22(2), 121–146.

Kimbell, L. (2011) 'Rethinking design thinking: Part 1', *Design and Culture*, 3(3), 285–306.

Kortzfleisch, H.F.O., Von Zerwas, D. and Mokanis, I. (2013) 'Potentials of entrepreneurial design thinking for entrepreneurial education', in *Procedia – Social and Behavioral Science 106*, 4th International Conference on New Horizons in Education, 2089–2092.

Liedtka, J. & Ogilvie, T. (2011) *Designing for Growth: A Design Thinking Toolkit for Managers*, New York: Columbia University Press.

March, J. (1991) 'Exploration and exploitation in organizational learning', *Organization Science*, 2(1), 71–87.

Martin, R. (2009) *The Design of Business – Why Design Thinking is the Next Competitive Advantage*, Boston, MA: Harvard Business Press.

Nielsen, S.L. & Christensen, P.R. (2014) 'The wicked problem of design management: Perspectives from the field of entrepreneurship', *Design Journal*, 17(4), 560–582.

Nielsen, S.L., Christensen, P.R., Lassen, H.A. & Mikkelsen, M. (2016) 'Opportunity design: Novel perspectives on design enabled entrepreneurial opportunity emergence', under review for the *Design Journal*.

O'Reilly, C.A. & Tushman, M.L. (2013) 'Organizational ambidexterity: Past, present, and future', *Academy of Management Perspectives*, 27(4), 324–338.

Rowe, P. (1987) *Design Thinking*, Cambridge, MA: MIT Press.

Sanders, E.B.N. & Stappers, P.J. (2008) 'Co-creation and the new landscape of design' *CoDesign*, 4(1), 5–18.

Sarasvathy, S.D., Dew, N., Read, S. & Wiltbank, R. (2008) 'Designing organizations that design environments: Lessons from entrepreneurial expertise', *Organization Studies*, 29(3), 331–350.

Schön, D. (1983) *The Reflective Practitioner: How Professionals Think in Action*, New York: Basic Books.

Shane, S. (2003) *A General Theory of Entrepreneurship: The Individual–Opportunity Nexus*, Cheltenham, UK and Northampton, MA, USA: Edward Elgar Publishing.

Shane, S. & Venkataraman, S. (2000) 'The promise of entrepreneurship as a field of research', *The Academy of Management Review*, 25(1), 217–226.

Simon, H. (1969) *The Science of the Artificial*, Cambridge, MA: MIT Press.

Verganti, R. (2009) *Design Driven Innovation*, Boston, MA: Harvard Business Press.

Section 4

The entrepreneurial context

11

Intrapreneurship

As promised in Chapter 1, we are now going to introduce you to intrapreneurship. In simple terms, intrapreneurship covers the phenomenon of entrepreneurship within the context of an existing business. Within this context, new opportunities are discovered or created which need to be evaluated and organised. The result may be new organisational units, strategic reorientation or innovations within the existing organisation. The driving force is still, as with starting up an independent organisation, based on a single individual or a group of people, often called 'intrapreneurs'.

However, intrapreneurship is very different from entrepreneurship. The existing corporate environment places certain conditions on the entrepreneurial process. The individuals who discover or create, evaluate and organise new opportunities within an existing corporate framework are dependent on the existing company accepting the presence of the new. The intrapreneur is thus constrained by the context of the firm. At the same time, however, the intrapreneur positively draws on the many diverse resources that are present in the existing business. Furthermore, it seems that the characteristics of intrapreneurs are in many respects similar to those of entrepreneurs (Bager et al 2010). This chapter provides you with an understanding of what intrapreneurship is and how the entrepreneurial process is created and run within the context of an existing business.

Intrapreneurship in practice

What follows is a story about intrapreneurship in a global company written by William B. Gartner and Ann Højbjerg Clarke. Since 2004 this corporation has attempted to foster new intrapreneurs among its staff and launch new innovative ventures by means of an internal business case competition.

CASE STUDY

Man on the Moon – a business case competition in a global company

(Devised by William B. Gartner and Ann Højbjerg Clarke)

Founded in 1933, the Danfoss Group is a family-owned corporation headquartered in Nordborg, Denmark and with operations in over 100 countries. Danfoss competes across global markets covering eight business areas: refrigeration and air conditioning, heating, frequency converters, industrial automation, water controls, high-pressure water solutions, geared motors and solar energy. In 2009, net sales for Danfoss exceeded 3.4 billion Euros, and the company employed over 25,000 people of whom fewer than 6,600 were based in Denmark.

Around the turn of the century, the Danfoss top management team realised a paradox existed between ways and incentives to develop incremental and radical innovations at the corporate and divisional levels of the organisation. At the corporate level, the creation of a centralised research and development centre could lead to the creation of radical innovations. However, such innovations were unlikely to be connected to business strategies within any of the existing divisions. By their nature, radical innovations are something different from the daily business of the divisions and therefore difficult to foster. Without direct links to a division's current operations and markets, radical innovations invented at the corporate centre were not likely to be pursued by the divisions. At the divisional level, the metrics of efficiency and profitability required a focus on existing customers, existing suppliers or other existing relationships so that innovative activities would aim at improving existing products or market shares, i.e. incremental innovation rather than radical innovation. The development of radical innovations required the investment of resources in new technologies and new markets which, in the short run, would not produce profits or efficiencies in each division's operations and markets. So, radical innovations were not pursued at divisional level. However, since most of the Danfoss divisions operated in mature markets with low growth and revenue, the future of the company required growth through the development of new products and markets. The primary question, then, for the top management team was: 'How might Danfoss go about creating new opportunities for growth while maintaining efficiencies and profitability in current markets and products?'

In 2004 Danfoss initiated a completely new organisational structure for pursuing incremental and radical innovations at the same time. The structure involved two primary parties:

- the Danfoss divisions, focused at existing markets and products through incremental innovation;
- the creation of Danfoss Ventures and the Danfoss Entrepreneur Park.

CASE STUDY *(continued)*

Danfoss Ventures would aim at radical innovations measured in terms of whether the innovations were new-to-market or new-to-company. The Danfoss Entrepreneur Park would support local entrepreneurs from inside and outside the corporation that have viable business ideas, which could benefit from the competences Danfoss already have, but which fall outside of Danfoss' current business scope.

The Man on the Moon competition is created

In order to generate both incremental and radical innovations within the Danfoss Group, the top management team decided, in 2004, to hold an annual internal competition for the creation of new businesses named 'Man on the Moon' (MOM), a title inspired by President J.F. Kennedy when he spoke of sending a man to the moon and returning him safely to the earth:

> I believe we possess all the resources and talents necessary. But the facts of the matter are that we have never made the national decisions or marshalled the national resources required for such leadership. We have never specified long-range goals on an urgent time schedule or managed our resources and our time so as to insure their fulfilment. (J.F. Kennedy, 25 May 1961)

Not only would such a competition be likely to identify innovations that the company might pursue, but the process would also identify employees within the company with intrapreneurial potential. These individuals could then be provided with skills and support to enable their intrapreneurial activities to occur within the company. While the company appeared to lack employees with intrapreneurial skills that could work with novel technologies and markets, managers at Danfoss were convinced that these entrepreneurial employees *did* exist within the company, but they had to be identified and encouraged to try. It was thought that there would then be a new career path for Danfoss' employees, a new path for intrapreneurs in addition to the traditional career paths for managers and specialists.

Danfoss sought a process that would identify these new intrapreneurs and then establish a

Figure 11.1 A playful man on the moon

CASE STUDY *(continued)*

talent pool that could later be used in their new established venture unit. Furthermore, they acknowledged that, in order to create such a pool, they needed the attention and commitment of the top management team, otherwise the initiative would die as employees would not be encouraged to take risks. During the process of developing this programme the venture group began to see this project as a human relations and culture change programme and, in addition, as a way to identify new business proposals with great potential.

From the beginning the goal of MOM was to 'aim high', the thinking being, 'we cannot do this in half measures as then we will never pull through'. It had to be world class. Consequently, the first competition had a budget that was quite large, especially in relation to Danfoss Ventures' own budget. Furthermore, in order to develop the competition and train the participants, Danfoss Ventures worked with researchers from American and European universities as well as external venture capitalists.

The Danfoss Venture division set the guidelines for team formation and rules for the contest, endeavouring to emulate the conditions of a start-up as closely as possible. Teams consist of two to five members. In order to cover vital aspects of a venture, different competencies have to be represented in each team, for example marketing, finance, engineering and distribution. The teams are free to utilise any contacts and resources, both inside and outside the Danfoss Corporation. Teams will be working on their business proposal in addition to their regular jobs. The organisers of MOM believe that those who aspire to become intrapreneurs within the corporation are willing to give +100 per cent to their work *and* venture efforts. By working on both projects and current jobs, without complaining, the MOM contest reveals who is really ready to put in the extra effort to engage in intrapreneurship. It is also important that the company's divisions where these employees work do not lose productivity because these individuals are involved in the MOM competition.

The MOM competition consists of the following phases:

1 The yearly MOM starts with a global invitation to participate. An important part of the competition is a top-management invitation to employees across the entire corporation.
2 Based on a strategic and operational assessment of the proposed business idea's potential by Danfoss Ventures, a number of promising teams are selected to join the next stage of the competition.
3 The selected teams participate in a two-day workshop that includes training in: team-building; venture creation concepts, skills, tools and activities.
4 One month later teams submit a summary of their business proposal and deliver a short presentation in front of a jury, which evaluates these projects. Normally half of the teams gain access to the final stage of the contest in which they receive one day of business coaching as well as mentoring from Danfoss managers. These mentors assist projects through the Danfoss system, ensuring that the teams are not held up by Danfoss policies and procedures. Teams are also given funds for expenses (e.g. travel, reports and consultants) and training.

CASE STUDY *(continued)*

5 After six more weeks, the finalist teams present their ideas and business proposals to the Danfoss top management team. The top three teams are awarded the opportunity to participate in an MIT entrepreneurship course in January/February the following year.
6 In a post-contest evaluation by Danfoss Ventures, all business proposals are assessed for further funding. The venture group also evaluates whether it is appropriate to place the project in an existing division or in the Danfoss-incubator unit. They also evaluate in which country the project is likely to be exposed to the most favourable conditions.

The MOM organisers do not expect participants in the competition to finish developing their ideas into specific products or services. Given that the competition lasts only three months, it is impossible to develop a finished product or service. Instead, participants are expected to state their business case clearly along with critical assumptions about the technology used. Winners should also clearly outline the areas that need to be investigated to determine whether the product or service is truly viable and profitable in the short and long term.

The MOM outcome
For the first competition held in 2004, three projects (nine participants in total, all from Denmark) were selected to participate in the final round in front of the Danfoss top management team. All participating projects were given funding of US$200,000 to continue the development of their ideas. Two of these projects are still running and one of these projects has entered the market. In the second competition held in 2005, there were 90 inquiries from Danfoss employees, which resulted in 40 applications; 20 individuals were interviewed, and 12 people were selected to participate in the competition (coming from Denmark and India). Four teams competed and two of these projects were funded. In 2006 there were 44 participants in 10 teams (from Denmark, China, India, France and Germany) of which four were funded. Each of the 10 projects had a business potential of over US$20 million. Three of these projects were absorbed by other divisions within Danfoss; two were shut down; and five were being developed further. Since 2006, the competition has stabilised at this level, engaging about 50 individuals yearly, divided into 10–15 venture teams. So, over the years a huge number of Danfoss employees have gained entrepreneurial experience and competence from this competition. In 2010 Danfoss decided to close down and reorganise some of its venturing activities, but MOM continues.

As the outcomes of the venture development competition vary from the successful creation of 'spin-ins' (projects that are absorbed into established Danfoss divisions); 'spin-outs' (projects that often are funded by outside investors and then sold-off); and 'stops' (projects that fail), the Danfoss Group sought to provide various pathways and incentives for employees who choose to be involved in these entrepreneurial ventures. All employees involved in the venture creation process had the opportunity to stay with their new ventures, and, if successful, earn bonuses based on the valuation of the project (either as an external exit or as an internal venture as valued by its profits to a division). Employees could also opt to

CASE STUDY *(continued)*

return to their respective divisions if they didn't want to continue with venture development efforts. When projects failed, managers could return to their divisions or find opportunities to work with other ventures.

The assumption that Danfoss had many entrepreneurial employees proved to be correct and MOM proved to be an efficient means of identifying these talents. Whilst not all MOM venture projects were successful, the venture competition did provide opportunities for employees at Danfoss to realise their intrapreneurial talents and direct the Danfoss Group into potential high-growth markets through the development of radical innovations.

Your immediate interpretation

What does the story tell you about Danfoss' experience with intrapreneurship in general? How would you immediately understand the development process historically? The following exercises can help you create an understanding of what is at stake in the story, and thus how you can comprehend intrapreneurship.

- Think about some of the challenges that confront Danfoss in their attempts to foster intrapreneurship within the organisation by way of the Man on the Moon competition. Then, prioritise the challenges depending on what you believe are most critical in relation to understanding intrapreneurship.
- Now, you should try to tackle and solve the challenge to which you accorded highest priority in the above exercise. First, put yourself in the place of an individual employee. How would he/she solve the challenge? Then adopt the role of the senior manager in Danfoss. How would the chief executive meet the challenge?
- Then reflect on how the two solutions found are influenced by each of the two roles you played. Did the two different roles make you handle the challenge differently? Why/why not?

Theories of entrepreneurship

Although the title of this section is 'Theories of entrepreneurship', the focal point is the theory of intrapreneurship. This theory will help you gain an understanding of the mechanisms that must be discussed when new opportunities arise that are to be evaluated and organised within the framework of an existing company.

The theory of intrapreneurship can be broadly divided into two perspectives. One perspective holds that intrapreneurship is initiated and driven by top management. Creation of intrapreneurship is thus top-down. The argument for a top-down process is that support and action from top management is essential if intrapreneurship is to become a reality. It is senior management's constant attention and monitoring that creates momentum and success. The other perspective takes the view that successful intrapreneurship is created by people with the enthusiasm and self-confidence to drive intrapreneurship forward. Here, intrapreneurship is created bottom-up. The argument is that intrapreneurship can only be cultivated through dedicated and enterprising people who in their daily work discover or create the potential for renewal. In this chapter you will therefore discuss intrapreneurship in terms of the paradox:

Top-down or bottom-up?

Background story

Before thoroughly exploring the paradox, let's delve into the background of intrapreneurship. Overall, intrapreneurship is a phenomenon that apparently is closely related to socio-economic development. Birkinshaw et al (2002) argue that the interest of US companies in intrapreneurship has, in historical terms, been fostered by three waves of popularity from 1960 to 2002. The waves show that it is particularly during periods of positive economic development that intrapreneurship is placed on the agendas of existing firms with a good economic situation, providing room for them to pursue new opportunities. Such interest does not appear during periods of economic recession. Birkinshaw et al talk of the three waves of popularity:

> The first ended in 1973 with the oil price shock and the ensuing recession. The second began in the early 1980s . . . and came to an end in the late 1980s (again because of recession). The third wave began during the great 1990s technology boom, and it peaked in 2000 before falling steeply. The third wave was driven by a combination of new technologies and also a bubble economy. (Birkinshaw et al 2002: 10)

In connection with each of the three waves, an increasing number of existing companies showed interest in intrapreneurship. The question is whether the experience of the three waves of popularity will influence how a fourth generation of existing companies engage in intrapreneurship. In other words, the question is: 'whether organizations will have learned the lessons in making the idea work' (Birkinshaw et al 2002: 10). There are indications that companies have not necessarily learned, as the financial crisis in 2009 again led to more companies downsizing their intrapreneurial activities. The Danfoss case study is a good example of this.

Other factors besides socio-economic development may also help to inhibit work with intrapreneurship. Birkinshaw et al (2002) list the following factors:

- Most companies work with multiple objectives rather than a precise measurement of intrapreneurship.
- There is no adequate managerial support. The result is that the skills required to develop intrapreneurial ideas and opportunities will not be developed.
- Remuneration systems, such as shares to employees, are not being implemented. There is simply no carrot that motivates the team behind the new opportunity.

So there are apparently many potential obstacles which must be overcome when working with intrapreneurship. This includes potential rivalry between new ventures and mature business lines in a company (Evald & Bager 2008). So, what are the success criteria? Critical success factors seems to be: 'develop clear goals – and a structure to deliver on them . . . build specialised capabilities . . . separate venture units and parent firm . . . committed sponsorship from the highest level' (Birkinshaw et al 2002: 12–15).

The prevalence of intrapreneurship internationally

There are few reports on intrapreneurship that compare the incidence of intrapreneurship between countries. A recent report by Bosma et al (2008) presents the results of an international study of intrapreneurship (defined as: employees developing new business activities together with their employer), carried out in 11 countries. The results show that intrapreneurship is not a very wide spread phenomenon: 'On average, fewer than 5% of employees are intrapreneurs . . . its incidence in the adult population is, on average, significantly lower than that of early stage entrepreneurial activity' (Bosma et al 2008: 5). The result provides clear evidence that even though we see independent entrepreneurship and intrapreneurship as being very similar activities, it is independent entrepreneurship that constitutes a more frequent expression of entrepreneurial behaviour. However, there are significant differences between low- and high-income countries: intrapreneurs seem to be roughly twice as prevalent in high-income countries as in low-income countries (comparing 11 countries, of which Brazil, Chile, Ecuador, Iran, Latvia, Peru and Uruguay are defined as low-income countries and where the Republic of Korea, Netherlands, Norway and Spain are defined as high-income countries). In another study comparing Denmark with other countries, Hancock and Bager (2003) find that Denmark is a country where one finds a high number of intrapreneurs. Not only is there a high level (46 per cent of the total entrepreneurial activity in Denmark), but also levels are slightly increasing over time. Denmark thus occupies a rare leadership position in terms of using employees in large companies as a springboard to discover/create new opportunities, evaluate and exploit them when compared with a number of other countries. Anyway, getting back to the Bosma et al (2008) study, there are various explanations for why there are differences in the level of intrapreneurship between low- and high-income countries: 'First, the level of economic development has a positive effect on the presence of larger firms, which negatively influences the prevalence of independent entrepreneurship in an economy. Second, large organisations in high-income countries may be more open to entrepreneurial behaviour than large firms in low income countries' (Bosma et al 2008: 5). Further, employees working in larger firms have relatively greater latitude in their daily work than is the case in other countries (Dobbin & Boychuk 1999).

A diverse concept

In terms of starting an independent organisation, the concept of intrapreneurship is a newer phenomenon than entrepreneurship. Therefore, intrapreneurship is not backed up by the same tradition that characterises entrepreneurship. Intrapreneurship is still a phenomenon in development. Even the term intrapreneurship is often debated because competing terms are used, such as 'corporate entrepreneurship', 'dependent entrepreneurship' or 'entrepreneurship in established companies' (Sharma & Chrisman 1999). We understand these terms interchangeably, but in this chapter use only the term intrapreneurship.

Branches in intrapreneurship

There are similarities between entrepreneurship as the start-up of an independent organisation and intrapreneurship. Both research fields are based on entrepreneurial behaviour and entrepreneurial activities, i.e. the activities that involve discovery or creation of opportunities and the evaluation and utilization of these through organising.

However, differences also exist. Whereas the process of creating something new in entrepreneurship involves all of the activities required to form a new independent organisation, intrapreneurship does not necessarily include all of the activities that an existing company is involved in. Intrapreneurship can thus appear as 'Dispersed' (= wide) or 'Focused' (= narrow) (Elfring 2005), which means that intrapreneurship can be both activities that involve all employees (dispersed), 'because each employee has the capacity for both managerial and entrepreneurial behaviour', or only involve a *few* employees (focused) who are considered to be particularly entrepreneurial. The Danfoss case study is a good example of a combination of the two, since Danfoss created the Man on the Moon competition, potentially involving all their employees, but at the same time puts its money on new ideas in a more focused way in their 'incubator' system through Danfoss Ventures.

But the most crucial difference between entrepreneurship and intrapreneurship is that entrepreneurship is the entrepreneurial process through which an individual or a group of people who are independent of connections to an existing business, establish one or more new independent organisations (Sharma & Chrisman 1999). On the other hand, it is characteristic of intrapreneurship that the process takes shape, when opportunities are developed by individuals or groups of people that are dependent upon a company's existing organisational framework (Collins & Moore 1970). Collins and Moore are among the first to divide the research in entrepreneurship into two main groups according to whether entrepreneurial activity is independent or dependent of an existing company (intrapreneurship). This is illustrated in Figure 11.2, which divides the intrapreneurship concept into three different branches.

The figure shows that intrapreneurship research is characterised by three different branches or trends. To begin with, Guth and Ginsberg divide intrapreneurship into two major subgroups, namely: 1) formation of a new organisational unit and 2) strategic renewal (Guth & Ginsberg 1990). The formation of a new organisational entity may include a new project, a new company or a new division. By strategic renewal we mean an organisational change strategy that may include changing core competencies, resource uses and competitive parameters at project, corporate, divisional or group level.

In 1999 the division was further refined when Sharma and Chrisman added a third subgroup: innovation. The addition occurs because existing companies can create new organisational units, or change their strategies without necessarily having to innovate: especially if innovation is viewed from a strictly Schumpeterian perspective. Additionally, a larger organisa-

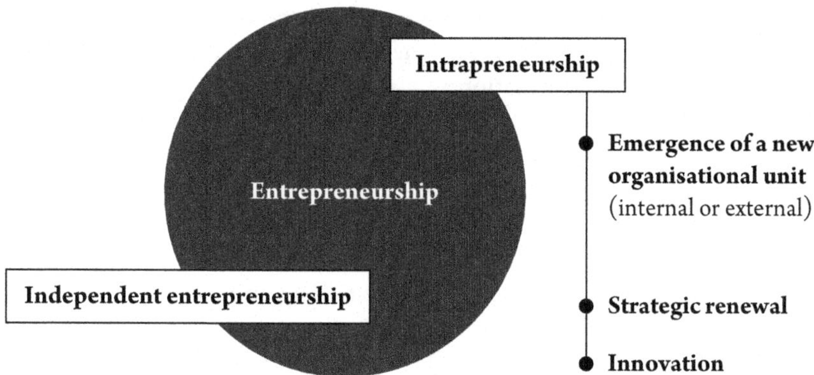

Figure 11.2 Ramifications in the research field of intrapreneurship

tion can innovate, without the other two elements necessarily being a part of the activity. For example, new combinations of knowledge occur without the combinations resulting in new units or strategic renewal. In most cases however, intrapreneurship involves all three aspects, as is the case in the Danfoss case study where Danfoss implements strategic renewal, innovates and creates new organisational units via the Man on the Moon competition and the incubator system.

The final refinement of intrapreneurship to which we will introduce you is that the formation of a new organisational unit can both be internal or external to an existing corporate organisational framework (Von Hippel 1977). The formation of a new organisational unit can occur internally, through the development of internal units such as new groups, projects or companies. The formation of a new organisational unit may also take place externally through the establishment of joint ventures and spin-outs. In the Danfoss case study both forms are combined, as Danfoss worked with spin-ins and spin-outs as a result of the Man on the Moon competition. In this chapter we confine ourselves to understanding intrapreneurship as creating new units internally. This is consistent with Burgelman's (1983a, 1983b) definition of intrapreneurship. He sees intrapreneurship as a process in which companies achieve differentiation through internal development processes. This focus really puts the paradox, 'top-down and bottom-up' on the agenda as internal intrapreneurship implies that innovation must either live side by side with the existing organisational structures, routines and strategies (focused intrapreneurship) or be adopted into the existing organisation structures, routines and strategies (dispersed intrapreneurship). The consequence of Burgelman's understanding that intrapreneurship is achieved through internal development processes can thus be very different processes according to whether intrapreneurship is assumed to be distributed across the whole organization, or if intrapreneurship is restricted to a particular unit or part of the whole organisation.

The degree of innovation in intrapreneurship

The forces and challenges that existing firms encounter in their establishment of intrapreneurship is dependent on the degree of novelty of the opportunities pursued. Are we talking about an opportunity that is new to the existing organisation, new to the market or new to the world? The more the opportunity can be described as innovative, the more the existing business faces the challenge of creating a new market for that opportunity.

To talk about the various degrees of innovation related to intrapreneurship we need to introduce the concept of incremental versus radical intrapreneurship. They must be understood as a continuum. The difference between incremental and radical innovations is plotted in Figure 11.3.

Incremental innovation refers to the idea that opportunities remain fundamentally the same, but are renewed gradually. Development of businesses therefore takes the form of a gradual process by which products, processes, etc. incrementally and slowly take new shape. This is the case for instance with the divisions in Danfoss, which itself stands for progressive innovations. At the opposite end of the continuum, radical intrapreneurship is concerned with how existing companies develop in leaps and bounds, coming up with potential opportunities that are completely different from existing ones. Here, the Danfoss case study is also illustrative, as Danfoss deliberately tried to establish an incubator system that has the opportunity to gamble on more radical ideas (Clarke et al 2012).

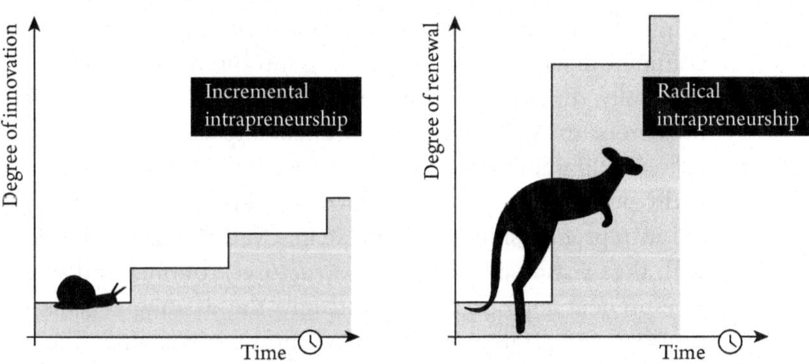

Figure 11.3 Incremental versus radical intrapreneurship

The process behind intrapreneurship

So, what characterises the entrepreneurial process that lies behind intrapreneurship? There are obviously many different opinions on how this process progresses. Figure 11.4 offers one model.

The figure shows what it takes for individuals or groups of individuals to take the initiative to undertake intrapreneurship, discovering or creating opportunities and perhaps ultimately translating these into concrete actions through evaluation and organisation. This figure focuses on what happens during the process behind intrapreneurship.

The figure particularly emphasises how intrapreneurship is a product of two factors, which are constantly interacting with each other, namely: individual characteristics and organisational characteristics. For these two factors to start interacting with each other there is often a catalyst or trigger event. 'The decision to act intrapreneurially occurs as a result of an interaction between organizational characteristics, individual characteristics, and some kind of precipitating event. The precipitating event provides the impetus to behave intrapreneurially when other conditions are conducive to such behavior' (Hornsby et al 1993: 33). More specifically, Zahra (1991) points to how the triggering event may, for example, be the development of new procedures or technologies, the replacement of management, a collaboration with, or acquisition of another company, a competitor's incipient takeover of market shares, efficiencies, changes in customer demand or economic changes. All this can lead to individuals in an existing company discovering or creating a new opportunity. The following explains the figure's content in more detail.

Individual characteristics

Over time, important individual characteristics have been shown empirically to influence the process of intrapreneurship. Many of the characteristics listed in Figure 11.4 are obvious, but two of them deserve elaboration. These are the need for achievement and internal locus of control. The need for achievement is, as mentioned in Chapter 1, one of the first traits associated with entrepreneurs in the field of entrepreneurship research. As a natural consequence, this trait is also incorporated within the literature on intrapreneurship. People who prefer to be personally responsible for solving problems, setting goals and achieving them are considered to have high achievement needs. Achievement needs are then closely related to other factors listed as individual characteristics, such as goal-oriented behaviour and the need for

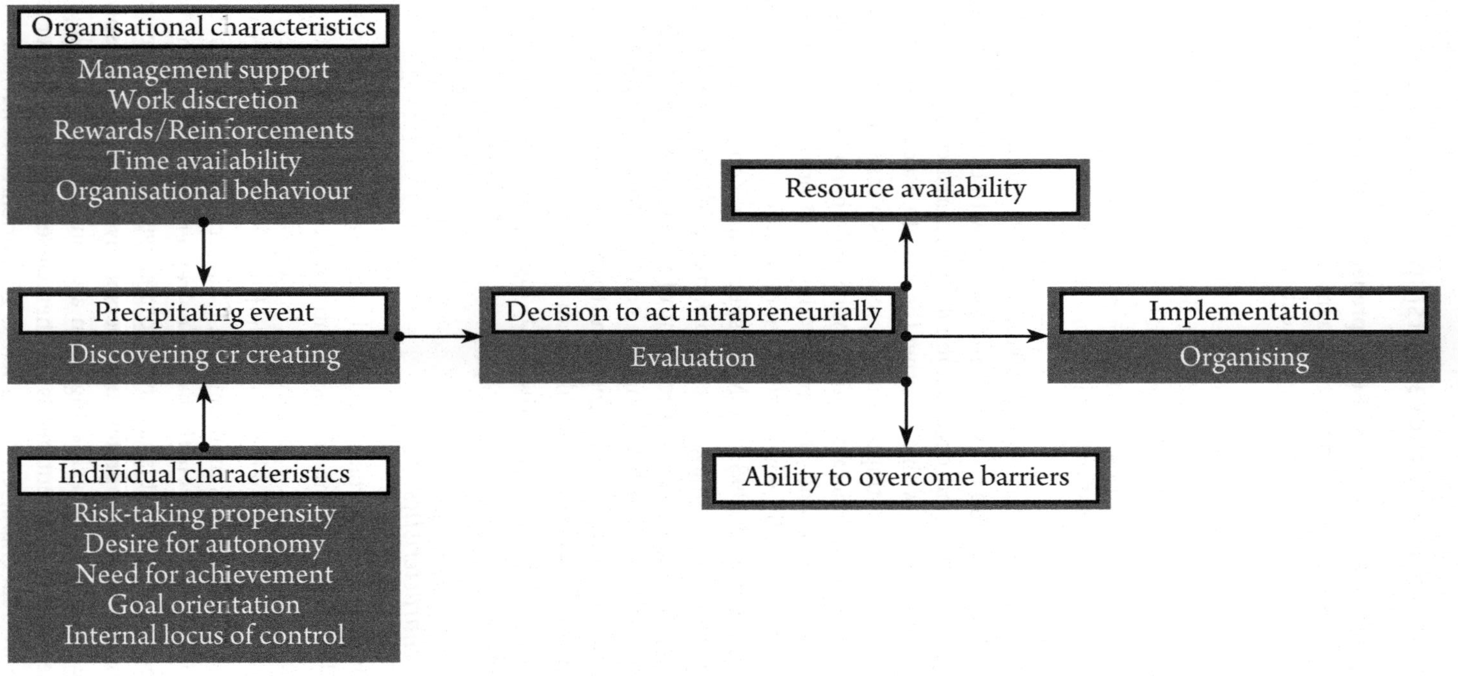

Source: Hornsby et al (1993: 31).

Figure 11.4 Intrapreneurship as a process

autonomy. Control over inner feelings is a different type of character trait associated with the intrapreneur. This factor refers to individuals or groups of individuals feeling that they themselves have control over what happens in the process of intrapreneurship.

Organisational characteristics

In the case of organisational characteristics a number of factors play a crucial role. These are, in contrast to the individual characteristics, less obvious and are therefore examined in more detail. Management support includes, for example, rapid adoption of potential opportunities identified by employees, appreciation of those who present new potential opportunities, support of experimental projects and the availability of venture capital. Job autonomy covers employees' ability to independently plan work and an absence of destructive criticism of employees' mistakes. Within reward/reinforcement, there is consideration of personal challenge and responsibility, financial remuneration depending on performance and raising awareness of the potential opportunities that employees have developed within the organisational hierarchy. The time factor refers to the time that is made available for employees to hatch new potential opportunities through, for example, moderate workloads, removal of deadlines on all aspects of a person's work and support for time-consuming problem-solving projects. Avoidance of rigid organisational boundaries is to avoid standard procedures for all work functions, reducing dependence on narrow job descriptions and rigid performance standards. All of these are assumed to be involved in promoting the process of intrapreneurship.

Activities in the process of intrapreneurship

If no obstacles arise in the interaction between organisational and individual characteristics, then according to the model, individuals or groups of people begin a series of activities. This can include preparation of business plans, market research and various meetings with the existing business concerning the size of venture capital support. In other words, a range of activities for the purpose of evaluating the opportunity is set in motion. Is it ready for the market and how? If the necessary resources are made available and the range of organisational, socio-cultural, business administration and individual barriers are overcome, then the process of intrapreneurship can result in proper organising of the opportunity.

Top-down intrapreneurship

Now you know what the term intrapreneurship covers, and you know the key events in the process of intrapreneurship. However, this chapter's paradox indicates that there are two different perspectives of what creates intrapreneurship.

Overall, top-down processes are described as being characterised by the management within existing companies taking the initiative through the formulation of strategies, action plans and commencement of actual operations in the field. Intrapreneurship is thus implemented from the firm's upper layer and passed down into the system, which according to Figure 11.5 suggests that the organisational dimension dominates the process of intrapreneurship. Top-down intrapreneurship means a controlled process, which manages and controls its development. Last but not least one can expect a close relationship between the existing company's management, the intrapreneurs and the development of the potential opportunity.

From the top-down perspective this close relationship is considered to be appropriate. The relationship creates the opportunity for formal and informal coaching (Thornhill & Amit 2001). Furthermore the intrapreneurs have easy access to the skills and resources built up by the existing company over time.

Bottom-up intrapreneurship

Unlike the top-down perspective the bottom-up perspective focuses on the situation in which intrapreneurship is created as a result of employee initiative. Intrapreneurship thus grows in existing companies from scratch. Figure 11.5 suggests that the individual dimension dominates in terms of explaining the generation of intrapreneurship within the organisation. Instead of control, the bottom-up perspective emphasises greater autonomy, since the

Figure 11.5 Top-down and bottom-up processes

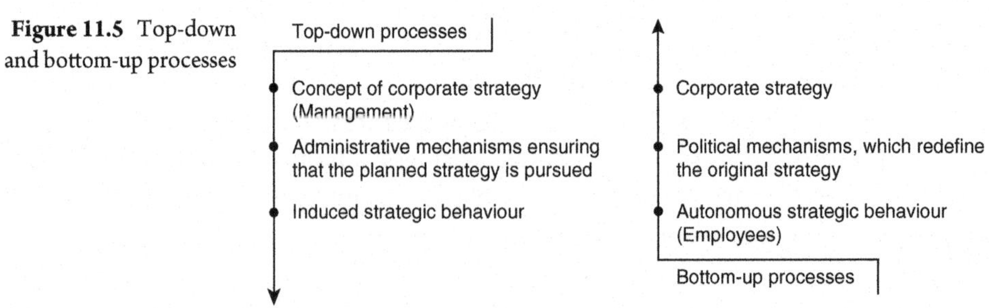

Source: Burgelman (1983a: 225).

employees, through continuous innovation, break with the management's guidelines and plans. The bottom-up perspective assumes, in other words, a loose coupling between the existing corporate governance, the intrapreneurs and the potential opportunities that are discovered or created.

Where the relationship between these actors is too close it is assumed by the bottom-up perspective to kill the entrepreneurial, dynamic working environment characterised by the team behind the potential new opportunity (Birkinshaw et al 2002). The reason is that it is explicitly or implicitly expected that existing corporate standards, structures, rules and values will be complied with when the new opportunity is being further developed (Day 1994). This can lead to a dimming of the creative development required for further development of the opportunity. A high level of autonomy in connection with intrapreneurship is therefore preferred.

Top-down and bottom-up

To clarify the difference between the top-down and bottom-up processes further, we introduce Burgelman (1983a and 1983b). He is concerned with how strategies of intrapreneurship emerge and are formed into larger existing businesses. Figure 11.5 shows the top-down and bottom-up perspectives in a single diagram.

As shown on the figure's left-hand side, the starting point for existing businesses is an articulate and official strategy, which informs the employees of the direction in which the company wishes to develop. To ensure that the employees in the existing company comply with the strategy, senior management can initiate a number of administrative mechanisms. As such, these mechanisms control the behaviour of employees so that they follow the direction identified in the strategy. These administrative mechanisms either motivate or punish employees to demonstrate the strategic behaviour that senior management wants. This is what Burgelman considers to be top-down-driven entrepreneurial activities and processes.

Now the figure's right-hand side. Since most employees are at the operational level where day-to-day decisions are made, they are constantly faced with new potential opportunities for how challenges can be resolved, improved, or attacked quite differently from before. The new potential can sometimes differ dramatically from the planned and intended strategy. If the new opportunities prove to be successful, a series of political mechanisms start up. The political mechanisms can be discussions concerning existing strategy so that senior management is aware that there are alternative ways to solve challenges. 'Political mechanisms through which middle managers question the current concept of strategy, and provide top management with the opportunity to rationalize, retroactively, successful autonomous strategic behavior' (Burgelman 1983b: 1352). The existing firm's official strategy is thus reconsidered and the new opportunities are integrated. Here, according to Burgelman, it is a bottom-up process that creates and forms the official strategy.

However Burgelman's (1983b) main argument is that strategies for intrapreneurship emerge and are shaped by interconnected activities that people at different hierarchical levels in the existing firm attend to. A combination of the conduct and actions exhibited by top managers, middle managers and employees helps determine strategies for intrapreneurship. Strategies for intrapreneurship are not just either planned intentions that are created and shaped top-down, or strategies that emerge and take shape from the bottom-up. They are a result of both top-down and bottom-up processes. Actually it is a widespread assumption within the intrapreneurship literature that the balance between top-down and bottom-up processes is central to successful intrapreneurship. 'Many ventures fail because parent corporations provide the venture with inadequate support or autonomy. Paradoxically, to surmount this problem, some corporations grant ventures so much free rein that the ventures incur large losses . . . how can corporations manage these extremes by providing autonomy while maintaining damage control?' (Simon et al 1999: 145).

How to create a balance

So, creating successful intrapreneurship is about finding a balance between top-down management and bottom-up initiatives (Heinonen & Toivonen 2008) and requires elements of both control and autonomy. Traditionally, the literature has focused on how larger companies can maximise the likelihood of the new opportunity's success through a high level of autonomy and thereby providing room for bottom-up processes. However, there are several examples of how existing companies that give 'free rein' to their new projects and companies have no guarantee of the venture's success. In fact, 'free rein' can be just as fatal for a new opportunity's future as too much control through top-down processes (Block & MacMillan 1993).

However, Thornhill and Amit (2001) stress that the need for social acceptance, commitment and control from top management should be viewed over time. For the majority of new businesses the need for economic control diminishes as they mature. Social acceptance and the support of senior management will, however, remain important regardless of the age of the new venture. But there are few empirical results that run counter to this idea. Over time, some new firms experience a greater focus on financial targets whilst at the same time, senior management become less involved. These results also make sense because more financial independence often leads to greater financial accountability. Finally, a company that achieves both independence and accountability generally has less need for senior management to provide 'air cover'.

The question is: how can a balance be struck between the top-down and bottom-up processes? There are many approaches. Simon et al (1999) recommend that existing companies appoint three people to handle the new business and existing business interests when intrapreneurship is being implemented. The combination of three persons should ensure that, on the one hand, new companies have sufficient autonomy to develop. On the other hand, the combination also ensures continuous control of the new companies. The three persons are, firstly, a 'venture manager' for the new company whose task is to run the new company and ensure that it procures the resources required for it to develop. The venture manager's purpose is thus primarily to safeguard the interests of the new company. Next, a 'venture godparent' is appointed. Typically this will be a centrally placed person appointed by the existing business to help the new company in its development. The venture godparent's mission is primarily to protect the new business from existing corporate bureaucracy and ensure that the resources that are central to its development are provided. Finally, the existing company appoints a venture ombudsperson. Typically this will also be a central person in the existing business – for example, a person from the existing company's management. This person's job is primarily to handle the existing business interests. This means that the investment that the new company reflects is continually assessed against the existing corporate interests. The roles that the three people fulfil are elaborated in Table 11.1.

Intrapreneurship: top-down or bottom-up?

You have now been presented with the processes and mechanisms involved in the creation of intrapreneurship. In particular we can identify two perspectives, each of which emphasises the advisability of adopting either a top-down or bottom-up approach in order to achieve successful intrapreneurship. The two perspectives are summarised in Table 11.2.

The source of the top-down perspective is at the top level of the organisation with the senior management being assumed to initiate the process

Table 11.1 Key people in the balance between top-down and bottom-up processes

Venture manager	Venture godparent	Venture ombudsperson
Runs the venture: needs autonomy	Protects the venture from organisational resistance: helps provide autonomy	Monitors venture progress: balances need for autonomy and control
Develops innovative, high-quality products	Argues for a high level of support and against removal of support during corporate downturns	Decides markets to enter based on fit with corporation
Pursues aggressive strategies	Blocks corporate interference in day-to-day activities	Determines the number and size of ventures in the portfolio
Moulds a culture based on creativity and a bias to act	Opposes inadequate rewards and unjust punishment	Uses milestones to provide venture support and manager compensation

Source: Simon et al (1999: 157).

of intrapreneurship. The process is a controlled process, ensuring that the official goal of management's plans and strategies are met. This takes place through various administrative mechanisms, such as various 'carrot and stick' approaches, thereby ensuring that the operational level listen to the senior level and understand the purpose of the official strategy. The success associated with the process of intrapreneurship is secured through control and minimal elbow room. In contrast, the bottom-up perspective supports the idea that the operational level is the key to understanding how the process of intrapreneurship occurs. It is the employees who take the intrapreneurial initiative; the process itself is controlled by autonomous behaviour. There is room for sudden impulses and innovative opportunities. Instead of administrative mechanisms, the process is con-

Table 11.2 The paradox: Top-down or bottom-up

	Top-down	Bottom-up
Hierarchical level	Top level	Operational level
Source of initiative	Top management	Employees
The process	Controlled behaviour	Autonomous behaviour
Tool	Administrative mechanisms	Political mechanisms
Mechanisms for implementation	Control and minimal autonomy	Autonomy and minimum control

trolled through political mechanisms through which people seek to create space, resources and support for the bottom-up process in the organisation. However, the prerequisite for a bottom-up process is that management is restrained and provides space for innovation through elbow room and minimal supervision.

A theoretical interpretation

In the following we give our interpretation of the Danfoss case study in light of the theory and the paradox presented in the chapter.

The top-down perspective

According to a top-down interpretation, we highlight the following in the Danfoss story. Over the years, Danfoss has experimented with various innovative approaches at the divisional and group level. At the divisional level small R & D departments have been attached to each division supporting the objective of creating innovation, and at group level a larger central research centre has taken care of innovation. Senior management in Danfoss have been dedicated in their efforts to support innovation, but have done so in different ways. Although the top leadership, through innovation strategies and associated administrative mechanisms, have got groups of their employees to comply with the two different innovation strategies, the results have not been satisfactory. Certainly, the innovation strategy to support radical innovation through a research and development centre at group level has resulted in radical innovations, but these have been so distant from the daily production in the divisions that this innovation has been poorly used. Moreover, the innovation strategy to support the divisions' own research and development of innovations also failed. No radical innovations have found a footing here, since the divisions' desires concerning what they innovated have been too narrow to fit directly into daily production – only incremental innovations have been achieved. However, the initiatives have convinced senior management that the staff involved in the activities have respected the various initiatives they have implemented. The administrative mechanisms have thus quite properly worked on controlling employee behaviour, but innovation strategies have lacked balance between the need for simultaneous incremental and radical innovations. After a period of years collecting experiences of how incremental and radical innovations are supported, the senior management then launched a system that supported both types of innovations simultaneously. The system included the Man on the Moon competition and the organisation of a venture company and an incubator environment.

When senior management launched the Man on the Moon competition in 2004, it did so with a certain amount of scepticism. There was anxiety about the system being launched and whether it was possible to really encourage the employees to think both incrementally and radically. However, a number of administrative mechanisms were implemented to monitor and back up intended and planned actions in accordance with the official strategy to ensure a steady course and inform employees what kind of behaviour they should exhibit. After a short test of the system senior management breathed a sigh of relief. The system worked and the administrative mechanisms they had put into play to control employees' behaviour also worked successfully.

On the basis of Figure 11.5, this can be interpreted as the administrative mechanisms operating and constantly keeping employees on track. The Danfoss story can thus be seen as an example of how intrapreneurship is constantly created top-down by senior management, who have an overview of what is needed for innovations to enhance the business of the group.

The bottom-up perspective

What if we look at the Danfoss story from a bottom-up perspective? This viewpoint would stress how it is only after several years with dedicated and ambitious employees that intrapreneurship was placed on the agenda of the senior management at Danfoss. The perspective will point out that it is the employees' own initiatives and commitment which ultimately convinces senior management that they are able to innovate both incrementally as well as radically and even at the same time.

The process at Danfoss, whereby senior management experimented with innovation at group and divisional level illustrates that the senior management had been unable to find out how they had to simultaneously create fertile ground for incremental and radical innovation. In cases of imbalance in the way innovation has been implemented at Danfoss, senior management has always taken action, but primarily in a lopsided/one-sided manner as they have focused on getting their staff to develop either incremental or radical innovation. Over the years, senior management began to see, through their employees' actions, that both types of innovation can occur simultaneously and that the combination of the two types of innovation is actually very useful for Danfoss: the existing business is constantly and incrementally renewed while Danfoss also ensures potential new business areas through more radical innovations that can evolve to become revenue sources, which are just as large as the 'old' business, in the future.

It is also why the senior management at Danfoss ultimately established the Man on the Moon competition, and even went a step further, establishing a venture department and an incubator environment. Senior management expected the Man on the Moon competition to draw on all employees' innovative capabilities throughout the organisation, whether this meant incremental or radical innovation. Moreover, the senior management also organised a venture department and an incubator environment for those employees who innovated more radically and therefore needed to isolate themselves from the rest of the company's everyday work in order to test the potential of radical ideas. Whilst they may have felt that they were on slightly shaky ground as initiatives started up and before they developed, the concerns and worries of the senior management were soon dispersed when employees exhibited enthusiasm and an overwhelming desire to participate in the Man on the Moon competition and other initiatives that were organised.

On the basis of Figure 11.5, this can be interpreted as individuals or groups of people with their autonomous behaviour having a positive effect on Danfoss' current and regularly changing innovation strategy. The Danfoss story can be seen as an example of how intrapreneurship is constantly created bottom-up before senior management shapes an official and intentional strategy.

Testing the theory

Now it's your turn to understand intrapreneurship. The following exercises are for inspiration.

 **EXERCISES**

1 **Offer a simultaneous bottom-up and top-down interpretation.** What happens to the Danfoss story, if you simultaneously try to identify the bottom-up and top-down processes? Which processes are in harmony with each other and which are in conflict with each other?
2 **Other companies that cultivate intrapreneurship.** Use the Internet to find material on other existing companies that make use of intrapreneurship. Search for words like 'intrapreneur' and 'intrapreneurship'. Next, discuss how different existing companies handle intrapreneurship, and in what areas they bear similarities to or are different from the Danfoss case study.
3 **Strengths and challenges associated with intrapreneurship.** On the basis of the material you have collected, you should now list the strengths and challenges that seem to characterise existing companies when trying their hand at intrapreneurship. What strengths and challenges recur regardless of size, age and industry association? Which seem to be specific to a small group of companies? Why is it apparently so?

4 **Introduce your new knowledge to a company.** Offer an invitation to or visit an existing company that would like to either experiment with intrapreneurship, or already have experience with intrapreneurship. Present the knowledge you have gained about intrapreneurship. Discuss with the company how best to handle intrapreneurship.

LITERATURE

Bager, T., Ottósson, H. & Schott, T. (2010) 'Intrapreneurs, entrepreneurs and spin-off entrepreneurs: Similarities and differences', *International Journal of Entrepreneurship and Small Business*, 10(3), 339–358.

Birkinshaw, J., Batenburg, R.B. & Murray, G. (2002) 'Venturing to succeed', *Business Strategy Review*, 13(4), 10–17.

Block, Z. & MacMillan, I.C. (1993) *Corporate Venturing: Creating New Businesses Within the Firm*, Boston, MA: Harvard Business School Press.

Bosma, N., Wennekers, S. & Stam, E. (2010) 'Intrapreneurship – An international study', Scales Research Reports H201005, EIM Business and Policy Research.

Burgelman, R.A. (1983a) 'A process model of internal corporate venturing in the diversified major firm', *Administrative Science Quarterly*, 28(2), 223–244.

Burgelman, R.A. (1983b) 'Corporate entrepreneurship and strategic management: Insights from a process study', *Management Science*, 29(12), 1349–1364.

Clarke, A.H., Evald, M.R. & Munksgaard, K.B. (2012) 'Exploring open innovation in a comprehensive innovation setup', *International Journal of Entrepreneurship and Innovation Management.*

Collins, O.F. & Moore, D.G. (1970) *The Organization Makers*, New York: Appleton-Century-Crofts.

Day, D.L. (1994) 'Raising radicals: Different processes for championing innovative corporate ventures', *Organization Science*, 5(2), 148–172.

Dobbin, F. & Boychuk, T. (1999) 'National employment systems and job autonomy: Why job autonomy is high in the Nordic countries and low in the United States, Canada and, Australia', *Organization Studies*, 20(2), 257–291.

Elfring, T. (2005) 'Dispersed and focused corporate entrepreneurship: Ways to balance exploitation and exploration', in T. Elfring (ed.), *Corporate Entrepreneurship and Venturing*, New York: Springer, 1–21.

Evald, M.R. & Bager, T.E. (2008) 'The problem of political rivalry among venture teams in corporate incubators: A case study of network dynamics in an advanced high-tech incubator', *International Entrepreneurship and Management Journal*, 4(3), 349–369.

Guth, W.D. & Ginsberg, A. (1990) 'Guest editors' introduction: Corporate entrepreneurship', *Strategic Management Journal*, 11.

Hancock, M. & Bager, T. (2003) *Global Entrepreneurship Monitor: Denmark 2003*, Copenhagen: Børsens Forlag.

Heinonen, J. & Toivonen, J. (2008) 'Corporate entrepreneurs or silent followers', *Leadership and Organisation Development Journal*, 29(7), 583–599.

Hornsby, J.S., Naffziger, D.W., Kuratko, D.F. & Montagno, R.V. (1993) 'An interactive model of corporate entrepreneurship process', *Entrepreneurship Theory and Practice*, 17(2), 29–37.

Sharma, P. & Chrisman, J.J. (1999) 'Toward a reconciliation of the definitional issues in the field of corporate entrepreneurship', *Entrepreneurship Theory and Practice*, 23(3), 11–27.

Simon, M., Houghton, S.M. & Gurney, J. (1999) 'Succeeding at internal corporate venturing: Roles needed to balance autonomy and control', *Journal of Applied Management Studies*, 8(2), 145–159.

Thornhill, S. & Amit, R. (2001) 'A dynamic perspective of internal fit in corporate venturing', *Journal of Business Venturing*, 16(1), 25–50.

Von Hippel, E. (1977) 'Successful and failing internal corporate ventures: An empirical analysis', *Industrial Marketing Management*, 6(3), 163–174.

Zahra, S.A. (1991) 'Predictors and financial outcomes of corporate entrepreneurship: An exploratory study', *Journal of Business Venturing*, 6(4), 259–285.

12 Social entrepreneurship

In this chapter we look at entrepreneurship in another context, namely that of social entrepreneurship. As is the case when building an independent organisation or with entrepreneurship in existing firms (intrapreneurship), social entrepreneurship is about discovering or creating new opportunities and evaluating them in order to finally exploit those opportunities through organising. In that way there's not much new under the sun. However, there are also differences between the forms of entrepreneurship that we have dealt with so far and social entrepreneurship. The goal of entrepreneurship in the private commercial sector is usually to create economic value for its owners – to make profits. In social entrepreneurship the primary goal is to create better conditions for people both locally and globally, while profit is merely a means to achieve social goals. Profit does not necessarily have to be the guiding goal. In other words, the guiding vision of social entrepreneurship is social and not economic in nature – although the second situation is also conceivable. It is precisely the balance between social and economic goals we discuss in detail in this chapter.

When we talk about social entrepreneurship, we apply a broader sense of the concept 'social' than one normally uses. We don't think only about the social sector and measures aimed at the socially disadvantaged. Social entrepreneurship can be created in many different sectors, through activities in the areas of culture and leisure, through relief efforts, aid and development projects aimed at people in the third world or by creating new commercial businesses that create better conditions for vulnerable groups.

Entrepreneurship in practice

In the following you will be presented with a parable, which is a short tale that illustrates universal truth. The parable is written by Kevin Hindle and can be taught in many contexts and interpreted in many ways. In this chapter the case illustrates how the distinction between 'for profit' and 'social' entrepreneurship is not an easy one to cope with.

The following parable refers to a community of indigenous entrepreneurship in the US. In common with nearly all indigenous communities in countries where they exist (Indians in the US, Aboriginal and Torres Strait Islander in Australia, First Nations in Canada, Ainu in Japan, Saami in Scandinavia, etc.) this community will be poorly resourced, probably on marginal land and the skills and educational levels of the members of this community will be lower than the average in the mainstream, all because of the massive disadvantage conferred on indigenous communities by the negative impact of colonial history. If the parable catches your interest then go to YouTube and listen to the video case by Kevin Hindle telling you personally about the idea of The Parable of the Teepee.

CASE STUDY

The parable of the teepee

(Devised by Kevin Hindle)

The Red Entrepreneur was making what the White Business Advisor called 'good money', but the Angry Group said it was very bad.

The business, called 'Redman Teepees', stood on a well-situated block of Reservation land leased from the Tribal Government, in an area zoned for commercial activity. Here, after some curves and go-slow warnings, the highway straightened again. The well-signed gas station, convenience stores, small museum and the casino were all designed to capture the attention of passing motorists, induce them to stop and spend a bit of time and money. A lot of cars, trucks and buses did stop on the commercial strip. A lot of drivers and passengers browsed the various stores. A surprising number bought teepees from the Red Entrepreneur. They bought them mostly as 'novelty items': something to put up in the back yard for the kids during summer maybe. They weren't that expensive, they kept the weather out and they were 'a bit different'.

In the room the meeting was hotter than the air-conditioning could handle. The Elder listened patiently to the Angry Group. They spat venom at the Red Entrepreneur. The best of their speakers called the Red Entrepreneur a 'thief of our culture; a man who degrades our heritage by trivialising the collective home of our ancestors for the cheap amusement of those who stole our land and our pride. He takes what belongs to all, the knowledge, the symbolism, the majesty of the teepee and sells cheap imitations of it, keeping the money for himself. This is wrong and must be stopped'. The Good Speaker had a deep, resonant voice. His anger was genuine and his words had power. The Angry Group was loud in support and the Elder listened carefully.

When the Red Entrepreneur spoke his anger was only just under control. But out of respect for the Elder he managed.

CASE STUDY *(continued)*

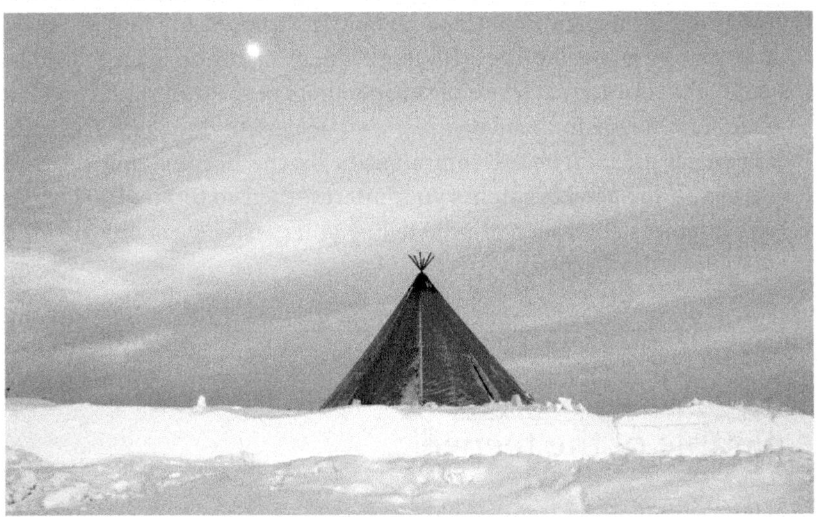

Figure 12.1 Teepees are used in very hot and cold environments

'I don't know', said the Red Entrepreneur, 'what is more contemptible in this Group: their hypocrisy or their laziness. Is it OK for our tribe to earn money from a casino that has nothing to do with the history of our people, owes its existence to a mere quirk in the White Man's law and teaches our young people only how to wear green eyeshades and deal cards, making them cardboard people? And it is not OK to keep alive the skills of teepee building, giving real jobs and real skills to real people?

Because', said the Red Entrepreneur, 'let me tell you that I do not make and I do not train people to make "cheap imitations". My teepees are authentically made, of good materials and made well. My sweat is in them. My heart is in them. They are sold at fair value. What do you do all day? Nothing. When you give back your government welfare checks and do something constructive, I will listen to you. I will hear you better when you talk less and do more. Until then, your words lack the weight of conviction. I have gone to many classes – paid for by the Tribal Government I might add – to learn business skills and technical skills. Why teach these skills if you do not want people to use them. I have built a relationship at the bank. I train young people. I pay them well. I pay rent. I pay taxes. And you say I give nothing. I give you your welfare checks'.

The Angry Group got angrier. At first the Elder's quiet voice was hard to hear. But quickly the room fell quiet. It was a strange thing many remarked upon: the Elder's quietness. It somehow made you listen. Very strange. And he spoke.

'This Angry Group fills me with sadness. Where is your true respect? Your respect for the warrior and the artisan, traditions our Brother here so proudly represents. I have seen his work. His teepees are good: not good enough but I will come to that. First, I must ask you a

CASE STUDY *(continued)*

hard question. We are people of the plains. In the days of defending our land and our nation in the old way, who was nobler: the warrior who rode to battle or the people afraid of combat who stayed by the warm fires and talked of how bad the world had become?'

The Red Entrepreneur smiled as he listened, but the Elder wiped his smile away.

'Why do you smile? You have no grounds to be smug. Be careful how you use your pride. There are good people in this group and some of their anger is justified. Though it should not be anger it should be sadness. It is sad that you do not make a full teepee; a true teepee, though our skills are such that you could. I say "our skills" because this group is right to say that the *idea* of the teepee, the *soul* of the teepee, belongs to us all. This is a story your work should tell. In our tradition, though construction was similar, every teepee was unique because, painted on it, was the life story, the life and distinctiveness of the family it housed. In this Angry Group, I know, are two superb artists. Why do you not use their skill? Offer to your customers the chance to have their life story painted on their teepees. They will like it. They will pay more. You *do* sell too cheaply and you do not share enough. What extra you make from this, put it toward strengthening the language programme that teaches our children the music of the ages. You do not speak our language and it is a shame that you do not respect this man, our Brother, who does – and speaks it majestically'.

Here the Elder directed his gaze and the gaze of all eyes to the Good Speaker.

'I have another question for you, Brother. Could you please write, for us all, the meaning of the teepee: its history, its role in the life and culture of our people? Write it well for two reasons. First, it is a great story and every buyer of a teepee must know it, understand it and, in doing so, they will come to understand us better. It is important work. Second, write it well because you will be well paid for your writing. No teepee will leave this reservation without your story, beautifully inscribed on parchment, being part of what the White Business Advisor might call the "product package". You will receive a payment every time a teepee is sold and you will deserve it because your words will add great value. They will be valuable to the buyers, enabling them to appreciate that the shelter they have bought is a noble thing, beautifully made and deep in significance as well as usefulness. They will add value to our community because every buyer will be keen to tell the story to all who see the teepee or share a night in it'.

And so it happened.

'Redman Teepees' changed its name. The White Business Advisor thought the new name, a name in the language of the people, 'made no marketing sense – and your new high-price, customization strategy will be the death of a good little business'.

The White Business Advisor was very wrong.

This was the birth – some would say re-birth – of a bigger, more profitable and growing business. The first customer of the re-born business was an Airline Pilot. He earned a lot of money and had a small property by the river where he loved to fish and invite his friends to stay. His story and his family history were carefully painted on the outside of his teepee. Where once, in the ancient days, the horse and weapons of a warrior might have been painted,

CASE STUDY *(continued)*

this man's life featured airplanes, his wife, his children and the fish that swam in the river he loved. It took a long time to finish this first teepee and it was very expensive. But the Pilot paid gladly and all summer the teepee was pitched on his land. It could be seen from a great distance. All summer it filled with a great variety of guests – who came to stay with the Pilot and his family. No-one who came into the teepee could resist reading the beautiful words inscribed on the sculpted buffalo-hide parchment which had pride of place as soon as they stepped inside. It told the story of the significance of the teepee in the life of the Tribe and how the concept of the teepee was not an old or dead thing but a vibrant tradition. A woman from Japan bought the next teepee. Artists from Japan came to join the artists of the Tribe and together their painting was truly beautiful.

Soon, from all over the world the volume of orders created the need for more artists, bigger premises, better training and all the things well known to go along with growing businesses.

The White Business Advisor was amazed. A national newspaper article and TV story ensured that demand outstripped supply dramatically. But the business will not compromise on quality. So, the opportunity will never be maximised. Once, this would have bothered the White Business Advisor but now, strangely, it does not. The Red Entrepreneur is very busy. The children's language school is flourishing. The Good Speaker has become a best-selling author. The Angry Group has changed its name to 'The Tribal Council for Cultural Dissemination through Native Enterprise'. (They have asked the Good Speaker to find them a better name and he is working on it.)

The Elder smiled. But the smile soon faded to a look of deep concern because this good story was submerged in too much tragedy. More good stories are needed urgently. Still, there had been a little learning. And that was very good.

Your immediate interpretation

What does the story tell you about social entrepreneurship? The following exercises can help you establish your understanding of what characterises the phenomenon and determine where the line between social entrepreneurship and other types of entrepreneurship may be drawn:

- Imagine that you want to start a commercial organisation, primarily with a view to making a profit. List the factors you think would be likely to drive your commitment. Then imagine that you want to start an organisation, preferably with a social purpose, and once again list the motivating factors. Are there clear differences between the two lists? Try to explain the similarities and differences.
- Look again at the teepee parable above. Discuss whether and how the

story shows social entrepreneurship as an activity that creates better conditions for people locally or globally.

- Social entrepreneurship is about creating better conditions for people through the creation or discovery of new opportunities that are then realised through the process of organising. Express your opinion as to how innovative and imaginative the story is. Is the teepee story a good illustration of how new innovative opportunities are created? Is it, in your opinion, a requirement that social opportunities must, by their nature, be innovative in order to be able to speak about social entrepreneurship?
- Do you know of other examples of social entrepreneurship than the teepee story, where individuals or groups of individuals through the creation or discovery of new opportunities have improved conditions for people locally or globally?

Theories of entrepreneurship

As mentioned, the main features of social entrepreneurship are similar to entrepreneurship that takes place in a commercial context. The main difference is that the driving force behind social entrepreneurship can often be a desire to ensure social justice, while entrepreneurship in a commercial context is directed primarily at profit (Johnson 2000).

There are a number of different perspectives on what social entrepreneurship covers. This chapter will focus on two perspectives that consider the social and the financial element of social entrepreneurship both as a means and as an end.

The first perspective on social entrepreneurship focuses on financial objectives as the ultimate goal and social objectives as a means to achieving financial goals. In other words, the focus of social entrepreneurship is to create a business and the social elements are a product in line with other commercial products. Since the ultimate goal is to create an economically sustainable and profitable organisation this kind of social entrepreneurship exists primarily in a commercial context, regardless of the social benefits produced in these organisations.

Perspective number two is primarily focused on social elements. Here, the social objectives are the ultimate goal, and any commercial exchanges take place only as a means of achieving social goals. Social entrepreneurship is therefore considered to be an activity that is fundamentally about creating a better world, and it takes place within what is often called the voluntary sector. The voluntary sector is so called because a substantial portion of the effort in these organisations comes from non-salaried workers. The voluntary sector is often referred to as the non-profit sector. In this chapter you will be introduced to social entrepreneurship in the light of the paradox:

Business or a better world?

Introduction to social entrepreneurship

Not many studies show how widespread social entrepreneurship is. A study of social entrepreneurship from the UK (Terjesen et al 2011) and one recently completed by the Global Entrepreneurship Monitor (GEM) in 2009 are the exceptions. Results from both studies are presented here to illustrate how different results for the prevalence of social entrepreneurship may be obtained, depending on how broadly the concept of social entrepreneurship is understood.

The prevalence of social entrepreneurship in Britain has been studied repeatedly (Harding & Cowling 2004; Harding 2006; Harding et al 2007). The latest survey from 2007 shows that nearly 1.2 million people in Britain were engaged in social entrepreneurship in 2005. Either the entrepreneurs were about to start a social activity (less than three months old) or led a fledgling social activity (between three and 42 months old). The start-up rate for social entrepreneurship is about half that of entrepreneurship as the building of an independent organisation (3.3 per cent of adults are active in social entrepreneurship compared with 6.1 per cent of those active in entrepreneurship to start up an independent organisation). In addition, a further 1.5 per cent of Britain's workforce operates well-established social activities which are more than 42 months old.

Social entrepreneurship thus seems to be a widespread activity in Britain. The impact of this on society is highlighted by calculations made by the UK government, which show that organisations with a social or environmental purpose account for a total turnover of £27 billion (Harding 2006).

The results from the UK indicate that social entrepreneurship in other countries can also be a major activity. The results from the GEM 2009 study show that 'the percentage of the population that is explicit about its involvement in social activities varies considerably around the world'. On average it seems that 2.8 per cent of the world's working age adult population is involved in social activities. However, the percentage ranges 'from 0.2 per cent in Malaysia to 7.6 per cent in Argentina'. The difficulty in capturing social activities is that variation is not only present across countries grouped by stages of economic development, but also by geographical region. 'Overall, very few consistent patterns of Social Entrepreneurship prevalence can be discerned at this point' (Terjesen et al 2011: 3). However, it is possible to point out that forms of social entrepreneurship 'manifest themselves in different ways – from a pure non-profit model to organizations that marry philanthropy with business models' (Terjesen et al 2011: 3). For example, the GEM study shows that it is possible to distinguish between companies which vary in the extent of their focus on social and commercial goals. Specifically, it is possible to distinguish between four categories:

> (1) Pure social entrepreneurial activity (where the individual launches or runs a social organization that has no commercial activities); (2) Pure commercial entrepreneurial activity (where the individual launches or runs a commercial organization that has no particular social goals); (3) Overlapping social and commercial entrepreneurial activity (where the individual launches or runs one and the same organization that is both commercial and social in nature); and (4) Simultaneous social and commercial entrepreneurial activity (where the individual launches or runs both a social and commercial organization which are different entities). (Terjesen et al 2011: 4)

The prevalence of social entrepreneurship reported in the UK and in GEM countries may, however, be debatable, because the volume depends greatly on the definition of social entrepreneurship used. As social entrepreneurship is an activity that has not yet been greatly explored, there is disagreement about how this phenomenon should be captured and defined. 'Social entrepreneurship . . . is not a tidy concept. Its untidiness has been argued to be a reflection of the way that the world is . . . It behooves anyone using the concept of social entrepreneurship to make clear the sense he/she attaches to it' (Peredo & McLean 2006: 64).

In spite of disagreement about the definition of social entrepreneurship, there is, however, a widespread consensus that social entrepreneurship is about achieving social goals, thereby creating better conditions for people locally or globally. However, that's as far as any agreement goes. The disagreement is about what priority the social objectives have in relation to financial objectives.

Social entrepreneurship as a continuum

Table 12.1 clarifies existing perceptions of social entrepreneurship. The continuum contains two extreme perspectives of social entrepreneurship. One defines social entrepreneurship as activities that are generally governed by social goals – a better world. The second understands social entrepreneurship as an activity in which social goals are present to some extent, but where business and therefore financial goals are the primary concern. In the centre is a third understanding of social entrepreneurship, which combines social and financial objectives in a more balanced relationship, although the social purpose is generally primary.

Creating a better world

One perspective shown in Table 12.1 strongly emphasises that it is only social goals that drive social entrepreneurship: 'At one extreme are those who hold that some goal(s) must be the "exclusive" aim of the social entrepreneur' (Peredo & McLean 2006: 59). The perspective is also expressed by Dees:

> For a social entrepreneur, the social mission is fundamental. This is a mission of social improvement that cannot be reduced to creating private benefits (financial returns or consumption benefits) for individuals. Making a profit, creating wealth, or serving the desires of customers may be part of the model, but these are means to a social end, not the end in itself. Profit is not the gauge of value creation; nor is customer satisfaction; social impact is the gauge. (Dees 1998: 5)

Table 12.1 Perceptions of social entrepreneurship – A continuum

	Priority of aims	The importance of commercial exchange and profit	Examples
A better world	The formulated, overall objective is entirely social (but subordinate financial objectives can be found)	Commercial exchange and profit are only created with the purpose of supporting the social objectives	Doctors without Borders (Médecins Sans Frontières) (www.msf.dk)
	The formulated, overall objective is primarily social	Commercial exchange and profit are created for supporting social objectives and making the business financially sustainable	The Danish Merkur Bank (www.merkur.dk)
Business	The overall objective is entirely financial (but subordinate social objectives can be found)	Commercial exchange and profit are created for making the business financially sustainable	Vestergaard Frandsen (www.vestergaard-frandsen.com)

Note: All websites last accessed 19 December 2016.

Source: Inspired by Peredo & McLean (2006: 63).

The organisation Médecins Sans Frontières (MSF, or 'Doctors Without Borders') is an example of a voluntary, non-profit organisation that is in line with Dees' definition of social entrepreneurship. MSF is a 'private, international, humanitarian organisation that provides medical relief to victims of conflicts and disasters around the world' (www.msf.org, last accessed 20 December 2016). The organisation was founded in Paris in 1971 by a group of French doctors who years earlier had worked during the civil war in Biafra in Nigeria, as well as journalists who supported the idea of independent and cross-border relief in areas that no one else could operate in. As a result of frustration at the strict rules and bureaucracy during the civil war in Nigeria and as a consequence of the doctors' feeling of being able to act, they wanted an independent organisation that could provide global relief and put the humanitarian debate about international solidarity on the agenda. In 2011 the organisation had offices in 19 countries and projects running in more than 60 countries.

At the intersection of social and financial goals

Table 12.1 is a modified version of the above perspective, which emphasises that in social entrepreneurship, social and financial goals can be combined with each other, although the social objective has primacy. It is thus wrong to limit the phenomenon of social entrepreneurship to the voluntary sector because social entrepreneurship can also be created in the commercial sector. In practice, social entrepreneurship can therefore involve social and commercial considerations at the same time, making the boundary between the two sectors 'not only vague but porous' (Peredo & McLean 2006: 61). Social entrepreneurship can thus be said to: 'blur the traditional boundaries between the public, private and non-profit sector, and emphasize hybrid models of for-profit and non-profit activities' (Johnson 2000: 1).

The argument for considering activities that combine social goals with financial objectives is that, 'a lack of financial resources or capital can constrain social entrepreneurship and restrict the ability of social entrepreneurs to create social capital' (Thompson et al 2000: 330). Therefore, the definition of social entrepreneurship is not about limiting social entrepreneurship to a specific context. Instead, this perception of social entrepreneurship focuses on whether the activities that people set in motion create better social conditions or not. A world-famous example demonstrating that it is possible to balance social and financial goals is the case of the Grameen Bank. Grameen Bank is a hybrid form of organisation, because it can be interpreted both as belonging to the for-profit sector and not-for-profit sector: The founder of Grameen Bank, Muhammad Yunus, says: 'Grameen Bank is at the forefront of a burgeoning world movement towards eradicating poverty through micro-lending: The microloan concept can be described as a simple concept that anyone can participate in, and thus make a real difference in alleviating poverty'. The Grameen Bank was founded in 1976 by Muhammad Yunus, an economics professor, with the idea that lack of capital was the primary obstacle to productive self-employment among the poor. Today, the Grameen Bank has more than 2 million members, better than 90 per cent loan recovery rates, and has been replicated in more than 40 developing and developed countries (including the United States) worldwide (McKernan 2002). The Grameen Bank does not provide credit alone; they bundle noncredit services along with credit. These noncredit services provide programme members with vocational training, organisational help, and social development inputs aimed at improving health, literacy, leadership skills and social empowerment (McKernan 2002: 94). The Grameen Bank tries to achieve a balance between the goal of creating a better world and creating a profitable economic business. The balance between social and economic goals is often called the double bottom line (Dees et al 2002: 173).

Social entrepreneurship as business

So far we have looked at two versions that agree that social objectives are more important than financial objectives in social entrepreneurship. The disagreement between them is illustrated by the degree to which they recognise the use of financial targets to meet social objectives.

However, there are also organisations where social objectives are not only blended with financial objectives, but are actually accorded a lower priority. The argument for also understanding this type of activity as a form of social entrepreneurship is that all activities which somehow improve people's social conditions are worthy of recognition, since this type of activity is ultimately instrumental in creating a better world (Austin et al 2006).

An example of a Danish organisation (which on one hand helps to create better conditions for people in the third world, but on the other hand does not hide the fact that the organisation is not an emergency aid project) is Vestergaard Frandsen. The products manufactured by Vestergaard Frandsen include, among other things, a mosquito net impregnated with chemicals that prevent the mosquito from flying and thus transmitting malaria. It is used, for example, in refugee camps. Additionally, Vestergaard Frandsen has launched a water-cleaning tool called LifeStraw. The suction tube is about 25 cm long and contains an advanced filter that purifies water. The filter makes it possible to drink from polluted rivers or ponds, which improves poor people's access to water significantly, especially in developing countries where lack of access to clean water is a major health problem. The CEO explains the balance between financial and social objectives:

> Our business is about 'doing business and doing good'. But business always comes first . . . You could say that we show that one does not preclude the other. But if the economy was of secondary importance, we might just as well hand over the keys to the Red Cross. There are plenty of problems in the world that call for more entrepreneurship. It is just a matter of rolling up our sleeves and getting started. (*The Economist*, 23 February 2007)

The emergence tradition and the opportunity tradition

So far in the discussion of social entrepreneurship we have mainly dealt with what is meant by the social element and with the weighting between the social and business elements. However, other discussions are essential. One of the things that we have discussed several times in this book is what is needed in order to describe something as entrepreneurial. In Chapter 1 we discussed two different traditions, each with their vision of what can be described as entrepreneurship: the emergence tradition and the opportunity tradition. According to the emergence tradition, the formation behaviour can be described as entrepreneurial if it relates to the formation of a new organisation, regardless of whether there is anything innovative involved. In contrast, the opportunity tradition considers behaviour to be entrepreneurial if it involves creation or discovery and exploitation of an innovative and ground-breaking opportunity, whether this results in a new organisation or not. This discussion also holds true in the theory of social entrepreneurship.

As with the emergence tradition Peredo and McLean define an activity as entrepreneurial if it is realised with social objectives in mind and results in the formation of a new organisation. 'Social entrepreneurship is sometimes understood merely as the initiation and/or management of a social enterprise' (Peredo & McLean 2006: 58).

However, some also believe that behaviour can only be described as social entrepreneurship when it involves activities of innovative social value. This thinking is equivalent to the aforementioned opportunity tradition. For example, Dees underlines that social entrepreneurs are innovative: 'They break new ground, develop new models, and pioneer new approaches . . . Those who are more innovative in their work and who create more significant social improvements will naturally be seen as more entrepreneurial. The truly Schumpeterian social entrepreneurs will significantly reform or revolutionize their industries' (Dees 1998: 4). In order for a new activity to be described as social entrepreneurship, that activity should be innovative and imaginative; it does not matter whether the activity involves the creation of a new organisation.

Social entrepreneurship: business or better world?

We have now discussed various perspectives of social entrepreneurship. These are brought together in Table 12.2.

We see from the table that the business perspective places emphasis on social entrepreneurship as an activity, which probably results in social benefits, but where the overall objective is financial; attempting to create a sustainable economic business. Here, it is the commercial exchanges which are considered crucial for success, and the social product is a product in line with other commercial products. On the other hand, the other perspective promotes the idea that the overarching objective related to social entrepreneurship is to create a better world. Financial targets are considered as ways to achieve the general social objectives. This type of social entrepreneurship belongs primarily to the voluntary sector, where the whole purpose is to create better social terms and conditions for the people. Besides these two perspectives there are innumerable variants, which to different degrees emphasise the relationship between social and financial objectives. This means that social entrepreneurship can actually take place anywhere in society. Activities

Table 12.2 The paradox: Business or better world

	Business	A better world
Primary objective	Financial	Social
Sector	The for-profit sector	The voluntary sector/non-profit sector
Motive	To create a financially sustainable business	To create a better world and better conditions for people
The relevance of commercial exchange	Crucial for the success and development of the organisation	Supporting the primary social objectives
The relevance of social output	A product similar to other commercial products	The deeper purpose of creating social entrepreneurship

do not take place solely within the voluntary sector or within the for-profit sector. There are countless hybrid forms of social entrepreneurship.

A theoretical interpretation

In the following we provide our interpretation of the teepee case that we examined at the beginning of the chapter. The Parable of the Teepee can be taught in many contexts and interpreted in many ways.

This book talks about 'the business perspective' versus 'the better world perspective', but how can this case be interpreted from respectively a business perspective and a better world perspective?

The business perspective

The teepee case fits well with the business perspective. Whatever his passion for his native heritage, The Red Entrepreneur has a world view of business that is more connected to the White Advisor and mainstream attitudes to commerce than the Good Speaker, who genuinely regards the earning of individual profits as community property – the heritage, intellectual property of the tribe's intimate connection to the teepee as a cultural artefact – as anathema.

The Angry Group's reaction to the new teepee venture can be seen as a collective protest against its for-profit and individualistic character. Moreover, it is commercialising a product loaded with collective, cultural symbolism, thereby seen by protesters as a venture which profits from something which belongs to the entire community. The Angry Group therefore sees the venture as much more aligned with white individualistic business culture than with their indigenous culture and egalitarian values.

Even after the reform it is questionable if the teepee venture becomes social. We have to presume that the Red Entrepreneur still owns and directs the teepee venture, possibly as a sole proprietor but almost certainly as a principal shareholder. From the perspective 'a better world', this does not indicate that the teepee case is an example of social entrepreneurship.

The teepee case does not specify exactly what kind of business we are talking about after the reform and, for some scholars and practitioners, this is decisive when evaluating the 'social' character of any venture: how is it organised, was its mission statement changed, how is power distributed, how are profits allocated etc.? Has the venture fundamentally turned into a 'social enterprise' or is the 'social dimension' merely rather a smart way for the Red Entrepreneur to make more money for himself?

The better world perspective

The teepee case also fits well with the better world perspective. The reformed teepee venture especially can be seen as an example of social entrepreneurship. The reformed business definitely embraces a wider range of stakeholders than the individualistic, for-profit venture as it started out. It involves more community people, enhances the knowledge level in the community, revitalises traditions, creates new relationships with outsiders and shares some of the profits with community members not actually involved in running the business.

But even before the reform there are elements that speak in favour of a better world perspective. For instance, the Red Entrepreneur defends himself by arguing that his venture has a positive community impact by employing and training young people and paying rent and taxes. He also argues that his teepees are of good quality and authentically made, paying due respect to indigenous traditions and culture. So, in his eyes it is not just an individualistic, for-profit business he is running, it is also a social enterprise in the sense that it is creating jobs and generating income in the community.

The teepee venture is definitely more socially oriented after the reform than in its previous individualistic, for-profit format. More of the community are involved and a school is supported, but the precise format is not outlined. Some would argue – this book does – that a fully-fledged social enterprise would have to consider a number of changes such as a new mission statement, specifying social goals, some kind of democratic rule, a changed ownership structure and new rules for profit distribution. In terms of overall sector position, such a deeply reformed social venture could then be said to 'belong' to the voluntary sector rather than the private for-profit sector.

For the author of this case, Kevin Hindle, the distinction between 'social' and 'individual' entrepreneurship is not seen as important. For Hindle the 'why' question – the motives and reasons for an entrepreneur starting a venture (for social good or personal profit) – is less interesting than the 'what, how and where' questions. 'What' and 'how' describe the entrepreneurial process (Hindle 2010b). 'Where' involves the vital importance of community factors to entrepreneurial process (Hindle 2010a). Whether you want to make a profit for yourself or be involved in an altruistic organisation for the benefit of others or anything in between, his argument is that you must do your best to understand the necessary mechanics of an appropriate entrepreneurial process; what will make the process 'appropriate' is a thorough understanding of the influence that community factors are likely to have on whatever it is that you want to achieve through your business. His diagnostic regime is a tool for facilitating that understanding. As such The Parable of the Teepee is a case that can be used beyond its indigenous specifics to demonstrate the highly generalisable analytical capabilities of Hindle's diagnostic framework for assessing how community factors are likely to affect any given entrepreneurial process. To further understand the 'diagnostic framework' concept go to YouTube and listen to the video case by Kevin Hindle, where the framework is summarised and applied to the teepee case.

Testing the theory

So, once again it's time for you to step into the entrepreneurial laboratory and try out another key topic in entrepreneurship, namely social entrepreneurship.

EXERCISES

1 **Media coverage of social entrepreneurship.** Find a series of articles on social entrepreneurship in various newspapers. Next, discuss the different attitudes that characterise the debate about social entrepreneurship. Which statements do you agree with and what do you disagree with? Argue why this is the case.
2 **Teepee videocase.** Watch the video case study on YouTube. The case is discussed in this chapter as an example of how social entrepreneurship is expressed; but do you agree? Is the story about social entrepreneurship? To what extent does the story meet the requirement of creating value for other people by creating or discovering a new opportunity and realising it through organising?
3 **Visit China.** In recent years, the Chinese government has invested trillions of dollars in new infrastructure, education, health and new welfare systems. Investment is expected to rise by 20–30 per cent over the coming years. China's next growth wave could create massive opportunities for many companies that can deliver solutions in the field. Your task is as follows: in light of developments in China, find a social idea from which you could benefit. Next, figure out how you will translate the idea into an opportunity, so it can form the basis for a viable organisation.

LITERATURE

Austin, J., Stevenson, H. & Wei-Skillern, J. (2006) 'Social and commercial entrepreneurship: Same, different, or both?', *Entrepreneurship Theory and Practice*, 30(1), 1–22.

Dees, J.G. (1998) 'The meaning of social entrepreneurship', available at https://entrepreneurship.duke.edu/news-item/the-meaning-of-social-entrepreneurship/ (last accessed 20 December 2016).

Dees, J.G., Emerson, J. & Economy, P. (2002) *Strategic Tools for Social Entrepreneurs: Enhancing the Performance of Your Enterprising Nonprofit*, New York: John Wiley & Sons Inc.

Harding, R. (2006) *Social Entrepreneurship Monitor: United Kingdom 2006*, Barclays, London Business School.

Harding, R. & Cowling, M. (2004) *Social Entrepreneurship Monitor: United Kingdom 2004*, Barclays, London Business School.

Harding, R., Hart, M., Jones-Evans, D. & Levie, J. (2007) *Global Entrepreneurship Monitor: United Kingdom 2007 Monitoring Report*, London Business School.

Hindle, K. (2010a) 'How community factors affect entrepreneurial process: A diagnostic framework', *Entrepreneurship and Regional Development*, December, 22(7–8), 599–647.

Hindle, K. (2010b) 'Skillful dreaming: Testing a general model of entrepreneurial process with a specific narrative of venture creation', *Entrepreneurial Narrative Theory Ethnomethodology and Reflexivity*, 1, 97–135.

Hindle, K. & Lansdowne, M. (2005) 'Brave spirits on new paths: Toward a globally relevant paradigm of Indigenous entrepreneurship research', *Journal of Small Business and Entrepreneurship*, Special Issue on Indigenous Entrepreneurship, 18(2), 131–141.

Johnson, S. (2000) 'Literature review on social entrepreneurship', White Paper, Canadian Centre for Social Entrepreneurship, University of Alberta, Canada.

McKernan, S.-M. (2002) 'The impact of microcredit programs on self-employment profits: Do noncredit program aspects matter?', *The Review of Economics and Statistics*, 84(1), 93–115.

Peredo, A.M. & McLean, M. (2006) 'Social entrepreneurship: A critical review of the concept', *Journal of World Business*, 41(1), 56–65.

Terjesen, S., Lepoutre, J., Justo, R. & Bosma, N. (2011) *Global Entrepreneurship Monitor Report on Social Entrepreneurship*', Global Entrepreneurship Research Association.

Thompson, J., Alvy, G. & Lees, A. (2000) 'Social entrepreneurship – A new look at the people and the potential', *Management Decision*, 38(5), 328–338.

13 Public entrepreneurship

So far, for the most part, we have given you the impression that entrepreneurship takes place only in the private sector, either by new businesses starting up, by existing companies cultivating intrapreneurship to reinvent themselves, or through social entrepreneurship. However, entrepreneurship also takes place in contexts other than the private sector (Drucker 1985). In the following you will become acquainted with entrepreneurship in the public sector, because new opportunities are discovered or created within public organisations and these also need to be evaluated and organised. The result could be new organisational units, new practices, products or services or innovative approaches to traditional welfare matters. Public entrepreneurship is thus created with the public sector in mind, but can be realised both by public actors and organisations and across sectors, e.g. through collaboration between private and public organisations.

One reason that many consider entrepreneurship to be highly relevant for the public sector is the scarcity of resources, and the consequent challenges public sectors typically face. Phrases such as 'leaner and fitter' (meaning, 'Do more with less, but better and cheaper') have almost become synonymous with most public sectors. Therefore, for most public sectors, rethinking welfare services, to a greater or lesser degree, is relevant.

Although public entrepreneurship shares many similarities with the kind of entrepreneurship with which you have been presented so far, with public organisations and actors also being able to act entrepreneurially you should take note of some fundamental differences. The public sector operates under a number of conditions that are specific to the public sector and it is important to be aware of these. Public organisations do not work in a free market, but operate within a political context. This means that public organisations, in addition to economic considerations, must meet the ideals of the common good, human dignity, integrity, equal rights and equal access for citizens to the welfare services that are produced. On top of these ideals, public organisations are also expected, as holders of authority, to control and supervise public use of, or private companies' production of, welfare services. This has to be done whilst at the same time being service oriented, professional, responsible and democratic.

Entrepreneurship in practice

You will now be presented with an example of public entrepreneurship. The example gives you insight into how an issue for all hospitals worldwide has been resolved by a public organisation and a private company joining together to develop a solution for the benefit of patients, different professional groups, hospital management, politicians and the private company.

CASE STUDY

Faster transport of blood samples from patients to the laboratory

(**Devised by the authors**)

When a patient is admitted to hospital, what is it that takes the most time? Is it the small prick in the arm when the nurse takes a blood sample, or is it the time it takes before the doctor receives the results of the blood test and can inform the patient of the diagnosis? Certainly patients today receive answers to such tests much faster than a few years ago, but few of them know that this is because of a special pneumatic pipeline delivery system. However, Ivan Brandslund, Head of Little Belt Hospital Laboratory Centre in Denmark, does know, because it was him who in 2007 came up with the idea for the system that has revolutionised the practice in hospitals in Denmark and other countries. This is because from the moment the test tube is filled with blood and the needle is withdrawn from the patient's arm, it is often important to get the result of the blood sample as soon as possible and this is a concern for all hospitals around the world.

Today, this pneumatic pipeline delivery system is known as Tempus600. It works by sending each small test tube directly to the laboratory for analysis, immediately after the sample is taken from the patient, in a sender robot driven by compressed air through a pipeline system.

Changing methods of analysis or transport?

The first seeds leading to the invention of the pipeline delivery system were sown much earlier. Vejle County Council introduced a common computer system for the county's institutions, and an enthusiastic Head of Department suggested that one laboratory would be enough for all of the county's hospitals, because they could now send test results electronically. Ivan, who was at this time the laboratory manager, pointed out to the Head of

CASE STUDY *(continued)*

Department that the results come from blood tests, and that blood cannot be sent electronically. However, the idea of being able to send blood electronically was implanted in Ivan's head.

For years, attempts had been made to try to obtain faster blood test results by adjusting the methods of analysis in the laboratory. What no one had thought of was changing the process of transporting the blood samples from where they are taken from the patient to the laboratory where bio-analysts are ready to analyse them. There would seem to be much greater benefit derived from changing the transport method than from changing the methods of analysis. This is because the transport of samples had always been a process of manual collection and transportation of the small test tubes of blood, which is relatively time consuming. Before the system was invented, a bio-analyst had to collect the small tube from the patient and deliver it to the laboratory. So that he or she wasn't constantly shuttling between departments and the laboratory, the bio-analyst would wait until there were plenty of samples to collect, but this meant that he or she would end up delivering a good deal of blood on each trip, and this delayed the analysis of each sample.

In 2009, the Region of Southern Denmark announced that it would establish the first joint emergency ward, and Ivan could see that the need for ever-faster test results would increase. At this point Ivan began working seriously on the idea of sending blood through a pipe delivery system: 'Actually, why not, I thought. Maybe we could actually send small test tubes in a kind of pneumatic system', says Ivan. He therefore tried to put the idea to different partners, but without success.

After a lecture, where Ivan had again spoken favourably of the idea of sending blood samples through pipelines, a man, Finn Dyhre Hansen, tapped him on the shoulder. He was the chairman of a small company that had developed a system to transport yoghurt through pipelines. Perhaps this company could help in implementing Ivan's idea for a pneumatic system? Ivan took the bait and talks about his first impressions of the private enterprise: 'So, I go to Bording to speak with the director of FagTek Ltd., as the company was called then (today the company is called Timedico Ltd.). It was a shabby factory building on a barren site, and I nearly turned around. However, director Daniel Blak liked the idea, so I gave it a try'.

Daniel Blak, a trained toolmaker and inventor of the Tempus600 system says: 'In 2008 when I made contact with Ivan, we already produced transport systems for the food industry, e.g. for Danone's bottled production. Originally we worked with ventilation, but a project for Danone led us to use air in a whole new way'. The assignment was to transport small plastic bottles of yogurt around the French food giant's factory in Valencia, and the system was the beginning of the firm Timedico. Based on this technology and know-how, Daniel and his partner believed that they could help Ivan solve the challenge of reducing transportation time, and so the partners began what was initially a financially free cooperation, purely based on mutual interests. After Timedico sought the first patents in 2008, they began serious development of the system that transports blood from hospitals' various departments to the laboratory.

CASE STUDY *(continued)*

Specifically, one of the coal-black blacksmith workshops that had been used in the ventilation department of the factory was transformed into a snow-white, bright room, which was to serve as a reminder of the sterile hallways and rooms in a hospital. Then Timedico constructed a test apparatus with a garden hose and blew some empty tubes through it. Little Belt Hospital was involved in several parts of the development, and as the system had to be tested, the hospital laboratory technicians contributed with blood tests, which were subsequently circulated along the ceiling in a thin plastic tube. Following this, the blood was tested to check whether it had been damaged. 'It went well with one pipe at a time, but we had to be able to run many pipes, and it was complicated. Nevertheless, it succeeded, and later in 2009 we set up the first system for testing in the Emergency Department at Kolding Hospital', says Ivan.

Noticeable reduced response time

Since then, the pneumatic pipe system has reduced the response time of the samples from about two-and-a-half hours to less than half an hour for urgent samples. The time saved did not happen overnight, partly because hospital staff had to adjust to a new workflow and send each sample off immediately after it was taken, and rounds were moved to take advantage of the shorter response time test results.

Previously, doctors and nurses were accustomed to the result of a blood sample taken within rounds in the morning coming back around noon. Now the analysis was ready during the rounds. This means that the patient can be treated and possibly discharged the same day if the treatment is working, or patients can be treated several times in the same day. The reduced response time has particularly improved the patients' comfort, since they no longer have to wait so long to get answers as to what is wrong. At the same time the patients progress faster and more efficiently through their treatment, saving bed days and eventually money for public hospitals. 'That's something the politicians understand', says Daniel Blak.

The system has also successfully modified workflows as the employees could see the benefit in using the system. For example, at Odense University Hospital the time spent by bio-analysts in collecting and delivering the samples has been reduced by 80 per cent, which means that they can use their educational expertise in blood analysis instead of transporting blood through the corridors.

With the pipe delivery system, samples are sent individually and immediately from each patient when they are taken, ensuring a faster turnaround time. At the same time the system saves the troublesome packing of the small glass tube, which earlier pipe delivery systems necessitated, because air transport is gentle and safe. 'In acute tests, we can now provide answers to the test in less than 30 minutes from the collection. Sub-acute tests we complete in a maximum of 40 minutes, and for the other samples we provide a response within 60 minutes. Previously it took between one-and-a-half to three hours', says laboratory manager Ivan Brandsund.

CASE STUDY *(continued)*

Tempus600 is a bestseller worldwide

Today, the system has spread, not only to almost all Danish hospitals, but also to hospitals in other countries, such as Norway, Finland, Germany, Holland, China, Taiwan, Kuwait, Israel, Sweden, England, Thailand, Saudi Arabia and South Korea. So it has grown rapidly since the idea was evaluated and organised. Today subcontractors in Denmark manufacture the Tempus600 system, so the company only consists of 13 employees who are mainly engaged in development and sales. And the sales side has experienced something of an unexpected bonus through formal collaboration with large companies such as Siemens, Roche, Abbott and Symex manufacturing machinery for the analysis of blood samples. Moreover, these four companies now market their analysis products as being compatible with Tempus600.

'It is obviously very valuable for us to gain exposure with such large and well-known companies. Our challenge is that we do not have competitors, and that means that there are still many hospital employees who do not know of the existence of a transport system for blood tests and other clinical samples', says Daniel Blak.

Figure 13.1 Tempus600

Your immediate interpretation

Based on the story, you should now focus on the impression you have achieved of public entrepreneurship. Prepare yourself to answer the following three exercises on the basis of your immediate understanding:

- Think about the challenges that the story addresses. Write down what diverse challenges affect the many different groups of actors who benefit from the reduction in transportation time from blood sampling to the laboratory. Who are the actors and what are the challenges that characterise them?
- Reflect on what generally seems to characterise entrepreneurship in the public, as opposed to the private sector. How is it perceived to be entrepreneurial in the public versus private sector, and do these views contradict each other, or is there an opportunity to reconcile perceptions?
- Reflect next on your first impressions of public entrepreneurship. Based on these, identify three recommendations you would make to government organisations who wish to make use of entrepreneurship, and to private companies who want to enter into cooperation with government organisations to develop welfare solutions – what should they be aware of?

Theories of public entrepreneurship

Before we continue with what we know about public entrepreneurship, we should first explain how public entrepreneurship can be understood. Public entrepreneurship can quite simply be defined as 'the generation of a novel or innovative idea and the design and implementation of the innovative idea into public sector practice' (Roberts 1992: 56). This way of defining public entrepreneurship is in line with the opportunity tradition we presented in Chapter 1, where entrepreneurship involves the creation of new targets, new products or new means–end chains. Moreover, the terms generation, design and implementation are identifiable because they are close to all the elements we presented as being constituent parts of the entrepreneurial process – namely, the terms opportunity emergence, evaluation and organising. However, be aware that the term 'design' in this context is not what has been presented in Chapter 10 – for now design should only be understood as translating an idea into an opportunity.

Another good idea for making a start, despite the fact that the area is still at the very early stage of development, is to divide the sparse literature available on public entrepreneurship into two main perspectives. One of the perspectives understands public entrepreneurship as activities initiated and operated within public organisations. Public actors guide the activities with minimal contributions from outsiders, because it is the public policymakers, managers and employees who have the technical, administrative and political expertise, along with insight into how the public system works. The prevailing belief from this perspective is in the sovereignty of the public sector and hierarchical management. Public entrepreneurship is therefore undertaken primarily in enclosed developments that limit the involvement of users or external partners. This we call the closed perspective of public entrepreneurship.

The second perspective takes the line that public entrepreneurship is best created by opening up knowledge and skills across government organisations and professional groups, or other sectors such as the private or voluntary sectors. Also, citizens are considered to provide valuable knowledge that can encourage new and better types of services or ways of organising. Heterogeneous fields of knowledge and skills help to ensure that more relevant information can be combined, and that challenges can be addressed from many different angles. Combining heterogeneous knowledge is often necessary if initiated changes are to create value not only for public organisations and their employees, but also more widely for the citizens and users of public welfare. The open approach believes that social management is a complex process that should involve numerous stakeholders – both external and internal. This perspective we will call the open perspective. In this chapter, you will therefore discuss public entrepreneurship in light of the paradox:

Closed or open?

The public sector's characteristics in Western countries

So what is the public sector really all about? Basically, you may want to distinguish between three models in regard to the organisation and financing of social services. These are ideal types, which you will not often find, empirically, in their pure form. The characteristics of the three models reflect historical traditions and the political struggle concerning welfare (Esping-Andersen 1996). The models are:

- the continental model;
- the liberal model; and
- the Scandinavian model.

The continental model is especially prevalent in Central Europe, in countries such as Germany and France. The ideology is conservative. This model is also referred to as the insurance model. The aim is to insure people on the basis of merit, i.e. it guarantees citizens' welfare through compulsory insurance schemes often linked to the labour market. The family is considered to have a central role when social problems have to be solved and the state plays a much smaller role. The liberal model is found in countries where there are strong traditions of limited government influence on civil society, such as the United States and to some extent United Kingdom. The ideology is liberalism, and the idea behind it all is that you make your own luck, so that the strong individual manages by him- or herself. Welfare benefits are only for the very weakest in society, and proof of poverty, through budgets, pay slips or other evidence is often a requirement. The Scandinavian model is most developed in the Nordic countries such as Denmark, Norway and Sweden. The ideology is more socialist. Its purpose is to insure everyone in society. It is based on high taxes and extensive redistribution through high transfer payments. The social benefits are universal and not selective, so that entitlement to the benefits is the same for all, regardless of income or preferences.

Regardless of which welfare model is adopted, the public sector, especially in Western countries, constitutes a large share of the national accounts (GDP). This is seen in Figure 13.2.

What also characterises most Western countries that have an extensive public sector is that the sector typically operates in the following areas: 1) the supply of services (typically in areas such as health, education, social care as elderly

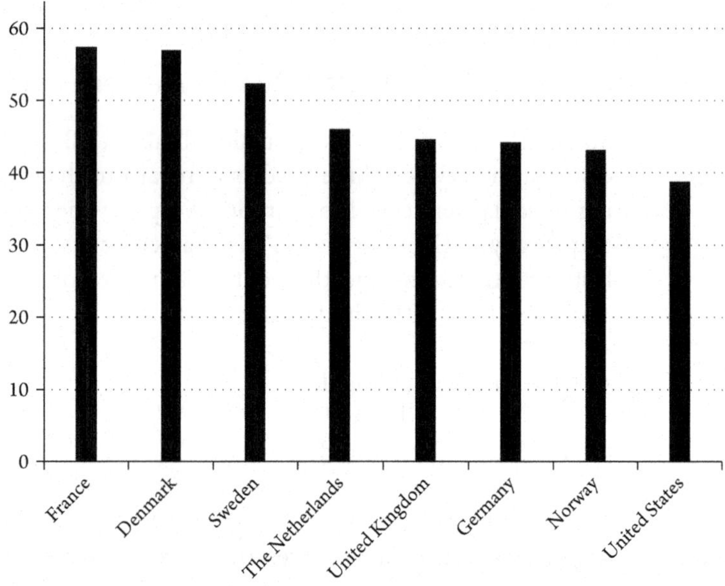

Source: OECD.

Figure 13.2 Public spending by GDP in 2013 in selected countries (%)

care and childcare, public transport, justice [police and courts], defence, foreign service and central and local administration), 2) planning and management (infrastructure, city and housing, business and competitive conditions, etc.), 3) the disbursement of transfer payments to households and subsidies to businesses, 4) tax collection and 5) the operation of publicly owned enterprises (water, electricity, public television and radio, infrastructure etc.).

To get a little closer to what characterises the public sector, we compare the public sector with the private sector. The comparison, presented below, gives you an insight into the fundamental differences between the two sectors.

Differences between the private and public sectors

Before you are presented with a number of fundamental differences between the public and private sectors (Table 13.1), it is important to understand that the differences can be used both as arguments for and against the respective closed and open perspective. However, please remember that we are simplifying reality here; the boundaries between sectors are far from always clear (Rainey & Bozeman 2000).

The difference between public and private organisations or actors becomes especially evident when partners cooperate with each other. Here, it is often clear that the actors may have different goals, values and strategies for collaborations undertaken with each other, while the parties also may want different results from working together. So the argument for establishing partnerships with each other, despite these potential differences, is the acquisition of heterogeneous knowledge that can more effectively solve a number of welfare challenges.

However, to get one step closer to an understanding of why entrepreneurship is increasingly used in the public sector, you need to know more about how the public sector operates today, especially in Western countries. We mention this because when public entrepreneurship first entered the political landscape there was a heated debate about the potential consequences of public entrepreneurship for democracy. For example, it was pointed out that there could be conflicts between:

- the need for entrepreneurial autonomy vs democratic accountability;
- the need for entrepreneurial secrecy vs democratic openness;
- the need for entrepreneurial risk taking vs democratic stewardship; or
- the need for entrepreneurial vision vs democracy's need for citizens' input and participation.

Table 13.1 Differences between the public and private sectors

	Private actors (firms)	Public actors (professions, politicians & users)
Goal	*Product & profit* Consistent & clear goal Typically low level of goal conflict	*Many, depending on the different actor groups* Typically high level of goal conflict
Incentives	*Mainly economic* Desire for competitive advantage Desire to limit knowledge sharing	*Many, social & political* Desire to improve the quality of welfare products and services, and to generate them more efficiently Desire for knowledge sharing
Output horizons	*Preference for quick results* Short-sighted goals Market-sensitive goals	*Preference for secure results* Long-sighted goals The process may also be a goal
Risk profiles	*Preference for low-risk projects* Appetite for risk is low Wants assurance about output	*Open to projects with high level of risk* Appetite for risk is relatively high Open to uncertainty about output
Decision-making speed	*Fast* Route to decision-making often short & unambiguous Tradition for involving few actors in decision-making and often closed	*Slow* Route to decision-making often long & complex Need for and tradition of involvement of many actors in decision-making and often open for input
Organisation types	*Responsive* Customer driven Market-oriented innovation	*Rights and statutory* Technology, expert, citizen & politician driven System-oriented performance management

Source: Inspired by Kearney et al (2008).

Scepticism towards public entrepreneurship hung, and hangs to this day, on the idea that entrepreneurship can be understood as being in conflict with basic democratic values (Bellone & Goerl 1992). Therefore, only a few decades ago, utilisation of entrepreneurship in the public sector was not as legitimate as it is, increasingly, today. So let's look at why entrepreneurship is increasingly used in the public sector.

Scarce financial resources call for entrepreneurship

We began the chapter by explaining that limited resources challenge the public sector in many countries. The challenge is linked to the fact that the public sector must, at the same time, meet constrained budgetary demands as well as increased demands for services and increasing levels of professionalisation and specialisation (Borins 2002), and this can be done by improving the entrepreneurial competence of the public sector. By increasing the public sector's entrepreneurial skills, the goal is to improve existing solutions and develop new ones. For example, it is desirable in order to obtain:

- better service and greater satisfaction with public services;
- better working conditions for public employees – through improved work processes, communication and management;
- efficiency and reduced public costs;
- more, and alternative, welfare services – as the population structure changes and better treatment becomes available;
- increased professionalisation and specialisation in treatments and services.

So, although scarce financial resources seem to be a basic situation for many public sectors today, it is hoped that entrepreneurship in the public sector can create continuous improvement that allows high-quality and improved welfare services. However, the way in which entrepreneurship is performed is different – this we look at in the following.

New ways to understand the public sector today

Public sectors are no longer what they were just 30 years ago; they have evolved like so much else. Many people still perhaps understand the public sector in line with the Weberian hierarchical bureaucracy (also called the 'old public administration'), which aims to ensure legal certainty, professional administration, manageability, reliability and separation between administration and politics, but this is not the whole story.

The public sector is currently characterised by several movements. In particular, 'new public management' (NPM) reforms have left their mark on the public sector and how public entrepreneurship is perceived. It is often said that it was the English scientist Christopher Hood who launched the concept of new public management in 1991 (Hood 1991). Hood used the concept to put into words the changes and modernisation of the public sector that occurred throughout the world from the early 1980s and which continue to affect public administrations today. The purpose of NPM is to adopt a kind of market-based system within the public sector in order to achieve more cost-effective management. The solution is thus increased competition, customer orientation and strategic management. A consequence of this is, for example, to see citizens as users or customers. In addition, NPM reforms meant that the government cautiously opened up more and more forms of cooperation with private companies. However, typically this is in the form of a supplier–customer relationship where the public sector continues to exercise a high degree of control and management. Moreover, it is often only in cases where the private sector can provide a specific known solution that the public sector opens up for cooperation. So although NPM has a different view of the environment when compared to how the public sector is characterised under the Weberian tradition, the NPM is still dominated by a relatively closed perspective of how public entrepreneurship can be created efficiently. Public entrepreneurship's tolerant look forward to new thinking is based on public control and management.

Apart from NPM, a different movement often expressed as a shift 'from government to governance, has also inspired the public sector' (Osborne 2010). 'Government' refers, here, to the formal institutions of government, while 'governance' refers to the complex and often interactive processes through which the economy and society are controlled. This movement has been given the name 'new public governance' (NPG). The purpose here is to try to promote trust-based management, interdisciplinary collaboration and active citizenship, while at the same time strengthening politicians' political leadership.

A more open and mutual interaction between the public sector and its environment is at play in NPG. In many respects, it provides opposition to NPM, as NPG calls on networked forms of cooperation, under which the controlling and steering role of the public sector is more like the role of a mutual value-adding party. So, there is a more interdependent relationship between public organisations and the external partners with which they collaborate. NPG is thus concerned with external collaboration as opposed to the intra-organisational approach and the input and output focus of NPM (Hodge & Greve 2010). In NPG citizens are thus not only considered to be recipients of a product (i.e. customers), but rather as co-producers of welfare benefits, as collaborators. The same holds true for private companies, as the public increasingly recognises the need to access the technological skills and know-how held by companies. Co-creation between the public sector and its environment is therefore considered to be a premise for creating a more efficient public sector. Through NPG the public sector can be included in

Table 13.2 NPM versus NPG

	NPM	NPG
Public employees	Public employees' own interest to be kept in check via control	Public employees' service motivation should be promoted through trust
The problem	The problem is the government monopoly on service	The problem is the complexity of what the public sector shall carry out
The solution	The solution is public–private competition via privatisation and contracting out	The solution is public–private collaboration through networks and partnerships
Citizens	Citizens are seen as customers	Citizens and volunteers are seen as co-producers of welfare
Managerial focus	Management of own employees with a focus on resources and performance	Management of interdisciplinary collaboration focused on process and effects
Politicians	Politicians seen as a board of directors that sets goals and parameters	Politicians are seen as political leaders of society
The goal	The goal is to increase efficiency through rationalisation	The goal is to promote efficiency and quality through innovation

Source: Inspired by Diefenbach (2011) and Ansell & Torfing (2014).

cross-sector collaboration, partnerships, and other types of relationships between relevant external actors. The aim with NPG is to contribute to the development and diffusion of innovation in public policies and services (Sørensen & Torfing 2012). Fundamental differences between NPM and NPG are illustrated in Table 13.2.

A number of movements have thus made their appearance in recent decades, which has led the public sector from a primarily closed approach to a more open, network-oriented approach, based on interaction and co-creation with external organisations and stakeholders (Sørensen & Torfing 2012). At present, there are a series of movements that figure in the public sector at the same time, but which attain different levels of dominance depending on the situation and the task at any given time. Thus, there are often great differences in how public organisations, politicians, managers or employees act as they continue to be heavily inspired by a view of the public sector based on NPM thinking, while others, depending on the situation, vacillate between several of the approaches. It is then complex to be a public politician, manager or employee today, with different views on the role of industry and an environment that may vary from situation to situation or task to task.

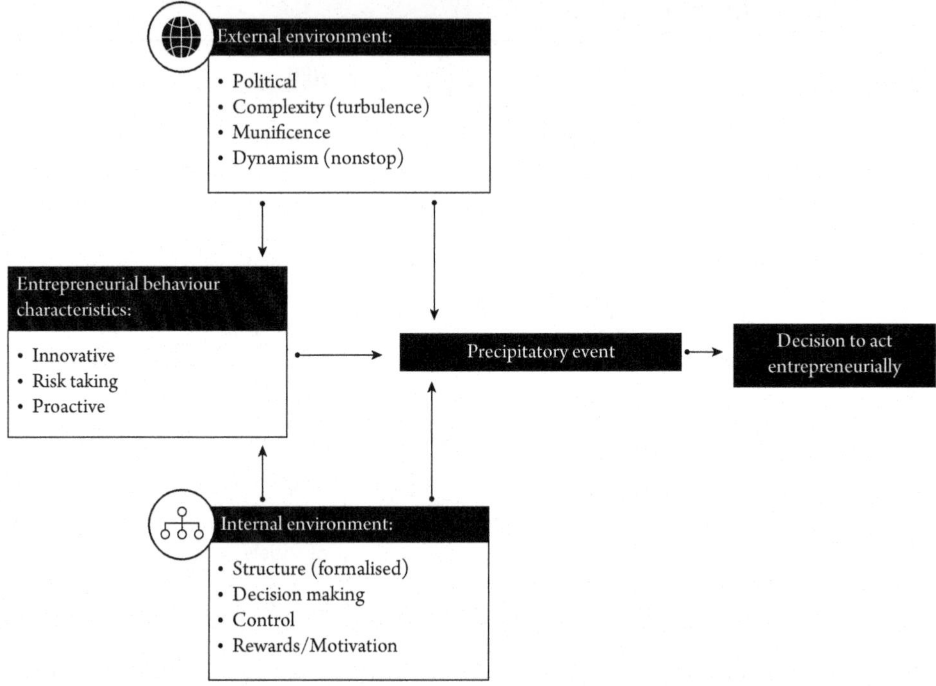

Source: Inspired by the conceptual model by Kearney et al (2008).

Figure 13.3 The public entrepreneurial process

Public sector entrepreneurship antecedents

So, what is it that drives public entrepreneurship? There are three key influences: 1) the external environment with which the public sector is associated, 2) the internal environment within which the public sector operates and 3) the entrepreneurial behaviour of internal and external stakeholders. Figure 13.3 illustrates these.

Often, the external environment for public organisations is relatively turbulent. Firstly, they are highly political, because the interest groups, lobbyists, opinions leaders and opposition politicians, etc. all attempt to influence and generate knowledge that is in favour of their own interests. However, these stakeholders are only a fraction of the other stakeholders that surround the public sector. Civil society (such as citizens, patients, volunteers and others) and the market (such as private organisations and NGOs) are also part of the public sector environment. Therefore, public sector environments are often perceived as complex and also dynamic. New technologies make their entrance, new political and regulatory changes occur, and social-demographic changes exert influence, such as urbanisation, population dynamics and educational infrastructure. All influence the action space of the various public organisations and actors.

The public sector's internal environment, i.e. the way the public sector is organised can also affect where and how many opportunities can be created or occur. Often the structure of public organisations is highly formalised to meet democratic requirements, such as accountability and openness. This also applies to decision-making processes, which are often long and complex, because many interests have to be considered. Checks are therefore also relatively high in many organisations. Hierarchical management and control is likely to ensure that the public services are provided in accordance with the regulations. Reward and motivation are often connected differently than in private companies. The reward is often not financially dependent, and many public actors can be motivated to maintain a zero-fault culture, because the fulfilment of laws and regulations equate to democratic values.

Additionally, actors who are in the government or external organisations demonstrate entrepreneurial behaviour that can be crucial to whether the opportunities that are discovered or created are taken (Morris & Jones 1999). The innovative readiness an organisation's stakeholders exhibit can easily be explained by an organisation's skills and willingness to engage in entrepreneurial processes, activities and collaborations. Risk taking involves a readiness to commit resources to address opportunities. It is also this dimension that clearly shows the differences in behaviour in the public versus private sector. Whilst those in the private sector may go bankrupt, there are other things at stake in the public sector: programmes and organisational units can be shut down, budgets can be cut and the quality of the services can be reduced, or can be completely removed (Morris et al 2008). To act proactively also points to the organisations' actors being action oriented, focused on implementing ideas, able to interpret rules, exhibiting adaptability, having networking capabilities and the ability to utilise the resources and expectations that exist so that challenges of a different nature can be overcome (Currie et al 2008).

The precipitatory event provides just the impetus to organisations and actors to behave entrepreneurially when a series of other factors contribute positively to launching and exhibiting this behaviour and way of thinking. Impetus that promotes or provokes actors or organisations to discover or create public entrepreneurship typically arises from the unclear and inconsistent goals inherent in the public sector (Ramamurti 1986). Unclear and inconsistent objectives thereby generate opportunities to exercise discretion and promote opportunities for flexibility. Sadler (2000) presents a number of other factors that can influence impetus: for example, 1) cohesive work groups, 2) participative decision-making, or 3) perceived competition.

However, apart from these antecedents, public organisations also run into other challenges when trying to evaluate and organise the opportunities generated. This is not shown in Figure 13.3, but they are nonetheless worth knowing about. For example, Borins (2001) undertook a study of various barriers that are created when ideas are to be implemented in the public system. At least three different types of barriers in the implementation process can be identified:

- barriers arising within public organisations, such as hostile attitudes, turf wars, difficulty in coordinating organisations, logistical problems, difficulty in maintaining the enthusiasm of programme staff, difficulty in introducing new technology, union opposition, middle management resistance and public sector opposition to entrepreneurial action;
- barriers arising in the political part of the public sector, e.g. inadequate funding or resources, law-making and regulatory constraints and political opposition;
- barriers existing in the external environment, such as when doubts are planted by civil society and the market, on the effectiveness of a particular programme, difficulty in reaching the programme's target group, opposition by those affected in the private sector (entities that would experience increased competition) and general public opposition or scepticism.

Even during the course of implementing public entrepreneurship, the internal and external environments continue to exert influence, which can make public entrepreneurship a challenging activity.

In the following, we summarise the discussions that characterise the closed and open perspectives of public entrepreneurship, to sharpen your understanding of the 'closed–open' paradox (Figure 13.4).

Closed perspective of public entrepreneurship

For the most part, research in public entrepreneurship within the closed perspective has been preoccupied with how individuals, so-called 'grand, forceful entrepreneurs', have challenged the rules and launched innovations for the benefit of public interest (Bernier & Hafsi 2007). The individual's performance is often emphasised, because when we experience a change that

Figure 13.4 Closed versus open approach to public entrepreneurship

has happened against all the odds we tend to be fascinated by the idea of the individual entrepreneur who single-handedly manages to transform a vague vision into success, even though the odds are against the enterprise.

Therefore, research into public entrepreneurship has also focused on identifying different types of such individuals. For example, four main types of public entrepreneur can be identified (Roberts 1992), which highlights the various levels at which public entrepreneurship can take place:

- Political entrepreneurs (politicians) hold elected leadership positions in government.
- Executive entrepreneurs (top and middle managers) hold leadership positions without having been elected, and face administrative responsibility.
- Service entrepreneurs (front-line managers/staff) are not elected, nor do they assume leadership, but face administrative responsibilities.
- Policy entrepreneurs (outsiders such as opinion leaders) – in contrast to the other three types – do not hold formal positions in government.

However, within the closed perspective we see a tendency for scholars to begin orienting themselves toward the kind of public entrepreneurship that is more systemic (Bernier & Hafsi 2007). The argument for moving from the individual to the systemic level is essentially as follows. In general, when the environment is homogeneous and stable, public entrepreneurship is often expressed in the classical form, where it is the individual and the exceptional that play the leading role (Dobell 1989). When the environment is more heterogeneous and turbulent, public entrepreneurship often manifests itself in a more systemic way. This means that public entrepreneurship is not limited to isolated individuals, but rather includes a large number of people, affects a large segment of the organisation's operations, and becomes institutionalised (Bernier & Hafsi 2007).

This understanding is consistent with entrepreneurship in general and is starting to be recognised as being a collective phenomenon. Some entrepreneurship researchers even go so far as to write that entrepreneurship in general is recognised as a collective rather than a singular activity (see, e.g., Wright & Vanaelst 2009, who are interested in entrepreneurial teams). When entrepreneurship is considered to be a systemic issue it becomes close to the mechanisms we see being utilised in intrapreneurship. There is a need for the top-down and bottom-up processes to be linked and coordinated. This we have already discussed in Chapter 11.

Open perspective of public entrepreneurship

The second perspective that characterises research in public entrepreneurship moves from researchers being primarily concerned with what creates entrepreneurship within public organisations, to considering forms of public entrepreneurship that take place across multiple sectors, organisations and actors. Traditionally, public entrepreneurship has been typically seen as processes and activities taking place within the walls of public institutions, either through the so-called heroic entrepreneurs or via systemic entrepreneurship. Focus on the spillovers of private actions into the public domain that have occurred, for instance through social entrepreneurship, has been limited (Klein et al 2010). However, in recent literature in the field, there is an increased attention to the collective efforts occurring inter-organisationally and cross-sectorally between public and private organisations. Thus, public entrepreneurship is also beginning to be perceived as activities and processes that take shape between different sectors. Whilst some researchers look, for the most part, at interaction and co-creation from the public side, others primarily investigate cooperation from the private sector (Miles et al 2006; Hartley et al 2013), but both

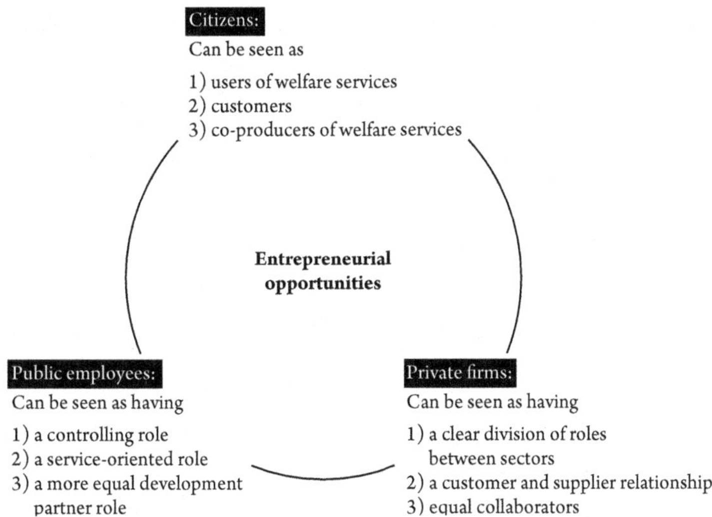

Figure 13.5 New roles for public employees, citizens and private firm actors

contribute with a common understanding of collaboration taking place inter-organisationally.

When talk turns to public entrepreneurship, it becomes more and more common to think in terms of three actors, consisting of public organisations, citizens and private companies. Interplay between these three parties is often seen as being necessary to improve the existing welfare solutions and develop new ones. This is known as the 'triple bottom line'. Figure 13.5 shows the diversity of roles that public officials, citizens and private companies may play – but take particular note of point 3 in each of the large circles that characterise the open perspective of public entrepreneurship.

Specifically, it is the idea that out of the interaction between the three bottom lines must be a number of advantages. For the public organisations there must be a far better use of the few resources the government has to create a lasting and sustainable organisation, for the citizens, quality public welfare services must be created, and for private companies there must be more growth and economic benefits. The idea is that when these three aspects are considered together, new resources are brought into play that enhance the development of new or existing welfare solutions. It can also be said that the development of new welfare solutions can flourish when all parties are on board – where each partner's contribution is limited. However, to open up a dialogue and for co-creation purposes, the different parties have to be aware of the new roles they must adopt.

Public entrepreneurship: closed or open perspective?

You have now been presented with what encourages and discourages public entrepreneurship. In particular we have identified two perspectives concerning the achievement of successful public entrepreneurship: closed and open.

The closed perspective understands public entrepreneurship as processes and activities initiated and operated within public organisations. Public actors guide the activities with minimal contributions from outside, because it is the public policy-makers, managers and employees who have the technical, administrative and political expertise and insight into how the public system works. This perspective highlights the sovereignty of the public sector and hierarchical management. Public entrepreneurship is therefore primarily undertaken in bounded developments that limit the involvement of users or external partners.

On the other hand, the open perspective emphasises the massive benefits that can exist by opening up knowledge and skills across government organisations and professional groups, or other sectors such as the private and voluntary sector or civil society. Heterogeneous knowledge and skills are therefore considered to be helpful in ensuring that more relevant information can be combined and welfare challenges can be addressed from many different angles. Therefore, there is also, in the open approach, a belief that social management is a complex process that should involve a number of stakeholders – both external and internal. These two perspectives are summarised in Table 13.3.

In most cases you should bear in mind that you will not find these pure perspectives when you encounter public entrepreneurship. Rather, you will probably experience a mix of perspectives, either from situation to situation or depending on who you are in dialogue with.

A theoretical interpretation

In the following we give our interpretation of the case with which we started the chapter. The case is interpreted in the light of the theory and the paradox that has been presented in the chapter.

The closed perspective

The pipe delivery system can be interpreted as a reality, because of a doctor's entrepreneurial setting, professional expertise and organisational

Table 13.3 The paradox: Closed versus open

	Closed	Open
Where does public entrepreneurship take place?	In-house between public sector management, employees and politicians	Across the sectors, organisations or groups of actors
Source of initiative	Public actors and organisations as well as experts (political, administrative or professional)	A diversity of users and organisations from different sectors
Type of solution	Solutions meet the public sector's method of functioning and thus democracy's fundamental premises	Ownership of solutions from many heterogeneous partners with extensive use of the voluntary principle
The process	Heavily influenced by professional in-house experts and politicians who see reality from their own professional viewpoint	Influenced by multiple heterogeneous sources of knowledge and is considered open to continual negotiation and accommodation between the parties
Type of knowledge	Expert knowledge (political, administrative and technical)	Tacit knowledge, often linked to very local situations and contexts

knowledge. The Head of Department challenges the existing rules and standards at the hospital and achieves success with his resourcefulness precisely because he possesses internal knowledge of how the public system works and can create professional coalitions across internal groups, such as nurses and laboratory staff and hospital management. The private company's role on the other hand, is minimal and they are involved only to the extent necessary. Moreover, their involvement is within a controlled environment where the primary control is retained by the public hospital and the doctor, so the public interest can be achieved.

Safeguarding of the public interest is underpinned by the documentation process, which is important for the Head of Department and the other professional personnel and hospital management. The solution can only be used when sufficient evidence is provided, and certainly after repeated control tests have taken place. It's for this reason that the system was only gradually introduced at the hospital. The pipe delivery system was installed on a step-by-step basis, so that any faults could be quickly detected and re-adjustments made. It was also important in the implementation phase that work routines, based on professional considerations were met optimally.

The entrepreneurial process is thus initiated and driven primarily by the public sector itself, as public actors guide the activities with minimal contributions from outside. The closed development process is preferred, because management and control can be established on the basis of professional expertise and insight into how the public system works. There is a belief in the sovereignty of the public sector and in hierarchical management. From the closed perspective, we see that the 'heroic entrepreneur', i.e. the Head of Department, was able to spot an opportunity, and against strong odds was thinking outside the box by beginning to question how blood tests were traditionally handled. At the same time, through evaluation and progressive organisation, he manages to implement the possibility systemically across several professional groups. The expectations of the public organisations, that they practice responsible authority in controlling and supervising the production of welfare benefits, while simultaneously being service oriented, professional, responsible and democratic, are fully met in the story.

The open perspective

The pipe delivery system came into being because a doctor and the other staff at the hospital were open to new knowledge and insights from an outside party. A more open approach to the development of the pipe delivery system gained momentum after the laboratory manager Ivan realised, over a long period of time, that the hospital's professional staff could not solve the various problems associated with treatment of blood samples. These problems led to patients receiving sub-optimal treatment that did not satisfy their needs or the professional pride of the hospital's staff.

Previously, skilled personnel collected blood samples and delivered them to laboratories for testing, which was time consuming. When the laboratory manager was confronted with a wealth of ideas from the Head of Department he began to break with his usual professional silo thinking. The solution did not lay in the actual analysis of the blood sample, but in the transport time. When the laboratory manager continued his search of the environment for new perspectives on the problem of the long wait for blood test results, he was finally successful. A board member from a small private company reacted and connected him with the technological knowledge required to be able to think outside the box and rethink how the welfare solution could be organised.

Up to this point, the hospital had not considered the possibility of using technological knowledge from an external source, to reduce the response time of blood samples. However, the private firm's know-how from transporting yoghurt through pipelines provides the impetus for the laboratory manager and other professional personnel to engage in collaboration with the firm. It is soon clear to the laboratory manager that the combination of his own professional expertise and the private firm's technological know-how is precisely the cocktail needed to devise a new efficient way of transporting blood samples.

The solution soon gained the support of numerous other stakeholders as it met several goals. Not only did the solution cater for the need for individual patients to receive faster treatment, but it also enabled the professional staff to provide the best possible treatment, whilst allowing the hospital's management to save scarce resources through shorter hospitalisation time for patients. Moreover, the politicians got what they wanted i.e. a solution that uses that taxpayers' money in a much more efficient manner. For the private firm the solution helped to create more jobs, more revenue and exports, thus meeting the company's desire to conquer new markets.

The story is a good example of the open perspective on public entrepreneurship because it makes visible the necessity of thinking across fields of knowledge, so that the diversity of knowledge and insight that exists among external and internal actors can come into play. However, it is not only necessary to meet and talk to each other. Only through a long process in which the parties co-create can they unearth different requirements for the solution. This requires not only openness to each other's differences, but also trust that all are contributing with valuable knowledge. The story also shows clearly that social management is a complex process and that democratic ideals of the common good, human dignity and integrity, and equal rights and equal access for citizens to welfare benefits are multiple requirements to be met at the same time. However, they managed to create value for numerous stakeholders, with the welfare solution being perceived as beneficial and successful by many heterogeneous organisations and actors.

Testing the theory

Now you can test your understanding of public entrepreneurship in a series of exercises designed to help you interpret how public entrepreneurship can take shape. The following suggestions are for inspiration.

? EXERCISES

1 **How can the interaction between individuals and groups of actors be illustrated?** How would you draw the network of relationships that take shape between organisations, individuals and groups of actors in the story of pipe delivery system? Do individuals dominate the

beginning, whilst the later stages of the story are characterised by several groups of actors and interaction between organisations? Or do you see the story begin and end in a completely different way? How do you illustrate the story based on your understanding of what happens in the key events?

2 **Consider the possibility of using public entrepreneurship in developing countries.** In this chapter we focused, mainly, on the range of benefits that public entrepreneurship can bring to Western developed countries. However, isn't it possible that public entrepreneurship can provide important benefits to the public sector in developing countries? What is your thinking about this?

3 **Experiment with your acceptance of the heterogeneous knowledge.** You know by now that there can be large differences that come into play between private and public organisations and actors when they enter a collaborative working relationship. You may already know this from when you have discussed politics or other value-based issues with your fellow students. Start a discussion with your fellow students, and be the person who constantly sees things from 'the other side'. As the discussion takes place, write down the different attitudes espoused about the items discussed, and process the subsequent arguments to find out whether there are different knowledge bases underpinning the various positions. Perhaps, these different knowledge bases are just different facets of the subject's complexity?

LITERATURE

Ansell, C. & Torfing, J. (eds) (2014) *Public Innovation through Collaboration and Design*, London: Routledge.

Bellone, C.J. & Goerl, G.F. (1992) 'Reconciling public entrepreneurship and democracy', *Public Administration Review*, 52(2), 130–134.

Bernier, L. & Hafsi, T. (2007) 'The changing nature of public entrepreneurship', *Public Administration Review*, 67(3), 488–503.

Borins, S. (2002) 'Leadership and innovation in the public sector', *Leadership & Organization Development Journal*, 23(8), 467–476.

Currie, G., Humphreys, M., Ucbasaran, D. & McManus, S. (2008) 'Entrepreneurial leadership in the English public sector: Paradox or possibility?', *Public Administration*, 86(4), 987–1008.

Diefenbach, F.E. (2011) 'Entrepreneurship in the public sector – when middle managers create public value', dissertation, University of St. Gallen, GWV, Fachverlage Gmbh.

Dobell, A.R. (1989) 'The public administrator: God? Or entrepreneur? Or are they the same in the public service?', *American Review of Public Administration*, 19(1), 1–11.

Drucker, P. (1985) *Innovation and Entrepreneurship: Practice and Principles*, New York: Harper & Row.

Esping-Andersen, G. (1996) *Welfare States in Transition: National Adaptations in Global Economies*, London: Sage.

Hartley, J., Sørensen, E. & Torfing, J. (2013) 'Collaborative innovation: A viable alternative to market competition and organizational entrepreneurship', *Public Administration Review*, 73(6), 821–830.

Hodge, G. & Greve, C. (2010) 'Public–private partnerships and public governance challenges', in Osborne, S. (ed.), *The New Public Governance? Emerging Perspectives on the Theory and Practice of Public Governance*, London and New York: Routledge, pp. 149–162.

Hood, C. (1991) 'A public management for all seasons?', *Public Administration*, 69(1), 3–19.

Kearney, C., Hisrich, R. & Roche, F. (2008) 'A conceptual model of public corporate entrepreneurship', *International Entrepreneurship and Management Journal*, 4(3), 295–313.

Klein, P.G., Mahoney, J.T., McGahan, A.M. & Pitelis, C.N. (2010) 'Toward a theory of public entrepreneurship', *European Management Review*, 7(1), 1–15.

Miles, R.E., Miles, G. & Snow, C.C. (2006) 'Collaborative entrepreneurship: A business model for continuous innovation', *Organizational Dynamics*, 35(1), 1–11.

Morris, M.H. and Jones, F.F. (1999) 'Entrepreneurship in established organizations: The case of the public sector', *Entrepreneurship Theory & Practice*, 24(1), 73–93.

Morris, M.H., Kuratko, D.F. & Covin. J.G. (2008) Corporate entrepreneurship and innovation: Entrepreneurial development within organizations, 2nd edn, Mason, OH: Thomson/South-Western.

Osborne, S.P. (2010) *The New Public Governance? Emerging Perspectives on the Theory and Practice of Public Governance*, London and New York: Routledge, 431.

Rainey, H.G. & Bozeman, B. (2000) 'Comparing public and private organizations: Empirical research and the power of the a priori', *Journal of Public Administration Research and Theory*, 10(2), 447–470.

Ramamurti, R. (1986) 'Public entrepreneurs: Who they are and how they operate', *California Management Review*, 28(3), 142–158.

Roberts, N.C. (1992) 'Public entrepreneurship and innovation', *Policy Studies Review*, 11(1), 55–64.

Sadler, R.J. (2000) 'Corporate entrepreneurship in the public sector: The dance of the chameleon', *Research and Evaluation*, 59(2), 25–43.

Sørensen, E. & Torfing, J. (2012) 'Introduction: Collaborative innovation in the public sector', *The Innovation Journal: The Public Sector Innovation Journal*, 17(1), 1–14.

Wright, M. & Vanaelst, I. (2009) *Entrepreneurial Teams and New Business Creation*, Cheltenham, UK and Northampton, MA, USA: Edward Elgar Publishing.

14

Entrepreneurship policy

Worldwide, governments have become increasingly aware of the importance of promoting entrepreneurial activity through policy actions. The underlying assumption is that a high level of entrepreneurial activity benefits the country's economic growth, strength of innovation and job creation. This strengthens the basis for maintaining or expanding the country's welfare system.

The growing political interest has led to researchers becoming increasingly interested in entrepreneurship policy. They do this both to fill the researchers' classic role – that of helping to explain and understand the phenomenon – and to engage in constructive and critical dialogue with politicians. The constructive aspect is that the knowledge developed by researchers could form the basis for more appropriate and effective policy measures, whilst the critical element lies in questioning whether entrepreneurship policy is appropriate or even justified at all. Critical questions might include:

- Does political intervention do more harm than good because it distorts the market conditions and the natural reproduction of great entrepreneurial talent?
- Is political intervention (at the end of the day) more of a support to the many consultants, trainers and consultants that feed on designing entrepreneurial projects than a support to entrepreneurs – and is it also a support to the politicians themselves who want to gain popularity by aligning themselves with the growing entrepreneurship field?

Entrepreneurship in practice

To better understand the political reality, this chapter provides an insight into a selected EU-funded project, Enspire EU, the aim of which is to develop entrepreneurial talents in socially disadvantaged and marginalised groups. The social objective of the project sought to establish a new agenda for entrepreneurship policy, which usually focuses on the most motivated, competent and best-integrated communities.

CASE STUDY

Enspire EU

(**Devised by Pia Schou Nielsen**)

This case is about policy-making and how policy is translated into initiatives that are designed to increase the economic wealth and social welfare in society. Every year, policy-makers allocate billions of taxpayers' money to support the general needs in, and development of society, at local, regional, national and international levels. Policy-makers are under constant scrutiny – are they administering the money in the right way, and what is actually coming out of their investments? An example of such an investment is the Enspire EU project, which was a project under the European Regional Development Fund. The project ran from January 2010 until December 2013, and had a total budget of 1.5 million Euros. The project was a so-called Regional Initiative Project, under the INTERREG IVC programme, meaning that the purpose of the project was to improve the effectiveness of regional policies in Europe, within the predefined subject of 'innovation and the knowledge economy'. Just under 180 million Euros were allocated to this area over a six-year period (2007–13), and these funds were distributed amongst 120 projects.

But for now, let's go back to the beginning of the Enspire EU project. In 2007, a group of people from across Europe met to discuss how to encourage and inspire more people in Europe to become entrepreneurs. These were representatives from business development organisations, chambers of commerce and local regions from across 11 different European countries (Denmark, Sweden, Romania, Czech Republic, Hungary, Slovenia, Poland, France, Spain, UK and Cyprus). The purpose of the meeting was to develop a trans-European project to help boost entrepreneurship and the entrepreneurial spirit, which had suffered a decline over recent years in spite of increased entrepreneurship policy investments. Research at the time showed decreasing desire on the part of Europeans to pursue a career in entrepreneurship. Despite growing investment in entrepreneurship policies in the EU, there seemed to be a gap between the efforts made by politicians to foster an entrepreneurial spirit, and the actual entrepreneurial activity taking place in local communities across Europe. Entrepreneurship was, without doubt, considered to be a driver for economic growth by the European Commission, by local authorities and by the research community – however, how to encourage entrepreneurship among ordinary people was apparently an underestimated challenge.

When discussing how to react to the decline in entrepreneurship across Europe, the group quickly agreed that a shift in the conventional way of thinking about entrepreneurs had to drive their new project. Many people across Europe have the education, the network and the knowledge to become entrepreneurs. Moreover, many were already either entrepreneurs, or subject to the many already existing political programmes designed to help potential entrepreneurs start their own business. In fact, the group argued, these were not the ones who needed the most help to become entrepreneurs. Instead the group asked: 'What about those people who are not already inspired to start their own business? What can we do for them?'

CASE STUDY *(continued)*

This question formed the foundation for the project later to be called Enspire EU. Changing the discussion from the original 'How do we create wealth through entrepreneurship', to 'How do we create wealth through entrepreneurship in marginalised groups?', the purpose of the project became two-fold: both to boost entrepreneurship as an economic driver, and also to introduce entrepreneurship as a way for marginalised people to be led back into society. The project partners agreed to focus their attention on three groups of Europeans, named the 3Ds:

- *the disadvantaged*: people without the same opportunities as the average European;
- *the disconnected*: people who are disconnected from the labour market (long-term unemployed, people with a low education);
- *the discouraged*: young people at secondary level of education discouraged with the education system.

The rationale behind these three groups was based on both an entrepreneurial mind-set argument and an unemployment argument. Members of the 3Ds are, to different extents, excluded from society, which make them less exposed to entrepreneurial role models, networks, resources and training. As a result, their entrepreneurial mind-sets are less developed than that of the average European, making them a good case for further political attention. From an unemployment perspective, the argument is to use entrepreneurship as a way back into employment, which has economic benefits to both the individual and society, as well as social benefits.

The Enspire EU project consisted of different components. One of the major components of the project was to identify best practice entrepreneurship programmes across the 11 participating European regions that were already in place to help these groups. These best practices were described and disseminated in a 'toolkit' to regions all over Europe, so they could be inspired to set up similar initiatives. Moreover, the project involved making transfer tests, where small-scale initiatives were transferred to other regions, to learn about the challenges of transferring initiatives from region to region. Finally a set of policy recommendations was presented to policy-makers all over Europe, to provide guidelines on how to formulate the best entrepreneurship policies at the regional levels.

Best practice examples

One of the best practices identified was the Prince's Trust Enterprise Programme in the UK. This is a great example of a political programme designed to encourage entrepreneurship, with the dual ambition of having both economic and social impact. The Prince's Trust enterprise programme (www.princes-trust.org.uk, last accessed 31 December 2016) is an initiative supporting unemployed young people aged 18–30 in assessing whether their business ideas are viable, and whether self-employment is right for them. The programme offers a range of different possibilities for support, such as mentoring, financial support, education and training.

Another best practice was the Assistance Centre to Support Female Entrepreneurship in

CASE STUDY *(continued)*

Zlín, in the Czech Republic. The Assistance Centre offers help for female entrepreneurs, both with regard to their business and their personal work–life balance, recognising that women have different prerequisites for entering into self-employment. The women are offered counselling, financial support and training in starting up a business. The centre is managed by the Zlín Chamber of Commerce and Industry.

Outcomes of the project

The big question in entrepreneurship policy, as well as in many policy areas, is whether the individual projects have made any difference to the participants and more importantly to society in general. When project manager Allan Ottesen was asked about the impacts of the Enspire EU, he answered:

> The Enspire EU project was considered a major success, both among the partners and by the project management. The project resulted in two key products that can be directly applied in all regions across Europe: a toolkit and a set of policy recommendations. Moreover, the Enspire EU proved that best practice transfer is in fact possible when taking into consideration the transferability of the individual initiative. What will be the impact of the project is still too early to tell. We already know that policies have been changed in several of the partner regions, based on the policy recommendations from the project. Moreover, specific initiatives have been initialised locally, for example the Office for Supporting Women and Young Entrepreneurs in Larnaca, Cyprus, and a plan for the development and promotion of entrepreneurial culture in the Andalusian educational system has been approved in Spain. The economic impacts of policy programmes are far more difficult to assess, and we can only anticipate the positive economic effects of programmes such as Enspire EU.

While the impact of the Enspire EU project on the wealth and welfare of the participants is difficult to verify, it can be concluded is that the Enspire EU project has helped policy-makers across Europe to make informed decisions when deciding how to design and implement policies and initiatives aimed at discouraged, disadvantaged and disconnected people.

For more information on the Enspire EU project, go to www.enspire.eu (last accessed 31 December 2016).

Figure 14.1 The logo of the Enspire EU project

Your immediate interpretation

What does the Enspire EU case tell you about policy-making in the entrepreneurship field? Do you have a spontaneous interpretation of the case? The following exercises can help you form an understanding:

- Imagine that you were present at the meeting where the Enspire EU project was initiated. What would your reaction have been to the idea on spending taxpayers' money on marginalised groups rather than the most willing and best-qualified potential entrepreneurs?
- What is your reaction to the idea of best practice? Are European countries so different that solutions must be tailored to the specific circumstances in each country, or can best practice solutions be applied successfully across countries?
- What do you think is your future role related to entrepreneurship policy? Do you aspire to be a policy-maker yourself, a recipient of policy initiatives and support programmes, or perhaps one of the many persons who are working with support and facilitation of entrepreneurial activities through advisory centres, educational institutions, incubators and other entrepreneurship promoting organisations?

Theories of entrepreneurship

Entrepreneurship policy views the entrepreneurship field from a different perspective than the individual actor perspective that has characterised the previous chapters. Politics is about creating the structural and economic framework for the activities of individual entrepreneurs and organisations, i.e. a macro-perspective rather than a micro-perspective.

Within the entrepreneurship policy field we find a variety of actors. There are politicians and officials at several levels: the supranational EU, national states, regions and communities. Many non-state actors also contribute, such as the financially strong Kauffman Foundation in the United States that initiates and drives many entrepreneurship policy initiatives, particularly in the education sector. Another example is the consulting and accounting firm Ernst & Young, which operates an annual Entrepreneur of the Year campaign in many countries with regional, national and international awards. A third example is the student organisation Venture Cup, which runs an entrepreneurship competition among university students in several countries. This interest from the private and voluntary organisations means, of course, that elected politicians are influenced from many sides in their decision-making about entrepreneurship policy.

Politicians and members of organisations that are dedicated to the entrepreneurship field operate from the basic conviction that entrepreneurial activity is good for society. In particular, the focus is on the economic side, thus contributing to prosperity and job creation. However, as the Enspire EU case shows, there is also some focus on welfare, both indirectly as economic progress creates the financial basis of the welfare system, and directly as specific programmes can move people from passive support to self-support benefitting both the citizens and public budgets. The two perspectives can be seen as competing – for example, when focusing on welfare becomes so strong that the business is neglected. However, they can also be viewed as complementary, as is typically the case for social entrepreneurs seeking to find a balance between business and social considerations. Therefore, in this chapter we focus on the following paradox:

Wealth or welfare?

The growth of the entrepreneurship policy field

The field of entrepreneurship policy grew in the late 20th century as an offshoot of the more established policy field for smaller companies, often referred to as the 'small business policy' (Gilbert et al 2004). It gradually became clear to politicians and others with political interests that policy measures aimed at the conditions for established small businesses are not identical to measures aimed at creating new businesses and new economic activity. This realisation, and the growing interest in job creation and entrepreneurship, eventually manifested itself in the field of entrepreneurship policy (Audretsch 2007).

Unlike small business policy, entrepreneurship policy focuses on the early stages of business life: the stages before the start, during the start and in the first years after start-up, including the early growth phase. The field also recognises the need for policy initiatives aimed at other types of entrepreneurial activity than the classic commercial start-up of new businesses, such as social entrepreneurship, intrapreneurship and public entrepreneurship.

The rise of the new policy field meant that Western countries allocated more public funding to promoting entrepreneurial activity. These funds were used to improve the information and advisory system, start entrepreneurship courses, affect the education system, improve access to finance for entrepreneurs, launch campaigns and much more. Overall, the public financial resources for this purpose have grown rapidly in developed countries since

2000, albeit with significant variation from country to country. However, compared to the total resources for economic policy, resources for entrepreneurship policy are relatively limited.

In the years since the millennium there has been a gradual change in politicians' focus on the field. In the years around the turn of the century political interest primarily focused on increasing the number of new companies. The assumption was that an increase in the number of new businesses would, in itself, result in job creation and affect the overall economic growth positively. This assumption was increasingly questioned by new empirical studies. Statistical data from nation states and the OECD showed that the number of start-ups in a country was relatively stable over a number of years and affected more by economic trends than by policy initiatives. The growing body of research also suggested that it was not the number of new companies as such that had a positive macroeconomic impact, but rather the start-up and development of companies with high growth potential, often called high-impact start-ups (Van Stel et al 2005; Acs 2008; Minniti 2008).

In the wake of this realisation the political focus shifted somewhat, away from volume and towards the quality of new companies (Autio et al 2007; Bager et al 2015). This led to new discussions concerning how we define quality and, from a political point of view, how can we identify entrepreneurs and start-up companies that have the potential to grow large, but have not yet proven that they can grow?

The rationale for entrepreneurship policy

Market failure is considered by many as the key factor in justifying or even requiring policy intervention: 'One of the first key challenges faced by governments whose aim is to produce higher levels of entrepreneurial activity will be to determine what systemic gaps or markets failures exist for individuals moving through the entrepreneurial process' (Stevenson & Lundström 2007: 104).

Historically, many governments have sought to counteract market failures, i.e. imbalances that the market economy cannot rectify by its own forces. As we saw in Chapter 3, where Kirzner's theory was mentioned, entrepreneurs perform an important function in a market economy by entering the market with new ideas, products and companies and fill gaps in the market when they occur. In this way entrepreneurs help to counteract temporary imbalances and reduce distortions in the economy.

These types of temporary 'holes' in the market do not justify political intervention, whereas market failure may justify or require intervention, for example, targeting large companies that abuse a dominant position in the market to keep the new firms out. The question is, how do you decide in practice that a bias or imbalance is so large and systematic that political intervention is reasonable or necessary? Theoretically, it is not difficult to justify the difference, but in practice it is.

Which systematic market failure is typically linked with the entrepreneurship field? The concept of 'liability of newness', as we explained in Chapter 4, seems to be part of the answer. Most entrepreneurs are young people without significant financial resources and without the financial means to buy adequate information, counselling and skills development in the free market to become competent entrepreneurs, and thus have a good chance of succeeding in realising their business idea. It is probably the reason why we see, all across the world, governments establishing free or cheap access to information, advice and training for entrepreneurs. Without that government intervention there would be less competent entrepreneurs to fill the many gaps in the market, or to create something radically new in the market; in other words, discovering or creating more Kirznerian and Schumpeterian opportunities in this way, for the benefit of the overall economic dynamic.

Another systematic market failure relates to new technological knowledge. In many countries, governments focus on developing and disseminating new technical knowledge and avoiding friction in the process of transferring new knowledge and technology from universities, laboratories and related knowledge-intensive institutions into practical use. However, for many different reasons systematic friction occurs in this process, a so-called 'knowledge filter' that inhibits or blocks the flow of technological knowledge. This inhibits the possibility of creating new high-tech companies or new business areas in existing companies, which justifies political intervention. In fact, political intervention in this area has been recognised for a long time in the form of the patent systems that all developed countries have built up over time. The patent systems can be understood as a tool for managing friction in knowledge flows by providing preferential rights in the market for inventors, entrepreneurs and innovative companies that come to the market with a major innovation. The rationale is that these people and companies would not be willing to invest sufficient resources in the development of new technologies and methods if it was easy for competitors to copy their solution as soon as it was developed.

In other areas of the knowledge-intensive and high-tech field, it is difficult to clearly determine whether it is merely a short-term 'hole' in the market or a systematic market failure. Therefore, in practice it may be appropriate to use a different rationale than the market failure rationale, namely 'additionality', which focuses on the marginal effect of a policy intervention: 'Does government involvement result in actions being taken that would not have been taken otherwise by private actors in the absence of policy?' (Auerswald 2007: 30). The essential criterion for assessing the merits of a policy intervention is therefore whether, overall, it leads to a better situation than that which would have developed without the intervention. In practice this additionality test is more manageable than the market failure test, but the additionality test can also be difficult to handle in practice, because one is trying to compare the current situation with an imaginary future situation without political interference. In retrospect, this can be tested by using control groups so that the group covered by the procedure, often referred to as 'treatment group', is compared to a similar group who have not been subject to intervention.

In addition to systematic market failure and additionality, political intervention can, in some cases, be justified by government failure. The thinking here is that over the years, politicians have introduced many laws and regulations that need revision in order to unleash entrepreneurial dynamism. This particularly applies to the regulations that governments have adopted to control access to the setting up a new business. In this area, according to the World Bank Group's global benchmark analysis (www.doingbusiness.org, last accessed 31 December 2016), considerable variation remains between countries in terms of how easy it is to register and start a new business, even among the most developed countries. In some countries it is still a time-consuming process to be approved and there may be costs associated with the registration process. In addition, there are restrictions on certain social groups in some countries, for example, on women in male-dominated societies like Saudi Arabia.

So far we have discussed the rationale for entrepreneurship policy on the basis of societal and market needs, thus it can be called the 'demand' side. However, there is also a 'supply' side that should be considered, i.e. whether there are enough motivated and competent entrepreneurs to meet the needs of society. This we also touched on in Chapter 3, where we demonstrated that significant parts of the population either lack the intention to pursue a business idea they have discovered, or alternatively want to become an entrepreneur but are lacking a good idea to pursue.

The 'supply' side affects the developed countries, dominated by a wage earner culture, where most young people are no longer brimming with the entrepreneurial inspiration they would previously have received from parents, relatives, neighbours, and which 'automatically' often provided inspiration for starting their own business. This is one of the reasons why entrepreneurship education with the active support of the authorities has been used extensively by educational institutions in developed countries in recent decades, from primary schools to universities. Furthermore, governments around the world support campaigns to encourage people to have a more positive view of entrepreneurship and a career as an entrepreneur.

The entrepreneurship policy field can therefore be seen, overall, as government attempts to control the balance between supply and demand for entrepreneurship through policy intervention. Some researchers are very optimistic with regard to controlling this balance: 'Public policy and governance can shape virtually all the contextual determinants of the demand for entrepreneurship and over a longer time, the supply of entrepreneurs as well' (Hart 2003: 8). Others see the entrepreneurial field as more unruly, diverse and influenced by society's informal institutions and culture, and only to a limited extent influenced by political regulation (Aldrich 1999).

The institutional anchoring of entrepreneurship policy

As we have seen in previous chapters, entrepreneurial activity develops in many forms. This applies to both constructive forms, such as commercial entrepreneurship, social entrepreneurship and intrapreneurship, and also to more destructive forms, such as drug trafficking and human smuggling. One can, therefore, see political regulation and entrepreneurship policy as an attempt to develop an institutional framework that promotes constructive and inhibits destructive forms of entrepreneurship (Baumol 1990).

This overall effort seems to be common to most governments around the world, but the precise institutional framework varies considerably across countries, even among the most developed ones. This variation stems from differences in political thinking in the countries, including the thinking behind industrial policy. In some countries the focus is on industrial policy to create favourable general conditions for the unfolding of economic activity, whilst in other countries there is more of a willingness to implement selective policy interventions to address specific needs, opportunities and groups. This also applies to entrepreneurship policy, where one pole of the political debate argues for a 'pick-the-winner' strategy where specific technologies, sectors or socio-economic groups and entrepreneurial types are political priorities, whilst the opposite pole is against politicians' attempts to select future winners, and therefore focuses on creating good general framework conditions. These poles in economic policy thinking are especially crystallised in the debate on the creation of favourable conditions for potential high-impact entrepreneurs, but there are also intermediate positions that argue that even if politicians can not 'pick' the best ideas and entrepreneurs, they can support promising entrepreneurs as they are making progress – sometimes referred to as 'retaining winners' (Autio & Rannikko 2016). With regard to this debate the Enspire EU case takes an intermediate position, because on the one hand it 'picks' certain socio-economic groups, but at the individual level their efforts were aimed at developing the participants rather than choosing 'the best'.

Target groups

As mentioned, entrepreneurship policy is, in principle, concerned about all types of entrepreneurial activity, and in virtually all countries worldwide governments offer free or low-cost information, counselling and training to prospective entrepreneurs. However, this general aim is supplemented, in many countries, by a focus and prioritisation of specific groups of entrepreneurs. This is either because they have a special potential, as is the case for highly educated people with technological expertise, or because political efforts towards socio-economic groups help to boost their entrepreneurial activity.

Technological entrepreneurs are supported in most developed countries, as politicians look at technological entrepreneurship as a pathway for the creation of innovative new businesses and jobs. Experience in recent decades, where IT giants like Microsoft, Apple, Google and Facebook have become some of the world's most valuable companies, are indications that this may be a way to create something great and valuable. Typically, such firms grow out of university environments, where students and researchers engage in converting their new technological knowledge into new businesses. Often, new technology entrepreneurs and teams grow out of a special entrepreneurial environment in the region, such as is the case in California with Stanford University and Silicon Valley. Therefore, more and more universities and the surrounding community are looking to support these processes by developing incubation systems for highly skilled entrepreneurs in collaboration with the technology transfer centres at universities and research institutions. Overall, however, only a small proportion of the many attempts at technology start-ups will be successful, but experience suggests, after all, that the provision of seed capital, support for patenting, mentoring, business incubation and similar efforts will strengthen the chances of success for these types of risky venture, which in the early stage often face great uncertainty about the technology, product and market opportunities (Byers et al 2014).

Whilst the political interest in creating new high-tech companies is driven by the desire to improve the economy and prosperity of the country, support for socio-economic groups is significantly driven by a welfare perspective. This can specifically relate to the support of particular projects and groups, e.g. female or ethnic entrepreneurs, which are believed to have the potential for increasing their participation in entrepreneurial activity for their own benefit as well as that of society. It can also be about people who desire to become entrepreneurs, even though they are starting from a disadvantaged position, e.g. the disabled and unemployed.

The welfare perspective concerns both the individual and society. At the individual level it may be engaging in an entrepreneurial project that increases welfare and well-being, whether or not it directly affects the person's income positively or negatively. For the community there is potentially a positive effect on well-being, as well as wealth, when weak socio-economic groups become involved in entrepreneurial activity, because the government typically saves social contributions to those concerned, whilst these entrepreneurs are helping to create new economic value.

Experience with policy programmes targeted at vulnerable socio-economic groups are mixed. Ethnic entrepreneurs, who are often immigrants or refugees, typically have a higher level of entrepreneurial activity than the majority population. This can be due to several factors, including their lack of opportunity to secure a job that matches their qualifications. All things being equal, the immigrants and refugees have a weaker personal network to draw on in the job search process, as they typically do not speak the language well and have difficulty in gaining recognition for their education and qualifications earned in their home country. The road to a well-paid job is difficult for this group, which makes a career as an entrepreneur fairly attractive from an opportunity cost consideration. Opportunity costs refer to the benefits a person can gain by choosing one action rather than an alternative action. Overall, one can say that the entrepreneurial motivation for immigrants and refugees is often relatively high; whilst at the same time they often have good academic qualifications from education and experience from previous jobs at home. The chance that governments, through policies, will be able to succeed in moving these groups from passive support to self-support is therefore relatively high.

For women entrepreneurs, who worldwide account for only about one-third of all entrepreneurs, it seems that specific policy programmes have had a rather limited effect. The Global Entrepreneurship Monitor (GEM) project has been following developments around the world for a number of years, and the big picture is that the gender difference appears to be slowly closing. However, it is uncertain whether this can be attributed to policies, or to other conditions, such as a gradual change in gender roles. A recent GEM report on women entrepreneurship, which is based on data from 61 countries, notes that 'the gender gap (ratio of women to men participating in entrepreneurship) has narrowed by 6%' in the period 2012–14 (Kelley et al 2015: 8). It should be noted here that the mentioned GEM report focuses on independent entrepreneurship, where the proportion of women is much lower than in intrapreneurial activity (Bosma et al 2011).

Entrepreneurship policy areas, objectives and measures

Many different policy factors affect entrepreneurial activity. Some instruments provide economic incentives, for example by providing tax benefits to entrepreneurs, improving financial opportunities and reducing costs for consulting and IP protection. Others reduce administrative barriers, such as facilitating the administrative and financial costs of starting a new business or reducing the costs associated with the termination of business operations. These economic and administrative measures have an immediate and powerful effect, while 'softer' measures such as education and campaigns are more indirect and longer term.

Among researchers there is an ongoing debate about the policy initiatives that should be counted as being within the entrepreneurship policy field. Hart (2003) excludes education, macroeconomic policy and other policies that do not directly affect entrepreneurial activity, while other researchers, such as Stevenson and Lundström (2007) include the more indirect and 'soft' measures. Other researchers go further and argue that entrepreneurship policy should pervade a very wide range of policy areas, rather than focusing on specific actions in a relatively small corner of economic policy, sometimes referred to as an 'add on' policy to the economic policy: 'Entrepreneurship policy may actually be less about specific new instruments or agencies and more about how traditional policies and agencies need to be redirected from their traditional role in the managed economy to a very different orientation in the entrepreneurial economy' (Audretsch et al 2007: 3).

An overview of the policy field's priorities, objectives and measures has been developed by Stevenson and Lundström (2007), who have studied entrepreneurship policy and measures in a large number of countries since 2000. Overall, they believe that entrepreneurship policy focuses on three key factors: motivation, skills and opportunities. The logic here is that there should be an opportunity that the entrepreneur can discover or create, but

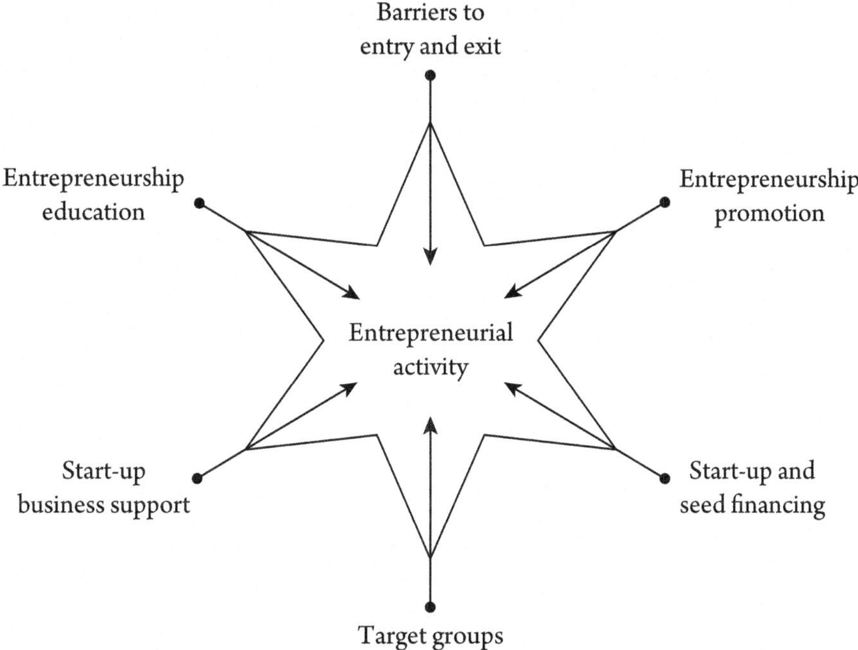

Figure 14.2 Six policy areas affecting entrepreneurial activity

which requires an actor with motivation and skills for the opportunity to be realised. Developing skills requires information, training and advice, and for developing motivation, entrepreneurship education and entrepreneurship promotion are important elements. Additionally, the existence of opportunities depends on barriers to entry and exit as well as the financial conditions. Overall, they conclude that the policy field is divided into six major policy areas that affect entrepreneurial activity (Figure 14.2).

Each of the six policy areas is accompanied by specific objectives and instruments, as shown in Table 14.1.

The range of objectives and resources in the entrepreneurship policy is therefore broad and complex. Some instruments are 'soft' psychological, educational and sociological, whilst others are 'hard' economic and technological. Typically, the 'soft' elements are expected to have an indirect and long-term effect on entrepreneurial activity, while the 'hard' are expected to have a more direct and short-term effect. In relation to the overall paradox in this chapter – wealth versus welfare – one can say that 'soft' measures such as campaigns, advice and training are aimed at both promoting wealth and welfare, whilst the 'hard' measures are primarily aimed at enhancing wealth.

Table 14.1 Policy areas, objectives and measures

Policy area	Policy objectives	Policy measures
Entrepreneurship promotion	Increase social value; create awareness; promote role models	Award programmes; profiling role models; mass media activities; entrepreneurship events
Entrepreneurship education	Increase opportunities to gain 'know-how'; integrate entrepreneurship into the formal educational system	Entrepreneurship adopted into national curriculum guidelines; development of entrepreneurship-related curriculum; train teachers to teach entrepreneurship; support youth entrepreneurship; sponsor business plan competitions; fund incubators and seed capital programmes
Barriers to entry and exit	Reduce time and cost of starting a new business; improve start-up and growth opportunities; remove 'disincentives' to the entrepreneurial career choice	Streamline business registration processes; remove 'quiet disincentives' in labour market; review competition law and other regulations; relax tax and administrative burden on new firms; offer tax breaks for new firms; implement 'better regulation' units in government
Start-up business support	Easy access to start-up information, advice, counselling; facilitate the transfer of 'know-how'	Enterprise and start-up service centres and one-stop shops; start-up web portals; mentoring and training programmes for new entrepreneurs; support for entrepreneurial networks; programmes to improve the quality of business advisory services
Start-up and seed financing	Address market failures and gaps in provision of appropriate financing; reduce information asymmetries	Micro-loan, pre-venture and starter funds; loan guarantee programmes; seed capital funds for techno-starters; incentives for angel and venture capital investments; access to information about available financing; partnerships with banks and financial intermediaries
Target groups	Reduce systemic barriers for groups underrepresented as business owners; reduce risks for high-growth technology start-ups	Target group-specific centres; awards; promotion advisory, training and mentoring services; procurement set-asides; incubators for techno-starters; venture capital, pre-seed funds, campus capital programmes

Source: Inspired by Stevenson & Lundström (2007).

Figure 14.3 Carrot rewards and policy

Entrepreneurship policy from a wealth perspective

Let us now return to the selected paradox, initially focusing on the wealth perspective.

Globally, interest in entrepreneurship among policy-makers has grown rapidly in recent decades. The primary reason for this is a political idea that links entrepreneurial activity with economic growth. The research in entrepreneurship since 2000 has shown that the relationship between entrepreneurial activity and economic growth is not as simple and direct as many politicians imagine. This has not reduced political interest, but politicians have become more aware of the importance of the balance between the quantity and quality of new ventures. In the most developed countries and regions, it is not the number of new businesses in itself, but rather the proportion of high-impact and high-technology ventures that have an effect on long-term economic growth. In the least developed countries, getting more people to start new businesses is not important, as the start-up rate in most developing countries is very high. In these countries political interest is therefore mostly concerned with developing, professionalising and internationalising existing businesses.

The policy instruments from a wealth perspective are particularly 'hard' economic instruments, such as subsidies and tax benefits, as well as regulation of the legal and administrative conditions for starting and running new businesses.

Entrepreneurship policy from a welfare perspective

Political interest in entrepreneurship policy is not, however, driven only from an economic perspective. As we have seen in the previous sections, politicians see entrepreneurship policy as a means for involving marginalised and disadvantaged populations in the economy. For these groups, engaging in entrepreneurial activity typically strengthens individuals' skills, confidence and self-esteem and builds social capital through new network relationships. So, these individuals potentially achieve much more than just economic success through their entrepreneurial commitment, and even if they end up not achieving economic benefits, the entrepreneurial experience may still have been the first step away from an isolated and weak position in society. Political interest in the weaker sections of the population shows itself in direct support for projects for these target groups, and in a growing political interest in supporting social entrepreneurs who start and run businesses that have a social purpose.

Entrepreneurship policy: wealth or welfare?

Table 14.2 summarises the key characteristics of the two perspectives presented above. At the macro-level the focus on the wealth perspective aims to achieve economic growth, whilst the welfare perspective seeks to assist in development of the welfare system and the involvement of disadvantaged and marginalised groups in the economy. This is reflected at the micro-level where we find a corresponding focus on strengthening the respective individuals' economic situation and their well-being and welfare. Methodologically, entrepreneurship policy from a wealth perspective specifically focuses on 'hard' economic incentives and statutory requirements and conditions for economic actors, whilst from a welfare perspective the focus is mainly on 'soft' measures that strengthen the population's interest in entrepreneurship and helps to develop entrepreneurial motivation and competence within the entrepreneurially active population. Finally, the wealth perspective is

Table 14.2 The paradox: Wealth or welfare

	Wealth	Welfare
Macro-goal	Increased GNP and more jobs	Improved welfare system
Micro-goal	Increased income	Improved well-being
Measures	Primarily 'hard'	Primarily 'soft'
Target groups	Technology and high-impact entrepreneurs	Social entrepreneurs and the 3Ds (disadvantaged, disconnected and discouraged)

particularly focused on high-impact entrepreneurs and technology entrepreneurs, whilst the welfare perspective seeks to involve marginalised and vulnerable social groups in entrepreneurial activity alongside support for social entrepreneurs.

Finally, it should be emphasised that the two perspectives cannot be seen as opposites. Historically, there is a clear link between society's economic growth and the building of welfare systems, and at the individual level there is a positive relationship between individuals' prosperity and welfare.

A theoretical interpretation

In light of the theory presented, we now return to the Enspire EU case that opened the chapter, on the basis of the posited paradox: wealth or welfare?

The wealth perspective

As we have seen in the theoretical section, entrepreneurship policy aims, primarily, at creating greater prosperity. It is also said in the case description that, 'entrepreneurship was considered a driver for economic growth by the European Commission, by local authorities and by the research community'. However, the case also says that European Union politicians have not, so far, been successful in creating the desired growth in the number of new businesses, and that there was therefore a need to explore new avenues. Basically, the case can be interpreted as an unconventional attempt to reach new groups of people – the 'disadvantaged', 'disconnected' and 'discouraged' – where there was untapped potential. The approach was unconventional compared to previous entrepreneurship programmes, but the goal is the same: to increase prosperity and strengthen the economy.

The project also aligns with Stevenson and Lundström's point about the importance of proper policies towards particular groups in order to 'reduce systemic barriers for groups underrepresented as business owners'; cf. Table 14.1. If, through policy measures one can raise the proportion of entrepreneurs active in selected, low-participation population groups, then there is potential for a major boost in these groups rather than in groups that are already heavily involved in entrepreneurial activity. These actions can be seen as a rational attempt to increase overall entrepreneurial activity for the benefit of the economy and raise living standards. The effect will be particularly evident with rising prosperity for the participants who successfully establish their own business, but indirectly there will be a positive effect on the overall economy.

The result of the Enspire EU programme is difficult to assess, as the project manager states: 'the economic impact of policy programmes are far more difficult to assess, and we can only anticipate the positive economic effects of programmes such as Enspire EU'. However, this does not imply that the ambition was not to create economic growth and prosperity.

The case also describes how the project tried to transfer successful experiences from one country to another via the best practice method. This can be seen as a rational attempt to maximise economic effect of the 1.5 million Euros that was invested in the project by the EU.

Finally, let's consider whether Enspire EU took action against a systematic market failure, which, if removed, would increase the overall prosperity in the EU. Was it a systematic market failure that the participation of vulnerable and marginalised groups in the EU was relatively low compared with other population groups? Not really. We see the same pattern in other parts of the world, for example in the US, and this is probably related to some of the key characteristics of entrepreneurs, e.g. a high degree of self-efficacy (see the discussion in Chapter 2), which seems relatively rare in the weak and marginalised social groups.

On the other hand one can also say that the EU's problem with low participation in entrepreneurial activity may be an indication of a market failure, but more likely to be a combined market and government failure. Indeed, the low participation could be due to relatively generous benefits and unemployment schemes in EU countries, which weaken the incentive for the vulnerable groups of people to take up work or start a business. Such a system error cannot be resolved, however, with a small project such as Enspire EU, but requires deep reforms of the countries' social and labour market policies.

The welfare perspective

From the start, the Enspire EU project had a welfare challenge, since it was directed at people in a weak social or marginalised position, living in relative poverty and often unhappy, because they do not feel like a part of society. The Enspire EU project's starting point was that although these populations overall are hardly in line with the most entrepreneurial parts of the population, it should be possible to activate some of these people through entrepreneurial projects and thereby increase their welfare. This applies regardless of the level of success of the entrepreneurial project, because during the project period they would have done something meaningful, created new relationships and developed skills and confidence.

If we look closely at the specific population groups considered under the Enspire EU project headings, i.e. the 'disadvantaged', 'disconnected' and discouraged', the welfare challenge is evident in all of them. Let's look at two major groups: immigrants and the unemployed.

Immigrants from outside the EU represent a growing group of citizens in EU countries. A significant proportion of immigrants lives in relative poverty and are marginalised from the greater society. This is due to many factors: from federal restrictions, discrimination in the labour market, weak network relationships, lack of recognition of skills and migrants' poor command of the language and cultural codes. Together, these conditions mean that it is more difficult for an immigrant, with the same qualifications as the majority population, to find a job. The situation can be so hopeless that it may tempt many immigrants to consider crime, prostitution and the like as a way out of their difficult situation, even if they are highly motivated to take a job or other forms of legal employment, so they can support themselves and their families. In this situation entrepreneurial activity with the support of a project like Enspire EU represents a welcome alternative, which can improve immigrants' welfare by providing them with a meaningful existence and the ability to self-support.

For the unemployed, benefit periods and economic conditions vary considerably from country to country, but all countries have restrictions on the time period for which unemployment benefit can be claimed and these also represent a relatively low level of income. The unemployed can therefore, especially if they have been unemployed for a longer period, find themselves in a situation similar to that of immigrants, because they find the labour market inaccessible, and must look for an alternative route in life. Here a helping hand, such as the Enspire EU project can be a first step out of the deadlock. Their participation will, regardless of the level of success of the entrepreneurial project, help to make them active and give them something meaningful to do. For this group, there is also a big plus in terms of welfare.

On top of these welfare improvements for those directly involved, Enspire EU may have a more indirect effect on the authorities, trade unions, job centres and other actors dealing with the weak and marginalised groups, by demonstrating an alternative to the role of employee. Often, the systems and organisations focus so much on jobs that they overlook the possibility that people in vulnerable groups might start their own business. This bias of authorities and organisations can be said to be a 'government failure', which the Enspire EU project can help to rectify. In this way a project like Enspire

EU has a potential effect for much more than the relatively few who have the opportunity to participate in the project.

Testing the theory

The theory and the practical reality within the field of entrepre-neurship policy, as we have discussed in this chapter, can be difficult to understand and empathise with unless you get closer to the political reality that surrounds you. Therefore, we suggest that you try the following exercises.

EXERCISES

1 **Mapping the entrepreneurship policy system in your locality.** Think of the city or community of which you are a part, then try to write down all the public, private and voluntary organisations that are directly or indirectly involved in designing or implementing entrepreneurship policy. There will certainly be some players you do not know of in advance, so make a systematic search through the Internet.
2 **Write a narrative.** Write a real or fictional story about an immigrant woman or unemployed person in your community who has had the opportunity to participate in a publicly supported entrepreneurial project aimed at starting their own business. Write about both the process and the results seen from her/his point of view.
3 **Interview a policy-maker.** Consult a politician or political actor who is active in the entrepreneurship policy field. Conduct an interview asking about his or her role and views on policy field. Take notes and write it into a case.

LITERATURE

Acs, Z. (2008) 'Foundations of high impact entrepreneurship', *Foundations and Trends in Entrepreneurship*, 4(6), 535–620.

Aldrich, H. (1999) *Organizations Evolving*, London: Sage.

Audretsch, D. (2007) *The Entrepreneurial Society*, Oxford: Oxford University Press.

Audretsch, D., Grilo, I. & Thurik, R. (eds) (2007), *Handbook of Research on Entrepreneurship Policy*, Cheltenham, UK and Northampton, MA, USA: Edward Elgar Publishing.

Auerswald, P.E. (2007) 'The simple economics of technology entrepreneurship: Market failure reconsidered', in Audretsch, D., Grilo, I. & Thurik, R. (eds), *Handbook of Research on Entrepreneurship Policy*, Cheltenham, UK and Northampton, MA, USA: Edward Elgar Publishing, 18–35.

Autio, E. and Rannikko, H. (2016) 'Retaining winners: Can policy boost high-growth entrepreneurship?' *Research Policy*, 45(1), 42–55.

Autio, E., Kronlund, M. & Kovalainen, A. (2007) *High-Growth SME Support Initiatives in Nine Countries: Analysis, Categorization, and Recommendations*, Helsinki: Finnish Ministry of Trade and Industry.

Bager, T., Klyver, K. & Nielsen, P.S. (2015) 'Special interests in decision making in entrepreneurship policy', *Journal of Small Business and Enterprise Development*, 22(4), 680–697.

Baumol, W.J. (1990) 'Entrepreneurship: Productive, unproductive and destructive', *The Journal of Political Economy*, 98(5), 893–921.

Bosma, N., Wennekers, S., Guerrero, M., Amorós, J.E., Martiarena, A. & Singer, S. (2011) *GEM Special Report, Entrepreneurial Employee Activity* (last accessed 31 December 2016 at http://

www.babson.edu/executive-education/thought-leadership/premium/Documents/90246%20EEA%20Report%202011.pdf).

Byers, T., Dorf, R. & Nelson, A. (2014) *Technology Ventures – From Idea to Enterprise*, New York: McGraw-Hill.

Gilbert, B.A., Audretsch, D. and McDougall, P.P. (2004) 'The emergence of entrepreneurship policy', *Small Business Economics*, 22(3–4), 313–323.

Hart, D.M. (2003) 'Entrepreneurship policy – What it is and where it came from', in Hart, D.M. (ed.), *The Emergence of Entrepreneurship Policy – Governance, Start-ups, and Growth in the U.S. Knowledge Economy*, New York: Cambridge University Press, 3–19.

Kelley, D., Brush, C., Greene, P., Herringtoon, M., Ali, A. & Kew, P. (2015) *GEM Special Report, Women's Entrepreneurship* (last accessed 31 December 2016 at http://gemorg.bg/reports/special-topic-reports/gem-2015-women-s-report/).

Minniti, M. (2008) 'The role of government policy on entrepreneurial activity: Productive, unproductive, or destructive?', *Entrepreneurship Theory & Practice*, 32(5), 779–790.

Stevenson, L. & Lundström, A. (2007) 'Dressing the emperor: The fabric of entrepreneurship policy', in Audretsch, D., Grilo, I. & Thurik, R. (eds), *Handbook of Research on Entrepreneurship Policy*, Cheltenham, UK and Northampton, MA, USA: Edward Elgar Publishing, 94–129.

Van Stel, A., Carree, M. & Thurik, R. (2005) 'The effect of entrepreneurial activity on national economic growth', *Small Business Economics*, 24(3), 311–321.

15

Synthesis and recap

As an entrepreneur you must be prepared to run the gauntlet between paradoxes. You must, for example, find a balance between planning and improvisation. One minute you are in the planning phase with its deskwork and calculation; then the next minute you set your inventiveness and improvisational behaviour free. Sometimes these processes occur synchronously, sometimes asynchronously. But whatever phase you are in, you as an entrepreneur must be able to walk a tightrope in a universe of paradoxes, because that is what is required for the entrepreneurial process to succeed. At this point, we finally want to cast a unifying glance at the paradoxes that we have dealt with along the way and ask: is there a connection between them? The entrepreneur certainly experiences a connection in the practical world, but is there also a deeper theoretical context? Perhaps paradoxes can be added together in groups, and maybe we can find a meta-paradox hidden in the pattern of the many paradoxes that we have presented in the preceding chapters.

The book's paradoxes

Being an entrepreneur is about balancing in the universe of paradoxes. Paradoxes are not then a matter of choosing one over the other, but about finding the right balance in your specific situation. This choice varies according to who you are and what process you seek to develop. However, you may as an entrepreneur safely assume that you cannot settle for either extreme, however much it may appeal to you. One entrepreneur may love the start-up phase where ideas are bubbling, there is room for improvisation, and nothing is firmly established. Another entrepreneur may be more comfortable when the project's basic idea is established, and it is important to realise the idea through action, planning and organising.

However, regardless of preferences, there are no entrepreneurial processes where only one side of the paradox is present. Ideas are barely conceived before the first immediate evaluation is made, and throughout the organising phase there is a constant need for new ideas as to how the product can be presented, how to cultivate customers, recruit staff, etc. So, irrespective of personal preferences and stages of the process, entrepreneurs operate in a universe of paradoxes, where there is a need for pragmatic 'both-and solutions' rather than 'either-or solutions'. One can therefore say that the entrepreneurs – or entrepreneurial teams – who master the paradoxes of the entrepreneurial process are the likely winners in the race between the many projects that are constantly being launched across all possible areas.

That's why we have chosen to build the chapters of this textbook around some key paradoxes. We believe that paradoxes are important, just as they are within the field of organisational and management theory in general (Hatch & Carliffe 2006; Scott & Davis 2007; De Wit & Meyer 2010). Moreover, we have, through the paradoxes, pointed out that whilst some paradoxes are central to the creation phase, others are important in a later phase or related to specific contexts. Finally, we have focused on the essence of entrepreneurship: the interplay between the discovery or creation of opportunities to be evaluated and exploited by the organisation, instead of more functional aspects such as finance and marketing.

Let us start by summarising the paradoxes, as they were presented in the book's introductory chapter. The summary is presented in Figure 15.1.

The paradoxes should not be understood as incompatible extremes. In our interpretation of the cases we emphasise that it's more a question of balance between seemingly contradictory perspectives on the same topic. It is not therefore a choice that has to be made between extremes, but rather a balancing act for the individual entrepreneur or team of entrepreneurs; a tightrope walk, between the extremes. Both perspectives of a paradox typically

Born	or	Made
Discovered	or	Created
Instrumental	or	Legitimate
Planning	or	Improvising
Necessity	or	Opportunity
Exploit	or	Explore
Rational	or	Embedded
Management tool	or	Creativity curb
Entrepreneurial thinking	or	Design thinking
Top-down	or	Bottom-up
Business	or	A better world
Closed	or	Open
Wealth	or	Welfare

Figure 15.1 The book's paradoxes

contribute to our understanding of what's happening in the entrepreneurial process.

A synthesis of the paradoxes

Is there a relationship between the paradoxes shown in the left- and right-hand sides of the table, i.e. between on the one hand born, discovered, instrumental, planning necessity, exploit, rational, management tool, entrepreneurial thinking, top-down, business, closed and wealth, and on the other, made, created, legitimate, improvising opportunity, explore, embedded, creativity curb, design thinking, bottom-up, better world, open and welfare. Is there a kind of meta-paradox hidden in this puzzle?

One can actually argue for the existence of a meta-paradox, although some of the paradoxes are better aligned with the meta-paradox than others. Where the left-hand side of the table above can be summarised as an objectivist approach, the right side is likely to be summarised as a subjectivist approach (Burrell & Morgan 1979). The objectivist and subjectivist approaches reflect two different theoretical directions. The former suggests that there exists an objective world independent of humankind and their actions, where the outside world, in terms of human action, can be known, described and predicted. In the subjectivist approach reality is not externally given, but is internal and based on the individual's subjective understanding. Reality is created through human actions, experiences and understanding: social reality is thus created rather than discovered.

In the following we will further explain how the aforementioned meta-paradox is embodied in entrepreneurship.

An objectivist approach

The left-hand side of Figure 15.1 summarises the objectivist approach to entrepreneurship. Here, individuals and groups of people behave in as economically rational a manner as possible. The connection on the left-hand side is that entrepreneurs discover an opportunity, evaluate it through the use of instrumental tools and start organising it: an almost linear process that can be plotted in advance. Among other things these activities include entrepreneurs adjusting their networks for the purpose and developing a business plan. This allows entrepreneurs to manage their way through the entrepreneurial process more efficiently and safely. The process is deliberate, systematic, and controlled through planning towards the achievement of a specific and predictable goal – a profitable organisation. It is therefore considered possible to manage the entrepreneurial process with only the right knowledge, which is why top-down management and control from upper management are the key to achieving entrepreneurial behaviour. This approach assumes that there are optimal recipes for how one or more entrepreneurs should approach the entrepreneurial process. All this can be termed an objectivist approach to entrepreneurship, as the entrepreneurial process is given and therefore independent of individuals. It exists 'out there in the real world'.

As actors, entrepreneurs are just a form of 'cog' in the wheels of a machine that attempts to reach goals as quickly and efficiently as possible. The project, not the person, is the key factor. The entrepreneur's function is to develop and manage the entrepreneurial machine, so as to reach the previously established goals. Through planning, control of machinery, coordination and analysis the entrepreneur is able to steer the machine in the desired direction. The born perspective emphasises how the entrepreneur is assumed to have been born for the purpose.

The objectivist approach also promotes the existence of a 'best practice' for developing a new organisation. The business plan, considered to be a management tool, is an example of such 'best practice' for organisational formation. The plan's objective nature is reflected by the fact that from the beginning of the entrepreneurial process it is, to a great extent, possible to predict what destinations the entrepreneur must visit in the process of realising the goal. The plan's various dimensions (financing, marketing, strategy, etc.) show that the entrepreneurial process consists of a set of activities which need to be planned and coordinated. Accordingly, it is central to the objectivist approach to present some universally applicable tools and structural regularities that can support the entrepreneur in directing the entrepreneurial machine.

Sarasvathy (2008) has characterised the objectivist approach as 'causal' since it is based on both the goals that the entrepreneur constantly aims at, and also the selection of means to achieve the goals. The entrepreneur is assumed to have access to the required means, such as resources and networks (more or less), or to rationally determine them at the start of the entrepreneurial process. They are taken for granted.

A similar causal approach is seen in classical organisation theory and the mechanical and rational approach to the formation and operation of organisations propounded by Taylor in the early 20th century (Scott & Davis 2007). Likewise, we find the approach reflected in decision theory, where the rational theory tradition is central, both historically and in modern decision theory. For organisations, however, it is bounded rationality rather than absolute rationality (Simon 1946). Bounded rationality implies that we are not aware of all the alternatives and consequences of the choices we make, just as in practice we accept satisfactory solutions rather than optimal solutions. Such an understanding also makes sense in entrepreneurship.

A subjectivist approach

The right-hand side of Figure 15.1 expresses a subjectivist approach to entrepreneurship. Here, the entrepreneur is motivated by, and acts from, many different logics that do not always fit into a traditional rational economic logic. The human being is at the centre, both at the individual level and at the group level. The individual becomes an entrepreneur through personal development, and he or she has a decisive influence on the design and shaping of the entrepreneurial process. Nevertheless, the person who creates opportunities and decides to pursue them is a holistic human being who also has other priorities in life. The entrepreneurial process is thus far from a fixed entity given by something 'out there'. Rather it is an entity created by the actions, thoughts, feelings, desires and experiences of the entrepreneur.

The subjectivist approach stresses, however, that the entrepreneur does not create the entrepreneurial process alone. The process is created and recreated through constant interaction with other people, which illustrates how the entrepreneurial process is socially constructed. Therefore, other people and networks are the basis within which the entrepreneurial process is embedded and constantly influence how the process works. So, far from being a linear process that follows predetermined phases and objectives, the entrepreneurial process is shaped by jumping back and forth and parallel sequences.

Another foundation of the subjectivist approach is scepticism about the value of planning and closely defined objectives. The future cannot be predicted, and both actions and decisions should depend upon what situations arise. This is true not only for entrepreneurs who find themselves in an early phase of the entrepreneurial process in which ideas and projects emerge and new organisations are being formed. In more mature and existing organisations where routines and systems have already, to a great extent, been determined, planning and the definition of objectives can be equally difficult activities to complete, especially if the goal is to create something new. It is not possible to predict everything, and therefore it is important to let the entrepreneurs who carry out everyday activities have room to move.

It is also crucial, according to this approach, to let innovation occur bottom-up, because the creation and design of new things can sometimes be a chaotic process, where objectives and planning do not always make sense and add value. Actually, one can argue that a highly rational and planned approach can destroy opportunities for the entrepreneur and weaken the development of new ideas. Therefore the business plan is often seen as a curb on creativity and design thinking is important to countervail the planned way of thinking.

Rather than planning at the desk, the subjective perspective is about moving into the world and being guided by the idea, but open to change or new directions. For example, an idea might be redirected to a completely different clientele. Instead of being predictable, universally valid and targeted, the subjectivist approach sees the entrepreneurial process as a unique process, the outcome of which is as yet unknown. As Steyaert writes: 'Every entrepreneurial endeavour follows and writes its own story' (Steyaert 1997: 15).

Only by acting and interacting with others can the entrepreneur figure out whether and how the opportunity can be organised – whether it is legitimate, and more precisely, how it should be carved out. Weick captured this with the phrase: 'How do I know what I think until I see what I say' (Weick 1969: 207). So, it is a case of first saying and doing something, and then interpreting and understanding it. This highlights how the starting point for the subjectivist approach, which has also been pointed out by Sarasvathy (2008), is not closely defined goals. On the contrary, the starting point is the actions performed by the entrepreneur and the means to which he or she has access. Sarasvathy calls this approach 'effectual' as opposed to 'causal' because the starting point is the means by which the entrepreneur mobilises in order to achieve an overall effect.

The relevance and possible combination of the approaches

Let's emphasise once again that both of the two broad approaches to entrepreneurship outlined here are important and should not necessarily be seen as competing opposites. There is a sound theoretical basis for both of them, and for the individual entrepreneur the key is to achieve a balance in any specific situation. Sometimes the balance leans towards the objectivist approach and at other times towards the subjectivist approach. Something similar applies when selecting study programmes and projects at the university. Here again there are objectivist and subjectivist sides which students should be able to handle simultaneously.

Both sides are therefore relevant. However, you can benefit from working with each of them separately, i.e. by choosing one side of the paradox and thinking through the project or the process from this angle. But it can certainly be valuable to see the project or process from both of the paradox's perspectives. With this method you can get deeper into the material and more effectively avoid the normative 'blindness' we all carry with us in terms of those particular angles that we find especially appealing. For example, when starting up, some people will be 'fired up' by the rational perspective, whilst others will be discouraged by such a 'calculative' approach. Both have, so to speak, a need to wear 'reverse spectacles' and see things from the opposite point of view. By considering entrepreneurship from multiple angles one can obtain a better understanding of why processes evolve, as they do, and not least, why success or failure is sometimes the result of an entrepreneurial process.

Your journey is just beginning

We are now approaching the end of our journey through this textbook and the learning universe associated with it. We hope you have enjoyed the journey, have been inspired and now feel better equipped to embark on your own entrepreneurial journeys in your own specific context. Whether you become an independent entrepreneur or go on to develop entrepreneurial projects within existing organisations or in your leisure time, we are fairly confident that you are, at some point in time, going to engage with new ideas, possibilities and their realisation, simply because it is so universal and important in people's lives and careers.

In going forward, we suggest that you, one way or another, get to grips with one or several entrepreneurial projects in practice. Only then will you really understand much of what we've written about and only in this way will you discover – perhaps hidden – talent and strengths that you have. It is in practical projects that you will experience just how difficult and frustrating it can be, not being able to find your way through the jungle of ideas, but on the other hand, the feeling of success that comes when the entrepreneurial project succeeds. It's a bit like watching a roller coaster from the ground: it is only when you've actually ridden on it that you know just how it feels.

Practical projects can be found in many ways. You can start a student business whilst studying, rather than having a student job, or together with others you can embark on a project in social entrepreneurship, for example, targeting the world's climate or poverty problems, or you can seek an internship in a company or organisation where you will work with the development of new opportunities in multidisciplinary project teams.

You can also develop your knowledge of the book's themes by pursuing them within the education system. If the book and its subject area has caught your interest, you can further your education at many universities around the world that offer courses focusing on the issues we have mentioned, e.g. innovation or creativity. A study in the US has shown that students who are trained to foster new ideas and find or create opportunities become better at it than students who have not undergone such training and education (DeTienne & Chandler 2004). Here then, the old adage, 'practice makes perfect' is appropriate. There are also advanced courses in specific subjects such as the financing conditions that apply to start-up companies, management of growth, or the special procedures and rules relating to intellectual property protection.

You can also choose to participate in the many extra-curricular activities offered by universities and further education establishments globally. These include innovation-camps that typically run for 48 hours with the participation of business leaders and other organisational representatives; business plan competitions and training courses; and mentoring in your local business incubator environment for students.

Perhaps you're not yet convinced that entrepreneurship is important to you. So, let us finally summarise three key arguments:

- Whether you want to get a job when you graduate, or want to start a new organisation, it strengthens your chances of success if you have already, as a university student, learned to master the key aspects of entrepreneurship, i.e. creation, evaluation and organising opportunities. Remember that in the modern world, the vast majority of jobs for the highly educated involve interdisciplinary project-based work on new ideas, opportunities and their realisation. Everything indicates that this will become increasingly important in the future because of the increasing pace of change and innovation levels in society.
- Should you wish to start your own organisation, possibly together with others, it is naturally important to prepare for it in college where you have chance to 'play' the role before it becomes serious and costs you a lot of money.
- A final argument is simply that it is fun to participate in entrepreneurial projects. As a student most of your time has been spent absorbing existing knowledge. Entrepreneurship is fundamentally different,

> although here too there is an academic field with established knowledge. It is basically about developing the ability to seize something that doesn't yet exist. And mostly it appears to be fun. The fun thing is that you are working to develop something new and typically do it in cooperation with people who have completely different experiences and academic backgrounds than yourself. It is often only in such contexts that we really understand the field we have learned and how it can be used.

Let's conclude with Harvard Professor C. Otto Scharmer's argument that entrepreneurship and a future orientation is important:

> We also pour considerable amounts of money into our educational systems, but haven't been able to create schools and institutions of higher education that develop people's innate capacity to sense and shape their future, which I view as the single most important core capability for this century's knowledge and co-creation economy. (Scharmer 2007: 3)

LITERATURE

Burrell, G. & Morgan, G. (1979) *Sociological Paradigms and Organisational Analysis*, London: Heinemann Educational.

DeTienne, D. & Chandler, G.N. (2004) 'Opportunity identification and its role in the classroom: A pedagogical approach and empirical test', *Academy of Management Learning and Education*, 3(3), 242–257.

De Wit, B. & Meyer, R.J.H. (2010) *Strategy Synthesis, Resolving Strategy Paradoxes to Create Competitive Advantage*, London: Cengage Learning.

Hatch, M.J. & Cunliffe, A.L. (2006) *Organization Theory, Modern Symbolic and Postmodern Perspectives*, Oxford: Oxford University Press.

Sarasvathy, S. (2008) *Effectuation: Elements of Entrepreneurial Expertise*, Cheltenham, UK and Northampton, MA, USA: Edward Elgar Publishing.

Scharmer, C.O. (2007) *Theory U – Leading from the Future as it Emerges*, Cambridge, MA: SoL Press.

Scott, W.R. & Davis, G.F. (2007) *Organizations and Organizing: Rational, Natural and Open System Perspectives*, Englewood Cliffs, NJ: Prentice Hall.

Simon, H. (1997[1946]) *Administrative Behavior*, New York: Free Press.

Steyaert, C. (1997) 'A qualitative methodology for process studies of entrepreneurship – Creating local knowledge through stories', *International Studies of Management and Organization*, 27(3), 13–33.

Weick, K. (1969) *The Social Psychology of Organizing*, Reading, MA: Addison-Wesley.

Index

achievement need 4, 29, 239
ADAM soap-making co-op, case study 113–116, 131–132
age and entrepreneurship 31
Ajzen, I. 35, 37
Aldrich, H.E. 10, 80, 82, 96, 98, 157, 163, 168, 170, 174
alertness 58, 63, 65
Allen, K.R. 75, 76, 89
Alvarez, S.A. 137
Amit, R. 128
Andersen, H.C. 29
antecedents, public entrepreneurship 282–284
Argentina 258
Armstrong, L. 77
Austin, J. 262
Australia 98
Autio, E. xix
autonomy 29, 39, 241, 244

Bager, T. 227
Baker, T. 152
Baker, W.H. 186
Baldwin, J. 48
Barney, J.B. 143, 144–145
barriers 284
Barringer, B.R. 51, 75–77, 188
Baum, J.R. 21, 33
Baumol, W.J. 8
Becker, G.S. 147
Berger, P.L. 95
best practice, objectivist approach 319
Bhave, M.P. 52, 98
Bhidé, A. 126
Biafra 261
Birch, D.L. 5
Birkinshaw, J. 233–234, 243
Birley, S. 163
Block, Z. 244
Boland, R.J. 218
Bolivia 7
Bolton, J.E. 5
Borins, S. 284
'born entrepreneur' 29
Bosma, N. 100, 234, 235
bottom-up process *see under* intrapreneurship
bounded rationality 194, 320
Bourdieu, P. 148
Boutaiba, S. 60
Bowker, G. 48
Brandslund, I. 270–272, 290
Brazil 149, 235
bricolage approach 152
Brown, T. 212
Brush, C.G. 100
Buchanan, R. 207
Bulgaria 6
bulletproof vest 55–56
Burgelman, R.A. 237, 243, 244
Burrell, G. 318
Burt, R.S. 148, 165–166
business angels 76
business cards 82
business cycle models 126
business model 84, 130, 180, 189, 190, 212, 217, 259
business plans 16, 149, 179
  background of individuals and 185
  case study 179–183, 197–198
  commitment and dedication 188
  concept statement 188
  contents of 191–192
  context, content and process 184–197
  creativity curb 184, 194–196, 197
  definition 184, 188
  experience-based logic 194–195
  flexible 189
  formats 188
  goals realistic 189
  instrumental evaluation 75–76, 83
  management tool 184, 192–194, 196
    case study 197–198
  milestones 77, 189
  objectivist approach 321

subjectivist approach 320
written document or thought process 186–188
Bygrave, W.D. 13, 168

Canada 98
Cantillon 8
capital 146
Carland, J.W. 10
Carter, N.M. 11, 12, 127
Casson, M. 27
Chell, E. 33
childhood 31, 35
Chile 235
Christensen, P.R. 218
Clarke, A.H. 238
closed perspective
case study 288–290
public entrepreneurship 284–288
co-creation 65, 213, 217, 280, 281
see also interaction, social
coffee, case study 47–50, 63–65
cognitive processes of entrepreneurs 33–34, 41, 147
discovering opportunities 59
evaluating opportunities 74
Coleman, J.S. 146, 148, 167
Collins, O.F. 236
commitment
and dedication 188
perspective 41
community factors 266–267
competitive advantage 142
resource theory 143, 144–145
complementary approach 12–14
complexity
evaluation of opportunities 74
improvisation perspective 94, 103
organisations 95, 96, 98
concept of entrepreneurship 8, 12, 18
complementary approach 12–14
elevator pitch 4–6
historical flashback 6–12
international variation 17–18
significance of context 16–17
concepts, key 18
concept statements 188
context
business plans 184–186
emergence of opportunities 60–61, 62
significance of 16–17
see also intrapreneurship; social entrepreneurship
continental model, public sector's characteristics 275–276
contingency theories 32–33
control, internal locus of 29, 40, 239
Cooney, T. 179
corporate entrepreneurship *see* intrapreneurship
cost–benefit analysis 73
Coulter, M. 8
craft businesses 185
creating opportunities *see under* emergence of opportunities
creative destruction 9, 27, 64
Cross, N. 207
culture 18
networks 170–171
see also international variation

Danfoss Group, case study 228–232, 234, 236, 237, 247–249
Davidsson, P. 12
Day, D.L. 243
De Bono, E. 195
debt capital 147
decision theory 319, 320
Dees, J.G. 260, 262, 263–264
Delmar, F. 80, 188, 192–193
demand and supply 302–303
demography 31
Denmark 7, 100
Danfoss Group: case study 227–232, 234, 236, 237, 247–249
fashion: case study 67–71, 84–87
intrapreneurship 235
Meyer Group: case study 89–93, 108–110
music industry: case study 157–161, 176–177
opportunities and intentions 52–55
Vestergaard Frandsen 262–263
dependent entrepreneurship *see* intrapreneurship
Designandelen, case study 201–204, 220–221
Design Economy Report (2015), *The* 205
design thinking 201, 215–218
case study 221
Designandelen, case study 201–204
designer view of 207
discipline view of 207–208
entrepreneurial 213–215, 218–220
case study 220–221

methods 212–213
organisational resource of 208–209
process 209–210
discovery of 'what is?' 210–211, 219
envisioning the future: 'What if?' 211
select futures: 'what wows?' 211–212
test futures: 'what works?' 212
three views 206–209
destruction, creative 9, 27, 64
DeTienne, D. 323
developed countries 309
developing countries 6, 98
intrapreneurship 234–235
opportunities and intentions 55
social entrepreneurship 261–263
starting a business 98
De Wit, B. 184, 317
DiMaggio, P.J. 120
discipline view of design thinking 207–208
discovering opportunities *see under* emergence of opportunities
Dobbin, F. 235
Dodd, S.D. 171
double bottom line 262
Down, S. 5, 34
Downing, S. 34
Dunne, D. 209
dynamic state model 127

eBay 61
Eckhardt, J.T. 11
economic growth 5
economic tradition 8–9
entrepreneur is born 27
Ecuador 235
effectuation perspective 65, 105
effectuation theory 217–218
elevator pitch for entrepreneurship 4
for existing organisations 5
for society 5–6
for you 4–5
Elfring, T. 236
emergence of opportunities 47
alertness 58, 63, 65
case study 47–50, 63–65
context 60–61, 62
creating opportunities 51, 60–63
case study 64, 65
discovering opportunities 51, 57–59, 62, 63
case study 63–64, 65
effectuation perspective 65
extent of intentions and capabilities 52–55
objectivity 57–68
opportunity vs idea 51–52
social interaction 60–62, 64
subjectivity 58, 60, 64
types of opportunities 55–57
emergence tradition 10–11, 13, 18
social entrepreneurship 263–264
energy, renewable 6
Enspire EU, case study 294–299, 311–314
entrepreneurial opportunities 213–215
entrepreneurial thinking 213–215, 218–220
Designandelen, case study 220–221
entrepreneurs 13, 21, 25–26
achievement need 29
autonomy 29, 39
born 26, 27–30, 37–39
case study 39–40
case study 21–25, 39–41
character traits 29–30
cognitive processes of 33–34, 41, 59, 74, 147
commitment perspective 41
contingency theories 32–33
control, internal locus of 29, 40
definition 13
demography 21
genes 29–30
identity and 34–35, 40–41
individual's process towards entrepreneurship 35–37
investor evaluation of 76
made 26, 30–37, 38
case study 40–41
objectivist approach 318
perceived instantaneous strategic configuration 41
risk, attitude to 29, 39, 74
self-efficacy 29, 40
social-psychological tradition 9–10
subjectivist approach 320
types of 26–27
upbringing 31
wider picture of 31–33
entrepreneurship in established companies *see* intrapreneurship
Entrepreneurship's Big Five 29
equity 147

Ernst & Young 298
ethnic entrepreneurs 305
Evald, M.R. 170, 234
evaluation of opportunities 67, 73–74
  case study 67–71, 84–87
  cognitive and emotional process 74
  complexity 74
  cost–benefit analysis 73
  definition 73
  ex-ante 73–74
  ex-post 73
  instrumental 72, 74–79, 83–84
    case study 84–85
  legitimate 72–73, 79–84
    case study 85–87
  liability of newness 72, 82
  risk 74
  social interaction 73, 80–91, 82, 86
events 124–125
ex-ante evaluation 73–74
executive entrepreneurs 285
experience-based logic 194–195
experimental prototyping 216
exploitation of opportunities 216
exploitative thinking 209
exploration 208–209
ex-post evaluation 73
external environment
  barriers 284
  for public organisations 282–283
external stakeholders 282

Facebook 304
fashion, case study 67–71, 84–87
Fayolle, A. 21, 35, 41, 96–97, 100
feedback 212
  creating a new organisation 94–95
  legitimacy 79, 82, 84, 86
Ferrazzi, K. 172
financial crisis in 2009 234
financial resources 146–147, 148–149, 154
  instrumental evaluation 75, 76–77, 79, 84–85
  legitimacy 80
  networks 148, 167, 168
Five Forces Model 76
Fletcher, D.E. 60
flexibility 105, 151, 197
  business plans 189
franchising 70, 85, 89
freelancers 125
French wine business, case study 21–25, 39–41
'fuzzy brains' 221

Gartner, W.B. 3, 10–11, 28–30, 32, 60, 94, 98, 127, 227
GEM (Global Entrepreneurship Monitor) 52–55
  age 31
  gender 31
  organising not always a success 98–99
  social entrepreneurship 258–259
gender and entrepreneurship 31
gender gap 306
General Theory of Entrepreneurship, A (Shane) 215
genetics 29–30
Germany 100
Ghana 149
Global Entrepreneurship Monitor (GEM) project 128, 305–306
Gnyawali, D.R. 17
Google 185, 304
Gordon, S.R. 127
Grameen Bank 261–262
Granovetter, M.S. 164, 165, 167
Greiner, L.E. 126
Grichnik, D. 74
Guinea-Bissau 99
Guth, W.D. 236

habitual entrepreneur 26
Hancock, M. 235
'hard' economic instruments 309
Harding, R. 258
hard measures 306, 307
Hart, D.M. 306
Hatch, M.J. 95, 102, 317
Haynie, M.J. 75
health insurance 100
Hébert, R.F. 27
Heinonen, J. 244
heterogeneous knowledge 275
Hindle, K. 73, 76, 77, 252, 253, 266–267
Hisrisch, R.D. 31
historical flashback 6
  economic tradition 8–9
  emergence tradition 10–11, 13, 18, 263–264
  opportunity tradition 11–13, 19, 263–264
  social-psychological tradition 9–10
Hoang, H. 34, 163
Hojbjerg Clarke, A. 227

Holland, J.L. 118
Honig, B. 185, 194, 195
Hood, C. 279
Hornaday, J.A. 10, 28
Hornsby, J.S. 239
Hull, D. 28
human resources/people 146, 147, 148–149, 153
  instrumental evaluation 76–77, 79
  legitimacy 80
hybrid entrepreneurship 125

ideas
  opportunities *versus* 47, 51–52, 67
  Venture Intelligence Quotient (VIQ) 78
identity and the entrepreneur 34–35, 40–41
improvisation perspective 93–94, 103–108
  case study 109–110
  effectuation perspective 65, 105
India 149
indigenous entrepreneurship, parable of the teepee 252–257, 265–267
individual factors, influence on nascent entrepreneurship 118, 120–122
industry/market, instrumental evaluation 75–77, 79
information
  absorptive capacity 59
  access to 59, 63
    evaluation and limited 74
  improvisation perspective 103
  planning perspective 102
institutional anchoring, entrepreneurship policy 303–304
institutional factors, influence on nascent entrepreneurship 118, 119–120
instrumental evaluation 72, 74–79, 83–84
  business plans 76–77, 83
  case study 84–85
  opportunities with great potential 77–79
  Porter's Five Forces Model 76
  procedural model 76
  scale, scope and span 77
  SWOT analysis 76
  Venture Intelligence Quotient (VIQ) 78, 83
insurance, health 98
intangible products 83
interaction, social
  emergence of opportunities 60–62, 64
  evaluation of opportunities 73, 80–81, 82, 86
  improvisation perspective 65, 105, 107, 108, 110
  see also networks
internal environment, for public organisations 283
internal stakeholders 282
international variation 17–18
  gender and entrepreneurship 30
  intrapreneurship 234–235
  opportunities and intentions 55
  organising not always a success 100
  resources 149
  starting a business 98–100
internet 82
intrapreneur 17, 27, 227, 229–230, 234–235, 239
intrapreneurship 227
  background 233–235
  bottom-up 233, 237, 242–243, 247–248
    case study 248–249
    creating a balance 244–245
    top-down and 243–245
  branches in 235–238
  case study 227–232, 234, 236, 237, 247–250
  critical success factors 234
  degree of innovation 238
  dispersed 236, 237
  diverse concept 235–238
  focused 236, 237
  incremental 238
  individual characteristics 239–241
  internationally 234–235
  organisational characteristics 241
  process behind 239–242
  radical 238
  spin-ins or spin-outs 231, 237
  theories of 232–249
  top-down 233, 237, 242, 245–247
    bottom-up and 243–245
    case study 247–248
    creating a balance 244–245
intuition 34
Iran 235
isomorphism 120

Johannisson, B. 163
Johnson, C. 80, 81
Johnson, S. 257, 261
Jones, C. 33

Katz, J. 11, 94, 95, 127
Kauffman Foundation 298

Keh, H.T. 67, 72, 74
Kelley, D. 6, 12, 18, 55, 100
Kennedy, J.F. 229
key concepts 18–19
Kierkegaard, S. 195
Kirzner, I. 55, 58
Kirznerian opportunities 56, 57, 62, 301
Klyver, K. 120, 169, 170
Knight, F.H. 8
'knowledge filter' 301
Kolb, D.A. xix
Korea 235
Kortzfleisch, H.F.O. 218
Korunka, C. 26
Kroeger, C.V. 12
Kuratko, D.F. 188, 192

Landström, H. 8
Larson, A. 169
Latvia 235
learning cycle xx
legitimacy perspective 72–73, 79–83, 84
  case study 85–87
  definition 80
  feedback 79, 82, 84, 86
  mentors 82
  organising not always a success 100
  our 'best' self 81
  process 81, 82–83, 84
  role models 80, 85
  strategies for building 81–83
  trust 82
letterheads 82
Levie, J. 100, 101
Levie, J.D. 127
liability of newness 72, 82
liberal model, public sector's characteristics 276
Lichtenstein, B.B. 127
Lichtenstein, B.M.B. 151
Liedtka, J. 209
lifecycle 122–124
lifecycle models 12
  networks 163
life events factor, influence on nascent entrepreneurship 118, 122
Lin, N. 162
Llewellyn, D.J. 28
Logopaint, case study 137–141, 153–155
Lundström, A. 306, 311

Madié, D. 187
Malaysia 258
management theories 76, 102
March, J.G. 94, 150, 151, 153, 193, 194
Margolis, R. 48, 49
market failure 300–303
market/industry, instrumental evaluation 75–77, 79
Martin, R. 208, 209
McClelland, D.C. 9
McKelvey, B. 95
McKernan, S.-M. 262
Médecins san Frontieres (MSF) 261
medical software industry, case study 179–183, 197–198
mentors 82, 100
Meyer, C., case study 89–93, 108–110
micro-lending 261–262
Microsoft 304
milestones 77, 189
mission statements, social entrepreneurship 265, 266
Mitchell, R.K. 33
Mobitrix, case study 179–183, 197–198
Morgan, G. 94
Muller, E. 128
Munthe plus Simonsen, case study 67–71, 84–87
Murphy, R.J. 8
music industry, case study 157–161, 176–177

Naffziger, D.W. 4
nascent entrepreneurs 12, 26, 98, 113
nascent entrepreneurship
  ADAM soap-making co-op, case study 113–116
  individual factors influencing 120–122
  institutional factors influencing 119–120
  life events influencing 122
  necessity perspective of 128–130
    case study 131
  opportunity perspective of 129–130
    case study 131–132
  self-employment and 118–119
necessity-based businesses 55
necessity perspective, of nascent entrepreneurship 128–130
  case study 131
Netherlands 235
networks 16, 148–149, 157, 162
  case study 157–161, 175–177
  elevator pitch 4

embedded 162, 173–175, 176
case study 176–177
help provided by 162–163
heterogeneity argument 163–166
homogeneity argument 166–167
legitimacy 81
lifecycle models 169
nascent entrepreneurs 98
organising not always a success 100
rational tool 162, 171–173
case study 176–177
situation dependent 169–171
social network theory 162–163
newness, liability of 72, 82
new public governance (NPG) 280–281
new public management (NPM) reforms 279–281
New Zealand 98
Nicolaou, N. 29
Nielsen, S.L. 218
Nigeria 261
Nike 50
non-profit/voluntary sector 257–258, 261, 264, 266
Nordström, K. 5
Norway 235
novice entrepreneur 26

objectivity
objectivist approach 318–320
opportunities and 57–58
Ogilvie, T. 209
Ohmae, K. 196
open perspective
case study 290–291
public entrepreneurship 286–288
opportunities
emergence of *see separate entry*
evaluation of *see separate entry*
organisation of *see separate entry*
opportunity costs 121, 125, 305
opportunity perspective, nascent entrepreneurship 129–132
case study 131–132
opportunity tradition 11–13, 19
social entrepreneurship 263–264
optimism 33, 59, 74
organisation
case study 89–93, 108–110
definitions 94–96
ease of start-up 98
feedback 96
five phases 96–97
improvisation perspective 93–94, 103–107
case study 109–110
instrumental evaluation 75, 76
international variation 98
intrapreneurship: organisational characteristics 241
key activities 98
networks 98
organisation of opportunities 89
organisation theory 11, 94, 319
organising not always a success 99–101
planning perspective 93, 102, 107–108, 184
case study 108–109
resources 98, 103, 105, 107–108, 110, 152
technology 98
organisational resource of design thinking 208–209
overview of key concepts 18–19

Pahl, N. 76
parable of the teepee 252–257, 265–267
paradoxes xxi–xxiii, 316–318
balance 321
objectivist approach 318–320
subjectivist approach 320–321
synthesis of 318–321
patents 55, 139–140, 153–155
Peet, A. 48, 64, 65
Penrose, E.T. 142
people/human resources 146, 147, 148–149, 153
instrumental evaluation 76, 79
legitimacy 80
Peredo, A.M. 259–261, 263
personality 26, 27–30
cognitive processes 33–59
entrepreneur is born 27–30
identity 34–35, 40–41
optimism 33, 59, 74
social-psychological tradition 9–10
personality traits 28
'person–job fit' model 118
Peru 235
Picasso, P. 195
'pick-the-winner' strategy 303
pipe delivery system 288–290
Pittaway, L. 11
planning perspective 93, 101–103, 107–108, 184
case study 108–109
policy entrepreneurs 285

policy of entrepreneurship 294
  areas, objectives and measures 306–309
  Enspire EU, case study 294–298, 311–314
  growth of 299–300
  institutional anchoring of 303–304
  politics 298
  rationale for 300–303
  target groups 304–306
  wealth perspective 309–311
    case study 311–312
  welfare perspective 305, 310–311
    case study 312–314
political entrepreneurs 285
Porter's Five Forces Model 76
portfolio entrepreneur 26
Powell, W.W. 120
private and public sectors, differences in 277–278
production sector, business plans 185
product/service
  instrumental evaluation 75–77
  organising not always a success 100
prototypes 83
psychology, research tradition 19, 163
public entrepreneurship 269–270
  antecedents 282–284
  characteristics in Western countries 275–277
  closed perspective 284–288
    case study 288–290
  defined 274
  differences between private and public sectors 277–278
  open perspective 286–288
    case study 290–291
  scarce financial resources call for 279
  Tempus600 system, case study 270–273
  triple bottom line 287
  types of 285
  understanding public sector 279–282
pull entrepreneurs 128
push entrepreneurs 128

Quinn, R.E. 80–81

rationale, for entrepreneurship policy 300–303
rationality, bounded 194, 320
recession, intrapreneurship and 233–234
reciprocity 167
Redzepi, R. 91
renewable energy 6
resource accumulation 124
resources 15, 98, 137, 141–142
  bricolage approach 152
  'capital' 146
  case study 137–141, 153–155
  definition 143–144
  differences and connections between categories 148–149
  exploitation 150–151, 152, 153–154
    case study 153–154
  exploration 151–153
    case study 154–155
  feedback 82
  financial 146–147, 148–149, 154
    instrumental evaluation 75, 76, 79, 84–85
    legitimacy 80
    networks 148, 167, 168
  human 146, 147, 148–149, 153
    instrumental evaluation 76, 79
    legitimacy 80
  improvisation perspective 103, 105, 107–108, 110, 152
  international differences 149
  from market to resource focus 142–145
  networks 98, 148–149
  organising not always a success 100
  planning perspective 102
  resource theory 143–145
  social 146, 148–149, 163
  three-way split of 145–149
  valuable 144–145
  see also networks
'retaining winners' 303
Reynolds, P.D. 80
risk
  attitude to 74
  instrumental evaluation 74
  and opportunity costs 125
  organising not always a success 100
  perception of 74
  planning perspective 102
risk willingness 124
role models 80, 85

Sadler, R.J. 284
Sanders, E.B.N. 217
Sarasvathy, S. 8, 34, 47, 60, 61, 63, 65, 102, 103, 105, 108, 110, 152, 217–218, 319, 321
Sauermann 2005 118

Saxe, G.J. 3
Scandinavian model, public sector's characteristics 276
Scharmer, C.O. 324
Schilit, W.K. 193
Schön, D. 207
Schultz, H. 48–50, 63–64, 65
Schumpeterian opportunities 301
Schumpeter, J.A. 9, 27–28, 55
Scott, W.R. 317, 319
self-efficacy 29, 40
self-employment, and nascent entrepreneurship 118–119
senior entrepreneurship 124
serial entrepreneur 26, 89
  Claus, M. 89–93, 108–110
service entrepreneurs 285
service/product
  instrumental evaluation 75–78
  organising not always a success 100
Shane, S. 4, 11–13, 29–30, 33, 37, 57, 58, 81, 94, 127, 141, 186, 206, 213–215
Sharma, P. 235, 236
Shaver, K.G. 33
shops 185
Shuman, J.C. 187
Siegl, Z. 48
Simon, H. 207, 209, 217–218
Simon, H.A. 194, 320
Simon, M. 244, 245
Simonsen, M. 158
Skype 79, 185
small businesses 5
  business plans 185, 186
small business policy 299
social entrepreneurship 252, 257–259
  as business 257, 262–263, 264
    case study 265–266
  case study 252–257, 265–267
  categories of 259
  as a continuum 259–260
  creating better world 257–258, 260–261, 264
    case study 266–267
  definition of 259
  double bottom line 262
  emergence tradition 263–264
  hybrid forms 261, 264–265
  intersection of social and financial goals 261–262
  opportunity tradition 263–264
  studies of 258–259
  voluntary sector 257–258, 261, 264, 266
social interaction
  emergence of opportunities 60–62, 64
  evaluation of opportunities 73, 80–81, 82, 86
  improvisation perspective 93, 94, 101, 105, 110
  see also networks
social-psychological tradition 9–10
social resources 146, 148–149, 163
soft measures 306, 307
Spain 235
Speisman, S. 172
spin-outs 231, 237
Stappers, P.J. 217
Starbucks, case study 47–50, 63–65
start-up business process 125–127, 130
start-up, ease of 98–100
Stepherd, D. 34
Stevenson, H.H. 137, 143, 146
Stevenson, L. 306, 311
Steyaert, C. 3, 321
strategic configuration, change in perceived instantaneous 41
subjectivity
  opportunities and 58, 60, 64
  subjectivist approach 320–321
  success or failure 101
Suchman, M. 80
'supply' side 302
sustained competitive advantage (SCA) 132
Sweden 100, 149, 276
Switzerland 31
SWOT analysis 76

target groups 304–306
technological entrepreneurs 304
technology 98
teepee parable 252–257, 265–267
Tempus600 system, case study 270–273
Terjesen, S. 258, 259
'thinking with the hands' 213
Thompson, J. 261
Thornhill, S. 242, 244
top-down process *see under* intrapreneurship
Tour de France 77
trade organisations 81
'treatment group' 302
triple bottom line, public entrepreneurship 287

trust 82
Trust Enterprise Programme 296

Ucbasaran, D. 26
Uganda 55
uncertainty 8–9
  business plans 185
  cognitive processes 33
  ex-ante evaluation 74
  improvisation perspective 93, 103
  instrumental evaluation 74
  planning perspective 102
  resources 141, 151
  tolerant of 29
unemployment 129, 312, 313
United Kingdom 100
  social entrepreneurship 258, 259
United States 6, 98, 100, 262, 276, 298
  female entrepreneurs 31
  indigenous entrepreneurship 252–257, 265–267
  intrapreneurship 233
  resources 149
university 17
upbringing 31
Uruguay 235

Van de Ven, A.H. 150
Van Gils, A. 179
Vecchio, R.P. 29
Venkataraman, S. 206, 213, 214
venture capital 76, 122, 168, 185, 241
Venture Cup 298
Venture Intelligence Quotient (VIQ) 78–79, 83
Vestergaard Frandsen 262–263
voluntary sector 257–258, 261, 264, 266
Von Hippel, E. 237

warfare 8
wealth perspective, of entrepreneurship policy 305, 309–311
  case study 311–312
Weberian hierarchical bureaucracy 279, 280
websites 82
Weick, K.E. 34, 94, 321
welfare model, public sector's characteristics 276
welfare perspective, of entrepreneurship policy 310–311
  case study 312–314
Wernerfelt, B. 143, 144
Western countries, public sector's characteristics in 275–277
wicked problems 207
Wickham, P.A. 27, 77, 101, 192
wine business, case study 21–25
women 18, 31
  entrepreneurs 305–306
World Bank 98–99, 302

Yunus, M. 261–262

Zahra, S.A. 239

GW01605936

PRINCE
EUGEN's
WORLD of
FLOWERS
AND THE WALDEMARSUDDE FLOWERPOT

AND THE WALDEMARSUDDE FLOWERPOT

Arvinius+Orfeus

CONTENTS

PRINCE EUGEN *& the Swedish design classic, the Waldemarsudde flowerpot* *6*

THE FLORIST'S JOB *BALANCE & HARMONY FROM THE WILD* *20*

KRISTINA'S TOOLS 26

SPRING PALETTE *With flowers on a bare branch & the first delicate greenery* *28-69*

BRANCHES 34

TULIPS 40

STEP BY STEP *TEN TULIPS in the No. 3 pot* 46

NARCISSI 52

STEP BY STEP *WINDING TULIPS in the No. 3 pot* 58

SETTING THE TABLE FOR A SPRING BUFFET 62

EARLY SUMMER *The sun warms & the fields are abloom with flowers* *70-91*

STEP BY STEP *VERTICAL IRIS in the No. 1 pot* 82

STEP BY STEP *EARLY SUMMER BOUQUET in the No. 2 & 4 pots* 88

SUMMER *Now is the time for flowers as far as the eye can see* *92-155*

PEONIES 96

GREENERY 106

POTTED PLANTS *Waldemarsudde's mainstay* 110

PELARGONIUMS 111

STEP BY STEP *SUMMER PASTELS in the No. 3 pot* 120

FROM PLANTING TO HARVESTING 122

RUDBECKIAS 126

STEP BY STEP *WHITE & TALL in the No. 4 pot* 132

STEP BY STEP *WARM & SUNNY YELLOW TONES in the No. 3 pot* 138

DAHLIAS 142

STEP BY STEP *A BALL OF PIPEVINE in the No. 3 pot* 154

HINT OF AUTUMN *Autumn approaches with rowan, rose hip, elderberry & snowberry* *156-181*

SETTING THE CRAYFISH TABLE 160

STEP BY STEP *NASTURTIUM, MARIGOLD & ROSE HIP in the No. 3 pot* 166

STEP BY STEP *LOW & COMPACT IN SHADES OF GREEN in the No. 3 pot* 174

STEP BY STEP *GREEN MOSS, IVY & PINE CONES in the No. 1, 2 & 5 pots* 180

WINTER *The frost spins white crystals round the vegetation* *182-220*

STEP BY STEP *SOFT LAMB'S EAR & SAGE in the No. 1 & 5 pots* 188

DINNERS AT WALDEMARSUDDE THEN AND NOW 190

CHRISTMAS DECORATING 196

AMARYLLIS 202

STEP BY STEP *AMARYLLIS & MOSS in the No. 3 pot* 210

DRIED PLANTS 218

PLANT INDEX *221-222*

THE ENTRANCE OF THE MANSION

PRINCE EUGEN & THE SWEDISH DESIGN CLASSIC, *THE WALDEMARSUDDE FLOWERPOT*

BY KARIN SIDÉN

"NEXT TO THE ARTS, I THINK FLOWERS ARE MY GREATEST JOY"
Prince Eugen

PRINCE EUGEN (1865-1947) is primarily remembered as one of Sweden's greatest landscape painters, and the founder of the popular art museum Prins Eugens Waldemarsudde on the lush island of Djurgården in central Stockholm. Less known to the wider public is that Prince Eugen was also one of the most significant art collectors of his era, a patron of the arts, an advocate for arts and culture, as well as a designer.

PRINCE EUGEN'S MOST FAMOUS decorative arts object is the Waldemarsudde flowerpot, which he designed in 1915 and which serves as the focal point of this book. Prince Eugen's flowerpot is a timeless Swedish design classic, which with its clean lines can be used in many different ways: as a vase for each season's plants, flowers, twigs, and fruits; for growing plants and flowers; and much, much more. In Sweden, where the growing season is short, flowers are a first harbinger of spring and the last delicate reminders that the long summer days must eventually come to an end. Within the pages of this inspirational book are exciting tips from Waldemarsudde's renowned florist Kristina Öhman on how to arrange flowers and plants in the Waldemarsudde pot – tips that we hope will trigger the reader's own creativity and creative desire, and serve as a sourcebook for anyone interested in Swedish floral design and traditions.

Prince Eugen harvesting HYDRANGEA, 1930s. Photographer unknown.

PRINCE EUGEN WAS BORN ON 1 AUGUST 1865 at Drottningholm Palace, home of the Swedish royal family both then and now. The fourth and youngest son of King Oscar II and Queen Sophia, the Prince was initiated early into the responsibilities expected of a Swedish hereditary prince. That role was not always easy to merge with his chosen path as a serious artist. The Prince studied art history and aesthetics at the University of Uppsala in Sweden with Professor Carl Rupert Nyblom from 1886 to 1887, and studied painting privately with among others Wilhelm von Gegerfelt and Gillis Hafström. The Prince's parents then somewhat reluctantly allowed him to travel to Paris in 1887 for advanced art studies. Once there, he came into contact with Swedish, other Scandinavian, and French artists. He was also able to study art at the Louvre, at the Paris Salon, and at the city's many galleries. In Paris, Prince Eugen studied with a number of important French painters in their studios, such as Léon Bonnat, Pierre Puvis de Chavannes, Alfred Philippe Roll and Henri Gervex. A dwelling was provided to him by Baron Gustaf Celsing and his wife Ulla, which facilitated a rich social life. The Prince also came in contact with several Swedish artists, among them luminaries like Carl Larsson, Ernst Josephson and Hanna and Georg Pauli. Swedish portrait painter Eva Bonnier was also among the artists the Prince met in Paris. Bonnier was an active member of the reformist artist organization Konstnärsförbundet, which stood in opposition to the Royal Art Academy in Sweden. She initially expressed a sceptical attitude towards Prince Eugen as an artist, something he would unfortunately face all too often during his early years as a painter. In one of her letters, she responds to an invitation to an artist party arranged by the Prince by saying she agrees with fellow Swedish painter Dick (Richard) Bergh that it was "inappropriate for members of Konstnärsförbundet to ingratiate themselves with a prince." In an ironic turn of events, Eva Bonnier would eventually come to collaborate with Prince Eugen, even electing him as a member in her arts endowment fund in the early 1900s. But by then the winds had long since turned, and Prince Eugen was well established as a serious and important artist among critics, artists and the public. After his breakthrough as a landscape painter in the early 1890s, the Prince would never again be dismissed as a dilettante royal amusing himself in his spare time by painting.

AFTER HIS RETURN HOME TO SWEDEN FROM PARIS IN 1889, Prince Eugen took on an increasingly important role in the Swedish art scene as a landscape painter, art collector and advocate for culture and the arts. One of the works that helped establish his reputation as a painter of note was Våren *(Spring)*, which the Prince painted at Balingsta, outside Stockholm, in 1891, and in which lessons from French plein air painting and detail realism were united with elements of a dawning National Romanticism. This was followed by works like Det Gamla Slottet *(The Old Castle)*, painted at Sundbyholm Manor outside Eskilstuna, as well as Molnet *(The Cloud)* in its multiple versions created with inspiration from Tyresö, Sweden. There, Prince Eugen became the central figure in an artist colony that included Swedish painters Richard Bergh, Oscar Björck, Gunnar G:son Wennerberg, Lennart Nyblom, author Helena Nyblom and her husband, aesthetics professor Carl Rupert Nyblom, as well as Danish painter Viggo Johansen. The Prince would spend 16 summers at Tyresö. At a comfortable distance from Stockholm and all its attendant obligations, the landscape was a vital inspiration for the Prince as a painter.

IN 1899, PRINCE EUGEN BOUGHT THE WALDEMARSUDDE PROPERTY from the Bergman Olson family, who had been running a shipping business and lumberyard on the site. The property was situated on the southern side of the island of Djurgården (The Royal Game Park), then outside Stockholm but today very much part of the city. The Prince immediately began planning the construction of his own home, which would include a park and gardens. He contracted the famous Swedish architect Ferdinand Boberg, with whom he would work closely to develop the site. The Mansion took two years to build. It was completed in 1905, and in 1913, a gallery building was added to house the Prince's steadily growing art collection. Further additions to the gallery were made in the 1940s.

IN HIS WILL, PRINCE EUGEN STIPULATED that his Private Apartments in the Mansion would remain intact and be shown to the public as they had looked in his time. To this day, the elegant and pleasant interiors of the Drawing Room, the Dining Room, the Flower Room and the Library are graced by significant pieces of furniture and decorative artworks by prominent Swedish artists such as the Prince himself, Ernst Josephson, Anders Zorn and Carl Larsson. And of course, the rooms are adorned with flowers. Prins Eugens Waldemarsudde is currently the only art museum in the country with an employed florist. The Prince's Private Apartments are decorated year round with beautiful flowers

THE CLOUD
by Prince Eugen 1896 (cropped)

THE LINSEED OIL MILL

from the greenhouses, park and gardens by the museum's skilled florist Kristina Öhman. The flower displays in the Art Nouveau vases and Waldemarsudde pots in the Drawing Room and Dining Room, and the Flower Room with its exuberance of blossoms, are beloved attractions for many visitors. Beneath Zorn's intimate portrait from 1909 of the Prince's mother, Queen Sophia, stand eleven or twelve Waldemarsudde pots of flowers, as they have since the days of Prince Eugen. His passion for flowers and garden art is evident in his park and gardens, arranged by the eye of an artist, and decorated with sculptures by among others the famous French sculptors Auguste Rodin and Antoine Bourdelle, and renowned Swedish sculptors Carl Milles and Carl Eldh. It is also evidenced by the strong floral presence inside the Mansion's beautiful rooms.

WHEN PRINCE EUGEN DREW THE MODEL of the Waldemarsudde pot in 1915, he had already designed decorative arts objects, primarily in silver and ceramics, intended as gifts among his circle of friends, the royal family and court. Prince Eugen also designed a number of chairs with links to the late Gustavian and Swedish Empire styles. At the turn of the century 1900, and influenced by the English Arts and Crafts movement, it was common for artists to engage in the decorative arts, decor and sometimes entire living environments alongside their painting. Swedish artists Gunnar G:son Wennerberg, Gustaf and Maja Fjæstad, Carl and Karin Larsson, Eva Bonnier and Ferdinand and Anna Boberg are only a few examples of this.

ON ONE OF THE OVERDOOR PAINTINGS in the Drawing Room, the Prince's close friend Georg Pauli has depicted the art form of decorative arts in a rendition of Prince Eugen in Alf Wallander's studio, a testimony of the Prince's passion for the design field. The Collections at Waldemarsudde also include around 900 applied art objects that the Prince received as royal heirlooms, or gifts that he himself had designed or acquired in Sweden and abroad.

AS AN 18-YEAR-OLD IN 1883, the Prince had already designed his first decorative arts object, a platter that was fired by Swedish porcelain manufacturer Rörstrand. The platter was decorated with a wooded landscape in blue. Several silver objects followed, of which the most famous is the Rowanberry Bowl *(Rönnbärsskålen)* in a distinctly Art Nouveau style. The outside of the low bowl is decorated with rowanberries and rowanberry leaves in cast, low relief. The ornamentation is

WOMAN'S HEAD
by Christian Eriksson

THE YOUNG LINNÆUS
by Carl Eldh

BOY WITH DOLPHIN
copy after the original by Andrea del Verrocchio

THE THINKER
by Auguste Rodin

Gate detail at entrance to Prins Eugens Waldemarsudde. Architect Ferdinand Boberg 1901.

reminiscent of the decorative expression of American architect Lois Sullivan, who in turn was a role model for Eugen's good friend, the architect Ferdinand Boberg. The Rowanberry bowl was made in 1897 according to the Prince's signed original, and was exhibited later that year at the major Arts and Crafts Exhibition in Stockholm. When the exhibition ended, the Prince gave the bowl as a gift to Ulla and Gustaf Celsing, whom he had come to know as a young man in Paris.

IN 1904, THE PRINCE DESIGNED THE MODEL for another silver bowl, this time with a completely different and more classic expression. The multifaceted vessel bears the Prince's monogram and the coat of arms of the province of Närke (Prince Eugen was Duke of Närke) in a beautifully elaborated frieze. The Prince's star silver piece is said to be a high bowl on a stand with twelve facets decorated with a waveband, an embossed angular pattern and a ribbon border. Jacob Ängman, the best silversmith in Sweden at the time, supervised and surveyed the actual execution. The Prince also designed jewellery in silver and enamel, such as brooches, rings, cufflinks and breastpins in a style reminiscent of Danish silversmith Georg Jensen's works from the same time. Prince Eugen donated one of the brooches, of gold and precious stones, to Emma Zorn in 1902 to show his appreciation for a lovely stay at the Zorngården in Mora with the artist couple Anders and Emma Zorn.

IN CERAMICS, THE PRINCE DESIGNED MODELS of decorated tableware, including a whole dinner service in white porcelain adorned with the province of Närke's coat of arms, a softly shaped wreath of laurel leaves and berries in relief on the brim, which had a thin gilt edge. The service was produced at Rörstrand in 1905. Prince Eugen also designed other flowerpots in addition to the Waldemarsudde pot, including one in Art Nouveau style with his crowned monogram and lancet shaped leaves around the mouth and base. The collections include two cobalt blue urns with gold decor and the words "From Eugen 1908", both signed Gustavsberg. The popular octagonal Waldemarsudde pot and the larger twelve-sided bowl, called a jardinière, were made after the Prince Eugen signed originals at Gustavsberg in 1915.

PRINCE EUGEN ONCE STATED THAT "Decorative arts objects should be based on geometric shapes." Several of the Prince's decorative arts objects are ßcharacterised by a geometrical design, as well as a clear, clean, classic and timeless look. The Waldemarsudde pot, with its slightly coned octagonal shape and simple decor in relief of vertical channels and horizontal wavebands in white glaze, is an example of this timeless, classic expression. The pot, which stands on eight feet, was produced for the home at Waldemarsudde, and also as a gift item. During the Prince's time, and to this day, there are always eleven or twelve Waldemarsudde pots with seasonal potted plants set beneath Anders Zorn's intimate portrait from 1909 of Prince Eugen's mother, Queen Sophia. The Prince preferred the flowers to be blue. However, white, yellow or light pink are also acceptable.

THE ARCHITECT AND FRIEND OF THE PRINCE, Ferdinand Boberg, was among those presented with a Waldemarsudde flowerpot by the Prince, which was later bequeathed to the Nationalmuseum (National Museum of Fine Arts) in Stockholm. In the archive at Waldemarsudde is a document stating that sculptor Axel Bruce was given the task of developing the mould and core for the pot for a fee of 200 crowns.

A POSSIBLE SOURCE OF INSPIRATION for Prince Eugen in the design of the Waldemarsudde pot is likely found in the circle of Josef Hoffmann and Wiener Werkstätte, and the so-called Counter-Art Nouveau style. The Waldemarsudde pot is undoubtedly one of Sweden's most famous and popular decorative arts objects, gracing institutions and homes all over the country. During the Prince's time, the Waldemarsudde pot was produced at the Gustavsberg porcelain factory outside of Stockholm. When production was resumed by the museum in 1952, it was at the initiative of the then museum director Gustaf Lindgren, who thought it would make a nice museum souvenir. Gustavsberg handled production until 1994, when it was taken over by Rörstrand until 2006. Gustavsberg then resumed production until 2015, at which point Lidköpings porslinsfabrik (the Lidköping porcelain factory) took over. The factory occupies the historic premises of Rörstrand, with a staff that has previously produced the pot during the Rörstrand days. The models, cores and production molds are based on the originals from 1915.

PRINCE EUGEN PERSONALLY DESIGNED the pot that is now known as No. 1 or "Ettan", and the low twelve-sided jardinière called "Trean" or No. 3. The

THE LINSEED OIL MILL

The Waldemarsudde pot in its various sizes, No. 5 (10 x 10 cm), No. 1 (13 x 13 cm), No. 2 (16 x 16 cm), No. 4 (19 x 19 cm) and the jardinière, No. 3 (13 x 25 cm).

other three sizes were launched later. The Waldemarsudde pot is only sold at Prins Eugens Waldemarsudde, in the museum shop or via the museum webshop. Waldemarsudde has exclusive rights to both the manufacture and sales of the popular pot. The unique handmade decorative arts object is produced according to the rules of applied art. The clay is fired and glazed, the outer surface polished, and each pot is examined at various stages in the production process in order to maintain the highest quality. Underneath the pot is a distinctive, unique bottom stamp with Prince Eugen's signature for originality and quality assurance.

IN HIS LIFE, PRINCE EUGEN WAS AN ARTIST, a patron of the arts and an advocate for arts and culture. On his death in 1947, his will decreed that the entire estate of Waldemarsudde be donated to the Swedish state. At the time, this was the single largest private art donation in Sweden. The donation included all of the buildings on the property, the beautiful park and gardens, an art collection of nearly 7,000 works of mainly Swedish, other Nordic and French artists, all fixtures and other personal property. When Waldemarsudde opened to the public in 1948, it became Sweden's first art museum with a focus on modern and contemporary art, and it also became a favoured place for visitors from all over the world. Today, Waldemarsudde is one of Sweden's most popular art museums, and regularly mounts ambitious exhibitions and programmes. Prins Eugens Waldemarsudde – with its captivating architecture, nature, park, gardens and art collection, situated with a beautiful view of the inlet to Stockholm – is a unique Gesamtkunstwerk. For the art museum, Prins Eugens Waldemarsudde, the Waldemarsudde pot is an invaluable and unique product whose returns are an important source of revenue for the museum.

THE FLORIST'S JOB *BALANCE AND HARMONY FROM THE WILD*

"WE CANNOT TAME NATURE," says Kristina Öhman, the florist and floral visionary responsible for the cut flower decorations at Waldemarsudde. Year round, she harvests plants from the cultivations and the park for her arrangements. To help her, she has a few tools, glass vases and urns – as well as the elegant Waldermarsudde pot designed by the Prince in 1915. Kristina Öhman shares Prince Eugen's passion for wild nature. During the Prince's time, the Private Apartments were decorated with fresh cut flowers and potted plants from private cultivations. There are descriptions preserved of which flowers were placed where and for which occasions during the year.

THE FLORAL ARRANGEMENTS AT WALDEMARSUDDE VARY. They are often unruly and deliberately asymmetrical, with garden character. The result depends on the availability of plants throughout the seasons, which means that there is sometimes a scarcity of cut flowers. "That characterises the arrangements and that is the way it is. Sometimes the potted plants and bulb plants play a more prominent role," says Kristina Öhman. "At the same time, it is a joy to work seasonally. There is always a plant that I long for: the first tulips in the greenhouses; when the flower clusters of wisteria colour the south wall behind the gallery blue. Or when the peony buds and dahlias bloom, and the amaryllis that pop up already in October."

IN ADDITION TO THE AVAILABILITY OF PLANT MATERIALS, there are other aspects to consider. The architecture of the rooms and the colour scheme that was designed by the Prince himself is a particular challenge. The Dining Room, for example, is a magnificent room with a coral carpet, turquoise walls and a number of artworks. At the same time, it is a large room that demands its arrangements.

"Some examples of flowers that work with this colour scale are dahlias, snapdragons, gladiolus and the Apricot Beauty tulip that has a scent of cardamom," says Kristina Öhman.

HER ARRANGEMENTS OFTEN TAKE UP A LOT OF SPACE, vertically or in formations that stretch out across the dining table. All around, on bureaus and small tables, single flowers are placed in smaller vases as complements. Perhaps the primary function of the floral arrangements is to inspire visitors who annually stream through the rooms of the Mansion. Many come particularly for the flowers, both for those that grow outside and for those indoors.

THE CLASSIC WALDEMARSUDDE FLOWERPOT is not only used for potted plants, as it was in the past, but also as a vase for garden flowers. The five sizes of the pot contribute to the whole with their different idioms. Sometimes the bouquets are built high, other times they are low and wide. The smallest pot is useful for single low flowers and for bouquets of meadow flowers. "The most beautiful is when many small pots are placed together," says Kristina Öhman. As one of the missions at Waldemarsudde is to preserve and manage the facility as it was at the time of the Prince, there is no use of oasis for the arrangements in the Prince's Private Apartments, a support foam that was not available then. Kristina Öhman uses more greenery, such as twigs, leaves and branches than they used in those days – a feature that gives a wilder impression. But the branches also have a supportive effect. "The goal with the flower arrangements at Waldemarsudde is that they will be perceived as balanced and harmonious in a wild way – no matter which pot, vase or urn the flowers are placed in."

KRISTINA'S TOOLS

1. PRUNING SHEARS *for tougher branches like chestnut.*
2. SMALL HANDY KNIFE *for cutting flower stems.*
3. THE FLORIST'S FAVOURITE PRUNERS *work for most jobs, such as the tulip harvest. Shown here is the tulip CARNAVAL DE NICE.*
4. SMALL HANDY PRUNING SHEARS *for thin stems. For example, the delicate, fragrant, yellow WILD TULIP that grows in the park at Waldemarsudde.*
5. KNIFE WITH REPLACEABLE BLADE *for cutting flower stems.*

1.
2.
3.
4.
5.

SPRING PALETTE *WITH FLOWERS ON A BARE BRANCH & THE FIRST DELICATE GREENERY*

OUTSIDE, WINTER MAY RAGE. But for Waldemarsudde's florist, spring starts in January when the first tulips bloom in the greenhouses. The earliest tulips have shorter stalks than those that bloom later in spring. At Waldemarsudde, both are used for bouquets in vases and for arrangements in pots. The spring season is a hectic time with continuous events like the spring market, musical concerts and dinners of various kinds. The Mansion is to be decorated with fresh cut flowers of the season, all to give visitors the feeling that someone is home. The flowers are an important part of the overall experience.

"At this time of year, I start almost every day in the greenhouse. I take the tulips that are in full bloom with me to a workroom in the Mansion where I place them in buckets of cold water before arranging them in different vases and pots," says Kristina Öhman. Just as important as the tulips during this season are twigs and branches. They provide support and structure in the arrangements. By late January and early February, Kristina harvests twigs and forces them indoors in buckets of warm water.

"Lilac and bird cherry bloom quickly and I often cut these branches first. The more branched they are, the better support for the sinuous tulip stalks." The delicate greenery and the sparse flowering of the branches make them the best dance partner for tulips in vases and pots. Red dogwood, currant twigs, chestnut, forsythia, blueberry sprigs and other branches are used in the arrangements. Chestnut and pipevines take the longest to bloom and one may need to wait three to four weeks.

"I use the branches as support for the stalks inside the vase. The weeping birch makes an excellent support, as the soft branches are easy to roll into a

20/2
20/2
20/2
20/2

wreath-like ball. The pipevine can also be used in a similar way." When the wildflowers bloom in the park, spring has properly sprung. The weather outside may still be erratic but that does not stop Kristina from picking what is blooming in the park.

The first winter aconites bloom early in the warm spring sun next to the gallery terrace. Yellow star-of-bethlehem and all anemones follow. For the spring flowers, the smallest Waldemarsudde flowerpot is useful.

"In the Prince's days, all the leaves of the wood anemones were removed and inserted in chicken wire in vases. It was a job that required nimble fingers and plenty of time, but the result was a perfect bouquet, round and voluptuous in shape." Today, simple and nicely sized bouquets that fit the smallest pots are preferred. She places these in windows and on low tables that are found in various places around the Mansion.

Thereafter, the spring flowers follow each other in bloom. Crocus, wood squill, snowbell, narcissus, snake's head, wisteria and clematis all embellish Waldemarsudde both outside and inside during spring. Even for potted plants, a lot happens in the first months of the year. Fairy primrose, which has been sown in November, starts to bloom in early spring. This is an unusual variety that for a long time could only be found at Waldemarsudde. However, lately it has been appearing in the flower shops.

"Cineraria is another important plant as it appears in old photographs from Prince Eugen's time. At Waldemarsudde, it is the high variety Masterpiece that is grown. It has daisy-like flowers that open in a cavalcade of colours such as pink, bright blue and violet. I often put them on the tables in the Flower Room in early spring."

BRANCHES
WHEN THE BRANCH BUDS START BURSTING, POTS & VASES SPROUT OPTIMISTICALLY

EVERYTHING IS USED, even the leftovers from when the arborist prunes the trees in the park. When the branch buds start bursting, the pots and vases sprout optimistically throughout the spring. Greenery can sprout in the dead of winter at Waldemarsudde. Twigs and branches that Kristina Öhman cuts in the park transform the winter into spring, at least indoors.

First, the bird cherry and lilac bloom. At the very darkest time, it takes two to three weeks until the buds burst after the pruned stalks have been placed in warm water. The pipevine and chestnut need four weeks. Everything in nature at this time can come to good use. When the arborist comes to prune the trees, Kristina takes branches from both oak and maple that sprout with delicate little flowers and leaves. The branches of the snowberry bush and twigs of blueberry are also useful for the tulips and narcissi of spring. Forsythia is special as the yellow flowers show first, followed by the leaves. The bird cherry gets tiny white flowers that help the warm spring sun feel less distant.

Kristina Öhman uses twigs and branches as support mass inside the pots. This way, they are practical while a part of the actual arrangement. Balls of weeping birch and pipevine together with twigs of lilac and rose hawthorn are placed in pots and vases. They provide a stable support for the plant stems throughout the entire flower season at Waldemarsudde.

PIPEVINE
CURRANT
BLACKTHORN
FORSYTHIA

CHESTNUT

BLUEBERRY

SIBERIAN DOGWOOD

BIRD CHERRY

IN POT NO. 3

Sprigs of LILAC, RED HAWTHORN and WEEPING BIRCH are examples of plant materials that facilitate flower arrangements.

The tulips ARMANI, BLACK PARROT, ÎLE DE FRANCE, WEBER'S PARROT, PEACH BLOSSOM, the hyacinth SPLENDID CORNELIA, and HONEYSUCKLE in the No. 3 pot. RED HAWTHORN is the base material.

TULIPS
THEY DANCE IN THE VASES UNTIL THE FIRST PETALS FALL

AT WALDEMARSUDDE, the greenhouses are in full bloom as early as December. This marks the start of the tulip season that lasts all the way into May.

The actual planting starts in September when the bulbs are placed in boxes of soil. Because tulips need a cold snap to bloom, they are put in the big tulip fridge at Waldemarsudde. This mimics winter, and they will start to grow. When they have grown a bit they are moved to bright greenhouses, and after about three weeks the first specimens are usually ready for harvest.

Kristina Öhman only harvests the tulips when the buds show colour. She often lets them stand and soak up water until the next day. That way, they have time to bloom and the stalks also become flexible and easy to work with. Tulips grow about a centimetre per day and drink lots of water. Making sure that the stalks are not without water is part of the florist's daily job during this period.

Waldemarsudde's greenhouse-grown tulips are at their loveliest when they bloom and they are kept at the Mansion until the first petals fall off. To keep tulips the same height, they need to be cut every now and then. Kristina Öhman likes to let the stalks grow and wander out across the tables as they like.

The dark red Black Parrot and Mount Tacoma, mixed with red dogwood, create a dramatic combination. Another is the mild yellow and citrus scented Verona with forsythia and budding Siberian peashrub.

2.
4.
5.
3.
1.

8.
10.
7.
9.
6.

11.
12.
13.
14.
15.

16.
17.
18.
19.
20.

TULIPS

1. PAKO
2. APRICOT BEAUTY
3. LYDIA
4. PRIMAVERA
5. JAN VAN NES
6. PEACH BLOSSOM
7. WHITE DESIRE
8. BLACK PARROT
9. WHITE PARROT
10. GABRIELLA
11. ÎLE DE FRANCE
12. BRUNO LILJEFORS
13. MICKEY MOUSE
14. ARMANI
15. DOUBLE DUTCH
16. ALADDIN
17. BALLERINA
18. CARNAVAL DE NICE
19. ESTELLA RIJNVELD
20. HELMAR

1.

2.

3.

4.

STEP BY STEP

TEN TULIPS

Arrange beautifully in the No. 3 pot with nature's materials

1. PICK A BUNCH OF BRANCHED TWIGS. Here we have used common snowberry twigs, but lilac is a good alternative. Cut to appropriate length. The tulips will grow, so leave a bit of length on the twigs.
2. LET THE CUT TWIGS SUPPORT THE OTHERS, which are then placed in water to form a support mass for the tulips.
3. STICK THE TULIPS DOWN LOW around the outer edge of the pot and continue up. Finish with the tulips at the top to make a nice shape.
4. USE DIFFERENT TYPES OF TWIGS, like blueberry or willow as shown here. If desired, more flowers, such as narcissi, can be added.

MATERIALS

TEN TULIPS used here are WHITE DESIRE

SNOWBERRY TWIGS

BLUEBERRY TWIGS
that have been forced indoors for two weeks and have started to bloom

PUSSY WILLOW

TULIPS, NARCISSI and PUSSY WILLOW in the No. 3 pot.

THE DINING ROOM, 18TH CENTURY FRENCH MANTEL CLOCK

Spring bouquet and tulips BRUNO LILJEFORS, PEACH BLOSSOM and WEBER'S PARROT, SNAKE'S HEAD, SNOWBALL TREE, RANUNCULI and SNOWDROPS in the No. 1 pot.

SUMMER BOUQUET

ZINNIA, MALLOW, HYDRANGEA, MARIGOLD

NARCISSI *ARE FRAGRANT POETRY THAT GRACE VASES AND POTS AT WALDEMARSUDDE*

NARCISSI EMBELLISH WINTER AND SPRING with their lovely fragrance. At Waldemarsudde, they are used in both vases and pots. Many different varieties are cultivated in the greenhouses, blooming successively. They are forced in the same way as the tulips and are planted in pots that Kristina Öhman places on the little flower table in the Drawing Room. They are often accompanied by ivy and fern of various sorts.

The big narcissus finale occurs when those under the apple trees by the greenhouses bloom. Kristina Öhman harvests different kinds that grow freely for the vases indoors. The fragrant drooping Cragford narcissus is mixed with various branches and twigs. When the corydalis blooms in May, Kristina mixes it with the poet's narcissus. It is also beautiful to mix narcissi of different sorts in the same vase.

Narcissi contain a plant secretion that has a toxic effect on other plants. They should preferably be kept in cool water for a few hours so that the secretions are washed off from the stalks. The florist changes the water several times to that the juices completely disappear. She avoids cutting the stalks again as then she would have to start over. It is therefore important that the narcissi are cut to a length that is suitable for both the vase and accompaniment from the start.

1.
2.
3.
4.
5.
6.

7.
8.
9.
10.
11.

NARCISSI

1. SAILBOAT

2. ABBA

3. GRAND SOLEIL D'OR

4. CHANGING COLOURS

5. SEGOVIA

6. VAN SION

7. SCARLET GEM

8. YELLOW CHEERFULNESS

9. BELLA ESTRELLA

10. SWEETNESS

11. WATERPERRY

STAIRS BY THE ORANGERY

NARCISSI in the No. 4 pot.
Including THALIA, PRIMEUR, POET'S NARCISSI and SIBERIAN CORYDALIS.

STEP BY STEP

WINDING TULIPS

Nest with eggs & spring flowers – an arrangement that fits nicely on a low table

1. POUR SOME WATER IN THE BOTTOM OF THE POT – used here is NO. 3 – and shape the branches of weeping birch into a nest and place in the pot.
2. USE TULIPS THAT HAVE GROWN in a vase for a few days. This makes them easier to bend and follow the shape of the pot.
3. PLACE SOME EGGS on top that have been dyed in the shades of the spring flowers.
4. ADD MORE SPRING FLOWERS that follow the birch branches.

MATERIALS

TULIPS used here are BLACK PARROT
WEEPING BIRCH alternatively, use BIRD CHERRY or HONEYSUCKLE
CROCUS
HYACINTH
DWARF IRIS
ANEMONE
COLOURED EGGS

2.

4.

THE SOUTH PORCH OF THE OLD HOUSE

Place some tissue or oasis at the bottom of the No. 1, 2 and 5 pots. Bind the flowers of FORGET-ME-NOT and HYACINTH on a sprig of ivy. Spray the wreaths with water, place in a plastic bag in the refrigerator until you are ready to decorate the table.

SETTING THE TABLE FOR A SPRING BUFFET

More than flowers in the pots

NEXT SPREAD

1. THE NO. 3 POT FILLED with eggs and twigs of dried climbing hydrangea.
2. BLUEBELLS AND CUCKOO FLOWERS in the NO. 1 pot.
3. SMALL WREATH OF HYACINTH AND IVY in the NO. 5 pot.
4. GRAPE HYACINTH AND BARRENWORTH in the NO. 5 pot.
5. COLOURED EGGS WITH SPRING TWIGS IN BLOOM. Cut the twigs and stick a water tube (or small bottle) on each, and let them frame the eggs in the NO. 3 pot.

TIP

Untreated wooden planks on simple stands make a great buffet table, and a lovely contrast to the white glossy Waldemarsudde flowerpots.

OPPOSITE PAGE

Spring buffet with herring, early potatoes, eggs, cheese, bread and spring vegetables. On the table are wildflowers of spring such as forget-me-not, barrenwort, bluebell and hyacinth.

MATERIALS

CLIMBILNG HYDRANGEA

BLUEBELL

FORGET-ME-NOT

CUCKOOFLOWER

IVY

HYACINTH

GRAPE HYACINTH

BARRENWORT

SPRING BRACNCHES

1.
2.
4.

The painting HYDRANGEAS by Prince Eugen. On the table are varieties of CINERARIA, low and old-fashioned high. All are forced in the greenhouses at Waldemarsudde.

THE DRAWING ROOM

FAIRY PRIMROSE in the No. 1 pot underneath Anders Zorn's portrait of Queen Sophia. The potted plants are altered according to season.

THE FLOWER ROOM

Prince Eugen in the 1910s, surrounded by stemmed PELARGONIUMS in pans on the floor. Photographer unknown.

EARLY SUMMER IS THE TIME OF SCENTS *THE SUN WARMS & THE FIELDS ARE ABLOOM WITH FLOWERS*

IF SPRING IS ALL ABOUT DELICATE GREENERY, then early summer is the time of scents. The fields are slowly coloured in a thin floral veil of blue, white and pink. Cow parsley, forget-me-not and barrenwort dominate the floral display in the early summer meadows.

"Meanwhile, all the more flowers are sprouting in the park. Bird cherry, lily of the valley, violet, wild tulip, daylily, starlight sensation, cowslip, lilac and roses are plants that I can pick for the Mansion arrangements," says Kristina Öhman. In the early summer at Waldemarsudde, the association Konstnärernas Vänner have their annual meeting with afternoon tea followed by a garden party. The association aims to enable artists to have a decent standard of living. The initial goal was to support and secure their lives in old age, and each year about 70 people are given assistance. Prince Eugen initially contributed to the fund's development by being active as the president of the association. Each spring he was also the host of the event.

"For me, it means that every nook of the Mansion must be decorated with the flowers of the season. Around 150 people come to drink tea and eat canapés, and Queen Silvia usually sits in the Flower Room together with the year's art prize recipients. I like to decorate the tables with flowers that match the rooms, even in the Prince's light blue kitchen." It takes a considerable quantity of

Early morning harvest of meadow flowers, CUCKOO FLOWER, FORGET-ME-NOT, COW PARSLEY, ahead of the Konstnärernas Vänner's annual event.

flowers. Wildflowers are the most reliable during this time. They also meant a great deal to the Prince, who was keen to preserve the meadows as a contrast to the more manicured gardens. Decorating with wildflowers indoors is a tradition at Waldemarsudde.

"Wildflowers take a long time to pick but over the years I have learnt a trick. Right in the meadow, I bundle them into good-sized bouquets. Then I strap a rubber band around the stalks and place them in buckets of water that I have with me." Thanks to this preparation, the work with removing leaves and unravelling stalks is not as extensive. Take a bundle, tear off most of the leaves and cut them to the right length before placing them in a vase. The rubber band is removed and complimented with the other flowers.

"I fill the large wide pot, No. 3, with forget-me-not. The flowers keep for a whole week if the water is changed regularly. The narcissi, which have at least as long a season as Waldemarsudde's tulips, come to good use on this day. There is a full narcissus field under the apple trees below the greenhouse where they are harvested. Narcissus works well with forget-me-not and meadow saxifrage, which make bouquets in blue, white and yellow." During this time, there is much happening and the Mansion needs to be kept in beautiful condition.

"I pick daisies, poor man's orchid, mountain cornflower, columbine, iris, Jacob's ladder, Solomon's seal, rodgersia leaves, starlight sensation and fragrant yellow daylily. If I'm lucky, I can also hear the nightingale sing for the first time as I work." When the tulip season comes to an end, the first peonies may have started to bloom, with a bit of luck. Together with columbine and lilac sprigs, they form a unique arrangement in the low wide Waldermarsudde pot. Besides peonies, the alliums also start to bloom. With their fluffy balls blooming on straight stalks in various shades of violet, they are bulb plants that create energy indoors. At Waldemarsudde, they work especially well with Gunnar Nylund's high cobalt blue ceramic vase. But it can be tricky to arrange the leafless stalks.

"My trick is to wrap a bergenia leaf around each stalk before placing them in the vase. Eventually, it will form a nice base down inside the vase that gives the stalks good stability." Until midsummer, the fragrant early summer flowers are in continuous succession in the arrangements. And as the season comes to a close, a new rich floral season approaches.

No. 5 pot with ALMOND BLOSSOM, COWSLIP, CUCKOO FLOWER and NARCISSI.

THE GRAVE OF PRINCE EUGEN IN THE PARK AT WALDEMARSUDDE

Wreath of THALIA NARCISSI, PEONIES, SPRAY ROSES, TULIPS, BLUEBELLS, HYDRANGEA and APPLE BLOSSOM.

THE FLOWER ROOM

Set for HRH Queen Silvia and the Konstnärernas Vänner scholars. FORGET-ME-NOT, SPRAY ROSES and CUCKOO FLOWERS.

HRH Queen Silvia's visit to Waldemarsudde for the Konstnärernas Vänner's annual event in May 2013.

THE DRAWING ROOM
The Prince's Private Apartment where Prince Eugen lived in the 1930s. On the table is a generous spring bouquet of DAISY, COLUMBINE and SNOWBALL BUSH.

THE DINING ROOM

The last TULIPS and the first PEONIES of the season meet in the same vase. COLUMBINE, BUTTERFLY BUSH in an Art Nouveau vase from the Gustavsberg Porcelain Factory.

STEP BY STEP

VERTICAL IRIS

Various covering materials in the No. 1 pot

On buffet tables, it is nice if the floral arrangements are tall and slim, so they are visible without taking up too much space. Iris goes well with Jacob's ladder and sheer light green pipevine. A few purple Mikado sticks will reinforce the shape of the arrangement and pick up the colour of the iris. The buds of the iris will bloom successively, so the wilted flowers can be carefully plucked out.

1. CUT A PIECE OF OASIS and let it soak up water in a bucket.
2. CUT THE OASIS SO THAT IT LEAVES about four centimetres from the top of the pot and fill with room temperature water.
3. VARIOUS MATERIALS CAN BE USED to conceal the oasis, such as bergenia leaves. Cut the stalk and insert between the oasis and edge of the pot so that it reaches the water. Fold the leaf over the oasis, make a neat incision in the leaf and fasten with the iris.
4. PRETTY PEBBLES OR DECORATIVE GLASS are other good mulches. When arranging in oasis, it is important to pick the plants and let them sit in a bucket to soak up water for a few hours, or overnight. Plants with soft stalks, such as pipevine, have a particular need for full saturation to be able to draw water from the oasis.

MATERIALS

IRIS
JACOB'S LADDER
PIPEVINE
BERGENIA LEAVES
MIKADO STICKS

1.

2.

THE DRAWING ROOM
ALLIUM, BERGENIA LEAVES, REEDS and PIPEVINE in Gunnar Nylund's ceramic vase.

PIPEVINE

STEP BY STEP

EARLY SUMMER BOUQUET

Classic Waldemarsudde flowers in the No. 2 & No. 4 pots

1. PLACE PEONY LEAVES IN THE POT with lukewarm water.
2. CUT THE FLOWERS and start with the shorter ones along the outer edge and build inwards towards the middle. Alternate the greenery and flowers.
3. NOW ALL THE STALKS have formed a good support mass. Insert the top flowers last.
4. MAKE SURE THAT NO LEAVES are under water, as this will start a decomposing process.
5. TRY MIXING DIFFERENT SHAPES, such as small flowers with the larger roundness of the peony or the pointy lupine. Grass is beautiful to insert into the bouquet to give it a delicate look.

Schizanthus is an old variety that has been cultivated at Waldemarsudde since the days of Prince Eugen. It is also known as poor man's orchid, and makes an excellent cut flower that lasts over two weeks in a vase. The fragrant stock is also part of the traditional range.

MATERIALS

DAISY
BUTTERCUP
SINGLE AND DOUBLE STOCK
SCHITZANTHUS
LILAC
LUPINE
PEONY
COLUMBINE
SNOWBALL BUSH
GROUND ELDER
VARIOUS GREEN LEAVES WITH STEMS

THE FLOWER ROOM
HYDRANGEA and IVY on the flower tables, SPRENGER'S ASPARAGUS, CISSUS, SWEDISH IVY in the alabaster urn.

THE FLOWER ROOM

Prince Eugen, late 1920s. Photographer unknown. On the flower tables are CHRYSANTHEMUM and SPIDERWORTS in the alabaster urn, to the right BEGONIA.

SUMMER
NOW IS THE TIME FOR FLOWERS AS FAR AS THE EYE CAN SEE

AFTER MIDSUMMER THE COLOUR OF THE OUTDOOR GREENERY deepens and stretches as far as the eye can see, while most is in full bloom.

"To me, summer is associated with a lot of work, as there are so many different plants to take advantage of. But what does that matter when I have such a beautiful place of work," says Kristina Öhman. For the visitors who pass through during summer, there is a calmness over the park. There are plenty of places to sit down – on a bench next to a fragrant lilac bush, a grassy slope towards the Saltsjön bay, on the hidden Kvarnberget hill with a view of the water, or on the dock below the old house.

"On Mondays, when the museum is closed to the public, the place is especially peaceful and I often see people camping on a bench for hours, enjoying a good book, or couples sharing dinner with proper china and glasses. In early mornings, I sometimes see canoe paddlers who have spent the night on the beach on the Ryssviken Bay." It is a beautiful place that Prince Eugen chose to settle in, and then left for us all to enjoy. In the summertime, the Museum often exhibits works from the collections, focusing on Prince Eugen's paintings along with those of his contemporary fellow artists. This is a good time to view the famous *Molnet (The Cloud)*, *Det Gamla Slottet (The Old Castle)* and *Våren (Spring)*, which are the Prince's most renowned works. During this time of year, Waldemarsudde offers a floral display like no other, even indoors. The start of summer is dominated by peonies that are grown by the greenhouse for the arrangements. The season starts about a week before midsummer and lasts for approximately three weeks.

"The unique thing with peonies is that you never really know how they will bloom. If it gets too hot, the loveliness can be over in a flash, while a sudden heavy shower can crush the flowers. It is therefore important to take advantage of them and utilise them while the flowering is underway."

Another plant that is in bloom at this time is the iris. Prince Eugen associated it with a garden that he fell in love with during a trip to Italy, and it is a classic flower at Waldemarsudde. A low variety creates a low border around the rose gardens and on the gallery terrace. There is also an iris garden that was recently recreated by the Round Temple. It is not only with the iris that the green leaves are used during the summer season. Kristina uses them abundantly, happily combining many different varieties.

"The heart-shaped leaves of the pipevine are nice when paired with peony leaves and strands of honeysuckle. The leaves give volume to the arrangements and set the style for the whole floral display." A strict arrangement becomes voluminous, vibrant and airy with the help of winding clematis twigs or honeysuckle. Other leaves work as a backdrop and to highlight the actual flowers in the bouquet, she says. Such as the dill-like leaves of the garden cosmos.

During summer, Kristina likes to use different shades of green. As autumn approaches, the leaves begin to change into many different colours, from yellow-green to purple. With the dawn of autumn, the floral arrangements at the Mansion also change.

COSMOS and LINDHEIMER'S BEEBLOSSOM

PEONIES
THE SEASON IS A THREE-WEEK-LONG COLOURFUL PERFORMANCE

WALDEMARSUDDE'S PEONY SEASON is a colourful performance that begins around midsummer and lasts for about three weeks. They first bloom in the field, where Kristina Öhman can harvest the very first specimens at an early stage.

There is also a 20-metre-long peony bed up by the greenhouse where she harvests peonies throughout the season. The bed is made up of plants that have been moved from different places in the park, as well as purchased varieties. Therefore it is not possible to determine exactly which varieties are grown there.

Kristina Öhman likes to make large, full bouquets of baroque character for any room in the Mansion. Some are all white based on the fragrant Festiva Maxima. The arrangements can also be colourful, like the dark pink Karl Rosenfeldt and Jacob's ladder, fragrant daylily, light green lady's mantle and the lacy flowers of the ground elder. Foxglove, ground elder and light pink peonies make a lovely pastel pink bouquet.

Another of the peony's many plant companions is the rhubarb. A variety called Victoria, whose light red stalks are beautiful in a clear glass vase along with peonies is grown on the peninsula. The result is a bouquet with a pinky red colour scale.

When they have finished blooming, the seedpods are a work of art in themselves if you look closely. Kristina Öhman likes to use these in the floral arrangements. Peony leaves are also used in the bouquets throughout the season, and indeed well into the autumn when the crisp greenery shifts to a purplish hue.

1.
2.
3.
4.
5.

6.
7.
8.
9.
10.

FRAGRANT PEONIES

All the fragrant peonies in the summer gardens have been moved from an older flowerbed, so some varieties may be old. All are fragrant peonies, which can vary greatly. The old varieties are unknown, but the newer ones are listed here.

1. SARA BERNHARDT

2. KARL ROSENFIELD

3. BOWL OF BEAUTY *Old variety*

4. FESTIVA MAXIMA

5. EDULIS SUPERBA *Old variety*

6. KARL ROSENFIELD

7. FESTIVA MAXIMA

8. SARA BERNHARDT

9. OLDER VARIETY *Unknown*

10. COMMON RED SCENTED PEONY *Old variety*

FAS-2

GARDEN REFRESHMENTS

The low pot acts as a bowl for the STRAWBERRIES, and the smallest pot as serving bowls. In the glass vase are red RHUBARB STALKS with PEONIES in shades of pink and cerise. Rhubarb lemonade made from the VICTORIA variety that grows in abundance in the nursery at Waldemarsudde.

1.
2.
3.
4.
5.
6.
7.

GREENERY AS BASE

When florist Kristina Öhman arranges flowers in vases and the Waldemarsudde pot, she not only thinks of the flowers in her bouquets, but also the greenery.

Here are examples of what is available in the park and gardens that she fills the vases with.

1. RUDBECKIA *Large dark seedpods give a lovely contrast in the vase.*
2. LILAC *Picked and forced indoors already in winter and used as support and company for tulips.*
3. HOSTA *Beautiful leaf in the summer bouquet.*
4. GRAPE VINE *Winding vines that give a wild expression in the summer floral arrangements.*
5. HONEYSUCKLE *Picked in early spring for vases with tulips and narcissi.*
6. SPRENGER'S ASPARGUS *Beautiful in the vase and keeps well.*
7. BERGENIA *These large leaves can clad the inside of a glass vase to conceal the stems.*
8. ALLIUM *Decorative even after blooming without wilting.*
9. HYDRANGEA *Useful as green accompaniment in the vases. Also has a nice autumn colour.*
10. CURRANT *Decorative with its green unripe berries.*
11. CLEMATIS *The vines are sustainable and beautiful.*
12. BRUNETTE *Lovely aubergine coloured leaves are nice in bouquets and its flowers have a wonderful scent of raspberry. Belongs to the perennials of late autumn.*
13. FORSYTHIA *Has a beautiful autumn colour in shades of burgundy.*
14. RHUBARB *Fabulous in a glass vase with its red stalk. Combine with tulips or peonies in shades of red.*
15. PIPEVINE *The florist's favourite with its winding vines. Grows on the Mansion's north side, several metres up the facade.*
16. HOSTA *Lovely lime green, large leaves from the round flowerbeds on the north side of the Mansion.*
17. COLUMBINE *Just finished blooming and decorative with its green seedpod.*
18. POPPY *Still beautiful despite having dropped its last petal.*
19. RASPBERRY *A favourite among the flower decorations all season, first as greenery and later in autumn when the leaves shift in reds and greens.*
20. IVY *The one that grows at Waldemarsudde is strong, and thus excellent for decorating Christmas moss wreaths.*
21. DAYLILY *The thin, long leaves are excellent in vases.*
22. HOSTA *Smaller variety with a white edge.*

9.
10.
8.
11.
12.
14.
13.

15.
16.
17.
18.
19.
20.
21.
22.

POTTED PLANTS *WALDEMARSUDDE'S MAINSTAY*

OF ALL THE POT PLANTS THAT ARE GROWN IN THE GREENHOUSES, it is primarily the pelargoniums that prevail in the Mansion.

At Waldemarsudde, the potted plants are as important as the cut flowers. Since the early 1900s, plants such as cineraria, primula, poison primrose, cape primrose, lady's purse, cyclamen, begonia, wallflower and pelargonium have been grown in the greenhouses. At the Prince's time, these were what decorated the Mansion. It is only in recent years that cut flowers have come to represent the greater part of the flower decorations at Waldemarsudde.

Potted plants do still play a key role, and during the year about 250 of them pass through the Mansion's rooms. All must be kept in good condition, which means that the yellow leaves and wilted flowers are removed regularly. The plants are turned periodically so that the leaves that have been exposed to light are turned inwards.

Today the pelargoniums have moved onto centre stage in the Mansion. Mårbacka, English, regal and various scented pelargoniums are part of the classic range of Waldemarsudde.

The Waldemarsudde pot is used diligently with the potted plants. It fits well with the Mansion and fulfills a practical function. The feet on which the pot stands raise it up a bit from windowsills and tables. This allows air to pass underneath so that no condensation occurs. Kristina Öhman also likes to put clay pellets, clay shards or oasis at the bottom of the pots before placing the plants in them.

2.

4.

5.
6.
7.
8.

PELARGONIUM

1. MADAME NONIN

2. SWEET MIMOSA

3. MADAME THIBAULT *Old variety*

4. SWEET JESS

5. EKEBY OLIVIA

6. CONCOLOUR LACE

7. MÅRBACKA

8. KARDINAL

TIP

Fill the bottom of the pot with CLAY PELLETS, CLAY SHARDS or OASIS so that the inner pot does not sit too low and in water.

Various PELARGONIUMS *in Prince Eugen's beloved pots.*

SOUTH PORCH OF THE OLD HOUSE

SCENTED PELARGONIUM

STEP BY STEP

SUMMER PASTELS

A lovely flower cushion in the No. 3 pot with flowers of round shapes

Place all plants in buckets of water for a while so that they become springy and easier to work with. Soak the oasis block.

1. CUT THE SATURATED OASIS BLOCKS. Place one piece at the bottom, about three centimetres high, and place two blocks on top of it on the side. Cut it to the shape of the pot, leaving a few centimetres around the edge. Splice if needed. Cover with hydrangea leaves that are fastened one after another with the flower stalks.
2. PLACE THE FLOWERS CLOSELY TOGETHER and keep in mind that the flower heads are to be placed inside the edge of the pot, so a good idea is to bevel the oasis.
3. SMALL APPLES ARE SECURED with flower sticks, twigs.
4. FINALLY, FRAME THE FLOWER CUSHION with some twigs of pipevine. Cut the vines, stick the ends into the oasis and wrap around, fastening with wire if needed. Fill the pot with water.

MATERIALS

GARDEN HYDRANGEA

ZINNIA

GLOBE THISTLE

DAHLIA

ELDERBERRY

PEPITA ROSE

PASHMINA SUMMERHOUSE ROSE

PIPEVINE

SMALL GREEN APPLES here from Waldemarsudde's ROSE APPLE

2.

3.

FROM PLANTING *TO HARVESTING*

WHEN THE TINY SEEDS HAVE GROWN TO FULL SIZE in the flowerbeds, the Mansion is flush with magnificent flower arrangements. From July, Kristina Öhman starts harvesting cut flowers in the flowerbeds by the garden nursery. They have been constructed specifically to supply the Mansion's flower arrangements, and this is where cut flowers are grown for vases both in the museum and at the Mansion.

The gardeners sow the first flowers in February. When they have grown into sturdy seedlings, they are moved from the greenhouses to the garden boxes, and then eventually planted in the flowerbeds. Thanks to the plantings in the flowerbeds, there are generous amounts of flowers to harvest throughout the summer. The range has barely changed from when the Prince lived. Marigolds, salvia viridis, alonsoa, zinnia, rudbeckias, scabiosa, cornflowers, sneezeweed, blanket flowers, whorled coreopsis, various types of sunflowers, snapdragon, fragrant tobacco flowers, cosmos, lovely dahlias, red majestic lobelia, baby's breath, flossflowers, poppies, verbena, Lindheimer's beeblossom, aster and gladiolus are still part of the traditional range.

During the summer, Kristina Öhman's days start in the flowerbeds. Equipped with filled buckets, she harvests flowers that are immediately placed in the water. Summer flowers droop quickly. By immediately placing them in water, they become easier to work with. A pair of sharpened pruning shears is the best tool for the job, and the creative process starts already in the flowerbed. Kristina Öhman chooses colours and flowers to harmonise with the Mansion's various rooms.

But it is not just a matter of cutting the plants. Kristina harvests the flowers so that they can shoot new stems and flower again. She cuts snapdragons a bit above ground, while cosmos and dahlias are snipped above the branching so that the side buds can bloom. Some vases, however, require long stalks.

In late summer, when everything has grown to full size, Kristina Öhman goes all out on the arrangements. Large flower arrangements are given plenty of space in the rooms with high ceilings. Kristina Öhman plays with proportions by creating generous arrangements in the Drawing Room while holding back on the bouquet in the Dining Room, or vice versa.

In June, the annual summer flowers are planted, such as DAHLIAS, RUDBECKIAS, TASSEL FLOWERS, MARIGOLDS and TOBACCO FLOWERS.

HARVEST

The flowerbeds can be harvested from July.

MARIGOLD

RUDBECKIA

MEXICAN SUNFLOWER

ZINNIA

RUDBECKIAS *LIKE HAPPY SUNS, THEY GILD THE VASES FAR INTO AUTUMN*

ONE OF KRISTINA ÖHMAN'S MANY FAVOURITE FLOWERS is the rudbeckia. At Waldemarsudde, it is grown in a handful of different varieties, annual and perennial, in a colour scale that shifts from yellow to burgundy and various shades of brown. One of the oldest varieties is grown down by the shore below Rodin's *The Thinker* and is called Goldquelle. It can grow to the height of a human in the right conditions, but at Waldemarsudde it competes with throngs of tree roots that have been allowed to spread out in the flowerbed.

During the Prince's time, it was most often from these flowerbeds that the flowers were harvested when his home was to be decorated. There is a film that shows gardener Gunnar Lövgren carrying an armful of flowers just picked from the flowerbeds. Old black-and-white photos show vases and flowers virtually everywhere, on Prince Eugen's desk, on chests of drawers and on the loggia where he ate lunch when the weather permitted.

Today, Kristina Öhman arranges rudbeckias with other flowers in shades of pink and cerise. The bouquets are filled out with sprigs of garden hydrangea whose leaves shift in reddish-purple tones at this time of year. They fit nicely, while giving the bouquet airiness and volume.

She fills the blue glass vase with yellow rudbeckias in different shades. The result is a colourful eye-catcher with blue larkspur and blue salvia viridis. To soften the colour mixture of the bouquet, Kristina adds lime yellow that can be found in tobacco flowers and anise hyssop leaves at Waldemarsudde. Finally, she adds light green leaves from pipevine and hosta. The blue and yellow arrangement fits best on the table in the Bernadotte Room with its ochre yellow walls.

1.
2.
3.
4.
5.
6.
7.
8.

10.
11.
9.
12.
13.
17.
15.
16.
14.

RUDBECKIAS

1. CAPPUCCINO

2. MOROCCAN SUN

3. CAPPUCCINO

4. ECHINACEA PARADISO

5. MOROCCAN SUN

6. CAPPUCCINO

7. CHEROKEE SUNSET

8. PRAIRIE GLOW

9. GOLDQUELLE

10. PRAIRIE GREEN EYES

11. GOLDSTURM

12. MAYA

13. RUDBECKIA NITIDA

14. GOLDSTURM

15. GOLDILOCKS

16. CHEROKEE SUNSET

17. CHEROKEE SUNSET

THE MANSION'S STAIRCASE

Kristina Öhman coming down the stairs with TOBACCO FLOWERS, DAHLIAS, PIPEVINE, COSMOS, LINDHEIMER'S BEEBLOSSOM, TRUMPET FLOWERS, RASPBERRY SPRIGS and YELLOW IRIS LEAVES in the No. 4 pot.

THE ENTRANCE HALL
Looking into the Library.

1.

STEP BY STEP

WHITE & TALL

Build with volume in the No. 4 pot

1. START WITH THE GREENERY, hydrangea and peony leaves. Pluck the lowest leaves off the stalks so that there are no leaves under water. Cut the stalks with a sharp knife.
2. FILL THE POT WITH THE LEAVES that will then support the flowers.
3. MAKE SURE TO ALSO CUT THE LOWEST LEAVES off the flower stalks. Place the flowers around the edge of the pot, and build up towards the centre.
4. FILL WITH FLOWERS AND GREENERY. Finally, insert the longest flower stalks. They will stand firmly now that all the stalks have formed a dense base.

MATERIALS

TOBACCO FLOWER
SNAPDRAGON
SCABIOSA
DAHLIA
LINDHEIMER'S BEEBLOSSOM
PHLOX
GARDEN COSMOS
Leaves of HYDRANGEA, CURRANT, PEONY, RASPBERRY, IRIS

THE DINING ROOM

The No. 4 pot with DAHLIAS, ZINNIA, SNAPDRAGON, SEEDPODS of MEADOWSWEET and PEONY in coral shades that harmonise with the Chinese carpet.

THE PRINCE'S KITCHEN

BASIL, THYME, OREGANO, MARJORAM, ROSEMARY and seed planted POT ROSES in the No. 1 and 5 pots.

STEP BY STEP

WARM & SUNNY YELLOW TONES

A simple arrangement in the No. 3 pot

1. PLACE FOUR WATER-FILLED glasses in the pot.
2. FILL WITH LEAVES of peony, hydrangea and fennel.
3. CONTINUE WITH THE FLOWERS, bush marigolds and various rudbeckias.
4. INSERT SO THAT THE FLOWERS form a nice shape and finish with a large sunflower as centrepiece.

The bush marigolds form tufts and are used as border plants on the gallery terrace at Waldemarsudde. This small-flowered variety has a pleasant citrus fragrance and one tuft is enough to fill the No. 3 pot.

MATERIALS

RUDBECKIAS

BUSH MARIGOLDS

SUNFLOWER

Leaves of PEONY, HYDRANGEA & FENNEL

2.

DAHLIAS *GENEROUSLY HARVESTED IN LARGE BUNCHES & COLOUR COORDINATED WITH THE VARIOUS ROOMS*

IN THE DAHLIA SEASON, nature is rich and generous. Even the flowerbeds at Waldemarsudde are bursting with flowers that have grown over summer. The florist makes arrangements for the Mansion that pour out, and with the help of vines, spread across the tables.

There are different varieties of dahlias in the flowerbeds on the Waldemarsudde peninsula, both sown from seeds and those that have grown from tubers. When they have properly bloomed, they are harvested in large bunches to be placed in vases of cool water.

Kristina Öhman now makes bouquets for the Dining Room in orange and apricot tones, as they harmonise with the room's carpet. Burgundy sunflowers break nicely with the yellow-red colours, while raspberry twigs and the dill-like leaves from cosmos make the bouquets airy and green. Orange marigolds are not only nice together with the other flowers in the bouquet, they are also very significant for the place, as they were among the Prince's favourite flowers.

Sometimes, when Kristina Öhman wants a mild and minimal arrangement, she may let a single large dahlia float on the water's surface in the No. 3 pot. To frame the flower, she lets a few vines of Virginia creeper twirl along the edge of the pot.

1.
2.
3.
4.
5.
6.
7.
8.
9.
10.

11.
13.
12.
14.
15.
17.
16.
19.
20.
18.
22.
21.

DAHLIAS

1-5. *Variety from the seed mixture* FANTASIA DAHLIA PINNATA

6. *Seedsown* DECORATIVE DAHLIA *from* DECORATIVE GIANTS

7. DAHLIA TAMBURO

8. DECORATIVE DAHLIA *Seedsown*

9. DECORATIVE DAHLIA

10. *Variety from the seed mixture* FANTASIA DAHLIA PINNATA

11. *Variety from the seed mixture* FANTASIA

12. *Variety from the seed mixture* FANTASIA

13. MIGNON DAHLIA *Variety from the Prince's time*

14. CACTUS DAHLIA LUDVIG HELFERT

15. BALL DAHLIA SUNNY BOY

16. DECORATIVE DAHLIA LEMON CANE

17. *Variety from the seed mixture* FANTASIA DAHLIA PINNATA

18. *Variety from the seed mixture* FANTASIA DAHLIA PINNATA

19. *Seedsown from the mixture* COLLARETTE DANDY

20. *Variety from the seed mixture* FANTASIA DAHLIA PINNATA

21. DECORATIVE DAHLIA HENRIETTE

22. MIGNON DAHLIA *Variety from the Prince's time*

HARVESTING TIP

When harvesting, be sure to do it above a branch so that the buds are kept for a later harvest.

THE POND BY THE WATER GARDENS
NÄCKROSEN (WATER LILY), *sculpture by Per Hasselberg*
DAHLIAS float in the water.

ROSES in the No. 5 pot on a Swedish-made faience tray from Marieberg, 1780s. A gift from The Prince's father King Oscar II.

ROSE
DOROTHY PERKINS

THE FLOWER ROOM

Summer bouquet with DAHLIA, LARKSPUR, SCABIOSA, PUSSY FOOT, TRUMPET FLOWER, SNAPDRAGON as well as PIPEVINE and LILAC beneath a triptych by Prince Eugen.

OPPOSITE PAGE

Rose, RED RIDING HOOD

2.

3.

STEP BY STEP

BALL OF PIPEVINE

The beautiful, winding pipevine has many uses

1. HARVEST A FEW METRES OF PIPEVINE and pluck the leaves off the stems.
2. INTERTWINE THE STEMS to form a round translucent shape and place it in the pot so that one half of it sticks out, and fill with water. The NO. 3 pot is used here.
3. THE PIPEVINE HAS NOW CREATED A MESH for the flowers to be inserted into. Pluck all the leaves off the stalks, cut with a knife and ensure that they reach the water. Let the flower heads rest on the mesh to form a nice round shape. If you do not fill the entire mesh with flowers, the pipevine will show through.
4. IF POSSIBLE, USE SEEDPODS AS WELL, or add a couple of beautiful white dahlias to contrast with the bright colours.

The Linseed Mill and Conservatory are visible in the background.

MATERIALS

PIPEVINE

LOVE-LIES-BLEEDING

DAHLIA

ZINNIA

GARDEN COSMOS

ROSA RUGOSA

TRUMPET FLOWER

RUDBECKIA

RUE seedpods

MEADOWSWEET seedpods

HINT OF AUTUMN

AUTUMN APPROACHES WITH ROWAN, ROSE HIP, ELDERBERRY & SNOWBERRY

WHEN THE MAPLE TREES in the park shift to yellows and reds, we know that autumn is on its way. The landscape at Waldemarsudde is slowly transformed and the plants that were recently used as cut foliage in vases change to a golden colour scale.

This is a rich time of year. Before the frost comes, there are still plenty of flowers. Kristina Öhman harvests elderberry, rose hips, crab apple, rowan, Virginia creeper and love-in-a-mist in the park. The plants add character and the scent of decay to the arrangements. Together with dahlias, rudbeckias, garden cosmos, marigolds, winding clematis and the last roses of summer, the result is lavish and full.

"Yellow is a dominant colour in the flowerbeds. Many people have a hard time with that colour. But in the autumn light, the yellow flowers are particularly beautiful, especially together with flowers of the same shade," she says. Dahlias and nasturtiums are the first plants to go with the first night frost. Some years we can be lucky enough to find nasturtiums that have escaped the cold. Those plants that grow protected by the wall just below the gallery terrace have a tendency to live longer.

"I often use them in the Library where the vines with both flowers and seed-pods meander out across the room's long table. The nasturtiums attract a lot of attention as they normally should not survive in areas visited by the year's first frost." There are other places in the park where the frost does not easily reach.

TEACUP *borrowed from Bacchus Antik.*

But you must know them, and Kristina, who through the years has combed through every thicket on the peninsula, knows where to find the goodies.

"The last cosmos of the season are usually found in the flowerbeds next to the gallery terrace. At this late stage in the season, the gardener gives me permission to pick the flowers in the beds." Cyclamen is part of the traditional potted range at Waldemarsudde and now the plants, which were sown in January, are starting to bloom. They need a long time to develop into fully grown plants. But in October, the first specimens are brought up to the Mansion.

"I like to mix various shades of pink and red cyclamen together in the low wide Waldermarsudde pot." After the summer's explosion of fragrant blossoms and the autumn's rich arrangements, it can be nice to rest the senses a little. Kristina likes to use flowers in white and green together with wild plants found in nature this time of year. One suggestion is to use the No. 3 pot as a base for a flower concoction consisting of various chrysanthemums and carnations, skimmias and hydrangeas.

"Sometimes I like to make low arrangements. I often work down inside the pot, which creates a feature that can be placed on a low level, such as a coffee table."

CEZA
CONSTA

SETTING THE CRAYFISH TABLE

The season's plants in shades of red & orange

NEXT SPREAD

1. MANY SMALL POTS LINED UP – here the NO. 5 – form a garland of flowers. Dahlias, the little coral bead plant with its orange berries, and virginia creepers make a colourful decoration.

2. LAY A SMALL FLOWER at each place setting on the table.

3. RED ROSE HIPS ARE BEAUTIFUL to cover the oasis with in the gladiolus decorations.

4. THE CRAYFISH ARE PLACED in the low NO. 3 Waldemarsudde pot.

5. NAPKIN RINGS OF PIPEVINE.

MATERIALS

DAHLIA
GLADIOLUS
VIRGINIA CREEPER
CROWN DILL
ROSE HIP
CORAL BEAD PLANT
PIPEVINE

BEER GLASSES *borrowed from Antique & Quriosashopen.*
SNAPS GLASSES *from Bacchus Antik.*

2.

3.

5.

STEP BY STEP

NASTURTIUM, MARIGOLD & ROSE HIP

Colour-bursting late summer flowers

1. INTERTWINE THE BRANCHES of pipevine, without leaves. Place them in the No. 3 pot, as support for the stalks. Add some green leaves such as peony or hydrangea leaves.
2. CONTINUE PLACING FLOWERS AT THE BOTTOM along the outer edge, such as bush marigold, nasturtiums, rudbeckias, dahlias and the like. The raspberry leaves now have shifting red tones and go beautifully with the other flowers.
3. FILL WITH GREENERY AND FLOWERS from the edge inwards. Insert the top flowers last.
4. PICK ROSE HIP TWIGS of some length and let them float out with the clematis vines.

MATERIALS

NASTURTIUM
RUDBECKIA
MARIGOLD
DAHLIA
CLEMATIS
ROSE HIP
Leaves of PEONY, HYDRANGEA, RASPBERRY

1.

2.

SOUTH PORCH OF THE OLD HOUSE

CYCLAMEN in the No. 3 pot on a bed of MAPLE LEAVES and PARADISE APPLES.

THE THINKER
by Auguste Rodin

THE PRINCE'S KITCHEN

Arrangement of sculptures and green plants. LACE FERN, PONYTAIL PALM, MOTHER SPLEENWORT, CLUBMOSS and CREEPING WIRE VINE. Sculptures, from left: NEAPOLITAN PRINCESS by Francesco Laurana, TORSO by Anders Jönsson, A YOUNG REVOLUTIONARY by Christian Eriksson, PORTRAIT OF THE AUTHOR VIKTOR RYDBERG by Per Hasselberg.

STEP BY STEP

LOW & COMPACT IN SHADES OF GREEN

A low and tight arrangement in shades of green makes a lovely centrepiece on the dinner table

1. SOAK THE OASIS. Cut to shape and place in the No. 3 pot, leaving five centimetres to the top of the pot. Let the plants soak up water for a few hours before they are placed in the oasis.

2. CUT THE FLOWER STALKS with a sharp knife to approximately five centimetres and insert straight into the oasis.

3. FRAME WITH IVY that runs along the edge. The black seeds of the sunflower become a centrepiece among the green and white flowers.

MATERIALS

CHRYSANTHEMUM

CARNATION

ROSE

HYDRANGEA

WINTERBERRIES

BERRIES OF ST JOHN'S WORT

SNOWBERRIES, SUNFLOWER SEEDS AND IVY
from the gardens of Waldemarsudde

THE STUDIO

Prince Eugen, 1910s.
Photographer unknown.

THE LIBRARY

AMARYLLIS and HAWTHORN SPRIGS.

THE OLD HOUSE
No. 1 pot with candle decoration of MOSS, IVY, CLUBMOSS and LARCH CONES.

STEP BY STEP

GREEN MOSS, IVY & PINE CONES

An arrangement that lasts longer, without potted plants or fresh flowers

1. FORM A ROUND BALL of newspaper and wrap with myrtle wire.
2. WRAP THE MOSS AROUND in an even shape. Wrap the wire tightly, as fresh moss will shrink.
3. PLACE A PIECE OF DRY OASIS in the NO. 1, 2 and 5 pots to hold the candle steady. Cut some pieces of thicker wire, about four centimetres long. Heat the end of the wire to make it easier to stick it into the candle.
4. PLACE THE BLOCK CANDLE in the oasis. Decorate with moss and form a simple candle ring of ivy and clubmoss. Decorate with a few cones, preferably of larch.

MATERIALS

GREEN MOSS

IVY

CLUBMOSS

CONES

OTHER

Block candle
Thick wire
Newspaper
Myrtle wire
Oasis

1.

2.

3.

4.

WINTER
THE FROST SPINS WHITE CRYSTALS ROUND THE VEGETATION

WHEN THE FIRST SNOW HAS COVERED THE FLOWERBEDS, both the gardener and the florist can breathe a sigh of relief. What remains to be harvested in the park are hawthorns with their red berries and dried seedpods of purple mullein. Now serenity spreads in the park. Winter has come to Waldemarsudde.

Even the boat traffic in the Saltsjön Bay decreases, but the greenhouses are abuzz with activity. The Christmas flowers are being prepared for the holidays. At Waldemarsudde, the seasons flow into each other and those visitors who have made it out to Waldemarsudde in autumn have already been able to enjoy the year's first amaryllis.

A lack of cut flowers typifies the floral arrangements throughout this period. The filled flower vases are replaced by potted plants. They are grown from seeds in the greenhouses and have a long tradition at Waldemarsudde, and were used already at the Prince's time as table decorations at the Mansion during the winter.

"Cyclamen, begonia and Christmas cactus are part of our classic winter range and there are several old photographs that show where and how they were placed," says Kristina Öhman. Many of the beautiful pots that were used at the Mansion are still there. The wide Art Nouveau pot from Gustavsberg in white is useful as it holds many plants, and Kristina likes to fill it with white, fragrant cyclamen.

The Waldemarsudde pot is diligently used, even for bulbs such as amaryllis and hyacinth. Tradionally, the year's first 12 blue hyacinths are placed on the chest of drawers beneath Anders Zorn's portrait of Queen Sofia that hangs in the the Parlour.

"The first hyacinths tend to bloom sometime at the beginning of December. Towards Christmas, the colour of the flowers changes at the Mansion. Even though the Prince did not celebrate Christmas at Waldemarsudde, it was to be beautifully decorated during the holidays."

"I get many pink flowers from our greenhouses this time of year, both bulbs and potted plants. I enjoy placing the Waldemarsudde pots of mixed sizes together, filled with hyacinth, amaryllis, Christmas begonia and cyclamen in varying shades of pink," says Kristina Öhman. Lily of the valley belongs to the traditional flowers at Waldemarsudde. In the early 1900s, it was a common flower at Christmas and Prince Eugen used it both as decoration at the Mansion and as gifts to family and friends.

"They are grown from sprouts that the gardener orders. When the first bells open on delicate stalks, I fill the No. 3 pot and cover the soil with moss. The lovely scent spreads all over." Because green moss is mainly what grows at Waldemarsudde, it is used to cover the soil that the lily of the valleys are planted in. If Kristina happens to find some Cladonia stellaris somewhere else, she alternates with that.

"The white moss goes nicely both with the pot and little bells of the lily of the valley. It brightens up the gloomy winter light." When Christmas is over, it is not long before the new season begins. In the garden nursery, the spring planting is already under way and hundreds of bulbs of tulip and narcissus are waiting to be brought from the fridges to the greenhouses. After about three weeks in the light, they can begin to be used in the flower arrangements.

"In anticipation of the first tulips, I usually use white amaryllis in the Drawing Room." Now it is a bit of a challenge to achieve the wild look that is a Waldemarsudde hallmark. With the help of dried plants and seedpods, Kristina achieves the right feel for this short period.

TILE STOVE IN THE OLD HOUSE

Wreath of SILVER DUST and CUSHION BUSH. In the No. 2 pot is WIRE-NETTING BUSH with CLADONIA STELLARIS. Candle rings of CUSHION BUSH, SAGE and SILVER DUST. Balls of LAMB'S EAR, SAGE and CUSHION BUSH.

1.
2.
3.
4.

STEP BY STEP

SOFT LAMB'S EAR & SAGE

An ambient still life

1. USE A PRE-MADE BALL of oasis, as a perfectly round shape is required when gluing leaves.
2. PICK LAMB'S EARS, both large and small. Place the smaller ones at the top of the ball, and the larger towards the middle. Remember to overlap the leaves, as they shrink when they dry.
3. CHRISTMAS BAUBLES are an alternative to paper and oasis. Wrap the cushion bush sparsely on the white and silver coloured baubles. Use silver wire to make it part of the decoration.
4. SAGE LEAVES HAVE BEEN USED for the smaller ball that fits in the smallest pot No. 5, and Lamb's ears in the No. 1 pot.

MATERIALS

LAMB'S EAR

SAGE

CUSHION BUSH

OTHER

Glue
Silver wire
Newspaper
Plastic baubles

THE DINING ROOM

Table setting with the Nobel dinner service, glasses and silverware by Gunnar Cyrén and china by Karin Björquist.

DINNERS AT *WALDEMARSUDDE THEN & NOW*

BY KARIN SIDÉN

PRINCE EUGEN HAPPILY INVITED HIS FRIENDS, the royal family and other guests for dinner to his lovely home at Waldemarsudde. Painters Anders Zorn and Carl Larsson, authors Verner von Heidenstam and Helena Nyblom, composers Wilhelm Stenhammar, stage luminaries Gösta Ekman and Karl Gerhard, explorer Frithiof Nansen and architect Le Corbusier, as well as many of the era's politicians, royalty and diplomats, were among the dinner guests. As an example of the extent of activity, it can be mentioned that in 1933, Eugen arranged a total of 46 dinners, nine lunches and one supper. Some of the truly significant events at Waldemarsudde included the great ball in the Gallery in conjunction with the Prince of Wales's visit to Sweden in 1931, and the lunch before Princess Ingrid's wedding to Crown Prince Fredrik of Denmark in 1935. On the menu at the official inaugural dinner party on 31 October 1905 to celebrate the completion of the Mansion at Waldemarsudde, was lobster, chicken, diplomat pudding, cheese, dessert and lovely wines.

"EVERYBODY FLOWERED AROUND THE PAINTER-PRINCE. Stiff, impossible justices became cheerful, awkward artists thawed in the grace of the sun, becoming spirited like at studio parties," concluded Karl Gerhard of the many events at Waldemarsudde during the Prince's time. Eugen's private secretary Gustaf Lindgren has in turn told that the Carl XIII glasses crowned the famous Brazilian imperial dinner service in the Mansion's dining room, and that magnificent flower arrangements were created for the events. For the finer dinners, the flowers were arranged by the Prince's butler Eric Ericsson, after gardener Gunnar Lövgren had personally selected all the flowers from the gardens and greenhouses. The floral arrangements were then placed in crystal vases on mirror trays with silver edges.

THE GREAT GALLERY

Lunch ahead of Princess Ingrid's wedding to Crown Prince Fredrik of Denmark, 1935.

NOWADAYS, DINNERS ARE HELD IN THE DINING ROOM only on special occasions. Since 2012, these include the annually organised dinner for the Nobel Prize laureates in physics or medicine. The dinner is held on 6 December, a couple of days before the big Nobel Prize Awards Ceremony, and is arranged in cooperation with the Nobel Committee for physics or medicine. With torches outside the Mansion gates and the red carpet in place, the medicine laureates, along with their partners and representatives of the Nobel Committee, are received by the Museum Director, who welcomes them and tells of Prince Eugen's Waldemarsudde, its history and activities. Champagne is served in the Drawing Room before the beautifully set dinner with the Nobel dinner service begins. A highlight of the dinner is the array of beautiful flower arrangements created by the museum's skilled florist. Waldemarsudde pots and vases in various sizes are adorned with beautiful arrangements of flowers that interact with the splendour of the room, the table settings and the menu.

THE DINING ROOM

TALEA ROSE, HONEYWORT, LONGLEAF PINE, ANEMONES and EUCALYPTUS in the No. 3 pot.

CHRISTMAS DECORATING

HOLIDAY FLOWERS WITH TRADITION ADORN THE MANSION IN DECEMBER

DECORATING THE ROOMS WITH PLANTS during the Christmas holidays is a tradition that lives on since the Prince's time. He himself would celebrate Christmas with the family at Drottningholm Palace, but still the Mansion was decorated for the holidays, not least for the staff who were allowed to use the Dining Room for a Christmas dinner.

Frozen lily of the valley were of great significance to Prince Eugen. They were used to decorate the Mansion and given as Christmas gifts. The Prince bought frozen sprouts that were forced to bloom in the greenhouse at Waldemarsudde. Then they were delivered to friends by the Prince himself along with a handwritten greeting.

The old bulb catalogues have been preserved and show how the gardener ordered huge amounts of hyacinths in various colours and sorts. Today, it is mainly the Roman hyacinth that attracts attention. It grows with small flowers, sparsely placed on delicate stems. The florist fills vases that spread a pleasant Christmas scent through the Mansion during the holidays.

In snow and freezing temperatures, Kristina Öhman looks for ivy under the snow. For the restaurant located in the Prince's former kitchen, she makes entirely green wreaths on straw frames clad with green moss and vines of ivy. During this period, amaryllises adorn the rooms of the Mansion and the Waldemarsudde pot comes to good use. Beautiful branches from the park replace floral sticks for support. Kristina Öhman covers the soil with green moss and other elements of Christmas. Larch cones, ornamental apples, hazelnuts, baubles and cuttings of red dogwood.

THE FLOWER ROOM

Low Christmas decoration with AMARYLLIS, SIBERIAN DOGWOOD, PINE, ASPIDISTRA LEAVES, LARCH CONES, PARADISE APPLES, HOLLY and STAR ANISE.

THE DINING ROOM

Low Christmas decoration with POMEGRANATE, ORANGES, CINNAMON and WALNUTS. In the background, red TULIPS, RANUNCULI.

ROMAN HYACINTH, WHITE MARVEL TULIP, CARMEN and RAPIDO AMARYLLIS, YEW, HOLLY, NORDMANN FIR and ILEX in the No. 3 pot.

Tip: Place a piece, about 4 cm, of an oasis block at the bottom of the pot for easy arrangement of the green sprigs.

THE PRINCE'S KITCHEN

Waldemarsudde's pink Christmas flowers: CHRISTMAS CACTUS, CYCLAMEN, CHRISTMAS BEGONIA, AMARYLLIS NEON and HYACINTH.

Wreaths bound with SILVER FIR decorated with cones of LARCH and HYACINTH FLOWERS on wire.

AMARYLLIS *WITH NEAT & DELICATE BELLS ADORNS THE MANSION ROOMS DURING WINTER*

ONE OF THE PLANTS THAT THE MANSION is generously decorated with during winter is amaryllis. They are grown from bulbs in the greenhouse, and in September the gardeners plant the first bulbs. These are often treated to sprout and flower as soon as possible, and at Waldemarsudde, they can bloom as early as autumn.

It is mainly the old-fashioned varieties that are cultivated. The flowers are neater and beautifully ornate, which goes well with Waldemarsudde's philosophy of flower decoration. The stalks vary in height, and when the flowers bloom they make burgundy, red, white and red, pink, lime green and white bells. The red ones are most often used at Christmas, while the lime green and white grace the rooms after the holidays.

When the colour of the flower is seen through the bursting bud, the amaryllis pots are carefully transported to the Mansion. When the first bell opens, they are placed in the various rooms.

The amaryllis is not demanding in terms of maintenance. While budding, they should be watered sparingly, and more after the flowers have bloomed.

Water them only when the soil has dried up, pouring about a cup of water round the bulb. If the amaryllis has been watered too much and grown too tall, it can be cut and placed in a vase. This is beautiful with pine twigs or other evergreens.

1.
2.
3.
4.
5.

7.
9.
8.
6.

AMARYLLIS

1. CARMEN

2. RAPIDO

3. LEMON LIME

4. VISION

5. DONAU

6. LUNA

7. NEON

8. BABY STAR

9. LOVELY GARDEN

THE LIBRARY

BABYSTAR AMARYLLIS in a row in the No. 2 pot.
SIBERIAN DOGWOOD supports the stalks.

In the background, THE YOUNG CARL VON LINNÉ by Carl Eldh.

Pot fillings: 1. Sprig cuttings of DOGWOOD. 2. STAR ANISE AND CLOVES. 3. HAZELNUTS 4. Small Christmas baubles.

A good idea is to cover the soil with MOSS before putting on the decorations.

1.

2.

Filling of CINNAMON which gives off a lovel fragranc

No. 3 pot with LUNA AMARYLLIS, green DOGWOOD, BRANCHES with LICHEN embedded in green MOSS.

STEP BY STEP

AMARYLLIS & MOSS

Wintery beauty in the No. 3 pot

Amaryllis can advantageously be planted in the Waldemarsudde flowerpot, but do water before planting in this case. As long as it is budding, it needs very little water. Many arrangements of this type grace the tables in the Prince's Private Apartments of the Mansion from October to February.

1. KEEP THE PLASTIC POTS on if they fit in the pot. The amaryllis will be steadier then, and it is better if the roots are not in water later on. It also works with clay pebbles, pottery shards or similar.
2. HERE TWO HAVE been kept in their pots while the third has been planted without. But do place a piece of dry oasis at the bottom so that it has the same height as the other two amaryllises.
3. FILL WITH SOIL to steady the bulbs.
4. COVER THE BULBS with beautiful moss. Insert sprigs of green dogwood and lichened branches.

MATERIALS

AMARYLLIS used here is the LUNA type
GREEN & WHITE MOSS
GREEN DOGWOOD
BRANCHES with lichen

2.

4.

THE LIBRARY
LILY OF THE VALLEY in a row nestled in green and white MOSS in the No. 5 pot.
In the background, the goddess of victory VICTORIA on a porphyry ball.

LILY OF THE VALLEY SPROUTS with their long roots are planted in pots of sand-mixed soil and covered in MOSS. They are then forced in Waldemarsudde's greenhouse. After three weeks, they spread their fragrance throughout the Mansion.

SALIX UDENSI

3.

CAFÉ EKTORPET

WHITE ORCHIDS on a bed of PUSSY WILLOW.
Here they are supported by various sorts of WILLOW in their pots.

THE FLOWER ROOM
Among HYACINTHS and CINERARIA. 1916, photographer C.G. Rosenberg.

OPPOSITE PAGE
Rose, AVALANCHE in the No. 5 pot.

1.
2.
3.
4.
5.
6.
7.
8.

DRIED PLANTS

1. PURPLE MULLEIN

2. MARTAGON

3. CHESTNUT

4. POPPY

5. RHUBARB

6. CLIMBING HYDRANGEA

7. HYDRANGEA PANICULATA

8. TREE PEONY

633

LA FLEURISTE
KONGL. HOF-BLOMSTERHANDEL

BUKETTER · KRANSAR · GIRLANDER · BLOMSTERKORGAR och BLOMSTERGLAS · KRUKVÄXTER · PLANTERINGAR · JARDINIÈRES · ALLA SORTERS FANTASI-ARRANGEMENTS · MIDDAGS- SUPÉ & COTILLONS DEKORATIONER ·

[illegible]MALMTORGSGATAN. 6
RIKS TEL. 2550 + ALLM. TEL. 6296

Stockholm, den 8 Nov. 19[illegible]

Herr K. H. Prins Eugén. De[illegible]

1907.			
Jan.	15	Av 2 Medeola	5
apr.	22	25 Tulpaner	62
Juni	3	1 Krans	30
"	"	frakt	1
		Kr.	42[illegible]

Räkningen torde kvitterad återsändas till:
H. K. H. Hertigens af Nerike[illegible]
Ekonomiförvaltning.
WALDEMARSUDDE, STOCKHOLM 1.

Betaldt
24 DEC. 1907.
LA FLEURISTE
[illegible]

[illegible]r kontant, av hålles vördsamt om likvid inom 30 dagar.

VERIFICATION
From the Bernadotte family archive, 1907.

PLANT INDEX

ALLIUM 73, 86, 107, 108
ALONSOA 122
AMARYLLIS 20, 177, 182, 185, 196, 197, 199, 200, 202, 203, 204, 205, 206, 208, 209, 210, 211
Baby Star 204, 205, 206, 208
Carmen 199, 203, 205
Donau 203, 205
Lemon Lime 203, 205
Lovely Garden 204, 205
Luna 204, 205, 209, 210, 211
Neon 200, 204, 205
Rapido 199, 203, 205
Vision 203, 205
ANEMONE 58, 59, 60, 195
ANISE HYSSOP 126
APPLE BLOSSOM 76
APPLE TREE 52, 73
ASPIDISTRA 197
ASTER 122
BABY'S BREATH 122
BARRENWORT 62, 63, 64
BASIL 136, 137
BEGONIA 91, 110, 182
Christmas Begonia 185, 200
BERGENIA 73, 82, 83, 84, 85, 106, 107
BIRD CHERRY 28, 35, 37, 58, 59, 60, 70
BLACKTHORN 36
BLANKET FLOWER 122
BLUEBERRY 28, 35, 37, 46, 47
BRUNETTE 107, 108
BUTTERCUP 88, 89
BUTTERFLY FLOWER, SCHIZANTHUS OR POOR-MAN'S-ORCHID 18, 73, 81, 88, 89
CAPE PRIMROSE 18, 110
CARNATION 158, 174, 175
CHESTNUT 26, 28, 37, 218, 219
CHRISTMAS CACTUS 182, 200
CHRYSANTHEMUM 91, 158, 174, 175
CINERARIA 31, 66, 67, 110, 216
CINNAMON 198, 208
CISSUS 91
CLEMATIS 31, 94, 107, 108, 156, 165, 166, 167
CLOVE 206, 207
CLUBMOSS 178, 179, 180, 181
COLUMBINE 73, 81, 89, 107, 109
CONE 180, 181
Larch Cone 178, 179, 196, 197, 200, 201
CORAL BEAD PLANT 160, 161, 162, 163
CORNFLOWER 122
CORYDALIS 52
COSMOS 94, 95, 122, 130, 131,132, 133, 143, 154, 155, 156
COW PARSLEY 70, 71, 72
COWSLIP 70, 75
CRABAPPLE 118, 119, 120, 121
CREEPING WIRE VINE 172, 173
CROCUS 31, 58, 59, 60
CROWN DILL 160, 161, 162, 163
CUCKOOFLOWER 62, 63, 64, 70, 71, 72, 75, 77
CURRANT 28, 36, 107, 108, 132, 133
CUSHION BUSH (SILVER GARLAND) 186, 187, 188, 189
CYCLAMEN 110, 158, 168, 169, 182,
DAHLIA 20, 23, 118, 119, 120, 121, 122, 123, 130, 131, 132, 133, 135, 142, 143, 144, 145, 146, 147, 148, 149, 153, 154, 155, 156, 160, 161, 162, 163, 165, 166, 167
Ball Dahlia Sunny Boy 145, 146
Cactus Dahlia Ludwig Helfert 145, 146
Dahlia Tamburo 144, 146
Decorative Dahlia 144, 146
Decorative Dahlia Henriette 145, 146
Decorative Dahlias Lemon Cane 145, 146
Mignon Dahlia 145, 146
DAISY 73, 80, 88, 89
DAYLILY 70, 73, 96, 107, 109
DOGWOOD 37, 206, 207
Green Dogwood 209, 210, 211
Red Dogwood 28, 40, 196
Siberian Dogwood 197, 206, 208
ELDERBERRY 118, 119, 120, 121, 156
ELEPHANT'S FOOT 172, 173
ENGLISH YEW 199
EUCALYPTUS 195
FAIRY PRIMROSE 31, 68
FENNEL 138, 139, 140
FERN 52
FIR
Nordmann Fir 199
Silver Fir 200, 201
FLOSSFLOWER 122, 153
FORGET-ME-NOT 61, 62, 63, 70, 71, 72, 73, 75, 77
FORKING LARKSPUR 126, 153
FORSYTHIA 28, 35, 36, 40, 107, 108
FOXGLOVE 96
GERALDTON WAX 195
GLADIOLUS 23, 122, 160, 161, 162, 163
GLOBE THISTLE 118, 119, 120, 121
GRAPE VINE 106, 107
GROUND ELDER 88, 89, 96
HAWTHORN 177, 182
Red Hawthorn 35, 38, 39
HAZELNUT 196, 206, 207
HOLLY 199
HONEYSUCKLE 39, 58, 59, 60, 94, 106, 107
HOSTA 106, 107, 109, 126
HYACINTH 39, 61, 62, 63, 64, 182, 185, 196, 200, 201, 216
Blue Roman 199
Bluebell 62, 63, 64, 76
Grape Hyacinth 58, 59, 60, 62, 63, 64
Roman 196
Splendid Cornelia 39
HYDRANGEA 8, 51, 66, 76, 90, 107, 108, 132, 133, 138, 139, 140, 158, 174, 175
Bigleaf Hydrangea 118, 119, 120, 121, 126, 165, 166, 167
Climbing Hydrangea 62, 63, 64, 218, 219
Hydrangea Paniculata 218, 219
ILEX 197, 199 (HOLLY BERRY)
IRIS 73, 82, 84, 94
Dwarf 58, 59, 60
Yellow Iris 130, 131, 132, 133
IVY 52, 61, 62, 63, 64, 90, 107, 109, 174, 175, 178, 179, 180, 181, 196
JACOB'S LADDER 73, 82, 96
LACE FERN 172, 173
LADY'S MANTLE 96
LADY'S PURSE 110
LAMB'S EAR 186, 187, 188, 189
LICHEN 209, 210, 211
Cladonia Stellaris 186, 187
LILAC 28, 35, 38, 47, 70, 73, 88, 89, 93, 106, 107, 153
LILY
Martagon 218, 219
Snake's Head 31, 50
Lily of the Valley 70, 185, 196, 212, 213
LINDHEIMER'S BEEBLOSSOM 95, 122, 130, 131, 132, 133
LOBELIA 122
LOVE-IN-A-MIST 156
LOVE-LIES-BLEEDING 123, 154, 155
LUPINE 88, 89
MALLOW 51
MAPLE 35, 156, 168, 169
MARIGOLD 156, 165, 166, 167
Bush Marigold 138, 139, 140, 141
Common Marigold 51, 122, 123, 125
MARJORAM 136, 137
MEADOW SAXIFRAGE 73, 75
MEADOWSWEET 135, 154, 155
MEXICAN SUNFLOWER 125
MOCK-ORANGE 18
MOSS 178, 179, 206, 213
Green 180, 181, 185, 196, 209, 210, 211, 212
White 210, 211, 212

PLANT INDEX

MOTHER SPLEENWORT 172, 173
NARCISSUS 31, 35, 47, 48, 49, 73, 75, 107, 185
Abba 53, 55
Bella Estrella 54, 55
Changing Colours 53, 55
Cragford 52
Grand Soleil D'or 53, 55
Poetnarciss 52, 56, 57
Primeur 56, 57
Sailboat 53, 55
Scarlet Gem 54, 55
Segovia 53, 55
Sweetness 54, 55
Thalia 56, 57, 76
Van Zion 53, 55
Waterperry 54, 55
Yellow Cheerfulness 54, 55
NASTURTIUM 156, 165, 166, 167
OAK 35
ORANGE 198
ORCHID 214, 215
OREGANO 136, 137
ORNAMENTAL APPLE 196
PARADISE APPLE 168, 169, 197
PELARGONIUM 18, 114, 115, 116, 134
Concolor Lace 112, 113
Ekeby Olivia 112, 113
English Pelargonium 110
Kardinal 112, 113
Madame Nonin 111, 113
Madame Thibault 111, 113
Mårbacka 110, 112, 113
Regal Pelargonium 110
Scented Pelargonium 110, 117
Sweet Jess 111, 113
Sweet Mimosa 111, 113
PEONY 73, 76, 81, 88, 89, 93, 94, 96, 98, 99, 100, 101, 102, 103, 104, 105, 107, 133, 134, 135, 138, 139, 140, 165, 166, 167
Bowl of Beauty 97, 99
Common Red Scented Peony 98, 99
Edulis Superba 97, 99
Festiva Maxima 96, 97, 99
Karl Rosenfield 96, 97, 99
Sarah Bernhardt 98, 99
Tree Peony 218, 219
PERENNIAL CORNFLOWER 73
PHLOX 132, 133
PINE
Longleaf Pine 195
Scots Pine 197, 202
PIPEVINE 28, 31, 35, 36, 82, 83, 84, 85, 86, 94, 107, 109, 118, 119, 120, 121, 126, 130, 131, 153, 154, 155, 160, 161, 162, 163, 166, 167
POISON PRIMROSE 110
POMEGRANATE 198
POPPY 107, 109, 122, 218, 219
PRIMULA 110
PURPLE MULLEIN 182, 218, 219
PUSSY WILLOW 214, 215
RANUNCULUS 50, 198
RASPBERRY 107, 109, 130, 131, 132
REED 85
RHUBARB 96, 104, 105, 107, 108, 218, 219
RODGERSIA 73
ROSE 18, 70, 94, 150, 152, 156, 174, 175
Avalanche 217
Dorothy Perkins 151
Pashmina Summerhouse 118, 119, 120, 121
Red Riding Hood 52, 153
Rugosa 154, 155
Spray Rose 76, 77, 118, 119, 120, 121
Spray Rose Pepita 118, 119, 120, 121
Talea 195
ROSEHIP 156, 160, 161, 162, 163, 164, 165, 166, 167
ROSEMARY 136, 137
ROWAN 16, 156
RUDBECKIA 106, 107, 122, 123, 124, 125, 138, 139, 140, 141, 154, 155, 156, 165, 166, 167
Cappuccino 127, 129
Cherokee Sunset 127, 128, 129
Echinacea Paradiso 127, 129
Goldilocks 129
Goldquelle 126, 128, 129
Goldsturm 128, 129
Maya 128, 129
Moroccan Sun 127, 129
Prairie Glow 127, 129
Prairie Green Eyes 128, 129
Rudbeckia Nitida 128, 129
RUE 154, 155
SAGE 186, 187, 188, 189
SALVIA VIRIDIS 122, 126
SCABIOSA 122, 132, 133, 153
SIBERIAN CORYDALIS 56, 57
SIBERIAN PEASHURB 40
SILVER BIRCH 31, 35, 38, 58, 59, 60
SILVER DUST 186, 187
SKIMMIA 158
SKIMMIA JAPONICA 174, 175
SNAPDRAGONS 23, 122, 132, 133, 135, 153
SNEEZEWEED 122
SNOWBALL BUSH 50, 80, 88, 89
SNOWBELL 31
SNOWBERRY 35, 46, 47, 174, 175
SNOWDROP 50
SOLOMON'S SEAL 73
SPIDERWORTS 91
SPIKEMOSSES 172, 173
SPRENGER'S ASPARAGUS 106, 107
ST. JOHN'S WORT 174, 175
STAR ANISE 197, 206, 207
STOCK 70, 73, 88, 89
STRAWBERRY 104, 105
SUNFLOWER 122, 138, 139, 140, 141, 143, 174, 175
SWEDISH IVY 90
THYME 136, 137
TOBACCO FLOWER 122, 123, 126, 130, 131, 132, 133
TRUMPET FLOWER 130, 131, 153, 154, 155
TULIP 28, 35, 47, 49, 73, 76, 81, 107, 185, 198
Aladdin 44, 45
Apricot Beauty 23, 41, 45
Armani 39, 43, 45
Ballerina 44, 45
Black Parrot 39, 40, 42, 45, 58, 59, 60
Bruno Liljefors 43, 45, 50
Carnaval De Nice 26, 44, 45
Double Dutch 43, 45
Estella Rijnveld 44, 45
Gabriella 42, 45
Helmar 44, 45
Île de France 39, 43, 45
Jan van Nes 41, 45
Lydia 41, 45
Mickey Mouse 43, 45
Mount Tacoma 40
Pako 41, 45
Peach Blossom 39, 42, 45, 50
Primavera 41, 45
Verona 40
Weber's Parrot 39, 50
White Desire 42, 45, 46, 47
White Marvel 199
White Parrot 42, 45
Wild Tulips 26, 70
VERBENA 122
VIOLA 70
VIRGINIA CREEPER 156, 160, 161, 162, 163
WALLFLOWER 110
WALNUT 198
WHORLED COREOPSIS 122
WILD APPLE 156
WILLOW 46, 47, 49, 214, 215
WINTER ACONITE 31
WIRE-NETTING BUSH 186, 187
WISTERIA 20, 31
WOOD ANEMONE 31
WOOD SQUILL 31
YELLOW STAR-OF-BETHLEHEM 31
ZINNIA 51, 118, 119, 120, 121, 122, 125, 135, 154, 155

TEXTS

Helena Kaasik
Karin Sidén
Kristina Öhman

PHOTO

Yanan Li

THANKS TO HASSELBLAD

EDITORS

Esther Whang and Julie Cirelli

FLOWER ARRANGEMENTS AND STYLING

Kristina Öhman

CREATIVE DIRECTION,
GRAPHIC DESIGN AND PHOTO DIRECTION

Maria Sånge

PHOTO P. 21, 30, 33, 36, 37, 48, 64, 72, 83, 87, 104, 111, 112, 125, 137, 141, 159, 181, 186, 207, 208, 214

Maria Sånge

TRANSLATOR

Bella Daniels Carlsson

PUBLISHER

Marie Arvinius

PRINT AND BOOKBINDING

Livonia Print SIA, 2015 Latvia

IMAGE REPRODUCTION

Olssons Grafiska AB

TYPOGRAPHY

Baskerville, Aktiv Grotesk

PAPER

COVER *Geltex*
INSERT *Munken Polar, 150g*

ISBN 978-91-87543-31-9

PUBLISHED 2015 BY

Arvinius+Orfeus Publishing AB

Olivecronas väg 4, 113 61 Stockholm, Sweden
+46 8 32 00 15
info@arvinius.se
www.ao-publishing.com

THE BOOK IS PUBLISHED BY ARVINIUS+ORFEUS IN COLLABORATION WITH PRINCE EUGEN'S WALDEMARSUDDE

GW01606034

THE JUDAICA IMPRINT
FOR THOUGHTFUL PEOPLE

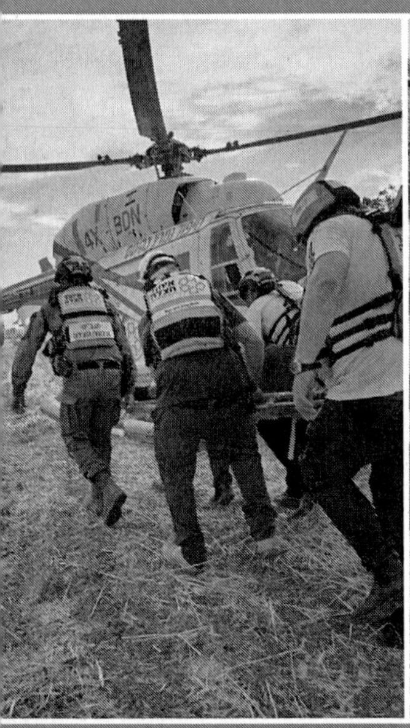

ANGELS

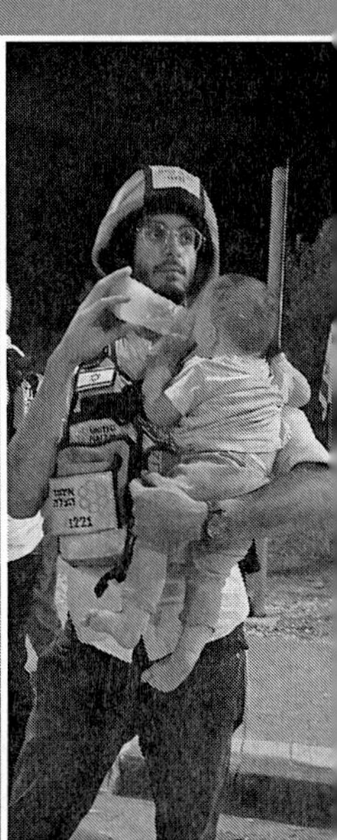

IN ORANGE

UPLIFTING STORIES OF COURAGE, FAITH, AND MIRACLES FROM THE UNITED HATZALAH HEROES OF OCTOBER 7TH

RABBI NACHMAN SELTZER

Author of the best-selling ***90 Seconds***

First edition – First impression / January 2024

Published by **SHAAR PRESS**
Distributed by MESORAH PUBLICATIONS, LTD.
313 Regina Avenue / Rahway, N.J. 07065 / (718) 921-9000

Distributed in Israel by SIFRIATI / A. GITLER
POB 2351 / Bnei Brak 51122

Distributed in Europe by LEHMANNS
Unit E, Viking Business Park, Rolling Mill Road
Jarrow, Tyne and Wear, NE32 3DP/ England

Distributed in Australia and New Zealand by GOLDS WORLD OF JUDAICA
3-13 William Street / Balaclava, Melbourne 3183 / Victoria Australia

Distributed in South Africa by KOLLEL BOOKSHOP
Northfield Centre / 17 Northfield Avenue / Glenhazel 2192, Johannesburg, South Africa

ISBN 10: 1-4226-3995-9 / ISBN 13: 978-1-4226-3995-9
ITEM CODE: ORANGH

Printed in the United States of America
Custom bound by Sefercraft, Inc. / 313 Regina Avenue / Rahway, N.J. 07065

This book was made possible thanks to the support of the following very special people:

Robert H. (Bob) and Amy Book

Douglas (Doug) Book

Neil and Sharon Book

Scott Book

Marci and Stephen Feinberg

Mark and Erica Gerson

Al and Chantal Gindi

Murray and Basheva Goldberg

Marcel and Coco Javor

Amy and Harlan Korenvaes

Miles Nadal and Family

Adele and Joel Sandberg

Jay and Jeanie Schottenstein

Jeffrey and Ariella Schottenstein

Joseph (Joey) and Lindsay Schottenstein

Sora and Jerry Wolasky

Aba and Pamela Claman Bs"D in the merit of the complete and speedy recovery of our beloved sister, Cheri Fox, Sarah Chana Pua Bat Mariossa

כי מלאכיו יצוה לך לשמרך בכל דרכיך

He will charge His angels for you
to protect you in all your ways.
— *Tehillim 91:11*

We danced 'round and 'round in circles,
as if the world had done no wrong,
From evening until morning, filling up the shul with song.
Though we had no sifrei Torah to clutch close to our hearts,
in their place we held those children —
the Jewish people will live on.

(Abie Rotenberg, *Journeys* 4, "The Man from Vilna,"
the classic song about the first Simchas Torah celebrated by
Holocaust survivors after the war)

Table of Contents

Tribute and Dedication 11
Acknowledgments 19
United Hatzalah and Unity for Redemption — An Overview by Rabbi Nosson Scherman 23
Introduction 33
Timeline 41

PART ONE: FIRST SHOCK WAVES

1: The Worst Kind of Déjà Vu 49
2: Eli's Vindication 58
3: A Patek Philippe With a Bright Red Band 63
4: Rav, Maggid Shiur, Hero 76
5: The Captive Doctor 84
6: A Toyota Pickup Truck 89

PART TWO: REALITY SETS IN

7: The Hardest Decision of His Life 97
8: "Is This 1943?" 108
9: Chassan Torah 2023 119

PART THREE: INTO THE WAR ZONE

10: Avi and Avi 129
11: Aharon's Finest Moment 138
12: "Al Abba Lo Sho'alim She'eilot" 144

PART FOUR: DOCTORS ON CALL

13: Invisible Wounds 153
14: Triage 163
15: Healing in the Air 169
16: Circle of Life 176

PART FIVE: ANYTHING TO SAVE A LIFE

17: A Different World 185
18: A Pile of Mattresses 191
19: Close Call 197
20: The Shabak Agent 208
21: The Helicopter Exit 215
22: To Hide or to Fight? 225

PART SIX: GEHINNOM ON EARTH

23: The Name on the Sticker 231
24: A Handful of Lollipops 238
25: The Reunion 242
26: Eliad's Trauma 251
27: The Ghost Town 260
28: Moshe Terror 266

PART SEVEN: AFTERSHOCKS

29: Fifty Million Dollars 277
30: Generosity! 283
31: Meeting the Wolves 287
32: The President's Tears 296
33: The Las Vegas Convention 308
34: Twin Rescue 317

Afterword 326

PHOTO CREDITS

Oren Cohen
Yechiel Gurfein
Shmulik Hershkopt
Shira Hirshkof
Yehuda Levi

Tribute and Dedication

While almost all of the courageous United Hatzalah volunteers who raced down to save lives came home safely, there were a few volunteers who, while serving in other capacities, did not return home. I dedicate this book to those "angels in orange" who lost their lives or were taken hostage on that dark day.

Dolev Yehud (Dolev ben Yael) was a very active volunteer in United Hatzalah. Dolev lives in Nir Oz, a kibbutz where one hundred and twenty-five people (a full one-third of the inhabitants) were either killed or kidnaped. One week before Simchas Torah, Dolev was honored by our organization as the number one volunteer in the Gaza area branch of United Hatzalah.

Dolev Yehud

On the morning of Simchas Torah, when the sirens began blaring, Dolev had no idea that terrorists had infiltrated the border and were literally attacking his kibbutz right at that moment.

After making sure that his three children and his wife, Sigal, who was close to her due date for birth, went into the shelter, Dolev ran out of the house to provide emergency assistance to anyone in need.

Dolev's family has not seen him since the moment he left them to go and help his people. His sister-in-law Arbel and her husband Ariel were also kidnaped and taken to Gaza.

Eight days later Sigal Yehud gave birth to a baby girl who has still not met her father.

I wrote a very strong letter to the Red Cross demanding that they fulfill their moral obligation and ascertain that Dolev is alive and well. After all — the Red Cross is officially committed to doing their utmost for the well-being of all lifesavers and reporters… To no one's surprise — the Red Cross did not reply to my letter.

Bar Kupershtein (Bar Avraham ben Julia) lives in Cholon. Bar's father, Tal, had been a volunteer with United Hatzalah for many years. Three years ago, Tal was driving on his way to save the life of a four-year-old girl who wasn't breathing, when he was hit by a car. On the day of the accident I went to visit him in the intensive care department of the hospital, where he was in a coma and in critical condition. There I met his wife, Julia, for the first time. I learned that they had a bunch of kids, that their oldest son was called Bar, and that he was seventeen years old. Like all the children, Bar was devastated by the accident, and I remember giving him a hug and trying to comfort him.

At some point in the conversation, I asked Julia what her husband did for a living.

"He owns a falafel shop."

"What are you going to do with the business while your husband is in the hospital and unable to work?"

"Bar will run the store until his father gets better. But that's only a temporary solution because he has school and anyway he's going to have to go to the army soon. This means that the store will probably have to close."

Bar Kupershtein

"Mrs. Kupershtein," I said, "you are not closing the store."

"What do you mean?"

"United Hatzalah is going to be taking over the running of your falafel store. Your business will continue. United Hatzalah volunteers will begin taking shifts in the store throughout the day."

This story happened a few months after I recovered from Covid and I was still very weak, but I decided that I wanted to take shifts myself for Tal — and so I began volunteering at Tal's falafel store at least once a week, in addition to taking on the overall responsibility of making sure that the store remained in business.

Bar taught me the recipe for the falafel and we had volunteers come from all over the country — from the Golan Heights, Haifa, Yerushalayim, Tel Aviv and as far away as Eilat. Religious, secular, and even Arab volunteers all took part. We built a website and people registered to take different shifts. We had one professional falafel maker on the payroll and all the rest of the workers were United Hatzalah volunteers.

Because this was happening during Covid restrictions, there wasn't enough business from people walking in off the street, so we started to advertise — telling people that they could do a mitzvah and order twenty or fifty falafels and that we would give them to soldiers, police, the fire department, or first responders. Hundreds of orders came in through the website and we were able to keep the store going for quite a while that way.

Unfortunately, Tal suffered a stroke a few months later. He was forty-six at the time and his youngest child, Yonatan, was just three. After the stroke he was never able to walk or talk again. Even though Tal is completely paralyzed, his mind is working and he understands everything. I felt very close to him and his family and took their situation to heart, doing my best to raise money for them.

One day Bar told me that he wanted to start training to become an EMT. He underwent EMT training in the army, and later we would sometimes send him to different places, such as events at the Kosel, or concerts or sports events where United Hatzalah had been hired to provide staff and emergency personnel. At these kinds of events the volunteers are paid, and since Bar's family needed the money, the army would allow him to do these kinds of jobs and we would try to send him to as many events as we could.

On the morning of Simchas Torah, Bar was down south doing

security and working as an EMT for a private ambulance company at the festival at Re'im along with five other EMTs.

During the course of the festival-turned-massacre, Bar became a genuine hero. Instead of escaping from the scene of the carnage, which he could have done, Bar stayed and rescued as many people as possible. Many people had been injured by the gunfire and couldn't move and he carried them to a nearby shelter/hiding place.

When the terrorists began getting even closer to where they were hiding, Bar took a gun from one of the policemen who had been killed and engaged in a gun battle with the terrorists until they overcame him, caught him, and kidnaped him to Gaza. We saw a video of him that was sent out by Hamas and we could see that he had been tortured by his captors.

Since the outbreak of the war, I have been in touch with Bar's parents and siblings, trying to provide as much support as possible.

Awad Dawarshe

Another United Hatzalah volunteer who was at the festival on medical standby, just in case someone got hurt, was an Arab volunteer by the name of **Awad Dawarshe.** Awad grew up in the city of Nazareth and wanted to become a doctor. He traveled abroad to attend university and get his degree, but when Covid broke out, the school he attended shut its doors and he was forced to return home before obtaining the degree.

Eventually Awad settled on becoming a paramedic, and he also decided to join United Hatzalah — an organization that he loved with all his heart. Awad was a very active volunteer. As a certified EMT, he was hired by a private company to help at the Re'im event.

When the carnage began, people screamed at Awad to run away. He chose to remain behind because he was providing medical treatment to a young girl who had been shot by the terrorists. He was caught by the terrorists early that day and brutally killed.

We organized a funeral for Awad a few days later. It was attended by hundreds of volunteers, many of them Jewish. I went to visit Awad's family, who couldn't stop talking about how much their son had loved United Hatzalah and how proud he had been to wear the United Hatzalah orange vest. He was twenty-three years old when he was killed, saving lives with no concern for his own safety.

Maor, the fourth volunteer this book is dedicated to, spent the majority of his life working for the Shabak (Israel's General Security Service), and was in charge of the entire southern part of the country when he retired a few years ago. His full name is still considered classified information even now, but I can tell you that after he retired from the Shabak, Maor decided to join United Hatzalah as a volunteer EMT, while remaining in the Shabak reserves, just in case he was needed. Even after he joined the ranks of United Hatzalah, nobody in the organization knew that he had been a key member of the Shabak in the not-so-distant past.

Maor lived in Kiryat Malachi, which is fairly close to Gaza, and he responded to the call along with many other volunteers from that city. He probably didn't know what he was getting into (like everyone else). Unlike many of the other volunteers, however, Maor had extensive battle experience, which is why when he realized that Israel was under attack, he shifted from focusing on giving emergency care to people and went into fighting mode instead. From what I understand, he killed a lot of terrorists that day and eventually he lost his life as well, dying *al kiddush Hashem*.

Maor Lavi was the third United Hatzalah volunteer to lose his life in this war. He had served in Gaza for 84 days, and every time he went home for a visit, he would go out on United Hatzalah calls. He and his wife Inbar have four daughters, the oldest of whom is six.

I was at a fundraising event in Miami when I heard that he had been killed in action. It was especially poignant to know he was gone, after seeing videos of Maor teaching his little kids how to perform CPR — all

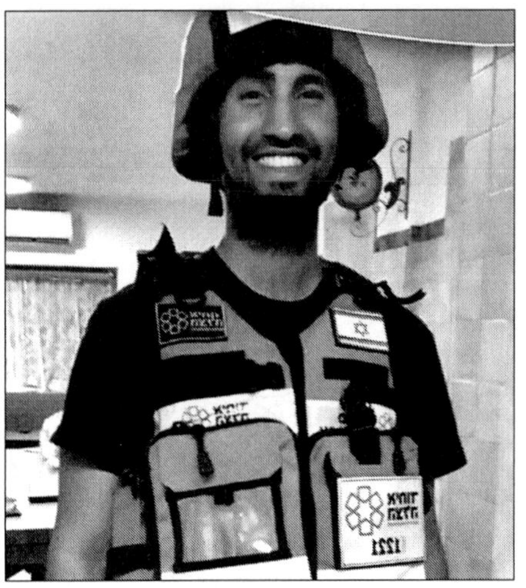
Maor Lavi

of them wearing Hatzalah jackets. It was obvious that United Hatzalah had been a major part of all of their lives.

I happened to have been standing near Miriam Adelson when I heard the sad news. I told her what happened and with tears in her eyes, she said, "Eli, I want to donate an ambulance to the city of Chevron in Maor's memory."

When I went to his house to pay a shivah call to Inbar and the kids, I gave the children small Hatzalah ambulances — the kids loved them — and I told them that there was going to be a big ambulance in Chevron with their father's name on it.

One of the kids had a question.

"What do you want to know?" I asked her.

"Can we get a ride in the ambulance?"

"One hundred percent..."

It was a very emotional visit.

Only a day before his untimely death, on Israel's main radio station, Maor shared that he had discovered a Chanukah menorah in a building in Gaza. He suspected it had been stolen during the October 7th attack. He requested that anyone who recognized it as their own contact him, so he could return it to its rightful owner. Maor and his comrades lit this *chanukiah* in Gaza on the 7th and 8th nights of Chanukah.

We established a fund at the beginning of the war to support our volunteers: those who were in the south and needed emotional and psychological intervention due to the traumatic scenes they witnessed; those who were evacuated from their homes in the south and north of the country and are out of jobs; and, of course, for those who had been injured, for the families of those who'd been killed, and for those who'd been financially affected by not being able to work for the months they spent fighting for their country.

We have already distributed millions of shekels to various families and plan on giving out much more. Since we have nine hundred volunteers serving in various positions in the army reserves right now, you can imagine how concerned we are for their well-being. We honestly believe that we owe them as much help as we can give them, since they are doing as much as they can for all of us.

As we were preparing this book for print, we received the tragic news that **Ro'i Avraham Meimoun** of Afula, another United Hatzalah volunteer, had fallen in battle in Gaza, protecting his people while in the reserves. Ro'i was twenty-four years old, full of life and passionate about helping others.

May the memories of all our fallen soldiers be a blessing.

Ro'i Avraham Meimoun

These are the people to whom I dedicate this book — the United Hatzalah "Angels in Orange" who risked their lives, and especially to those who actually gave their lives, for the Jewish people.

Eli Beer — President of United Hatzalah
Yerushalayim
2024

Acknowledgments

By Eli Beer

With immense gratitude to Hashem for bringing me to where I am today:

I would like to start off by thanking the spouses, children, and families of the United Hatzalah volunteers. Your unwavering support serves as the backbone for the vital, 24/7 lifesaving work carried out by our volunteers, your loved ones. The encouragement and understanding you provide within the walls of your homes are critical for our volunteers to wholeheartedly continue their daily commitment.

A special acknowledgment of course goes to every single United Hatzalah volunteer, whether serving as an EMT, nurse, paramedic, or doctor, and those serving in various behind-the-scenes roles whose efforts ensure the safety of our volunteers and the seamless flow of medical equipment. It is through your collective dedication that United Hatzalah can consistently be where it needs to be at the right time, and fully equipped.

On October 7th and the days that followed, we had many types of heroes. Thank you to those who stayed on the alert in their home neighborhoods, ready to protect their own communities. Also, to those in the south, as well as those who traveled down south, whose remarkable acts of heroism may have not been documented in the pages of this book. You are all integral partners in every encounter mentioned here.

I would like to acknowledge and thank all the incredible organizations and personnel who took part in the battles and lifesaving efforts on Simchas Torah and the days that followed — the IDF, the police, fire department, Magen David Adom, Zaka, Natali health services, and the emergency squads of all the kibbutzim and cities. Many were on the front lines of the battle and some lost their lives to protect others, *Hy"d.*

My daily work would not be possible without the incredible partnerships I've cultivated along the way. Specifically, I want to recognize the outstanding contributions of our board chairman, Mark Gerson, and his remarkable wife, Erica, and their children: Joshua, Elijah, Talia, and Aviva. Joshua, the eldest, has come to Israel twice since the onset of the war to help in any way he could. Mark's unwavering commitment to pushing United Hatzalah forward, chairing many various internal and external meetings, introducing us to new partners, and being available for every need is truly commendable.

A heartfelt thank you to our inspiring and incredible International Board, Executive Committee, and Young Leadership Board for their genuine care and personal involvement. Thank you to all those who opened their hearts during this very difficult time, giving so generously to ensure that United Hatzalah can continue to save lives. Special appreciation goes to Robert and Amy Book and Jay and Jeanie Schottenstein for their ongoing support, and particularly for establishing the Fallen Heroes Fund to aid the families of fallen soldiers.

Thanks to Marcel and Coco Javor, Paul and Lynn Leight, and David and Julie, whose care and concern for United Hatzalah volunteers goes way beyond supporting our ongoing lifesaving activities.

To Danny and Alicia Yacoby for ensuring the safety and protection of our volunteers.

To Alan Tisch, Ron and Pam Rubin, Keith Rosenbloom and Laura Rand, David and Allison Blitzer, Sidney and Phyllis Bresler, and to our partners in Australia — the Lowy family and the Lew family.

Thank you to Bruce and Amy Gelb for chairing our very successful Evening of Unity in Miami during these difficult times, and many others — your support and friendship mean the world to me.

I also want to express gratitude to our corporate partnerships, Jefferies, Salesforce, Deloitte, UBS, Mercedes, Harel, GT Law, and so many others who have reached out and supported us.

United Hatzalah's achievements on October 7th and in its aftermath were made possible by the incredible partnerships with federations such as JFNA, UJA NY, Keren Hayesod, and foundations that have supported us over the years, including the Helmsley Charitable Trust, Crown Family Foundation, Dell Family Foundation, and so many others who stepped up to help us during this critical time of need in Israel.

I am indebted to our VP Michael Brown and Batsheva Lovy for their dedication.

Thank you to Eli Pollak, Dovie Maisel, Laiser Heyman, Moshe Levi, Shai Jaskoll, and Batya Avidan — along with my entire team on the ground in Israel, as well as Jerry Silverman and the entire international team, for enabling this incredible operation to continue and save lives every single day.

A very special thank you goes to Rabbi Nachman Seltzer who immediately understood why this book was so important and who once again put everything aside to write it — with his trademark stamp of excellence and in the quickest amount of time possible.

A tremendous thank you to him and the entire ArtScroll team who stood at his side throughout the process — Rabbi Gedaliah Zlotowitz, Miriam Zakon, Suri Brand, Shmuel Blitz, Mendy Herzberg, Eli Kroen, Yisroel Perkowski, Estie Dicker, and everyone in the New Jersey office.

My incredible children, Avigail and Aharon, Penina, Libby and Meir, Yisrael David, Adina, and grandchildren Gabi, Itamar, Halleli, and Emily; I am so grateful.

Yisrael, I am so proud of you; you are the source of my strength. You are fighting evil and sacrificing so much to protect us.

To the one and only, my wife Gitty, my inspiration; if it weren't for you, nothing would be possible.

United Hatzalah and Unity for Redemption — an Overview

By Rabbi Nosson Scherman

When inhuman murderers burst into Eretz Yisrael with their guns blazing, determined to kill, maim, torture, and kidnap, thousands of unarmed and defenseless Jews were forced to run for their lives, with more than 1,200 falling victim to butchers masquerading as humans.

One thousand seven hundred civilians ran as well. They ran from the safety of Jerusalem, Tel Aviv, Modi'in and Bnei Brak, racing to the south, to the danger, not to take lives, but to save them. They were the "angels in orange," the volunteers of United Hatzalah.

These are some of their stories, collected and told masterfully by ***Rabbi Nachman Seltzer****, a brilliant writer, whose pen records the unparalleled ahavas Yisrael, whose ear captures every detail, and whose eye sees below the surface.*

In an era rife with discord, distrust, and disunity, ***United Hatzalah*** *epitomizes the unity and love of fellow Jews that, as we will see below, is the attribute that will bring the Final Redemption, with the coming of Mashiach, may it be speedily, in our time.*

ONE UNIT

In 1913, Mendel Beilis, an itinerant Jewish handyman, was arrested in Russia and accused of killing a Russian child to use his blood to bake matzos for Pesach. The charge was false, and the accusers knew it, but it was a time of upheaval and imminent rebellion against the Czar, and a blood libel against a Jew was a time-tested tactic to divert dissenters' attention from the source of their suffering.

Torah leaders knew that anti-Semites would dredge up "proofs" that Jews felt no compunction when taking the life of a non-Jew. A prime source would be the Talmudic text (*Yevamos* 61a) that Jews are referred to as "*adam,*" a human (and therefore are subject to the laws of ritual impurity), but non-Jews are not referred to as *adam* (and are therefore exempt from these laws). *Aha!* Perversely misinterpreting that ruling, anti-Semites would use it against Beilis and all Jews: If a non-Jew is not an *adam,* he is not human, so of course Mendel Beilis would feel justified to murder a non-human child to enable the baking of matzos.

Two great Torah leaders gave interpretations of the Talmudic dictum. Both interpretations are correct and both are epitomized by the heroic response of United Hatzalah's volunteers on that awful day.

The Chortkover Rebbe said that all Jews, wherever they are, are one *adam*, like one person. Unlike the other Hebrew words for a man — *ish, enosh, gever* — the word *adam* has no plural form. Jews are unique, because although we are scattered all over the world, we remain a single entity. A Jew in Australia, a world away from Russia, feels as one with Mendel Beilis.

Rav Meir Shapiro, the future Rav of Lublin and founder of the Daf Yomi phenomenon, added another element to the Talmudic dictum. If an Englishman embezzles on Wall Street, no one says all Englishmen are swindlers. But if a Jew is accused of murder in Moscow, anti-Semites claim all Jews are criminals. (As an interesting aside, Rav Shapiro revolutionized this concept with his Daf Yomi initiative, which unites us all as one *adam* in the same *blatt Gemara.*)

United Hatzalah, as this inspirational book shows so clearly, embodies these concepts. Its volunteers are chareidi, chiloni, and a virtual cross-section of Israeli society, but they are all united, not merely in the title "*United* Hatzalah," but as a single unit in the service of all who need them.

THE COST OF STRIFE

King David was one of the greatest of all Jewish leaders, one of the "seven shepherds," the master of repentance, author of *Tehillim* and progenitor of Mashiach. The notorious King Achav was one of the most wicked kings of the Northern Kingdom of Israel. He instituted idolatry throughout his kingdom and, with his evil queen Izevel, murdered hundreds of righteous prophets of Hashem. Nevertheless, there was an astounding difference between the armies of David and Achav. Achav's army was always victorious in battle, and suffered no casualties, while David experienced an occasional defeat and there were casualties among his warriors. Astonishingly, in military matters, Achav the wicked was more successful than David the righteous.

Talmud Yerushalmi (*Peah* 1:1) wonders how this was possible. The Talmud answers that, although the people of David's generation were righteous — idolatry did not exist in his kingdom — his nation was beset by strife and malicious talebearing. Two of his leading generals were disloyal, two of the wisest people in the land conspired against him, and the citizens of two towns tried to hand him over to King Shaul, who sought to kill him. His own son rebelled against him, and a leading sage cursed him. When there is internal strife, God withdraws His total protection.

In Achav's reign, evil though the people were, they were unified, so God protected them. Such is the power of unity and mutual respect and regard for one another.

Meshech Chochmah applies this observation to his own era. The author, Rabbi Meir Simchah of Dvinsk, Lithuania, was one of the greatest *Gedolei Torah* and thinkers of his time. He cites the well-known teaching (*Yoma* 9a) that the First Beis HaMikdash was destroyed because the people violated the three cardinal sins, idolatry, immorality, and bloodshed. But in the time of the Second Bais HaMikdash the people were righteous; why was it destroyed? The Talmud answers that the Beis HaMikdash was destroyed because of *sinas chinam,* baseless hatred. Which was worse, the Talmud asks, baseless hatred or the three cardinal sins? The Talmud says that history gives us the answer. The exile after the first destruction lasted only seventy years, but the current exile goes on and on and on.

Meshech Chochmah applies this teaching to his own generation. In the 1920s, religious observance had weakened very substantially in Western Europe and America, and even in the big cities of Eastern Europe — but Hashem is patient and loving even when Shabbos desecration is rampant. However, the author warned, when strife is everywhere and peace, or at least respect for opponents, is lacking, Divine protection may be removed. He writes that the Jewish world in his time was torn by angry competitiveness and animosity between communists, socialists, nationalists, atheists, and so-called "enlightened" Jews. Virtually the only thing that united all those "isms" was opposition to Torah Judaism — and this hatred could bring catastrophe.

His prophetic warning was published in 1926, seven years before Hitler came to power and thirteen years before the Holocaust began.

TRAGIC BREAKDOWN

In our time, animosity is everywhere. In political life, the norm used to be partisan rhetoric on the surface and behind-the-scenes friendship, collegiality, respect for tradition and protocol, and bi-partisan compromise for the common good. In the United States, for example, the most significant legislation was often fashioned jointly by political opponents, "working things out." The same was generally the case in the struggles for human and civil rights. The colleges were places for research, inquiry, challenge, and free expression of a broad range of opinions. No more. In America, Israel, and elsewhere, partisanship has descended into intolerance, animosity, and even threats of violence. And the worldwide Jewish community — which should have been a single, unified *adam* — has not been immune to the moral pandemic.

Jewish history shows that the effects of breakdowns in unity among us are frightening and tragic. Maharal explains that even when the multitude is sinful, the innate sanctity of the Jewish nation as a whole — when it is united — inspires Divine mercy. As we find in the story of Megillas Esther, the turning point came when Mordechai and Esther brought the people together in fasting, prayer, and, as the Sages teach, in Torah study. But when the nation is torn apart by disputes and hatred, the merit of the disunified nation falters and Hashem judges the people as individuals. How many individuals can claim to be so righteous that they can survive Divine scrutiny?

SHOCK OPENS EYES

And then, after a year of shrill and savage contention and divisiveness in the Holy Land, came October 7th, the Simchas Torah massacre. The Jewish people in Israel and elsewhere became united as never before in contemporary memory. Reservists converged at the Gaza border and former soldiers left the safety of America and Europe to rush back home and put their lives on the line.

The Torah community, including the much maligned chareidim, responded fervently. They came with truckloads of home-cooked food for the troops and set up tables and buffets fit for weddings. One group of these "caterers" was composed of chassidim, many with *peyos* down to their shoulders. A no-longer hungry soldier and a chassid-turned-cook-and-waiter hugged each other like reunited brothers. The soldier said, "I never knew any chareidim, but I hated them. Now I love them." A tireless and imaginative religious Jew came to the front with a truckload of washers, dryers, and a generator, so soldiers could wash their clothes. Non-kosher restaurants in Tel Aviv koshered their kitchens so that they could send food that all the soldiers could eat. A leftist Knesset member made a speech declaring that her opposition to religious Jews had been misplaced. Now she admired them and was grateful to them.

As happened many times in our history, crisis awakened the dormant spark of holiness in many hearts. Soldiers and civilians asked for tzitzis, and yeshivah students spent nights twisting the strings *l'sheim mitzvas tzitzis,* for the sake of the commandment of tzitzis. Soldiers put on tefillin, many for the first time, others for the first time since their bar mitzvah, and generous Jews contributed and raised money to provide them with tefillin. Soldiers wanted to learn, but where could they get a Chumash and a Gemara? Thanks to the Schottenstein family, ArtScroll/Mesorah printed Daf Yomi booklets and Chumash pamphlets — 80,000 by the time of this writing — and soldiers could take the holy words with them in their tanks and backpacks, as they advanced through the dangerous streets and tunnels of Gaza. Yeshivos canceled their intersessions so that their increased Torah study could be a source of merit for the soldiers. Typical of the response was a noteworthy and revered Rebbe who went to the front to encourage soldiers, visited wounded fighters in the hospital, attended a military funeral, and paid condolence calls to grieving families.

This manifestation of unity was astounding, coming on the heels of a time when societies in Israel and countries all over the world were tearing themselves apart and pessimism was the order of the day. It took the shock of Simchas Torah, October 7, to reverse the strife and bring the Jewish people together.

Pele Yoetz (*Ahavas Re'im*) cites *Midrash Tanchuma* (*Tzav* 7) that the *Shechinah* rests upon the Jewish people only when they are united. Elsewhere he writes that it is human nature for people to be motivated by self-interest, and this naturally leads to conflict, as everyone knows from personal experience. But there rarely comes an unforeseen occurrence that opens eyes and moves hearts and convinces people that the pettiness or trivialities that controlled their lives should be swept aside. It makes them realize that, after all, we are a single *adam,* Hashem is our Father, and Torah is our heritage.

Such a shock came on Simchas Torah 5784. It was more than the unspeakable cruelty of the savages, horrific though that was. Many comforting illusions were shattered. The world's greatest intelligence service was blind, an impregnable barrier was breached, and the vaunted IDF was caught completely by surprise. How could it happen?

Hundreds of thousands of Jews everywhere suddenly recognized that Hashem runs the world and that our security is in His hands. Suddenly, the contention between the Knesset and the court, antagonism between secular and religious — all these so-called "existential issues" faded into insignificance, replaced by the recognition that we are all Jews. And that brought a huge upsurge of support for the survivors of the carnage, the bereaved widows, orphans, and parents, the wounded, and the hostages. Ultimately, we are all one *adam.* And more than in many decades, we sense a growing and widespread recognition that we have One Creator.

RELIGIOUS REVIVAL

Baruch Hashem, in addition to a newfound sense of Jewish unity, there is wider recognition by many that the Torah is not only the soul of our people, but also our protector. Fifty years ago, after the Yom Kippur War, there was a ceremony in Israel dedicating a military cemetery where fallen soldiers had been interred. It was a secular event. The speakers were from the government, the military, academia, and community leadership. The only Orthodox speaker was Rav Shabsi Yudelevitz, a much beloved and respected scholar and speaker. Late in the program he was called to the podium.

He noted that all the speakers had effusively praised the heroism, bravery, and self-sacrifice of the soldiers, and yes, he said, every word was true. He continued, "You're probably wondering what the yeshivah students and *kollel* fellows did for the war effort." Most listeners smirked. What indeed did the Torah students do in their study halls while young men their age were risking and losing their lives?

Rav Yudelevitz recalled the early days of the war, when the enemy was advancing and Jewish prospects seemed worse than dire. Quietly, the military summoned the heads of the *Chevrah Kaddisha* burial societies and told them to be prepared for 80,000 graves! When the war ended, 2,700 soldiers had lost their lives — 2,700 too many — but nowhere near the grim expectations. And that, declared Rav Yudelevitz, is what the merit of Torah study accomplished.

That recognition is not yet universal, but it is far greater than it was fifty years ago. And it is growing.

THE KEYS TO REDEMPTION

Torah study and Jewish unity are extraordinary sources of merit, the merits that can hasten the coming of Mashiach. In our weekday *Shemoneh Esrei* we beseech Hashem, "*Teka b'shofar gadol l'cheiruseinu*, Sound the great shofar for our freedom." That blessing concludes, "gather us **together** from the four corners of the earth to our land." Note the word "together." It is a key to our redemption. God wants to gather us and bring Mashiach, but for that to happen it is up to us to be "together," to be united.

It is human nature that unity dissipates when the crisis is over. Let us not let that happen.

The Second Beis HaMikdash was destroyed because of disunity and strife; the Third Beis HaMikdash, as many commentators have taught, will be built when we eradicate the sins that brought the destruction. Let us resolve to strengthen and build on our current unity.

United Hatzalah lives up to its name. Its thousands of volunteers are "united" in commitment, courage, and readiness to save lives and preserve the well-being of every caller every minute of every day and night. This book is only a small part of the story. We are all a part of it, the story that has not yet reached its glorious conclusion. We can each choose to strengthen our unity, to be a proud part of the united entity that is *Klal Yisrael.*

Read ***Angels in Orange*** and be uplifted. Strengthen the unity of our people. Help bring Mashiach. Merit the *Geulah Sheleimah.*

Rabbi Nosson Scherman
Shevat 5784 / January 2024

On October 7, 2023 — Simchas Torah 5784 — over one thousand seven hundred volunteers of United Hatzalah willingly chose to put themselves in danger and entered the war zone to save countless lives literally under fire. Miraculously, almost every single one of the "angels in orange" who were down south that morning saving lives returned home alive.

This is their story.

Introduction

Simchas Torah 2023 is a day none of us will ever forget.

When I left home that morning to walk to shul with my son and son-in-law, I could already hear the muffled booms of rockets being deflected by the Iron Dome. The roads were empty, as they usually are on Shabbos morning, but the sounds of those rockets were unnerving.

A little voice inside my head whispered, "You should have davened in the shul near your house today…"

In the middle of davening, the sirens began to wail, and we had to leave the *beis midrash* and go downstairs to one of the nearby preschool classrooms that doubled as a bomb shelter.

It was hard to know what to do. Some people stayed behind in the shul. Most went downstairs. Some felt we should finish davening downstairs. Others wanted to wait until the sirens stopped wailing and continue when we were back in the shul.

It was a crazy morning.

Eventually things calmed down, and we were able to continue davening in shul. We were in the middle of *hakafos* when one of the neighbors walked into the shul, his face white. I don't remember how he had learned of the attack, but he was going around the neighborhood, from shul to shul, telling everyone that Hamas had broken through the border fences of Gaza and was racing through the south murdering Jews.

My friend Moshe Erenfeld went over to the *amud* and began to lead the *kehillah* in the recital of *Tehillim*. The emotion in his voice sent tremors through us, though no one was prepared yet to give voice to their fears. When we finished saying *Tehillim*, we went through the motions of a Simchas Torah davening, but it was a pale version of the day we all know and love.

When we left shul that afternoon, the streets were deserted and the twenty-minute walk didn't feel safe. For the rest of the day everyone waited to hear what was going on down south. We all sensed that there was something terrible happening, but since we didn't know exactly what, we waited anxiously to hear the news. None of us could have imagined the magnitude of what had actually occurred.

A relative of mine was staying at my house for Yom Tov. He works for the army in a medical capacity, managing medical personnel who deal with the soldiers, and his phone rang in the middle of the day. When he answered, he was told that he needed to be ready to come in if he was called.

"What happened?" he asked.

"Israel is at war," was the response.

Then came Motza'ei Yom Tov, and we learned that Hamas had attacked the country from the air and the sea and through the border fence. We learned that they had gone from kibbutz to kibbutz murdering anyone they were able to kill, and that they had taken more than

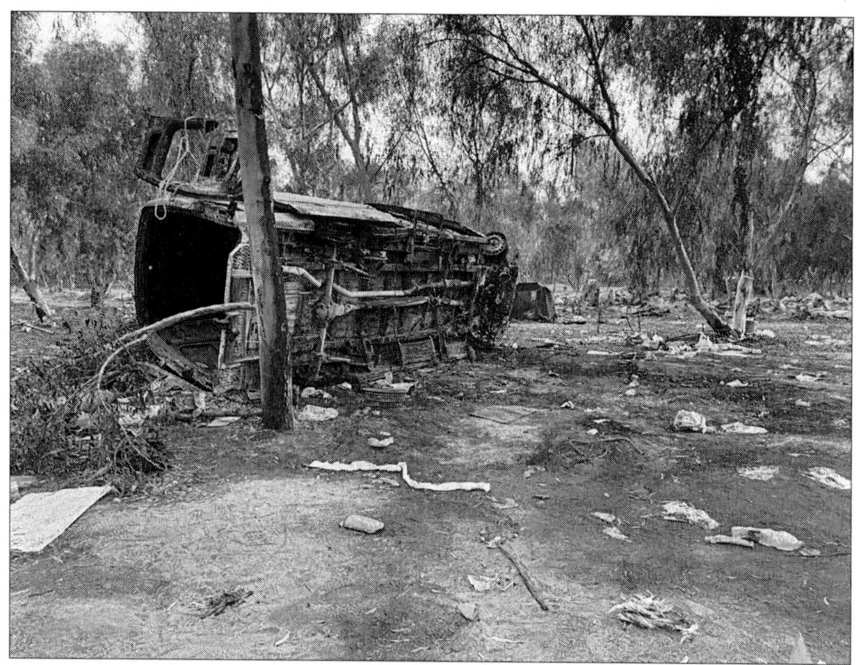

A burned-out ambulance at the site of the music festival

200 hostages. We learned that they had attacked the people who had attended a music festival near Kibbutz Re'im.

We learned that they had infiltrated the cities of Sderot and Ofakim.

And we understood that something happened on that day that had changed the world as we knew it.

From now on, our lives would be divided between life as it was before October 7 and life after that day. And we knew that just as people living in November 1963 remembered where they were when they heard that JFK was assassinated, and those living in September 2001 remembered where they were when the Twin Towers came down on 9/11, so, too, we would recall what we were doing and where we were doing it when we heard about the attack that happened to *Klal Yisrael* on Simchas Torah 2023.

Two weeks after the outbreak of the war, Eli Beer and I were speaking. Somewhere in the middle of the conversation we realized that although *90 Seconds* had been published quite recently, the time had come to write another book — a book about what happened on Simchas Torah and about what United Hatzalah did for *Klal Yisrael* on that day.

We met later that day for a few hours, and for the rest of that week I interviewed the volunteers who had put their lives in danger and headed south to save the lives of their fellow Jews, without a thought for their own safety. The more I spoke with the volunteers, the more I realized what an amazing story was waiting to be told.

Amazingly, almost every single volunteer who risked their life and went to help treat the victims lived to tell the tale. Indeed, barely any of them were wounded.

It was an incredible story, and I put aside everything I had been doing to write it. The result is in your hands.

The story of the "angels in orange."

This is a book about one never-to-be-forgotten day — a day that displayed both the best and the worst that mankind has to offer, a book about modern-day heroes. And most importantly, about the kind of *ahavas Yisrael* that sends people to a war zone to save a Jewish life.

It's about *mesirus nefesh* pure and simple.

Volunteers doing their holy work

Unless they've done their army service and are called up as part of the army reserves, United Hatzalah volunteers are not trained soldiers. They join United Hatzalah to provide medical assistance to those in need. Car crashes, household and work accidents, women giving birth with no time to get to the hospital — those are daily occurrences. But while the volunteers of United Hatzalah are always ready to drop everything to save lives, no one said anything to them about risking their own lives under fire.

And yet that's exactly what happened on the day of Simchas Torah and in the week that followed. The volunteers of United Hatzalah willingly placed themselves in danger time and again, exhibiting the kind of *mesirus nefesh* that went way beyond what anyone could have expected of them.

In their minds, there was never any question of whether they would put their own lives on the line. As far as they were concerned, they were trained to save lives, and that's what they were going to do.

Amazingly enough, the Master of the world safeguarded this incredible group by ensuring that almost every volunteer who traveled down south to save lives survived to tell the story.

Some were shot at.

Some encountered terrorists.

One was almost crushed by a tank.

But almost every one of those heroic tzaddikim made it home alive.

Because this isn't only a book about *mesirus nefesh* — it's also a book about some of the miracles that happened on that tragic day.

Including the miracles that Hashem performed for His "angels in orange."

I'm no military expert, but I have written many books, some of which have involved various battles fought and won, and I can say that the fact that Israel was attacked on October 7, 2023, on the morning of Simchas Torah, doesn't make sense.

It doesn't make sense that in the month prior to the attack, the Israeli radio stations devoted countless hours to the Yom Kippur War, relating over and over how the country had been taken by surprise. Yet somehow, virtually the exact same thing took place again.

It doesn't make sense that the army leadership ignored the fact that hundreds of Hamas members had been training heavily — and in many cases out in the open — in the months leading up to the October 7 attack.

It doesn't make sense that the army disregarded the intensive training exercises that Hamas was conducting on the Gaza beaches just across the border — in full view of Israel — even though the soldiers whose job it is to let the higher-ups know about such occurrences kept warning them over and over.

It doesn't make sense that the Arabs were able to keep such a secret for so many months without Israel's vaunted security agencies finding out every detail. Since when are Arabs able to keep a secret? And yet they did. And it doesn't make sense.

Nothing about what happened makes sense.

And yet it happened.

In a stunning surprise attack, reminiscent of Japan's attack on the US Navy fleet stationed at Pearl Harbor on December 7, 1941, Hamas terrorists breached the fence separating Israel from its neighbor, took out Israel's warning systems, effectively paralyzing the flow of vital information, and slaughtered soldiers in the nearby bases. Then they went on a rampage of brutal killing, torture, and kidnaping. It was the worst day the Jewish people had experienced since the Holocaust.

How all this could have possibly occurred will be discussed for years to come, when the dust of this war finally settles. But to my mind there seems to be only one possible explanation.

For reasons known only to Him, the Master of the world decided that our forces would be oblivious to what was happening right before their eyes. And so they didn't see.

On that day of infamy, Simchas Torah turned into a day of mourning in the truest sense, and the words of the Tishah B'Av *kinnos* came true before our eyes.

אֱלִי צִיּוֹן וְעָרֶיהָ, כְּמוֹ אִשָּׁה בְצִירֶיהָ, וְכִבְתוּלָה חֲגֻרַת שַׂק עַל בַּעַל נְעוּרֶיהָ.

Let Zion and her cities lament like a woman in the pangs of birth and like a young woman girded with sackcloth [in mourning] for the husband of her youth.

עֲלֵי שִׂמְחַת אוֹיְבֶיהָ, שֶׂחֲקוּ עַל שִׁבְרֶיהָ, וְעַל עִנּוּי בְּנֵי חוֹרִין נְדִיבֶיהָ טְהוֹרֶיהָ.

For the rejoicing of her enemies, who laughed at her destruction and for the suffering of her freeborn sons, so noble and so pure.

עֲלֵי קוֹלוֹת מְחָרְפֶיהָ, בְּעֵת רַבּוּ פְגָרֶיהָ, וְעַל רִגְשַׁת מְגַדְּפֶיהָ, בְּתוֹךְ מִשְׁכַּן חֲצֵרֶיהָ.

For the voices of those who abused her when her corpses fell thick and fast, and for the tumult of her revilers within the courtyard of her Sanctuary.

אֱלִי צִיּוֹן וְעָרֶיהָ, כְּמוֹ אִשָּׁה בְצִירֶיהָ, וְכִבְתוּלָה חֲגֻרַת שַׂק עַל בַּעַל נְעוּרֶיהָ.

Let Zion and her cities lament like a woman in the pangs of birth and like a young woman girded with sackcloth [in mourning] for the husband of her youth...

There is no question that in the last year the fabric of Israeli society has been decidedly weakened, virtually coming apart at the seams, as brother turned against brother — right fighting left, secular battling religious — and Israeli citizens inexplicably did their utmost to weaken the government any way they could. There is no question that Israel was harmed by these developments, and there is no question that our enemies took note (Hamas terrorists stated this clearly during their interrogations). The infighting, the lack of unity, gave them the impetus to attack us in the most brutal ways.

Once again it became clear that we, the Jewish people, do not have the liberty of fighting among ourselves. What the enemy didn't realize was that their attack on our nation would do more to repair the fractures than anything we could have done. In one day, we went from a state of terrible infighting to a state of true brotherhood, as everyone in the country united against the common enemy. Suddenly there was *achdus* and fellowship in our ranks again.

But at what a cost…

With all the horror, there were also the miracles.

Miracles on top of miracles.

During the early hours of Simchas Torah morning, there was a very limited police presence on the highways between the southern city of Sderot and the rest of the country. The roads were more or less open. Had the terrorists continued onward, they might have swept through the countryside, and there would have been little that anyone could have done about it. If even one hundred Hamas terrorists had reached Yerushalayim, who knows how many would have been killed?

It was Succos. Every hotel in Yerushalayim was filled to capacity with Jews who were unprotected. If the terrorists had continued on their rampage, the results would have been catastrophic. Yet they didn't even try to go there. Instead they killed, tortured, maimed, stole, kidnaped, and kept themselves occupied by committing terrible evil — but they didn't continue onward even though the roads were open and they could have gone anywhere they wanted.

Is this not a miracle?

The terrorists could have attacked the yeshivah in Tifrach, which was packed with fifteen hundred bachurim celebrating Simchas Torah. No one had a gun.

But they didn't go into the yeshivah.

A miracle of epic proportions.

And there are countless stories of other such miracles.

Stories of terrorists shooting at people at point-blank range — and nothing happened to them.

Stories of terrorists choosing one particular person and telling them to run — allowing them to live for no apparent reason.

So many miracles and so much pain — side by side.

As time passed and the fog that surrounded the first days of the war began to clear, stories began circulating not only about the horrific things that had happened and all the people who had been kidnaped and murdered, but also stories about the miracles that took place. So in addition to telling the stories of the courageous and dedicated United Hatzalah volunteers, I'll also be sharing some of those "miraculous moments" throughout the book. I heard some of these stories from the protagonists themselves. Others I heard from people who learned about them firsthand from the protagonists, while others came from reliable sources who researched the stories for accuracy.

One final message:

In general, I try to write books that everyone can read, from relatively young children to the most mature of adults. While writing this particular book, I tried to maintain sensitivity and avoid describing in minute detail the atrocities that occurred. This means that I omitted much of what I was told by the people I interviewed. At the same time, I felt that I needed to give an accurate and honest portrayal of the events that happened.

None of us likes reading about massacres and murder, and yet that is exactly what happened to our nation. Not in the distant past. Not a thousand years ago. Not five hundred years ago.

Now.

In our time.

To us.

And we need to know what happened. So choose what you want to share with your children. But read it yourself. Because you need to know what happened to your brothers and sisters in Eretz Yisrael on Simchas Torah 2023.

Rabbi Nachman Seltzer
Ramat Beit Shemesh
2024

Timeline

The first hours of the war were extremely chaotic. We have depicted the chronology to the best of our ability. Some of the times are approximate.

October 7, 2023

6:25 a.m.

- First reports of rocket sirens in Israel
- Dispatch alerts operational managers to a barrage of rocket fire and dispatches EMS volunteers to respond

6:45 a.m.

- Report from dispatch to operational managers that many terror attacks are taking place throughout the cities of the south
- United Hatzalah volunteer EMT Dolev Yehud is kidnaped by Hamas terrorists together with many other members of Kibbutz Nir Oz, and taken into Gaza. At the time of this printing, he is still being held hostage.

7:00 a.m.

- Representatives from the operations department arrive at United Hatzalah headquarters
- Rabbi Chaim Sassi is shot in Sderot while trying to save the life of a fallen police officer

7:30 a.m.

- By this time, 3,000 Hamas and Islamic Jihad terrorists have attacked over twenty-five kibbutzim and three cities in the Gaza periphery. Some of the kibbutzim managed to defend themselves in the face of the onslaught without any terrorists succeeding at infiltrating.
- Dozens of ambulances and ALS (Advanced Life Saving) vehicles have been dispatched by United Hatzalah to the south to respond. Simultaneously, volunteers from the central and Jerusalem regions of the country head south.
- The logistics center in Beit Shemesh opens and volunteers/staff head to the center to begin collecting and loading equipment to be sent south
- Dr. Tarek Abu Arar, a doctor and volunteer with United Hatzalah, is held captive by Hamas at gunpoint and used as a human shield for two hours while being forced to watch the execution of hundreds of Israelis driving on Highway 232

8:00 a.m.

- Situational operations room opens in an auditorium for the concentration of tasks and events
- United Hatzalah volunteer EMT Awad Dawarshe is shot and killed at the music festival near Kibbutz Re'im while trying to save the life of a woman who was shot as well
- United Hatzalah volunteer Bar Kupershtein, who was hired by an outside organization to serve as an EMT at the music festival, is kidnaped to Gaza. At the time of this printing, he is still being held hostage.

8:30 a.m.

- First emergency vehicles dispatched from Yerushalayim and the center of the country arrive in the south

9:00 a.m.

- First logistics truck with medical equipment to set up field hospitals and triage centers departs from the logistics center. It heads to Cheletz Junction as well as other locations to establish initial triage centers.

- United Hatzalah volunteer EMT Maor (for reasons of security, his last name may not be printed) is shot and killed by a Hamas terrorist while performing his duty as part of Israel's security forces.

9:15 a.m.

- Massive IDF call-up of reservists is in full swing, as people leave shuls, homes, their Yamim Tovim, and their families to join the IDF.

12:21 p.m.

- Medical supplies unloaded from logistics trucks at Cheletz Junction. These supplies, as well as bulletproof vests and helmets, are distributed to all volunteers who have arrived and to IDF soldiers who ran out of supplies of their own. Logistics trucks continue operating to resupply the forces in the field throughout the day.

1:00 p.m.

- The first helicopter receives permission to deploy to Cheletz to perform medical evacuation of critically injured patients. (Until then it was too risky due to rocket barrages and forces on the ground not having a clear enough picture of what was happening.) Two United Hatzalah helicopters were used throughout the day, making continuous trips back and forth from the Gaza border region carrying seriously injured and critical patients to various hospitals, including Tel HaShomer and Hadassah.

6:55 p.m.

- Shabbos and Yom Tov ends, and anyone who has not seen or heard the news about the war in Israel suddenly becomes aware of the situation. Hundreds of additional volunteers head down south to assist.

8:00 p.m.

- 26 ambulances already in the south are centralized and begin cycles of 12-hour shifts with armed volunteers on board

9:00 p.m.

- IDF forces finally arrive at Kibbutz Nir Oz and manage to kill all of the terrorists. Over 100 people were killed on the kibbutz, with terrorists setting fire to homes in order to smoke residents out of their safe rooms. The 160 residents who survived had all managed to stay in their safe rooms and survived the smoke. They are evacuated to Eilat on Sunday.

October 8, 2023

- Police and IDF special forces, who had been fighting with terrorists in the city of Sderot for over 20 hours, decide to destroy the police station that had been taken over by Hamas early on October 7th. The Hamas terrorists are too well fortified in the building for the security forces to neutralize them. The decision is made to bring the entire building down on top of the terrorists to end the bloody attack. At least 20 police officers are murdered by Hamas terrorists in the attack on the station.

- In Kfar Aza, where 72 residents were murdered, the IDF manages to eliminate the last ten terrorists, after nearly two full days of fighting. Most residents of the kibbutz who survived had been confined to their safe rooms for two days.

- Sdei Yoav logistics base is established in a parking lot, including an equipment center, vehicle operations center, command and control unit, as well as a mobile dispatch center to manage the operation in the Gaza periphery. Food and a makeshift kitchen are set up as well.

- The operations team sets up supply drop-offs in Yerushalayim, Bnei Brak, Beit Shemesh, and other areas of the country, for the public to donate food and medical supplies to be used in the field by United Hatzalah volunteers, IDF, etc. Civilian volunteers from all across the country begin arriving at United Hatzalah supply centers to volunteer with packaging and delivering supplies.

- Work is begun to deliver tons of United Hatzalah medical equipment and safety equipment to the IDF

- Daily debriefings and situational assessments are held internally, and regular briefings are held with security agencies

October 9, 2023

- After two days of fighting, the IDF and the counter-terrorism Yamam unit of the police succeed in eliminating all of the terrorists in the city of Ofakim. There were fifty civilian deaths in the city, and numerous people abducted as hostages. (One older couple from Ofakim managed to survive being captured by terrorists for 19 hours in their home by feeding the terrorists a meal and some cookies.)

- United Hatzalah volunteers and ambulance teams begin driving around cities where terrorists are still holed up, to deliver medications and food to residents who were told not to leave their homes

October 12, 2023

- Two terrorists are found near the Sdei Teiman airstrip (where emergency medical evacuation helicopters from MDA and UH are stationed, among other aircraft) and eliminated by security forces. The airstrip is 35 kilometers away from the border of Gaza.
- United Hatzalah begins the purchase of $15 million worth of medical supplies to begin restocking, as more than 90% of medical supplies saved up for a year were used in the first two days of the war

October 13, 2023

- United Hatzalah volunteer EMT Moshe Weitzman is injured by a rocket blast in Sderot while handing out food and medical supplies to people who were too frightened to leave the city

October 20, 2023

- Israeli police apprehend four Gazans hiding in an apartment in Beersheva. These are the last of the Gazans to be found from the October 7th incursion.

October 22, 2023

- Eli Beer is invited to meet with President Biden during his 8-hour visit to Israel
- The first mass psychotrauma debrief for operations managers and volunteers takes place at Sdei Yoav. Smaller individual debriefs and treatment had been ongoing since the war broke out.

October 27-28, 2023

- Eli Beer flies to Las Vegas to speak at the RJC and meet with many American politicians, including former president Donald Trump, presidential candidates Nikki Haley and Ron DeSantis, Speaker of the House Michael Johnson, and others to garner support for Israel amid the war effort

PART ONE
FIRST SHOCK WAVES

How much longer will there be weeping in Tzion and mourning in Yerushalayim? Have mercy upon Tzion and rebuild the walls of Yerushalayim.

— ***Tishah B'Av Kinnos***

"How I wanted to stay with this Jew and give him the respect he deserved, but there was nothing I could do for him because there were other patients who were still alive who we needed to treat."

— ***Charles Gros,***
Volunteer for Hatzolah of New York

CHAPTER ONE

The Worst Kind of Déjà Vu

Succos 2023 was Eli Beer's nicest Succos ever. In the years that followed Covid, fewer people than usual had been coming to Israel, but that Succos Yerushalayim was packed with American Jews — all happy, all celebrating. Every hotel was full, and people were thrilled beyond words to be back in the Holy Land surrounded by friends and family. It was a time of joy, a time for rejoicing. The streets were filled with the sound of music, and everywhere one went there was singing and dancing.

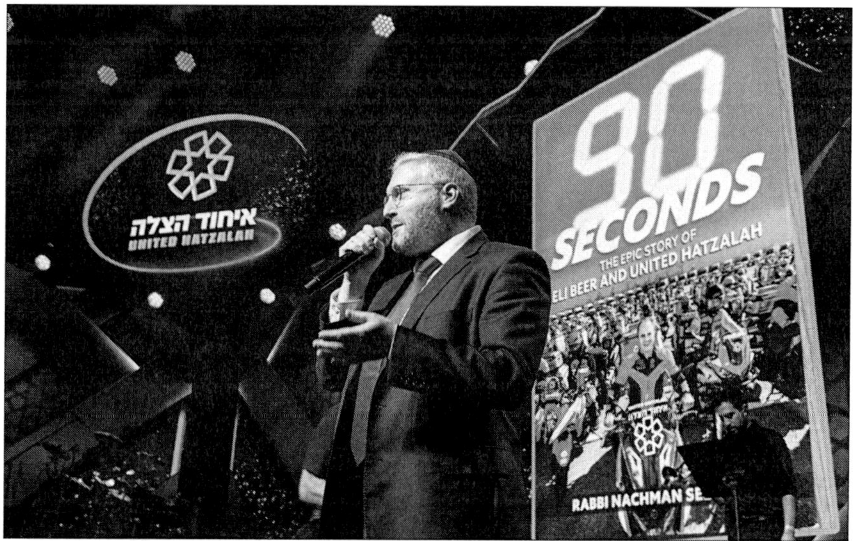

The author, Rabbi Nachman Seltzer, at the United Hatzalah concert speaking about the process of writing 90 Seconds and its worldwide success

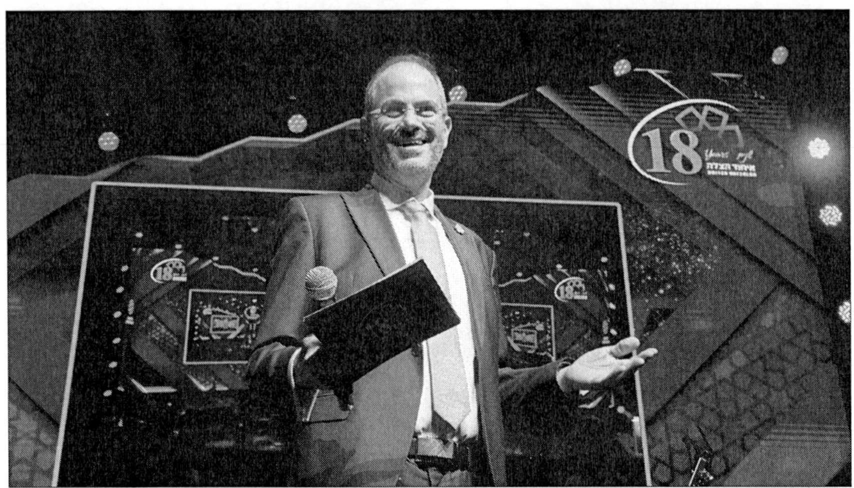

Eli raising money at the concert

Though busy with the annual United Hatzalah concert, Eli Beer somehow found time to go on quite a few calls in Yerushalayim. He had learned long ago that it was important for him to keep his own medical skills sharp. More than that, going on calls kept him connected to the thousands of Hatzalah volunteers.

On the Wednesday of Chol HaMo'ed, United Hatzalah held its annual Succos concert. It was a sold-out evening with fantastic performances by Akiva Turgeman, Mordechai Shapiro, and Ishay Ribo. The

Mordechai Shapiro at the show

Ishay Ribo performing

concert hall at Binyanei Ha'uma was packed with thousands of people who had come to show their support for United Hatzalah. In the middle of the concert, Eli held an appeal to raise money for the best defibrillators available on the market. Such quality doesn't come cheap, and they cost thirty-six thousand dollars each. Fifteen people answered his call for new defibrillators, while others donated funds for less expensive equipment.

All in all, the evening was a smashing success.

On Hoshana Rabbah, Eli joined a minyan organized by his friend David Geffner. Pinny Einhorn was the chazzan, and Eli found himself getting into the zone that morning in a way that hadn't happened to him in a very long time. They davened, sang, and danced for hours. Then there was a festive meal that lasted until close to Simchas Torah.

It was a beautiful time. An uplifting time. No one dreamed that a cataclysmic storm was brewing down south.

Eli and his family stayed at the David Citadel Hotel for Simchas Torah. He enjoyed the davening on the night of Simchas Torah, surrounded by good friends, everyone singing, dancing, and enjoying Yom Tov in the wake of the excitement and success of the concert. By the time the family went to sleep that night, it was very late.

His phone rang at six thirty the next morning. Since it was his special Hatzalah phone he knew that it was ringing because of an emergency and that he had to answer it.

It was his son-in-law Aharon. If Aharon was calling him at six thirty on Simchas Torah morning, it was clearly an emergency.

Eli answered the phone. "What's happened?"

"They're calling from the dispatch center," his son-in-law replied. "They're looking for you."

"What's going on?"

"One of our volunteers was shot."

"It's six thirty in the morning on Simchas Torah," Eli said. "How did one of our volunteers get shot?"

The whole scenario sounded strange, almost sinister, and he was overcome with a deep sense of foreboding.

"There are missile attacks right now in the southern part of the country."

The sense of foreboding grew worse.

"How many people do we have on call at the dispatch center right now?"

"We're on Shabbos mode. There are just ten people there."

Though he still didn't know exactly what had happened, it was clear to Eli that this was a major *pikuach nefesh* situation, and they would need all hands on deck.

"Put out a call to all our volunteers. Tell them we need more people and make it clear that this is a priority."

Usually on Shabbos there was no reason to have more than ten people at the dispatch center. Even on Simchas Torah, calls usually began coming later in the day, after people drank and took part in the general merriment. But all that was applicable on a regular Simchas Torah, and there was nothing regular about that morning.

Eli put on his suit. It was Shabbos and Yom Tov, after all. Turning to his wife, Gitty, who'd been awakened by the call, he asked, "What are you going to do?"

"People are being injured," she replied. "I'm going down south."

They said goodbye and Eli left the room to head for the Hatzalah headquarters, while Gitty prepared to head south. On the way down to the lobby, he ran into a paramedic from New York who was spending

Yom Tov in Yerushalayim. His name was Charles Gros, and he had been a paramedic with Hatzolah in New York for thirty-six years. Eli asked Charles to come with him to help. Charles immediately agreed, understanding that there was a good chance that they were going to need every available hand.

Even so, Eli didn't dream that he was about to experience a day he would remember for the rest of his life.

It took them just a few minutes to get across the city to United Hatzalah headquarters. The city was still quiet, and there was no traffic. Very few people knew what was going on just an hour and a half away in the south. Soon Eli parked the car across from Center One and was walking through the doors of United Hatzalah headquarters, where he made his way to the dispatch center.

The dispatch center is the pulsing heart of Hatzalah, the place where they receive the emergency calls and volunteers are given instructions and details of where they have to go. Eli immediately sent out a repeat of his message: they needed another fifty people to get over to dispatch — and they needed them now.

The message was sent out to the volunteers, many of whom were already in shul. The moment they looked at their phones and saw the messages that had been sent, people began to move. Since they were in

At the dispatch center

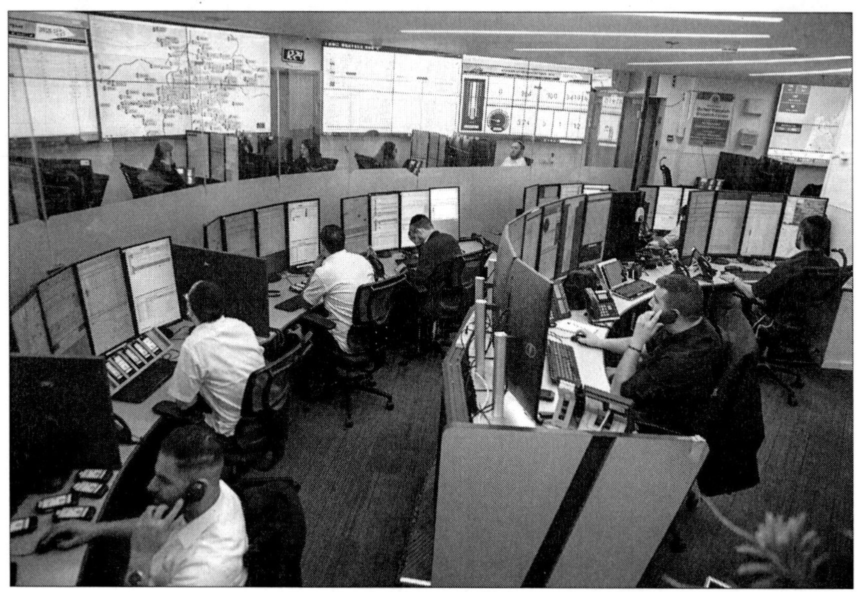

All hands on deck at the dispatch center

the middle of davening, those in shul were immediately alerted that the country was under attack and that this was no ordinary situation.

Leaving the building, Eli saw Yidden converging on the Hatzalah building. Volunteers were coming from all directions — chassidim still in their talleisim, others carrying them in their hands — running, running, everyone grasping that there was no time to waste.

Standing on the street, watching the sight, Eli was reminded of pictures he had seen of the outbreak of the Yom Kippur War in 1973, fifty years earlier. Then, too, Yidden had been forced to leave shul in the middle of davening to go to the front and defend their country from the enemy who was attacking them for one simple reason: because they were Jews. Now once again Yidden were leaving shul, determined to do whatever they could to help.

The scene was like the worst kind of déjà vu imaginable.

"I watched as my volunteers came running up to the building and began donning bulletproof vests and helmets before getting into the ambulances that were waiting to go down south," Eli relates. "While alarm sirens were wailing in Yerushalayim as well, the main threat was in the southern part of the country, and that was where the majority of our ambulances were needed. And so we watched as team after team were outfitted with equipment, boarded the ambulances, and drove off to war.

"We already knew from our own volunteers who lived in the south that people were being slaughtered down there, and I was informed that volunteers were on their way south from Bnei Brak, Tel Aviv, and even Haifa. United Hatzalah was mobilizing its troops and going to war."

By the end of the first day, United Hatzalah had 1,700 volunteers down south, where they operated with complete selflessness, saving lives literally under fire.

When Eli arrived at United Hatzalah headquarters, one of his calls was to Moshe Levy, VP of logistics.

"Do you know what's going on?"

"Yes."

"Where are you now?"

"I'm already in Beit Shemesh. We're opening the main warehouse."

Eli could picture the warehouse in his mind. The huge open space. Forty-five thousand square feet packed with every type of equipment a volunteer could possibly need, from bulletproof vests and helmets to medicines of every type, defibrillators, monitors, stretchers, oxygen tanks, trauma equipment, IVs, saline — anything and everything you can imagine was packed and ready to use. It was from this room that equipment was sent out to every part of the country so that the ambulances and volunteers had whatever they needed to do their jobs.

"For years," Eli says, "I insisted that we keep our warehouses fully stocked with equipment — just in case a war broke out and we needed access to a lot of equipment at once. I wasn't surprised that we were suddenly looking at a war, but I was surprised at the direction it was coming from. I had always envisioned an attack from Hezbollah in the north. But the threat was coming from the south, and from what I was hearing, it was clear that the country had been taken by surprise."

It wasn't long before Eli learned that Hamas terrorists had broken through the barrier separating Gaza from the southern part of Israel and were speeding around the region on black motorcycles, leaving a trail of death everywhere they went.

His son-in-law Aharon called to give him an update on the situation. Eli learned that one of the volunteers, who actually lived down south, had been injured, and another resident of the south who lived in Sderot, Rabbi Chaim Sassi, had been shot several times. Later they would learn about the courageous actions that Rabbi Sassi — a *rav*, yeshivah principal, and *maggid shiur* — had taken while under fire. (More about Rabbi Sassi later…)

Then Eli heard from the dispatch center that the head of United Hatzalah in Sderot, Nehorai Darshan, had been attacked while he was on his way to a call in the city. His vehicle had been riddled with gunfire from a passing Toyota pickup truck filled with terrorists. Nehorai barely survived.

Events were happening fast and furious, and they were still missing details on what was going on, but it was becoming clearer by the moment that they were facing something that was much bigger than they had initially thought. They still didn't know that the attack was unprecedented in scope, but that comprehension would be setting in as hundreds of calls came in to United Hatzalah in the next few hours from those who were hiding in their cars, between cars on the street, in their homes, and under bushes. People were reporting that they had left their babies hidden in their homes and were about to give themselves up — but they wanted someone to know that they had left their kids behind so that the children would be found when it was safe to get them.

The whole situation was unbelievable, and no one knew what the next second would bring.

Meanwhile, Gitty arrived at United Hatzalah headquarters, where she joined an ambulance crew heading down south. It was hard for Eli Beer to know that his wife, the mother of his children, the woman who had stood at his side and partnered with him in building United Hatzalah, the organization they both loved with all their hearts, was getting into an ambulance and heading straight into a war zone. He said goodbye and watched as the ambulance took off down the street, sirens wailing and lights flashing. Then he turned and reentered the building.

Shortly afterwards his son-in-law Aharon also headed south to run the entire operation on the ground. Later still, Aharon's wife, Avigail — Eli's daughter — went as well. Now there were three of his closest family members working under fire to save the Jewish people.

Eli didn't allow himself to think about the danger they were in. Instead, he threw himself completely into the tasks at hand. Hundreds of calls were coming in to the dispatch center, and they kept hearing of yet another town, another moshav or kibbutz, and even cities like

Sderot and Ofakim, that were under attack. He stood in the dispatch center listening to some of the conversations coming over the phone, to the people crying and begging United Hatzalah to please come and save them. And his heart broke as he heard parents tearfully begging Hatzalah to rescue their children.

"I don't care about myself, but please save my children..."

So it went, on and on and on.

It was too much. No one was equipped to deal with fighting in twenty-something locations, spread out over such a large area.

Events were happening at dizzying speed and it was virtually impossible to keep up. Eli Pollak, the CEO of United Hatzalah, was on the phone with the police and different government offices dealing with a million details, including the logistics of getting equipment, ambulances, and volunteers to where they had to be. Dovie Maisel, the chief of operations, was making sure that all the pieces of his puzzle were in place for the war ahead of them. It felt like the entire world was falling apart around them, but at least at their headquarters the people in charge were doing their jobs without hesitation and in the most professional way possible.

When they realized that they were going to run out of ambulances, the order was given from headquarters that any volunteer who was still determined to go down south should take his own car. In normal times, it's illegal to transport patients in privately owned vehicles, but this wasn't a normal time. That decision saved countless lives because they were able to bring more people to the hospital who would otherwise have been forced to wait — injured and in pain — in the middle of a war zone until an ambulance was free to transport them. It was yet another example of how United Hatzalah was thinking out of the box even as the crisis was squeezing the entire country in a vise.

CHAPTER TWO

Eli's Vindication

From the moment Eli had arrived at the dispatch center a few hours earlier, they had handled one crisis after another non-stop. He now understood that what he'd instinctively sensed earlier — that they were in the opening stages of another Yom Kippur War — had been accurate. After hearing what he heard over his communication device, the most prominent being the words *mechablim*, "terrorists," there was no question that the country was facing its greatest challenge of the last few decades.

It seemed to him that there was somewhere in the range of four hundred terrorists rampaging through the south, and in the meantime the army was having a difficult time getting its troops to where they needed to be in order to combat the threat. Had Eli known that it was actually close to three thousand terrorists who had infiltrated the country, he is not at all sure that he would have allowed Gitty to board an ambulance that morning. But he hadn't known, and now she was down there, in the middle of the worst kind of war zone, as were his daughter and his son-in-law.

"We told our volunteers to count how many dead they were seeing," Eli says. "But the numbers we were getting didn't seem real. They couldn't be real. How could it be that there were forty, fifty, sixty, seventy, a hundred people lying dead in their cars in the same strip of highway in Israel? How could it be that so many innocent civilians had been murdered and their bodies abandoned?"

Little did they imagine that the number of dead was going to total well over a thousand, while thousands of others would be wounded and more than 200 would be kidnaped and held hostage. Who could have ever imagined that Hamas terrorists were running loose and executing Jews in the street and even in their own homes?

It was unthinkable, and yet it was happening.

It was like the Yom Kippur War meeting the *Einsatzgruppen* — the teams of SS troops who roamed the countryside of Eastern Europe, gathering Jews from every village, forcing them to dig mass graves, and then gunning them down. And like the Nazis decades before, the attack by Hamas was a battle, not against soldiers, but against old men and women, mothers and babies, parents and children.

From the moment the volunteers of United Hatzalah arrived down south, they worked to save as many people as they could.

Under a sky filled with rockets that were exploding in every direction.

Under the constant threat of terrorists hiding a few meters away on the side of the road, ready to fire at them at will.

When the time came and the Jewish people needed United Hatzalah — they were there. Nothing stopped the volunteers of United Hatzalah. Nothing deterred them. They weren't afraid for their own safety and they threw themselves on the mercy of Hashem, confident that He would look after them as they went in. They stepped up to the task and performed like superheroes.

So it was that the volunteers of United Hatzalah treated thousands of people and saved their lives, driving many to hospitals and transporting others by helicopter, while the One above made sure they survived intact.

As Eli Beer stood in United Hatzalah headquarters in Yerushalayim, doing his best to manage the situation from there, his mind took him back to the year 2006 — to another time when Israel found itself at war.

He remembered it clearly. The enemy had started shooting rockets across the Israeli border with Lebanon, at cities in the northern part of the country. Eli Beer sent members of his team to the organization's warehouse that morning to see how much equipment they had in stock and how much needed to be purchased. To his shock and dismay, he was informed that the warehouse was more or less empty of equipment and that the funds that he'd collected for years to ensure that they would be equipped for such a situation had been allocated elsewhere, for other lifesaving purposes.

This was not the time to point fingers and there was no point in wasting energy assigning blame. There was one thing to do and Eli did it: he went into action and purchased a million dollars' worth of equipment on credit. Since the debt would have to be paid fairly quickly, he also bought a ticket for an El Al flight leaving that same day, landing in New York the next morning to solicit the needed funds. When Eli returned after his lightning-quick visit, Dovie Maisel, the COO of United Hatzalah, met him at Ben Gurion Airport with a convoy of trucks and ambulances stuffed with the equipment that Eli had just raised one million dollars to pay for. They immediately drove north to dispense vital equipment to Hatzalah volunteers, other first responders, and even soldiers.

Now, on October 7, 2023, war had broken out once more. A terrible, catastrophic war that had the potential to engulf the entire country and maybe even the entire Middle East. Yet this time something was very different than during the last serious war. This time trucks, ambulances, and volunteers were able to pull up to the main United Hatzalah warehouse near Beit Shemesh, or at one of the many other United Hatzalah branches around the country, and stock up on all the equipment they needed before heading into the field.

Eli as a young volunteer

This time there was no need for Eli Beer to get on the phone and buy equipment on credit. This time the warehouses were stocked with every piece of equipment that was needed. For years Eli had thrown his

Preparing equipment to be taken out to the field

heart and soul into fundraising for United Hatzalah. He never stopped, never rested, never ceased asking those who loved him and the organization to donate another ambulance, defibrillator, ambucycle, or first-aid kit.

Some thought him obsessive. Some couldn't understand why virtually every conversation ended with a request for more support for United Hatzalah. But the truth is, all of that — all those requests — were merely preparation for the one crucial moment that Eli feared was going to come.

On the day Israel was attacked, Eli's hard work was vindicated. Because that was the day when the warehouse was full of equipment and United Hatzalah was able to outfit every first-aid responder who needed it. They were also able to help equip many soldiers who had been called up to the front and were lacking the proper equipment, and offer expensive and vital medical equipment to the IDF.

The United Hatzalah warehouse near Beit Shemesh

On that fateful day — a day of rejoicing that had turned into a day of mourning — Eli was able to watch as his volunteers dropped everything they were doing and went off to save *Klal Yisrael*. The *mesirus nefesh* they exhibited will never be forgotten by the people they saved and by every grateful member of our nation.

A Miraculous Moment

There was a family who lived in the Ramat Eshkol neighborhood of Yerushalayim, while their landlord's family lived in Ofakim. For years the family who lived in the Ramat Eshkol apartment invited their landlord to come and spend Shabbos with them, but somehow it never worked out. Then, a few days before Simchas Torah, the Ramat Eshkol family called their landlord and informed them in no uncertain terms that they were coming to spend Simchas Torah with them in Ramat Eshkol, and they wouldn't take no for an answer. The family from Ofakim accepted the invitation.

Many people in Ofakim were murdered in the ensuing attack, but the owners of the Ramat Eshkol apartment, who were not in Ofakim, were spared. Someone asked the mother of the family from Ofakim to what she attributed the miracle they experienced.

"We have owned the apartment in Ramat Eshkol for many years," she answered. "In the beginning, rental prices were fairly low, and we rented it out to a *kollel* family. Years passed and we heard that owners in the neighborhood were starting to raise the rent. At first we didn't pay attention, but after a while, we decided that the time had come for us to raise the rent as well.

"We told the father of the family renting our apartment that we planned on raising the rent. 'That's your right," he said, 'but if you do raise the rent, we'll have to leave the apartment since we are not able to afford a higher rent.'

"Hearing this, we asked him if he is a person who learns three *sedarim* a day. He confirmed that he was. We decided that if this was the case, we weren't going to raise the rent. And we didn't."

It was to this that the woman from Ofakim attributed their being spared from harm that Simchas Torah — that they had enabled a *kollel* couple to afford their rent so that the husband could learn with peace of mind.

CHAPTER THREE

A Patek Philippe With a Bright Red Band

Charles Gros, a volunteer for Hatzolah in New York, was in Israel for Succos, like so many other Americans. The last thing he expected was to be caught in a war.

This is his story:

I was in my room in the David Citadel overlooking the Old City on Simchas Torah morning when I heard a noise. At first, I wasn't sure what it was, but then I heard the loudspeaker of the hotel kick in, and a voice said, "All guests in the hotel, please make your way out of your rooms and into the fortified stairwells. All guests from the ninth and tenth floors, please go down to the eighth floor and make your way to the fortified stairwell."

There was no question that the situation was dire if the hotel was waking the guests and telling them to leave their rooms and go to a reinforced safe area. My first thought was to check on my children, who were on a different floor. I left my room, and as I was walking down the hallway, I ran into Eli and his son-in-law.

"It's bad," Eli said. "Come help us."

"I'd be happy to come with you. I just need two minutes to make sure that my children are safe."

"Meet us in front of the hotel."

I let my family know that I was going to the United Hatzalah dispatch center. Then I went downstairs and met Eli underneath the grand arches of the David Citadel.

The next thing I knew we were driving with lights and sirens on through the deserted streets of Yerushalayim, toward United Hatzalah headquarters. Minutes later we were pulling up outside the United Hatzalah building, and moments after that, we were entering the dispatch center. I had never been there before.

The first thing I saw was a dispatcher on the phone with someone down south who had been shot in the leg. It was clear that events were moving rapidly. A few minutes later Eli informed me that the decision had been made that volunteers would be able to transport patients to the hospital in their private cars. He explained that this had never been done before.

Driving with a gun

Turning to me, he said, "Are you ready to go down south?"

"If I'm needed, I'll go."

Eli pulled over a guy named Avi, who was carrying a gun.

"Avi is going to be your driver," he said to me. "He's one of the best."

He called over someone else.

"He's going along to protect you."

Seconds later we were running outside to an ambulance. Before we could get in, there was a siren and we were forced to return to the building, where we waited for the all-clear and then returned to the ambulance. In no time, we were on our way out of Yerushalayim, lights flashing and sirens wailing as we navigated the steep curves of the Jerusalem–Tel Aviv highway.

It was Simchas Torah morning, and I was on my way to a war zone.

Our first stop was at United Hatzalah's main warehouse located in a forty-five-thousand-square-foot building not far from IKEA on Route 38 near Beit Shemesh. When we pulled up outside the warehouse, there was a truck being loaded with pallets of equipment that was needed down south. The moment we arrived, the staff stopped loading the truck and began turning our ambulance from basic-life-support capacity to advanced-life-support capacity. This meant that we would now be able to administer medication, intubate the wounded, and insert an IV line if needed. For a paramedic like myself, being in that warehouse was something akin to being a kid in a candy store. Every type of medical equipment that a medical professional might need could be found there in abundant quantities.

As we were getting into the ambulance to leave, someone handed me a box.

"Charles, this is for you."

I didn't know what to expect when I opened the box, but when I looked inside, I saw a brand-new bulletproof vest and helmet.

"This equipment may save your life today," the person who'd handed me the box said.

They took a few moments to adjust the vest and helmet to my size. When everything fit properly, I was taken over to a little desk. The top of the desk was covered with various patches, denoting the different jobs and responsibilities that a person might have in the organization: *Paramedic. Medic. Driver. EMT. Doctor.*

They picked up two patches with the word *paramedic* on it. The first one was attached to my chest. I felt a slap on my back as the second one was put in the right place. I wasn't sure if the slap was just to make sure that the Velcro was on well and wouldn't come off, or if it meant, "Let's be on our way. There's no time to waste!" Either way, the next thing I knew we were speeding down the highway in the direction of Sderot.

Fifteen minutes later, we received our first call. Someone had been injured in a missile attack. Missiles were falling around us as we drove further into dangerous territory. There were fires burning where they

Damaged cars on the road

landed, causing smoke, devastation, injuries, and death. While the Iron Dome was working overtime to prevent as many missiles as possible from entering Israel, the bombardment was too much for the system, and it wasn't able to stop everything from flying in.

We saw fields on fire and a house burning where it had been struck. There was no question that we were literally driving straight into a war zone. On the way, we were stopped by a nurse and a doctor who requested medical supplies so that they would be able to treat patients who had been wounded in earlier attacks.

Soon we arrived at our first call. A missile had fallen right in front of a building. There were a bunch of cars on fire, and since people were already dealing with the situation, we continued on our way.

I've been a paramedic for over thirty years and have seen many things in my life, but the situation we faced here was absolutely horrific. We passed cars that had been riddled with bullet holes and cars with people inside them who had been killed. Some of the cars on the road were still running, but they were empty.

Soon we came across army vehicles on the road. They were also empty — all the soldiers were gone.

One of the most frightening parts of the drive was that every time we saw a vehicle coming toward us from the other direction, we didn't know if it was our people or the enemy. We were getting reports of stolen police cars, stolen ambulances, and terrorists who were disguised in IDF uniforms, so whenever we saw any type of vehicle coming in our direction, both my driver and the other EMT made sure their guns were ready to fire — just in case.

It wasn't long before we began receiving patients, brought to us by soldiers who had rescued them from the music festival that had taken place right near the border with Gaza, as well as from nearby moshavim that been attacked. Soon I found myself in the back of the ambulance with four patients in various levels of pain and injury.

The patient in the worst shape was about twenty-four years old. He had been shot in both his hands and was lying on a stretcher, doing his best to cope with the pain and agony on the twenty-minute drive to the closest hospital. He had put both his hands in the air — in the classic pose of surrender — and begged the terrorist not to shoot. Surrendering didn't have the hoped-for effect on the terrorist, who promptly shot the young man in both his hands. Though in tremendous pain, the man was doing his best to hold on to his watch — a Patek Philippe with a bright red band. It was clear that he was worried about losing his watch, and at one point he said to me, "Please hold on to my watch for me. I trust you."

The watch

I took the man's treasured watch, and since I already had my own watch on my left wrist, I put the watch I'd been handed for safekeeping onto my right arm. Then I continued treating the injured man.

One of the patients spoke up to recount the miracle that happened to him.

Terrorists had shot him three times in the stomach. He explained that not being a skinny person had finally come in handy.

"It literally saved my life," he said. "The bullets that passed into my stomach didn't touch any major arteries because my fat protected me. That's what I was told by the first EMT who treated me."

Of course, it wasn't quite that simple and he didn't get off easy since some of his fat had literally melted from the heat of the bullets. Yet he was alive, and that was all that mattered.

Another injured patient tried to flee from a terrorist by running into a house. The terrorist followed him inside. He got on his knees and put his hands up in the air. "Please don't kill me," he begged. "My wife and children still need me!"

For no obvious reason, the terrorist decided to spare his life.

"Give me your wallet," the terrorist demanded.

He handed the Arab his wallet.

"Your phone."

He handed the terrorist his phone.

Suddenly he heard the sounds of Arabic coming through the walkie-talkie the terrorist was using to communicate with his commanding officers. Hearing the words coming at him, the terrorist turned on his heels and left. My patient wanted to be relieved, but he wasn't sure if the terrorist was coming back or not. He stayed inside the house for a long time, and the terrorist never returned.

Another wounded patient had been driving through the streets when terrorists began shooting at him. He pushed the friend who was with him off the passenger seat and into the car's footwell. Then he moved his seat as far back as it would go and used the reverse camera to drive backward until he reached a place of safety.

One woman they transported later that day wouldn't talk — not one word. Her husband had been killed in front of her eyes, and she was incapable of speech.

When we arrived at the hospital, the doors were opened, and the patient who had been shot in both hands was whisked off the ambulance and into the hospital. By the time I finished briefing the hospital staff on the condition of the patients, the man who had asked me to hold on to his watch was long gone, and the hospital wasn't allowing people to walk around inside unless they had a really good reason for doing so. I guessed that returning the injured man's watch didn't qualify, so I wasn't able to give him back his watch on that same day.

While I was disappointed that I hadn't been able to return the man's precious watch before parting ways, I knew that he was going to look for me when the situation calmed down. People asked me how I was going to make sure that the watch would be returned to the right individual. I told them that there was a very simple answer to that question.

"What's that?"

"The man to whom I will return the watch with the red band will have a very clear sign on his person."

"What kind of sign?"

"He will have been shot in both hands. No one else need apply."

The afternoon of that never-to-be-forgotten day found us in the southern city of Ofakim. We set up shop near the police station, where we treated about fifty people who had been mildly hurt or injured but didn't require hospital care. A little later we received a call to drive to a street where a man had been spotted lying on the ground. When we arrived, we could see that that the man, who was dead, was wearing a white shirt and black pants and appeared to have been a religious Jew. Most probably he had been on his way to shul that morning when he was shot and killed by a passing terrorist.

As a member of Hatzalah for so many years, I had long been taught about *kavod hameis* — of treating a deceased person with the proper respect. Even if you weren't able to save his life, at least you were able to give him the dignity he deserved.

How I wanted to stay with this Jew and to give him that respect and dignity, but there was nothing I could do for him and there were others who were still alive whom we needed to treat.

"Please forgive me," I entreated the man on the ground, "and try to understand that I can't bring you anywhere right now because I have to do my best to save as many lives as possible."

Then I got back into the ambulance, and we drove away.

A little later we ended up at a nearby army base that had been infiltrated by terrorists that morning. Soon we heard the sound of honking as a car approached the base very quickly. The soldiers guarding the base went on full alert. Moments later, a small white car came to a stop right near the base.

There were soldiers inside. Every one of them had their guns pointed out the window beside them. Some were literally hanging out of the window with their guns ready to shoot. They had a soldier with them who had just been shot in the head. The soldier who was holding on to him yelled to me, "He's still breathing! He's still breathing!"

I ran over to examine him, but immediately realized that he was unfortunately no longer alive despite his friends doing their best to get him to us as quickly as possible.

"What happened?" I asked them.

"We were going from house to house in one of the moshavim looking for terrorists. He was our leader — the soldier who went in first. In one of the houses, we walked into a room, and there was a terrorist waiting inside. He shot our friend before anyone could react."

It was obvious that all they wanted to do was stay with their friend. But after a few minutes, one of them said, "We have to go."

Turning to me, he said, "We have to go back. There's no time to cry. The rest of our platoon is still sweeping the area where we were and they need us."

I watched as they bade farewell to their friend. Then they got back into the car, his blood still on their uniforms, and drove back in the direction from which they'd come.

It was probably the most frightening day of my life, and the scariest part about it was the constant feeling of facing the unknown. It was clear that there were terrorists lurking alongside the roads and hiding in the nearby orchards. But we didn't know where, and just driving down the road was a terrifying experience.

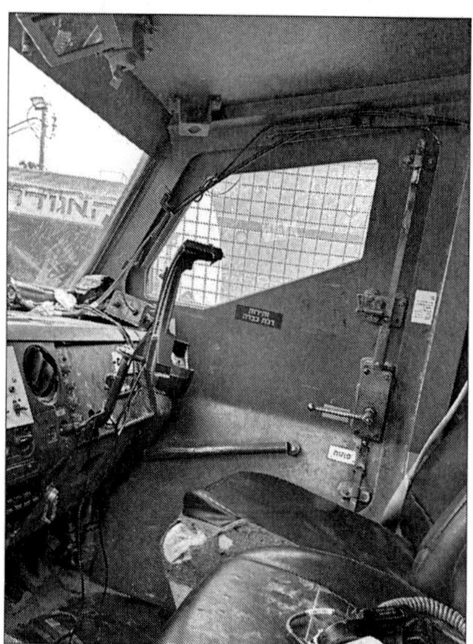

Army vehicle with equipment ripped out

Another terrible thing was seeing all the abandoned army vehicles. In one Humvee, all the soldiers were gone and the radio equipment had been ripped out of the console. It was clear that the soldiers had been abducted — and their computers and equipment had been stolen as well. Seeing the inside of the vehicle was heartbreaking beyond belief.

At one army checkpoint that we passed, we saw a number of vehicles — but not a soldier in sight.

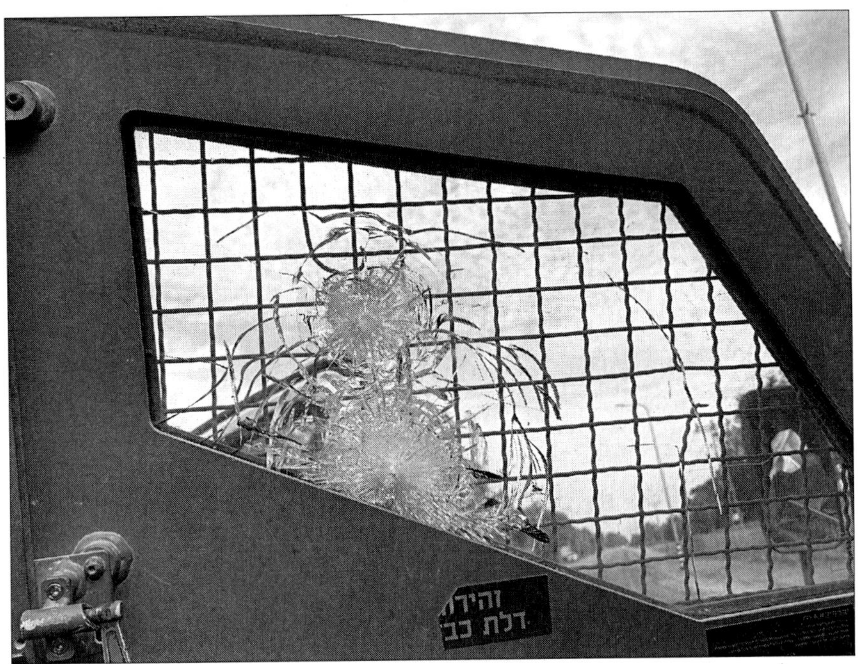

Army vehicle shot at

We were driving to our next call when we hit a traffic jam on the highway. The driver slowed down and tried to figure out why traffic was at a standstill.

None of us got out of the ambulance. It wasn't safe, and we couldn't take the risk. Instead of getting out, we looked through the windows trying to ascertain whether there had been an accident of some kind.

We saw a man standing nearby. He was outside, though it was extremely dangerous. The driver opened his window, and the man told him that there were terrorists hiding on the side of the highway who had ambushed the ten cars we could see in front of us, which had been riddled with bullets. He explained that it had taken people time to understand what was happening, and by the time they figured it out, many cars had already been attacked.

It was clear that no one could continue driving on the road until the army came and cleaned out the pocket of terrorists. We couldn't even get out of the ambulance to treat the wounded for fear that the terrorists were still there, waiting to shoot anyone who walked into their line of fire.

All of a sudden, our driver yelled to nobody in particular, "Everyone, stay in the ambulance!"

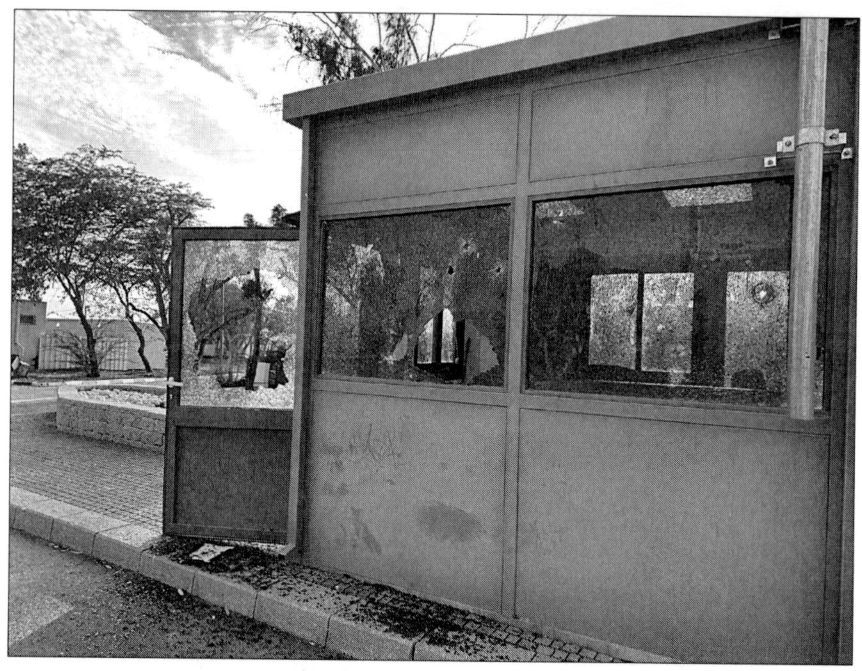

Abandoned army checkpoint

He immediately made a U-turn, and as he turned the ambulance around, I caught sight of eight fully armed terrorists dressed in black (what a fearsome sight!) emerging from a ditch beside the road and starting to run across the highway about fifty feet in front of us. I saw them jumping the barrier in the middle of the highway. All of them had guns, and they were intent on their mission.

It was clear that they had seen that the cars were no longer driving in their direction, and they wanted to attack more innocent people. They had emerged from their hiding place and were moving in our direction.

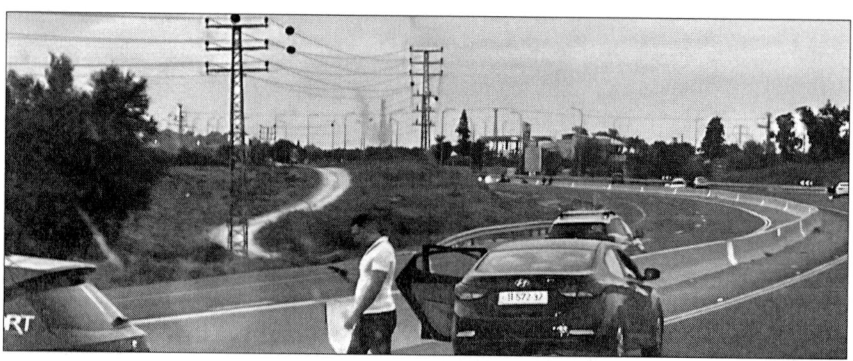

Terrorists crossing the highway in the distance

The driver didn't waste any time getting away from there. Moments later, the ambulance had been turned around, and we were driving as fast as we could on the wrong side of the road, our lights and sirens going full blast, and swerving to avoid the oncoming cars. Our windows were open, and we waved our arms at all the cars nearby, telling them to turn around and drive away immediately, making it clear that the road ahead was filled with danger.

You can see the terrorists on their way to kill more people.

We continued driving from place to place, treating people until close to nine o'clock that night, when we headed back to Yerushalayim. Though there had been a lull in the missile attacks in the afternoon, they started up again full force as night fell. We could see the explosions in the air, fireballs flashing through the atmosphere, while down on earth a long line of cars were heading our way, all filled with soldiers from around the country reporting to their units.

At ten in the evening, the ambulance dropped me off in front of the David Citadel, and I walked through its glass doors. The lobby was shockingly quiet and peaceful after the day of absolute madness I had just experienced. People sat in the coffee shop, and music played softly in the hallways and in the elevator. None of the people in the hotel could ever imagine what I had seen or experienced that day.

In all honesty, I myself could barely process what I went through that day.

And yet I was there, and I saw things that I'll never forget.

The missiles, the wounded and the dead, the fires, the fear of the unknown, the terrorists in the streets — and the man who gave me his watch for safekeeping. Although I wasn't able to get him that watch before he went into surgery, I knew without a smidgen of doubt that I was going to track him down and make sure that he received his beloved Patek Philippe with the bright red band.

As I said, there is no question that I'll recognize him when we meet.

A Miraculous Moment

Rabbi Boruch Rosenblum is a well-known speaker in Eretz Yisrael, and so he's someone many call when they have a good story to share, so that he in turn can share it with his audiences. One day his phone rang. A high-ranking army commander was calling him from Gaza.

"Rabbi, I had to call you with this story. It just happened, and we're still in shock."

Needless to say, Rabbi Rosenblum was very curious to hear the story.

"This morning," the commander began, "I walked into HQ for the morning briefing. This is when we finalize our missions for that day. The moment I entered the room and saw the faces of the rest of the commanders sitting there, I knew that something terrible had happened.

"The reason I knew this was because their faces were white.

"'What happened?'

"One of them pointed at a screen, where I could see footage of three tanks. The tanks were burning and entirely engulfed in flames.

"'This footage was taken by one of our drones,' an officer said.

"There were twelve soldiers in each of those tanks. If all three were on fire and the soldiers hadn't managed to escape, the army was going to have to inform thirty-six families that they had just lost their sons — thirty-six families in one day.

"The feeling of loss was staggering, and none of us knew what to do or say. Then someone's phone rang. It was a soldier from one of the tanks.

"We didn't understand how he could be calling us. Wasn't he dead? Hadn't we lost all thirty-six soldiers in one day? Yet he was on the phone.

"Of course, we had a million questions for him. How was he alive? Why were the tanks on fire? How had they known to get out in time?

"'We were driving in Gaza,' the soldier explained, 'when we suddenly realized that there was a problem with one of the tank's parts. It didn't take us long to determine that the part was broken, and we wouldn't be able to continue using the tank. Rather than remain in the tank until the problem was fixed, which would only have made us into sitting ducks, we got out of the tank and ran to find cover. When the soldiers in the second tank saw us leaving our tank, they came to the conclusion that there was a security issue and that they should also get out of their tank and run for cover.

"'The same thing occurred in the third tank when they saw the soldiers in the second tank exiting their tank and running for cover. Seeing something big happening, they, too, got out of their tank and ran for cover. Moments later all three of our tanks were hit by enemy fire, and all three tanks instantly went up in flames.

"'Had we still been inside, the outcome would have been catastrophic. But none of us were inside.'

"Rabbi Rosenblum," the commander concluded, "please tell everyone you know that there is no question why such incredible stories keep happening. They are happening because of all the *tefillos* and the Torah learning that is being done by so many people. Please tell everyone to continue praying, because without question it's the most powerful weapon at our disposal."

CHAPTER FOUR

Rav, Maggid Shiur, Hero

Rabbi Chaim Sassi was getting ready for the big day. It was Simchas Torah, and he and his *kehillah* — the shul was known affectionately by one and all as "Sderot B'Park" — had been planning a major celebration as a way of inaugurating the fairly new *kehillah*. Davening the night before had been an epic experience, and the singing and dancing in honor of the Torah had spilled out of the shul and into the nearby park. There had been tremendous growth as of late in the city of Sderot, and many of the newcomers had joined Rabbi Sassi's shul.

The new shul

Rav Chaim's Torah center

On the night of Simchas Torah, the *rav* had looked around him at those streaming toward the shul, at the men holding the *sifrei Torah* in the air, the women congregating alongside amid baby carriages and a sea of children, and he felt optimistic about the future of the shul.

The excitement had filled the air with a sizzle that drew people from the nearby high-rise buildings whose porches overlooked the park where the celebration was going on in full force. The joy that was exhibited that night seemed to overflow from those dancing onto those watching, until it felt like the entire city was caught up in the festivities.

It had been a night of genuine rejoicing with the Torah, and now Rabbi Chaim Sassi was looking forward to the morning prayers. Shacharis had been called for seven in the morning to be followed by a gala *kiddush* in honor of the *Chassan Torah* and the first Simchas Torah celebration in the new shul.

As an active volunteer for United Hatzalah, and hearing the non-stop sirens, the *rav* quickly realized that the country was under attack and that the volume of rockets being shot at the south was way more than they had ever encountered before. In addition to all the rockets, there was the sound of gunfire in the streets, which was even more unsettling than the rockets because it signified something unknown and ominous.

It sounded like there were terrorists in the streets attacking the city, but Rabbi Sassi found that almost impossible to believe.

Besides his responsibilities as a shul *rav* and principal of a yeshivah in Sderot, Rabbi Sassi was also a member of the city's "*kitot konanut*" (civilian rapid response security teams). The team had spent a lot of time practicing for different scenarios where the city was under attack and civilians were needed to help protect the inhabitants. Unfortunately, in yet another tragic twist, the army had taken back the team's weapons a short while before the attack. The army had told them that they didn't need to worry because of the very expensive high-tech fence that had been built between them and the enemy in Gaza. This left them and many other security teams in the south of Israel without any real way to defend themselves. Even if some of the team members, like Rabbi Sassi, had their own guns, a handgun isn't much of a defense against enemy rifles or RPGs.

And yet that was the situation on the day of Simchas Torah 2023.

When Rabbi Sassi realized that the city was under attack, he took his gun and the bulletproof vest and helmet he had been given by United Hatzalah and went downstairs to load his ambucycle with all the medical supplies he had at hand. He turned on his radio and kept it on so that he could stay informed about where the various attacks were happening. Moments later, the radio was filled with the voice of

Rav Chaim in Hatzalah gear

the dispatcher reporting a bunch of shooting incidents on several streets not far away.

Rabbi Sassi mounted his orange ambucycle and drove off to help. He knew by now that a band of terrorists was rampaging through the city, so he stayed away from the main arteries and drove through the smaller side streets that the terrorists were less apt to use as they drove from neighborhood to neighborhood. Eventually he reached the entrance to the city, where he heard the sound of gunfire coming from the direction of the nearby gas station.

As the rabbi drew near to the scene of the battle, he began to pass car after car where the people inside had been shot dead — car after car of people who had been executed with gangster-style shots to the head. Driving onto the main road leading toward the exit of Sderot, Rabbi Sassi came across a group of policemen and stopped beside them.

"They're shooting by the entrance to the city right now," he told them. "Go there right away and close off the area! This way no one will try to drive out of the city and get shot at."

Moments later, a vehicle pulled up. At the wheel was a member of the Sderot security team, and he offered the rabbi an extra vest that he happened to have. Rabbi Sassi accepted the vest and put it on under his United Hatzalah vest. On top of that he wore a coat. There was no question in his mind that the more protection he had, the better.

He drove on and soon arrived at the scene of another damaged car, this one stranded in the middle of a roundabout. The driver was critically injured, and Rabbi Sassi removed him from the vehicle and began treating him, but he soon realized that there was little he could do. The man's injuries were too serious. Calls to passersby to help went unheeded, and with no other options, Rabbi Sassi left him there and went to get more equipment. He later found out that the injured man was picked up by a United Hatzalah ambulance and was still alive and under intubation a few days later.

As he drove along one of the main roads, people shouted at him that a policeman had been shot close by. On the way to treat the police officer, he saw a van parked on the street and intuitively grasped that the van had brought a group of terrorists to Sderot.

Rabbi Sassi got off his ambucycle and carefully approached the van to check whether his assumption was correct. Gun out and ready to shoot, he opened one of the van's doors and saw a curly black wig lying on the floor. He wasn't sure what the significance of the wig was but figured that the terrorists were using wigs as a disguise.

Next he went around to the back of the van and opened the doors to find himself face-to-face with a veritable arsenal of weapons. The space was filled with RPGs and sniper rifles and all sorts of other military equipment. But he didn't have time to do anything about the weapons because people were still yelling at him to drive over to the wounded policeman and treat him.

Rabbi Sassi continues the story:

"At a nearby bus stop not far from the city's police station, I saw three policemen and another volunteer from United Hatzalah — Yaakov Bar Yochai. The wounded man was one of the commanders of the Sderot police. He had been shot, and Bar Yochai had treated his wound and bandaged it neatly.

"I noticed another policeman lying on the other side of the street. He had been shot by a Hamas sniper who was shooting at people from the window of the police station. I could see that the policeman on the floor was still moving, though he had been shot in the hand and back.

"'He's still alive,' I told the other three policemen. 'I need you to cover me while I run to his side and bring him back here. As soon as I start running, shoot full blast at the police station. Don't stop shooting until I'm back here!'

"The policemen snapped to attention. Pointing their guns at the police station, they began shooting in the direction of the sniper. While they blasted away, I ran as fast as I could to the wounded policeman.

"The next few moments would be forever seared in my mind.

"Seconds after I reached him and began trying to help him up, the sniper shot me in the knee. A moment later I was shot in the hand, and shrapnel cut into my jaw. I was also shot twice in the head, but my United Hatzalah helmet protected me from the bullets.

"Ignoring the excruciating pain, I threw myself on top of the policeman to shield him from the sniper. Then I dragged him behind a dumpster, where I checked his pulse and realized that the chances of him surviving were very low. He was critically wounded, and I could see his life slipping away before my eyes.

"Knowing I had done all I could for the policeman, I got to work putting a tourniquet on my knee, which had all but collapsed and was bleeding heavily, and then I turned my attention to my jaw. Blood was gushing out, and I put on one bandage and another, but I could tell that it wasn't enough. A little voice in my head suggested that maybe this was a good time to recite *Vidui*, the prayer one says on his deathbed, but I ignored the voice and chose to optimistically recite *Tehillim* instead."

Rabbi Sassi stayed where he was for the next hour and a half, trapped in his spot behind the dumpster because of the flying bullets. There was an officer from the Shabak (Israel's General Security Services) taking cover nearby whom Rabbi Sassi knew. The Shabak officer promised to come rescue him and didn't stop encouraging him to hold on, until they could take the sniper out and it would be safe for him to move. He didn't content himself with words, throwing bottles of water that he had with him in Rabbi Sassi's direction, as well as more bandages, so that Rabbi Sassi could use them to stem the heavy bleeding.

But even after he applied the bandages, it was clear that he needed more. "I need you to get me more bandages!" he called out to his friend.

"Where from?"

Suddenly Rabbi Sassi had a great idea. "I'm sure you will be able to find plenty of bandages in the terrorists' van."

He didn't know how he had the foresight to think of this solution after having been shot four times, but Hashem put the idea into his mind and he knew it was a good one.

"What van are you talking about?"

Rabbi Sassi told his friend about the van filled with military equipment that he had seen earlier.

"I imagine you'll find plenty of bandages there as well."

He gave the officer directions to the van, and the officer returned a short while later with plenty of bandages — courtesy of Hamas. They were very good-quality bandages, perfectly sterile and previously untouched, and they served him well. And although he wasn't using his phone to talk to anyone without a valid *pikuach nefesh* reason (it was Shabbos, after all), he turned on his phone's video and focused it on his head injury so that he would be able to apply the bandages properly to the wound.

Here's a truly amazing thing.

When the Shabak officer opened the door of the van and began searching for a first-aid kit, he discovered plenty of bandages — and something else as well. There, lying on the floor of the van, was a radio, the kind that the terrorists were using to communicate with one another as they rampaged through Sderot killing and maiming innocent people. Since the officer worked for the Shabak, he was fluent in Arabic and understood everything the terrorists were saying to one another over their radios.

Suddenly our side was being given a direct view into the mind of the enemy. The officer heard them when they said which floor they were on in any given building, and he knew what they could see and what was out of their line of vision.

From that moment on, the officer listened in on the terrorists' radio communications and used the information he heard for our benefit. Many, many lives were saved in the merit of Rabbi Sassi's lightbulb moment.

How's that for a miraculous turn of events?

Finally, when the sniper's gunfire ceased, United Hatzalah volunteer Yaakov Bar Yochai came with his private car to evacuate Rabbi Sassi from Sderot and take him to the hospital. A wounded policeman sat in the front seat, and the *rav* lay down in the back. Soon an armored vehicle pulled up, and another wounded police officer was transferred

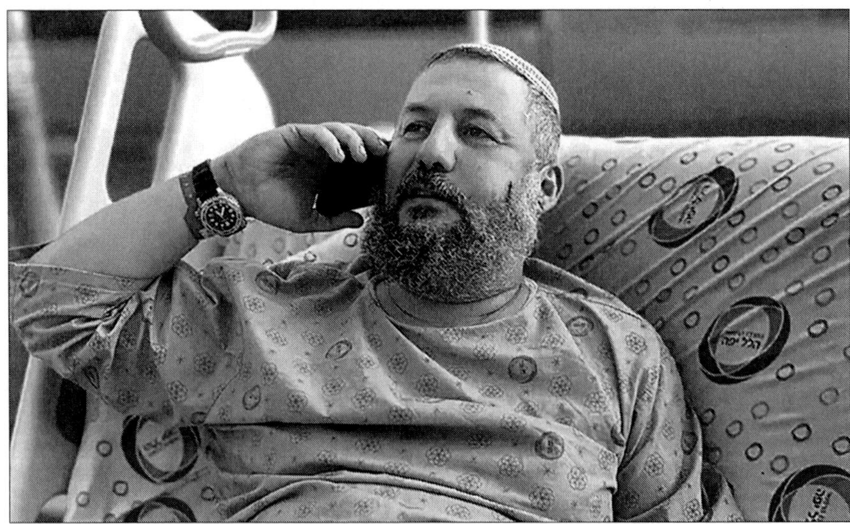

Rav Chaim in the hospital

into the back seat of Bar Yochai's car right beside Rabbi Sassi. The officer had been shot — he had an exit wound in his back — and he was in bad condition.

"I looked at the police officer," Rabbi Sassi remembers, "and saw that the man was bleeding heavily from his back. I knew I had to do something for him before he bled to death. Suddenly I had an idea.

"Unwrapping the edge of one of my own bandages, I stuffed it into the hole in the officer's back, keeping my finger inside the hole and making sure that the piece of bandage didn't slip out. There was no choice but to hold my finger right there in his back. Otherwise the blood would have begun spurting out all over again.

"An ambulance was waiting for us outside the city. When the medics wanted to move me, I told them that they couldn't take me out.

"'Why not?'

"'Because I'm currently connected to this police officer.'

"'What do you mean?'

"'Exactly what I said. One of my fingers is situated inside his back right now. You're going to have to get us out together.'"

Somehow they managed to get both Rabbi Sassi and the police officer out of the car and into the ambulance with Rabbi Sassi's finger still lodged in the officer's back. It was somewhat of a miraculous feat.

"Once we were settled and driving to the hospital," Rabbi Sassi continues, "the medic helped me remove my finger from the policeman's back and treated the wound. When we were together in the ambulance, I really thought that he wasn't going to make it, but I heard later that he survived.

"That was the kind of news that really made my day. And even though right now we are living in a hotel in Caesaria, I'm hoping to return home to Sderot as soon as possible, to my home, my yeshivah, and my shul, 'Sderot B'Park.'"

So went the story of a *rav, maggid shiur*, and hero.

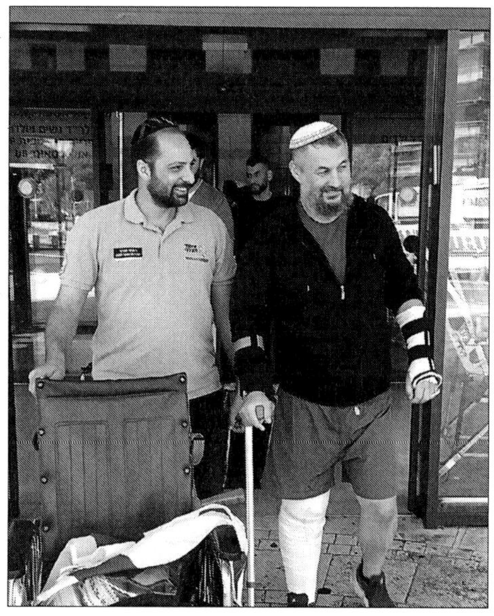
Rav Chaim being released from the hospital

CHAPTER FIVE

The Captive Doctor

It was October 7, 6:20 in the morning, in the Bedouin city of Arara BaNegev, and Dr. Tarek Abu Arar was getting ready to leave for work.

Tarek Abu Arar is a doctor of internal medicine at Barzilai Hospital in Ashkelon, as well as a devoted volunteer for United Hatzalah. He got into his car at six thirty and drove out of Arara in the general direction of Ashkelon. It was a beautiful day, and Tarek Abu Arar was enjoying the balmy weather.

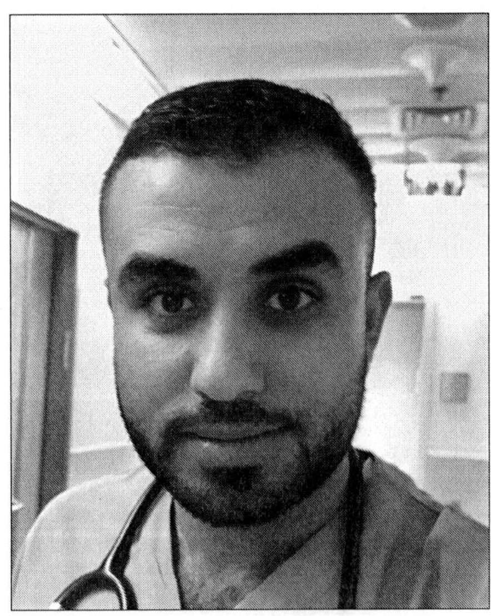

Dr. Tarek Abu Arar

It was about six forty when his wife called. Later he would remember that he had stopped the car in the vicinity of the city of Rahat to answer the phone.

"Hamas is shooting missiles at Israel," she informed him, "and a bunch of them landed here in our city!"

He thanked her for calling to let him know what was going on back home and told her to be very careful and to make sure to stay in a safe area. Then he put on the bulletproof vest he had received from United

Hatzalah. If rockets were falling in the Negev, they were definitely falling in Ashkelon and he had better be prepared. Then he got back into the driver's seat and continued his journey. Everything seemed normal until he reached Sapir Junction just outside the city of Sderot.

All was quiet. He didn't even hear any sirens. Nothing. It was just a regular Shabbos morning.

Had he known that terrorists had infiltrated the country, maybe he would have behaved differently when he saw a person lying on the side of the road seemingly wounded in a car accident. But he didn't know, and because he hadn't heard news of any terrorists infiltrating Israel, Tarek had no reason not to get out of his car. As a doctor, it's very hard to ignore such a sight. He had no inkling that he was about to have one of the worst experiences of his life.

"I began walking toward the man lying on the ground," Tarek recounts. "From where I was, he appeared to be a soldier, and I started walking a little faster in his direction. I was about fifty meters away when I suddenly saw what appeared to be an Israeli soldier motioning me to walk over to him. I thought that he needed my help and began walking toward him. When I was about ten meters away from him, the 'soldier' lifted his gun and shot me point blank in the chest.

"There was no reason for him to have done this. I wasn't a threat to him — the two of us hadn't even exchanged a word. Yet for some unknown reason the soldier had just shot me in the chest!"

Tarek collapsed on the ground from the impact of the shot. No doubt he would have died on the spot, but he was wearing his Hatzalah vest, and it stopped the bullet and saved his life.

"I started to scream and pray, certain that I was about to be killed and I had no idea why. I uttered the prayer that a Muslim recites on his deathbed, since it seemed clear to me that there was no way I was making it out of the situation alive.

"Just then I heard another voice screaming at the soldier. For some inexplicable reason, the person was screaming in Arabic.

"'Don't shoot! He's an Arab!'

"At that moment I understood that I had just been attacked by a group of Hamas terrorists. I also understood that the chance of escaping with my life was slim."

Looking behind him, Tarek saw what looked like ten men emerging from behind a row of bushes. They were dressed in army uniforms. First they removed his vest and shoes. Then they confiscated everything he had in his pockets.

Right away they began interrogating him in Arabic. They asked him questions, wanting to test his knowledge of Islam, making sure he was an Arab and not merely a dark-skinned Israeli who spoke the language.

"What's your name?" one of the terrorists barked.

"Dr. Tarek Abu Arar."

"Where are you going?"

"To Barzilai Hospital in Ashkelon."

"Recite verses from the Koran."

He did.

"Tell us the names of some of the important people in the Koran."

He gave them several names, including that of Mohammed's wife.

Tarek could see that his captors were outfitted with rifles and high-quality military equipment, and the uniforms they were wearing were very similar to the uniforms worn by soldiers in the IDF. The next thing he knew, they manhandled him over to the middle of the junction. There was a pole there, and they tied him to the pole with a rope. Tarek's arms were maneuvered behind his back, and he hung in the air unable to move.

"Now we have a hostage," they said.

"At that moment, I realized that the 'dead' man on the ground had been a trap set by Hamas — and I had fallen right into it. They were ecstatic that they had caught me and could use me as a hostage, because now the army wouldn't be able to kill them from the air, but would have to carefully engage them in battle on the ground so as to avoid killing me. This would buy them more time to do whatever it was they had come to accomplish.

"Moments later, hanging from the pole, I saw exactly what they planned on doing because they started shooting at passing cars. They shot at every single car that drove by, making sure to kill every person in every vehicle. They left no one alive. It was a horrifying scene to watch — made all the more so by the fact that it lasted for two long hours.

"Those were two of the worst hours of my life.

"Two hours in which I was forced to watch the worst kinds of animals killing innocent people for no reason at all."

When officers from the Yamam, Israel's counter-terrorism unit, a branch of the Israel Border Police, finally arrived at the junction, a fierce battle broke out between them and the terrorists, who were still using Tarek as a human shield. When the officers spotted him, he tried to show them with hand gestures where the terrorists were hiding.

Some of the terrorists were close by, and his punishment wasn't long in coming. Seeing what he had done, one of the terrorists shot him in the foot because he had shown the Yamam officers where their friends were hiding. The same terrorist also made a motion in his direction, which he took to mean that the next bullet they shot at him would end his life.

"I was in terrible pain and losing massive amounts of blood from the bullet wound in my foot. My chest was also aching from the bullet my vest had stopped. There was no question in my mind that the only thing I could do was pray for a miracle.

"The truth is, I had been praying since they took me captive. Yet I couldn't help but feel that there was no way I would survive this. My foot was still bleeding profusely and I was rapidly losing blood.

"But eventually the Yamam unit succeeded in wiping out the group of terrorists and were able to save my life. They cut me down from the pole and wrapped a tourniquet around my foot. An ambulance from United Hatzalah, the organization for which I volunteered, came and transported me to Soroka Hospital in Beersheva, where the medical staff treated me and allowed me to leave a few hours later.

"It was the worst experience of my life by far," says Tarek. "It was especially difficult for me because of the choices I have made and the way I live. I have dedicated my entire life to helping other people, to saving lives, both as a doctor and through the work I do for United Hatzalah. But on that day, not only was I not able to help any of the people who passed by and were killed by Hamas, I couldn't even help myself. It was a truly horrific experience, one that I don't even have the words to accurately describe."

A Miraculous Moment

A rebbe related how a student from his yeshivah who was called up as a reservist in the Givati unit called him and told him the following amazing story:

"Last night during the fighting, I found myself in the war room. The commander there came up to me and said, 'I have a mission for you.'

"I was intrigued and curious.

"'You're religious, right?'

"I nodded.

"'Good. Please go and pray.'

"I was completely taken aback. The commander was a nonreligious guy from Tel Aviv — not the kind of person I would have expected to be asking me to go and daven. Seeing how surprised I was, the commander explained.

"'The situation is very serious, and we need *tefillot*. There are multiple armored troop carriers that have broken down and are stuck in an exposed area in Gaza. We haven't been able to fix them, and this could turn into a catastrophe very quickly. Please pray that we will be able to fix them or that Hamas won't attack now. This is an emergency!'

"Of course, I agreed to go and pray for the troops. I left the war room and found a more private spot and began davening.

"'Hashem,' I implored, 'those soldiers are Your sons. Please have mercy on them and save them from our enemies.'

"I tried my best to give it my all. It was hard for me to focus, but I did what I could.

"Fifteen minutes later I returned to the war room. As I walked through the door, I asked Hashem to accept my prayers though they hadn't come easily to me. The moment I entered the room, the commander approached me. His eyes were shining with happiness.

"'You don't understand what happened here! A minute after you left to go and pray, the first troop carrier was fixed. Shortly after that, we were able to fix the next one, and now they are all ready to continue fighting.'

"Then he uttered a line I will never forget.

"'You aren't going back into Gaza. I need you here to pray!'"

CHAPTER SIX

A Toyota Pickup Truck

While Dr. Tarek Abu Arar was experiencing the worst day of his life, a young man named Nehorai Darshan, the head of United Hatzalah in Sderot, was preparing for the long day that lay ahead of him.

He, too, woke up early that day — it was six thirty when he got out of bed — on the morning of Simchas Torah. The southern part of the country was being bombarded by an unending stream of missiles, and his phone was buzzing nonstop. A few minutes later he received a message that a lot of people had been wounded in Sderot, and he left his home to go and help. In his wildest dreams, he didn't imagine that the falling missiles were the smallest part of the story and that the situation was a million times worse than anything they had encountered before.

He got in his car and began driving in the direction of the calls that had come in. As he approached the end of his block and was turning at the corner, his phone rang. It was the wife of a volunteer. She was hysterical.

"Nehorai, what on earth is happening in Sderot?!"

"What do you mean?"

"My husband left the house earlier this morning. There are missiles flying in every direction, and now I heard that there are terrorists all over the place!"

"I don't know about any terrorists. Right now I'm on the way to take care of people who were hurt from the missiles."

"But what about the terrorists?"

"I'm sure there aren't any terrorists."

Nehorai was the voice of order and reason, confident that everything was fine and people were overreacting for no reason. He could hear the sound of gunfire, but he didn't pay attention to it. He had heard gunfire before — this was Sderot, after all — and he tried his best to calm the panicked woman, telling her that he was sure everything was going to be fine and it wasn't as bad as she thought.

Then he saw the Toyota pickup truck right in front of him.

The human mind is a complex piece of machinery, capable of truly incredible feats. At the same time, it's very difficult sometimes for the human mind to comprehend things it is seeing with its own eyes if those things don't make sense. For Nehorai Darshan, this was one of those times.

Part of his brain took note of the Toyota pickup truck with the flatbed filled with people, and even though part of him knew that he was seeing something that didn't belong in Sderot, another part of his brain didn't allow him to fully process the sight, particularly since an Israeli police car was speeding along right beside the truck.

He saw the Toyota. He saw the driver and the people sitting next to him. More than that, he saw the people standing on the flatbed. They were dressed in black from head to toe, and each had a strip of green cloth tied around their heads.

The scene was not a common sight by any stretch of the imagination and should have caused Nehorai Darshan to make a U-turn on the spot and run for his life. But sometimes what a person sees is so far out and outlandish, so far-fetched and impossible, that he can't reconcile it as truth.

At the same time, there is also a limit to how much a mind can fool itself, and Nehorai's mind switched on moments later when he realized that there were rifles sticking out of the Toyota's windows. He suddenly grasped that the people in the back of the vehicle were terrorists.

Seconds later a number of things happened almost at the same moment. Nehorai's window had been opened, and he suddenly felt the whistle of wind zipping past his head. Seconds later he realized that a bullet had just flown right by his head.

Moments later his foot was pressing down on the gas pedal, and he was flying past the Toyota. The terrorists opened fire on him — a withering barrage of gunfire aimed at his ambulance with pure intent to maim and kill — and the window shattered. Nehorai Darshan put his head down and stepped on the gas pedal with as much force as he could muster, and he sped down the street and away from the Toyota full of terrorists who were shooting at him.

At the end of the block, he arrived at a traffic circle and he turned right, wondering what to do and where to go. Wondering if he would still be alive at the end of the day to tell the tale of what he'd seen on the streets of the city he loved with all his heart.

Driving down the block, Nehorai saw a man coming toward him. The man was carrying a gun in his hand. For a second, Nehorai thought about using the ambulance as a weapon and crashing it into him, but at the last second he just passed him by. He couldn't do it for the simple reason that he wasn't sure whether the man was a Jew or a terrorist.

"If I'd been sure that he was an enemy," Nehorai says, "I would have hit him without another thought. But I couldn't be sure, and I continued driving with one thought in my mind.

"I kept on thinking that I wanted to go home to take stock of the situation. I also needed to gather some more volunteers to come with me, and I needed to put on a bulletproof vest and helmet. There was no question that I needed to get off the street and into my house to take time to rally."

But this was easier said than done. The city of Sderot was infested with terrorists.

Nehorai continued driving down the street. He took another right in the direction of his house, when he saw a motorcycle heading toward him. Two people were sitting on the motorcycle, and they both had rifles. They were obviously terrorists, and Nehorai now understood that there were many more terrorists running free in the city than he had imagined. He couldn't continue driving in this direction and take the risk of getting shot at again, so he took the next immediate left, turning onto a little street (more of a lane) that led him toward a big open, grassy area.

On the radio he heard his volunteers letting dispatch know that they were leaving their homes to go on calls. Nehorai got on the radio and said, "No one leave your homes! Terrorists are running loose around the city. I repeat: No one leave your homes!"

As he was getting out the message on the radio, he saw a man outside the ambulance. He was out running with his dog as if all was right with the world and the city hadn't been overrun by terrorists with rifles.

Nehorai got out of the ambulance and went over to the man. "There are terrorists in the city," he said. "You can't be outside now. You need to find a safe place and stay there."

The man was absolutely shocked.

"I heard gunfire," he said, "but I never dreamed that the enemy infiltrated the city!"

Nehorai brought him up-to-date on the situation.

"I live a minute from here," the man said. "Come with me to my house."

Nehorai looked around them. The area was empty.

"Okay, let's go."

Minutes later they were relatively safe in the man's apartment. Nehorai let dispatch know that he was safe and told them where he was. He stayed with the man until a team of United Hatzalah volunteers came to get him an hour and a half later.

"Driving through the streets of the city I love," Nehorai says, "I saw sights that I will never be able to forget. I saw shocking sights: people lying dead on the street as if tossed there with no explanation. People who had been shot in the head. I was shaken to the core by everything I saw and was still in shock from having been shot at by terrorists earlier that day.

"Even now, weeks later, our families are still incredibly traumatized by everything that happened. At the same time, I can't help but thank Hashem for His kindness because it could have been much, much worse.

"If the terrorists would have arrived in Sderot an hour later, thousands of people would have already been in all the shuls — easy targets for the shooters. It's clear that the whole story was one big miracle, both collectively for the city and personally for so many people as well. I myself was in the worst kind of danger and felt a bullet whiz past my head. They shot my ambulance with a slew of bullets. But Hashem was on my side, and I escaped without a scratch. It was one miracle after another."

When later asked whether he would return to Sderot (at present his family is staying with their grandparents in Netanya), he says, "One hundred percent. My plan is to build a house right on the border!"

To the vision of that future home, I could only lift my cup and say *"L'chaim..."*

PART TWO
REALITY SETS IN

For these things I weep, my eyes shed tears, for the comforter to restore my soul is removed from me. My children are desolate, for the enemy has prevailed.

— Eichah 1:19

The decision to allow our volunteers to go into the war zone to save lives was the hardest decision I ever made in my life. But I had to do it. I had to allow them to go and save the Jewish people. For one simple reason: because we are United Hatzalah and this is what we do.

— Dovie Maisel,
COO of United Hatzalah

CHAPTER SEVEN

The Hardest Decision of His Life

While Rabbi Chaim Sassi was busy rescuing wounded policemen under fire in Sderot, Dovie Maisel, COO of United Hatzalah, was dealing with the fact that his son's bar mitzvah had fallen out on the same day that the world seemed to be coming to an end.

Dovie has been a close friend of Eli Beer's since they were kids. They are also first cousins. Dovie is a founding member of United Hatzalah and has been with the organization — and with Eli — through thick and thin. He is in charge of all United Hatzalah operations, in Israel and around the globe.

Unlike Eli, who had been in Yerushalayim on the morning of the attack, Dovie and his family were at his parents' home in Efrat that morning. Simchas Torah 2023 was a big day for the Maisel family, because they were celebrating the bar mitzvah of one of Dovie's sons, and the family had been eagerly looking forward to gathering together at the neighborhood shul and listening to their bar mitzvah *bachur* read *Parashas V'Zos HaBerachah* from the Torah, which was something he'd been practicing for the past six months.

By six forty in the morning, Dovie's radio was practically exploding with notifications of missile attacks all over the country. He immediately jumped out of bed and contacted the heads of the various United Hatzalah departments, trying to assess a situation that was changing from second to second. As soon as he developed some level of clarity, he gave the order to begin moving as many ambulances as possible from the center of the country to the south. The entire time he was on the phone, he kept hoping that events on the ground would start to stabilize and that he would soon be able to leave for shul with his family and attend his son's bar mitzvah.

But that was not to be.

As time passed and he kept receiving new information and the calls kept coming in from Ofakim, Sderot, Netivot, and other cities and towns in the south, Dovie understood that he wasn't going to be spending much time in shul that day. This was really brought home when dispatch received a call about a car accident involving some ten vehicles. It wasn't long before videos were coming in of terrorists driving around in Toyota pickup trucks and shooting people, and they understood that it wasn't a car accident and had never been a car accident, but rather a massacre executed by Hamas terrorists and that it was taking place in cities, towns, and villages all over the southern part of the country.

By the time the reports starting coming in from volunteers telling them that they were being shot at, it was becoming clear that while they still didn't really know the magnitude of what was happening, there was no question that it was way bigger than anything they had seen in the past. Dovie touched base with Eli Beer, who was on his way to the dispatch center from the David Citadel, and began sending out messages to let people know that more staff was needed at dispatch. He also contacted his logistics staff, explaining that they needed to get ready to move tons of equipment out of the main warehouse and into the field.

Dovie Maisel

"You heard what's going on in Sderot?" Eli asked.

"Yes," Dovie answered, "I already spoke with Nehorai, and he told me how the terrorists shot up his ambulance and he miraculously survived."

"When are you coming in?"

"It's my son's bar mitzvah today," Dovie explained, "and I

just want to hear him *lein* — even just one *aliyah.* I will come to HQ right after that."

"Got it."

That might have been the plan, but sirens started going off in Efrat right after Dovie got off the phone. Within minutes the shuls had emptied out as people started running for home and soldiers began jumping into their cars and heading out to their army bases. It was an authentic emergency, and there was no time to waste.

"I ran to the nearby shul," Dovie says. "There I grabbed one of the *sifrei Torah* and brought it home to my parents' apartment. The next hour passed in a blur. We made an express minyan. My son *leined* from the Torah, I hugged him tight, we did a little dancing, and then I said goodbye to my family, got into my car, and left Efrat for United Hatzalah headquarters in Yerushalayim.

"It was Simchas Torah morning, and I was in my car driving through the Gush Etzion tunnels as fast as I could. I could feel the urgency in the air, could almost taste the terror. Had we come this far only to be beaten fifty years after the Yom Kippur War?"

Shortly after nine in the morning Dovie was at United Hatzalah headquarters, where he was briefed on everything they knew so far. There was a flow of information coming in via an assortment of WhatsApp groups and other media sources.

"I was on the phone with one of the volunteers on site — David Bader [more on David and his incredible story later] — and I had him show me a visual of the scene around him. In those few minutes we counted more than twenty bodies lying on the street where David was standing.

"It was while we were taking stock of the scene that we caught sight of a United Hatzalah vest lying on the ground and we understood that there was a very real possibility that one of our volunteers had been kidnaped by Hamas.

"'David,' I said, 'get over there and read the name written on the vest so we'll know whose it was.'

"That's how we learned that one of our volunteers — a Bedouin doctor from a city in the Negev called Arara who works at Barzilai Hospital in Ashkelon, had been kidnaped by Hamas. We had no idea if he was alive or dead.

"'David, is there anyone alive where you are?'

"'Anyone who was still alive was already taken away by an ambulance — everyone else is dead.'"

For Dovie Maisel, pacing back and forth at headquarters in Yerushalayim, the words "everyone else is dead" hit him right in the gut. United Hatzalah is an organization dedicated to saving lives, and hearing that there was nothing they could do for the many people who had been massacred in their cars on an Israeli highway was incredibly painful.

Ever since he had been a little boy and witnessed a child run into the street where she was hit by a car, Dovie had known that he was going to save lives when he grew up. And that's exactly what he did. He kept the promise that he made to himself back then when he was just a little kid, and had been involved in saving thousands of lives ever since.

But now he felt helpless. So many people had been killed, and there was nothing he could do for them.

And he was faced with a difficult dilemma. What should United Hatzalah do with the bodies? They were a lifesaving organization, but how could they just leave the bodies lying there? Zaka, the search-and-rescue organization whose members were risking their lives to retrieve

The Cheletz intersection

the bodies so they could be given a proper burial, were working at the site of the festival near Kibbutz Re'im. But what if Hamas would take the bodies of the people they had killed in the cities and villages back to Gaza with them? That alone could cost Israel more Jewish lives, if they were forced to exchange live Hamas prisoners for the dead.

Dovie went into problem-solving mode.

Eventually he hit on a solution.

He had already sent down a logistics team run by Benny Lofez with a number of trucks to set up a staging area at the Cheletz intersection.

Cheletz was fairly close to where everything was going on and an easy location for ambulances to reach, but not so close that it was in danger of being attacked by terrorists (although missiles were a different story). Now Dovie decided to use those trucks as a place to store the bodies until they could be identified, transported and given a proper burial. It was unconventional and out-of-the-box thinking — which meant that it was a classic United Hatzalah move.

Benny Lofez and his team ended up gathering around sixty bodies that had been lying on the roads. They were deeply saddened by the terrible sights they saw, but gratified at being able to do the ultimate *chesed* for so many Jews by providing them the dignity they deserved instead of leaving them to just lie there in the sun for the next few days.

Once the staging area was set up — and it was done very rapidly — all ambulances and private cars that were transporting wounded people were able to bring them to Cheletz, where a team of doctors, both those of the army and those from United Hatzalah, determined who should be sent to the hospital in an ambulance and who was in such danger that they needed to be sent via helicopter.

Dovie would have loved to be able to liaison with Magen David Adom so that both organizations could work together and have as many ambulances as possible at their disposal to transport the wounded — but MDA personnel had been given strict instructions to stay away from the hot zones. He had understood that the order had been given after one of their members who lived down south had been killed during those first hours of the war.

Regardless of the reason, MDA's decision meant that when it came to offering emergency medical care in the areas down south where people were wounded or dying, United Hatzalah was more or less on its own.

At some point during the morning it was becoming more and more obvious to Dovie and his team that the amount of heavily wounded people who needed to be transported to hospitals was way more than they had anticipated and that it would probably be a good idea to start transporting those in the worst condition to hospitals via helicopter. There was one problem: the Ministry of Health didn't want to give them permission to use their helicopters for the task, though they were staffed with fully qualified flight EMTs. Unfortunately politics and bureaucracy was getting in the way of saving lives here.

Eventually, seeing that permission wasn't going to come and knowing that not using their helicopters might very well spell the difference between life and death for some of the wounded, Dovie made the decision to activate both of their helicopters with or without permission and send them to the landing area near Cheletz. It proved to be a good decision, because within a short time critically injured soldiers and civilians began pouring into Cheletz and the United Hatzalah flight teams began flying them to various hospitals for emergency lifesaving treatment.

"There is a time to be concerned about regulations," Dovie says, "but this was not it. This was a time to save lives, and that's all we cared about."

Which was why, when they were later contacted by the Ministry of Health, who admonished them for flying their helicopters against regulations, Dovie instructed his team to ignore the calls and to continue flying the patients and saving lives. If they got into trouble for disobeying regulations later, so be it. But he wasn't going to allow Israeli bureaucracy to get in the way. Not now.

It was a day Dovie Maisel would never forget. With all his experience — and he had been everywhere and seen everything, from collapsing wedding halls to major terrorists attacks, from national disasters in Nepal and Turkey to the calamity at Meron — absolutely nothing compared to what he was seeing from the live feeds being sent to them from the cameras on the front and back of every United Hatzalah ambulance.

Yet the biggest and most challenging decision of the day still had to be made.

By midmorning, Dovie had their logistics department set up an EOC — an emergency operations center — in the United Hatzalah building's auditorium. This way they would be able to get to work without

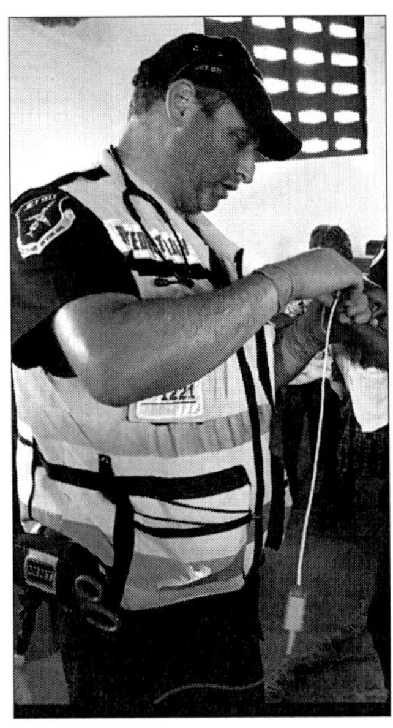

Dovie in Haiti

disturbing the volunteers in the dispatch center. There was also the benefit of the big screens on the walls, which provided clarity when watching footage.

"Get me all the pictures and data," Dovie ordered, "so we can start making decisions on how best to move forward."

Matters quickly grew heated between Dovie and his two deputies, Elad Bachar and Rochel Zubeta. Bachar and Zubeta were well trained in the art of dealing with emergencies, and staying in Yerushalayim instead of going down south to personally manage the operation went against their nature. But Dovie insisted that he needed them at HQ. There were enough people down south. Right now they belonged at the hub.

In the end, they gave in, but it was very difficult for them.

On the agenda for Dovie and his team was dealing with possibly the biggest dilemma of their lives: Should they or should they not allow their ambulances to operate near dangerous areas like Kfar Aza and Kibbutz Be'eri, which were still overrun with armed terrorists?

Bachar and Zubeta weren't at all sure that United Hatzalah should take the risk of sending their people to these places, and they presented all the arguments against going in.

"Dovie," Zubeta said, "how can we take the risk of sending our people into what amounts to a war zone?"

Dovie looked at her. "If you could, wouldn't you be going in this second to save lives?"

Rochel Zubeta admitted that she would be doing exactly that

Elad Bachar

if she could. At the same time, she felt that it was important for them to consider the matter strongly before giving their consent to their volunteers going in to dangerous areas.

But Dovie was adamantly in favor.

"Our guys are tough," Dovie argued, "and it's not right to stop them if they want to go in."

"But it's dangerous!"

"I know that, you know that, and so does every single one of our volunteers. They know the situation better than we do because they're the ones on-site. They're the ones seeing all the dead bodies!"

"So what's our official policy?"

Dovie stopped talking for a minute as he formulated the words. The decision he was about to make would have major ramifications. It had the potential to save countless lives, but at the same time there was a very good chance that many volunteers might not come home.

Finally he spoke.

"Our official policy is this. We will make it clear to every volunteer that the entire area near Sderot and the kibbutzim down south is dangerous. They need to know this. There is a real risk in entering any of those areas. That said, I will not order my volunteers to stay away.

"I won't tell them to stay away for two reasons: One, I have a feeling that even if I forbid it completely, many of them will go in anyway. That's the kind of guys we have. Two, our people won't be able to hear their fellow Jews — whether civilians or soldiers — calling for help and not go and help. They won't be capable of ignoring the distress of others who are injured or dying.

"Let me be clear: Every volunteer needs to know exactly what he or she is getting themself into. I'm not telling them to go in or not to go in. This is a matter of life and death. I'm leaving the decision up to them, because this is the kind of thing every person needs to decide for himself. Remember, the volunteers of United Hatzalah have operated in the Ukraine, helping thousands of people under enemy fire. We have traveled to Turkey and Haiti and Nepal and provided assistance to countries suffering from the worst kinds of natural disasters. We have gone to so many places and done so much training. And now the time has come to put all that training to use and to help the people of Israel!"

During the heated discussion, Eli Beer was working on something nearby. At some point he stopped what he was doing and got involved in the conversation — agreeing with Dovie. When one of the others continued to protest, Eli couldn't contain himself. He yelled, "And what if it was your mother who was trapped down south? What would you say then?!"

There were no more questions.

"My decision to allow our volunteers to save lives under fire was probably the most difficult decision I ever had to make in my entire life," Dovie says, "and I told that to my deputies. I knew the dangers. I knew that there was a good chance that some of the volunteers might get hurt or worse. At the same time, I knew that putting ourselves in danger to save lives is in our blood. It's in our DNA. This is what United Hatzalah stands for. This is our mission, and we could not and would not abandon it.

"I get goosebumps on my arms when I remember that moment. Because while I said those words and stated our official policy for the record, I remember thinking about the very distinct possibility of having to pay shivah calls to the wives of our precious volunteers — the heroic members of Hatzalah whom I loved with all my heart and soul. At the same time, I knew that this was what they wanted to do. I knew that this was what they would demand from us: to give them permission to go in and provide them with the backup they needed to do their job — even if terrorists were shooting at them and even with missiles flying overhead and exploding nearby.

"Because we are United Hatzalah, and that's what we do."

A Miraculous Moment

As many people know, the enemy was able to infiltrate almost every moshav and kibbutz that they tried to enter, only failing when they arrived at the settlements that kept Shabbos and whose gates were locked shut.

Without question, more than we keep Shabbos — Shabbos keeps us.

More than we protect Shabbos — Shabbos protects us.

In one kibbutz there was a family who had started keeping Shabbos. It was the mother who was mainly interested in becoming more religious, while the father was more or less going along with his wife. Since they lived in a kibbutz that was not religious at all, none of their neighbors kept Shabbos, which meant that the atmosphere on the kibbutz wasn't very conducive to keeping Shabbos properly. For this reason, the family began leaving their home and spending Shabbos in other communities.

Prior to Simchas Torah of 2023, the parents decided that they weren't up to going away for Shabbos and Yom Tov that week since the mother was expecting a baby soon. Instead of traveling to another community for Shabbos, they would host a religious family at their home instead.

On the morning of October 7, they started hearing gunshots in the kibbutz and the sounds of people yelling at one another in Arabic. It was clear that something terrible was going on. Like most people who lived in that part of the country, they knew what they were supposed to do in the wake of an attack, and they quickly ran into their safe room, hoping and praying that they would make it through the day alive.

As the hours passed and the sounds of shooting still had not abated, they kept expecting the enemy to come crashing through their door. But no one came. No one even tried to see if anyone was there.

It was as if the terrorists couldn't see their home, as if they were surrounded by a special protective cloud — a cloud called "Shabbos."

Eventually, after many hours, IDF soldiers arrived, and a fierce battle ensued. When it was over, the family was finally able to leave their home.

They were incredulous when they grasped the full extent of the miracle they had experienced, when they realized how many people had been killed while they had been spared by the hand of Hashem. But even then, they still didn't know the extent of the miracle.

Over the next few days, maps and other intelligence were discovered on the bodies of the terrorists who had been dispatched from Gaza to kill as many people as they could. On one terrorist, a map was found that included every single house in that family's community — along with information about the family who lived there, such as how many people lived in the house and other relevant information that the terrorist would need to know. The information came from Arabs who had been working on the kibbutz and had been spying on the residents so they could pass on the information to Hamas.

Next to the line on the map that included information about this particular family, it stated, "They are never home on Shabbos."

And so, even though they were home that Shabbos, Shabbos protected them, just as Shabbos has protected the Jewish people since the beginning of time.

CHAPTER EIGHT

"Is This 1943?"

Gitty Beer will never forget the moment her daughter knocked on her hotel room door that Simchas Torah morning. It was six thirty in the morning, just as her husband Eli was getting the phone call from his son-in-law.

Gitty opened the door, surprised to see her daughter standing there that early, especially after they had all gone to sleep quite late the night before after the *hakafos* and spirited dancing.

"What happened?"

"Mommy, a war broke out!"

"What do you mean?"

"They're shooting rockets everywhere, and there are reports of terrorists inside the country."

Somehow Gitty had a feeling that this wasn't going to be a regular terrorist attack or a minor skirmish. She didn't know how she knew, but it was clear to her that Israel was about to become embroiled in something major.

Her fears were soon confirmed, and she decided to go down south along with two of her sons-in-law, Aharon and Meir, who were both EMTs. She still didn't know the true magnitude of what had happened, but there was no question that emergency assistance was going to be needed, and since medical assistance was their field, they decided that they must go where needed — to the Cheletz intersection down south.

By the time we arrived (Gitty relates), it was midmorning, and quite a few United Hatzalah ambulances were already in the area. We left our car at the designated meeting spot for United Hatzalah personnel and got into an ambulance. This was where I separated from my two sons-in-law. Aharon stayed at the staging area in Cheletz to manage operations, while Meir joined an ambulance crew and drove off to take a call.

On the ambulance that I joined was a volunteer medic named Kfir. He lived in Sderot and had left the city earlier that morning. He would later find himself returning to a city he didn't recognize.

Since the first reports of the attack were coming in from Sderot, that was where we headed. We still hadn't heard the news that the southern part of the country had been invaded. At this point, we seemed only to be facing a well-planned terror attack on the city.

On the way to Sderot, the highways were completely empty. It felt like Yom Kippur. I didn't see any police or security of any kind. Then we reached the outskirts of the city and soon came across what seemed like hundreds of cars all in a jumble. Some were just sitting in the middle of the road, while others were on the sidewalk. We paramedics looked at each other in trepidation. We had no idea what was happening, but we began to understand that it was bigger than we initially thought.

The ambulance made its way slowly down the road as we peered into every car that we passed. This was the moment when the shock and the horror really set in.

In every single car that we passed, we saw a dead body.

I couldn't believe what I was seeing. I remember thinking, *Are we still in 2023, or is this 1943?* There were dead people everywhere. Everywhere!

We got out of the ambulance and started checking people's pulses. But, of course, there was no pulse. No one was alive. We saw a dead soldier in one car, a dead baby in another. They had all been shot.

Soon more information came in, and we found out that there was still shooting in the city. Suddenly Kfir, the EMT from Sderot, turned to me and said, "We need to go to my house right now!"

"What happened?"

"I've been trying to reach my wife on the phone, but she isn't answering. I'm afraid that something happened at my house!"

On the spot we began driving toward Kfir's house.

It didn't take us long to reach his neighborhood. Once again, it was a very difficult drive because so many of the cars we passed along the way had people inside who had been shot. I kept looking for some sort of security presence on the streets, but we didn't pass any police cars or army vehicles.

We stopped outside Kfir's building and got out of the ambulance. Since I'm licensed to carry a gun (as a medic, you never know where you're going to end up), I took it out and made sure that it was loaded and ready, just in case. The other medic had his gun out as well. Obviously we were hoping that we wouldn't have to use them, but we were prepared for anything.

Kfir was terrified that terrorists had managed to infiltrate his home, and his fear was contagious. He unlocked his door, and we went inside. My heart was beating rapidly. It was an incredibly frightening moment. I was sure we were going to find a massacre within.

Kfir went from room to room, calling his wife's name, but there was no answer. Finally he got to the apartment's safe room. He knocked on the door, and his wife opened it. The moment he saw her, Kfir broke down completely and started to cry.

I had never seen something like that before. I'd never seen someone lose control like that and cry as if his entire world had fallen apart.

"Why didn't you answer me when I called you?" he asked. "Why didn't you answer the phone?!"

"We didn't hear the phone," she replied. "There's no reception in the safe room."

Even after his wife's explanation, he was still hysterical.

We went around the house and barricaded all the windows so that no one would be able to get inside. Finally, we left the apartment and returned to the ambulance, driving through the streets of Sderot in search of anyone who needed help.

It was Simchas Torah morning. A few hours before I had been sleeping in a beautiful room in the David Citadel Hotel. Now I was driving through the streets of the Wild West with a loaded gun and a prayer on my lips.

When reports began filtering through that terrorists had attacked multiple communities along the Gaza Strip, our ambulance left Sderot and began heading in that direction. We knew that there was going to

Near Kfar Aza

be a lot of wounded people there who would need to be transported to the hospital.

Eventually we reached the entrance to Kfar Aza. The sounds of shooting from inside the village were very loud. We didn't attempt to enter the village — that would have been pure suicide — but soon the

Kfar Aza

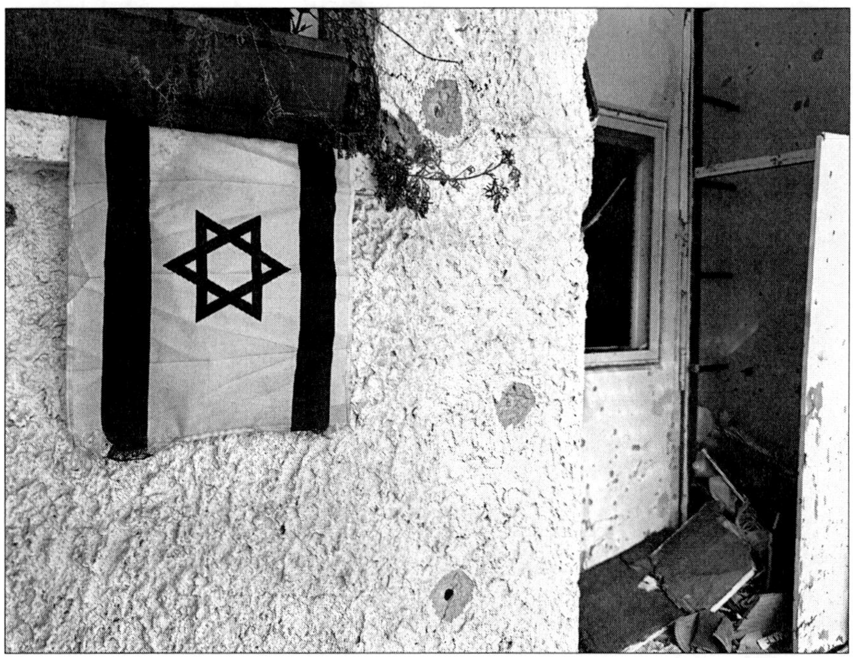

Kfar Aza

army began bringing out wounded people and moving them to the ambulance. From that moment on, we began making trips back and forth to transport the wounded to safety.

Sometimes we had three patients, sometimes two, sometimes one. We took some of the wounded to ambulances that were waiting outside the more dangerous areas so that they could transport the patients to the hospital (it was still relatively early in the day, and most of the ambulances hadn't yet gone into the actual war zone), and we drove the severely wounded patients to the United Hatzalah helicopters for transport to the various hospitals.

I returned home later that night, after hours of treating and transporting patients. I had seen the worst things that day. At one point I saw a person who had been shot while riding on a bike. He had fallen in a tangled jumble together with the bike, but even worse, he and the bike had somehow caught on fire. I had no idea what had caused the fire, but that wasn't the issue. The issue was that a fellow Jew's body was being burnt in front of my eyes.

We stopped the ambulance.

Got out.

Another volunteer named Moshe Weitzman and Kfir joined me, and we got to work pulling the body out of the fire. At least this way they would be able to identify him when there was time to figure out who had been killed.

In all honesty, I never imagined — not in my wildest dreams — that I would be spending Simchas Torah pulling a Jew out of a fire in the south of Eretz Yisrael when it was under attack. But that was the situation, and we did what we needed to do.

Now it was Motza'ei Yom Tov. I went to sleep for a few hours, and in the morning I went back down south. There were still plenty of wounded people to bring to the hospitals. On one ride we took two people. One had been shot and was badly injured in the leg. The other had been shot in the shoulder.

"What happened?" I asked.

"When the terrorists came to our neighborhood," the man replied, "we barricaded ourselves into our safe room. At a certain point, we heard the terrorists breaking down the front door and crashing into the house looking for people to kill. They went through all the rooms, and eventually they reached the safe room and realized that's where everyone was.

"Of course, they tried to get inside. They pulled the handle and tried to turn it, and I fought against them with all my strength. The struggle went on for forty minutes as the terrorists tried to get into the room

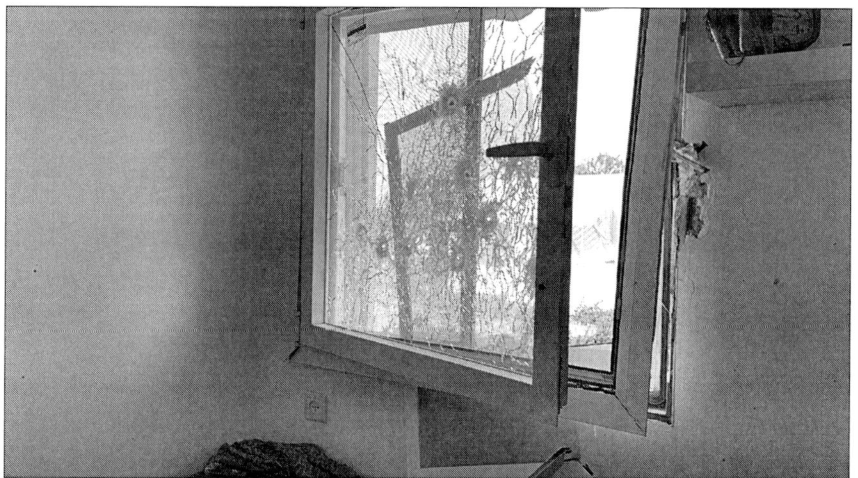

Broken safe room window

while I held on to that door handle and used every last vestige of willpower that I had to keep them out.

"After fighting for forty minutes, I couldn't hold them off any longer. Moments later, the door came flying open and the Hamas terrorists entered and started shooting at everyone at point-blank range. You can't even imagine what it's like to hear the sound of guns firing inside a small room."

"How did you two survive?"

"It was a miracle. Pure and simple. The terrorists were shooting, and our friends were falling. In the middle of all the craziness, everyone in the room landed in a heap on the floor. We were shot and wounded, and I guess we landed first.

"I don't know exactly what happened next. All I can tell you is that we landed on the floor, and our friends landed on top of us. Their final act in life was to shield us from the terrorists, who thought we were dead and didn't bother to shoot us again.

"We lay there for a very long time. An eternity. It took hours for the army to show up. Finally we heard the sounds of the soldiers arriving at the scene. Then the battle commenced. Still we stayed on the floor and didn't dare to leave the room. We stayed there, surrounded by our dead friends.

"After a long time we realized that the terrorists had been killed and that it was safe to come out. But there is no question that the fact that we are talking to you now — the fact that we are breathing — is a genuine miracle."

Besides transporting the wounded, we also drove from place to place to distribute food to soldiers, since the army hadn't had time to organize it. At one of the bases, a soldier gratefully accepted the food I brought him — and then he had a question for me.

"Do you by any chance have a pair of tzitzis I could have?"

I didn't have any pairs of tzitzis with me in the ambulance, but I resolved to try to return with as many pairs as I could find. When we returned to Cheletz, I asked logistics if there were any extra pairs of tzitzis around.

"Yes, we brought hundreds of pairs of tzitzis from Yerushalayim." Amazingly, someone there had thought that the soldiers might want some.

Tzitzis donated for soldiers

More tzitzis for soldiers

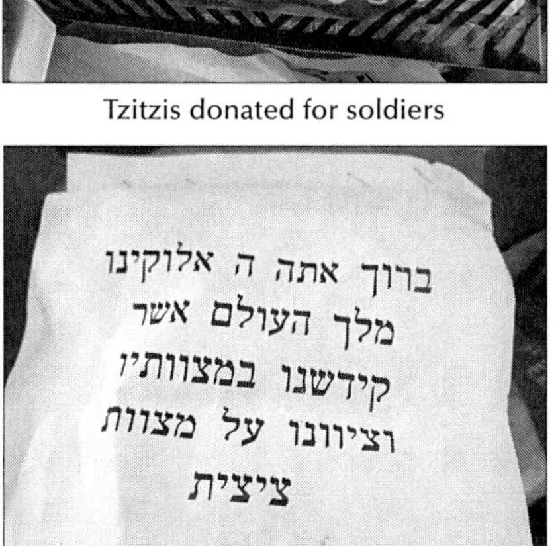

And more...

I took a hundred pairs of tzitzis, some white and some army green, and put them in the ambulance. I wasn't sure if that was too much or too little. Just because one soldier asked me for tzitzis didn't mean that other soldiers were also going to want a pair.

On Monday night, we reached Be'eri. There were hundreds of soldiers in the area. It was very late, and the only light came from the headlights of the army cars. We distributed hot food and drinks that United Hatzalah had sent from Yerushalayim to Cheletz — schnitzel and rice and kibbeh and vegetables and salads, along with plates, silverware, cups, and drinks.

After I had given out all the food, I asked if there was anyone there who wanted a pair of tzitzis. To my happy surprise, two hundred soldiers immediately responded with an enthusiastic yes. Which meant I didn't have nearly enough pairs for all of them.

After that, I started bringing tons of tzitzis with me wherever I went along with the food. And anytime I offered the soldiers tzitzis, their response was overwhelmingly positive and enthusiastic.

Giving out food

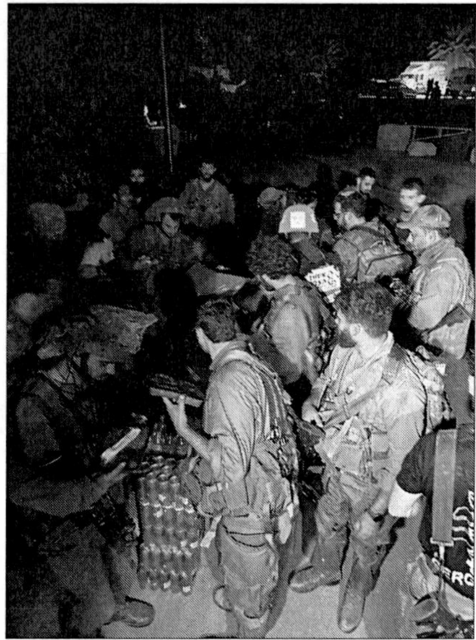
And more food...

As for me, all I'm thinking is, *Mi k'amcha Yisrael*...

Near the entrance to Kfar Aza — the scene of so much drama, pain, and miracles — there is a gas station. Inside the station, there's a convenience store whose shelves had been emptied by soldiers who took whatever there was and left notes with their contact information so that the owners could follow up with them later and receive payment.

When we pulled into the gas station on Tuesday afternoon, I saw an old man sitting near one of the outside tables and eating a yogurt. By this time it was rare to see civilians in the area, and he was so out of place that he caught my eye. His clothing was shabby and tattered, and he had a very neglected appearance about him. He seemed to be about eighty years old.

I approached him and asked gently, "What are you doing here?"

"I got hungry so I came to look for food," he replied.

"Where did you come from?"

"I was in the safe room in my house in Kfar Aza."

I was shocked. "But there's no one here anymore. Everyone was already taken from Kfar Aza!"

"I don't know anything about that. My wife and I came outside, and we didn't see anyone, but I was hungry so I went to look for food."

When I heard the old man's words, my heart broke. The world had just come to an end in their village, and suddenly these two old people just appeared out of nowhere, roaming around, with no idea of everything that occurred in the last few days. It was mind-boggling.

I took the couple to an ambulance and gave them something to eat and drink, and then we sent them to the hospital, letting the people there know that they should make sure the old couple met with a social worker who could take charge of their case.

For me, the most emotional moment of my time down south would always be when I accompanied Kfir into his apartment, both of us sure that we would find a massacre, and seeing him break down out of sheer relief.

But there were other moments that also made a deep impression. One of them was when we were down south in the beginning of the war, and soldiers were arriving at the United Hatzalah headquarters from all over the country. Many of them approached us and asked if we had any extra bulletproof vests and helmets.

At the time I remember thinking, *I don't understand. Why doesn't the army have enough equipment for the soldiers? Why is it that United Hatzalah is prepared and the army isn't?!*

We couldn't give them United Hatzalah vests because those bright orange vests would have turned them all into easy-to-spot targets for snipers, but we were able to give them United Hatzalah helmets, and I'm sure that that alone saved many lives.

But the scariest moment for me was when I saw all those cars on the first day and had no idea what I was seeing, and

The United Hatzalah warehouse filled to the brim with equipment

then I realized that there were dead bodies in every single car. I couldn't believe that it was real. I thought I was in a dream — a nightmare. And I couldn't stop asking "Where is everybody? Where are the police? The army?"

But there was nobody there. That scene still flashes through my mind whenever I think about it and probably always will.

There were frightening moments and emotional moments, times when I was moved and times when I was shocked and scared. But through it all, I'm happy and proud that United Hatzalah was there for *Klal Yisrael* when they needed us most. We made countless trips to the hospital, and we saved hundreds of lives and treated thousands of people. Hashem gave us this opportunity, and we accepted it with open arms.

CHAPTER NINE
Chassan Torah 2023

That entire Simchas Torah, Eli Beer was involved in matters of *pikuach nefesh*. When the phone rang, he made sure to answer it only if the call was related to saving lives. Otherwise he let it go to voice mail. When journalists from every television station called because they knew that the volunteers were down south saving lives, he didn't answer.

The rest of the team also worked without pause from morning till night that day. With mere minutes to go before sundown, Eli Pollak, the CEO of United Hatzalah, approached Eli Beer.

"Eli, it's Simchas Torah!"

"I know."

"None of us got an *aliyah*."

"I know."

Eli Pollak

Normally they would have been in shul that day and would have been called up to the Torah when the *baal korei* read the *parashah* of *V'Zos HaBerachah*, the final chapter that's read before concluding the Torah and starting the cycle again. But that day they had all been too busy dealing with life-and-death matters, and none of them had even thought about receiving an *aliyah*.

"Listen," Eli Pollak said, "we have a *sefer Torah* here in the building." It had been donated to the organization by the Hofbauer family years earlier. "Let's take a break for a few minutes. We'll *lein V'Zos HaBerachah*, we'll get *aliyos*, and we'll celebrate Simchas Torah."

By that time, the situation had calmed a little, and Eli knew that they could allow themselves a few minutes to read from the Torah scroll. Moments later, the *sefer Torah* was lying open before them, and Eli Pollak was reading from the final *parashah* of the Torah. He did it quickly, since the day was almost over, and every member of the team received an *aliyah* right there in United Hatzalah headquarters. Eli was called up last, and it was he who received the *aliyah* of the *Chassan Torah* that Simchas Torah. It was probably the most emotional *aliyah* of his life.

So that was that. Yom Tov was over. The team made Havdalah at the dispatch center. Moments later, Eli was in an ambulance on the way to Sderot. The region was still very dangerous. Though the army had succeeded in killing many of the terrorists who had infiltrated the country, a large number of them were still on the loose. And yet, as the president of United Hatzalah, Eli needed to see what was going on down south with his own eyes. He also wanted to relieve those who had been there since the morning because they were exhausted.

So he went.

On the way down south, he was finally able to take calls that didn't directly have to do with matters of life and death. Now he was able to take calls related to funding and much-needed support for United Hatzalah. On that journey to Sderot alone, the night after one of the worst days in recent history, there were donors who contacted Eli because they wanted him to know that they grasped the seriousness of the situation, and they were going to help United Hatzalah in any way they could.

Bob Book was one of those donors, offering a very generous donation. "And if you need more, Eli, call me."

Someone else called a few minutes later. He, too, made a generous pledge. As did Eli's long-time friend and partner Mark Gerson, as well as Jay Schottenstein, a longtime friend of the organization.

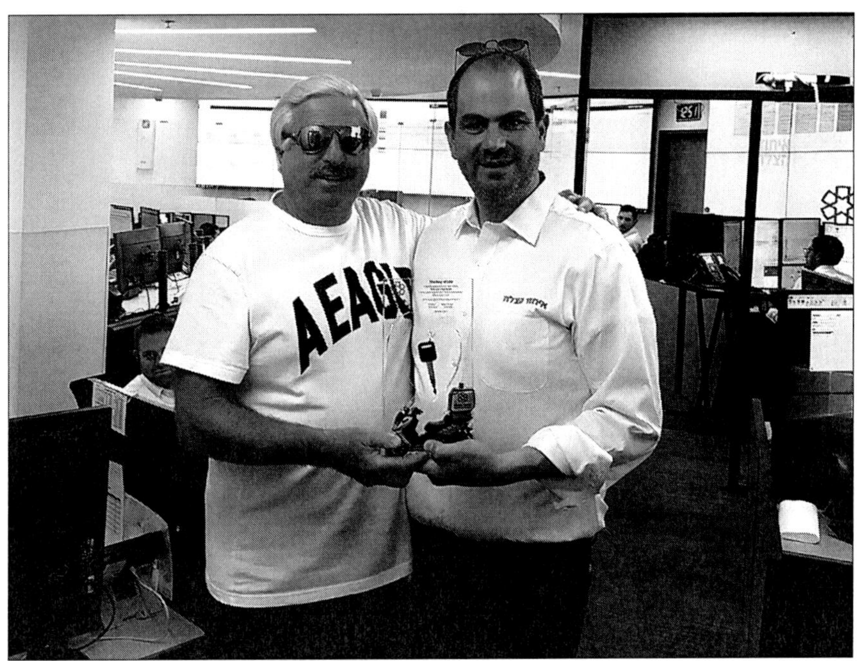

Eli and Bob Book

All in all, at least five major donors called after Yom Tov.[1]

It was an amazing start and the funds would be put to good use, but Eli knew that the real challenge still lay ahead.

"The southern part of the country was still in complete disarray when I arrived," Eli says. "I saw the bodies that were still lying on the roads. Though many of them had been picked up by volunteers of United Hatzalah" — Zaka, which had been busy dealing with the victims from the festival, would begin operating down south in the days to come — "there was still a very large number that needed to be collected and brought to burial. Aside from this, people were still being found alive. Many of the victims from the festival had been in hiding the entire day and were only now emerging from their hiding places.

"Suddenly, as the ambulance I was in was heading closer to our destination, we saw something moving on the side of the road. Our first

1. Since the donors owned property in Eretz Yisrael and regularly spent the Yamim Tovim there, they kept one day of Yom Tov.

The scene of the music festival at Kibbutz Re'im

thought was that it was a terrorist emerging from the forest to shoot at us. Every one of us was carrying a gun, and we took them out and got ready to shoot if necessary.

"It didn't take us long to realize that this was no terrorist. The man had come out of the forest with his hands up in the air, and we immediately stopped the ambulance and went out to see who he was. He looked like a beggar. His clothing was torn and ripped, and he had scratches on his face from crawling through the brush and brambles. Afraid that there might be terrorists behind him in the woods, we grabbed him, helped him onto the ambulance, and quickly left the area."

The man turned out to have been at the music festival near Re'im. Eli asked him if there was anyone with him.

"Not anymore. Everyone who was with me disappeared hours ago."

When questioned where he had been the whole day, he said, "I escaped from the music festival and ran for hours. I was exhausted, but I didn't let myself stop running. I must have run for five hours straight. Then one second I was running, and the next moment I collapsed. When I finally regained consciousness, it was getting dark, but I was still too frightened to move and leave my hiding place. Still, I realized that I couldn't remain there any longer. I needed to put something in my stomach, and I needed medical assistance.

"Knowing that I had to get out of the forest, I began crawling through the darkness toward the road and the lights of passing cars."

The man was starving and dehydrated, not to mention exhausted. It was tough seeing him and knowing what he'd been through. They delivered him to Cheletz, where there were people who would be able to take care of his physical needs and his emotional needs, as well.

At Cheletz, Eli tried to take it all in, to process and absorb the situation, though it was, in truth, impossible to digest. Still he tried. He needed to get a handle on everything so that he and United Hatzalah could do their work effectively.

The victims kept arriving in droves. If anyone thought the flow was drying up, minutes later another batch of wounded arrived.

He hadn't seen Gitty since she had headed south on Simchas Torah. He would only see her the next day, and when he did, her appearance shocked him. He didn't know that the way he looked was shocking, too.

By the middle of the night, he was ready to return to Yerushalayim for some much-needed sleep. He was more than ready to take a break from dealing with a world that had gone insane.

But he couldn't go home just yet, because he was still technically a guest at the David Citadel, and he needed to collect his stuff and check out of the hotel. His kids had already checked out of their rooms, but they hadn't taken everything and he needed to go back there himself. He got a ride back to Yerushalayim and was dropped off outside the Citadel.

Before he went inside, he gazed at the hotel's iconic arches, at the Waldorf Astoria across the street and Mamilla on the other side. Everything looked so charming and beautiful and majestic. It was hard to believe that nothing was normal anymore and that so many people had been killed in the worst ways devised by man in the last twenty-four hours.

So many important people had stayed at hotels such as this one over the past seventy-five years, coming and going as they tried to foster peace or suggest a deal that would satisfy the Palestinians. But nothing had ever been enough. And while many had dreamed and hoped that one day the perfect plan would be suggested and the Palestinians would agree to lay down their weapons, it had taken one day in the month of Tishrei for the vast majority of the Jewish people to understand that the

Palestinians didn't want to make peace, that they had never wanted to make peace, and that it would take an outright miracle for them — the miracle of *geulah sheleimah* — to ever want to make peace.

Suddenly the question was a question no longer. It had been answered in a murderous rampage that could never be forgiven by the people of Israel, who would never allow themselves to get over the atrocities that were perpetrated on October 7, 2023.

For the thousandth time, Eli thought about what he had seen that day, and he knew that the images would never leave his mind. Then he wiped away a few tears, nodded at the doorman and the security team that had been hired by hotel management, and headed to the front desk to check out.

It was close to two in the morning. He felt more tired then he'd ever felt in his life. Bone-numbingly tired.

He could hear the sound of music playing softly through the hotel's recessed speakers. After the things he had seen that day, the idea that music should be playing was almost obscene.

He met someone he knew in the lobby. The man started asking him about his day. Eli told him a fraction of what he knew and saw. On the spot, the man told Eli that he wanted to donate a defibrillator, valued at thirty-six thousand dollars.

Eli also touched base with Charles Gros, the Hatzalah volunteer from New York he had sent down south that morning. Gros was still trembling from the shock of everything he'd been through that day.

Once in his room, Eli realized that there was no way he was going anywhere. He'd been up for too long and needed to go to sleep. He decided to spend what remained of the night at the Citadel and to check out in the morning.

The next thing he knew he was out like a light. When he opened his eyes, it was 6:45 in the morning and rays of sunlight were streaming into the room.

It was hard to believe that the earth was still turning.

It was the day after Simchas Torah — Isru Chag for the Israelis, Simchas Torah for those who were visiting. There were a bunch of minyanim for anyone who was keeping the second day of Yom Tov being held at the Citadel and at the Waldorf across the street.

Eli walked across the street and spent some time telling the people who had shown up for davening about the events of the day before. He did the same thing at the various minyanim at the Citadel, speaking to the packed room just before the *aliyos* were sold.

He told his fellow Jews from America that Hamas had somehow managed to take Israel by surprise, how Israel had been brutally attacked and were currently fighting their second War of Independence. (He would later use that phrase — "Second War of Independence" — when interviewed on CNN and a host of other news shows, and it would be repeated by many others, maybe because it was so true.)

While normally the people davening at the minyanim at the Citadel and the Waldorf are in a very good mood and exhibit the highest of spirits — it's Yom Tov, after all — there was utter silence as Eli told them about the tragedies that had occurred in the last twenty-four hours.

Utter silence followed by the kind of bidding that had never been seen before.

When the *gabbai* stepped up and the bidding began, someone bought an *aliyah* for the price of an ambulance. Another *aliyah* went for a hundred thousand dollars. People wanted to contribute. Everyone's hearts were broken.

By nine in the morning, Eli had raised another nine hundred thousand dollars for United Hatzalah. It was clear to him that people were grasping the magnitude of the tragedy, and they wanted to help. And while part of his heart was shattered by the events of the previous day, another part of his heart swelled with love for his fellow Jews who had heard what he had to say and eagerly and enthusiastically responded by opening their wallets in ways no one would have ever been able to imagine just two days earlier.

PART THREE
INTO THE WAR ZONE

When I think how delicate women were seen walking in fetters at the hand of the chief executioner, woe is me.

— ***Tishah B'Av Kinnos***

It was like we were surrounded by the Ananei HaKavod — the Clouds of Glory — and they were protecting us from all danger and harm.

— ***Avi Yudkowski,***
Volunteer for United Hatzalah

CHAPTER TEN

Avi and Avi

I first met Avi Yudkowski when he was a kid who wanted to join the choir I headed. He sang in the choir for a while, and I became close to his wonderful parents as well. Today Avi is all grown up and a valued member of United Hatzalah, among other things. Tall, well built, formidable, and kind of fearless, Avi was a force to be reckoned with on the day *Klal Yisrael* needed their medical volunteers more than ever.

This is his story:

I woke up at seven o'clock on the morning of Simchas Torah. My phone was screaming, "*Tzeva adom, tzeva adom.*" Red alert, red alert. I understood that something major was happening and that I was probably going to have to go and help in whatever way I could.

I called Avi Gian, another volunteer who also lives in Givat Ze'ev, and asked him what he was planning on doing. I knew that he had an ambulance that Shabbos and figured that he would probably drive it over to wherever we needed to go.

"I'll let you know as soon as I figure it out," he said.

Twenty minutes later I called another volunteer, who told me that he had been just about to leave. I jumped into my car and drove over to his house, where his ambulance was waiting to go. On the way down south, we made a stop at the United Hatzalah warehouse near Beit Shemesh, where we stocked up on as much medical equipment as we could possibly take with us.

Loading a truck outside the warehouse

Just in case.

We still didn't know exactly what was going on, but it sounded serious, and there was no question that we wanted to be prepared for any scenario. As soon as we were packed and loaded, we drove down south to an intersection called Cheletz, which was where United Hatzalah had set up temporary headquarters.

While we had been loading equipment at the warehouse in Beit Shemesh, Avi Gian had already driven down south, entered the war zone, and was now on his way back to Cheletz with seven wounded people in his ambulance.

Avi Gian returned to Cheletz, the wounded in his ambulance were transferred to ambulances that were heading to hospitals, and Avi Gian was ready to return to the war.

Taking my bulletproof helmet and vest, I joined Avi Gian in his ambulance along with another EMT named Emanuel, a great guy and someone you can rely on in any situation.

It was barely morning, and already so much had happened.

As we drove toward Gaza, we asked dispatch for instructions as to what to do and where to go.

"Everyone should stay near Cheletz right now," we were told. "Don't go anywhere else until you're given further instructions."

They could understand why the dispatch center was hesitant about sending anyone in. No one really knew what was going on there yet. No doubt the higher-ups of United Hatzalah were trying to formulate policy at that very moment.

But here's what you have to know about my friend Avi Gian: He's not the type of guy to sit around and wait when he knows that there are people who are injured and dying and need his help.

The truth is, I felt the same way.

So we kind've ignored the instructions, left Cheletz and headed into the unknown. I'm not saying this was a smart move. I'm not justifying our decision. I'm just saying that *Klal Yisrael* needed us, and there was no question of our not going to help.

We had no idea what awaited us on the other side. We simply hoped for the best and prepared for the worst as we drove off in the direction of the Sha'ar HaNegev intersection not far from Sderot.

There were three of us in the ambulance. All of us were wearing bulletproof helmets and vests. Avi Gian and Emanuel were both armed. We hadn't been driving for long when a car came speeding over to us, motioning to us to stop.

"I have wounded people!" he yelled.

We stopped and helped two girls into the ambulance. They had been at the music festival at Re'im and were in bad shape. One had been shot in the shoulder and leg. She was also missing a finger. The other had been shot in the hand. We drove back to Cheletz with our passengers and transferred them to another ambulance, which would take them where they needed to go for treatment. Then we turned around and headed back to the Wild West.

We took the road to the left, driving on Route 232 — the Avenue of Death. We kept our eyes out for other ambulances, but it seemed like we were the only ambulance on the road.

I'd grown up in a regular family in a regular neighborhood. In my wildest dreams, I never imagined that I would see the things I saw on that road. So many cars had been shot at; so many people were dead. It was impossible to process what we were seeing on a normal Israeli highway.

It looked like hundreds of cars had been attacked, and there was nothing we could do for any of them. We kept looking into the cars to

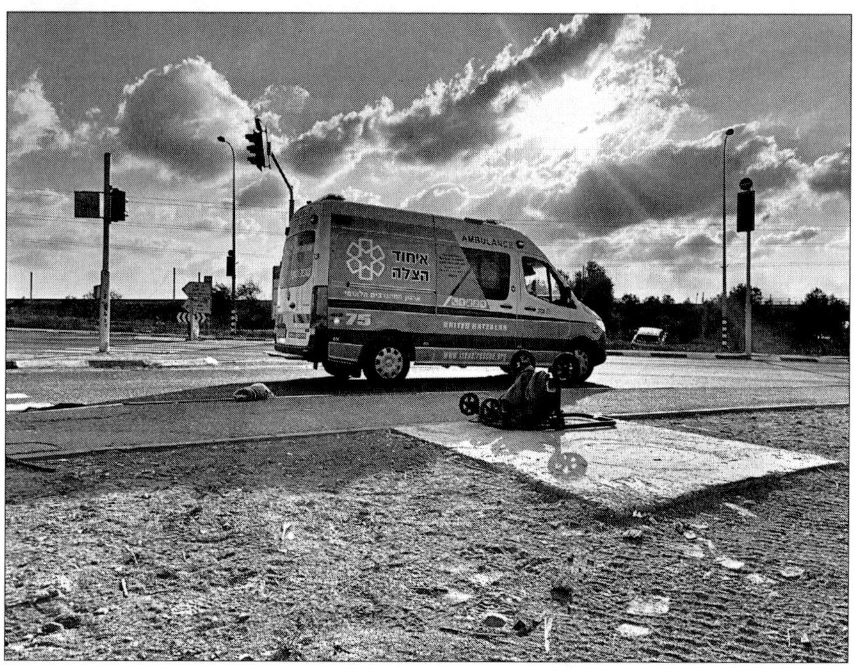

Avenue of Death

see if there were any wounded to treat. But it was clear that everyone was dead, and we were too late to help.

In one of the cars we saw a dead soldier still holding his gun. We knew that we couldn't leave the gun in the car. Not when there were still terrorists running around the area who might take it and use it against us.

Avi stopped the ambulance, and the three of us got out. Avi Gian had his gun out, standing guard, while Emanuel and I removed the soldier from his car and loaded him onto a stretcher in the ambulance. Then we got back into the ambulance and drove along the road until we met a few Israeli soldiers.

"We picked up a soldier from one of the cars," we told them. "He's no longer alive. Where should we bring him? Where are all the bodies being taken?"

The soldiers exchanged glances. They didn't know what to say.

One of them spoke up. "No place has officially been designated yet for bodies."

The entire country had been caught unawares. Nothing was operating properly, and all systems were down. In the end, we drove to Sderot and left the soldier near a small police station by the entrance to the city.

His gun was now in the hands of the police, and he was one step closer to a proper burial. In a way, it was like we had just been involved in the mitzvah of taking care of a *meis mitzvah* — a body that had no one to take care of it.

Just that morning, I had been looking forward to a day of dancing with the Torah in shul. Instead I now found myself doing the kind of mitzvos I never imagined would come my way.

We were still in Sderot when we caught sight of another army jeep heading our way. When it drew closer, we saw something we had never seen before. There was a wounded soldier lying on the hood of the jeep. Another soldier was sitting on him to make sure he didn't slide off, and he was administering some sort of emergency field treatment while they drove. They must have been going over fifty miles an hour.

No doubt the soldier would have been in the back of the jeep under normal circumstances, but the back was jammed full of soldiers, and there was no room. That explained what he was doing on the hood.

The jeep pulled up near the ambulance, and we transferred the soldier from the hood onto our stretcher. Then we put him into the ambulance and took him back to Cheletz, where we handed him over to one of our special intensive care ambulances for the ride to the hospital.

The next few hours were a blur of activity. We went back and forth seven times, each time meeting vehicles on the road carrying the wounded who needed to be brought to the ambulances at Cheletz. Sometimes we would meet a car who had someone for us to transport almost immediately. Other times we waited at the Sha'ar HaNegev intersection until a car or jeep arrived.

During one of the times that we pulled up to wait at Sha'ar HaNegev, we noticed the bodies of two officers from the special police forces lying on the ground. Though there were dead people everywhere, we felt that we couldn't leave police officers or soldiers on the road.

We had a good reason for this.

We didn't want the soldiers who would be coming in to fight to see the soldiers who had been killed. We had a feeling that seeing such a sight would be demoralizing and would take the edge off their ability to fight the enemy. That was the last thing we wanted to happen, so we made sure to bring them to the entrance to Sderot as well. It was a *chesed shel emes*, the most authentic act of *chesed*, and the least we could do for Jews who had given their lives for their country and for *Klal Yisrael.*

It was closing in on two in the afternoon. We hadn't had any time to think since we had arrived at Cheletz that morning and had been working on what seemed like autopilot for hours. Though it was all incredibly scary, we weren't focusing on that part of it at all. There would be time for that later. Right now we were just trying to save as many lives as we could. To get the wounded people into the ambulance and over to Cheletz, where they would be transported to the hospital. We never managed to actually enter Sderot, though we knew there was a lot of furious action happening there, because every time we arrived at Sha'ar HaNegev, we were stopped by a car or jeep with a wounded patient who needed to be transferred to the hospital.

On one of our trips, we were transporting a woman who had been critically injured when terrorists attacked her car. Sadly, her husband had been killed. As we drove, the woman kept begging us to promise her one thing.

"Please go back to our car and cover my husband!"

It was such a human moment.

At first, we were reluctant to give our word. There were so many wounded who needed us. How could we take the time to fulfill her request when we were sorely needed elsewhere?

But the woman wouldn't relent, and in the end we agreed, touched by her devotion to her husband. We took down the license plate number of her car and its general location and promised her that we would go back to see what we could do for him.

It was a moment of beauty in a sea of raw pain.

After yet another run back to Cheletz Junction, we returned to Sha'ar HaNegev, where we waited for more wounded to arrive. We were there for about fifteen minutes without any movement. This was strange. Until that point we hadn't had to wait more than a few minutes before we were given more wounded to bring to Cheletz.

Avi Gian looked at me. I could see his mind working. I had a feeling I knew what was coming next.

"Avi," he said, "until now all the wounded were coming to us from that direction, right?" He pointed.

"Right..."

"Well, then, what are we waiting for? Let's go to them!"

He pressed down on the gas pedal, and off we went.

As we drove, we constantly heard the sounds of gunshots, sirens wailing, and missiles exploding. But all that was nothing compared to what we saw on the road in front of us.

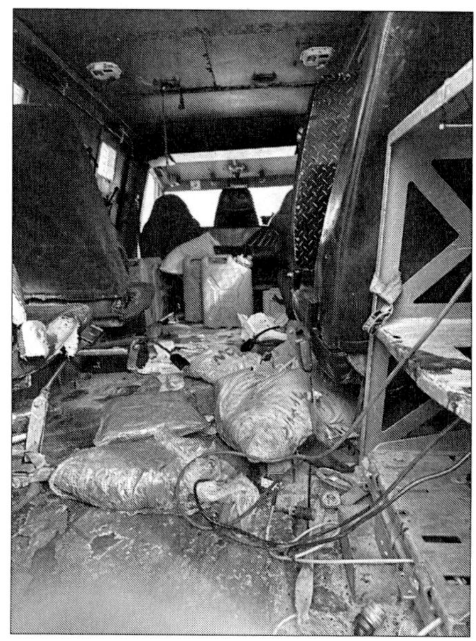

An ambulance awaiting cleanup after transporting the wounded

We had already seen many terrible sights that day. But now, as we drove down Route 232, the things we were seeing were worse than anything we had seen up until then. It was like experiencing a nightmare while wide awake. I was reminded of the words from davening: *"Habeit miShamayim u're'eh ki hayinu la'ag vakeles bagoyim…* — Look from Heaven and perceive: we have become an object of scorn and derision among the nations. We are regarded as sheep led to slaughter, to be killed, destroyed, beaten, and humiliated. But despite all this, we have not forgotten Your Name. We beg You not to forget us…"

This is what I saw that day on Route 232.

I could see trees and fields on the side of the road burning fiercely. On the other side, I saw car after car filled with people who had been killed point blank. There were also some black motorcycles lying on the ground, with the dead bodies of Hamas terrorists on the road nearby. A police car with a shattered windshield, the officers inside murdered.

On and on and on. It was so bad that the ambulance had to swerve between the bodies.

And then we arrived at the entrance to Kfar Aza.

The sound of shooting was much louder now that we were so close to the scene of one of the major battles taking place. To the side was a

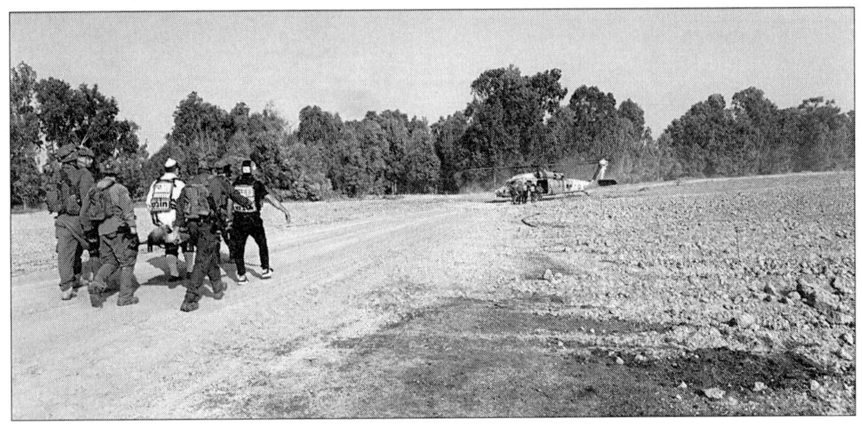
Transferring a patient onto a helicopter

gas station, which was being used as a staging area for the soldiers to get ready before going into the village. All of a sudden, an army jeep came zooming out of Kfar Aza. There were four wounded soldiers in the jeep.

We didn't even have time to think. We just loaded the wounded into the ambulance and drove back to Cheletz as quickly as we could. We did this for the next few hours, making trip after trip between Kfar Aza and Cheletz, trying to get the wounded soldiers to the ambulances and helicopters as fast as we could so that they could get to the hospitals

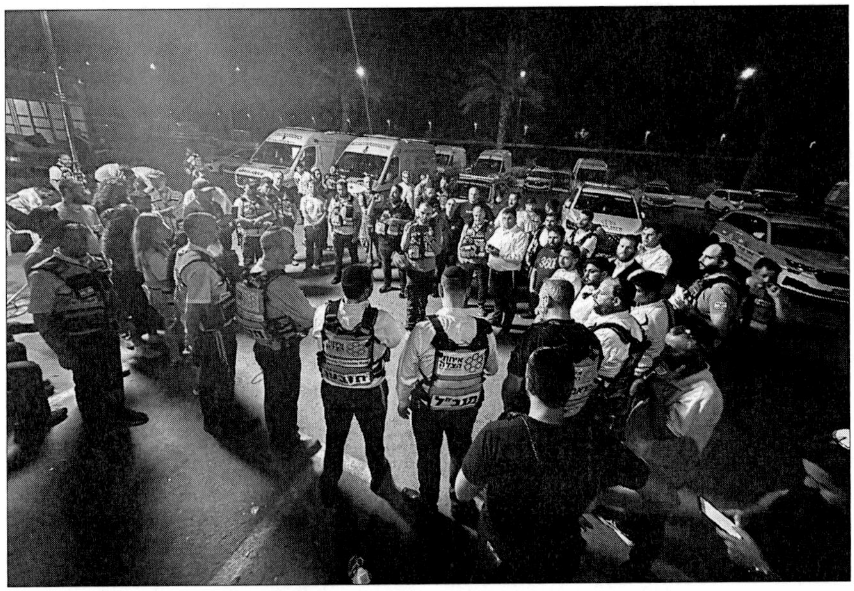
Briefing for volunteers

in time to save their lives. There was no time to waste. Every second counted.

No thinking, just reacting, years of experience kicking in.

Transfer patients from the jeep.

Hit the road.

Get them out of the danger zone.

Clean the ambulance so it can be used again.

Then repeat. Over and over. Again and again.

CHAPTER ELEVEN

Aharon's Finest Moment

They were doing their best. They couldn't have done more if they tried. But it wasn't nearly enough. There were still very few ambulances that had managed to make their way to the entrance to Kfar Aza. Even if Avi Gian and Avi Yudkowski made the trip fifty times, it wouldn't be enough. More ambulances were needed.

The fighting was still going on, but the moment it stopped the army was going to start bringing the wounded out of the village. If there weren't enough ambulances waiting to transfer the wounded out of the area, many more people would die. At this point, they were the only ones transporting the wounded from Kfar Aza. The fact was, they needed more ambulances. Otherwise they were going to drown under the load.

Eventually Avi Gian went to see Aharon Ben Haroush.

Aharon is Eli Beer's son-in-law, and he was one of the people that United Hatzalah had sent down south to run operations.

"Aharon," Avi argued, "you need to send in more ambulances to Kfar Aza. There's about to be a flood of wounded people coming out of there, and there aren't any ambulances waiting for them. Having all our ambulances at Cheletz isn't enough. We have to get the wounded from Kfar Aza to our ambulances here. We need to bring our ambulances right to the gate of Kfar Aza so that they can take the wounded soldiers and civilians straight to the hospital the second they're brought out from inside."

Aharon looked Avi in the eye.

"If you want to go into a war zone and put yourself in danger, I can't stop you. But I can't send the other ambulances to a place where they could be shot at and possibly killed."

"Our job is to save lives," Avi insisted. "That's what we were trained to do. Right now our people need the United Hatzalah ambulances at the entrance to Kfar Aza. If we don't do this, more people will die because they won't get to the hospital in time. That's the reality. I don't see that we have a choice in the matter!"

Everyone was getting worked up, and everyone had good arguments. Avi Gian wanted to save the lives of the soldiers and civilians from Kfar Aza. Aharon Ben Haroush was worried about putting the volunteers of United Hatzalah in danger.

Both were right. Avi Yudkowski watched as all this unfolded before his eyes, happy that he wasn't the one who had to decide.

At that moment, Aharon Ben Haroush made a decision that he will probably relive for the rest of his life. "All the ambulances that are here at Cheletz," he ordered, "follow Avi Gian to Kfar Aza!"

That was it. United Hatzalah was going in. One hundred percent.

"I can't tell you how proud I was at that moment to be a member of such an organization," Avi Yudkowski says, "an organization where each and every volunteer was ready to show the most incredible *mesirus nefesh* for their fellow Jews. It was as if Avi Gian had called out, '*Mi laShem eilai!*' and all the ambulances were following him into the wilderness to make a *kiddush Hashem* and protect *Klal Yisrael*.

"Moments later, I watched as three regular ambulances and two intensive care ambulances (like emergency rooms on wheels) began following us. A convoy of ambulances was on its way."

At Kfar Aza all the ambulances were parked in a row with their backs to the village. This way they would be able to pull out and leave as soon as wounded victims were placed inside.

They could hear the battle raging inside Kfar Aza — the unending gunfire, the screams of the soldiers and the terrorists, the explosions — and all of it accompanied by the sound of rockets flying overhead and landing nearby. The explosions were incredibly loud and so forceful that the ground shook.

Sitting in the midst of the war zone as they were, it would have made sense if there would have been serious casualties among the United

Ambulances at Kfar Aza

Hatzalah volunteers. But no. Very few volunteers got hurt, and almost no one had been killed.

When he thought about it later, Avi Yudkowski felt as if the members of United Hatzalah had been surrounded by a modern-day version of the *Ananei HaKavod*, the Clouds of Glory that had protected the Jewish people as they traveled through the desert on their way to Eretz Yisrael. He had no other way of explaining how everyone was able to stay safe.

Outside Kfar Aza

The shelling in the kibbutz intensified, but for some reason the gate to Kfar Aza remained closed and no one was coming out.

Ten minutes passed.

Twenty minutes.

Half an hour.

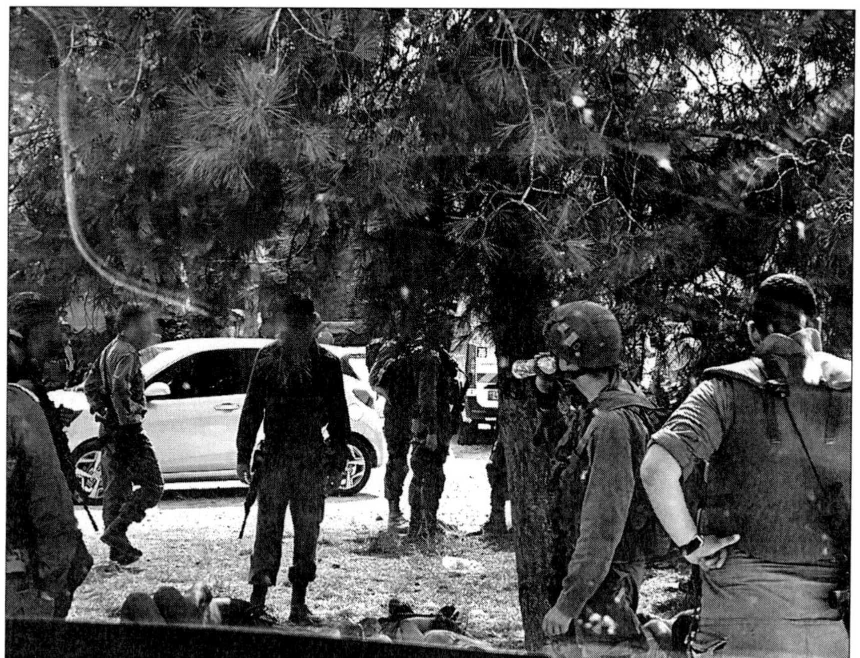

Terrorists caught by soldiers...

What was going on?

Meanwhile, they were sitting ducks. They knew that there were terrorists hiding in the orchards and fields right across from where the ambulances were situated.

Then, suddenly, the United Hatzalah volunteers heard soldiers shouting right beside them. It seemed that the soldiers had just caught three fully armed terrorists who had emerged from one of the fields and were on their way over to where the ambulances were waiting to pick up the wounded — determined to kill more Jews.

The terrorists were caught at the last second — mere feet from the United Hatzalah volunteers.

Another miracle...

"Seeing this," Avi Yudkowski said, "Avi Gian didn't know what to do with himself. He came over to me and said, 'I convinced Aharon to send all the ambulances into a war zone because I claimed there will be a flood of wounded people, but we've been waiting here for half an hour without any signs of activity. And now we almost got killed by three terrorists. He's going to say that I led everyone into danger for no good reason.'"

Avi Gian was a little distraught.

"He was still talking to me," Avi Yudkowski says, "when the gate of Kfar Aza suddenly opened, and a huge tank came rumbling out at top speed. It was going so fast that it drove over an army vehicle with its treads, crushing the car like it was a plastic bag. Thankfully no one was in the car. Looking at the tank and the way it was driving, we immediately understood that there was someone in the tank who was heavily wounded and needed emergency assistance right away."

The first soldier who was taken out of the tank was no longer alive.

The second soldier had been badly injured. He was transferred into one of the intensive care ambulances and driven full speed ahead to the hospital.

Now there was one intensive care ambulance and four regular ambulances waiting for the flood of wounded — which had still not arrived.

Another ten minutes passed, and still nothing had happened. Aharon Ben Haroush, who'd come to the area to assess what was happening, approached Avi Gian and said, "Listen, I don't want to keep the drivers here any longer. It's too dangerous. I'm going to send them back."

For his part, Avi Gian apologized for insisting that Aharon send in the ambulances when they hadn't been needed in the end. While they were still in the middle of their conversation, the gate opened and five army jeeps came speeding out of Kfar Aza one after the next. They made a beeline for the ambulances and began transferring their wounded from one vehicle to the other. Each jeep held at least four critically wounded soldiers. All were bleeding profusely. From one second to the next, they went from having way too many ambulances to not having enough. Every ambulance now had one critically injured soldier on the stretcher and another three or four soldiers all with gunshot wounds.

"When we arrived at Cheletz with our soldiers," Avi Yudkowski says, "there were no ambulances left, so we drove them all the way to Barzilai Hospital in Ashkelon. That was the only time that day that we drove all the way to the hospital ourselves."

They were about to leave the hospital and drive back to Cheletz when someone banged on the ambulance window. They opened the window to see who it was. It turned out to be an officer from the Sayaret Matkal, one of the army's special-forces units.

"My hand was injured a few hours ago," he said. "They took care of me, and now I need to get back to my team at the front. Can I get a ride with you?"

In awe of his *mesirus nefesh*, they obliged.

"Jump in!" Avi said.

In he went and off they drove.

Avi Yudkowski continues the story:

We exited the hospital and started driving back in the direction of Kfar Aza. The officer put on his helmet. Then he opened the ambulance window, stuck his gun outside, and peered through the sights, on the lookout for the enemy.

"Relax," I told him. "We already made the drive forty times today. You don't need to stick your gun onto the highway. None of the terrorists are in this area."

He looked at us as if we were crazy.

"Are you kidding? I was driving on this same route three hours ago, and a group of terrorists tried to attack me from the side of the road."

"What are you talking about?"

"You see that tree over there?"

The soldier pointed to a tree on the side of the road.

"The terrorists jumped down from the tree and attacked."

His answer made a deep impression on us. We understood yet again that Hashem was looking after us and protecting us from all the dangers around us. It was brought home yet again how easily we could have been shot that day. How we could have ended up in the hospital. Or worse.

Then the officer received a message on his phone.

"Change of plans," he said. "I need you to drive me to the police station in Sderot. There's a gun battle. My team is already there."

"Your wish is our command."

Just like that, we were headed back to Sderot.

CHAPTER TWELVE

"Al Abba Lo Sho'alim She'eilot"

When they arrived at the police station in Sderot, they heard gunshots and realized that the enemy was shooting at their ambulance from inside the police station.

"We weren't interested in being used for target practice," Avi Yudkowski says, "and decided to get away from that spot as soon as possible. We couldn't go to the right and we couldn't go to the left, because both of those directions would have left us exposed to the enemy. But Avi Gian was as cool as always. He made a U-turn and drove into a small parking lot nearby. There we jumped out of the ambulance and crouched behind it, keeping the ambulance between us and the terrorists.

"What a different kind of Simchas Torah this was turning out to be. Instead of singing *"Toras Hashem Temimah"* and dancing around the *bimah, sifrei Torah* in our arms, we were dodging bullets in a Sderot parking lot.

"The scene was absolutely surreal.

"Bullets flying in every direction. Screaming. Shouting. Explosions. In the middle of all the craziness, one of the commanding officers approached us, a determined look on his face.

"'I need help from you.'

"'What do you need?'

"'One of my soldiers was killed a few hours ago. The body is lying on the street, and we haven't been able to get to him until now. Can you help us get him out of the street?'

"We didn't hesitate.

"Taking the stretcher from the ambulance, we ran into the street in the direction of the fallen soldier. Running in front of us were three Yamam — police special forces — all shooting at the window in the police station from where the terrorists were firing a constant barrage of gunfire.

"We reached the fallen soldier. No time to think. The commandos beside us shooting for all they were worth.

"We laid the stretcher on the ground and moved the soldier onto it. Meanwhile, the police commandos kept shooting at the police station. Keeping our minds completely focused on what we were doing, we lifted the soldier on the stretcher, turned around, and ran back in the direction of the ambulance.

"Mission accomplished — under fire!

"I never imagined doing something like this when I woke up that morning.

"It was like a lifetime had passed since then."

They loaded the murdered soldier into the ambulance. A few minutes later the army gave them permission to leave the area, and they drove off as fast as they were able. They brought the dead soldier to a place set up on the side of the road, where they had already brought way too many of their fallen brothers that day. They would have liked to take him to be buried but they had to deal with the people who were still alive and whose lives could still be saved.

It was a good ten hours after Avi Yudkowski and Avi Gian had first driven into the war zone.

A few minutes later another car stopped them. There was a wounded man in the car. The driver told them that the man had been at the festival and had been shot in the stomach.

"Take good care of him," the driver said. "He's in bad shape."

They started driving back to Cheletz where a helicopter from Unit 669, the army's search-and-rescue unit, was waiting. Since there were many wounded people arriving at Cheletz at the same time, the doctor was going to have to decide who would be flown to the hospital and who would be taken by ambulance.

Dr. Adam Ballin was in charge of triage — of deciding which patients were in worse or better condition and who should be treated first and how. When the next ambulance arrived, he examined the patient with the stomach wound and gave his ruling.

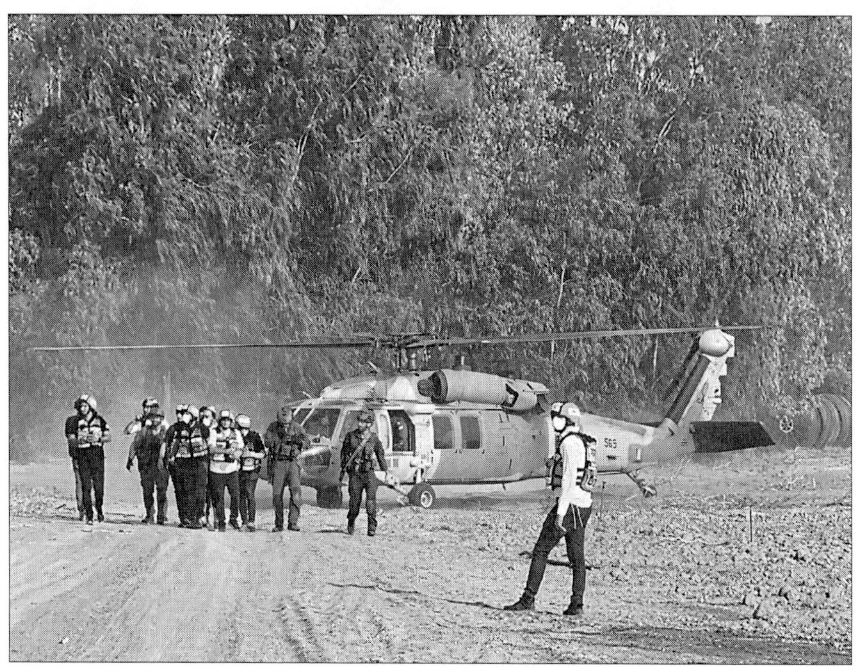

Soldiers and volunteers by a United Hatzalah helicopter

"Put your patient into the helicopter," he told Avi and Avi. "The other patient is in much worse condition. The chances of him making it are very low. Your patient should be the one to go by helicopter. At least this way we will be able to definitely save his life."

"We began moving the patient into the helicopter," Avi Yudkowski says. "We were already under the helicopter when we heard the sound of sirens rising and falling for the thousandth time that day and saw about thirty missiles cruising toward us through the pitch-black sky.

"We ran back to the ambulance and lay on the ground. Moments later, the missiles exploded — way too close for comfort. Seconds later, the helicopter took off. We got back into the ambulance and headed back into the war zone to see who else needed our help."

They ended up taking one more critically wounded person to Cheletz. He kept losing consciousness in the ambulance, and Avi Yudkowski kept talking to him, asking him questions about his family, trying to keep him awake. He would answer while at the same time apologizing, saying that he couldn't help himself, that he couldn't stop falling asleep…

They brought him to Cheletz, and an ambulance took him to the hospital.

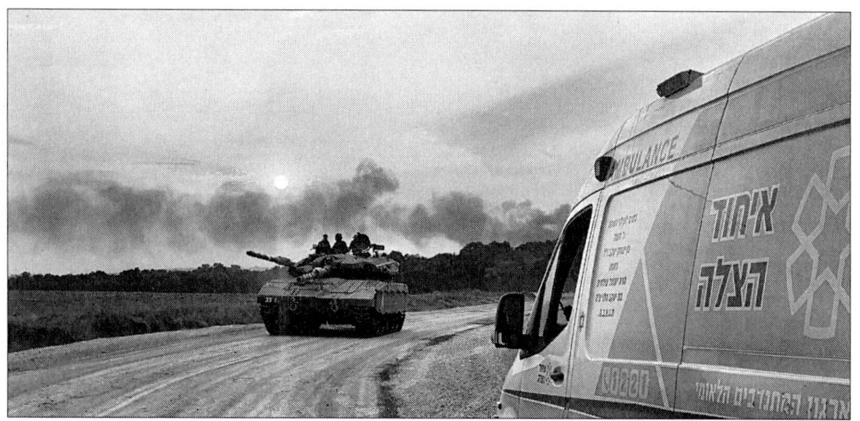

Driving in the combat zone

That was the end of their first day in the war zone. They drove back to Yerushalayim, and the entire way Avi Gian insisted on listening to one song and one song only. It was called *"Al Abba Lo Sho'alim She'eilot,"* by Moti Weiss. We don't ask questions on our Father.

It was exactly what they all needed to hear.

On Sunday the team was back, transporting the injured and wounded to Cheletz. On Monday afternoon they were at the entrance to Kfar Aza when a soldier approached them, asking if anyone had a sandwich or something else for him to eat. They didn't have anything, and they felt terrible.

It wasn't that there wasn't plenty of food for the soldiers — just not near Kfar Aza, which was still a hot zone. Leaving the soldier behind, they drove the ambulance to the entrance of Sderot, where they picked up six hundred portions of food, and brought it back to the very appreciative soldiers who couldn't get enough.

The next day, Tuesday, Avi Gian and his wife managed to raise twelve thousand shekels — enough to pay for seven hundred delicious meals — which they picked up from Yerushalayim and delivered to the soldiers at Kfar Aza. They made sure that the food was steaming hot, and the soldiers said that this was the first time they were eating hot food since Friday night.

"We served them pasta and meatballs," Avi Yudkowski says, "and I have a feeling that if you ask one of those soldiers in twenty years' time to tell you what was the best meal they ever had, that Tuesday

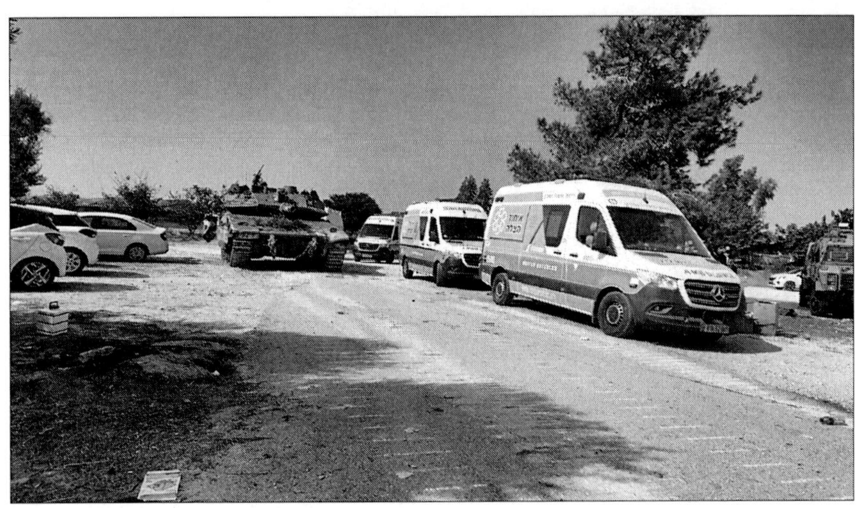

Working together to save lives...

afternoon lunch will definitely make it high on the list."

And here's something Avi Yudkowski's father later recounted that his humble son "neglected" to mention:

"Avi had saved one meal for himself. He, too, was hungry and hadn't eaten a hot meal in a while. After all the meals had been distributed and everyone was enjoying the delicious food, Avi sat down to eat his pasta and meatballs. At that moment a soldier approached him.

"'I just got here. Is there anything left?'

"Avi didn't blink an eye.

"'Sure,' he said, handing the soldier the food he had just been about to eat. 'This is for you.' "

By Tuesday night Avi Yudkowski had come to the end of his rope. He was exhausted — physically, mentally, and emotionally — and he really needed to go home. He and his fellow volunteers had saved many lives and made sure that many bodies would receive *chesed shel emes*. They had risked their lives for the sake of their people multiple times. Now Avi needed to get some sleep.

It was three in the morning, and the ambulance was passing Kibbutz Be'eri, the scene of another incredibly brutal massacre. This wasn't a great place to be driving through in the middle of the night, not with so many terrorists still on the loose.

Complete darkness on the right. Complete darkness on the left.

"Suddenly something happened to me," Avi says. "I was fine one second, and then a second later I felt a surge of the most intense feeling of fear shooting through me, and I knew — I don't know how I knew, but I knew beyond a shadow of a doubt — that we had to get away from where we were right away.

"Avi," he yelled, "get the ambulance out of here! Step on the gas and get us out of here immediately!"

As all this was going on a message came in from dispatch.

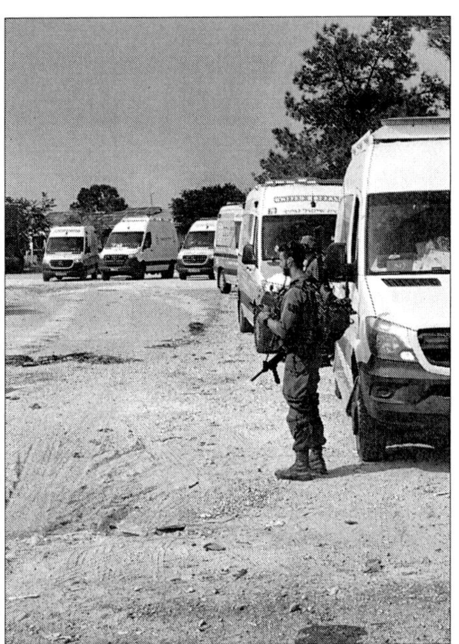

Ambulances at Be'eri

"Are you near Be'eri?"

"Yes, why?"

"Terrorists have just infiltrated the area. Get out of there now!"

Avi Gian needed no more urging. Seconds later, they were speeding away from the area.

They passed Be'eri.

They passed Sa'ad.

They passed Kfar Aza.

Soon they were pulling up at the Sha'ar HaNegev intersection near Sderot, where about forty soldiers were standing in the middle of the road with their guns pointed in their direction. Not the kind of thing you want to see when you're driving down the street.

They pulled up next to the soldiers.

"What on earth are you doing here?" their commander shouted. "Do you know the kind of danger you're in? Get out of here now!"

Later the medics found out that four cars filled with terrorists had come in from Gaza that night. There was a gun battle right outside Kfar Aza two minutes after the ambulance passed that spot.

One of the cars was shot up. All the terrorists inside were eliminated. The other three managed to turn around and went back to Gaza.

"All this meant that the terrorists had been driving behind the ambulance for a long time," Avi Yudkowski says. "If we had remained where we were for even a minute longer, I probably wouldn't be talking to you right now. But Hashem was protecting us. As I said, we felt the Clouds of Glory surrounding us, and we were able to help so many people who desperately needed us."

A Miraculous Moment

Aharon Ben Haroush was the one in charge of managing the volunteers on the ground throughout that endless Simchas Torah — the one who had to implement the decisions made at headquarters back in Yerushalayim. There was nothing simple about this because he was sending volunteers into dangerous places without knowing whether they were going to survive.

While he was making life-and-death decisions at Cheletz, and later at Kfar Aza, there was something else weighing on his mind: His grandmother lived in Sderot, which meant she was in danger from the double threat of missiles and terrorists.

"My mother's entire family lives in Sderot," Aharon says. "Every time something major happens in the city, my wife and I go to pick up my grandmother and bring her to us."

Now it was Simchas Torah, and under normal circumstances Aharon would have never dreamed of calling his grandmother, but with terrorists running around the city, it had become a matter of *pikuach nefesh*. So he called her, but she didn't answer the phone. He called again and again, but still no answer.

It was only on Motza'ei Yom Tov that he was finally able to get through to his grandmother's aide.

"I've been trying to reach my grandmother the whole day," he said. "Why didn't anyone answer the phone?"

"We were in the safe room," the aide explained, "and there's no reception there."

"Please let me speak with my grandmother."

Aharon's grandmother got on the phone. "Aharon, when are you coming to get me?" she asked.

By then, it was already midnight. Dozens of wounded people were pouring out of Kfar Aza and Be'eri, and now his grandmother wanted him to come and pick her up.

He sent a team into Sderot to pick her up, while he remained behind to manage the situation at Kfar Aza for a while longer. When he was finally able to leave, he drove to Cheletz, where he met his grandmother, who had been brought there. It turned out that she had been staying at his uncle's house in Sderot that day.

"Where were you all day?" his grandmother complained. "Why didn't you come to get me until now?"

Then she started to cry. Like a baby.

"Why didn't you take care of me? Why didn't you come to get me? People died on my block!"

She had managed to keep it together the entire day, but when she saw her grandson, she finally allowed herself to break down. She didn't stop crying the entire way to Yerushalayim. Seeing her in such a state tore Aharon's heart.

"I told my uncle that he also needed to leave Sderot," Aharon relates, "but he didn't want to leave, stubbornly insisting on remaining at home. After rescuing my grandmother, I sent in more teams to get the rest of my family members out of the city — everyone except for my uncle, who wouldn't hear of leaving no matter what I said.

"On Sunday morning, there were still terrorists running around the city and rockets flying everywhere, and I let him know that the conversation was over. I was coming to get him, and he would be leaving with me. End of story.

"Seeing that I was serious, that I wouldn't take no for an answer, he finally agreed to leave Sderot. He left the city at two in the afternoon. Just a few hours later, at six o'clock in the evening, a rocket came flying out of the sky and struck my uncle's home.

"Half an hour later another rocket landed in the courtyard of my grandmother's home. But she had already left, and so had he."

Not a miracle?

PART FOUR
DOCTORS ON CALL

O that my head were water and my eyes a fountain of trickling tears, that I might weep all the days and nights of my life for the slain children and babies and the old men of my congregation.

Alas for the house of Israel and for the people of the L-rd, for they have fallen by the sword.

— ***Tishah B'Av Kinnos***

United Hatzalah is Israel, and Israel is United Hatzalah.

— ***Dr. Shlomo Gensler***

"Before I left the house, my father, who was with us for Yom Tov, put his hands on my head and blessed me with the timeless words of "Yevarechecha Hashem v'yishmerecha... May Hashem bless you and watch over you..."

— ***Yoni Rosenfeld,***
Flight EMT for United Hatzalah

CHAPTER THIRTEEN

Invisible Wounds

By the day after Simchas Torah, United Hatzalah headquarters had come to the conclusion that they needed to build a field hospital down south at a location that would be close enough for the ambulances to bring the injured and wounded and far enough away to keep everyone relatively safe.

They chose Kibbutz Sdei Yoav, located between the cities of Kiryat Gat, Kiryat Malachi, and Ashkelon.

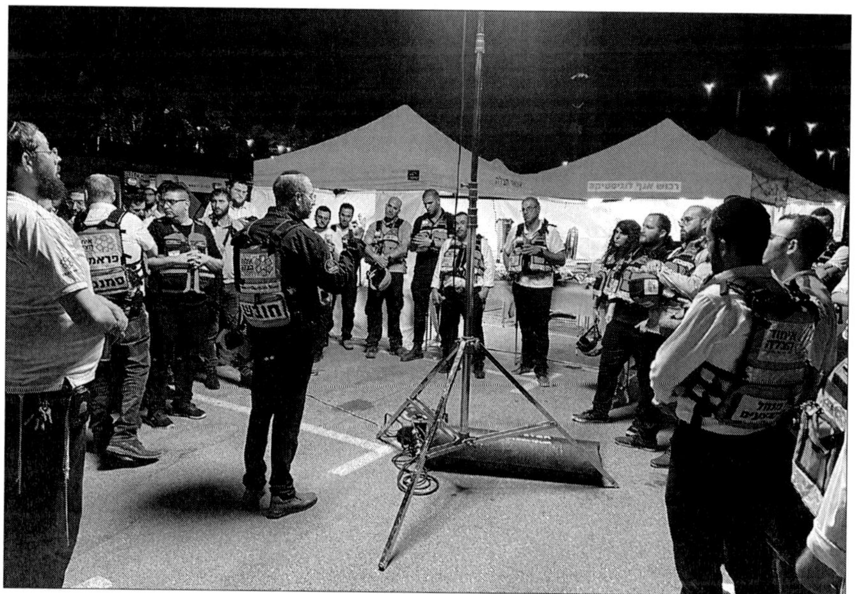

Eli delivering a briefing at Sdei Yoav

Decision made, trucks were loaded with equipment from the United Hatzalah warehouse, and by nightfall ten large tents had been erected, along with bomb shelters, bathrooms, and even showering facilities. Some of the tents were used as makeshift kitchens where volunteers could prepare something to eat or have a hot cup of coffee. There was plenty of food for both volunteers and soldiers and anyone else who found himself in the area and was in need of a square meal. Another tent was used as a command center and others for conference rooms and for medical centers. There were also tents filled with beds for volunteers who needed to catch a few hours of sleep.

With huge *siyata d'Shmaya*, the Sdei Yoav command center became fully operational virtually overnight.

To anyone looking at the setup at Sdei Yoav, it's very clear that one of the reasons United Hatzalah is so successful at carrying out its mission is because of its incredibly motivated and professional logistics department. No army can fight a war without good logistics. An army can have the best fighters in the world, but without enough food, water, and fuel, they won't be able to achieve victory. Soldiers can't win a war when they're hungry.

It's for all these reasons that United Hatzalah invests so much in their

Minchah at Sdei Yoav

logistics department, intent on making sure that the volunteers receive whatever they need to fulfill their mission.

All this was happening as other Hatzalah teams were working feverishly at the Cheletz intersection not far from Sderot, which was the staging area for all ambulances coming in and out of Gaza. The doctors there performed triage and made snap life-and-death decisions regarding which patients were to be sent to the hospital by ambulance and which by helicopter.

Equipment at Sdei Yoav

Many of both volunteers and wounded ended up at Sdei Yoav. Some of the wounded had no physical signs of damage. They were shattered on the inside, from what they'd witnessed or endured themselves. Those suffering from trauma were not only greeted with warmth and open arms and given a hot meal, they were also given

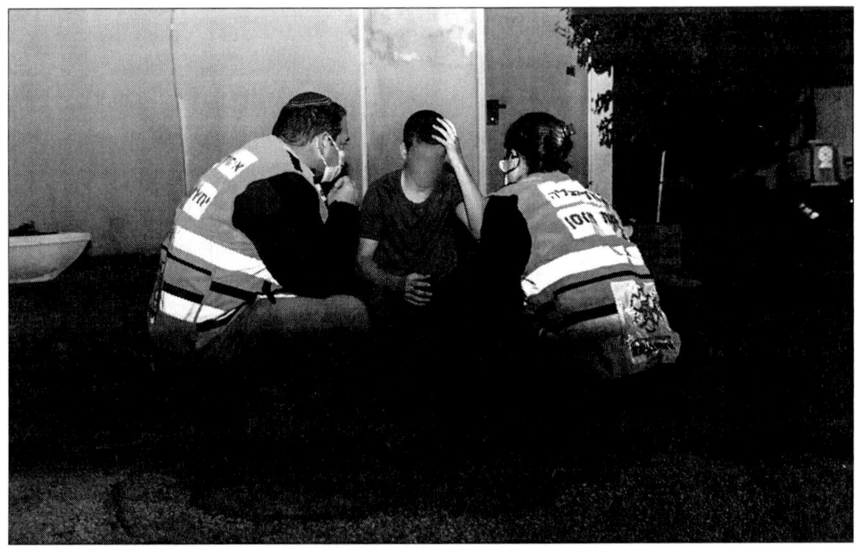
The Psychotrauma and Crisis Response Unit volunteers doing their holy work

treatment by United Hatzalah's Psychotrauma and Crisis Response Unit.

The unit is comprised of psychotrauma specialists, who provided on-site counseling to those who were still in shock, as well as to the volunteers who were returning from the front lines with fresh memories of death and destruction filling their minds. Many were in such a state of shock that they couldn't even speak, and it was up to the skilled Hatzalah teams to bring them back from where they'd been with the entire arsenal of psychotrauma tools that they had at their disposal.

The main job of these Hatzalah professionals is to help release the person they're working with from the feelings of hopelessness that have ensnared them, that make them feel as if the world is coming to an end and that nothing will ever be okay again. Such a person has entered what's termed "survival mode," and it's the team's job to draw the person back to a place where they cease feeling lonely and helpless and instead feel that they are surrounded by love, that they are not alone.

When a person afflicted with such feelings hears "I'm with you — you're not alone," it can make a real difference to their state of mind. It's imperative that the person actually feels the truth of that statement in their heart and soul, because it will help them take the first step to recovery. The idea is to take the person away from the feeling that something so terrible happened to me that I'm not capable of dealing with because it's too big and too traumatic, over to the stage where they can relate to what happened to them as their story. When someone relates to an experience as their story, the person is now in a place where they can learn how to deal with it.

While the majority of the volunteers were focusing on the physical injuries of the thousands of victims who were continuously arriving to their doorstep, the psychotrauma unit focused on their state of mind, on their mental and emotional ailments. Their goal was to help those who had been traumatized by what they had seen and experienced return to the healthy person they were before they were exposed to the horrors perpetrated by some of the worst people the world has managed to produce in decades.

By two weeks into the war, the psychotrauma teams had already conducted more than 1,600 conversations, both in person and on the phone, with people seeking reassurance — both during the daytime hours and at every hour of the night as well. Since each conversation on average takes between fifteen to forty-five minutes, one can imagine how incredibly challenging was the workload the volunteers willingly took on themselves.

Another very important decision, made a few days into the war, was that all volunteers were treated to a dose of trauma therapy before leaving for a shift on the ambulance. They were also met with a professional trauma expert upon their return.

Looking at the members of the teams, you will see regular people living regular lives. And yet there is nothing regular about the holy work the psychotrauma professionals were doing.

Eli Roth is a volunteer who was at Kfar Aza on Simchas Torah. "We had been waiting at the entrance to the village for the wounded soldiers to be taken out for a long time," he says. "For some reason, nothing was happening, and we began to think that we couldn't stay there any longer. You could almost feel the danger in the air.

"Right across from where we were waiting there were fields, and we had been told that they were filled with terrorists. Standing there in the open, we felt as if every second could be our last.

"Suddenly a soldier opened the door of my ambulance and climbed inside with all his gear. This was very unusual, and I asked him what he was doing.

"'I need to get out of here!' he said, clearly troubled.

"I understood that something had happened to him — maybe not physically, but emotionally he was damaged. I asked him what had happened to make him feel this way.

"'We went into a house in Kfar Aza,' he said. 'There were four of us. Suddenly a terrorist shot the soldier in front of me. I turned around and saw another terrorist shooting the two soldiers behind me. Somehow I managed to fight my way out of there.'

"He was in one of the top units in the army, but he was very shaken by his experience. One of the women who was with us was a member of our psychotrauma unit, as well as being an EMT, and I asked her to speak to him. She also spoke with two other soldiers who had seen their friends getting killed before their eyes.

"Meanwhile, the soldier was refusing to get out of my ambulance.

I had no problem getting him away from the area, but I had to inform his commanding officer that I was taking him with me. Otherwise, they would think that he had been kidnaped by the enemy.

"'Give me your commander's number,' I said.

"'My commander and all the other top officers are still inside Kfar Aza,' he answered. 'You won't be able to speak to them.'

"'Okay,' I said. 'I'll go over to the army HQ in the area and let them know the situation.'

"Temporary headquarters had been set up for the high-ranking officers who were running the entire operation from outside Kfar Aza, and I went over there. Once inside, I told them about the soldier who wanted to leave the area and asked who was responsible for him.

"No one wanted to take responsibility for signing off on him. They were busy with a million things right then and couldn't deal with it. And just then the gate of Kfar Aza opened, and a tank came rumbling out with wounded soldiers, and there was no longer any question of taking the poor guy anywhere, not when we needed to use the ambulance for soldiers who had been physically wounded in battle.

"I went over to the soldier and said, 'I'm very sorry about what you went through, and I think you really need to see a doctor, but I won't be able to take you away from here right now. There are too many people who will die if we don't get them to the operating room at the closest hospital immediately.'

"I had another EMT walk the soldier over to the army headquarters and find him a seat. We ended up taking four wounded soldiers from Kfar Aza to the hospital. One of them sat beside me, drifting in and out of consciousness. The entire way, I kept calling his name and telling him to stay with me.

"While I wasn't able to take that emotionally wounded soldier with me at the time, I was glad that at least I'd been able to send someone from the psychotrauma unit to speak to him and begin the process of healing."

A Miraculous Moment

One of the heroes of Simchas Torah — and the recipient of a major miracle — was First Sergeant Igor Pivenev, a police officer stationed in Chevron. Igor was on the job when Hamas attacked. His wife called him from Yated, the village in the western Negev where they lived, and told him that they were constantly hearing sirens. He told her to go into the safe room and to please be careful.

Igor had originally planned to remain in Chevron that day, but when he heard that terrorists had entered Sderot, he realized that his family was in danger and asked for permission to go and be with his family.

As he drove south, Igor found that the road was closed in the vicinity of the city of Ofakim. He approached the police who had closed the road and asked them to please allow him to go through so he could get to his family.

"You can go," they said, "but you should know that there are terrorists on the loose, and the area is extremely dangerous."

Igor thanked them for their concern and continued on his way.

Soon he found himself at Urim Junction.

Igor saw a car over a hundred meters (a little more than 100 yards) ahead lying at the side of the road. He pulled up by a bus stop and got out of the car to see if the driver needed help. He had to walk through brush to reach the car, and there he saw a dead soldier lying on the ground. Another dead soldier was in the car. Seeing that there was nothing he could do for them, he turned around and went back through the brush. That's when he saw two terrorists firing at cars on the road. He took up a position and fired at both terrorists, killing them on the spot.

A few minutes later two more terrorists arrived on the scene, and Igor opened fire on them as well. Hashem was with him, and he managed to kill them, too. He checked that the terrorists were dead and then tried to save two women who had been driving down the road, but they had already been murdered.

Having successfully dispatched four terrorists, Igor returned to his car and began making his way slowly down the road. Soon he heard more shooting and noticed a suspicious motorcycle parked nearby.

Igor parked his car and quietly got out. He moved forward silently until he located the terrorists, who were shooting at innocent people. He found a good position and eliminated them. When he saw that they weren't moving, he drove toward them to check whether they were dead.

They were.

As he made his way home Igor succeeded in outwitting still

other terrorists, eventually eliminating thirteen terrorists all on his own. All he could think about that entire day was surviving and getting to his family.

"I tried my best to destroy as many of our enemy as possible while not getting hit myself," Igor says. "I needed to get home, and that meant I needed to kill terrorists along the way."

Igor doesn't consider himself a hero. When asked about his actions that day, he said, "I did what any policeman would have done. Now I'm back in Chevron, the heart of the country — and one of the most important places for a Jew to be."

Igor's journey home: yet another miracle on a day that was filled with them.

CHAPTER FOURTEEN

Triage

Dr. Adam Ballin works at a medical clinic during the day and as a first responder for United Hatzalah after hours. He's also one of the doctors that volunteers in the field are told to call if they're not sure what to do when treating a patient. He isn't usually on call on Shabbos and Yom Tov, which was why he was surprised when his United Hatzalah phone rang at eight o'clock in the morning on Simchas Torah. It was the dispatch center on the line.

"Doc, there's a big problem down south. Rockets have been falling here all morning, terrorists have been riding around on motorcycles, and there are vans filled with terrorists driving through the streets shooting people. We're clearly in the midst of a national emergency."

Dr. Ballin was a doctor, and he kept his cool and focused on what needed to be done.

"Okay, what's the question right now?"

"We have a responder out in the open in Sderot who has been working on someone who was shot in the chest. He's been with him for forty minutes by himself. There are no police and no ambulance services available. What should he do?"

"Tell him to call me."

When the volunteer called, Dr. Ballin asked a few questions to clarify the situation.

"He's been shot in the back, he doesn't have a pulse, and he's not responding."

"I think that you did your best. Right now you need to cover him and get yourself to a safe place as quickly as possible."

That was how it all began for Dr. Adam Ballin.

"I got in touch with dispatch and asked them if our group of doctors should get ready to go down south. 'There's the threat of missiles falling in Yerushalayim, too, at the moment,' dispatch said. 'Right now stay in Yerushalayim. We'll be in touch.'

"An hour later, the call came asking me to head down south. By then we knew that the situation there was as bad as a situation could be, and it was clear that my services were needed. My wife was worried about my safety, and I told her that I would go and consult with my *rav*, Rav Binyomin Moskowitz, the *rosh yeshivah* of Midrash Shmuel.

"There was a whole back and forth and then he said, 'If you're needed to save lives, and no one else can do what you can, then you need to go.'

"That was it. I had asked a *shailah* and had been given an answer.

"It was time to go."

United Hatzalah had purchased several jeeps, which had been outfitted with an extensive array of top-quality medical equipment, turning them into mini-hospitals on wheels. These are the vehicles that doctor volunteers such as Dr. Ballin use when they go out on calls. United Hatzalah also has a truck that contains all the components needed to set up a field hospital.

"The truck accompanied us on the journey down south, following the directions we were given, until we arrived at the designated location, a place called Cheletz. It was the perfect location for our setup. It was fairly close to the front, making it easy to bring wounded people there, but it was far enough away to be a safe place where we could operate (aside from the 'minor' issue of approaching rockets that didn't stop blasting off the entire time)."

They got to work setting up a field hospital immediately. Unfortunately, the first people who were brought to them were deceased, and the doctor was forced to pronounce them DOA (dead on arrival). Since Zaka wasn't operating in the area yet, it had been decided to utilize one of the Hatzalah trucks that had been used to transport equipment as a temporary morgue until they could be identified and buried.

Soon another ambulance arrived with two women. They had been at the music festival near Re'im. One of them had been shot in the arm, and she and her friend had hidden in the bushes for six hours straight playing dead. Her upper arm was in very bad shape — she'd had the foresight to take a picture of the wound before tearing off a piece of her dress to use as a bandage. That was a good thing because the picture would be able to provide the doctors who eventually did her surgery with important information about the wound.

"The question now became where to send her for surgery," says Dr. Ballin. "We realized that if we sent her to Soroka Hospital, close though it may be, there was a good chance that she wouldn't be able to get the reconstructive surgery she needed so desperately because there were already so many people there waiting for the doctors to take care of them. In the end, an ambulance driver who had just arrived was told to drive her to Hadassah Ein Kerem in Yerushalayim.

"'There's no traffic on the roads today,' I told him. 'You'll be back very soon. Just get her there as soon as possible.'

"I didn't speak to her after Simchas Torah, but from what I was told, the staff at Hadassah were able to save her arm. That would have been amazing for anyone, but it was especially important for her since she told me when we met that she needed three things: pain relief, fluids, and her arm to be saved, since she works as a personal trainer.

"I promised her that we would try our best, and to the best of my knowledge things worked out for her in the best possible way considering the terrible circumstances."

When the next wave of injured soldiers was brought to their doorstep, it was obvious that the soldiers were going to need to be airlifted to a hospital. Soon it was decided that Unit 669 — the army's emergency search-and-rescue unit — would send helicopters and that United Hatzalah would use its helicopters as well.

Since the area at Cheletz was the size of five or six football fields, there was plenty of room for the helicopters to land. The drivers moved their ambulances out of the way, while the logistics team got to work setting up a landing zone for the helicopters to use.

The moment it was ready, the helicopters began landing, and not a minute too soon, because a group of injured soldiers had just been brought in and one of them was in really bad shape and needed to get

Getting patients onto a helicopter

to the hospital as quickly as humanly possible. That was just the first. After that, about five helicopters just came and went, taking the soldiers who were most grievously injured to the hospital.

"The decisions we doctors were forced to make grew harder. One soldier had been shot in the head, and I wasn't sure if he was going to make it. At the same time, there was another soldier who had been shot in the stomach. With the second soldier, I knew that if he was brought to a hospital quickly, he would make it, and if not, he would die. We were all leaning toward sending the soldier with the stomach wound — but then, at the last second, we found a way to fit them both onto the helicopter with barely an inch to spare."

While Dr. Ballin and his team were making instant life-and-death decisions throughout the day, rockets were flying above their heads. The helicopter pilots displayed immense bravery at their willingness to fly in and out under the threat of approaching missiles.

"I couldn't help but marvel at their genuine skill, at how they were able to navigate their aircraft under fire. Lest you think that this isn't a big deal, you need to understand that even one piece of shrapnel hitting a helicopter is sufficient to put it out of business even if it doesn't destroy it completely."

Despite the obvious risks, the pilots spent the entire day flying back and forth, avoiding missiles and landing their helicopters between power lines and trees, absolutely determined to save as many lives as they could, missiles or no missiles.

Since Cheletz is located on a main artery, as the hours passed the volunteers observed more and more soldiers arriving at the scene of the fighting. They came in army trucks, and they came in small cars with five officers shoved into one vehicle.

There were police cars loaded with cops and what looked like old, run-down vehicles (with powerful engines) coming in from the West Bank, driven by undercover officers of the Shabak, who normally were stationed in places like Jenin, Tulkarem, and Shechem, but were now here to fight.

One lady was brought to Cheletz from a kibbutz. She came with her two kids and didn't know where her husband was. She explained that she had barricaded herself with her kids into the safe room in their house.

"The terrorists tried breaking in for a long time," she said. "When they saw that they weren't being successful, they decided to burn the house down. The entire house burned down around us — except for the safe room where we were hiding."

"They had been in their safe room for about fourteen hours straight," says Dr. Ballin. "She was black with soot and suffering from serious smoke inhalation. But they were alive! It was yet another clear and obvious miracle in a never-ending chain of miracles."

Another father and daughter were stuck in their safe room for a very long time. Dr. Ballin asked him how he had kept the terrorists out.

"I did the only thing I could think of."

"What was that?"

"I sat beneath the handle of the door and didn't allow them in. They tried for hours to break down the door. They even used tools. But I sat against that door, and I held on to the handle with all my might. Hashem was on our side because they couldn't break in and we survived."

"Is there anything we can get for you?" Dr. Ballin asked him.

"Two things. A drink and a charger for my phone so I can call my family and tell them we're okay."

The doctor handed him a Coke, a bottle of water, and a few bags of potato chips.

"Sit down, take a drink, and relax a little," he said. "You saved your own life and your daughter's life. You're a hero! Now take a few minutes and catch your breath."

The next time there was a lull, the team at Cheletz heard that another wave of wounded would soon be coming in, this time from Kibbutz Be'eri. In the wake of this report, they decided to move closer to the patients' location and set up a mini-triage area at Kibbutz Shuva.

"It was quiet and dark when we arrived at close to three in the morning. There were a couple of soldiers standing guard, but otherwise we were very much on our own. All of a sudden we heard a single gunshot ring out. Everyone hit the floor, and whoever had a gun immediately chambered a round.

"Soon we heard that there were armed terrorists on motorcycles in the area, hiding in the nearby orchards and fields. Later we would learn that this was absolutely true and that we had been in genuine danger the entire time we were there."

Dr. Ballin realized that they couldn't remain there any longer. It was just too dangerous. Moments later, they began packing up their gear and left as soon as they could.

"Until this day we still don't know who fired the shot. We don't know if it was a terrorist or a soldier who shot a bullet by mistake. But one thing seems fairly certain: The shot that was fired made us conclude just how much we didn't want to remain at Shuva and convinced us to leave a place of certain danger. There's a very good chance that we owe our lives to that bullet."

CHAPTER FIFTEEN

Healing in the Air

Yoni Rosenfeld is a flight EMT, an EMT who specializes in transporting patients by helicopter. He lives in the Pisgat Zev neighborhood of Yerushalayim.

This is his story.

I received a phone call from Aharon Ben Haroush early on Simchas Torah morning informing me that there were major developments in

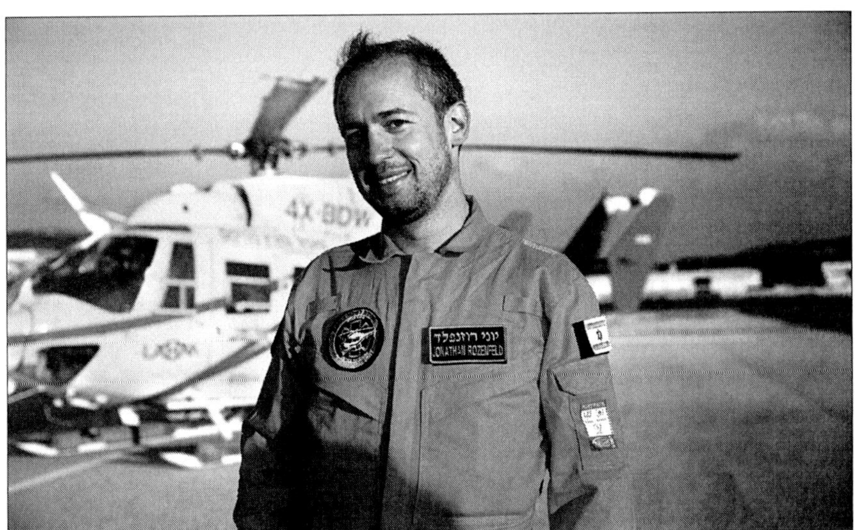

Yoni Rosenfeld — flight EMT

the south. Missiles were flying into Israel from Gaza, and I was needed there as soon as possible.

At first, I didn't understand the severity of the situation, and I told Aharon that I couldn't come. It was Simchas Torah, and I wanted to spend it dancing with my children in shul. Instead of going myself, I contacted a group of volunteers — a doctor, a paramedic, and a driver — and put together a crew for one of the intensive care ambulances.

Then I received another call. A volunteer was calling for medical advice, and dispatch put the person through to me.

"For the last hour and a half, I've been taking care of someone who was shot!"

He described the wounds to me.

"I gave him oxygen and now all my oxygen is finished, as are my liquids. What should I do with him?"

I didn't understand the question.

"What do you mean, what should you do with him? Get him into an ambulance and over to a hospital!"

"That's impossible."

"Why is that?"

"Because they're shooting at us!"

"Who is shooting?"

"Listen, we're under attack and can't go anywhere right now."

Suddenly I understood that this was no normal emergency. Something big was going on.

Then I received another call, this time from the woman in charge of United Hatzalah's helicopter division.

"Yoni," she said, "I'm sure you know that one of our helicopters is always on standby and ready to go. But it seems to me that we're going to need to prepare our second helicopter to fly critically wounded patients from the war zone to different hospitals. I'm currently putting together a flight crew, and I've already spoken with the pilot. Are you available to be the flight paramedic for the second helicopter?"

There were no more questions on my part. No more dilemmas. "Yes, of course."

"Thank you. Avi Marcus is the other flight paramedic on your helicopter. Drive down south now. You'll meet him there."

"And the helicopter?"

"It will be waiting for you."

I got my gear together as fast as I could. Then I gathered all the kids together and gave each of them a long hug. It was obvious that I was leaving them and going into a dangerous situation. I looked at my kids and told them that I loved them. My oldest son was crying as I said goodbye. He had heard the sirens all morning in Yerushalayim and was smart enough to understand that this was no simple matter. A day that was supposed to have been joyous — a day of dancing with the Torah — had turned into a day of sadness and sorrow.

My wife was anxious, to say the least, and I tried to reassure her.

"I'm going to be on a helicopter. We're not going to land anywhere dangerous. We're not going to land under fire. I'll be safe."

"How do you know?"

"Because they told me that the helicopters are mainly going to be used for flying patients from hospitals that are already full to hospitals that still have the space and medical staff to handle more patients. No one will be shooting at us."

Before I left, my father, who was with us for Yom Tov, put his hands on my head and blessed me with the timeless words of "*Yevarechecha Hashem v'yishmerecha...*" May Hashem bless you and watch over you...

I walked out the door with tears in my eyes.

Needless to say, my instructions changed rapidly, and instead of meeting the helicopter at a hospital, I was instructed to drive to the Cheletz intersection. I drove there as fast as I could and arrived at the same time as the helicopter, which was just landing. Wearing my bulletproof vest and helmet, I ran to the helicopter, and moments later we were in the air and flying to the hospital with our first two patients of the day. One was bleeding heavily from his wounds and wasn't in stable condition. There was nothing we could do to stop the bleeding. It was obvious that we needed to get him into an operating room — the quicker, the better. For this patient, every minute was critical and would literally spell the difference between life and death. The other was also severely wounded.

We couldn't fly them to Soroka Hospital in Beersheva or to Barzilai Hospital in Ashkelon even though they were closest to our location, because both of those hospitals were already in the midst of other surgeries and the wounded men we were transporting wouldn't receive the care they needed. Instead we flew them to Hadassah Ein Kerem Hospital in Yerushalayim.

Whereas chaos reigned at Soroka, with many patients forced to wait just to receive basic treatment, Hadassah had a lot of staff available and were waiting for us at the helipad. Within moments, the hospital staff had unloaded the patients from the helicopter, and shortly after, they had already been moved to the operating theaters for emergency surgery.

I made sure to follow up on both of them later on and learned, to my joy and relief, that with *siyata d'Shmaya* we had gotten them to the hospital in time and their lives had been saved.

This piece of news was a ray of bright sunshine in an ocean of darkness and gloom.

By now the helicopter needed to refuel, and we flew to our helicopter base, Sdei Teiman, situated between Beersheva and Netivot. This area wasn't exactly safe either. In fact, the next day a missile fell on the helicopter's landing area. Not only that, two terrorists managed to infiltrate the base. They were outfitted with plenty of weapons and could have killed many people, but *b'chasdei Hashem* they were discovered and eliminated before they were able to carry out their plan.

As soon as we refueled, dispatch told us to fly to Soroka, where another wounded patient was waiting for us who needed to be flown to Hadassah. The patient turned out to be a doctor from Shayatet, one of the navy's toughest commando units. He had been wounded by a grenade, and a tourniquet had been wrapped around his right leg. It was clear that unless he reached an operating room in the near future, he could lose his leg. That was the last thing we wanted to happen, and we were determined to get him onto the operating table as soon as humanly possible.

In the end, we were able to fly him there in time to save his leg, but it was a close call. Tragically, there were many who lost vital limbs because they were waiting to be treated in hospitals where the staff was unable to get to them in time due to the overwhelming number of wounded they had to treat. But this doctor's leg was saved, and he will walk again in due course, and that was cause for celebration. Yes, even amid the intense sadness and pain.

So it went throughout the day.

Pick up a critically wounded patient.

Loading a patient onto a United Hatzalah helicopter

Fly him to the hospital to save his life.
Refuel the helicopter.
Fly back to pick up another patient.
Again and again.

We continued flying patients and saving lives until we were ordered to stop our lifesaving missions for political reasons — and with that our helicopters were grounded. I know it sounds insane that people in positions of power would put political considerations before saving lives, but that is unfortunately what occurred.

What happened was this:

On Sunday morning I flew to Soroka Hospital in Beersheva to pick up an officer from the Sayaret Matkal elite commando unit whose hand had been badly wounded in battle and needed emergency surgery. We had already arranged to have the surgery done at another hospital, this one in Kfar Saba, where doctors were ready and waiting for his arrival. But when we landed at Soroka — two paramedics and a pilot — we were met by a woman from the Ministry of Health who informed us that we didn't have the proper permits required to fly patients from one hospital to another.

The officer was waiting for us, his release letter from the hospital in his good hand, but we were told by the Ministry of Health representative, "You cannot transport this man..."

In all honesty, we couldn't believe that this was actually happening, but nothing we said made any difference, and in the end, we were forced to take off from Soroka without the officer on board.

There was no reason to stop us from doing our job. We were simply saving lives when all the other helicopters used by the army or Magen David Adom were busy flying other seriously wounded patients.

It made us very sad to know that we were being stopped by the very ministry whose job it is to save lives. Even if they didn't want to thank us for our work, they shouldn't be getting in the way. But our helicopters were grounded at the expense of those who could have been saved.

And while this will no doubt make people uncomfortable to hear, it's the truth and the story must be told.

At the same time, I know that in the merit of the flights we made, there are Jews who will be healed of their wounds and other Jews who will live to tell their children the story of Simchas Torah 2023. And for that alone, everything we went through was more than worth it.

I will never forget the way some of the wounded asked me to hold their hands during the flights, how I could feel their vulnerability and pain. I will never forget how we flew those brave soldiers and officers — men who had done whatever they could to fight off the worst kind of enemy imaginable, men who had seen many of their friends and comrades falling in combat all around them.

I know that for those wounded people, the United Hatzalah flight crew were like angels of kindness and hope. I know this because they stood up — and they barely had any energy to stand — and hugged me with their last vestiges of strength to convey their gratitude and thankfulness for what we were doing for them.

(Author's note: Following the incident, United Hatzalah turned to the Supreme Court about the aviation issue and after two long hours of hearings, the Supreme Court ruled in favor of United Hatzalah and its ongoing aviation services.)

A Miraculous Moment

As everyone knows, this war is far from the first time Israel has had to fight in Gaza. And every time the army is forced to go into that den of beasts, *Klal Yisrael* hears of miracles that happened to the soldiers there at the front, because the days of each war were also filled with countless miracles, and in truth, we will never really know the full extent of the miraculous events that occurred. Here is one incident that occurred in one of the previous Gaza operations — and I am reminded of it now.

One unit had a contingent of troops inside Gaza. Their mission: to find a particular house that the terrorists had been using to store a large cache of weapons. It was a few days into the war, and the streets of the city were dark, empty, and abandoned, the windows of the destroyed homes looking at the world through hollow eyes. Not a person was to be seen, and even the animals had vanished.

The platoon of soldiers moved quietly through the streets, the hand of each soldier on the shoulder of the one in front of him. They moved with care and precision, knowing that they could be ambushed at any second by terrorists who were hiding in the area.

Suddenly, a white dove took off from the rooftop of one of the nearby houses. Instead of flying away, the dove plunged toward them and came to a halt midair, hovering directly in front of the first soldier in the line, the soldier who was leading the group.

The lead soldier didn't know what to do. He didn't want to make noise in order to shoo the dove away, which would alert the terrorists to their position. At the same time, the dove was in his face and he couldn't move forward. He lifted his rifle and tried to move the dove aside. Finally, the dove flew off.

A moment later, the second soldier in the line grabbed his friend and pulled him backward. There was no time for explanation, no time to tell him why. It was only later that the second soldier explained that when the dove had flown off, he had been able to see that it had been perched on a very thin wire that had been tied in such a way as to ensure that the first soldier in the line would walk into it — setting off a series of explosives that would have obliterated them all. Hashem in His infinite mercy and kindness sent a white dove to stop His children from tripping the wire.

This was just one of the many stories I remember from back then — along with many stories of soldiers who were stopped from entering certain booby-trapped buildings, sometimes by old men with long white beards and other times by an elderly woman who came just at the nick of time and saved many lives with her warnings.

Interestingly enough, the woman's appearance coincided with the yahrtzeit of Rachel Imeinu...

CHAPTER SIXTEEN

Circle of Life

Dr. Shlomo Gensler's day began much the same as that of his friend and colleague, Dr. Adam Ballin. A resident of the Maalot Dafnah neighborhood of Yerushalayim, he, too, was asked by the organization to take calls from people down south seeking medical advice.

In short order, he found himself talking to the daughter of a man who had been struck by an RPG. He had been grievously wounded in the attack, and she explained that they had applied tourniquets to the worst of the patient's wounds, but he was losing consciousness. Since United Hatzalah didn't have anyone in the area yet, Dr. Gensler called the army and asked the person who answered the phone what they could do for the injured man.

"We're very sorry, but at this point in time we don't have the ability to help anyone," was the answer. "Tell the people to try to get to the hospital themselves."

Dr. Gensler got off the phone and called the people back. When they answered, he heard the sound of rapid machine-gun fire.

He told the daughter what the soldier he'd spoken to had said.

"There's no way we can leave right now," she replied. "We're under attack."

They ended the conversation soon afterward, and Shlomo Gensler knew that the chances of these people receiving the help they needed or even surviving the day were minuscule. It wasn't a very encouraging way to start the day.

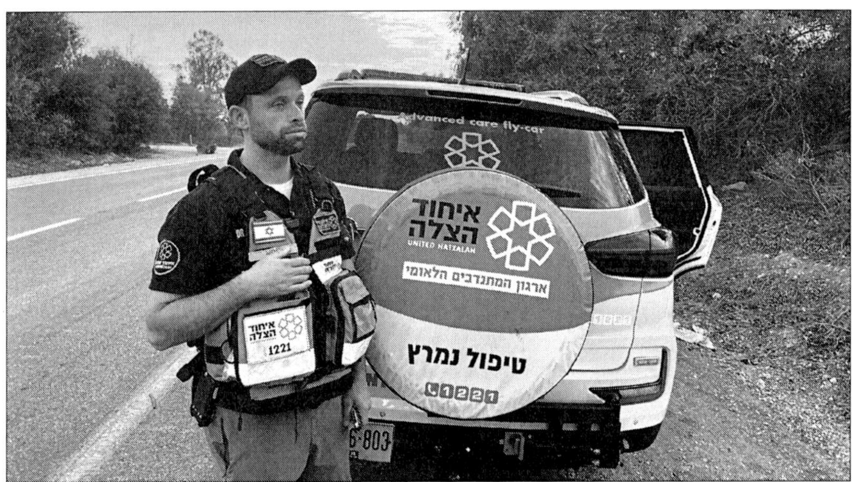

Dr. Gensler with his United Hatzalah jeep

Shortly afterward Aharon Ben Haroush called him and asked if he would be willing to go down south to help.

"I just have to ask my wife," was his answer.

He told his wife what was going on, and she told him to go and help. Then, taking another EMT with him, Dr. Gensler drove down south to the Cheletz Junction.

That day Dr. Gensler found himself in different places at different times. At some point, he ended up on the outskirts of Netivot, where a United Hatzalah volunteer was treating people. From then on the team of doctors kept moving closer to the hardest hit settlements and setting up mini-field hospital triage points everywhere they went.

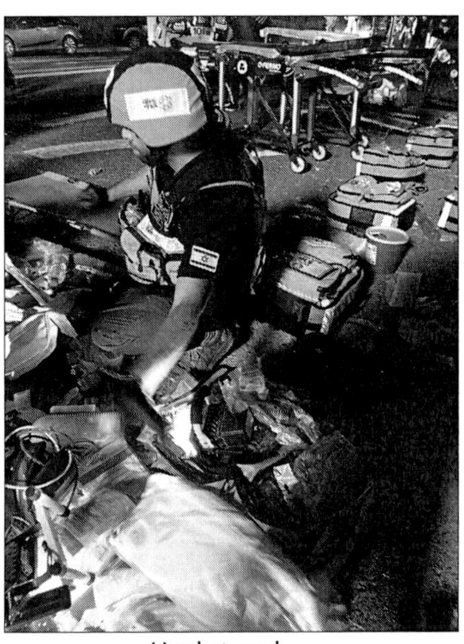
Hard at work...

They were kept constantly busy, whether intubating a patient, decompressing a person's chest, providing pain relief, or just assessing a patient's medical status. They also had

Lying on the ground when hearing the red alert

to decide who would be sent to the hospital via a basic ambulance, who with an intensive care ambulance, and who with a helicopter because that was the only way to save their life.

"I saw so many people who were shot that it's difficult for me to recall everyone who went through our care that night," Dr. Gensler says. "We were dealing with every type of injury and had to make quick decisions under intense pressure. It was absolutely insane.

"As I stood there going from one injured person to another, I was struck by the sheer number of United Hatzalah volunteers who had willingly put their own safety aside to go and help their fellow Jews. What was interesting was that while Magen David Adom EMTs hadn't been given permission by their higher-ups to enter the more dangerous areas, because a number of their EMTs had been killed earlier that morning, many of the MDA staff stayed close to the United Hatzalah teams at the triage stations (which were somewhat removed from danger), moving closer to the front as we moved."

The entire time he worked, Dr. Gensler heard the sounds of rockets exploding and people screaming that terrorists were infiltrating the area not far from where the medical teams were situated. Soldiers were running from place to place, and the general feeling was one of danger and uncertainty.

Then a rocket landed two blocks away, and the explosion literally shook the ground with a kind of ferocious intensity that would send many people into shock under normal circumstances. But there was nothing normal about these circumstances, which meant that as soon as the medical teams were allowed to rise from the ground, they got back to work.

"Our next triage station was near Shuva," says Dr. Gensler, "where United Hatzalah once again set up a mini field hospital and got to work. Shuva is a religious kibbutz and was one of the very few places that the terrorists hadn't managed to infiltrate. There were a number of doctors with different specialties living there who joined us in setting up a clinic of sorts near the kibbutz entrance. Any patient who wasn't in a stable condition was taken out of the ambulance that had brought them and was administered lifesaving treatments. We set up another helipad so that helicopters from Unit 669 could land and fly those in critical condition to the hospital. Other patients were taken by our ambulances to a location where the Magen David Adom ambulances waited to take them the hospital."

Soon a system was in place: United Hatzalah ambulances went into places like Kfar Aza and Be'eri, picked up the wounded, and either drove them straight to the hospital or transferred them to a Magen David Adom ambulance, which made the drive.

"The dynamic between United Hatzalah and Magen David Adom during that first day was an interesting one," Dr. Gensler recalls. "When we first started treating patients on the morning of Simchas Torah, there were still some higher-ups from Magen David Adom in the area reviewing the situation, and we sometimes got into arguments over diagnoses. There were cases in which we felt we needed to perform emergency life saving techniques immediately, while some of their people insisted that the patients be taken to the hospital right away.

"There was something of a power struggle at first, but when they realized that the system we had set up was working and that we had the staff and resources, they left the area with United Hatzalah clearly in charge, leaving many of the MDA volunteers and ambulances there to help us. At that point, we began working together, and we were able to develop what was to me nothing less than an amazing rapport between the two groups of medical responders. Some of the Magen David Adom EMTs even left their own ambulances and joined United Hatzalah medics on theirs."

Many of the responders from Magen David Adom complained to their bosses for not allowing them to take the ambulances to places like Kfar Aza the way United Hatzalah was doing. "United Hatzalah was saving people all day," they said. "Why didn't you give us permission to do the same? You claimed that we weren't allowed to do so due to safety reasons, but no one is safe right now. You should have let us go in to save lives!"

The relationship that developed between the groups during that first day was so powerful that when the United Hatzalah team drove up to the Magen David Adom Headquarters in Netivot the next day, they were greeted by a real hero's welcome.

Dr. Gensler saved many lives throughout that endless night. Unfortunately, there were also times when there was no choice but to pronounce a person dead. Dr. Gensler later learned that one of the people he pronounced deceased had been a United Hatzalah volunteer, as well as a member of the Shabak. This particular victim arrived at the Cheletz clinic along with another member of the Shabak, who was not allowed to leave his side. This was common practice for people who possessed secret intelligence. The person accompanying the patient, who was also a United Hatzalah volunteer, was wearing an army uniform without any markings and a mask over his face that covered everything but his eyes.

When the patient was brought in, the accompanying agent approached Dr. Gensler and said, "This man is very important. Please do whatever you can to help him."

The doctor tried to do what he could, but he had already passed away. It was quite a depressing moment. The victim had come down south not as a United Hatzalah volunteer, but as a member of the Shabak, to fight Hamas. And while a number of United Hatzalah volunteers were killed or kidnaped that day, none of the volunteers who came south specifically to save lives were killed. Every one of them returned home alive.

The sun finally started to rise after an endless night of dealing with life-and-death situations. Dr. Gensler was exhausted, his energy levels totally depleted. Suddenly and unexpectedly an elderly woman showed up. When asked why she had come, she said, "My two grandchildren called me. They told me that they're hiding in a closet in a safe room in Kfar Aza. Can you please convince the army to send in soldiers to rescue them?"

How can you say no to a grandmother?

Immediately the United Hatzalah team got in touch with the army and relayed what the grandmother had reported about her grandsons.

The army reacted with alacrity and immediately sent soldiers to the house where the children were hiding. They succeeded in rescuing them, and they were eventually reunited with their grandmother.

Volunteers asked the children to tell their story. They described how their parents had been murdered in front of their eyes.

"It was like we were listening to kids who had been rescued from the Nazis," says Dr. Gensler. "When I heard their story, I had to leave the area and walk away to cry by myself. When I got control of myself again, I returned and continued treating patients."

Then a woman was brought to the field hospital. It was clear that she was going into labor. One of the doctors who lived nearby brought her to his home, made her comfortable, and gave her something to eat after the night she'd been through.

She had the baby shortly afterward in his house.

"If there was one thing that could give us hope on that dark day, it was the knowledge that a brand-new baby had entered the world on the morning after Simchas Torah," Dr. Gensler says. "When I finally returned home, it was with a tremendous appreciation for the incredible work that had been done by so many amazing and selfless people. I have been a part of United Hatzalah for many years, but to me Simchas Torah stuck out as proof of an idea that had been percolating in my mind.

"It's a simple truth — but one that is true on so many levels: United Hatzalah is Israel, and Israel is United Hatzalah. And the more we grow, the more the country as a whole will understand that we're here to help and to save lives.

"Because that's what we do."

A Miraculous Moment

As time passed, more stories of personal miracles began emerging. One family related how their son had been planning to go down south to attend the music festival at Re'im, which would be taking place on Simchas Torah.

"I'll be home for most of Succos," he told his parents, "but I want to go with one of my friends to this music festival that's being held near Kibbutz Re'im."

"The festival is being held on Simchas Torah?" his parents asked, dismayed.

"Yes."

"And what kind of a festival is it?"

When he told them, his parents didn't like what they were hearing. Since they were the kind of parents who had managed to retain a close connection with their son even though he had chosen a different path from theirs, the father tried to come up with a way to convince his son to stay home. Finally, he thought of something.

"I know of a shul not far from here," he said, "where the people enjoy their whiskey and vodka on Simchas Torah. There's plenty of booze, and the dancing will be off the charts. You want to go to this music festival in Re'im. You want to drink and you want to dance. I know it's not the same thing, but what do you say? Would you consider staying home and go to that shul for me instead? Please?"

And the son agreed.

But he had one request. "I want to invite the friend who was supposed to go with me to the music festival to spend Simchas Torah with us here instead."

"By all means," his parents said, happy to accommodate if it meant their son was staying home for Yom Tov.

On Simchas Torah morning the sirens sounded in their neighborhood, and it soon became clear that something terribly wrong was happening in their small and somewhat fragile country. The friend, who wasn't religious, decided that he had to check his phone to see what was going on. His host — his friend's father — begged him not to open his phone, but the friend couldn't help himself. He had to know. When he returned to the room, he looked shell-shocked.

He went over to his friend's father and began hugging him, thanking him over and over for convincing them not to go to Re'im. His friend's parents had literally saved their lives.

As for the son, well, let's just say that he decided to stay home that Motza'ei Simchas Torah as well…

PART FIVE
ANYTHING TO SAVE A LIFE

The joy of our heart has ceased, our dancing has been turned into mourning.

— Eichah 5:15

The pasuk states, 'Ki malachav yetzaveh lach lishmorcha b'chol derachecha — He will charge His angels to protect you in all your ways...'
That's the way it was for us, for all the volunteers of United Hatzalah, on the day the world lost its mind.

— David Bader,
United Hatzalah volunteer

Ribbono shel Olam, why are soldiers from our side shooting at me?

— David Bader,
United Hatzalah volunteer

CHAPTER SEVENTEEN

A Different World

Chezi Rosenbaum spent Simchas Torah with his fellow volunteer, David Bader. It turned out to be a harrowing day, but when their phones first started buzzing, neither of them dreamed of what lay in store for them and the rest of the volunteers.

Chezi is the chapter head of United Hatzalah in Kiryat Malachi. He had gone on rescue missions to Turkey and Ukraine, in addition to his volunteer work in Israel. That day, Simchas Torah 2023, dispatch called him early in the day, letting him know that there were reports of gunshots in Ofakim and Sderot, twenty minutes from Kiryat Malachi.

Chezi Rosenbaum

Before doing anything, Chezi left to go to shul for davening. It was very important for him to be in shul that morning because he had to say *Yizkor* for his mother, something he always did his best not to miss. He was about to walk into shul when his phone rang. It was Aharon Ben Haroush.

"Chezi?"

"Yes?"

"I'm at the Cheletz intersection now. Go right now to the warehouse in Kiryat Malachi and take all the equipment we have there — everything: bandages, tourniquets — and meet me at Cheletz."

Chezi followed instructions and drove to the warehouse where he gathered together everything they had. Then he drove down to Cheletz, where Aharon Ben Haroush was waiting for him.

"Chezi, you're going out together with David Bader. You have a gun, so at least you can protect yourself to some degree. Drive around and see if you can get a handle on the situation."

David Bader was asked to report to United Hatzalah at six thirty in the morning. He woke up his wife, explaining that there was a situation in the south and he was needed.

It wasn't easy for him to leave home. Simchas Torah is a Yom Tov where children are a focus. It's a day of singing and dancing and *pekelach* for the kids. Though he takes his responsibilities at United Hatzalah very seriously, David is equally serious about his responsibilities as a father, which meant that he really didn't want to miss spending the day with his kids in shul.

In response to his wife's question of when he would be back with the family in shul, he said, "Eleven thirty at the latest. I'll be back in time for *Kol HaNe'arim*."

His wife looked at him, seeking reassurance. "You promise you'll be back by then?"

"I promise. When it's time to leave, I'll appoint someone to take command in my place and I'll come home."

"I had been in Sderot many times before that day," David says. "It's generally a happy place filled with happy people going about their business. The people who have made Sderot their home are used to

David Bader

missiles flying overhead and wailing sirens and don't scare easily. Missiles and sirens are simply business as usual.

"But not that day. On that day I saw a whole different Sderot. I saw dead bodies lying on the ground. It was hard to process the sight of so many dead people. At first we got out of the ambulance and started checking people's pulses. But it quickly became clear that they were dead, and there was nothing we could do for them.

"A little further in, I caught sight of a Toyota pickup truck. The word 'Toyota' was painted on the back in red. There was a group of terrorists standing on the flatbed, rifles in their hands and strips of green cloth around their heads.

"When they caught sight of the ambulance, they opened fire and shot at us. The sound of the attack was loud and frantic. Luckily we were still far enough away from them, and I was able to turn around and flee from the deadly Toyota that was stalking the streets of Sderot.

"When I was out of their range, I slowed down a little and tried to process what I had just seen — and how I had just been on the receiving end of an entire array of weaponry.

"What on earth was going on here? This wasn't the world I knew. It felt like I had suddenly found myself in the middle of a movie showing what it would look like if the world was coming to an end. It was clear that I was going to have to look for another way into the city. Fortunately, such a road existed, and I took it."

Chezi and David ended up staying together for the rest of that endless day. Soon they came upon one of the wildest sights they had ever seen. Terrorists had shot the driver of a car. The door was still open; the driver, who was dead, was still sitting in the driver's seat, and since the man's foot was still pressing on the gas pedal, they watched the car move of its own volition across the road, up onto the median, and then on to the other side. It eventually stopped when it hit an impediment that forced it to stop. Otherwise it would have kept going until it ran out of gas.

The car was still there days later.

Driving down the Avenue of Death, it didn't take David and Chezi long to understand that they couldn't keep what they were seeing to themselves: cars upside down, everyone inside dead, a car that had crashed into a wall. More dead.

On the Avenue of Death...

David called the dispatch center.

"I'm driving on Route 232, and we have counted at least seventy dead."

"Are you sure that your numbers are accurate?"

They understood why the dispatcher was skeptical. It didn't sound like such a thing could be true. Instead of arguing with them, David opened a Zoom call with the dispatch center and used his phone to count the bodies with them so that they would see the situation for themselves and understand the severity of what was transpiring a mere hour and twenty minutes from where they were. They were also able to get an image from the camera on the front of the ambulance.

While David was on Zoom with headquarters, Chezi continued going from car to car to see if anyone was still alive. Suddenly a warning siren went off. Missiles would be falling in their general location in a matter of seconds.

Chezi saw a shelter on the side of the road — the kind of shelter that the government put up in public areas throughout the south so that people would have a place to go in case of an attack. When he arrived at the shelter, he saw that there were people inside. Unfortunately, terrorists had thrown a grenade into the shelter, and they had all been murdered.

A little later an army vehicle pulled up to a stop near them. "We have a badly injured soldier who needs to get to the hospital!" the driver said.

Moments later the wounded soldier was in the back of their ambulance, and Chezi was giving him first aid. The soldier had been shot in the head — there was an open wound and Chezi could see into his skull — and the soldier needed an emergency operation as soon as possible. Chezi did what he could for his patient, but he was limited since they weren't equipped for such an emergency. The soldier needed to be transferred to an intensive care ambulance.

Chezi called dispatch. "Where's the closest intensive care ambulance?"

"The closest intensive care ambulance is situated at the entrance to the Magen David Adom station in Sderot."

"By then we knew what was happening in Sderot," Chezi says. "We knew about the shootings and the terrorists. There was no question that Sderot had turned into a very dangerous place to be. But there was a soldier lying on the stretcher in my ambulance, and I didn't want him to die. So David and I decided that we were going to take him to the Magen David Adom station, come what may.

"'David,' I said, 'when we get into Sderot, press that gas pedal to the floor. Do not stop for anything. Got it?'

"'Got it.'

"'Then let's go.'"

Waze wasn't functioning, making it more difficult for David to figure out the way. Meanwhile, Chezi was busy using something called an "ambu bag," or a self-inflating bag. This is a handheld device that's commonly used to help patients breathe when there is no access to a ventilator or other source of oxygen.

They could hear the shooting. There was no question that fierce battles were being fought close by.

"David, listen," Chezi said. "Floor the gas pedal and drive straight down the road as fast as you can!"

"Waze isn't working," David shouted back. "How will I know whether to make a right or a left?"

"I'll look out the window and tell you when to make a turn."

"When we reached the entrance to the MDA station," Chezi says, "the soldier was still breathing. He was still with us. I felt like he was talking to me with his eyes. He was staring at me, and it was clear that he was trying to communicate something to me. An intensive care ambulance from United Hatzalah was waiting right where we had been told it would be, and we transferred the patient into the next ambulance, where a paramedic immediately began intubating him. Moments later they drove away with the patient, probably heading to one of our helicopters.

"We spent a few minutes cleaning up the ambulance before turning around and driving back to Cheletz to do it all over again."

CHAPTER EIGHTEEN

A Pile of Mattresses

On the way to pick up more wounded soldiers, Chezi and David stopped at a junction. There were two Yamam (special-forces police) officers standing there. Not far away, an army tank was stranded at the side of the road. They had seen it on one of their earlier trips that day, but they hadn't paid it any attention. On a normal day, seeing a tank just sitting on the side of the road would have made a big impression. But there was nothing normal about that day.

Chezi and David got out of the ambulance. Chezi went back to looking at the cars and bodies, hoping to find someone still alive that he could treat. David meanwhile struck up a conversation with the Yamam officers.

"I was still schmoozing with the officers," David says, "when I noticed a high-ranking army officer standing a little farther down the road. He was standing behind the tank — the tank that had broken down — and motioned at me to walk in his direction.

"I remember thinking at the time, *He probably got hurt in the tank accident. He obviously needs my help.*

"I had no idea what was going on behind the tank. It was very wide and obstructed my view completely. But I wasn't thinking about that. The only thing on my mind right then was walking down the highway and over to the army officer so that I could find out what he needed and help him.

"I was about to start walking. But then, for no real reason that I could put my finger on, I turned to the two Yamam officers.

David Bader

"'Hey, guys, you see that officer standing there behind the jeep?'

"'Yes, what about him?'

"'He's motioning me to come over to him. Can you come along with me for protection? From what I understand, there are a lot of terrorists running around in this area.'

"The three of us began walking in the direction of the army officer.

"The next thing I knew someone was shooting at me."

The shots were coming from a machine gun that was mounted on top of a car that had been concealed behind the tank.

A fraction of a second later, David realized that all of those bullets were aimed at him, and he couldn't understand why soldiers in the Israeli army were shooting at a medic who had arrived at the scene in an ambulance.

Ribbono shel Olam, why are soldiers from our side shooting at me?

David called dispatch and yelled at the top of his lungs, "They're shooting at me! They're shooting at me!"

"Who is shooting at you?"

David had no way to explain who was shooting at him or why. He himself didn't understand what was going on. It took about fifteen seconds for him to grasp that he had read the situation wrong and that the high-ranking army officer motioning him over on the road wasn't an officer at all, but a terrorist, and the soldiers surrounding the car also weren't soldiers; they, too, were terrorists. And they were all shooting at him because he was a Jew and they were terrorists who wanted to kill as many Jews as they could.

"I have no way to explain why the bullets didn't hit me," David says. "I have no way to explain it because there's no clear explanation, and yet nothing happened to me, and none of the bullets caused me any harm."

While David was disoriented when he suddenly found himself under fire, the officers beside him maintained their composure and started giving David clear orders.

"Run to your left!" they shouted. "Stay near the tank. That way the tank will be between you and the terrorists, and they won't be able to hit you."

David obeyed immediately and ran as close as he could to the side of the tank. Meanwhile, the police officers swung into action. There's no question that Hashem was on their side. They fought the terrorists with bravery and professionalism, and the entire battle barely lasted a minute or two. When the dust cleared and the fight was done, there were two special-forces police officers standing on the road and five dead terrorists — including the one who had been pretending to be a high-ranking officer. He would never pretend to do anything ever again. His days of acting on the stage of terror were over, and his day of judgment had arrived.

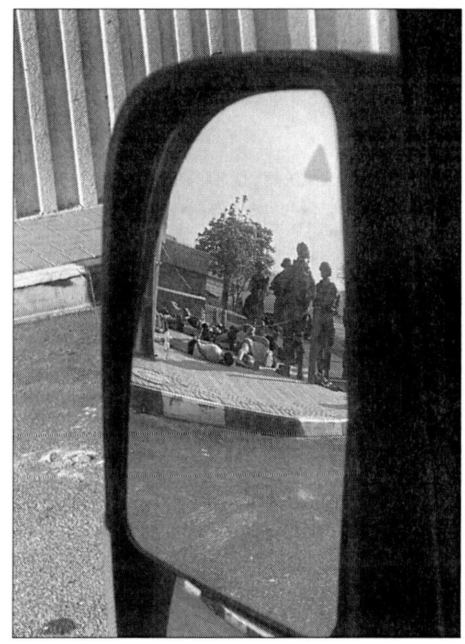
Terrorists in the rear-view mirror

"Had I not asked those two Yamam officers to join me on my walk," David says fervently, "I would have been killed by terrorists masquerading as members of the IDF. But Hashem in His infinite kindness and wisdom put a dose of fear in my heart and I made my request to the Yamam officers, and they agreed to come with me — and somehow all the bullets that were shot at us missed and nobody got hurt…

"This, my friends, is what is called a miracle. Plain and simple.

"The *pasuk* states, '*Ki malachav yetzaveh lach lishmorcha b'chol derachecha* — He will charge His angels to protect you in all your ways …' That's the way it was for us, for all the volunteers of United Hatzalah, on the day the world lost its mind."

"All of us knew that we were taking a chance. It's not that we didn't understand what we were doing. We weren't oblivious to the dangers. All of us wanted to return home to our families. At the same time, we felt that the risks we were taking were acceptable because it was those risks that were giving us the opportunity to remove four critically wounded soldiers at a time from danger and save their lives.

"Yes, we knew it was dangerous, but we couldn't turn away when Hashem was giving us the chance to save so many of our brothers and sisters."

On a normal day such an adventure would have put an end to any other plans a person might have. But it wasn't a normal day, and there was no time for them to go into shock. Not with the mission they had been given from above.

For the next few hours, they ferried wounded soldiers to the hospital. At first they were stopped, and four injured soldiers were transferred into their ambulance.

"We drove them to Soroka Hospital in Beersheva," says Chezi. "I will never forget that ride because the soldiers were in terrible pain and begging us for relief, but there was nothing I could do for them because only

Chezi

paramedics are allowed to administer drugs and we had only basic first aid with us."

They tried taking the soldiers to Cheletz, where Dr. Adam Ballin was in charge of operations. Chezi briefed him on the situation, but he was all out of medicine and had nothing left to give them. Hearing that, Chezi and David immediately left Cheletz for the hospital. Fifteen minutes into the journey, Chezi asked David to switch places with him. He just couldn't bear to listen to their cries anymore. David agreed, and Chezi took his place at the wheel while he took Chezi's place in the back of the ambulance.

After they dropped off the soldiers at Soroka, they were sent to Netivot and once again were asked to take four soldiers to the hospital. This time they were female soldiers, and each of them had been wounded from fragments of a grenade that had been thrown at them.

Chezi asked them when the attack happened.

"At seven in the morning," one of them answered. "That's when the terrorists came."

They recounted that they had done their best to hold off the terrorists, but at some point the enemy succeeded in breaching their lines, and that's when they threw the grenade at them. They had been injured by the fragments all over their bodies, from head to toe.

"What did you do then?" Chezi asked.

"It was obvious that the terrorists were going to kill every soldier, so we ran into one of the rooms and hid under a huge pile of mattresses. Then we heard the terrorists entering the building. We heard them singing and dancing. We also heard them shooting our friends. We stayed hidden beneath the pile of mattresses and prayed to G-d to save us from the animals who wanted to kill us.

"They were laughing and we were crying. Silently."

The soldiers stayed under the mattresses for hours until they felt it was safe to come out. Since they had been hiding until then, they hadn't been able to let their families know that they were okay. They didn't have their phones with them, and Chezi and David were more than happy to give them theirs.

"I don't need to describe the happiness, relief, and gratitude that their families felt when their phones rang and their daughters were calling to let them know that they were still alive," Chezi says.

Another moment of pure beauty in a day of stormy darkness.

Fifteen minutes later Chezi and David dropped them off at the hospital. Then they turned around and went back in again.

Soon they picked up two more soldiers — one with a bullet hole in the stomach and another with a bullet hole in the back. They drove them to the helicopter base at Sdei Teiman so that they could be transported to the hospital by helicopter.

They ended up driving back and forth for hours, doing their utmost to save as many lives as they could.

On Sunday morning Chezi and David were driving down the highway in the middle of the day when a car stopped and the passengers asked for assistance. Their friend had been at the festival and they had been looking for him for hours.

"We managed to locate his car using the GPS chip that insurance companies use to locate a car when it's been stolen," they said.

"Where is it?"

"Near here, right at the edge of the forest."

"Is your friend inside?"

"No, but we know that his phone isn't far away."

"Where is it?"

"A short distance inside the forest."

"Why don't you go to it?"

"We're afraid to go by ourselves. There's been a lot of shooting in the area, and terrorists could be hiding in the bushes."

Chezi and David agreed to go with them. The four of them went into the forest and managed to find the friend's body lying not far away, and they carried it back with them to the ambulance.

"If we hadn't gone in that day," says Chezi, "there's a good chance that no one would have been able to find him afterward because he was lying in the middle of nowhere. But his friends cared enough to go searching for him, and we cared enough to go with them and bring him out. Now at least he would merit a Jewish burial.

"This is what I meant when I said that the risks were worth it. Yes, it was dangerous. But on the other hand, how many times in life does a person get a chance to fulfill the mitzvah of dealing with a *meis mitzvah*?"

CHAPTER NINETEEN

Close Call

On Tuesday Chezi was on an ambulance shift to the city of Ashkelon. That morning, another volunteer, who lives in Sa'ad, a religious kibbutz near Kfar Aza and one of the only places in the area that survived intact on Simchas Torah, asked if he could borrow Chezi's Hatzalah vehicle. He had to bring medicine to survivors of the Hamas attack who had been evacuated to hotels in the Dead Sea area. Since he was joining an ambulance crew, Chezi agreed.

Car damaged by rocket

Miraculous moment...

The volunteer drove over to Kfar Aza to retrieve the medicines that people had left in their homes and parked the car in what he imagined was a safe spot. A short while later, a fierce battle broke out between the soldiers outside Kfar Aza and a group of terrorists who hadn't yet been eliminated.

It wasn't long before a tank arrived at the scene of the battle. Chezi's friend was still sitting in the car with another volunteer when the tank suddenly began backing up toward them without any warning. The driver of the tank was moving quickly and was unable to see the car behind him. Chezi's friend realized that he was in real danger of being crushed alive by an Israeli tank.

As the tank continued backing up, inching closer and closer, they were sure that the tank was going to crush them to death.

But no.

The tank crushed the front of the car but stopped short of crushing the rest of it — mere millimeters from where the two of them were sitting.

It was yet another miracle in a war that was filled with miracles from start to finish. If the tank had moved any faster and gone just a little further, the two of them would have been killed.

But the driver didn't back up quickly, and the story ended as it did — with the sole damage being to Chezi's United Hatzalah vehicle.

"Looking at the picture of my crushed car," Chezi says, "I couldn't help but remember how many calls I had gone on with that car and how many times it had helped me carry out my missions.

"There was another thought coming through as well: the fact that the car had come to me through the efforts of my good friend Yaakov Shwekey. Our friendship goes back many years — back to when he was just starting out in the music business, and I was working as an event planner who organized a lot of events in Israel for the Syrian community in the States. During those years, we did a lot of work together and became close.

"Yaakov also developed a beautiful relationship with Eli Beer and United Hatzalah, performing at several of the organization's Chol HaMo'ed concerts. But it wasn't only about the concerts. It was a real relationship — a real connection.

"Let me give you an example of what I mean. It's a story about Yaakov, his wife, Jenine, and the connection between what they do and United Hatzalah."

The story begins with a wonderful individual and a real *baal chesed* named Simcha Shain. Simcha is a paramedic and a Lakewood Hatzolah volunteer who is constantly busy saving lives. He lives in Lakewood and owns a company called Paraflight, which transports patients to the best medical care anywhere in the world. When someone needs to get to another city or country and can't travel on their own because they need constant medical care and attention, Simcha Shain will make sure that they reach their destination in the best condition possible. (He's also the paramedic whom Eli Beer asked to accompany him back to Israel after he recovered from Covid.)

Simcha accompanies patients because that's his job and *parnassah*, but he also does this on numerous occasions for *chesed*, which is why at times he serves as an air-based paramedic for Hatzolah, as well as for Chai Lifeline. Since Simcha is always flying, it makes sense that many of his stories happen to him while in the air or in foreign countries.

Like the story that involved the Shwekey family, the bar mitzvah of a boy named Eli, and a breathing tube.

But it would probably be a good idea if we just started at the beginning, and the beginning in this case starts with the Special Children's Center in Lakewood.

The Special Children's Center is based in Lakewood, New Jersey, and was founded by Jenine Shwekey, Chaya Bender, and Mimi Bloch. It's a place where parents of special needs children can send their kids with complete confidence that they will receive incredible care and love. And every year The Center takes a group of children on a trip to Eretz Yisrael, and Simcha Shain accompanies them as the in-house paramedic.

In the summer of 2017, everyone was looking forward to the trip even more than usual because they were going to be celebrating the bar mitzvah of a boy named Eli. Eli has Down syndrome, and he had been waiting for a very long time to be able to put on his tefillin for the first time at the Kosel. His father was planning to fly in from the States together with Eli and his mother, intent on being there with his son when he donned tefillin while standing at the Western Wall. But Eli's grandfather passed away just after they left for the trip, and Eli's father learned of his own father's passing right after his arrival to Eretz Yisrael on Tuesday.

Eli's father stayed in Eretz Yisrael for the burial, which took place the next night, and then returned to the States to sit shivah with the rest of his family members. Since Eli's father couldn't be at the Kosel to help his son put on tefillin for the first time, Yaakov Shwekey stepped in.

When the children arrived at the Kosel, they danced to the accompaniment of singing, shofar blasts, and musical instruments. Once they had made their way to the Kosel, they began their own minyan. The plan was to celebrate the bar mitzvah at the Wall, and then they were scheduled to drive to an army base about forty minutes away.

The trip was planned down to the minute, which meant that they were going to leave exactly when scheduled so that they would be able to get to the next stop on their itinerary on time.

"The davening was almost over," Simcha says, "when I happened to turn around, and noticed a young boy standing with his father not far away. The two of them were clearly not religious, but the boy was wearing tefillin and had a tallis wrapped around his shoulders. It was obvious that he, too, was there to celebrate his bar mitzvah, but unlike Eli, who was accompanied by a group of friends and well-wishers, this boy and his father seemed to be alone."

It was clear to Simcha that they didn't know what to do, and since no one had approached them and offered guidance, they were just going to leave and that would be the end of the boy's big religious moment. He would probably never put on tefillin again or find out what being a bar mitzvah really meant. Action was needed and Simcha took it.

"How are you doing?" Simcha said to them after introducing himself.

"Today is my son's bar mitzvah," the father replied. "But we were just about to leave."

"You can't leave," Simcha said. "Your son should have a real bar mitzvah celebration!"

"That's okay. We're good."

"No, you really have to have a proper bar mitzvah celebration. Don't go anywhere!"

Simcha ran over to Yaakov and said, "We have to make this kid a proper bar mitzvah. Let's invite him to join our minyan and give him an *aliyah*."

"No problem," Yaakov said. "Let's do it!"

This was no simple matter because it meant pushing off their departure time — which played havoc to the way the trips were run — but everyone understood that this was a once-in-a-lifetime opportunity. So it was that they didn't leave on time and instead spent the next forty minutes singing and dancing with the boy and his father, intent on giving him a bar mitzvah celebration that he would remember fondly for the rest of his life.

When the second bar mitzvah was winding down, Simcha Shain went outside the Old City walls to wait for the bus. It wasn't long before someone came running over to him to call him back. Something had happened and he was needed immediately!

One of the boys on the trip — his name was Baruch — needed to be on a ventilator wherever he went. Without it, he couldn't breathe properly. Something had happened to his ventilator, and it wasn't working. Simcha came running, examined the ventilator, and saw that the plastic tubing that connected the breathing tube to the ventilator had been nicked (probably by a passerby who had unknowingly brushed up against Baruch) and was now cracked and unusable.

"How much time can you manage being off the ventilator?" Simcha asked Baruch.

"Ten minutes."

"No problem. We can get to the Inbal Hotel from the Kosel in ten minutes."

Baruch had a spare breathing tube back at the hotel. The clock was ticking and they were off.

Simcha scooped Baruch into his arms and ran out of the Kosel area, together with Baruch's father, who'd also come on the trip. When he reached the street, he saw an older couple getting into a taxi cab. He told them that he and Baruch had to take it because it was a matter of life and death.

"Inbal Hotel," he told the driver. "And you have to get us there in under ten minutes!"

Simcha and Baruch got into the back seat, Baruch's father sat in the front, and off they went.

They drove through the gates of the Old City, made a right, and drove about two hundred feet, where they promptly came to a halt — because traffic was at a complete standstill. Baruch was showing signs of having difficulty breathing, so Simcha took out what is commonly known as an "ambu bag," or a self-inflating bag — a handheld device commonly used to help patients breathe when they don't have access to a ventilator or other source of oxygen. Baruch took a little breath every thirty seconds, but there was no question that they needed to get him to his hotel quickly.

Simcha got out of the cab and ran a little bit up the road. It didn't take him long to see that it had been shut down completely and that there was no chance of the traffic easing up in the near future.

Not knowing what else to do, Simcha called Dovie Maisel.

"Dovi, I need your help!"

"Sure, what do you need?"

"I need you to send an ambucycle to the Inbal Hotel. The driver will need to find a way into this room" — he gave Dovie the room number — "and pick up a suitcase on the bed that has ventilator tubing inside it. The second he has the suitcase, the driver has to hurry to where I'll be waiting, two hundred feet from the gates of the Old City leading to the Kosel."

Suddenly Simcha heard sirens from behind them. He turned around and saw a police vehicle approaching. The police officer was driving on the sidewalk and cut in front of the taxi. It was then that Simcha saw that in the back seat of the vehicle were Jenine Shwekey and Chaya Bender. In the front seat was sitting the chief of the police station at the Kosel.

It seemed that the Shwekeys had met the police chief the night before, when Yaakov had performed at a concert at the Kosel in honor of Yom Yerushalayim, and he was more than happy to do anything he could to help the young boy who couldn't breathe.

"Bring the boy into the police car," they told Simcha.

"Baruch is staying in the taxi," Simcha said. "You can lead us out, but he is not getting out of the taxi. It's too dangerous to move him!"

While all this was happening, Dovie sent a volunteer from United Hatzalah over to the Inbal Hotel to pick up the breathing tube. Later the people at the front desk related how a man had suddenly come running into the hotel wearing a motorcycle helmet on his head and screaming that he needed to get into a particular room immediately.

"You can't get into the room," they tried telling him, but the volunteer from United Hatzalah wouldn't take no for an answer and told

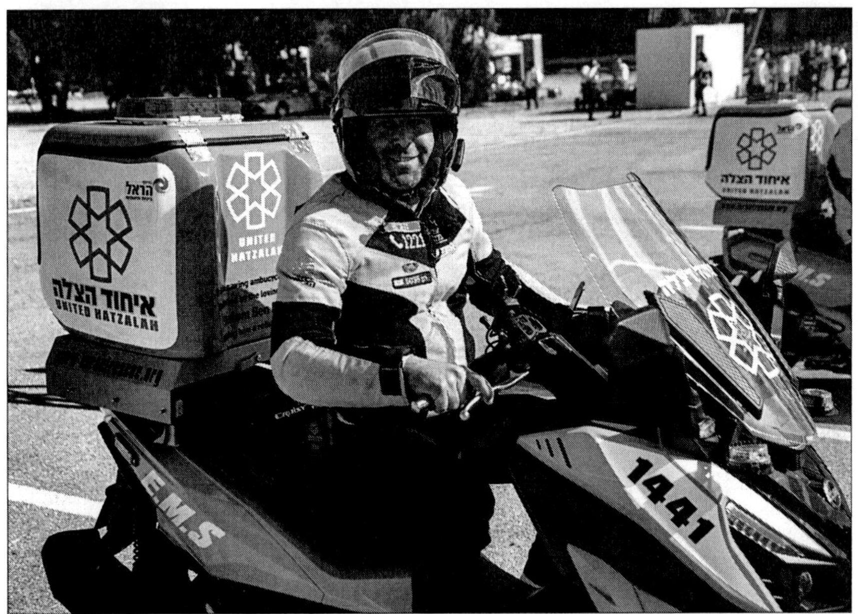

United Hatzalah volunteer

them that they had better open the door and help him get the breathing tube that he needed — unless they wanted their guest to die.

In the end, the hotel staff opened the door to the room and allowed the man from United Hatzalah to take the equipment he needed.

Traffic was still at a complete standstill when the ambucycle came speeding toward them, sirens blaring, lights flashing. Where the police were stuck in their place, United Hatzalah was able to move — and able to move fast.

"Had we left the Kosel when we were originally supposed to," Simcha says, "there is a good chance that we would have been on the highway, far from the Inbal Hotel and the extra breathing tube. While it's possible that Baruch might have recognized the problem before we left, it's also possible that he would have figured it out when it was too late.

"But because Yaakov and Jenine had agreed to push off the visit to the army base in order to provide a nonreligious boy with the bar mitzvah celebration of a lifetime, we were still within driving distance from the hotel when we realized that there was something wrong, and we were able to send a Hatzalah volunteer to pick up the equipment we needed.

United Hatzalah volunteer on his ambucycle

It was a true example of the importance of caring for another Jew. It was also a beautiful example of how United Hatzalah can be counted on to get anything done — even entering a hotel room when needed."

Getting back to Chezi's car — a car that he had driven to go out on more than a thousand emergencies, a car that was always being utilized for important mitzvos — you could say it was a real mitzvah mobile.

"I want you to understand something," Chezi says. "The car I drove had been donated to United Hatzalah by a donor named Sam Rosenberg and his wife, who give a lot of money to the Children's Center of Lakewood, which is run by Jenine Shwekey. That it came from such a source meant that the car possessed the kind of merits that would protect its driver — tank or no tank, war or no war. And that is exactly what happened on the day it was almost crushed by a tank. Because that story could have easily ended in the worst kind of tragedy. But it didn't. And I attribute that to the source of the car and where it had come from."

When asked what he felt were the scariest moments of their time down south, Chezi and David gave it a few seconds' thought before answering.

"For me, there were three very scary moments," Chezi replied. "The first was when we were driving through Sderot on the morning of Simchas Torah. There was so much shooting around us and it seemed like every second might be our last.

"The second moment that shook us up was when David almost got killed by the Hamas terrorist who was impersonating an IDF officer. Besides the fact that he was almost killed, we had driven along the same road earlier. We had seen that tank and had passed by it, and we realized that they could have tried to kill us then. But they didn't succeed because Hashem didn't allow it."

"And the third scary moment?"

"That happened at the entrance to Kfar Aza. A group of ambulances were parked there, and we were just standing around, when a car driven by a Shabak agent pulled up. The driver told us to get out of the open because there were about fifty terrorists across from us hiding in the orchard. I remember the soldiers taking up positions and pointing their guns toward the orchard. Then another car driven by an agent pulled up, and the driver told the soldiers that there were terrorists hiding on the other side as well. I remember thinking, *What on earth are we doing in such a place?*

"The rest of the time we didn't let ourselves think too much. Besides, we were too busy to think."

Chezi and David would undoubtedly be talking about what happened on Simchas Torah for the rest of their lives. When they will be eighty years old, they will tell their grandchildren and great-grandchildren about what happened on Simchas Torah 2023.

"You know what *was* going through my mind the entire day?" Chezi adds. "The fact that I hadn't been able to go to shul to say *Yizkor* for my mother."

It was true. He had been just a little busy. But there is no doubt at all that his mother up in Heaven was very happy that he spent the entire day saving lives even though it meant he couldn't be in shul to say *Yizkor*. Saving Jewish lives is the greatest *zechus* that a son could do for his mother, and there is no question in my mind that Chezi made his mother very proud that day.

A Miraculous Moment

The person who related the following story heard it from the protagonist himself. This is the way the man told his story:

I was at the festival in Re'im along with twelve of my friends. An hour and a half before Shabbat started, I began having this really bad feeling. You see, after Yom Kippur this past year, I resolved to keep every Shabbat until the end of Simchat Torah. The

Shabbat of Simchat Torah was the last one that I had committed to keep.

I said to myself, *This is what you promised Hashem, and you must keep your word like a real man!*

I decided that I was going to keep my word, come what may.

I turned to my friends and told them that I was going to leave. Then I begged them to come and celebrate Shabbat with me — at my expense. I'm talking about a group of guys of whom not one was *shomer Shabbat*. For some inexplicable reason, seven of my friends agreed to come with me and get a taste of what it means to keep Shabbat.

Now the challenge became finding an apartment that we could book so close to Shabbat.

I quickly did a search on Booking.com and found an apartment that was located in nearby Ashkelon. The owner even offered to order catered food for us as well.

We left the festival and arrived at the apartment just thirty minutes before sundown. That night I had a dream. A dream that shook me to the core.

In the dream I saw a childhood friend of mine. His name was Yitzchak Ben Yosef and he was from Yerushalayim. Yitzchak drowned in the Kinneret in 2017. Now he was coming to me in a dream.

"Daniel," he said, "you should know that what you did today — leaving the festival and going to Ashkelon for Shabbat — caused such an uproar in Heaven and that it's only because of your adherence to Shabbat that you were saved!"

Obviously I didn't really understand the meaning of the dream when I woke up, but it would all become clear very soon.

In the morning we were awakened by sirens, but I still didn't understand the full implications of what my friend had come to tell me. It was only later that we heard about the massacre, and then I understood beyond a shadow of a doubt why I was still alive. To my great sorrow, five of my friends remained at the festival. Two of them were taken hostage by the terrorists. The other three were killed. I attended their funerals.

Today my friends and I are keeping Shabbat. We were fortunate to see the power of Shabbat, and we can say in the clearest way that "More than we safeguard Shabbat, Shabbat safeguards us."

CHAPTER TWENTY

The Shabak Agent

Yisroel Biton and Akiva Kaufman both live in the city of Bnei Brak. Both are married with children. Both are hardworking young men in their twenties. And both are volunteers for United Hatzalah.

Yisroel Biton had been away with his family at a bed and breakfast up north during Chol HaMo'ed Succos and only returned home right before Simchas Torah so they could spend Yom Tov in their friendly neighborhood shul. Yisroel was looking forward to dancing and singing with his friends, having a little *l'chaim*... But the Simchas Torah he was so anticipating turned out to be a very different Simchas Torah than expected.

"The first siren started to wail at six thirty in the morning," Yisroel says. "I didn't hear it. I woke up an hour later, and from the sound of things, I figured there was a good chance that rockets might end up falling in the Tel Aviv area and I should be ready for anything.

"I got out of bed and got dressed. My first instinct was to put on my Yom Tov clothes. Then I decided that maybe that wasn't such a good idea, and I put on weekday clothes instead. Somehow I knew that I was going to be working very hard that day and needed to be wearing the kind of clothing that would give me freedom of movement."

When he heard from someone that a rocket had landed in Tel Aviv, Yisroel called his friend and fellow volunteer Akiva Kaufman, and they drove together to Tel Aviv on his Hatzalah ambucycle. When they arrived, they could see that one building where the rocket had fallen had suffered immense damage, but thankfully, only the building had been affected and no one had been hurt.

"While we were very happy that nothing serious had occurred," Yisroel says, "I was feeling unsettled by the constant sirens and the booms coming from the Iron Dome shooting down the rockets. Even more unsettling was when we discovered that members of Hamas were riding around the south attacking every town and village where they could gain entry. Soon we learned that vans filled with terrorists were driving through the streets of Sderot!

"It sounded like something out of a war movie. But it was unfortunately all too true.

"I looked at my friend Akiva. 'We need to get over to the Hatzalah warehouse on Jabotinsky Street and pick up bulletproof vests and helmets. Then we need to go down south as soon as possible!'

"He agreed. I called another volunteer who owns a van, and we discussed the situation. In the end, we decided that we would all meet and then drive down south together in his van. A fourth volunteer found out and asked to join us."

Three of the four volunteers driving together had guns, and at first, as they drove from the center of the country toward the south, the guns were still in their holsters. They tried to imagine what they would be seeing when they got there, but whatever they imagined ended up being light-years away from the reality.

They were driving on Route 34 toward Sderot when they saw an army jeep coming toward them. Recognizing them as medical personnel from the light on their roof, the driver of the jeep stopped, and they found themselves treating their first patient of the day. He had been shot and was seriously injured. They immediately got to work, bandaging him and administering first aid. They reported the incident to the United Hatzalah dispatch center, and an ambulance arrived to take the wounded man to the hospital.

Having dealt with their first emergency, they were ready to continue onward, but they had barely gotten back into the van when another jeep pulled up next to them. This time the patient had been shot in the legs. Once again they sprang into action and treated him until another ambulance arrived.

"Under normal circumstances," Yisroel says, "every one of these incidents would have been major news — gunshot wounds are taken very seriously. But this wasn't a normal situation, and there were way too many such events for each of them to be publicized."

Standing on the highway, the four United Hatzalah volunteers deliberated over their next move. The jeeps they were encountering were obviously coming from somewhere. Should they head in that direction or stay where they were? Akiva wanted to stay. It was quiet and safe, and they were able to do good work without endangering themselves. The other three were having none of that. They wanted to get into the van and drive to wherever it was all happening.

It was three against one.

So they went.

It wasn't long before they arrived at the Sderot intersection. A fierce battle was taking place at the Sderot police station a hundred yards away. By now the only patients who were being handed over to medics were those who had been heavily wounded. Everyone else was told to sit down and wait until someone was free to take care of them. It was a chaotic scene, and everyone was making decisions on the spot.

Yisroel Biton joined a police ambulance and accompanied a heavily wounded patient out of the area. His friends did the same for other wounded people. Everyone was doing their best to help whoever they could. About two hours later the team got back together, and they left Sderot and headed further south for the Sha'ar HaNegev intersection.

"It was at that point," Yisroel Biton says, "that everything we thought we understood about what was happening blew up in our faces. Suddenly we realized that everything we had seen until now was just the preamble to what was to come.

"As we drove in the direction of Gaza, we saw what looked like a convoy of about fifty cars. Inside and around every car there were dead bodies. Later we figured out that all these people had been at the music festival near Kibbutz Re'im and had managed to get to their cars. The terrorists, pretending to be soldiers, blocked the road and created a traffic jam so that no one was able to move forward. When the terrorists felt the time was right, they gave an order and the terrorists opened fire on all the cars and the people standing outside on the street. Since they were coming from the festival, most of those who had been killed were young, and here and there you saw children as well. And in the middle of the road was a tank that had been hit by an RPG.

"There was also a vehicle with eight dead Arabs inside. They had obviously been workers with permits to work in Israel, and the terrorists had murdered them. No one was spared. They had come to kill, and that's what they did. And the entire time we were gaping at this hellish sight, not quite able to believe what our eyes were telling us, we could hear the sound of shooting and the rockets exploding everywhere. We could smell the nearby fields burning and taste the acrid flavor of the smoke billowing in the air. It was as if we had somehow stumbled into the middle of the war between Russia and Ukraine.

"The whole scene was like a glimpse of the apocalypse, the end of the world as we knew it. That all this was happening within the borders of Israel made it a million times worse.

"That's what we saw, heard, felt, smelled, and tasted at 10:50 on the morning of Simchas Torah 2023."

From Sha'ar HaNegev they continued driving on the highway. Up ahead they saw a Yamam vehicle. Suddenly the vehicle turned right, then left, before coming to a halt on the side of the road. The doors opened, and eight officers jumped out and took up fighting positions, their guns out and ready to shoot. Seconds later, another van came from the opposite direction. This van was filled with terrorists. Clearly, the officers had been told that the terrorists were heading in their direction, and seconds later a very fierce but very short-lived battle broke out between the Yamam officers and the terrorists, right in front of the team of United Hatzalah volunteers.

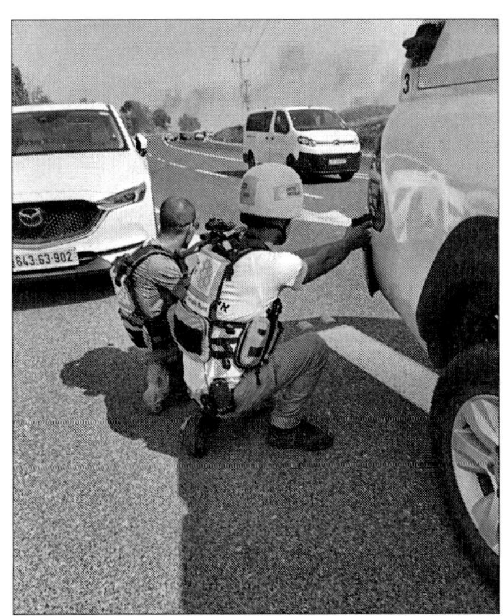

United Hatzalah volunteers in gunfight with terrorists

Yisroel, Akiva, and the other two volunteers who were with them got out of their van and got as low to the ground as possible. Just then one of the

Yamam officers shouted at them, "Be careful! You're exposed to the field on your left!"

There were open fields on both sides of the road. The volunteers who had guns shot in the direction of the field to their left, just in case. Meanwhile, the Yamam officers killed the group of terrorists, and moments later the battle had come to an end, and all the terrorists had been eliminated.

When the dust settled, the Yamam officers turned their attention to the volunteers from United Hatzalah. "*Chevrah*, you shouldn't be here now," one of them said. "This is a very dangerous area."

"We're medics," Yisroel explained, "and we're here to do our jobs — the same as you. You know how to fight, and we know how to treat people medically. We're here to do our duty as citizens of Israel."

"Alright, then, if you insist… Continue straight from here. Guns in your hands, bullets in the guns, and make sure you're ready for anything."

At Shuva Junction, the volunteers saw ten stretchers lying on the ground. They were occupied by soldiers, civilians, and foreign workers. It was a mini field hospital but lacking sufficient manpower to treat anyone who had been seriously injured.

"We got to work immediately," Yisroel says. "We treated anyone who had been lightly injured — and by lightly I mean they were bleeding but not heavily, or they had been grazed by shrapnel or bullets — and then we instructed them to sit on the side and wait until we dealt with those who were critically injured. We had to focus primarily on those who had been heavily wounded and were hovering between life and death.

"We turned to the medical personnel on the scene and asked them what the plan was for getting the wounded to the hospital. 'There is no plan,' we were told. 'We don't have any ambulances.'

"I looked at Akiva and the rest of my crew. 'If that's the case, then we'll just have to do it ourselves.'

"Now it was their turn to ask what I meant.

"'We have a van,' I said. "We'll take wounded patients to the hospital. It's not an ambulance, but we're trained medics and we'll do what we can to keep the patients alive until we get them to an ambulance or to the hospital.'

"Next I turned to Akiva. 'This is what we're going to do,' I said. 'We're four volunteers. Two of us will sit in the front. One will drive the van, and the other will have his gun out, ready for anything. The other two will get in the back with the patients.'

"Akiva got in the back. Then we moved the first stretcher into the van. It was too long and stuck out, which meant we couldn't close the door.

"'I'll also sit in the back,' I said. 'I'll keep my right foot on the stretcher to keep it from sliding out of the van. My other foot will be on the floor so that I can keep my balance while I point my gun outside the van.'"

Besides the soldier on the stretcher, Yisroel and the rest of his team took three other wounded soldiers. They would sit in the van's second row of seats.

Yisroel turned to one of the policemen in the area.

"Do you have any extra bullets for me?"

He looked at Yisroel. "Did you serve in the army?"

"Yes."

"You know how to shoot?"

"Yes."

"Okay, here are some bullets. If anything moves on the side of the road — shoot. Don't ask questions. Just shoot."

"Got it."

That was it. The plan was in place, and the United Hatzalah volunteers, in their makeshift ambulance, made the trip back and forth to various hospitals several times, with four wounded patients in the van each time.

At one point they returned to Shuva and found twelve women soldiers waiting there. They were barefoot and could barely move. It was obvious that they were in shock. Terrorists had attacked their base, and many of their friends had been killed. It was evident that the girls had been through a terrible trauma. There was no question that they needed to be taken to the hospital as quickly as possible.

Yisroel told them all to get into the van and they drove all twelve girls to the hospital at one time.

Wounded people kept appearing from different directions. One of the main sources were two cars that belonged to the Shabak — one a Volkswagen, the other a Mercedes. The cars had been bulletproofed, and were able to enter the battles zones and rescue wounded people under fire. They kept returning to Shuva with yet another group of seriously wounded soldiers, whom the volunteers transported to the hospital.

At one point, Yisroel approached one of the Shabak cars. He knocked on the window, and the Shabak agent looked at him through the bulletproof glass.

"He looked like the scariest guy you can imagine," Yisroel recalls. "He wore black from head to toe, and his face was covered with a ski mask so that only his eyes were visible. This way no one would be able to identify him. He was also outfitted with an array of weapons. The other Shabak agents all looked the same.

"They were fearsome creatures, and I was glad they were on our side.

"Under normal circumstances, I wouldn't have knocked on the car's window. Normally I would have stayed away from an agent of the Shabak. But these were not normal times, and so I knocked."

The Shabak agent opened the door. "What do you want?"

"You keep bringing wounded soldiers. I wanted to know where they're all coming from."

"I would be happy to take you guys along with me," the Shabak agent said, immediately understanding where the conversation was going, "but the area is too dangerous for me to allow it."

The agent left, pulling out into the road in a cloud of dust. Yisroel turned to the other volunteers on his team.

"Guys," he said, "get in the van. We're going in."

No one argued. They all knew that it was the right thing to do.

That was it.

They got into the van.

And then the angels in orange hit the road.

CHAPTER TWENTY-ONE

The Helicopter Exit

They turned right in the direction of Kibbutz Sa'ad and Kfar Aza, eventually coming to a halt not far from the entrance to the village. The sounds of battle were deafening. They could hear gunshots, explosions, anti-tank missiles, and who knew what else, and the smoke was thick and it was hard to breathe.

The Shabak agent who had refused to take them was standing at the entrance to Kfar Aza. The man was looking at him, and Yisroel Biton turned his head in the other direction because he didn't want the man to come over and scream at him for disobeying him.

The agent didn't scream at him. Instead he walked over to Yisroel and asked, "How long will it take you to drive to Shuva?"

"Six minutes."

"I need you to get a patient out of here. Take him to Shuva and hand him over to an ambulance. Then turn around and come back. I want you back here in twelve minutes!"

And Yisroel understood that the Shabak agent wanted them on his team.

It wasn't long before they fell into a rhythm. The two Shabak cars went into Kfar Aza, driving through the streets under heavy gunfire, and returned, again and again, with heavily wounded soldiers.

They were wounded in the worst ways. It was heartbreaking to see it. But Yisroel and his team didn't have time to focus on that. They had a job to do, and they were going to do it, come what may.

The wounded were transferred into their van, and they left for Shuva.

United Hatzalah vehicle and IDF tank — side by side...

Then they returned. Then they left again, making the journey over and over, delivering patients to the waiting ambulances and saving lives in the most literal sense of the word.

"One of the times that we were standing in front of the entrance and getting ready to load another patient," Yisroel recalls, "a tank came barreling out of Kfar Aza, clearly in a rush to get one of the crewmen to an ambulance. I don't know how it happened, but the tank driver must have been a little out of his mind with worry, because he released a bullet from one of his guns in the direction of the ground not far from us. Tank bullets are not like regular bullets and if that piece of metal had been any closer, we wouldn't be alive to tell the story. As it was, the bullet hit the ground, throwing up rocks and dirt in all directions.

"It was a very close call. Another beautiful miracle to inscribe on our minds for the rest of our lives."

Everything about the situation was insane. At one point, when Yisroel was busy with a patient, he heard the sound of shooting from about thirty yards away. He was focused on the patient, so he wasn't paying attention to what was going on around him — to the fact that a fully armed terrorist had somehow managed to approach and start shooting not far from where they were.

When Yisroel finally grasped what was happening, he called to his fellow volunteers, "Guys, is everything okay?"

They gave him a look — as if everything that had just occurred was the most normal thing in the world.

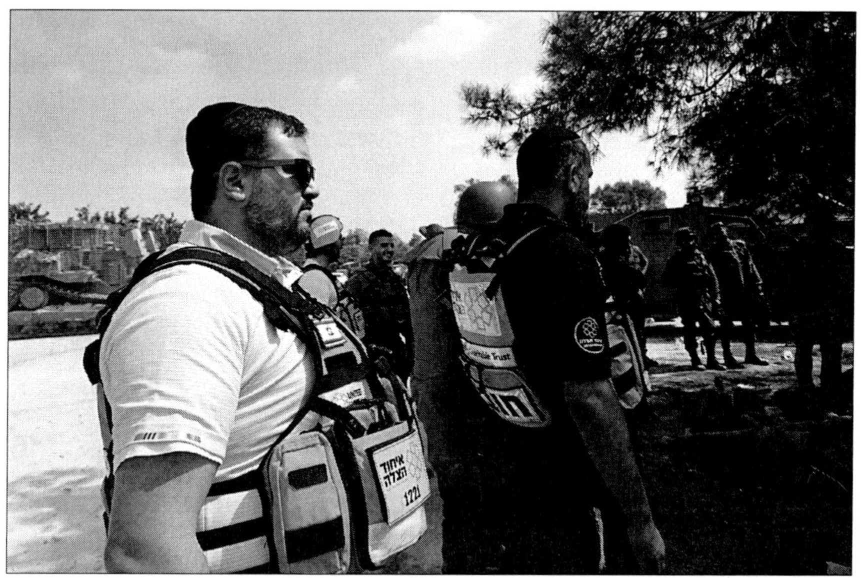

Terrorists under arrest

"He's been terminated."

"Who?"

"A Hamas commando."

It took Yisroel a few seconds to regain his composure after hearing that a fully armed terrorist had just been terminated so close to where they were situated.

Another miracle?

It certainly was.

"Many of the wounded were too far gone to help," Yisroel recalls. "So many brave soldiers were no longer alive when they were brought through the gates of Kfar Aza. So many soldiers who couldn't be taken to the hospital because they were no longer among the living. Do you know what it's like to see such young faces that would never grow old?"

Seeing those soldiers demonstrated to the United Hatzalah volunteers the immense *mesirus nefesh* of those fighting inside the village — and how so many were giving up their lives to protect their people.

Yet they had no time to mourn. They needed to work. They needed to become machines.

They needed to do the job.

With more wounded beginning to pour out from Kfar Aza, they were soon extremely busy. They worked in tandem with soldiers from Unit 669, the army's search-and-rescue unit, and did whatever they could to help.

"At some point," Yisroel says, "I reached out to Yoni Martin, the spokesman for United Hatzalah, and told him that we needed more ambulances and stretchers so that we could get the wounded out of the area and over to the hospitals. Otherwise, many more people were going to die. From what I understood, Eli Beer and Dovie Maisel were with him when I called and heard our conversation. I wasn't the only one begging the bosses at United Hatzalah to send in the troops, and not long afterward Aharon Ben Haroush gave the order, and a whole convoy of ambulances led by Avi Gian and Avi Yudkowski, who were riding in ambulance number one, came pulling up to Kfar Aza.

"Later I heard that the commander of Unit 669 sent a message to Eli Beer telling him that he had just had a meeting with other commanders and that he wanted to let Eli know how impressed they all were with the volunteers from United Hatzalah and he felt that they should be given commendations for valor shown under fire — like any other soldier who shows great courage and bravery on the battlefield."

At 6:50 p.m. a *Namer* (Leopard) emerged from Kfar Aza. A *Namer* is an armored personnel carrier, a large bulletproof vehicle that essentially looks like a small tank, and this particular *Namer* was carrying a man with a large hole in his shoulder and a terrible wound in his hand. He was in very bad shape. Yisroel decided that there was only one thing to do for him, and that was to use a technique known as packing. This means using a special pressure bandage that the medic needs to apply with his hand and can't release until he delivers the patient to the operating table.

They needed to take the patient to Cheletz, but all the ambulances had already left with other wounded. Someone had even taken their van to transport patients. Yisroel looked around, trying to figure out a solution. Then his eye fell on an army vehicle, the kind that's open at the back.

"Drive over here," Yisroel called to the soldier behind the wheel.

Moments later they were loading the stretcher with the wounded

An army jeep

soldier into the back of the vehicle. It was no simple matter because the stretcher was longer than the back of the vehicle, which meant that that the soldier's head and feet were sticking out of the two sides of the jeep. Akiva got on to hold on to the stretcher, while Yisroel kept his hand on the pressure bandage with one hand and held on to the other end of the stretcher with the other. With that, the driver took off down the road, driving what felt like a hundred miles an hour all the way to Cheletz.

As the jeep barreled down the highway, Yisroel looked at his friend and said, "Akiva, do you believe what we're doing right now?! Did you ever imagine us doing anything like this in our wildest dreams?"

"You have to understand something," Akiva said later. "Today, anyone working in the medical arena knows how many protocols there are in place for any move you take with a patient. There are a million rules dictating what a medic is allowed to do and what he's not allowed to do. In many cases, the protocol demands that a critically injured patient is allowed to be taken to the hospital only in an intensive care ambulance.

"In this case, Yisroel and I had a patient in the most serious condition — suffering from a near-fatal gunshot wound, unconscious, intubated. Yet here we were, two medics taking him to the hospital without a paramedic (whose training is more intensive than a medic's) in a vehicle in which the stretcher didn't fit. On top of all that, the sun was starting

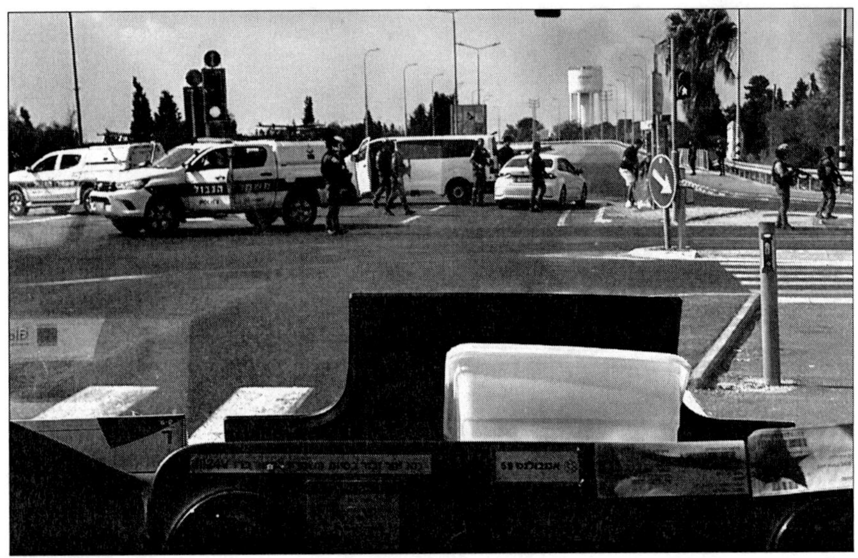

Down south — war time

to set, and darkness was beginning to settle down around us, and the driver was driving that jeep faster than a race car while swerving left and right so that he wouldn't drive over any of the bodies strewn on the road or hit any of the cars that would suddenly loom in the middle of the road. And all this was accompanied by the sounds of gunshots from the distance, as well as rockets landing and exploding, fields going up in flames, and clouds of smoke stinging our eyes.

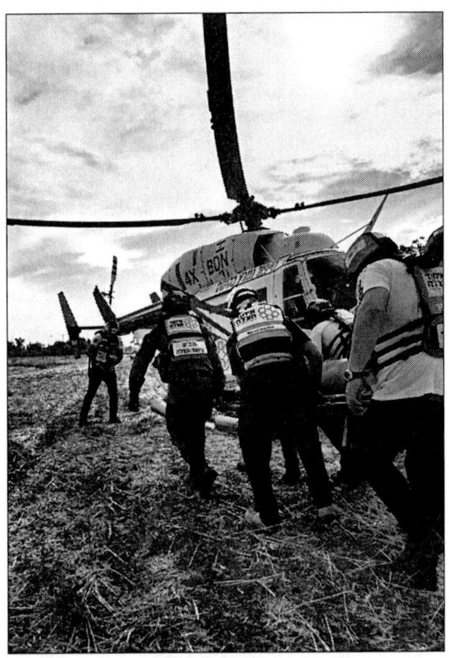

Ready to go...

"That ride felt like it took hours when in reality it was probably more like fifteen minutes. But that was our reality right then. A reality where we were occupying a whole different dimension, where time seemed to slow at times and fly by too fast at others, while the entire time we were trying to keep the injured man alive.

He was our patient, our responsibility, and we were determined to do whatever we could to keep him with us.

"And then finally there were lights in the road, and we could see the Cheletz intersection up ahead. A helicopter was ready and waiting for our patient. The engine was on, the rotors were turning, and everyone was ready to go. It was just that kind of night."

Soon the jeep pulled up alongside the helicopter, and people came rushing over to help unload the stretcher. The helicopter was making a lot of noise, and Yisroel had to yell at the top of his lungs just to be heard.

"Nobody take off the stretcher until I can come down with it!"

They took down the stretcher slowly and carefully, and then, when they were on the ground, Yisroel checked his vest to make sure that the gun he'd been carrying all day was still on his person and hadn't fallen. It was.

A paramedic appeared at his side. "What's his status?" the paramedic yelled over the noise of the helicopter.

Yisroel gave him an update. All the wounds and everything that had been done for the wounded man. It was very difficult to be heard.

"Okay, bring him onto the helicopter!"

Five people helped Yisroel and Akiva lift the stretcher and carry it onto the helicopter.

"It was my first time in one of Unit 669's helicopters," says Yisroel. "It was a huge monster of a helicopter. A massive, gigantic beast, capable of swallowing up large numbers of people and equipment. As we were setting down the stretcher, I could see that the ramp at the back of the helicopter was starting to close in preparation for takeoff.

"Suddenly I looked down at my vest and my heart almost missed a beat because I could see that my gun wasn't there. It must have fallen out of my vest as we were moving the stretcher from the jeep onto the helicopter. It was noisy as the engines warmed up and the propellers whirled around, and I hadn't heard the gun drop.

"'My gun fell out of my vest!' I shouted to the soldiers over the noise of the helicopter. 'My gun is missing!'

"We searched the helicopter. It wasn't there.

"'Listen,' I said, 'we're in the middle of a war. I need my gun. I can't afford to lose it. The police will give me a hard time, and I won't be able to get another one so easily. I have to get off the helicopter right now!'

"It was one of those moments in life when you have a split second to make a decision and you have to make the right one. I made my decision. I was getting off the helicopter.

"Grabbing the hand of the paramedic closest to me, I pressed his hand on the spot where I had been applying pressure on the soldier's wound and told him to take over for me.

"'Do not stop applying pressure for even a second!' I yelled.

"He nodded. He understood.

"Then Akiva and I jumped out of one of the side doors, because the back door was already closed, and immediately began searching for the gun. Suddenly an officer approached. He was holding a gun in his hand.

"'I think this is yours,' he said.

"I looked at the gun. It was an army-issued Glock 19. 'It's not mine,' I said. 'I have a Glock 43.'

"We continued searching. Thankfully we found my gun a few minutes later. The helicopter was long gone, winging its way through the air on the way to the hospital. I looked up at the black sky, periodically illuminated by a flash of red when a rocket was struck down by the Iron Dome, and I hoped that they would get there in time and save the soldier's life. We had done all we could. Everything that Hashem had given us the ability to do. The rest was up to Him."

Talk about anticlimax. Their hearts didn't stop racing for a long time after the helicopter took off. From Cheletz they returned to Kfar Aza and continued bringing out wounded patients until about five in the morning. They had been on their feet from seven thirty the previous morning — almost twenty-four hours straight.

At one point, a huge army vehicle pulled up nearby. It was almost as big as a truck. The driver called to Yisroel and Akiva in their ambulance.

"I need you to park in front of my vehicle," the driver requested when they had driven closer. "I don't want any of the soldiers here to see this."

"Why not?" Yisroel asked. "What's inside the truck?"

"Bodies of soldiers who were killed in battle."

"Why can't we leave them in the truck?"

"We need the stretchers for other patients."

They couldn't argue. It was true.

When they had parked according to the soldier's satisfaction, they all got out of their respective vehicles and the driver opened the back of his truck, which was filled with bodies. Bodies that had come from the battlefield. Bodies that had been hit by grenades and RPGs.

It was one of the worst sights a person can see. Israeli soldiers — soldiers from the best commando units in the IDF — dead in the back of the truck, and the driver didn't want the other soldiers to see them, because he knew it would destroy their morale. So instead he asked the members of United Hatzalah to help him take them off the truck and transfer them to a temporary holding area for bodies until they would be taken care of by the army's *chevrah kaddisha* unit.

Just when they thought they had seen everything there was to see, something else happened that made them realize that, no, there was more.

Yisroel turned to his friend Akiva (and there was no question that after their shared wartime experiences they would be best friends for life), and he said, "Akiva, when we take the stretchers off the truck, don't look at the bodies. Look at me and I will look at you."

"When we reached the spot that was designated for us to leave the bodies," Yisroel says, "we laid them on the floor and asked *mechilah* from each one because we didn't have time to lay them down as gently as we would have wanted and because we were leaving them there, even if temporarily, instead of bringing them straight to burial.

"'I'm sorry, my friend,' I said over and over. 'I'm sorry that we're in such a rush. Please forgive us if we didn't treat you with the dignity you deserve. You are a *gibbor Yisrael*, a hero of Israel, and I'm sure you'll be given a warm welcome up in Heaven. . .'

"One thing that really affected me was when Ro'i, one of the other volunteers who had come along with us, handed me a bag and told me to place it on top of one of the soldiers. I asked him what it was.

"'It's a part of his body that was detached from the rest during the battle.'

"There was nothing to say to that. I laid the bag on its owner and whispered a heartfelt apology. Then I leaned over him and I said, 'Goodbye, my friend. *Tzeischem l'shalom*.'"

That's the way it went for a while. So many bodies and so many rockets flying above them, and from time to time a rocket landed only a short distance away. They would hear shooting, and sometimes the soldiers there yelled at them to move because the terrorists were shooting from the bushes. But they continued doing what they had to do and didn't stop, despite the danger.

Yisroel was in the midst of treating one wounded soldier when a siren went off, and he knew that he needed to run to a shelter so that he wouldn't be hit by shrapnel.

"It was just me and him," Yisroel recalls. "Everyone else was in the shelter. I looked at the soldier and he looked at me. Then he opened his mouth and said, 'You're not going to leave me, right?'

"There was real fear in his eyes, and my heart went out to him. To be so wounded and so vulnerable… I gave him a clumsy hug — not easy with a bulletproof vest — and said, 'I'm with you until it's over. Don't worry.'

"And I stayed with him until everyone else came back."

Not long after that Ro'i told Yisroel Biton that he needed to go because his army unit was calling him to report to the field. So Yisroel and the rest of his team left for a few hours, promising themselves that they'd be back on the morrow.

And they were.

CHAPTER TWENTY-TWO

To Hide or to Fight?

They returned to Kfar Aza the next morning. Once again they were parked near the entrance to the village, and every so often more wounded soldiers were brought out and they had to decide whether to drive them to the hospital or whether they needed to be transported via helicopter because they were critically injured.

So it went for several hours, and then something frightening happened. Yisroel, Akiva, and another volunteer — also named Yisroel — were at the gas station just outside Kfar Aza, along with a group of soldiers. The soldiers explained to the United Hatzalah volunteers that twenty of them had gone into Kfar Aza to fight the terrorists earlier that morning and seven of their friends had been killed. The fighting was so bad that they lost the commander of their unit and his second-in-command as well.

"When we came out of Kfar Aza," one soldier related, "one of the commanding officers on the scene told us to come here and try to recover after what we just went through."

Meanwhile, Yisroel Biton was on the phone with his brother Moshe. While he was still on the phone, two soldiers suddenly came running and started screaming, "Everyone take cover! There's a group of terrorists heading in this direction!"

"Moshe," he said, "something is happening! I have to go!"

Yisroel hung up on his brother, and it goes without saying that Moshe called back a hundred times over the next twenty minutes. Meanwhile, both the United Hatzalah volunteers and the soldiers ran into the gas station coffee shop, heading for the store's safe room, which was filled with merchandise. Now it was absolutely packed with Hatzalah volunteers, four civilians who had been in the area, and about thirteen soldiers.

"I looked around me at all the people who had crammed into the safe room," Yisroel says, "and I realized that this was all wrong. What happened next was amazing — all the more so because it wasn't planned. In fact, I have no idea where it came from. Maybe it had to do with all the stories I had heard the day before about people who were killed while hiding in their safe rooms, and I understood that hiding from the enemy was not an option. The only choice was to stand and fight bravely with the help of Hashem.

"'*Chevrah*,' I called out, raising my voice above the din.

"Everyone looked in my direction.

"'*Chevrah*, what's going on here? Did we come here to hide or to fight?!'

"I pulled the gun out of my vest and loaded it. I made a thing out of it, instinctively knowing that seeing me get ready to fight would lift their morale. Then I said, '*Chevrah*, let's go. Everyone is going out! Five soldiers on the right. Five soldiers on the left. Three in the middle. I'm going with you. And, boys, if anything happens and anyone threatens us, we're going to take them down without asking questions!'

"For the next twenty minutes, we were each down on one knee, everyone on full alert, weapons out and ready for anything."

"I don't have a gun permit," Akiva later related, remembering the incident, "which means that I don't have a gun. When Yisroel gave that incredible speech, and everyone went with him to stand up to the threat and fight off the terrorists, I went into the manager's office. The computer that was sitting on the desk showed footage from the various cameras on the property.

"When I saw what was on the screen, I was literally shaking with fear. I took out my phone and typed out a short message to my father, telling him that he should start saying *Tehillim* right away. He responded immediately and asked where I was and what was happening.

"I tried to marshal my thoughts. The truth is, they were the thoughts of a person who feels like he's going to die at any second. I remember looking up at the ceiling and wondering if I could find a place to hide between the actual roof and the plaster work. Without a gun to protect myself, I felt like it was just me and the One above and that He was the only one I could rely on."

This soldier carried a small *Tehillim* with him. It stopped a bullet from hitting him.

They all waited, guns at the ready, and there was no question that if a terrorist would have approached them at that moment, he would have been welcomed with hundreds of bullets. Seconds later, they heard the sound of an army helicopter flying low over their heads. They barely had time to process what they were seeing when the helicopter sent missiles aimed at two vans filled with terrorists who had been making their way through the nearby orchards.

The missiles scored direct hits on the vans and blew them up on the spot. A few minutes later, another soldier came running over to report that the threat had been neutralized and that everyone could relax.

At that moment, Akiva exited the gas station store. "Yisroel," he said, "it's eleven o'clock at night, and I've had enough. Let's go home."

So they did, returning home to Bnei Brak and their wives and kids. But they came back the next day and the next, until the situation started to stabilize and their help was needed elsewhere.

There was no question in any of their minds that the things they saw and the miracles that happened to them would remain with them until the end of their days. It was just that kind of situation. And while those few days were some of the hardest and most challenging they would probably ever experience, there is no question that they would do it all over again.

"Because," Yisroel says, "we're United Hatzalah and that is what we do."

PART SIX
GEHINNOM ON EARTH

Why do You forget us forever, forsake us for so long?

— Eichah 5:20

Route 232 reminded of a computer game
where people kill other people and flip over their cars —
because that was exactly what we were seeing.

— Naomi Galeano,
United Hatzalah volunteer

CHAPTER TWENTY-THREE

The Name on the Sticker

Caryn Gale and Sergio Garelnik are a married couple who live in Modi'in in central Israel. They are also volunteers for United Hatzalah. They woke up at six thirty on the morning of Simchas Torah to the sound of thunderous explosions as the Iron Dome shot down a steady barrage of missiles. Being attacked by enemy missiles is unfortunately part of life in Israel, so they weren't overly concerned, though Caryn Gale didn't feel comfortable going for her morning walk that day. Instead she kept herself busy cutting up some vegetables for the *kiddush* that was going to be served later that day at their shul.

It wasn't long before both of them received messages from the head of their branch of United Hatzalah, Itzik Kara, instructing them to be on high alert. Since Itzik never sent out messages on Shabbos or Yom Tov unless it was absolutely necessary, they understood that the situation they were facing was very serious, and with missiles possibly landing in Modi'in, they needed to be available in case they were needed. Since all their children are married and out of the house, Caryn Gale and Sergio are free to do whatever they need to do without having to worry about the kids. This makes it easier for both of them to serve as volunteers.

When davening started, Caryn Gale told her husband to go to shul. "If a call comes in, I'll come with the car and pick you up."

"Don't you have to say *Yizkor*?" he asked her.

But Caryn Gale just asked him to take her vegetable platter to shul and said she would be in touch depending on the situation.

In the middle of Shacharis, Sergio felt his phone start to vibrate.

He went outside to check the message. It was from a paramedic who said that he was looking for an ALS (advanced life support) qualified driver to go down south. He also needed two EMTs.

Just to clarify how things work in the world of the medical support team, there are EMTs, there are paramedics, and then there are people who take a course that allows them to assist paramedics. It's the paramedics who are ALS qualified. Sergio had taken the course that put him between EMT and paramedic, which meant that he was an extremely qualified EMT who could assist a paramedic with an intubation or, if need be, administering lifesaving drugs to a patient.

Sergio has devoted much of his life to helping people and is a volunteer for both United Hatzalah and for Magen David Adom. He has years of experience, having been a member of Hatzolah when he lived in the United States. Caryn Gale is also a volunteer for United Hatzalah and has also undergone significant training. Of course, all this is in addition to their regular jobs. Bottom line, both Caryn Gale and Sergio are very busy people who go out of their way to contribute to the people of Israel in any way they can.

"When I saw the message," Sergio says, "I let Caryn Gale know what was needed, and we both decided to join the team and head down south."

"If I'm going to be honest," Caryn Gale said later, "we had no clue what we were getting ourselves into. If I had known what was going on down south...well, I don't know what I would have done."

But they didn't know, and off they went.

Caryn Gale and Sergio were instructed to drive to a United Hatzalah warehouse where they would pick up bulletproof vests and helmets. Caryn Gale thought that they would be heading to Ashkelon or Kiryat Gat to help extricate survivors from a building that had been hit by a rocket. They didn't fathom the truth about what awaited them down south on October 7. It was beyond imagination, beyond anything that anyone could ever conceive. At nine o'clock in the morning they were still blissfully unaware of the reality and the part that they were going to play in that reality.

"I had been dressed for Yom Tov," Caryn Gale recalls, "and I changed into something more practical for the day that lay ahead. Later I was very happy that I had chosen to wear black.

"The only food in the house was whatever I had cooked for Yom Tov, since I had used up all the nosh to make Simchas Torah *pekelach* for my grandchildren before Yom Tov. This meant that there were no cookies or potato chips for us to take, but I found a bag of lollipops in the closet and threw a huge handful of them into my bag, along with two bottles of water. I wasn't even sure why I took them. I had this vague thought that maybe I'd need some energy later on and the sugar would help. But the truth is, we weren't thinking much at the time. We were just going into action mode and trying to get ready as quickly as possible.

"We drove over to meet the ambulance and got suited up in our bulletproof gear. You can't imagine how heavy it felt on our shoulders and heads, but we ignored the discomfort and got in the ambulance. Moments later, Sergio had turned on the ignition, and we drove to pick up another volunteer. Then, all preparations done, we exited Modi'in and began driving south.

"It was the morning of Simchas Torah 2023, and we were about to pay a visit to Gehinnom on earth."

They were given instructions to rendezvous with the rest of the United Hatzalah teams at an intersection called Cheletz, which none of them — not even Itzik Kara, the head of United Hatzalah of Modi'in — had ever heard of. That, of course, would soon be remedied, and they would come to know it all too well.

A short while after they had begun driving, they removed the vests and helmets. They were just too uncomfortable to wear. But as they drove closer to Cheletz, they could literally see the rockets flying overhead, and they realized that they'd better pull over so that everyone could put their flak jackets and helmets back on.

"As soon as we arrived at Cheletz," Sergio says, "we were told to follow another ambulance in the direction of Sderot. Soon we were met by a team of Yamam officers, who told us to follow them to Sderot. The officers had a machine gun welded to the top of their vehicle, which made us realize that the situation was more serious than we thought. But the reality still hadn't registered."

That was about to change.

As they entered the city of Sderot, they saw dead bodies strewn on the side of the road.

"Itzik and I were sitting in the front of the ambulance," Sergio recalls, "which is why we were able to see the corpses on the sidewalks of a residential area. Caryn Gale was sitting in the back and couldn't really see anything, and I didn't tell her what we were passing right then."

Eventually, though, Caryn Gale peeked out and saw a dead body, wearing an IDF uniform. To her surprise, no one was covering the body or doing anything about it. But it didn't take them long to understand that no one was covering the body because there were too many people who had been killed.

"It was so bad," Sergio says, "that at some places I had to drive over the median in the middle of the road and drive down the wrong direction because there was a car with people who had been shot inside blocking traffic."

It was a war zone in every sense of the word. They followed the Yamam officers through the streets of the city and over to the police station. As they drove they saw bodies lying on the ground and soldiers running through the streets. The sound of shooting served as the soundtrack to it all.

They parked their vehicle and made their way to an area where a group of United Hatzalah volunteers had gathered, all still dressed in their Yom Tov clothing — white shirts and dark pants visible under their flak jackets. A few minutes later, a barrage of missiles started flying in their direction and everyone crammed into one of the public shelters on the road. When the sirens stopped wailing, they waited for another few minutes, then emerged.

"Once we were back on the road," Sergio said, "we met a vehicle that had a wounded patient for us. He was in critical condition."

"The ambulance was driving so fast that we couldn't even sit on the seats," Caryn Gale says, picking up the thread. "Instead I sat on the floor at the head of the patient. My job was to set up the oxygen for him — two bullets had struck him in the head (miraculously missing his brain), and it was very difficult to place the oxygen mask on his head because of all the bleeding. Meanwhile, Itzik and Naomi, another volunteer who'd joined them, were setting up IV lines and trying to get some meds into his system. The entire time we were being tossed all over the place, but we persisted and tried our best to keep him stable.

"I had never dealt with such a critically wounded patient before, but

I found that I was completely focused on saving his life to the exclusion of everything else: Stop the bleeding. Make sure he's breathing. Check his vitals. Get the blood pressure cuff on…"

At the hospital, the trauma team was waiting outside, and they immediately transferred the wounded man over to them. Then they washed down the ambulance and headed back into the war zone to save another life.

Once back at Cheletz, dispatch sent them to the Kfar Aza intersection. It was twelve thirty in the afternoon, and they were burning rubber. As they approached an intersection where they spotted one lone army jeep and two soldiers, the siren went off. They pulled the ambulance over to the side of the road, jumped out, and rushed into a nearby shelter. A few minutes later, they got back into the ambulance when they were informed that a critically wounded soldier was being brought to the junction at Netivot.

Waze had taken them on a roundabout route in order to avoid Route 232, which was how they found themselves near the Netivot junction. They headed toward Netivot, and almost immediately were flagged down by the army ambulance carrying the wounded soldier. They made a U-turn, pulled up alongside the army ambulance, and five seconds later, he had been transferred into the ambulance, and they were on their way, with the soldier's commander sitting in the front passenger seat. It had been a rapid transfer, and there hadn't even been time to process the soldier's condition.

In moments, they were back on the road. Destination: Barzilai Hospital. Soon afterward they found themselves driving down Route 232 — the Avenue of Death.

Cars all over the place. Bodies all over the place. It was literally an obstacle course. Sergio was trying to get to the hospital as fast as he could, and they were zigzagging from one side of the road to the other, while everyone in the back of the ambulance was trying to treat the patient while trying to avoid crashing into the sides of the ambulance.

The twenty-one-year-old patient had a bullet wound in his shoulder and shrapnel in the back of his head, as well as many other injuries. He

On the Avenue of Death

was still conscious, and to the team treating him, had the look of a little boy.

He kept on repeating in a plaintive voice, "Put me to sleep, put me to sleep, it hurts so bad, put me to sleep. . ."

"The single most important thing you can do for a person in trauma or a person who has been shot," Sergio explains, "is to stop the bleeding. If they're still bleeding, anything else you do isn't going to help."

The soldier had been injured at 8:30 in the morning, and the ambulance had only gotten to him at 12:45, which explained his terrible state and the excruciating pain. He had been bleeding extensively for many hours, and his blood pressure was dangerously low. He was in such bad shape that Caryn Gale didn't see how he could possibly survive.

Caryn Gale tried to bandage his wounds and stop the bleeding. At the same time, she needed to get an oxygen mask on his face. They were also trying to find a vein to insert an IV into his arm — and all this while Sergio was driving like a maniac to the hospital. Finally Naomi successfully inserted the IV into him, and they tried to get as much liquid as possible into his body.

By the time they arrived at the hospital, Caryn Gale's clothing was soaked with blood. Later she reflected that it was a good thing that she had changed into black clothing before leaving the house that morning.

The soldier was still alive (that alone was a miracle) when he was brought straight to the trauma unit. They didn't know what was in store for the young, beautiful boy whose life they had put so much effort into saving. They didn't have his information, they didn't know his cell phone number, and at that moment there was no time to do anything but clean out the ambulance and get back on the road. But before they left the hospital, one of the crew managed to see the name on the sticker that the hospital had printed out with the patient's information and had been stuck onto his in-patient bracelet. They stored away the information for later, hoping that they would be able to track him down and find out what had happened to the young boy they had come to love in the short while that they had made every effort to save his life.

Caryn Gale was still wearing the same bloodstained clothing when they left the hospital. There simply hadn't been any time to find something to change into. Her tennis shoes were also soaked through with blood. At least she had been able to change her gloves.

I asked her if she still has the shoes.

"Yes," she replied, "but I can't wear them."

CHAPTER TWENTY-FOUR

A Handful of Lollipops

By now it was already afternoon, and the ambulance crew from Modi'in were on their way back to Cheletz. When they arrived, they were informed that there were a lot of injured people at Kfar Aza and that as many ambulances as possible should head in that direction. So it was that they joined the convoy of United Hatzalah ambulances driving down Route 232.

It was pretty clear to the volunteers that at that point very few people in Israel actually understood what was going on. They themselves couldn't figure out whether missiles had landed on so many cars and that was why so many people had died or whether they had been killed by some other means. At that time, they still couldn't have envisioned what had really occurred early that morning.

There were so many cars still burning, and they felt a sharp pang when they passed one car and saw a United Hatzalah vest hanging inside. This turned out to be the car of the Bedouin doctor who had been taken hostage by Hamas earlier that morning and somehow lived to tell the tale.

There was a baby stroller dangling from another car, a discarded car seat lying in a jumble — testimony to inhuman behavior of the worst kind — and bodies just about everywhere.

At first, Caryn Gale suggested that they stop and cover the bodies, but they realized that there were so many that it would have been impossible to handle even a fraction of them. They had been so busy since they arrived down south that they were finding it challenging just to remember all the people they had taken to the hospital or to a helicopter for transport.

On the way to Cheletz, they had passed another intersection where many Magen David Adom ambulances were parked and waiting for patients. Later they realized that only United Hatzalah was operating in the dangerous areas, while the MDA ambulance drivers had been given strict orders from above to stay out of danger. And so they were waiting at that intersection for the United Hatzalah ambulances to bring them wounded people to transport to the hospital.

"While I can understand why such a decision was made," Sergio says, "I know that by going into the places that others wouldn't enter, we were able to save hundreds of lives."

By the time their ambulance arrived at Kfar Aza, busloads of soldiers were pulling up outside the village. They could see soldiers lying on the ground around the perimeter, their guns up and at the ready, their body language focused and alert. It was obvious that the army knew that the surrounding fields were filled with terrorists, and the soldiers were ready for anything.

The ambulance was parked with its back facing the entrance to Kfar Aza and its front facing a nearby orchard, which was also potentially filled with terrorists. It was a very frightening place to be, all the more so when Itzik instructed the crew to wait behind the ambulance because he didn't want them standing in the open where they were exposed to the threat hiding in the orchard.

Suddenly, an army jeep emerged from Kfar Aza carrying two families, each with two young children. They had no shoes on their feet. They had no purses, no phones. Not only that, the jeep that had driven them out of the village had clearly been

United Hatzalah volunteers engaged in gunfight with terrorists

United Hatzalah logistics truck

occupied by someone who had been mortally wounded, because there was blood all over their bodies and clothing.

"When I saw the three-year-old boy covered in blood," says Caryn Gale, "we rushed over to make sure that he wasn't wounded, and we asked them if any of them had been hurt. They confirmed that they were merely shaken up. The blood wasn't theirs.

"Both families were transferred into an ambulance for their protection, and a thought suddenly flashed through my mind: *I have lollipops in my bag!*

"I went to my bag, unable to believe that I had taken those lollipops with me when we left the house that morning. I took out the lollipops, put them in my pocket — and right then a red alert siren went off."

Immediately the two families, along with the United Hatzalah crew, threw themselves on the ground, the parents lying on top of their children. The three-year-old boy started crying — and Caryn Gale reached into her pocket and pulled out a lollipop.

"I have a lot of grandchildren," she says, "and when you offer a lollipop to a child, his eyes light up. It doesn't matter that we were surrounded by smoke and that there were sirens wailing. There I was passing out lollipops to him and his little sister, and their father looked at me and he was so touched. I almost couldn't believe that G-d had given me the idea to take lollipops with me so that I would have them at the exact moment that we would need them.

"I moved over to the other two kids and handed them lollipops as well — and gave a few extra to the parents, because it was clear this wasn't going to be over anytime soon.

"I felt such gratitude to Hashem for allowing me to have this *zechus*. I was so thankful that I had put those lollipops in my bag in the first place and thankful that I had remembered that I had put them there at the moment I needed them so much. I had saved many lives that day. But when I handed those lollipops to the children, it felt just as meaningful as when I had been able to stop the bleeding of wounded soldiers in my ambulance."

CHAPTER TWENTY-FIVE

The Reunion

After the sirens had quieted, Caryn Gale noticed a young man sitting on the sidewalk not far from where she and the crew were situated. He was stone silent, his face as pale and gray as cement. It was clear that the man was in shock.

Caryn Gale had received some training with United Hatzalah's psychotrauma unit, so she went to sit down beside him. He didn't look at her or acknowledge her. She tried talking to him, and eventually he responded. He told her that he had been at the music festival near Re'im, which had been raided by Hamas terrorists that morning.

"I've been hiding in the orchards all day," he told her. "I crawled from place to place on my stomach, hoping that I wouldn't be caught by a terrorist. When I saw your ambulances, I knew that you were Jewish and that I would be safe if I came out."

Caryn Gale gave him an extra flak jacket and helmet. Though she had managed to hear part of his story, he could barely talk the entire time they were together.

"I got him to the point where he was willing to drink some water," says Caryn Gale. "He was very thankful for the drink. (Maybe I should have given him a lollipop…) He could barely function. They tell you as part of your training that you need to try to get people in shock to move. You need to get them to help you, to do something. But I couldn't convince him to do anything. Then he said, 'Can I come in your ambulance with you? I really need to get out of here.'"

Caryn Gale gently explained that they could only take physically wounded people in her ambulance. "But we do have an extra seat, and

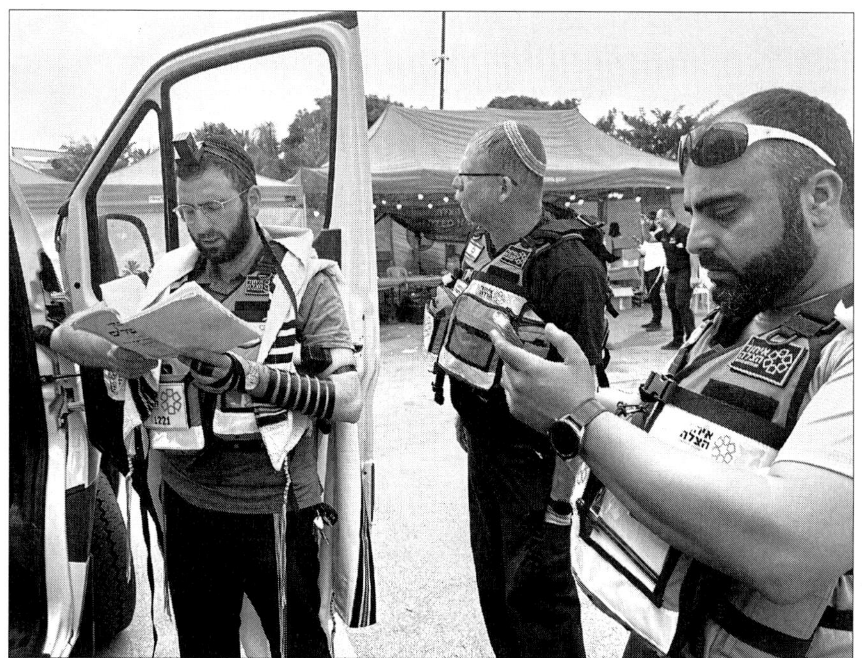

Davening Shacharis at Sdei Yoav

if I have only one wounded person to transport, I'll put you in my extra seat."

"Thank you, thank you!"

"Remember, even if we can't take you out because we're too full, the army is here and they'll take you out. You won't be stuck here. Just make sure to keep on wearing the flak jacket and helmet, and you'll be okay."

The fighting was fierce inside the village, and many had been wounded in action while others had died. It wasn't long before they left the entrance of Kfar Aza with two soldiers — one in critical condition and the other in bad shape but not as bad as his friend. Unfortunately, this meant that Caryn Gale was unable to take the young man who had escaped from the festival.

When they left the area, Itzik and Naomi went in the back of the ambulance with the two soldiers, while Caryn Gale sat beside her husband in the front. Once again they found themselves driving down the Avenue of Death.

"Until then, I had been in the back," Caryn Gale remembers, "which meant that I was seeing the terrible sights on that road for the first time. Now I understood why we were zigzagging on the road and driving on the median. It finally hit me that we were literally driving through a war zone and rescuing people while under fire.

"It had been a long, long day, and I watched as the sky began changing color and slowly shifted from day to night. We hadn't eaten, but there was blood on my hands, body, and shoes, and I wouldn't have been able to eat anything even if I would have wanted to. It was still Yom Tov, and no one really knew what we'd been through.

"It was getting late and I was worried about my children and grandchildren, so I told Sergio that it was time for us to go home for the day after delivering the wounded soldiers to the helicopter so they could be transported to the hospital.

"We made sure that the ambulance was restocked, which meant searching through the many boxes that had been brought to Cheletz and were still unsorted and in a jumble. Eventually we found new sheets for the bed, more saline, and new gloves, and we cleaned out the ambulance. Then we said goodbye to Itzik and Naomi, who decided to stay longer with two new crew members, and we began searching for a way home.

"We were still wearing our flak jackets and helmets."

They were sitting on the side of the road by Cheletz, waiting for a ride, when Caryn Gale caught sight of someone carrying bottles of water to give to the volunteers. When she took another look, she saw it was the young man who had been sitting on the sidewalk near the entrance to Kfar Aza, the man who had crawled through the orchard for hours and who had been in such shock he could barely move.

Now, two and a half hours later, he was up and about.

And he recognized her.

He came running over to her and called out, "You helped me! You helped me, and now I'm here to help people. Let me give you a bottle of water."

Would there be no end to the surprises of the day?

Caryn Gale couldn't drink right then — and besides, she had water in her own bag. But she accepted the bottle because she knew that it would help him feel like he was making a difference, and that is so incredibly important with trauma patients.

She called Sergio over as well and said to the man, "Look, he was also on my ambulance. Give him a bottle of water, too."

Just a short while before, the man had been in shock and unable to speak, and now he was passing out water to all the volunteers at the Cheletz intersection. It was incredible to see. And while the moment that Caryn Gale had given out the lollipops would forever rank as the most unique moment of that day, seeing that young man returning to himself was something that she would also never forget.

It might have been time to leave, but getting home wasn't going to be easy. They couldn't use the ambulance to get home, since it was needed at Cheletz, and there weren't any people around to give them a ride. Then they heard the rise and fall of the siren's wails again, and everyone there immediately lay face down in a muddy field that was filled with straw and stayed there until they were told that they could get up.

Eventually they found an ambulance that was going to Yerushalayim. There was a wounded soldier in the back, and Caryn and Sergio were able to sit there with him. The entire way home the soldier sat on one of the ambulance seats and sobbed. He didn't stop crying from the start

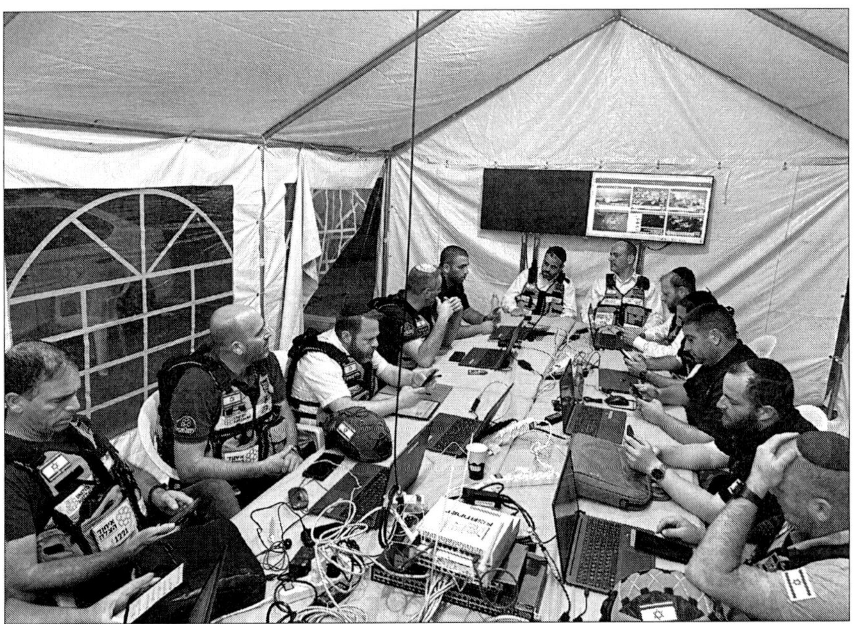

Dispatch center at Sdei Yoav

of the journey until they got off. He had been through a horrific day: all the soldiers who had been in his jeep had been killed. Somehow his life had been spared. It was a miracle, but he couldn't fathom how all his friends were dead while he was left alive, and he couldn't stop crying. There was a professional from the psychotrauma unit with them, and he spoke to the soldier the entire way home, but he didn't stop crying — even for a moment.

It wasn't long before the ambulance dropped them off on the road near Yad Binyamin, close to where Caryn Gale's daughter lived.

Soon everyone piled into their daughter's car. The grandchildren were traumatized after the day they'd had, and it was decided that they would all return together to Modi'in because Caryn Gale and Sergio had a safe room and their kids didn't. The Yom Tov food was still on the hot plate, and all Caryn Gale wanted to do was take the shower of a lifetime after that endless day. But how could she do that when she had to help take care of six grandchildren, whose eyes were still huge and scared to death?

Thankfully, there were still some of the magic lollipops left, so she lined them up on the couch and gave one to each. Then she gave them some pictures to look at and went to take a shower, trying to wash an incredibly traumatic day away.

Sergio found her afterward, and Caryn Gale was looking at her hands and saying, "I can't get the blood off!"

Sergio looked at her hands. "The blood is off," he said. "Your hands are clean."

She shook her head. "I can't get it off. I just can't get it off."

She had seen the blood on her hands the entire day — and she saw it still and it wasn't going away. It was as if she couldn't unsee the things she had seen.

Sergio immediately messaged one of the higher-ups in the psychotrauma unit and told them that Caryn Gale needed to speak to someone because she was in shock after everything she'd been through that day.

It wasn't long before someone called.

Although Caryn Gale herself had been trained in how to speak to people in shock, and even though she had been using those techniques throughout the day and she knew what the volunteer was doing — the person on the other end of the line began using the very same techniques on her, and they really helped. At first, Caryn Gale said, "I don't want to tell you about the things I saw today because it will traumatize you."

"That's okay," the other person said.

Feeling that she was being given the space, Caryn Gale was able to speak, and she told the other person about some of the atrocities she had witnessed. She described how she had been face down in the dirt in front of the entrance to Kfar Aza while the siren wailed and the rockets flew way too close, the smoke burning her eyes. She related how her hands had been slippery with the blood of a twenty-one-year-old soldier and how she'd had the taste of metal in her mouth all day and couldn't eat or drink, and she explained how she had heard the explosions all around her until the point where it felt like her own ears were going to explode.

Ambulances lined up at Sdei Yoav

Then the other woman said, "When someone is traumatized, often one of their senses is affected."

And Caryn Gale understood that because of everything that had happened that day, every one of her senses had been affected. She had been so overwhelmed by all the trauma that she hadn't been able to pull herself out.

The volunteer from the psychotrauma unit made some suggestions, which helped. And while Sergio also spoke to the volunteer, it was clear that he hadn't been affected the same way. But the psychotrauma expert reassured them that every person has their own set of experiences. Every person reacts to things differently.

And it was at that point that Sergio opened up to the volunteer on the other end of the line and started telling her about his experiences on September 11, when America was attacked and the Twin Towers collapsed.

"On the morning of 9/11," Sergio began, "I was a volunteer for both the Bergenfield, New Jersey ambulances and their fire department. I was then working for a software company that tracked the plays for the NFL, and we had two huge screens on our walls. A few minutes after I got to work someone said, 'A plane just crashed into the World Trade Center.' We all ran into the room with the screens and started watching — and a few minutes later we saw the second plane hit the second building. The moment I saw this, I knew beyond a shadow of a doubt that America had been hit by the worst terrorist attack ever.

"I left work and went home to speak to my wife. Our children were little back then, and I had to decide whether I was going to go out with the fire department or on an ambulance. I ended up being on the first ambulance that was sent to Giants Stadium, where we were supposed to be given further instructions. But on the way there, we were told to proceed to Liberty State Park in Jersey City, which was directly across from the Twin Towers on the other side of the Hudson River.

"Many people don't know this, but 9/11 (the day terrorists destroyed the Twin Towers) was also the date when a very large flotilla of boats came across the Hudson, many of which were transporting wounded people, and we were waiting on the other side to treat them and to take them to the hospital."

Sergio shared all this with the volunteer. Then he said something else.

"You know what the difference is between today's attack and 9/11? On 9/11, after the terrorists flew the two planes into the buildings, the attack was over. Sure we could see the smoke, and we knew that the Twin Towers had come down, but for us the terrorist action was over.

"When we drove down south on Simchas Torah, the action was far from over. There were still rockets exploding everywhere and terrorists running around and shooting people, and we had to operate under fire."

And while Sergio hadn't been thinking about 9/11 throughout the day, for some reason it came up when he was speaking to the psycho-trauma expert — and then he let everything out.

He returned to the south the next day, together with Itzik and Naomi.

Caryn Gale didn't go.

In the days that followed, Sergio and Caryn Gale found themselves wondering over and over what had happened to the soldiers they'd delivered to the hospital or driven to a helicopter for transport. They had been in critical condition, and there was a good chance they were no longer alive, but they wanted to know.

About two weeks later, Caryn Gale received a call from Naomi, who informed her that they had managed to track down one of the soldiers whom they had driven to Barzilai Hospital in Ashkelon.

"How is he doing?"

"He is alive and in rehabilitation."

This was outstanding news.

"Where is he?"

"Tel Aviv. And we're all going to visit him tomorrow."

At eight thirty in the morning, they met up with Itzik and rode in the ambulance to the hospital and rehab center in Tel Aviv. The four of them located the soldier, and when they walked into his room all wearing their United Hatzalah vests, he was sitting up in bed. His arm and hand were bandaged, and he looked at them and they looked at him. It was a charged moment — their just seeing him alive.

They introduced themselves. "We're the ambulance crew who drove you to the hospital."

They spent about twenty minutes talking. They told him about the journey to the hospital (he'd been unconscious at the time), and he told them about his recovery, and then they took a picture together — and they all felt a little bit of closure after the experiences they had been through on Simchas Torah.

"In retrospect," Caryn Gale says, "there's no question that our volunteers were surrounded by special protection from Heaven, because there were so many times that day that we drove down roads where terrorists had been operating minutes before or minutes after we passed through.

"No, it is obvious that there were angels escorting us every minute of that day and keeping us safe. There was one time when we had to get out of the ambulance yet again because of another siren. We jumped out of the ambulance and laid flat on our faces on the side of the road in an open field, still wearing our flak jackets and helmets. Seconds later the rocket landed in the field where we were, and the ground shook from the explosion, and part of the field went up in flames and I'm thinking, 'I can't believe I almost got killed by a rocket!"

It would have been something if there were terrorists hiding in the field, and the rocket hit them when it landed. . .

"I wouldn't be surprised if that actually happened," Caryn Gale replied in response to the suggestion, "and we just didn't know about it..."

Between me and you — that wouldn't have surprised me either.

Not after the kinds of miracles that happened on 10/7.

CHAPTER TWENTY-SIX

Eliad's Trauma

Naomi Galeano, who lives in Ramat Beit Shemesh, will never be the same after Simchas Torah 2023. This is her story:

We were getting ready to leave to shul that Simchas Torah morning when the sirens started going off. I ignored them at first, but after they had been wailing on and off for about an hour, I knew that I needed to turn on my United Hatzalah phone.

I joined the organization a few years ago and have been an active volunteer ever since. I also work at a number of different jobs. One of them is for Sherut Leumi, helping place girls and boys with disabilities, whether autism, CP, or Down syndrome, finding the right Sherut Leumi job for them. I also work as a doula. Oh, and I'm also a mother.

It wasn't long before I saw a text from the head of United Hatzalah in Beit Shemesh: *Something terrible is happening down south. Will probably need medics to go and help. Please stay in contact with the group.*

Ten minutes later he was back.

We need medics. We need people!

"I'm going," I said to my husband. He wasn't sure it was a good idea.

"What's the worst that can happen?" I responded. "We're trained to deal with all kinds of situations."

"I don't know," he said again. "It's probably going to be dangerous."

Then he reconsidered.

"If I was in the army," he said, "I would probably run down there the second they need people…"

That was it. He was in, and so was I. From one second to the next, we had made the decision. I would go and help our people in their hour of need. Little did we dream what my help would entail or what the hour of need would be like.

Then again, neither did anyone else.

I let the head of the branch know that I was free to go.

"We don't know exactly where you'll be going," he said. "We have no real idea of what's going on down there. Are you okay with that?"

I told him that I was.

In the end, three of us drove down south in a private vehicle, planning on joining an ambulance crew when we arrived. It was me, Avi Bar Lev, and another volunteer who lived in Ashdod and happened to have been in Beit Shemesh for Yom Tov. I said goodbye to the kids with big smiles and hugs. I wasn't nervous at all. Something was happening down south, but we were used to this kind of thing. This is Israel. Something is always happening here.

We had no idea how clueless we were.

When we arrived at the Cheletz intersection, it was filled with United Hatzalah volunteers. I couldn't get over seeing the *chassidish* guys in their Yom Tov clothing unloading the trucks that were arriving in a steady stream from the main warehouse. We were told to open one of the boxes so that we could each take a helmet and bulletproof vest. "Be ready."

We looked at one another — and it was as if we could read each other's thoughts.

"Ready for what?" I asked.

No answer.

In short order, we opened the boxes and took what we needed.

"Is one of you armed?" we were asked.

Avi was armed.

"Make sure you have your gun out and ready to use."

Now we were starting to get really scared. What on earth was going on there?

That's when we were told that since the terrorists had taken out most of the electric lines in the area, internet service was down and we

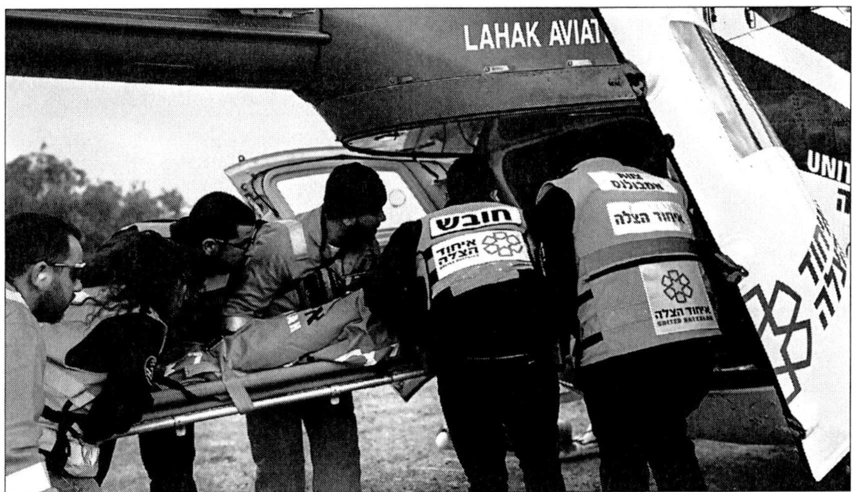

Volunteers loading patient onto United Hatzalah helicopter

should take pictures of the map that showed the places where we'd be driving so we would know where to go. We were also given some phone numbers of local security and army people — just in case.

Our first mission was to bring supplies to one of the helicopters that was transporting the critically injured people to the hospital. They had just returned and needed more supplies. The helicopter was situated at a junction that was closer to the actual war zone. Minutes later, we were in the ambulance and driving down Route 232.

Route 232 — the Avenue of Death — reminded me of a computer game where people kill other people and flip over their cars, because that was exactly what we were seeing.

We seemed to be surrounded by fog. It took me a few moments to comprehend that it wasn't fog but smoke. Then we saw the fires burning. We thought that maybe a rocket had fallen, which would explain the fire and the smoke. But then the ambulance drove past one of the cars, and I was able to see that the smoke was coming from the cars. And then I realized that there had been passengers in those burning cars, Jews who had shared the same kind of death as the Jews in the Holocaust. Only this time it was happening here, in the land we loved so much.

Every mile brought more bodies, more cars flipped upside down, on that Avenue of Death. And it was becoming harder to drive because we didn't want to hit any of the bodies that were strewn all over. So we kept the speedometer at about ten miles an hour and cautiously made our way through that terrible obstacle course.

We could hear the sound of gunshots the entire time, but other than that, it was absolutely quiet. Complete silence punctuated by gunshots. We had been told not to put on any of our ambulance lights, so we didn't. Later we learned that the terrorists had tried to ambush many of the ambulances.

A friend of mine, also a volunteer, told me later that they had been driving down that road when the medics saw a pile of bodies at the side of the road. Suddenly they noticed one of the bodies lifting its hand, and they realized that someone might still be alive and need help. They slowed down and had an argument about whether or not they should get out of the ambulance despite the danger. Thankfully, they didn't get out because a terrorist jumped out of a car that was right next to the bodies and started shooting at the ambulance.

The hand that they had seen belonged to a terrorist. They were deliberately trying to ambush the ambulances and kill the teams of people who were coming to treat wounded civilians. They knew that the ambulance crews had nothing to do with politics, and they weren't soldiers, but they didn't care. We were Jews, and they were trying to kill as many Jews as possible.

We continued driving. In one car I saw a man who had been shot. His body was resting on the steering wheel. In the back seat, a woman — also shot — was sprawled over a baby seat. The baby had been shot as well, and it looked like the mother had been killed trying to protect her child.

Smoke rising in the distance

The reason we could see what had happened so clearly was because the doors of the car had been left open for all the world to see the atrocities that had taken place inside. I remember seeing the baby carriage lying on the floor of the car along with a pile of baby paraphernalia, and from the way it was all jumbled together, it was obvious that the terrorists hadn't only killed them, but had robbed them as well.

I didn't know it at the time, but the sight of that family would keep visiting me in my dreams.

I don't know if they will ever stop.

A few minutes later, we saw the welcome lights of a police car ahead of us on the road. You can't imagine how happy this made us. But then, when we got closer, we could see that the car was upside down, and there were dead soldiers and police officers all around. Those who volunteer for United Hatzalah have been well trained. We live in a country where terrorists attack innocent people all-too-often. But when we think of injuries, we think of a stabbing or someone who was injured from a piece of shrapnel. I never fathomed in my worst imaginings that I would see a massacre like this on an Israeli highway.

At one point we started to count the dead bodies we had seen. Eventually we reached a number that was so high that we just stopped counting. There was no point.

When we reached Sdei Teiman, the helicopter was waiting, and we

Another driverless car on the Avenue of Death

delivered the supplies we had brought: two ambulance bags to replace bags that were now soaked with blood from the victims who had just been flown to Soroka in Beersheva. We cleaned up the interior and stocked the helicopter with the supplies we had brought, and then returned to the Cheletz intersection. From there, the dispatcher told us to drive to Kibbutz Sa'ad.

Kibbutz Sa'ad, located not far from hard-hit Kibbutz Be'eri, was one of the few towns in the area that were completely under the control of Israeli forces. Most of the others were still overrun by terrorists, and driving past them was a life-threatening matter. We were told to wait at Kibbutz Sa'ad for the wounded to be brought to us for transport and treatment.

Though it was no more than a five-minute drive to Sa'ad from Cheletz, everything felt like it was taking much longer than usual that day. When we reached the entrance to the kibbutz, soldiers were there standing guard, and the next thing we knew we heard someone shouting at us over a loudspeaker.

"Get out of the ambulance with your hands over your head! If you are armed, put your weapons on the floor immediately. If you do not follow instructions, you will be shot!"

We got out of the ambulance, literally shaking from fear. The situation around us was tense — the kind of situation where anything could happen.

Avi started screaming "*Shema Yisrael*" at the top of his lungs. After that he called out, "We're volunteers from United Hatzalah!" The whole scene was beyond terrifying.

Our identification confirmed, we were allowed into the kibbutz. As we drove through the entrance, we suddenly heard an immensely loud barrage of gunshots. They were clearly coming from somewhere very close by, and the security forces grabbed us and quickly moved us into a nearby shelter. If we had had any questions before, there were none now: We were in a fire zone.

We were in the midst of a war.

We were tasting Gehinnom.

Soon we got another call from the dispatcher telling us that there were four critically wounded soldiers waiting for the ambulance at the Shuva intersection. This meant that we were now going to be driving

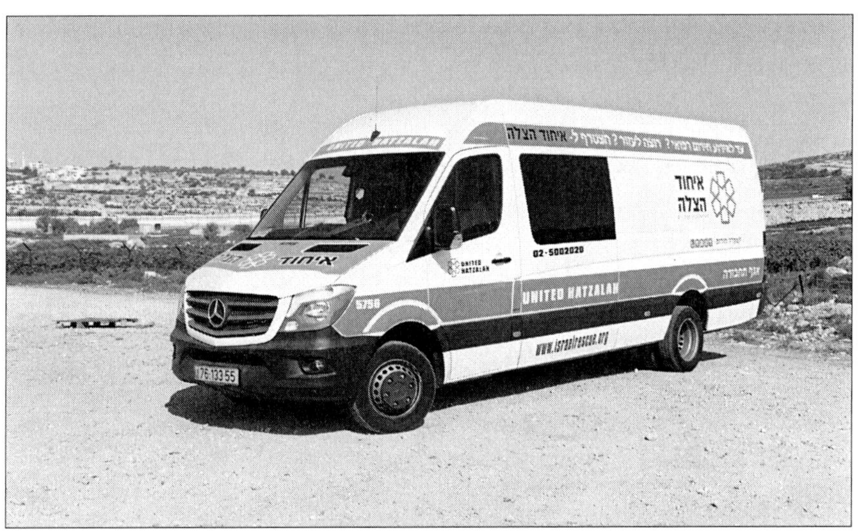

Logistics vehicle

closer to Gaza. When we arrived at the intersection, two people came over to the ambulance. One was an army paramedic. The other was an army doctor.

"Go to the next call," they said.

"What about the soldiers? We were told that there are four wounded soldiers that we need to pick up."

They shook their heads. "We just confirmed their deaths."

It was like pouring salt on an open wound. We looked at the soldiers lying on the floor. They looked like they were sleeping. So young, and nothing to do for them.

One of the soldiers who had greeted us asked if we could take the bodies of his friends, but his commander intervened.

"They can't move the bodies now. Right now we are not dealing with the dead. Right now our job is to try and save the living."

We drove back to the Cheletz intersection, I had never felt so helpless. As we pulled into the intersection, an army jeep dropped off two wounded people whom they had rescued from the music festival near Re'im. They had been hiding in the bushes under a car. One of them had shrapnel in his head and a bullet in his back. The other hadn't been physically injured, but there was no doubt that whatever he had seen would remain with him for life.

We drove the injured person to one of the helicopters, and the other was put on an ambulance. Then one of the soldiers said to us, "Don't worry. We already took the body of the girl."

Hearing those words, the young man in the ambulance started to cry. "Why did he say that?" he yelled. "That's my *kallah*! We're supposed to get married in a month. I kept her alive for eight hours under that car. Tell me she's still alive! Tell me she's alive!"

We started driving to the hospital, and the entire time he kept saying, "Please, you have to tell me she's alive!!! I kept her alive. I talked to her just an hour ago. She's alive, she's alive! Tell me she will live!"

He opened his phone and showed me their wedding invitation — for a wedding that was never going to take place. And as much as I wanted to reassure him that, yes, his bride was indeed alive, it just wasn't possible.

When I tried to examine him, he refused to allow it.

"I don't want you to examine me," he said. "I kept her alive for eight hours. No one came to rescue us for eight hours!!! I called and I called and I called. I sent my location and no one came, and all I want you to do is to tell me that she is alive!"

Then he punched the number of the girl's mother on his phone and shoved the phone at me. "Tell her that she is alive!" he demanded.

But I couldn't do that as much as I wanted to.

"I'm with Eliad," I told the mother. "We're on the way to Kaplan Hospital in Rechovot. Please come and bring him some clothing and

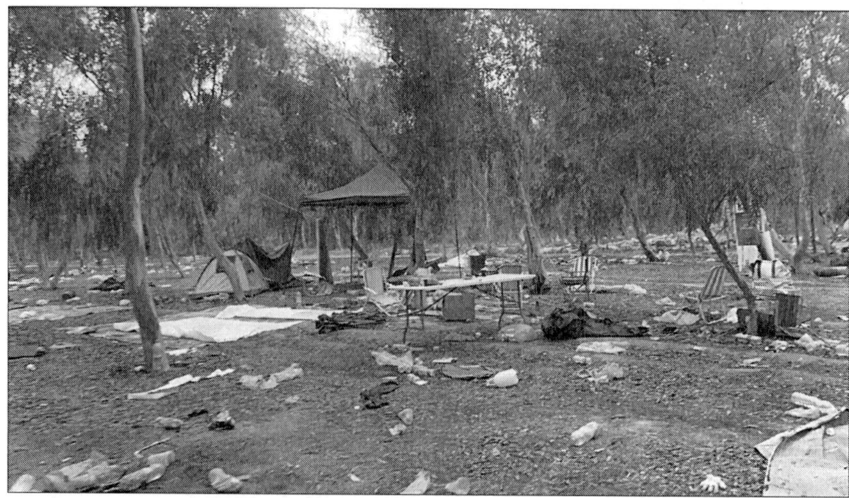

The scene of the music festival after the Hamas attack

anything else he might need. He'll be waiting for you."

"What about my daughter? Where is Rachel?"

"I don't know. I have Eliad with me. He's alive. Please come to see him at the hospital. We'll meet you there."

The mother started to cry. "Please tell me where they took my daughter."

"I don't know," I repeated. "But I have Eliad and he's alive and he's with me. Please come to the hospital. He's waiting for you."

I repeated those words over and over, unable to bring myself to say anything else. Somewhere deep inside I held on to a seed of hope that maybe Rachel was alive and the soldier had made a mistake. Maybe Eliad and his *kallah* would have their happy ending. But the rest of me knew that the chances of that happening were beyond small.

So I told Rachel's mother whatever I knew I could say and tried my hardest not to say the things I knew I wasn't allowed to say, even though I wanted to say those things and make those promises — perhaps more than I wanted to do anything else in my life. But I couldn't.

Throughout that drive I knew that as soon as we dropped off Eliad at the hospital, the ambulance was going to turn around and head back to the war zone, to Route 232.

Here's the thing: You can't allow yourself to break down or cry, because you don't know how many more hours you're going to be there in the middle of that war zone and you don't have the luxury of losing it and breaking down. You need to remain strong for all the people who need you.

All I could do right then was pray that Eliad and all others would heal and be okay one day.

CHAPTER TWENTY-SEVEN

The Ghost Town

At some point, the dispatcher instructed all the ambulances that were available to go to Kfar Aza. The army hadn't gone in yet when Naomi's ambulance arrived, and the village was still under control of terrorists. They found the village encircled by troops from various army commando divisions.

The army still hadn't been able to send any of their ambulances to the area, nor were Magen David Adom ambulances allowed to venture so close to Gaza, which meant that United Hatzalah had the only ambulance teams on the ground to take care of the wounded.

"So many *yishuvim*, moshavim, and kibbutzim under attack," Naomi says, "and only our teams of medics and paramedics were there to transport all the wounded. The whole thing made no sense. But that was the situation. As we say in Ivrit, '*Zeh mah sheyeish*' — that's how it is, so deal with it."

The United Hatzalah ambulances were parked side by side and were facing outward so that they could drive off as soon as the wounded were placed inside. There was a gas station to the right, a huge field on their left, and surrounding the village there was a forest. It was clear that all the open areas were hiding armed terrorists poised to attack.

There were also dead bodies everywhere. Some were soldiers. Others were civilians who had died at the entrance to their village. There was also a stack of dead terrorists, and soldiers had to move bodies to the side so that the ambulances could park.

Like the Holocaust...

"I looked at the scene before me," Naomi recalls, "and I thought, *It's just like the Holocaust. Just like the Holocaust...*"

But this time the Holocaust was taking place not in Poland, but in Israel.

There were also a few families at the site, those who had somehow, miraculously, been rescued. The families were waiting for someone to get them out of the area, but they would have to wait a little longer. The medical teams had to give precedence to the injured whom they knew were going to be brought out at any moment.

Every ambulance was allocated a team for the wave of wounded that was about to come crashing upon them. Each team consisted of three people: a medic, a driver (who was also a medic), and a doctor. The doctor on Naomi's team was an orthopedic surgeon.

Once they were divided into teams, the commanding officer on the scene said, "Now everyone has to be quiet."

The order was given, and on the spot the hundreds of commandos who were there fell silent. It was a silence accompanied by nonstop shooting coming from the village and the sound of rockets, which were either blown up by the Iron Dome or managed to get through and hit their targets.

Then the gate of Kfar Aza opened, and the army vehicles began going in.

"The next thing we knew," says Naomi, "we were hearing gunshots. Much worse than before. A barrage of gunfire that seemed like it was never going to end."

"Get on the ground!" the commander ordered.

Everyone lay on the ground. The soldiers were on one knee, their guns pointing in every direction, in case terrorists hiding in the fields and forests chose that moment to start shooting.

When the shooting inside the village finally died down for a short while, the commander got on the radio and asked each of the units who had entered in army vehicles if they were alright. Then he began asking about the civilians sheltering in their houses.

"House number 50?"

"X."

X meant they had been killed.

"House number 51?"

"X."

"House 20?"

"X."

"House 30?"

"X."

He asked about house after house for five long minutes, and all he received in response was confirmation that no one inside was still alive. Finally, the answer came that the people inside one of the houses was still alive.

There was silence for another five minutes. Then the gates opened again, and the cars started emerging. Naomi and the doctor on her team went to the first car. They opened the door.

"Is anyone here injured?"

"No."

They closed the door and the vehicle continued driving.

It was the same story with the next army vehicle.

The third car was a different story. They had injured soldiers with them.

"Usually one critically ill patient is assigned to an ambulance," Naomi says. "Never more than that. Now there were three or four. Three or four critically wounded patients and one medic."

The wounded soldiers were placed in the ambulances, which

immediately pulled away, driving down the road in the darkness — down the road leading away from a place that had been a vibrant community and was now one big cemetery.

A few families survived the massacre and were brought out of Kfar Aza. They weren't physically hurt, but their eyes were hollow, and they told us about their relatives who had been kidnaped and taken into Gaza. "It was hard to believe that we were talking to people who had been trapped for the past twenty-four hours," Naomi says. "They had been under attack from six in the morning and had seen mankind at its absolute worst. They asked us how they should break the news to their families because the country still didn't know the extent of what had happened over the course of that Simchas Torah.

"It was at this point that the dispatcher told us to drive to Be'eri, where we would be given patients to take to the hospital. But then, on the way, dispatch told us that there were too many terrorists for us to drive to Be'eri and that we should stop at a *yishuv* called Alumim and wait there.

"We pulled into Alumim. It was an absolute ghost town. The gate at its entrance was wide open, and there were bodies of murdered foreign workers everywhere.

"It took about five minutes for the injured from the area to arrive. We were given three patients, and we left Alumim moments later.

"The drive was more dangerous now because it was already well into the middle of the night. There were no lights on the road, and we weren't allowed to turn on the ambulance's lights, so the driver turned on the flashlight on his phone to light up the road ahead of us. The driver concentrated on getting through the obstacle course ahead of him while I sat in the back of the ambulance to monitor the patients. One of the patients was a woman about ninety years old. She had dementia and didn't know what was going on. There was also a father there whose fifteen-year-old son had been kidnaped and taken to Gaza. His agony was indescribable.

"After making sure that our patients were in good hands, the hospital asked us to help them prepare fresh beds, among other things, because they were short-staffed. We also had to clean our ambulance, which meant that it was a while before we were back on the road.

"When we arrived back at Cheletz, we were given a load of body

United Hatzalah volunteers in one of the villages after the attack

bags — boxes and boxes of them — to transport to Be'eri. Back we went on Route 232 on what was turning into the longest day of my life. At that point, I turned to Avi and said, 'I cannot drive down Route 232 again tonight. That's it. No more for now.'

"That road and the sights I had seen there had been seared into my brain. I was able to tell him where to drive — right or left — because I remembered every spot on the road where a body was lying. I also remembered whether they were old or young, male or female, and what had happened to them. It was all there in my head and probably always would be.

"By then it was close to five in the morning, and the sun was starting to rise over a world that seemed to have gone completely insane. We had been active for fifteen hours straight, and we were exhausted beyond all comprehension. Since I didn't want to get back on the road, I stayed in Cheletz. For the next few hours I remained there and helped out wherever I was needed."

For the next twenty-four hours, the volunteers of United Hatzalah provided medical support and served as a backup team for the army, working tirelessly and unceasingly to save as many lives as they could. After making rounds in the danger zone and dropping off wounded patients at the hospital, they chose to return and do it all again, time after time.

"Despite the danger, despite the bullets whistling past our heads and the boom of rockets exploding on the ground, in a strange way we felt safe and protected, as if Hashem Himself was watching over His volunteers and protecting them while they went about saving their fellow Jews. It was incredible to learn how team after team went into the most dangerous places and emerged safe and unharmed.

"It was a clear and open miracle. No question about that."

CHAPTER TWENTY-EIGHT

Moshe Terror

Naomi continues sharing her story:

I returned to Beit Shemesh at around eight o'clock in the morning. Avi said that he was going to try and get some sleep and that we would speak in a few hours. There were people on the streets. They knew terrible things had happened down south, but if you hadn't been there you really couldn't visualize the horror. I couldn't look at anyone. I couldn't talk to anyone.

I lay down and fell asleep for two and a half hours.

When I woke up I called Avi.

He didn't even ask. He knew that I wanted — needed — to go back.

"I'm coming to get you," he said.

I got in the car and we drove back to Cheletz where I joined a different crew that was heading to Be'eri to assist with the evacuation of all the people who miraculously were still alive there. The last civilians left the area at about one or two in the afternoon — at which point dispatch told us to drive to the city of Sderot.

There are two entrances to the city of Sderot — the north entrance and the south entrance. We first entered from the north, but we were then told that there was a battle going on right then in the south side of the city between our forces and a group of terrorists, and we were needed there.

We drove into the city. The road is wide and spacious. There is a train station there, and a sign that reads "Welcome to Sderot."

There were two safe places that we could enter in case of rockets — one with a door that locked, the other without. In the middle of the road a gun battle was taking place. I could see about a hundred and fifty soldiers and police shooting at a group of about ten terrorists wearing blue and green clothing. Some of them could have been mistaken for soldiers. Because this was Sderot, there are safe places all over the city and the terrorists were using two of them for cover, as well as a car.

The police ordered us to get out of the ambulance and to go inside one of the safe places and lock the door. We followed orders and were soon inside. Being inside that room was scarier than being outside because we could hear what was going on but couldn't see. We heard the gunshots and the screams — the thunderous sounds magnified in the tiny space.

After about ten minutes — it felt like an eternity — silence settled on the street and the police told us to open the door. We then watched as the army sent up two drones into the sky. This way we could see the entire area and would know if there were more terrorists hiding who would attack us if we went to attend to the wounded.

The drone showed that the area was clear — which meant that we could begin taking care of the wounded. Several soldiers had been killed. Another soldier was severely wounded and was transported from the area by helicopter.

The rest of the day passed in a haze of battle. I watched as soldiers fought terrorists another four times in the same area. Two more soldiers died and two more were injured. We were forced to stay inside the safe area during each of the battles — and it never became less frightening.

We ended up remaining in Sderot until the next day. Then we drove to the command center which United Hatzalah had set up in Sdei Yoav. I found a corner in a tent and went to sleep for a few hours. Part of me wanted to go home, but another part felt that I couldn't leave while so much was happening and my fellow Jews were being killed and so many people were needed.

No.

I couldn't leave.

Not when I knew what to do and was able to help save lives.

So I stayed.

By now the days had started running into one another and I wasn't even sure what day it was.

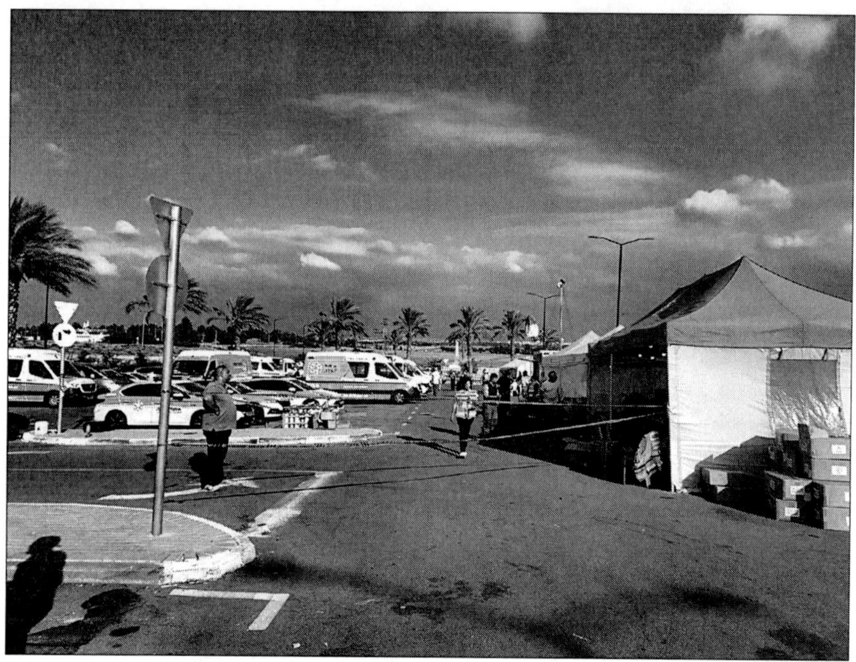

Sdei Yoav

I did another twelve-hour shift the next day. I texted my husband from time to time letting him know that I was fine. He knew that I needed to do this and he supported me one hundred percent. I couldn't go home right then. It would have been like traveling from one dimension to another, from one reality to another completely different form of existence. From a place where people were living with gunfights in the middle of the roads to a city where people were living a normal existence. No. I had to stay at least until things began to calm down.

Eventually they sent me home to go to sleep for another few hours in my own bed. I obeyed orders and went home. I woke up the next morning at six and returned to Sdei Yoav and took another shift with an ambulance.

As the days were passing I found myself thinking more and more about my brother Moshe Chaim.

My brother is in a very special combat unit in the army (it's so secret we don't even know what it is) and during the first days of the war I called my sister-in-law and asked her where he was.

"Two soldiers came looking for him on Simchat Torah," she replied. "I told them that he went to the Kotel for *hakafot*. They went to look for him."

My brother called me a few days into the war.

"Naomi, can you do me a favor?"

"What do you need?"

He explained that he needed ointment and bandages for a severe rash he'd developed from walking around with his weapons for the last few days without having been able to change his clothing. I bought everything he needed and then I told one of the people in charge at Sdei Yoav that my brother had asked me to meet him in Sderot in a few hours' time.

"They are shooting again in Sderot," he protested.

By then I was way past worrying about another gunfight. Not after the things I'd seen over the past days.

"I will stay away from the fighting, but I need to go see my brother."

And that's exactly what I did.

My brother sent me the location where he was staying. It was a school building — nothing fancy — nondescript and perfect for his unit. When we finally saw one another I gave him a hug and I started to cry, which caused him to start to cry.

"When did you get here?" he wanted to know.

"Simchas Torah afternoon. Around two or three."

He thought for a second.

"The army only arrived at about four thirty in the afternoon on Simchas Torah. That means that United Hatzalah was here even before the army."

"I know."

Then he asked me, "Where have you been?"

I told him the list of places we had been. Near Be'eri, Alumim, Kfar Aza.

Then my brother started crying again.

He looked at me.

"You saw."

His words were laden with meaning and echoed with thousands of years of Jewish history.

I nodded. "Yes."

"Please don't tell my wife."

His wife just gave birth two months earlier to their first child. A daughter. They had been waiting a long time for that child.

I looked at his pants and shoes. They fairly crackled from stiffness. It was obvious that they had been soaked with blood.

I pointed at the blood. "Is that yours?"

He looked where I was pointing.

"Not mine. It's the blood of a terrorist."

"What happened?"

"I'll tell you.

"It happened in Kibbutz Re'im. We knew of a house where there were five living people sheltered in their safe room. There were also four terrorists in the house — who for some reason were unable to break into the room where the Jews were taking refuge. Our mission was to take out the terrorists while making sure the Jews stayed alive. I found a person from the kibbutz who was able to tell me exactly how the house was built. Now we knew where to shoot and which part of the house to stay away from.

"We shot from the side of the house where we knew there was no danger to our people. We shot for ten minutes straight. Then we threw two grenades into the house and went in.

"There were two rooms — one on either side of the safe room. I went into one of the rooms. There were closets all along the walls. I shot into them all — making sure that if any terrorists were hiding inside, they were now unquestionably dead. Then I went into the next room. As I walked inside, I felt someone grabbing my pants. I looked down at the floor. There was a terrorist lying there. He was badly wounded.

"Barely alive. Almost dead.

"Yet with his last bit of strength, he was trying to stab me with a knife. The animal was using his last moments on earth to try and kill another Jew."

"What did you do?"

"I shot him. That's where all the blood came from.

"Then the family was able to leave the safe room for the first time in many, many hours. Two parents. Three kids. All alive."

We spoke for a long time and I told my brother about the things that I'd seen over the last few days.

"We should stop crying now," he said to me. "I can't allow myself to cry right now. We'll have enough time to cry after this is over. Then the two of us will sit together and cry our eyes out."

My brother is a real hero. His unit remained in Sderot until the next day, and I went back to see him because I didn't know the next time we were going to see one another again. When I got to the school there were two soldiers standing guard at the entrance of the building.

"Who are you looking for?"

"My brother, Moshe Chaim."

"Who is Moshe Chaim?"

Seeing that they didn't know who I was referring to, I showed them a picture that I had of him.

"Oh, you mean Moshe Terror."

"Moshe what?!"

"Moshe Terror."

"Terror? Like terror?"

"Yes — your brother is the kind of soldier who causes terror to the enemy. You don't understand. Your brother is a genuine hero around here. He has saved so many of our lives. He's so sharp. So many times he is able to see and identify terrorists before the rest of us."

Turning to some of the other soldiers, the soldier said, "This is Moshe Terror's sister."

Soldiers began gathering around. Each of them had their story of how my brother saved his life. It was incredible to hear — and I realized that while I had thought I knew who my brother was, I really didn't know anything at all!

And I thought to myself, "I don't want my brother to have to fight and be a hero. I want him back home where he belongs, with his wife and baby daughter… and on the benches of the kollel where he sits, learning Torah from morning till night…

"And when we can finally sit together a little and cry it all out."

Not long ago I had a conversation with my husband. I said to him, "You know something — when our children are old enough to understand what happened to the Jews of Europe, none of the Holocaust survivors will be alive anymore. When I was growing up, every Holocaust memorial day we were able to see and meet a living survivor. Our children will not have that opportunity." But now I realize that I was wrong. Because they will have the chance to meet many of the survivors of our very own, personal holocaust.

A Miraculous Moment

I heard the following story from the protagonist himself, a young man named Ro'i, who had attended the music festival with his wife. This is how he tells it:

During the music festival, I remember standing there, filming everything going on. Suddenly, I noticed that there were rockets flying in our direction.

I didn't waste any time. Grabbing my wife's hand, I said, "We're running to the car this second. We need to leave right now!"

We started running and all I could think of was how the music was still playing. Rockets flying in our direction and the music is still playing.

Crazy.

"This could be our last moment together," I remember saying.

My wife said, "Don't talk *shtuyot*. Hashem is watching over us!"

Suddenly we passed a car, and I saw a man sleeping inside. I knew that if I didn't alert him, there was a good chance he was going to die.

I knocked on the window and yelled, "Get up! Get up!"

I kept knocking and yelling for half a minute — a very long half a minute — until finally he woke up.

(He called me five days later and left me a message: "I remember how you woke me up when I was sleeping. It is in your *zechut* that I am still alive. You saved my life, and I want you to know — I have three children...")

The moment I saw he was awake, we continued running to our car. We jumped inside, and I started driving away from there. As we drove, my wife saw two pickup trucks, one black, the other white, and each had about eight terrorists standing on the truckbed. I looked at the terrorists just as they aimed their weapons at us and started shooting.

I pushed my wife's head down below the window, and, lowering my own head, I continued driving, all the while screaming, "*Shema Yisrael...!*" That scream was strong and loud — I don't even know where it came from.

Meanwhile, the terrorists were shooting at us and I was driving. I remember looking up for a second and seeing the bullets coming from every direction, but none of them hit us.

A few seconds later, I raised my head and I looked in the rear-view mirror, watching as the two pickup trucks turned left in the direction of the festival. I kept on driving. I drove past Ofakim and didn't stop until we arrived in Beersheva. At that moment, a rocket landed, and a house nearby went up in flames.

It's been five days since we almost died, and I find myself asking Hashem, "Who am I? And what do You want from me?" Because of everything we went through and the miracles that happened to us, we have decided — me, my wife, and our children — to start keeping Shabbat. And I feel that all of us need to work on our *emunah*, our *tefillah*, and our *shemirat Shabbat*. All of us need to pray to Hashem to redeem us from this *galut*. But most of all, we need to remember that *Am Yisrael* is strong when *Am Yisrael* is united.

PART SEVEN
AFTERSHOCKS

Restore us to You, Hashem, that we may be restored!
Renew our days as of old.

— *Eichah 5:21*

I took the baby from the soldier's arms,
and it was like holding Jewish history in my arms.

— ***Tal Lalum,***
United Hatzalah volunteer

CHAPTER TWENTY-NINE

Fifty Million Dollars

For years, practically since the moment he founded United Hatzalah, Eli Beer has had to work hard fundraising. It isn't only him — everyone who runs an organization is confronted with the same challenge and needs to raise funds to finance their cause and achieve their goals.

In the face of the massacre on October 7, a group of United Hatzalah's most faithful supporters called Eli immediately after Yom Tov to pledge large donations, but it simply wasn't enough. From the way United Hatzalah had burned through equipment on the first day of the war, it was clear that they were going to have to replenish their entire stock of equipment at the cost of tens of millions of dollars.

The day after Yom Tov, the United Hatzalah leadership held a meeting in Eli Pollak's office to make key decisions as to how to proceed. They were four on the team: Eli Beer, Eli Pollak, Moshe Levy, and Dovie Maisel. They were the same four who had been part of the dream from the very beginning. The same four who had helped build United Hatzalah into the organization it had become — who had helped Eli Beer turn the dream of a few *yeshivah bachurim* into an organization that is respected by millions of people around the globe.

They were his team. His friends. The people he could depend on through thick and thin. And now they were facing a situation that was worse than anything they had seen since they started.

The air was charged as they sat in Eli Pollak's office and tried to figure out what United Hatzalah had to do to weather the current storm.

"The big question is this," Eli Beer got right to business, "what exactly are our needs right now?"

The team jumped in.

"We need twenty-five more ambulances at the minimum, especially since the IDF has been borrowing ambulances from us. There's a good chance that this war could last six months or even a year — and we don't have enough ambulances right now. We also need more trucks to deliver equipment where it's required."

"What else?"

"Tents. To use for temporary ER centers and field hospitals. We're going to need a field hospital in the south and another up north."

"And satellite phones, which will work everywhere. We've been needing them for years."

Eli was taking notes. Then he began calculating how much money they had in the bank against everything they needed to buy and estimated what it was all going to cost. At that moment, there was no way they could afford such an outlay. Yes, they were solvent. They were even in good shape financially. But to make the kinds of purchases that the team was telling him they needed was a whole different level — a level that had been out of their league until now. Yet now there was no choice but to make it happen.

The team had been telling him that they needed all this equipment for years. He had never been able to make it happen. Now it seemed that the time had finally arrived — and from the way people had reacted upon hearing what was going on down south, it was clear that their supporters and donors would feel the same way. They were facing an emergency and would have to act accordingly.

By the time he had finished writing everything down and tallied it all up, the number came to an astounding forty-nine million dollars. In the past, it would have been considered an unattainable dream. Not anymore. Not in a time like this.

Suddenly the dream had become a reality.

There was no question that the challenge would be great. The United Hatzalah budget for 2023 had been fifty-five million dollars. Yet now from one day to the next, he was almost doubling his budget. But what choice was there? The country was at war, and they needed the equipment. Bottom line: It would have to be done, and with the help of Hashem, it would.

Close to six million dollars had already been raised since the outbreak of the war through his regular donors and by selling the *aliyos* at minyanim held at the hotels the morning after the massacre. This meant that they were missing "only" forty-three million dollars. The question now became how to proceed.

In the past, Eli's first move would have been a lengthy fundraising trip to cities around the world, but the country had just been attacked, and in the current situation, he didn't feel that leaving was the right thing to do. His volunteers needed him, and his family needed him. Israel was at war, and Eli Beer would not be flying to Miami.

Not now.

Not when his son was fighting the enemy in Gaza.

Not when his son-in-law was managing the United Hatzalah field hospital down south.

There was a time and a place for everything, and now was the time to stay home.

So travel was out.

But what to do instead?

Sitting at his desk, Eli remembered something his father had told him years earlier. In 1948, his father had raised money for Israel and helped obtain weapons for the fledgling state. He had helped build Moshav Kommemiyus with his bare hands and lived there for a year. This was a father who had shown Eli that talk is cheap and action is what counts.

Eli remembered a conversation with his father as if it had taken place only the day before. "Eli," he said, "during Israel's War of Independence back in 1948, everyone helped in whatever way they could. People came out of the woodwork looking for ways to help the brand-new country. And let me tell you something: It was easier to raise money during the War of Independence than it had been to raise funds during the Holocaust. When I tried raising money to help the Jews in Europe, I ran into a brick wall. Nobody believed that millions of Jews were getting killed in concentration camps. And because they didn't believe it — or didn't want to believe it — they didn't give.

Eli meeting with Minister of Defense Yoav Galant

"In 1948, the situation was different. There was no question of whether or not Israel was fighting for its very existence. There was no question that they were fighting for every inch of land, and no one had to be convinced of the validity of the cause. After what had happened in Europe and the loss of six million Jewish lives, Jews around the world understood the need for a Jewish country. So did non-Jews. And the moment the new country was being threatened, millions of people resolved to do their utmost to help.

"And they did."

"As I replayed my father's message to me," Eli says, "I suddenly felt a sense of déjà vu, as if I was reliving history. A sort of Holocaust had just been replayed on the soil of Eretz Yisrael, the land I loved with all my heart and soul. And I knew that I was going to do what my father had done, that all I needed to do was to give people the opportunity to help, because that was what they wanted to do.

"At that moment, I made a decision. Instead of flying around the world, I would host meetings on Zoom. And I was going to invite famous and influential people whom I respected to address my donors and supporters."

Really, it was a very simple plan. Instead of having meetings with five or ten people, they could meet with fifty or more people at a time. They'd send out mass invitations and host the meetings online, and people were going to help, because they would understand that there was no choice but to do so. Israel and United Hatzalah needed their support.

The first Zoom meeting was arranged. Instead of the expected fifty people, Eli was joined by over one thousand supporters and friends of United Hatzalah, including two former ambassadors, David Friedman and Michael Oren, who were the keynote speakers. Eli opened the proceedings by giving everyone a rundown of the situation on the ground. He hadn't planned on breaking down, but it wasn't long before he was wiping away tears as he described the atrocities that had been committed by the enemy.

"My friends," he said, "I saw terrible things that I never imagined seeing in my life. Everything I saw in the last thirty-five years doesn't compare to the things I saw in that one day."

He told them about the never-ending phone calls coming in from people in the south begging them for help, telling them that they were being attacked and shot at, that their houses were being burned down, or that they had someone with them who was injured and they didn't know what to do.

Moments later he was crying, and so was everyone listening. When he finished speaking, he said, "Okay, so what now?"

He gazed into the camera — at the images of dear, beloved faces who had been supporting United Hatzalah for so many years and had joined the Zoom meeting because they wanted to continue doing so. He said, "I have a list of equipment that we need to buy. That's what's next for us. We need to restock our shelves with millions of dollars' worth of medical supplies that were already used on the first day of the war.

"But that's just the beginning, because it's clear that this is not going to be a short fight. And if the war continues for a long time, there will be a constant need to replenish our supplies — and that's going to cost money and a lot of it."

He could see people nodding, and he knew that the message was getting through.

"Back in 2006, I flew to America to ask our donors to support us during the Second Lebanon War. At that time, our good friend Mark Gerson opened his house to me and helped me raise a million dollars in one evening. But today a million dollars isn't enough. The organization has grown and is twenty times the size it was back then.

"Moreover, the war Israel is fighting now is very different. We aren't only facing missiles — there are terrorists running around the south as we speak, still looking for Jews to kill. And there's a very good chance that we will soon be attacked from the north as well, and then we will officially be fighting a multifront war. I say officially because it's already happening unofficially. And what if another battlefront opens up in the center of the country? What then?

"So we need to purchase as much equipment as we can now so that we will be prepared. This is not a joke. It's not a game. This is one of the most serious moments in this country's history, and we dare not shy away from shouldering our share of the burden.

"My friends, as much as I might want to, I cannot fly across the ocean right now. Maybe in a few weeks, but not now. And because, as much as I want to, I can't fly to you and take the time to visit each one of you personally, I'm turning to you as a group, and asking you to step up to the plate and join me just because you understand that this is the right thing to do for the Jewish people at this point in history. We need your help. Please do whatever you can!"

As Eli spoke, he was picturing his father, and Gabi Beer was talking to him. "See, Eli?" he was saying. "People want to help. They understand what needs to be done. You don't have to do it all by yourself anymore. Everyone is ready to help you now..."

And it was true. On the spot, people began pledging their support. They raised another two million dollars right then and there. Over the next few months, Eli raised over fifty million dollars and spent seventy percent of the money to replenish their depleted shelves. But the warehouses were filled with equipment and United Hatzalah was now the grateful owner of as many satellite phones as they needed. New trucks had been ordered and were on the way, as were more ambulances and ambucycles.

People pledged and people matched and people gave and people opened their hearts, and it was incredible to see — because it was the kind of scene where the only response a person can have is *"Mi k'amcha Yisrael!"*

CHAPTER THIRTY

Generosity!

Joe Teplow is a volunteer EMT with the New York branch of Hatzolah. Joe had been visiting Israel for Succos, and as soon as he heard news of the massacre on October 7, he went to the United Hatzalah headquarters to help.

Joe would never forget what he saw in the first few days of the war. One of the things that made an impression on him was everyone's willingness to contribute to the war effort. As soon as they sent out a message saying that the soldiers needed something — toothpaste, for example — a truck would pull up outside the United Hatzalah building and a hundred boxes of toothpaste would be deposited on the pavement, there for United Hatzalah to transport to the soldiers in need. Two tons of water were delivered by water companies. It was the same with other goods and supplies.

When Joe, who had been making himself indispensable, was ready to return home a few days after the war started, he went to say goodbye to Eli. "Listen," he said, "I wish I could stay here longer, but I need to get back to New York."

"Okay, but I'm going to need you to continue helping me from there."

"What do you need me to do?"

"I need you to be my man in America to ensure that we have access to supplies that we need. Although today things have changed and we can buy a lot of supplies and equipment in Israel, there is a shortage of certain supplies. I can't get enough bandages here because they've all been sold to other countries like America and Ukraine. There's also a shortage of tourniquets and special medical scissors.

"Of course, there are also plenty of things that Israel doesn't manufacture. I need to know that I have someone like you in place to help us obtain those supplies. You will serve as our purchasing agent in the States. You'll meet with the companies and negotiate good terms and, most importantly, serve as the liaison with the New York branch of Hatzolah (Rabbi Yechiel Kalish, the CEO of Hatzolah in America, was very happy to help), which also purchases a lot of equipment and will be able to get us good deals. Can you do this for me and for United Hatzalah?"

To his credit, Joe agreed. Little did he know what the job entailed. Though it wouldn't have mattered. Once he agreed, he never wavered or backtracked. He was in — one hundred percent.

Practically from the moment Joe landed in New York, people started calling Joe. The word was out: He was the man to speak to if you wanted to help Israel and United Hatzalah.

Caller: "How can I send diapers to Israel?"

Joe: "We don't need diapers."

Another caller: "I want to send a batch of undershirts."

Joe: "We don't need undershirts."

Joe was on top of the situation, only accepting gear and equipment that was on the list and nothing else. Dovie Maisel, too, arranged for more bulletproof vests and helmets — the kind of stuff they really needed.

Over the next few weeks, Joe was responsible for sending three El Al cargo planes loaded with an immense supply of medical equipment and other vital things to Israel. The first two flights were free of charge — courtesy of El Al. Upon landing at the airport, they were met by United Hatzalah staff who made sure that customs allowed everything through without taxation, in accordance with a special wartime amendment that was passed in the Knesset. From there, the equipment was loaded onto United Hatzalah trucks and driven to the main warehouse on the outskirts of Beit Shemesh.

Not only did Joe work nonstop as the liaison between United Hatzalah and what seemed at times to be a million people, he also arranged a really good deal for the organization, reaching out to a businessman named Josh and asking for his support. Josh was familiar with United Hatzalah and wanted to help in a big way.

"Joe," Josh said, "I'll make you a deal. You work for one of the most successful Jews in the world. Tell him that if he donates a million dollars to United Hatzalah, I will match it."

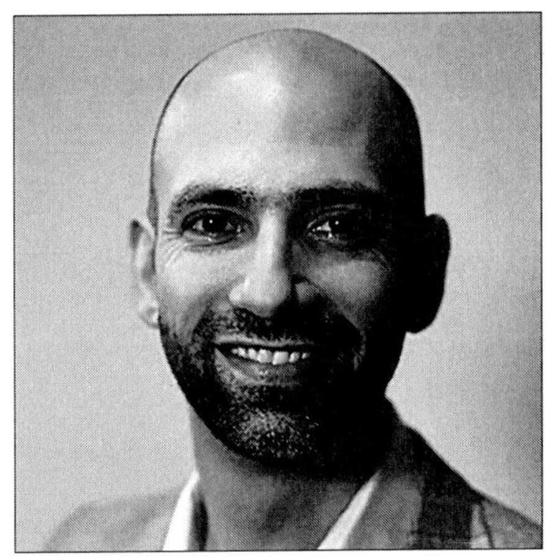
Michael Brown

Joe relayed the message, and his boss agreed without hesitation.

Joe now had two million dollars to spend on purchasing equipment, and was able to tell Eli and Michael Brown (the indefatigable and hardworking VP of United Hatzalah) to use the money they were raising for other things because he had raised a lot of the money he needed to purchase supplies himself.

No matter how much money was coming in, endless amounts were flowing out, to the extent that it was hard for Eli and his team to keep up with their very real needs.

The cost of operating the ambulances on a daily basis was one hundred and fifteen thousand shekels.

One hundred fifteen thousand shekels a day.

That kind of money adds up very quickly. That is not to mention the cost of operating the command center at Sdei Yoav, the supplies and equipment, and the million other things involved in running an operation like United Hatzalah in wartime.

If phase 1 was making sure that everyone had what they needed in the first few days of the war and phase 2 was replenishing the warehouses after all the equipment and supplies had been exhausted, now they were at phase 3 — which meant doing their best to assess their needs for the long haul — or, at least, however long the war would last.

There was another factor that Eli and his team had to take into consideration: training all the new volunteers who wanted to join the organization. When *90 Seconds: The epic story of Eli Beer and United Hatzalah* was published in the beginning of 2023, there were about 6,300 volunteers in United Hatzalah. The goal was to reach 12,000, which would allow them to respond to every emergency in the country in less than ninety seconds.

Since that time, the organization has grown. There are now more than 7,000 volunteers — with another 2,500 waiting to join. People around the country have been lining up to join the organization, especially after seeing the volunteers' heroic actions on Simchas Torah and the number of lives they had saved. They, too, want to join in the effort and do their part.

Though United Hatzalah normally trains 700 volunteers a year, the plan right now was to train another 2,100 volunteers in the coming year. But for that to happen, United Hatzalah needed to be able to pay for it: the cost of training and fully equipping one volunteer is ten thousand dollars. This means the budget just for training volunteers was projected to reach twenty-one million dollars in 2024.

Aside from all this, United Hatzalah is constructing a new three-story building in Sderot — no more temporary structure. And then there are all the new vehicles that need to be purchased for the coming year and the upkeep, as well as the new medical machines, the epipens, the defibrillators. The expenses never stop.

But unlike in the past when this would have made Eli extremely nervous, now he is confident that the money will arrive — because, as he says, "our people know what's going on, and I know that they're going to be there for us."

In his mind, it's very clear: "If people are sending their children to fight for the country and volunteers are putting their lives in danger, then the donors of United Hatzalah will be grateful for the opportunity to partner and save lives."

Sometimes Eli will look at a group of donors meeting with him on Zoom and say, "Right now we need to raise money for more bulletproof vests. I know that you are people who care about Israel and want United Hatzalah to be able to deal with emergencies under fire. But for that to happen, we need more vests. This is the situation. Are you in?"

And time after time they are. Because they really care.

CHAPTER THIRTY-ONE

Meeting the Wolves

The first few weeks of the war that broke out on October 7 took a major toll on United Hatzalah. Over 1,700 volunteers had spent significant amounts of time saving lives in Gaza and had seen the worst atrocities known to man. They had evacuated thousands of wounded Israelis under fire and provided the finest medical backup possible for the Israeli army. They were heroes of the first degree, but now that they had overcome the initial shock and the army had entered Gaza to fight Hamas, Eli Beer knew that they had a long, arduous road ahead of them.

Aside from the physical and emotional toll the war had taken, there was also the logistics. During the second Lebanon war, Eli spent a million dollars on needed equipment. This time around, United Hatzalah had spent fifty million dollars and counting. Since the moment the war started, Eli has kept his phone on at all hours of the day and night, making himself available to deal with any pressing matter that arose. Branches from around the country were constantly reaching out to him to request more equipment. Everyone needed more medical supplies, more bulletproof vests and helmets. The country was at war and everyone needed something urgently.

It wasn't only the volunteers of United Hatzalah who needed equipment. In the chaos of those first days the IDF also was missing vital equipment, and many army bases contacted Eli for United Hatzalah's help. The army even requested that United Hatzalah loan them ten ambulances — and they did.

Eli was receiving calls from officers and from bases and from individual soldiers. Then one day an IDF sniper got in touch. He had recently flown in to Israel to take part in the battles as a member of the Givati Brigade. He called Eli Beer and told him that the helmet he had been given wasn't the best quality, and since they were about to enter Gaza, he needed another one — as did the rest of his unit. Eli didn't know the young man. He had never spoken to him before. But here was a soldier who had flown in from Florida to fight for his people, and there was no way that Eli could even consider turning him down. In his mind, it was like his own son was asking him for a tactical helmet, and just as he would never consider turning down a request from his son, neither could he turn down a request so that another young soldier could stay safe.

"How many tactical helmets do you need?" Eli asked.

"We need ten helmets."

Eli promptly called Eli Pollak and asked him to arrange for ten helmets to be supplied to the sniper's unit. Pollak called the factory in Raanana that supplies United Hatzalah with helmets. The factory opened at eleven o'clock at night to fill the order and promised to deliver ten tactical helmets directly to the troops at the front.

United Hatzalah would end up supplying over two hundred army bases and brigades with urgently needed supplies. Though they were well stocked, and this was something they were in a position to do, getting the equipment to the bases wasn't simple. Since many of them were located in dangerous areas, it was hard to find people who were willing to make the trip. Eli decided to set an example and deliver equipment to some of the bases himself.

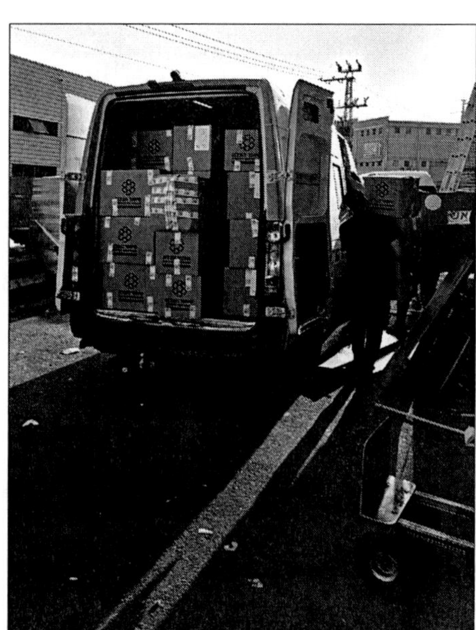

Loading more equipment to send out

Later during the first week of the war, Eli headed south. His son-in-law Aharon Ben Haroush was behind the wheel, while Aharon's wife, Avigail, sat in the back seat. There was another United Hatzalah vehicle following behind them, also filled with equipment designated for the soldiers.

Besides delivering the equipment to the bases situated in the south, Eli was also hoping to see his son Yisrael, whose unit was stationed in the area. But when he arrived at his son's base, he was informed that he wouldn't be able to see him because the soldiers were busy training.

Curious, he asked one of the officers, "What kind of training are they doing?"

"Today they've been learning how to jump out of helicopters during combat."

Somewhat disappointed that he hadn't been able to see Yisrael, Eli left the base and drove to his next stop, his car filled with equipment and medicine that still needed to reach their destination. Soon they were driving down Route 232 — the now infamous Avenue of Death.

Driving down that tragic road evoked somber thoughts and memories as they recalled the hundreds of dead bodies that had been lying on that very stretch of road just a few days earlier.

Kfar Aza was situated on one side of the highway, emptiness on the other. Utter darkness everywhere. Darkness so thick it smothered them like a blanket. No one else was on the road. Not even an army vehicle

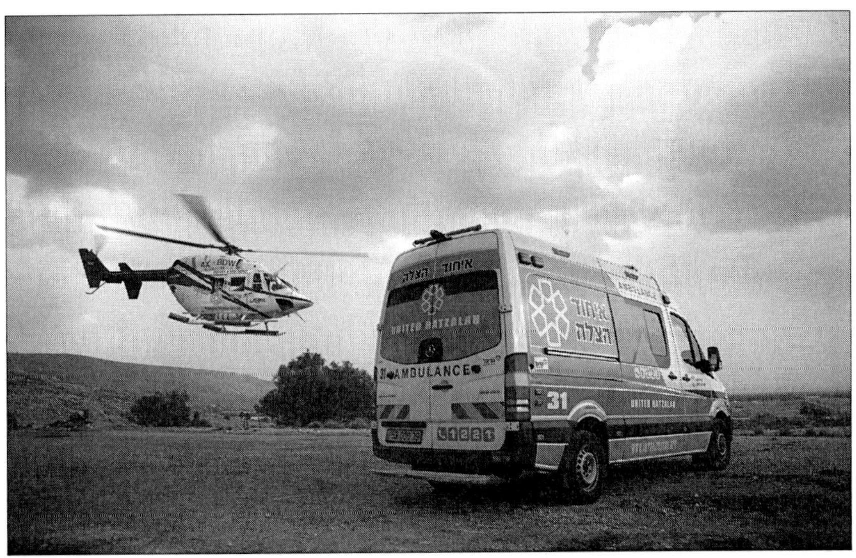

was to be seen. The feeling of sheer loneliness was intense. There was also a sense of fear at being back there again, in a place that had seen such carnage, where we had lost so many of our people to the murderous hordes of Hamas terrorists.

It was ten thirty at night and they were all alone. They would have felt a lot better if they had been able to turn on their lights, but there were still terrorists on the loose and a car's lights would give them an accurate target. With no choice, both cars continued to drive in abject darkness.

At one point, Eli looked behind him, and all he saw was empty road. He didn't want to be an alarmist, but the United Hatzalah vehicle that had been following them had just disappeared without any explanation.

"I tried reaching the other car by phone," Eli recalls, "but there was no reception in the area. We had just passed the entrance to Kfar Aza, and no one was answering my repeated calls. You can imagine how I felt as we continued driving down that road in darkness so complete it felt like *choshech Mitzrayim* had descended on the world again."

"Maybe something happened to them," Eli's son-in-law, Aharon, said. "Should I turn around?"

Working together for a common goal

Turning around in the middle of that pitch-black road would have been incredibly dangerous so they continued onward. Suddenly they saw six monstrous and amorphous shapes parked across the road directly in front of them. A few seconds later they could see that the highway had been blocked off by six gigantic vehicles known in the army as *Zevim* — Wolves.

Zevim are fearsome vehicles that are as large as tanks and come equipped with massive weaponry. Under normal circumstances, Eli would have welcomed the sight of an army presence in such a dangerous area. But this wasn't a normal time, and Eli understood that they were in terrible danger because the soldiers didn't know whether they were Jews or terrorists, and their guns were all pointed directly at their car.

Aharon was still driving, and they were getting closer and closer to the army vehicles.

"Aharon," Eli cried, "stop driving this second!"

"Why?"

"The army doesn't know who we are. They might shoot at us. Stop now!"

Moments later, the *Zevim* shone their powerful lights directly at them, and Eli was able to see the guns pointed at them.

"Aharon," he called out, "switch on the ambulance lights!"

Aharon turned on the lights, and the vehicle was immediately recognizable as belonging to United Hatzalah. But the soldiers on the road — all special forces — remained on high alert. Every single one of them had his gun up and aimed right at their windshield, and Eli suddenly found the words of the *Shema* emerging from his lips almost of their own accord.

The fear was intense. Beyond intense. Eli had a sudden thought that there was a possibility that the soldiers in front of them weren't really soldiers but terrorists who had somehow managed to take control of the army vehicles and were about to mow them down. It was also possible (actually probable) that the soldiers were actually soldiers who might end up shooting them down by mistake before giving them a chance to identify themselves.

The next thing Eli knew, the soldiers were screaming, "Get out of the car! Get out of the car!"

Aharon was so confused that he didn't understand what the soldiers were saying and thought that they were ordering them to turn around.

He began turning the car around, and the soldiers yelled even louder. "Get out of the vehicle!"

Suddenly, one of the soldiers started shooting in the air as a warning. No one was playing around here. This was as serious as it gets.

"Aharon," Eli shouted, "stop driving now!"

Eli finally got through to his son-in-law, and Aharon pressed the brakes. The moment the vehicle came to a halt, Eli's daughter Avigail, an EMT with United Hatzalah who was about to complete her training to be a paramedic, opened the door of the car. In her bulletproof vest and helmet, she began walking toward the soldiers with her hands up in the air.

"We're from United Hatzalah," she yelled.

The soldier yelled back. "What are you doing here?"

Moments later Eli was out of the car and approaching the soldiers. He explained that the vehicle was full of equipment and medical supplies for the soldiers in the nearby army bases. The reason they were on the road was because they had been driving from base to base to deliver the equipment and make sure that they arrived at the right address.

"Are you the car that stopped to pick up passengers in the middle of the road not far from here?"

Suddenly Eli understood what was going on. A group of terrorists must have infiltrated the area shortly before, and the army was under the impression that a car, assuming the people on the side of the road were Jews, had stopped for them. Now he understood why the army was on such high alert.

"It wasn't us," he reassured them.

Later on they found out that the United Hatzalah car that had been following them had seen people crossing the highway. It didn't take them long to figure out that there was a good chance that they were terrorists. They promptly turned around and kept driving in the opposite direction, putting space between them and the murderers. That was why the car had disappeared — because his volunteers had had the good sense to flee the scene as fast as they could. They, too, had tried calling Eli, but reception was down in the area and no one could get through to anyone else.

"You need to get away from this place as fast as possible," the soldiers said.

Eli was more than happy to follow orders. He gave the commanding officer a hug, thanked him profusely, and he and Avigail got back in the car. The army let them pass, and then Aharon stepped on the gas.

"It felt like he was doing 125 miles an hour," Eli says. "I don't think I was ever in a car driving at that speed. It was insane."

It was only when they arrived at the gas station outside Sderot that they began breathing normally once again. Reflecting on the events of the past hour, Eli couldn't say what had been the most dangerous part — the terrorists who had been running around in their area, a hundred special-forces soldiers with their guns pointed straight at them, or the way Aharon drove that night…

As soon as they had recovered somewhat, Eli insisted on being driven home.

"The following Shabbos morning," he says, "I went to shul, and when I received an *aliyah,* I recited the blessing of *hagomel* three times (one time with the Name of Hashem and the other two times without) — once for being saved from the terrorists, once for being spared by the soldiers, and once for surviving Aharon's driving.

A Miraculous Moment

Rabbi Shlomo Landau related the following two incredible stories:

A *yeshivah bachur* went to Ashkelon to visit a friend in Barzilai Hospital. In the bed next to his friend was a wounded soldier, who also had a friend there with him. The *bachur* was conversing with his sick friend when the soldier's friend interjected with a question.

"Why aren't you in the army?"

"I'm not in the army," the *bachur* replied, "but I'm doing a lot for the army."

"Really. What are you doing for the army?" The soldier's friend was clearly skeptical.

"I adopted a soldier."

"You adopted a soldier? What does that even mean?"

"When I pray and study Torah and perform good deeds, I do these things on behalf of my soldier, keeping him in mind and praying that he should be protected."

The friend began to laugh.

"So you're doing everything for a soldier, right?"

The *bachur* nodded.

"You're probably making all this up to make us feel good — or to make yourself feel good. Tell me something. What's the name of the soldier that you adopted?"

The *bachur* didn't miss a beat.

"Itai Yehuda ben Keren."

As soon as the *bachur* uttered the name, the wounded soldier lying in the bed turned pale.

"That's my name," he said. "I'm Itai Yehuda ben Keren."

For a second, everyone in the room was stunned when they realized that the visiting *bachur* had been davening for his friend's roommate.

But the soldier's friend wasn't finished.

"If you're praying and studying Torah for Itai, how is it possible that he was injured?"

"The ways of Hashem are complicated," the *bachur* replied, "but your friend is still alive. He survived."

As the conversation ensued, Itai told the *bachur* that he'd been injured on Tuesday.

"What time?"

"It happened at 4:40 in the afternoon."

Now it was the *bachur* who turned pale.

"I want you to know something," he said. "I try very hard to come on time to *seder*. On the day that you were injured I didn't manage to get to the *beis midrash* until five o'clock. You didn't have the usual protection you normally did."

By the time the *bachur* left, he and the soldier had become best friends and he knew that the two of them would be deeply connected forever.

And all four of the people there that day understood that Torah and mitzvos protect *Klal Yisrael* in ways that we can't even fathom.

And here is the second story:

One commando unit spent a very busy morning fighting terrorists in the streets of Gaza. After fighting nonstop for many hours, successfully eliminating many terrorists, the unit needed to take a break and eat lunch to recharge.

Of course, in the midst of the war zone, while they were on active duty, a break wasn't really a break. They held their sandwiches in one hand while still holding their guns with the other.

Suddenly, they heard the sound of a gunshot. Their first thought was that someone was shooting at them, but a second later they realized that one of the soldiers had accidentally fired his gun.

They looked around the area trying to determine where the bullet had gone. None of them had been hurt, but they wanted to know where the bullet went. They searched the area and didn't find it, so they broadened the perimeters of their search.

Not far from where they had been sitting and eating lunch, they came upon the entrance to a tunnel that they had previously overlooked. The reason they were able to identify the entrance now was because there was a dead Hamas terrorist lying across the entrance. He was holding an RPG in his hand and had clearly been in the process of seeking to kill the unit in its entirety.

But he wasn't able to complete his mission. Because there was a bullet hole right between his eyes — a bullet hole that had been made by the bullet that the soldier had fired by mistake, killing the terrorist before he had been able to cause the unit harm.

It's said that every bullet has an address. Obviously there is truth to these words.

CHAPTER THIRTY-TWO

The President's Tears

In the weeks that followed the brutal Simchas Torah massacre, Eli Beer walked around enveloped in a fog of incredible sadness and pain. After seeing the sights he'd seen, he was extremely depressed.

In his youth, Eli had spent a lot of time roaming the hallways and exhibits of Yad Vashem, which was situated in the forest right across from Bayit Vegan, where Eli grew up. He had come of age with a thirst to save six million lives — one life for every Jew who had been murdered by the Nazis. And he had gone on to do just that, building an organization that had been instrumental in treating countless residents in Israel.

Yet now he felt as if he couldn't go on. He didn't know if he would ever be able to recover after seeing such horrific sights. It was as if the Jewish people were experiencing a horrific taste of the Holocaust — after all, since the end of World War II there had never been a day like October 7, 2023, when so many Jews were killed in one twenty-four-hour period — and Eli had the feeling that he would never be the same again.

"I'll never forget my father-in-law's reaction when we spoke on Simchas Torah after he had sent me down south," Aharon Ben Haroush says. "He had remained behind in Yerushalayim to manage the situation from United Hatzalah headquarters and he came down south after Yom Tov was over. I remember him asking me, 'How many people were killed?'

"'More than eight hundred,' was my answer. Of course, now we know that the number turned out to be much higher than my initial estimate, but even that was too much to handle.

"'It can't be,' he screamed. 'It can't be! This is *Am Yisrael*! It can't be true! Don't say such a thing!'

"'I myself saw at least four hundred who'd been killed,' I told him. He couldn't accept what I was saying. He just repeated, 'It can't be! Don't say such a thing. This is *Am Yisrael* we're talking about! Don't you dare say such a thing!'

"Later that night my father-in-law came and saw the truth with his own eyes. But his reaction to my words is something I'll never forget."

For weeks Eli walked around like he was in a nightmare. Almost getting killed by the Israeli army while delivering medicine and supplies to the soldiers didn't help matters. It was like he was back in the dark days of Covid, when he almost died in a Miami hospital. At that time he had also felt like giving up.

Despite all that he'd been doing to raise funds for United Hatzalah, since the morning of the massacre, Eli had been walking around feeling more lost than he'd ever felt in his life.

"I felt so frustrated and angry at everything that happened," Eli says. "For two weeks straight I couldn't focus or concentrate. I found myself thinking over and over, *What would have happened if Hamas had sent twenty thousand soldiers into Israel instead of three thousand?*"

Nothing was important and he couldn't even seem to be able to find the time to sleep, shave, or shower. Like many of his volunteers, Eli Beer was depressed without even knowing it.

Eli needed a jolt in the arm to wake him up and help him focus on the future. Luckily for him the jolt was soon in coming. When he later reflected on what happened, the whole story seemed kind of miraculous to him.

While there are some miracles that are obvious and overt, there are other miracles that seem to be part of life — they seem "normal" — but when you think about it, you realize that they are also miracles.

Such was the story of Eli's meeting with President Joe Biden.

Many newspapers and television stations called United Hatzalah and asked if they could interview Eli Beer in the weeks following the war. Eli had been at the dispatch center from the very beginning. He had heard the calls from those whose homes were invaded by terrorists. Many of the calls had been terminated in the middle of the conversation, and when the volunteers called back no one answered. He had heard the crying and the screams and the gunshots. When the news outlets called, Eli gave as many interviews as he was able, knowing how important it was for the world to know what Israel was facing.

Still, even he was surprised when the phone rang one day and the caller said he was from the American Embassy in Yerushalayim.

"Mr. Beer," said the voice on the other end of the line, "President Joe Biden is coming to Israel in the near future and has requested to meet with you and a number of other key people during the short amount of time that he will be in the country."

Eli's first reaction was that someone was making a prank call, that the person was scamming him. The reason he assumed it was a joke was because the caller said that she knew how busy Eli was and she was hoping that he would be able to find the time to meet with the president despite his busy schedule. If he had thought the call was a joke before, the line about him being too busy to meet with the president clinched it, because who in his right mind turns down a meeting with the president of the United States no matter how busy he is?

He decided to play along.

"I'm very busy," he said, "so give me the exact date and let me check my calendar to see whether I am free at that time. I might have to reschedule some meetings to make this work..."

It turned out that the invitation was genuine. The president's team had chosen a number of people whom they thought President Biden might want to meet during his short visit to Israel. They suggested that the president meet with the representatives of the parents of the children who had been taken hostage in Gaza. They also invited the elderly couple whose home had been infiltrated by terrorists and who had managed to survive due to the wife's brilliant tactical maneuver of continuously offering food to the terrorists. The head of Zaka, too, was invited, and so was Eli Beer.

So it was that Eli Beer was scheduled to meet with President Joe Biden on October 22, 2023.

Meeting with President Joe Biden

The president's visit was scheduled to last for a mere eight hours before he took to the air again, which meant that the meetings were going to have to be brief. The president's entourage included well over one hundred vehicles, including armed vehicles, limos, and ambulances. From the airport the president was driven to the David Kempinski Hotel in Tel Aviv, which the Americans took over completely to use as their base.

All this because the president wanted to show his support for the State of Israel and its people at this critical time.

Eli left Yerushalayim with time to spare for his meeting with President Biden. When he arrived at the hotel, it was about ten in the morning. The place was teeming with police officers, Secret Service agents, and Israeli security guards. All the roads for five miles around had been closed by security, and Iron Domes had been set up all around

Ten Aviv as a precaution, just in case Hamas was crazy enough to attack the president of the United States as he drank a cup of coffee in the presidential suite of the Kempinski Hotel.

When Eli arrived at the security checkpoints, his United Hatzalah vehicle ensured that he was allowed to proceed relatively quickly. He showed his ID to the security personnel, who checked the list of expected guests for his name, and he was allowed through. After passing all five layers of security and finally pulling up outside the hotel, Eli parked his car, went inside, and touched base with the people from the American Embassy.

The meeting had been scheduled to begin at eleven, but President Biden had only arrived at the hotel at nine, which meant that all his meetings had been delayed. That, coupled with the fact that his meeting with Prime Minister Netanyahu, Minister of Defense Galant, Benny Gantz, and other cabinet members lasted for four hours, meant that everyone ended up sitting around and waiting for quite a while.

So it was only around one in the afternoon when they were ushered in to meet with President Biden.

Officially the meeting was supposed to last for fifteen minutes, which gave every person in the room one minute to speak with the president. In reality, the meeting lasted much longer since the president indicated his desire to speak to the people who had come to meet with him. The fifteen-minute meeting lasted one hour and fifteen minutes.

Biden was introduced to Rachel, the woman from Ofakim who had been holed up in her apartment with a group of terrorists for twenty hours until she and her husband were rescued by Israeli special forces. She explained how she had kept offering them food and drinks and even bandaged one of the terrorist's hands, doing whatever it took to keep them focused on anything other than her and her husband.

Eli attended the meeting wearing his orange Hatzalah vest — something he wears proudly wherever he goes — and President Biden devoted a lot of time to speaking to him, particularly since he was one of the few people in the room who was able to converse with Biden in fluent English.

After they were introduced, Joe Biden said, "I appreciate all the work you and your organization have been doing."

When Eli heard those words, he felt Biden was being sincere and that he really did appreciate everything that United Hatzalah had been doing for the people of Israel.

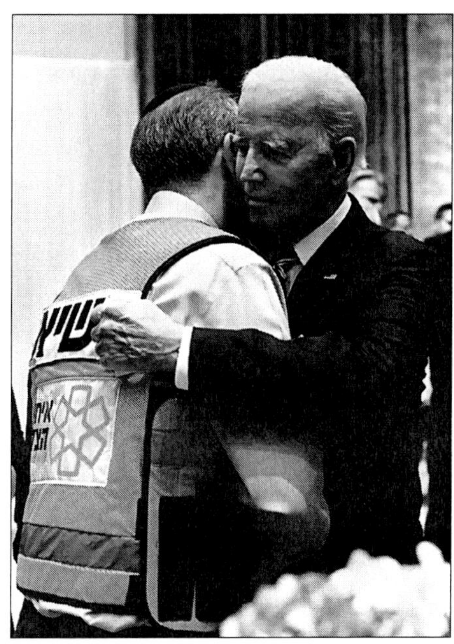

Sharing a hug with President Biden

"Mr. President," Eli said, "this visit is a historical moment, and I'm proud to be here to welcome the president of the most powerful country in the world, who has come to visit Israel at such a difficult time. You have lifted our spirits here in Israel and around the world."

The president asked Eli what he had seen on October 7, and Eli described it all, sparing no details.

"I broke down a minute into the conversation," Eli later said, "but I didn't let that stop me. I was speaking to the president of the United States, and I was determined to share the real story with him for as long as they gave me.

"I told the president that United Hatzalah has over seven thousand volunteers throughout the country and that they were comprised of all types of people. 'We have Jews and Muslims and Christians,' I told him. 'And we have volunteers who live in the south and saw the terrorists entering their villages and neighborhoods. Two of our volunteers lost their lives that day — one a member of Israel's security service, who died fighting the terrorists (I'm still not allowed to mention his name) and another, an Arab named Awad, who was working as security at the music festival near Re'im and did his best to save as many people as he could. Other volunteers were kidnaped from their homes. United Hatzalah is suffering along with the rest of the country in a very personal way. But our volunteers didn't allow anything to stop them, and they went into the most dangerous places to save as many lives as possible.'"

Eli described some of the worst sights that the volunteers had seen — things that would shock anyone with even the tiniest vestige of humanity.

"And as I spoke to him," Eli says, "I started crying, and so did he. I saw the tears welling up in his eyes, and he needed a tissue to wipe them away.

"'Eli,' Joe Biden said, 'I grew up as a big believer in G-d. My father always told us that we needed to protect the Jews, we have to protect the Jews. As a child, my father told me many times that the Jews are the Chosen People and that we need to make sure they are safe.

"Eli" — the president kept saying his name, almost as if the two of them were old friends — "Eli, I had four children. One died along with my wife in a car accident. A really, really bad car accident. It was the most painful thing ever. Another one of my children died of cancer. That, too, was an incredibly painful time for me. I lost two kids and my wife," he said, "and the pain that I feel now for Israel is like the pain I felt then when I lost the members of my family. The pain I felt when I lost my kids is the pain I feel now. The pain all of you are suffering now is also my pain. You don't have to be Jewish to be a Zionist. You don't have to be Jewish to be a lover of Israel."

The president repeated this line several times, and all the while he was holding Eli's hand. They also hugged a few times.

"I feel your pain," the president continued. "I'm totally with you, and I came here to Israel, not to command your army or to tell the prime minister what to do. I came here just to show my love and support for Israel.

"Eli, what United Hatzalah did was so honorable. I and so many other people watched what happened on television and saw your volunteers working to save lives. I am so proud of you!"

"Mr. President," Eli replied, "I want you to know something. A lot of our volunteers are American. I am so proud to be a Jew! I am so proud to be an Israeli! And I am so proud to be an American! I cannot tell you what it means to us to see the most powerful leader in the world coming here to support our country.

"On behalf of all the volunteers of United Hatzalah, on behalf of the people of Israel, and on behalf of all Jews around the world, I cannot thank you enough."

At this point the two of them shared another meaningful embrace.

Eli couldn't help but notice that President Joe Biden was still crying and that some of his tears had fallen onto Eli's jacket.

Some might say that President Joe Biden truly stepped into the position of a leader on the morning of October 7 and in the aftermath of the horrific attack on Israel. Because it was then that he stood with Israel in the most genuine way and did what he could to show a broken people that he felt their pain and was standing by their side. It was almost as if he had been chosen president for this moment — and he executed his mission and made every moral person proud.

In the wake of his meeting with President Biden, it seemed like every media outlet wanted an interview with Eli. He spoke with CNN and Fox News and was interviewed by Ben Shapiro.

What was interesting was that every person he knew, from the most right wing to the most liberal, felt gratitude to him for the way he represented the Jewish people during his meeting with the president. Everyone understood that the powerful connection that had been forged between the president of the United States and the president of United Hatzalah had nothing to do with politics and everything to do with expressing *hakaras hatov* to the leader of the free world for having the moral courage, fortitude, and bravery to stand up for what was right while unequivocally condemning the evil that had been perpetrated on the Jewish people.

Most importantly for Eli, it seemed to him that Hashem was speaking to all of them through the president, telling us that we don't have to worry, not only because "America has our back," but because Hashem has our back.

And that's really the only thing that counts.

Eli being interviewed by Ben Shapiro

A Miraculous Moment

Back in the days before the world had gone completely off the rails, a chareidi Jew from Bnei Brak named ma was driving on the Tel Aviv–Jerusalem highway when he suddenly noticed a car sitting on the side of the road with its hazard lights blinking. Inside the car were two parents, a child, and a dog. He pulled up behind the car and got out to ask what the problem was.

"We ran out of gas," the father explained. "We've been waiting here for half an hour. You're the first car that stopped."

"Don't worry about a thing," Yehuda reassured them. "I'll drive over to the nearest gas station at Motza and bring you back enough gasoline so you can get back on the road."

Yehuda gave them his phone number, they gave him theirs, and he promised to return as quickly as possible. He was back shortly afterward with a full jerry can of gasoline.

They offered to pay him for his help, but he refused.

"It's on the house."

"What do you mean? You drove to the gas station, you went out of your way and you spent money on me. What do you mean, 'It's on the house'?"

"Thank you for wanting to pay, but I did a mitzvah and I don't want payment for it."

"I don't believe this."

"What's so hard to believe?"

"Come here a second. I want to show you something."

The father led Yehuda around to the back of the car. On the trunk there was a bumper sticker.

"Do you see that sticker?" the man asked him.

Yehuda looked. The sticker said, "*Dros kol dos.*" Roughly translated, this means, "Run over every religious person."

"This is the first time in my life that I'm meeting a religious person," the man confessed, "and suddenly I find myself incredibly ashamed at the sticker on my car. I'm going to remove it."

"Tell me," Yehuda said. "Where are you from?"

"We live in Kibbutz Be'eri. It's situated down south, near Gaza."

"Interesting, I've never heard of it. At any rate, I hope you have a great trip and nothing else should go wrong."

They bid each other good night, went back to their respective cars, and drove off.

The next morning the man who had run out of gas on Highway 1 heard his phone ringing. He answered it.

"Hello? It's Yehuda."

"Yehuda who?"

"Yehuda. I met you last night on the highway when you ran out of gas."

"Yes, yes, of course. Hello and thank you so much for what you did. You really saved us!"

"You're welcome. I was just calling to make sure you got home safe and sound."

"Yes, after you left we drove to the gas station, filled up, and were able to get home just fine. Thank you very much!"

"My pleasure. Now I'm calm. *Kol tuv.*"

A few days later, on Friday afternoon, Yehuda called again. He had a story to share with the couple's young son, if they didn't mind.

"A story? Sure. Why not? What's the story?"

And so it began. Every *erev Shabbos* Yehuda would call the family from Kibbutz Be'eri and tell them a story. It usually wasn't longer than two minutes, and within a short time, this became their weekly tradition.

Half a year passed. One Friday, the man from Kibbutz Be'eri asked Yehuda a question.

"Tell me, Yehuda, aren't you bored on Shabbos?"

"Why would I be bored?"

"I don't know. You pray and you eat, and that's pretty much the whole situation, no? You can't speak on the phone or watch TV or work on the computer or go for a drive. That's why I'm asking. Aren't you bored?"

"It's funny you should think that I would be bored on Shabbos when it happens to be a day where I find that I am very busy."

"How's that?"

"Look, it will be difficult for you to understand without experiencing it for yourself. So here's what I suggest. Why don't you come and join me and my family for Shabbos? Then you can come and see how it is for yourself."

The man from Be'eri was taken aback.

"You're not serious! Me keep Shabbos? In Bnei Brak?! Are you forgetting that I'm chiloni?"

"I didn't forget for a second," Yehuda reassured him. "You will be my guest, and everything will be fine. We'll find an apartment for you to stay, and you will make us very happy if you accept our invitation."

"It seems kind of crazy to me, but I'll ask my wife and I'll get back to you with an answer."

In the meantime, Yehuda called his *rav*. He explained the situation and asked the *rav* for his advice on when might be a good time to invite the family from Be'eri to his house for Shabbos. The thing is, it was almost Tishrei. First there was Rosh Hashanah — two full days of intense davening. Yom Kippur, of course, was a fast day. Then there was Succos, when they'd be eating and sleeping in the succah.

"I can't really see them going for that," Yehuda said.

"What about Simchas Torah?" his *rav* suggested. "People will throw candies at them, and they'll have a chance to dance with the *sefer Torah*."

"I can't have them on Simchas Torah."

"Why not?"

"My father lives in Sderot, and all my siblings take turns going to spend Shabbos and Yom Tov with him. Simchas Torah is my turn to go."

"Why don't you invite your father to come and spend Simchas Torah with you in Bnei Brak? Then, in addition to experiencing a real Simchas Torah, the family from down south will also be able to see how beautifully your family treats your father, too..."

It was a good idea. There was just one glitch:

"We can only come to you if we can bring our dog," the man from Be'eri told Yehuda when he called to invite them for Simchas Torah. "Is that a problem?"

"Not at all. Bring your dog."

So it was that Yehuda's father, who lived across the street from the police station in Sderot, wasn't home when the terrorists took control of that part of the city, killing many people. Not only was he saved, but so were his son Yehuda and Yehuda's family, who were supposed to spend Simchas Torah with him in Sderot.

Then there was the family from Be'eri. They, too, were saved. They remained alive and well while the terrorists set their house on fire and their home went up in flames. And since they had to remain in Bnei Brak for a while (there was a war going on, after all), it made sense to send their son to a local Shuvu school.

And to think that it all began one evening on the highway when a *frum* guy stopped to help someone who ran out of gas…

CHAPTER THIRTY-THREE

The Las Vegas Convention

Israel had been heavily engaged in the war for several weeks when Eli Beer received a call from former United States Ambassador to Israel David Friedman, who also happened to be a good friend.

"Eli," he said, "I was invited to speak at the Republican Jewish Coalition, which is scheduled to take place in Las Vegas in a few days. All the Republican candidates for president are going to be there, including Donald Trump. It's a big deal."

Ambassador David Friedman

Eli waited in silence to hear where this was going.

"The thing is," David continued, "I can't make it, and I was wondering if you would agree to go and give a speech in my place. It's for the Motza'ei Shabbos event — the main event of the convention."

Eli's initial reaction was to turn down the invitation. He was busy with a million things in Israel and felt that his place was at home in Yerushalayim during *Klal Yisrael*'s time of need. But David pointed out that this was Eli's chance to present Israel's side of the story to the most powerful members of the Republican Party. It was an opportunity that shouldn't be missed.

There was no denying this logic, especially since Israel was fighting an uphill battle in public relations, with so many voicing loud and fierce opposition to the war in Gaza, and it needed all the help it could get.

In the end, Eli agreed to go.

Eli spoke with Matt Brooks, the chairman of the Republican Jewish Coalition and one of the most powerful and well-connected Jews in the United States.

"Eli," he said, "you need to say the truth about what happened on October 7. This is a major opportunity for key people to understand what occurred and why Israel must fight this battle to the end."

Eli agreed with Brooks and promised to deliver the speech of a lifetime.

At the conference

His flight was leaving Thursday morning, destination Vegas with a stopover in Los Angeles. He went home to pack for the relatively quick trip. When he walked through the door of his Ramot apartment, he ran into his daughter Adina. Seeing Eli with a purposeful look on his face, Adina could tell that her father was getting ready to leave the country.

"Where are you going?" she asked suspiciously.

Eli looked her in the eye. "Adina," he said, "I have a mission. Part of my job as the head of United Hatzalah is to go and give speeches about the situation in Israel so that everyone in the world can understand what's really happening here."

The problem was that Adina was fifteen years old and having a hard time, like so many other teenagers. The tragedy that had struck the country on Simchas Torah had turned many confident teens into pale shadows of their former selves, and Eli's daughter Adina was now afraid to leave their apartment — afraid to go to school, afraid to even go downstairs to the grocery store. With her older sisters already out of the house and her brother in the army, Adina was more or less on her own, especially since her mother was nearing completion of her paramedic course and was required to take many ambulance shifts.

With mother and siblings out of the house for the most part, Adina was disappointed to hear that her father was now packing to leave her as well, even if it was just for a few days.

Eli heard her out as she voiced her thoughts. "You know what?" he said at last. "You should come with me to Las Vegas."

"Really?!" A gleam of excitement and gratitude suddenly shone in Adina's eyes.

"Really. You're coming with me."

"Thank you so much!"

"You deserve it. You've been through a lot in the last few weeks, just like everyone else."

It was great to see the smile that crossed his daughter's face.

"Go pack. But do it fast. We have a flight to catch."

There was no question in Eli's mind that he had just made the right move. Sometimes a father needs to take his daughter along with him on a trip — and this was one of those times. To make it even sweeter for her, Eli handed Adina five hundred dollars.

"What's this for?"

"For you to go shopping when we get to Las Vegas. There are some great malls out there, and I'm sure you'll find some great stuff."

For a fifteen-year-old girl, that was like the cherry on top of the cake.

Once in LA, Eli had a Zoom meeting with the board of United Hatzalah and nearly one thousand of their major supporters. They started the Zoom call, and Adina was there, listening to what was being discussed. Mr. Robert Kraft, who, together with his family, have been extremely helpful and involved with United Hatzalah's efforts after October 7th, was one of the speakers on the call, and Adina was especially touched by what he had to say. She was also moved by numerous others on the call, because people started speaking up and making pledges. One person pledged ten thousand dollars, another eighteen thousand dollars, someone else fifty thousand dollars, and another a hundred thousand dollars. Suddenly Adina leaned toward her father and said, "Abba, I want to donate something, too."

"Go right ahead," Eli told her.

Adina looked into the camera and announced, "I want to donate three hundred sixty dollars."

She had decided to take most of the money that her father had given her to go shopping and donate it to *tzedakah.*

At that moment, Eli couldn't have been prouder of his daughter.

One of the people on the Zoom call — his name is Hersch — said, "If Eli Beer's daughter is donating three hundred sixty dollars, I'm going to donate three hundred sixty thousand dollars."

It turned out that bringing Adina along on the trip had been very much the right move to make for many reasons...

After breakfast, Eli and Adina went to the airport to catch their flight to Las Vegas. The conference was taking place at the Venetian, and that was also where they would be staying. The food at the convention would be kosher, and there would be a shul with minyanim for all the religious Jews in attendance.

Over one thousand people had arrived in Las Vegas to attend the convention, and soon Eli was in the thick of things, touching base with old friends and being introduced to new ones. Friday was set aside for meetings with many of the Republican politicians who had come to speak at the conference. The main attraction was former President Donald Trump, the man everyone wanted to meet.

It seemed to Eli that people were literally lining up for a few minutes of his time.

Eli went in with the famed philanthropist and physician, Dr. Miriam Adelson, to meet the former president. Since she is a loyal Trump supporter, no one would be rushing their meeting, and they would have as much time as needed to speak with Trump.

Donald Trump was meeting people in a beautiful office. Behind him was a row of American and Israeli flags — a clear reminder that this was the Republican Jewish Coalition. Eli reminded Trump that the two of them had previously met in 2016 and that Trump had even pledged to donate a couple of ambucycles to United Hatzalah.

"Yes, yes," Trump said, remembering the meeting and his donation. "I love Hatzalah…"

Donald Trump had a lot of questions about what exactly had transpired on October 7, and Eli was able to answer them all. He also told Trump what the United Hatzalah volunteers had done on the day of infamy, how over a thousand of them had entered the most dangerous places without regard for their personal safety. He also told Trump about the volunteers who had been killed — one of whom lived down south and had taken part in the fighting in his role as a member of the Shabak and not as a United Hatzalah volunteer.

Eli with President Donald Trump

"This is all Iran," Trump said. He expounded on his theme for a few minutes explaining what America needed to do about the Iranian threat. At the end of the conversation, Eli said, "I have one request from you."

"What's that?" Donald Trump asked.

"That the next time you come to Israel, make sure to visit us at United Hatzalah."

He agreed.

Eli Beer and Donald Trump shared a hug before Eli left the office.

From there he went to meet with Nikki Haley, former governor of South Carolina and another presidential candidate for the Republican Party.

"I ended up meeting with Nikki Haley for about twenty minutes," Eli says. "She wanted to hear all the stories, and she had a lot of questions for me. I showed her the footage of the October 7 massacre — distressing scenes that were very difficult to watch, but she wanted to see what really happened — and her reactions were incredibly sincere and heartwarming.

"Nikki had seen a lot of footage but not the material I had. I had footage that my volunteers had shot and footage from my ambulances, as well as the worst atrocities that Hamas had livestreamed as they went about acting like insane animals. A lot of material that had been seen by very few people. I showed her pictures of children that would break any heart.

"She was very emotional, and there were tears in her eyes. Then she looked at me and said, 'I love Israel. I'm hurting for Israel.'

"And it was clear that she was."

Eli met with a lot of people at that convention — congressmen, senators, and other candidates such as Florida Governor Ron DeSantis, who reminded Eli that he had been the one to help authorize and establish Hatzalah in Florida.

Eli's speech that Motza'ei Shabbos was very powerful and touched the hearts of many people in the audience, but in some ways the speech he gave the next evening was even more meaningful to him.

Because it was about his father.

The Sunday night speech was delivered at a pro-Israel rally attended by a few thousand supporters of Israel who had gathered to daven for Israel and recite *Tehillim* for the success of *Klal Yisrael* against their enemies. When Eli rose to speak, he stood behind the lectern and looked out at the giant crowd in front of him. The crowd waited expectantly to hear what he had to say.

"When I was a young teenager," he told the hushed crowd, "my

Eli at the conference

father told me that when he was a teen in the middle of World War II, he went to many rallies to demonstrate against the American government, which hadn't done a thing to help the Jews stuck in Europe. The rallies were held on Wall Street in Manhattan.

"My father told me that the government chose not to help the Jews and didn't even bomb the tracks to Auschwitz, though it would have been very easy for them to do so. Even worse in a way, they turned away boats filled with Jews who had made it out of Europe and were hoping to be welcomed to American shores. Instead of a welcome, they were denied entry and forced to return to the arms of the Nazis, who sent them to their deaths.

"My father told me how he and his friends used to stand on Wall Street holding signs informing passersby that Jewish people were being murdered by the Nazis in the concentration camps. 'Eli,' he said to me, 'I remember how people walked by without even looking at the signs in my hand or acknowledging the terrible truth of what they said. I couldn't believe it at the time. How could it be that my fellow Americans didn't care about the massive tragedy that was happening across the ocean? How could it be that no one cared about the mass murder of an innocent people?'"

Eli paused for a second before continuing, letting his words hover in the air.

"That, my friends, was the question that so bothered my father eighty years ago. And that is exactly what's happening right now before our eyes. Here we stand, in the middle of Las Vegas, with pictures of babies who were killed or kidnaped in our hands, and people are just passing by and turning the other way. None of them are even saying that they care. Because they don't. They just don't care.

"Now I understand what my father told me when I was just a kid: We have to care about the Jews! We have to care about our brothers and sisters! We have to unite!

"Because no one else cares.

"It's not like during the Holocaust, when no one really knew what was going on in Europe. Today we know exactly what happened in Israel. And if people don't want to listen to what you're saying — yell louder! Yell until they listen. Yell until people start to understand that if the enemy would, G-d forbid, win in Israel, they will move on to Europe and America. There is no choice but to stop them."

On Monday night, Dr. Miriam Adelson had an airplane from her company's fleet filled to capacity with supplies for United Hatzalah that had been purchased by Joe Teplow, Eli's representative in New York.

"Eli," she said, "I'm returning to Israel on this flight. Why don't you and Adina join me instead of flying back commercial?"

So it was that Eli Beer returned to Israel on a plane that was loaded with pallets of equipment, medical supplies, and one thousand trauma kits. Most of the equipment was designated for United Hatzalah. Some of it would go to the army.

Not long after they landed, Hamas sent about fifty rockets in the direction of Tel Aviv and Ben Gurion Airport. This meant that they were under great pressure to unload everything as quickly as possible so that the plane could take off again. United Hatzalah trucks were waiting to be loaded under the threat of yet another missile attack and the ominous, ongoing sound of wailing sirens.

Before they could unload the plane, Eli went to speak to the customs agent. The man recognized Eli, and when he explained that the equipment the plane was carrying was for United Hatzalah and the IDF, the man said, "You know what? Just go through..."

Eli recalled how it had been back in the early days when he had to take apart the radios he was smuggling into the country so that the customs agents wouldn't confiscate them — and here the man was allowing him to pass through with fourteen tons of equipment.

The thought made him smile.

After all the equipment had been cleared through customs, Eli and Adina left the airport and were soon on their way back to Yerushalayim. Both of them were looking forward to a restful night after the long flight. But the excitement wasn't over, because the sound of still more warning sirens had caused one of the drivers on the road in front of them to become so discombobulated that he crashed his car into the bus in front of him.

Immediately the highway was filled with smoke and fire from the totaled vehicle, and people on the highway naturally assumed that the car had been hit by a missile. There was a group of soldiers in the midst of a drill on the side of the highway, and they came running.

The moment Eli heard the boom when the car hit the bus, he also thought the car had been struck by a Hamas missile, and he quickly put on his bulletproof vest and helmet. Then he weaved his way between the cars separating them from the accident. Seconds later, he came to a stop near the car. Smoke was billowing from the engine, and Eli rushed to get the people out of the car.

"We got out our supplies and began treating them," Eli says. "Thankfully they were only suffering from shock, but they could have easily died in the accident."

Once at home, exhausted beyond measure, Eli found that he was too tired for sleep, so he did what he had done so many times before and walked out onto his porch. There he stood at the railing, taking in the absolutely breathtaking view of Yerushalayim, the city he loved with all his heart. And then, with what seemed like a million stars twinkling in the heavens far above him, Eli could finally get some much-needed sleep.

CHAPTER THIRTY-FOUR

Twin Rescue

A few days after meeting with President Biden, Eli received a call from Channel 12 of Israeli TV.

"We know that United Hatzalah volunteers were part of the team that saved two ten-month-old twins from Kfar Aza," the caller said.

"That's correct."

"We would like to meet their family."

"I'll see what I can do."

What happened at Kfar Aza was a massacre of historic proportions. Over sixty percent of the population were brutally murdered. The atrocities that occurred in the homes and streets of Kfar Aza mirrored the worst moments of the Holocaust and other horrific tragedies in Jewish history.

In one home, the parents were hiding in their safe room along with their twin baby boys. After being inside for a few hours, during which they called the police, the army, and anyone else they could think of, begging for someone — anyone — to come to their rescue, the mother finally felt like she had no choice but to leave the safe room and try to obtain some food for the babies, who were crying from hunger.

Upon exiting the room, she was caught by the terrorists, tortured in the most despicable ways, and then murdered, as was her husband, who tried to come to her aid and was brutally murdered as well.

It was an incredibly emotional moment for all the United Hatzalah volunteers waiting outside Kfar Aza when the twins appeared in the arms of the soldiers who found them. The soldiers weren't equipped to take care of the babies — they were busy fighting a never-ending stream of terrorists — and they were very relieved to be able to hand them over to the members of United Hatzalah, who couldn't believe that they were holding two babies who were miraculously alive after crying for fourteen hours with no one able to answer their cries.

Shalom Avitan, Chaim Attias, Sivan Mashiach, and Tal Lalum were the members of the team of medical professionals who treated the twins. Each of them knew that it would take them a very long time to recover from what they saw that day.

Tal Lalun is twenty-eight years old and grew up in the city of Ramla. She works as a website developer and volunteers as an EMT for United Hatzalah whenever possible. On Simchas Torah morning, Tal woke up to the sounds of the sirens like everyone else. Later in the day she joined United Hatzalah ambulance number 33 when it left Ramla and drove south. She hadn't given much thought as to what she would be facing when she arrived, but on the way she heard the chatter on the ambulance radio and understood that this was a desperate moment for Israel — maybe one of the worst moments in its history.

The Cheletz intersection was hopping when they arrived. Ambulances

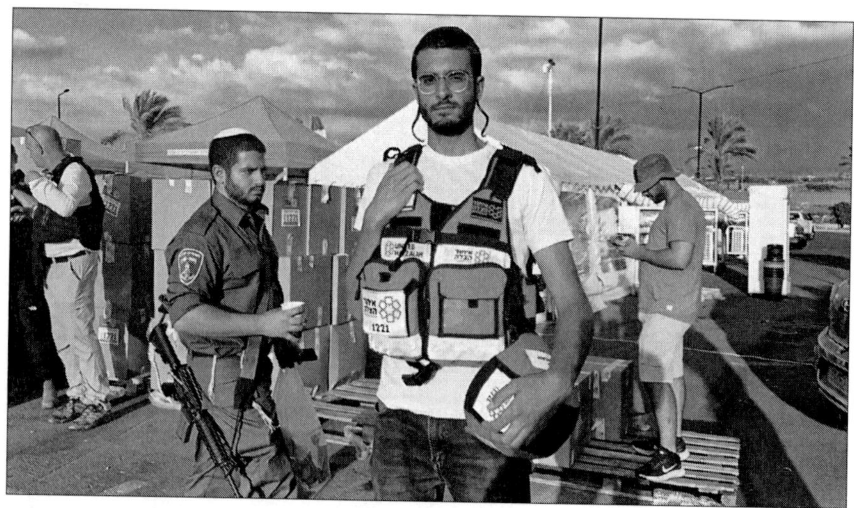

Shalom Avitan

were coming and going, transporting the wounded from Gaza to hospitals around the country. Those who had been grievously wounded were taken to the helicopter pad where United Hatzalah and Unit 669, the army's search-and-rescue unit, took turns landing and taking off.

By the time Tal's ambulance arrived, the army had already been battling the terrorists in the various kibbutzim that had been attacked. Tal and the rest of the ambulance crew were kept very busy transporting wounded soldiers, mainly to the two helicopter landing sites.

Though she witnessed numerous heartrending events throughout the course of her time in the south, the moment the twin boys were brought through the entrance of Kfar Aza was perhaps the most poignant.

"Shalom Avitan held one of the babies," she relates, "and a soldier was holding the second baby. 'Do you want me to hold him?' I asked the soldier.

"'Yes, please.'"

Shalom Avitan later told Eli Beer that standing outside Kfar Aza holding the baby in his arms, he felt like they had just rescued two babies from an extermination camp during the Holocaust. This had even more import considering that the twins' great-grandparents were Holocaust survivors.

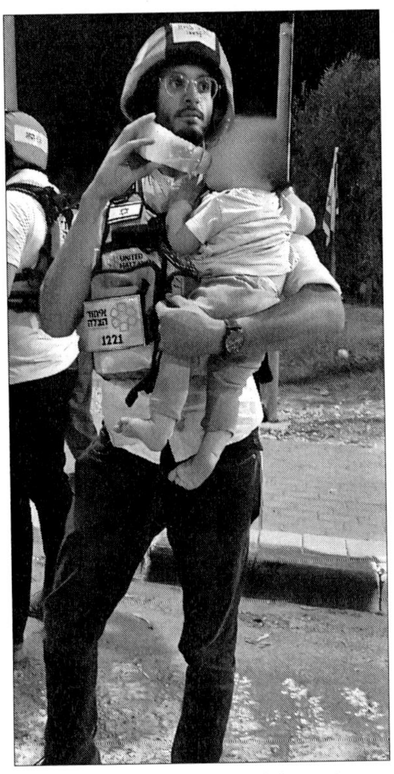

Shalom holding one of the twins

"I took the baby from the soldier's arms," Tal continues, "and it was like holding Jewish history in my arms. Until then we had all been working like robots, doing our best to keep our emotions at bay. But then the gate opened, and there were the two babies, safe and sound. At first I thought they were part of the same family, and I was so happy and excited that another family had somehow managed to escape the carnage. You have to remember that barely anyone was emerging alive from that place.

"Yet here were two babies. Two breathing twin boys. Proof that *Am*

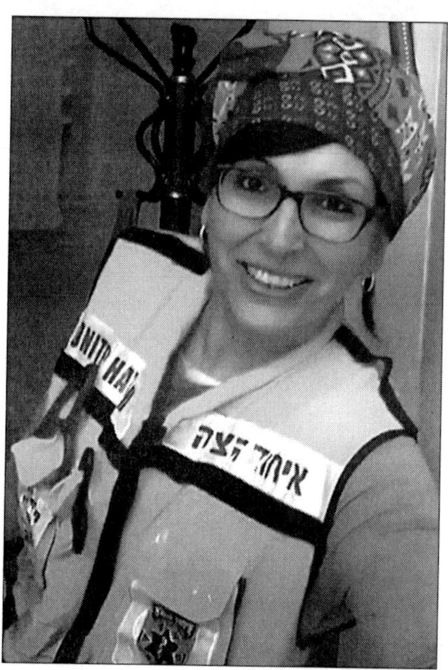

Sivan Mashiach

Yisrael would continue for eternity."

The baby she was holding was wrapped in a blanket, and somehow he came along with a bottle, and the blanket was clean without a sign of blood on it. But a clean blanket wasn't enough for the baby who kept on sucking on his bottle — clearly hungry and thirsty and wanting to eat and drink. Tal asked someone to fill the bottle with water, and the second she placed it into his mouth, he began drinking as if he would never stop.

The paramedic on her team, Sivan Mashiach from Elad, took the other twin from Shalom Avitan.

"It was clear that she knew exactly what to do with babies," says Tal, "and I gladly followed her instructions. When we brought the babies into the intensive care ambulance, Sivan told me to take off their clothing so that we could make sure that they hadn't been injured over the course of what had been an absolute day of insanity.

"We were in the middle of checking them from head to toe — they were so cute and oh-so-vulnerable at the same time — when the commander of the troops who had rescued the babies and brought them out of Kfar Aza climbed into the ambulance.

"That's when we found out that the twins' parents were no longer alive.

"Sivan and I stared at each other in utter shock. It was as if we suddenly understood what we were holding in our hands. We looked at one another and didn't know what to say or do. At the same time, we knew that we couldn't afford to fall apart — not when there were babies to look after, babies who had been on their own for fourteen hours after their parents were killed and had been left to cry and cry and cry — until they were finally rescued."

It was ten at night, fourteen hours after the start of the living nightmare, when the babies were rescued from Kfar Aza. They barely had the strength to cry by then after the traumatic day they'd had. The babies were clearly starving, but what to feed them? Water wasn't enough. They needed food as well.

A few volunteers went into the store at the nearby gas station to see what they could find. It was open, and soldiers had been taking things from the shelves that entire day and leaving IOU notes near the cash register to inform the owner how much they owed. The volunteers found diapers for the twins and formula. The moment they began feeding the twins, the babies latched onto the bottles and wouldn't stop sucking. They needed to make up for the past fourteen hours.

The army told the ambulance crew that they wanted to get the babies away from Kfar Aza and to a safe location as soon as possible. The medics quickly examined them, making sure that they were healthy and had no injuries.

"As soon as we finished doing a basic check," says Tal, "we brought the babies over to a waiting jeep. It was filled with soldiers, one of whom told me that he was a paramedic. I laid my hand on the head of the baby I had been holding for a moment, and then the twins were driven away from Kfar Aza to the hospital. Saying goodbye to those babies was by far the most emotional moment of the day for me.

"When I finally returned home, it all started to sink in and I thanked Hashem for keeping me safe and for keeping all the United Hatzalah volunteers safe while surrounded by terrorists who wanted nothing more than to kill every Jew they found. Later I learned that a commanding officer sent a letter to Eli Beer in which he wrote that if United Hatzalah hadn't been there to treat the wounded soldiers and transport them to the hospitals and helicopters, there is no question that the death toll would have been much higher.

"Hashem was there for us, and we survived our mission. And all the volunteers who went down south to help save lives came home alive and well.

"What a complete and utter miracle!"

Days later, Channel 12 called Eli, asking about the twins who had been treated by his volunteers.

"They were delivered to their relatives," Eli told the person on the other end of the call.

"We want to meet their grandmother, but she won't talk to the media."

Eli understood her completely. The grandmother of the twins had been through so much tragedy. Her daughter and son-in-law had just been killed in Kfar Aza, and her husband had died in a fatal car accident not long before. United Hatzalah volunteers had responded to that accident and had treated her wounded husband. That's how she had come to know Eli Beer.

He called her and they spoke for a while. At the end of the conversation, he said, "I know that you aren't feeling up to speaking with the media. But I think it's crucial for your family's story to be told. People should know about the twins and how they almost died and were miraculously saved. Please allow us to share your story."

Eli suggested that the United Hatzalah volunteers who had been part of the team who had rescued her grandchildren come and meet with her in Kfar Aza, with Channel 12's staff on hand to film the event.

So it was that a reunion was arranged between Shalom Avitan, tall, skinny, long *peyos*, originally from Stamford Hill, London, living today in Yerushalayim; Sivan Mashiach, with a *tichel* on her head; Chaim Attias, with his long *peyos* and large, knitted *kippah* from the city of Chevron; Tal Lalum, who'd cradled one of the twins so lovingly in her arms; and the family of the twins they had saved. There wasn't a dry eye in the room during that reunion, which lasted for hours.

The grandmother told those assembled that when she finally heard that the ten-month-old twins were in the hands of the United Hatzalah volunteers, she knew that they were going to be alright.

As the reunion neared its end, one of the uncles mentioned that the family of the twins' father was sitting shivah in another house on the moshav. The volunteers went there as well and sat with the family for about three hours, each group giving *chizuk* to the other. They learned that the twins' father had grown up in Kfar Aza and that he and his wife had been raising their children in close proximity to their grandparents. There were other relatives living there two doors away.

Listening to the tragic story, Eli Beer had a question he had to ask the family.

"Why did the terrorists decide to keep the twins alive when they killed so many other babies?"

The answer was chilling:

"The terrorists heard the babies crying, and they were hoping that people would come to rescue them so that when they arrived, the terrorists would be waiting to ambush them. Because there were some who understood the terrorists' plan, they sent out messages to everyone still alive in the village not to go to the babies under any circumstances, even though hearing them cry was the most heartrending sound in the world."

Chezi Rosenbaum

Eventually the soldiers arrived and fought off the terrorists. In the middle of the battle, one of the soldiers grabbed both babies, jumped into one of the jeeps, and drove away from the scene of the battle. He emerged from the entrance of the village right into the middle of a crazy scene where volunteers were treating an unending stream of critically injured people.

"When we saw those two babies," says Chezi Rosenbaum, one of the volunteers who was at the scene when those babies appeared, "I don't think there was one volunteer who didn't lose it. We had been operating on autopilot for so many hours. But seeing those babies, we could no longer hold back the tears."

During the height of the action, one of the commanding officers on the scene yelled at some of the United Hatzalah volunteers, "Why are you here now? Don't you know that you are endangering your lives?!!"

"What are you doing here?" the volunteer shouted back. "You're also putting your life in danger!"

"That's my job," the officer said. "I'm a soldier."

"We're soldiers too," the volunteers replied. "Soldiers of United Hatzalah!"

A Miraculous Moment

The story of Ori Magidish, the soldier who was captured by Hamas, taken into captivity in Gaza, and was miraculously rescued, gave hope and *chizuk* to the entire nation.

Morris Elul is Ori's uncle. Unlike many who heard the tragic story but didn't know what they should do about it, Morris decided to do something concrete for his niece.

"I was sitting together with Ori's parents," Morris recalls, "and I said to her father, 'Yossi, I have a feeling that Ori has some sort of protection from above."

Ori's mother, Maggie, performed *hafrashas challah* in her daughter's merit, and something incredible occurred as she was performing the mitzvah.

Ori's mother looked heavenward and began to pray. "I am doing this in the merit of my daughter and all the people who were taken captive," she said. "Please, please, *Borei Olam*, I love You, I love You! Please don't forsake me, Master of the world!"

The entire country was overcome when they saw the video of a mother begging Hashem for her daughter's safe return and in the same breath telling Hashem how much she loved Him. It was an incredibly spiritual moment and a huge *kiddush Hashem*.

The family took a *sefer Torah* around the city, dancing with it in honor of the captives, and then the *sefer Torah* was brought to Ori's home and carried into her room.

"It was at this point," Ori's uncle continued, "that my children said to me, 'Abba, do something for Ori!' I couldn't refuse. So many people were doing things in her *zechus*. How could I say no? On the spot I decided to keep Shabbos as a *zechus* for Ori to return home. Then I took it a step farther and I said, 'If Ori comes home healthy and well, I will continue keeping Shabbos — every single week!'

"On Sunday I was at work, and I told one of my coworkers about my niece who was taken into Gaza. He looked at me in shock. 'Morris,' he said, 'I just heard on the radio that the army brought Ori out of Gaza!'

"I thought he was joking, so I turned on the news. A minute later the announcer said, 'Just to recap what we were talking about a few minutes ago, the army just let us know that they rescued a soldier named Ori Magidish from Gaza. Again, one soldier — Ori Magidish — was just rescued from Gaza!'

"I burst into tears. When I managed to get myself under control, I called my son. The moment he heard my voice, he exclaimed,

'Abba, do you see what *shemiras Shabbos* can do? Hashem heard your prayers!'"

Almost immediately the streets near Ori's home in Kiryat Gat were filled with dancing people and the sound of music. Cars drove down the street honking with happiness.

"When I walked into Ori's home," her uncle said, "I went over to Ori's father and said, 'Didn't I tell you that Ori had a special protection from above?'

"He grabbed my head, kissed me, and said, 'It's all from Hashem!'

"When I saw Ori, I told her the story and the promise that I had made. Then I told Ori, 'Now I have to keep Shabbos forever.'

"Since then I have kept Shabbos and will continue doing so. I also started putting on tefillin every day. An open miracle happened to me. There's no other way of looking at it. We need to believe in Hashem. We need to daven to Hashem. He loves us and He hears our prayers!"

Afterword

And so, my friends, now you know some of what happened to *Klal Yisrael* on Simchas Torah — October 7, 2023. You know that the volunteers of United Hatzalah made a momentous decision that created a wonderful *kiddush Hashem*.

Because on that day they chose not to think about themselves and only to focus on their brothers and sisters. And wonder of wonders, almost every single person who risked their lives for *Klal Yisrael* and went down south to save lives returned home to their families. This is without question an incredible miracle.

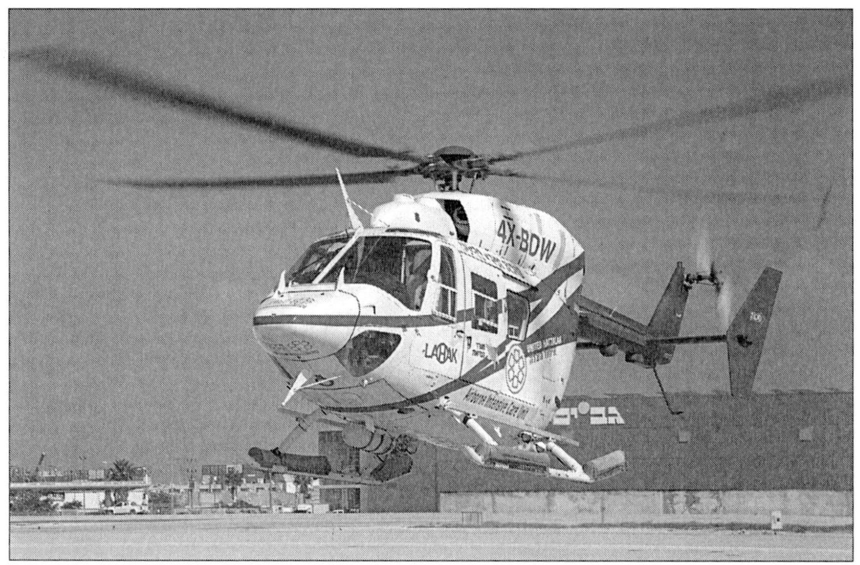

And while there is no way to know what the future holds for our unique and special nation, one thing seems fairly certain: As much as anything is certain in this world of ours, the orange ambucycles of United Hatzalah will continue riding forth to save lives whenever and wherever they can.

They will do this no matter what.

Through the heat and the cold.

Through good times and bad.

Through sickness and health.

And whether they are feeling optimistic or feeling low.

There is a reason this is so — a reason that applies now more than ever.

They will never stop riding because they are the soldiers of United Hatzalah — and saving lives is what they do.

For Hashem shall comfort Zion.
He will comfort all its destroyed places,
and He will make its wilderness like Eden,
its desert like the garden of Hashem.
Joy and gladness will be found in it,
thanksgiving and the voice of song.

— ***Tishah B'Av Kinnos***